The New Zealand
Bed &Breakfast
Guide
2008

Pelican editions
        First edition, January 2005
        Second edition, January 2006
        Third edition, January 2008

ISBN-13: 978-1-58980-524-8

Prices in this guide are quoted in New Zealand dollars.
All information in this guidebook has been supplied by the hosts. The
publishers will not be liable for any inaccuracies or any damages arising
from reliance on any contents of this publication. Infor mation about the
homes listed is subject to change with out notice. Readers are asked to
take this into account when consulting this guide.

Printed in China
Published by Pelican Publishing Company, Inc
1000 Burmaster Street, Gretna, Louisiana 70053

Cover illustration *From My Window, Oriental Bay* from an original
acrylic painting by Shona McFarlane .... of Millwood Gallery,
Wellington, New Zealand

Welcome to this edition of The Bed & Breakfast Book. Bed & Breakfast in New Zealand means a warm welcome and a unique holiday experience. Most B&B accommodation is in private homes with a sprinkling of guesthouses and small hotels. Each listing in the guide has been written by the host themselves and you will discover their warmth and personality through their writing. The New Zealand Bed & Breakfast Book is not just an accommodation guide – it is an introduction to a uniquely New Zealand holiday experience. The best holidays are often remembered by the friends one makes. How many of us have loved a country because of one or two memorable individuals we encountered? For the traveller who wants to experience the real New Zealand and get to know its people, bed and breakfast offers an opportunity to do just that. We recommend you don't try to travel too far in one day. Take time to enjoy the company of your hosts and other local people. You will find New Zealand hosts friendly and generous, and eager to share their local knowledge with you.

We have carefully inspected every property;

B&B Approved; All B&Bs in The Bed & Breakfast Book have been inspected on joining. They conform to the Schedule of Standards following. As important as the requirement of meeting a physical standard, we expect that all of our properties will offer excellent hospitality. Some hosts who are members of associations or marketing groups, which also undertake inspections, have chosen to display the logos below.

The **@home NEW ZEALAND** logo represents the largest organisation of hosted accommodation providers in New Zealand. It assures you of a warm welcome from friendly, helpful hosts. Accommodations displaying this logo are regularly assessed every two years and have met the quality standards set by the Association.

Qualmark™ is New Zealand tourism's official mark of quality. All Qualmark™ licenced accommodation listed in this directory means they have been independently assessed as professional and trustworthy, so you can book and buy with confidence. They will meet your essential requirements of cleanliness, safety, security and comfort; and offer a range and quality of services appropriate to their star grade.

Heritage Inns; A collection of luxury historic hosted character bed and breakfast lodges across NZ, are superior and often recommended by tourists. Our B&Bs have knowledgeable and friendly hosts. Our luxury accommodation ranges from the quiet honeymoon lodge in boutique romantic locations to central city accommodation - rivaling superior apartments, hotels or motels. Alternatively, enjoy the genuine NZ experience of an idyllic farmstay, lodge or luxury country B&B.

Superior Inns; Superior Inns of New Zealand properties are specially selected. All offer a true bed and breakfast experience, highlights of your visit to New Zealand. The specially selected bed and breakfast properties offer spacious bedrooms with bathrooms, luxury fittings, private guest lounges, fabulous delectable breakfasts and a chance to meet other visitors or be on your own. Our hosts can organise airport pickups, rental cars, restaurant bookings, honeymoon packages and short stay options.

Finding your way around
We travel from north to south listing the towns as we come to them. In addition, we've divided New Zealand into geographical regions, a map of which is included at the start of each chapter. In some regions, such as Southland, our listings take a detour off the north to south route, and follow their nose - it will soon become obvious.

Happy Travelling
The B&B Book Team

Our Guarantee

Hosts in The New Zealand Bed & Breakfast Book are committed to offering quality hospitality. If you receive hospitality which is less than you expected please discuss your concerns with your hosts at the time. If you are not satisfied you should contact the publishers who will take up the matter with the hosts. If you are still not satisfied the publishers will refund their assessment of a fair proportion of the tariff you paid.

Your comments

We welcome your views on The Bed & Breakfast Book and the hosts you meet.
Please visit our website **www.bnb.co.nz** or write to us at,
PO Box 6843, Wellington, New Zealand.

Comment Forms

Please help us to maintain our high standards by sending us comments about where you stayed. Guest Comments forms are available from your hosts.

- You may submit your comment on our website **www.bnb.co.nz**

- Or your hosts will give you a comment form.

- Or simply cut one from the back of the book.

- Each comment returned will be in our ongoing monthly draw for a free night's B&B.

- Each person staying can submit a comment for an increased chance of success.

- Guest comments are displayed on the hosts' pages at **www.bnb.co.nz**

About Bed & Breakfast

Our B&Bs range from homely to luxurious, but you can always be assured of generous hospitality.

Types of accommodation
Traditional B&B
Generally small owner-occupied home accommodation usually with private guest living and dining areas.
Homestay
A homestay is a B&B where you share the family's living area.
Farmstay
Country accommodation, usually on a working farm.
Self-contained
Separate self-contained accommodation, with kitchen and living/dining room. Breakfast provisions usually provided at least for the first night.
Separate/suite
Similar to self-contained but without kitchen facilities. Living/dining facilities may be limited.

Bathrooms
Ensuite and private bathrooms are for your use exclusively.
Guests share bathroom means you will be sharing with other guests.
Family share means you will be sharing with the family.

Tariff
The prices listed are in New Zealand dollars and include GST. Prices listed are subject to change, and any change to listed prices will be stated at time of booking. Some hosts offer a discount for children - this applies to age 12 or under unless otherwise stated. Most of our B&Bs will accept credit cards.

Reservations
We recommend you contact your hosts well in advance to be sure of confirming your accommodation. Most hosts require a deposit so make sure you understand their cancellation policy. Please let your hosts know if you have to cancel, they will have spent time preparing for you. You may also book accommodation through some travel agents or via specialised B&B reservation services.

Breakfast & Dinner
Breakfast is included in the tariff, with each host offering their own menu. You'll be surprised at the range of delicious breakfasts available, many using local produce. If you would like dinner most hosts require 24 hours notice.

Smoking
Most of our B&Bs are non-smoking, but smoking is permitted outside. Listings displaying the no smoking logo do not permit smoking anywhere on the property. B&Bs which have a smoking area inside mention this in their text.

Accessibility
    Certified as being wheelchair accessible.

Schedule of Standards

General

Friendly, warm greeting at door by host
Local tourism and transport information available to guests
Property appearance neat and tidy, internally and externally
Absolute cleanliness of the home in all areas used by the guests
Absolute cleanliness of kitchen, refrigerator and food storage areas
Gate or roadside identification of property
Protective clothing and footwear available for farmstay guests
Hosts accept responsibility to comply with local body bylaws
Host will be present to welcome and farewell guests
Hosts' pets and young children mentioned in listing
Smoke alarms in each guest bedroom and above each landing
Evacuation advice card displayed in each bedroom (recommended)
Working torch beside every bed
Suitable fire extinguisher in kitchen and on landing of each upper floor (recommended)
Fire blanket in kitchen (recommended)

Hosts accept responsibility to comply with applicable laws and regulations

Fire safety laws and requirements
Insurances
Swimming and spa pool regulations
Other laws impacting on operation of a B&B

Bedrooms

Each bedroom solely dedicated to guests with...
Bed heating
Heating
Light controlled from the bed
Wardrobe space with variety of hangers
Drawers
Good quality floor covering
Mirror
Power point near a mirror
Waste paper basket
Drinking glasses
Clean pillows with additional available
No Host family items stored in the room
Night light for guidance to w.c. if not adjacent to bedroom
Blinds or curtains on all windows where appropriate
Good quality mattresses in sound condition on a sound base
Clean bedding appropriate to the climate, with extra availabl

Bathroom & toilet facilities

At least one bathroom adequately ventilated and equipped with...
Bath or shower
Wash handbasin and mirror
Covered wastebasket in bathroom
Extra toilet roll
Lock on bathroom and toilet doors
Electric razor point if bedrooms are without a suitable power point
Soap, towels, bathmat, facecloths, fresh for each new guest
Towels changed or dried daily for guests staying more than one night
Sufficient bathroom and toilet facilities to serve family and guests

New Zealand and Regions

Northland

Whangarei

Auckland

Coromandel

Bay of Plenty

Tauranga

Waikato, King Country

Hamilton

Rotorua

Gisborne

Taranaki, Wanganui,
Ruapehu, Rangitikei

Gisborne

New Plymouth

Napier

Manawatu, Horowhenua

Hawkes Bay

Nelson, Golden Bay

Palmerston North

Wairarapa

Masterton

Nelson

Blenheim

Wellington

West Coast

Greymouth

Marlborough

Canterbury

Christchurch

Timaru

South Canterbury,
North Otago

Queenstown

Dunedin

Otago, North Catlins

Invercargill

Southland,
South Catlins

Stewart Island

Contents

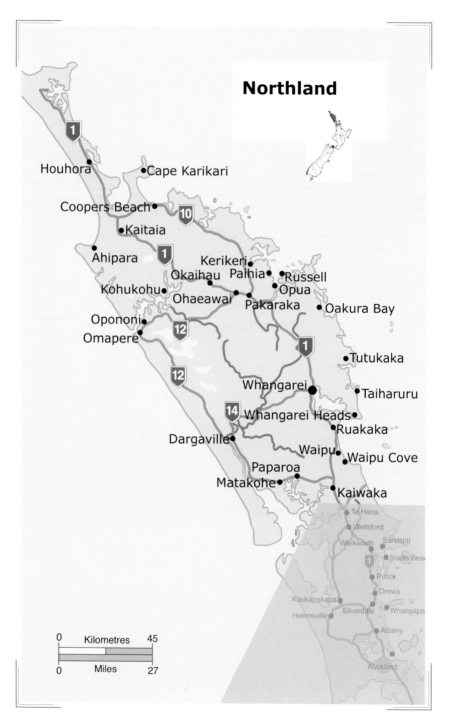

Northland

Houhora
•Cape Karikari
Coopers Beach•
Kaitaia
Ahipara
Kerikeri
Okaihau Paihia•
Kohukohu•
Ohaeawai
Pakaraka
Opononi•
Omapere
Opononi•

Russell
Opua
Oakura Bay

Tutukaka
Whangarei
Taiharuru
Whangarei Heads•
Dargaville•
Ruakaka
Waipu
Waipu Cove
Paparoa
Matakohe•
Kaiwaka
Te Hana
Wellsford
Warkworth Sandspit
Snells Bea
Puhoi
Orewa
Kaukapakapa•
Helensville Silverdale Whangapa
Albany
Auckland

0   Kilometres   45
0   Miles   27

Houhora *44 km N of Kaitaia*

Houhora Lodge & Homestay *Homestay*
Jacqui & Bruce Malcolm
3994 Far North Road, Houhora, RD 4, Kaitaia

Tel (09) 409 7884 or 021 926 992
Fax (09) 409 7801
houhora.homestay@xtra.co.nz
www.topstay.co.nz

Double $130-$180 Single $100-$110 (Full breakfast)
Dinner $45 by arrangement
Visa MC accepted Children welcome
3 King/Twin 3 Single (3 bdrm)
Bathrooms: 2 Ensuite 1 Private

We have fled our largest city with Rusty our Red Heeler dog to live on the shores of Houhora Harbour, and look forward to sharing this special part of New Zealand with you. Come and enjoy remote coastal walks, shell-collecting, Cape Reinga, 90 Mile Beach and other attractions. We can arrange 4x4 trips, sport or game fishing and provide relaxed and quality accommodation on your return. Home-made bread, home-grown fruit, home-pressed olive oil, vegetables and eggs. Email, internet, fax and laundry facilities available.

Cape Karikari - Whatuwhiwhi *30 km SE of Kaitaia*

Riviera Lodge *Luxury B&B Apartment with Kitchen*
Janine & Rex Honeyfield
69A Whatuwhiwhi Road, RD 3, Cape Karikari, Kaitaia

Tel (09) 406 7596 or 021 277 2510
Fax (09) 406 7581 riviera.lodge@xtra.co.nz
www.rivieralodge.co.nz

Double $130-$180 Single $120-$150
(Continental breakfast)
Children over 12 $40
High rate 10 Dec-28 Feb including public holidays
Visa MC accepted Children welcome
1 Queen 1 Double 1 Single (1 bdrm)
Bathrooms: 1 Ensuite Shower

Riviera Lodge is a Luxury B&B and semi self contained unit nestled on the edge of Doubtless Bay set alongside native bush, 15 minutes off Highway 10 Whatuwhiwhi, Cape Karikari. Recreational activities: rock fishing, diving, swimming, also fishing trips arranged. Walk to Perihipi Bay, handy to Matai Bay, Rangiputa and Tokerau beach. Just minutes to Carrington Resort which has a 18 hole golf course, winery and restaurant. Close to dairy. Janine, Rex, our dog Duke and cat Brandy welcome you to the winterless north.

Coopers Beach *3 km N of Mangonui*

Mac'n'Mo's *B&B*
Maureen & Malcolm MacMillan
PO Box 177, Mangonui 0442
104 State Highway 10, Coopers Beach, Mangonui

Tel (09) 406 0538
Fax (09) 406 0538
MacNMo@xtra.co.nz

Double $100 Single $60 (Continental breakfast)
Pet free home
Not suitable for children
2 Queen 1 Double 1 Twin (4 bdrm)
Bathrooms: 2 Ensuite 1 Private

Enjoy a million dollar view of Doubtless Bay while you enjoy Mac's smoked fish on your toast. The bus to Cape Reinga stops at our gate, you may go on a craft or wine trail, swim with dolphins, go fishing, diving or just relax on our unpolluted uncrowded beaches, there's one across the road. There are several fine restaurants and the world famous fish and chip shop nearby. Have a memorable stay with Mac'n'Mo, they will take good care of you.

Coopers Beach *4 km N of Mangonui*

Doubtless Bay Lodge *B&B*

Barbara & Ian Easterbrook
33 Cable Bay Block Road, Coopers Beach, Mangonui

Tel (09) 406 1661 or 021 824 571
Fax (09) 406 1662
enquiries@doubtlessbaylodge.co.nz
www.doubtlessbaylodge.co.nz

Double $85-$110 Single $65-$80 (Full breakfast)
Children $20
Visa MC Eftpos accepted
Children welcome
3 Queen 1 Twin (4 bdrm)
Bathrooms: 4 Ensuite

Enjoy your breakfast on the balcony or in the dining room and experience the panoramic views over Doubtless Bay and surrounding countryside. Short walk to the golden sands of Coopers Beach and local shops. Each room has its own ensuite, Sky TV, fridge, tea/coffee making facilities. Guest laundry and barbeque available. Cape Reinga tours, fishing trips and golf games can be arranged. Visit the many historic places, isolated beaches and local wineries in the area. Let us help you make this the perfect holiday destination.

Kaitaia - Pamapuria *10 km S of Kaitaia*

Plane Tree Lodge *B&B Homestay Cottage with Kitchen*

Rosemary & Mike Wright
Pamapuria, RD 2, Kaitaia, Northland

Tel (09) 408 0995 Fax (09) 408 0959
reservationsplanetreelodge@xtra.co.nz
www.plane-tree-lodge.net.nz

Double $150-$175 Single $100-$125
(Special breakfast) Children negotiable
2 S/C cottages, sleep 4 & 6 $180-$220
Visa MC accepted
Children welcome
5 Queen 2 Twin 1 Single (8 bdrm)
Bathrooms: 3 Ensuite 2 Private

Rosemary, Mike & Polly, their golden retriever welcome you to Northland, where summer lingers longer. Experience the beauty & tranquility of sub-tropical NZ. Enjoy the difference of receiving great hospitality in a quiet, peaceful rural setting with large relaxing gardens. Rosemary & Mike, your friendly knowledgable hosts love helping to plan your activities or adventures from their architectually designed home. Relax in the evening with a spa and complementary glass of wine. Wake each morning to birdsong and the aroma of a delicious breakfast.

Ahipara *15 km W of Kaitaia*

Beachfront *Luxury Apartment with Kitchen Self-contained & Serviced*

Paul & Jenny Steele
14 Kotare Street, Ahipara, 0551

Tel (09) 409 4007 or 021 256 4555
Fax (09) 409 4007
pauljenny@beachfront.net.nz
www.beachfront.net.nz

Double $150-$300 Single $150-$300 (Full breakfast)
Dinner $60pp by arrangement
Breakfast extra
Visa MC Eftpos accepted
Children and pets welcome
4 King 2 Double (2 bdrm)
Bathrooms: 4 Ensuite All bedrooms ensuite

Upmarket absolute water front self-contained seviced, private apartments. A studio covered patio with a second bedroom option. A two bedroom apartment with balconies. All bedrooms ensuite, surf views from every pillow. Paul and Jenny are fifth generatiion New Zealanders and have a cat called Sunshine who is not allowed in the apartments.

Kerikeri *3 km E of Kerikeri*

Matariki Orchard *B&B Homestay*
Alison & David Bridgman
14 Pa Road, Kerikeri, Bay of Islands

Tel (09) 407 7577 or 027 408 0621
Fax (09) 407 7593
matarikihomestay@xtra.co.nz
www.kerikeri.co.nz/matariki

Double $140-$160 Single $100 (Full breakfast)
Children negotiable
Dinner $50pp
Visa MC accepted
Pet free home Children welcome
1 King 1 Queen 2 Single (3 bdrm)
Bathrooms: 1 Ensuite 1 Private 1 Guest share

We welcome guests to our home, large garden, swimming pool and subtropical orchard, walking distance to historic area. 3 km to township David has a vintage car that is used for personalised tours. A short complimentary tour is offered of historic area We are retired farmers and David a local tour operator for nine years loves to help with where to go and what to do. Can arrange tour bookings. We enjoy providing dinner with NZ wine. No pets or children. Phone for directions.

Kerikeri - Okaihau *12 km W of Kerikeri*

Clotworthy Farmstay *B&B Farmstay*
Shennett & Neville Clotworthy
914 Wiroa Road, RD 1, Okaihau, Bay of Islands

Tel (09) 401 9371 or 027 494 1759
Fax (09) 401 9371

Double $90 Single $65 (Full breakfast)
Dinner $25 by arrangement
Visa MC accepted
1 Queen 2 Single (2 bdrm)
Bathrooms: 1 Guest share

We farm cattle, sheep and horses on our 310 acres. There are panoramic views of the Bay of Islands area from our home 1000 feet above sea level. Of 1840's pioneering descent, our interests are travel, farming, genealogy and equestrian activities. We have an extensive library on Northland history and families. Directions: SH10 take Wiroa/Airport Road at the Kerikeri intersection. 9 km on the right OR SH1, take Kerikeri Road just south of Okaihau. We are fourth house on the left, past the golf course (8 km).

Kerikeri *8 km SW of Kerikeri*

Puriri Park *B&B Cottage No Kitchen Orchardstay*
Charmian & Paul Treadwell
Puriri Park Orchard, State Highway 10,
Box 572, Kerikeri

Tel (09) 407 9818 or 027 471 4932
Fax (09) 407 9498
puriri@xtra.co.nz

Double $105 Single $85 (Full breakfast)
Children $35
Dinner $35
Children welcome
1 Queen 2 Double 2 Twin 1 Single (4 bdrm)
Bathrooms: 2 Private 2 Guest share

Puriri Park has long been known for its hospitality in the Far North. Guests are welcome to wander around our large garden, explore the kiwifruit and avocado orchards, sit by the lilypond or feed our flock of fantail pigeons. We have five acres of bird-filled native bush, mostly totara and puriri. We are in an excellent situation for trips to Cape Reinga and sailing or cruising on the beautiful Bay of Islands. We can arrange tours for you or pick you up from the airport.

Northland

Kerikeri *10 km N of Kerikeri Central*
Kerikeri Inlet View *B&B Homestay Farmstay*
Trish & Ryan Daniells
99C Furness Road, RD 3, Kerikeri

Tel (09) 407 7477
Fax (09) 407 7478
kerikeri_inlet_view@hotmail.com

Double $75 Single $45 (Full breakfast)
Children $15
Dinner $18 by arrangement
Backpackers $15 (no breakfast or water view)
Children and pets welcome
1 Queen 2 Double 2 Single (3 bdrm)
Bathrooms: 1 Ensuite 1 Private 1 Guest share

We welcome you to our spacious home on top of our 1100 acre beef and sheep farm. Enjoy the superb views of the Kerikeri Inlet and the Bay of Islands while you relax in our spa pool. Join us for breakfast consisting of seasonal fruit, home-made bread and butter, free-range chook eggs, and our own sausages, before exploring the many attractions around Kerikeri. Backpackers has private lockable bedrooms, lounge, kitchen/laundry. Note: please phone first in case we are overseas. We can speak Japanese.

Kerikeri *2 km W of Kerikeri*
Palm View *Luxury B&B*
Judy & Tony Pratt
Kotare Heights, Kerikeri, Bay of Islands

Tel (09) 407 6883 or 021 024 50615
palmview@xtra.co.nz
www.palmview.co.nz

Double $185-$300 Single $175-$295 (Full breakfast)
Dinner by arrangement
Visa MC accepted
Not suitable for children
1 King/Twin 2 King (3 bdrm)
Bathrooms: 3 Ensuite

Palm View is presently under construction, but will be open for guests December 2007. We are set in an acre of garden also under construction, but with many native shrubs and bushes.All bedrooms have luxury bathrobes, fridges, TV, electric blankets, hair dryers, iron and ironing board, coffee and tea making facilities. Your rooms have spectacular inlet views .We are 2 km from Kerikeri township where you will find many cafés, restaurants and many attraction.

Kerikeri *20 km N of Paihia*
Glenfalloch *B&B Homestay*
Keith
48 Landing Road, Kerikeri

Tel (09) 407 5471 Fax (09) 407 5473
glenfall@ihug.co.nz
www.kerikeri-accommodation.co.nz

Double $90-$115 Single $80-$90 (Full breakfast)
Children $25
Dinner $30pp by arrangement
Visa MC accepted
Children welcome
1 King 1 Queen 1 Double 1 Single (3 bdrm)
Bathrooms: 2 Ensuite 1 Private

Venture down Glenfalloch's driveway to our secluded bed and breakfast, nestled in a garden paradise. Enjoy the hospitality of Keith. Relax in the spa and swimming pool and on teh decks, or for the energetic there is lawn tennis. Glenfalloch is just 500 metres from Kerikeri's Stone Store and Kemp Mission House, and adjacent to the lovely Rainbow Falls walking track. Kerikeri is unique and offers some good golf courses within short distances, lovely shops and excellent restaurants.

Kerikeri *2 km N of Kerikeri*
Birchwood *Boutique B&B*
Pamela & Ian Adams
11 Maraenui Drive, Kerikeri

Tel (09) 401 7961 or 027 268 4848
Fax (09) 401 7962
info@birchwoodbedandbreakfast.co.nz
www.birchwoodbedandbreakfast.co.nz

Double $120-$160 (Special breakfast)
Visa MC Amex Eftpos accepted
Not suitable for children
1 King/Twin 1 Queen (2 bdrm)
Bathrooms: 1 Ensuite 1 Private

B irchwood offers the luxury of a beautifully appointed B&B in a relaxed charming country setting. Purpose built - privacy is assured with your own entrance which opens onto sunny decks where you can enjoy our popular breakfast basket each morning. A perfect base from which to explore the Bay of Islands and in walking distance to Kerikeri Village, yours hosts Pamela and Ian will happily provide you with local knowledge and at the end of the day our hot spa pool awaits you.

Paihia *7 km N of Paihia*
Lily Pond Estate B&B (Est 1989) *B&B*
Allwyn & Graeme Sutherland
725 Puketona Road, RD 1, Paihia
Lily Pond Estate sign at gate

Tel (09) 402 7041

Double $90-$105 Single $60 (Full breakfast)
1 Double 1 Twin 1 Single (3 bdrm)
Bathrooms: 1 Private 1 Guest share

D rive in through an avenue of mature Liquid Amber trees to our comfortable timber home on our five acre country estate growing citrus and pip fruit. The guest wing has views of the fountain, bird aviary, small lake and black swan with the double and twin rooms having private verandah access. Fresh orange juice, fruit and home-made jams are served at breakfast. We are born New Zealanders, and will gladly share our Bay of Island knowledge to make your visit most memorable.

Paihia *1.5 km S of Paihia*
Te Haumi House *B&B Homestay*
Enid & Ernie Walker
12 Seaview Road, Paihia

Tel (09) 402 8046
Fax (09) 402 8046
enidanderniewalker@xtra.co.nz
www.bnb.co.nz/tehaumihouse.html

Double up to $100 Single up to $70
(Continental breakfast)
Visa MC accepted
2 Queen 1 Single (2 bdrm)
Bathrooms: 1 Guest share 1 Family share

M illennium Sunrise. Welcome to our modern waterfront home, set amongst subtropical gardens with expansive harbour views, just minutes from tourist activities and town centre. Guests enjoy privacy through a clever split-level design. Buffet breakfast with a choice of dining room, garden deck or courtyard. Laundry facilities, ample off-street parking and courtesy pick up from bus available. Descendants of early settlers, we have a good knowledge of local history. Ernie is a Masonic Lodge member.

Paihia *0.5 km SE of Paihia Wharf*

Craicor Accommodation *Apartment with Kitchen*

Garth Craig & Anne Corbett
PO Box 15, 49 Kings Road, Paihia, Bay of Islands

Tel (09) 402 7882
Fax (09) 402 7883
craicor@actrix.gen.nz
www.craicor-accom.co.nz

Double $160 Single $120 (Breakfast by arrangement)
Continental breakfast optional $7.50pp
Visa MC Amex accepted
Not suitable for children
2 King 2 Single (2 bdrm)
Bathrooms: 2 Ensuite

The perfect spot for those seeking a quiet, sunny and central location. Discover the Garden Suite and Tree House. Self-contained modern apartments nestled in a garden setting with trees that almost hug you, native birds and sea views. Each apartment has ensuite bathroom, fully equipped kitchen for self-catering, super king bed, TV, insect screens and is tastefully decorated to reflect the natural colours of the surroundings. Safe off-street parking, all within a five minute stroll to the waterfront, restaurants and town centre.

Paihia *0.5 km NW of Paihia*

Windermere *B&B Apartment with Kitchen*

Richard & Jill Burrows
168 Marsden Road, Paihia, Bay of Islands

Tel (09) 402 8696 or 021 115 7436
Fax (09) 402 5095
windermere@igrin.co.nz
www.windermere.co.nz

Double $120-$220 Single $100-$180
(Continental breakfast)
Children $25 Extra adult $50
Visa MC accepted
2 Queen 2 Single (2 bdrm)
Bathrooms: 2 Ensuite

Windermere is a large modern family home set in a bush setting and yet located right on one of the best beaches in the Bay of Islands. Superior accommodation is provided with suites having their own ensuite and kitchen facilities. For longer stays one suite has its own laundry, dryer and fully equipped kitchen. The other suite has microwave and fridge only. Each suite has its own decks where you can sit and enjoy the view enhanced by spectacular sunsets. Sky TV. Outdoor Spa.

Paihia *6 km W of Paihia*

Appledore Lodge *Luxury B&B Separate Suite Cottage with Kitchen*

Janet & Jim Pugh
624 Puketona Road, Paihia, Bay of Islands

Tel (09) 402 8007 Fax (09) 402 8007
appledorelodge@xtra.co.nz
www.appledorelodge.co.nz

Double $120-$250 Single $120-$180
(Continental breakfast)
Unsuitable for children under 12
Minimum 4 nights over Christmas & New Year
Visa MC Amex accepted
2 King/Twin 1 Queen (3 bdrm)
Bathrooms: 3 Ensuite Large ensuites

Miniature waterfalls and rapids await your discovery as the Waitangi River gently tumbles past your bedroom window. Tranquillity and peace is here to rediscover with our spellbinding riverside setting where you can fish for trout or stroll the riverbank. Set in two acres all our accommodation have magnificent views up & down the river, are self-contained with ensuite and private decks where Janet's special home-made breakfast basket is provided for your enjoyment. Janet, Jim & Misty our golden retriever look forward to meeting you

Paihia *0.2 km N of Paihia Central*

Allegra House *B&B Apartment with Kitchen*
Heinz & Brita Marti
39 Bayview Road, Paihia, Bay of Islands

Tel (09) 402 7932 or 027 470 1137
Fax (09) 402 7930
allegrahouse@xtra.co.nz
www.allegra.co.nz

Double $125-$210 Single $120-$210
(Continental breakfast) Children negotiable
Apartment $165-$240
Visa MC accepted
1 King/Twin 1 King 1 Queen (3 bdrm)
Bathrooms: 3 Ensuite

Allegra House, our spacious, modern home is centrally located, just up the hill from Paihia's wharf, shops and restaurants. Spectacular views from all rooms. B&B rooms have ensuite bathroom, tea/coffee making facilities, fridge, TV and balcony. Self catering apartment with separate bedroom, large bathroom, fully equipped kitchen and spacious lounge opening onto a large balcony. Each room has its own air conditioning and the whole house is smokefree. BBQ, laundry facilities and internet access. Plenty of good local information.

Paihia *0.5 km SW of Post Office*

Decks of Paihia *B&B Country B&B*
Philip & Wendy Hopkinson
69 School Road, Paihia, Bay of Islands

Tel (09) 402 6146 or 021 278 7558
Fax (09) 402 6147
info@decksofpaihia.com
www.decksofpaihia.com

Double $145-$220 (Continental breakfast)
Visa MC accepted
Not suitable for children
3 King/Twin (3 bdrm)
Bathrooms: 3 Ensuite

Newly constructed purpose built home incorporating three guest suites with private ensuite bathrooms. Quiet peaceful central Paihia location, stylishly furnished very comfortable interior with ample living space. Beautiful sun drenched decks offer a relaxed outdoor living area. Philip and Wendy have enjoyed many years in the hospitality industry and are happy to share their extensive knowledge of the Northland region with you. Philip has strong links to the area - his great grandfather Patrick McGovern was Russell's police constable during the 1880s.

Paihia *1 km N of Information Centre*

Strawberry Fields B&B *B&B*
Sandy
26 Seaview Road, Paihia, 0200

Tel (09) 402 5128 or 027 280 8960
sandysea@xtra.co.nz
www.strawberryfields.net.nz

Double $110-$180 Single $90-$110 (Special breakfast)
Visa MC accepted
Not suitable for children
Pets welcome
2 Queen 1 Single (2 bdrm)
Bathrooms: 2 Ensuite

Lace, fine linen and lavender greet one in our very private and quiet home in a bush setting with scenic sea views. Large guest lounge with all amenities, private entrance. BBQ and spa pool available. Local art work adorns the walls. Well travelled Kiwi/American and Dutch hosts welcome you, also one cat and a dog. Large home baked and local treats for breakfast and afternoon teas. Off-street parking, ten minute walk to town. Laundry and internet available.

Paihia *0.2 km S of Paihia Wharf*

Chalet Romantica *B&B Apartment with Kitchen*

Ed & Inge Amsler

6 Bedggood Close, Paihia, Bay of Islands, 0200

Tel (09) 402 8270 or 027 226 6400
Fax (09) 402 8278
info-chalet@xtra.co.nz
www.chaletromantica.homestead.com/accom1.html

Double $135-$210 Single $125-$210
(Continental breakfast $ 15pp)
Children $ 15 when sharing room with parents
Apartments $155-$255
Visa MC Eftpos accepted
2 King/Twin 1 Queen (3 bdrm)
Bathrooms: 2 Ensuite 1 Private

Spoil yourself and experience the magic of Chalet Romantica. Each room has its own balcony with superb seaviews, quality furnishings and fittings, wireless internet, crisp linen and extra comfy beds. Central town location within a stroll to shops, wharf, restaurants etc. In house pool, spa, gym and laundry facilities. Gourmet breakfast served in stunning conservatory overlooking the Bay. We'd love to welcome you and to share our slice of paradise with you!

~

Paihia *7 km N of Paihia*

Quilters Rest *B&B Separate Suite*

Sue & Andy Brown

41 Retreat Road, Paihia, Bay of Islands

Tel (09)402 6047 or 021 164 7483
a.s.brown@xtra.co.nz

Double $120-$180 (Breakfast by arrangement)
Visa MC accepted
1 Queen (1 bdrm)
Bathrooms: 1 Ensuite

Enjoy the peace and tranquility at our private located home. Set in three acres of English style gardens, situated in beautiful countryside. Minutes from the waterfront of Paihia and within easy reach of all that the Bay of Islands and Northland offers. Relax by the pool and spa, for your exclusive use or just watch the sunset. A slice of paradise in your private suite with husband and wife hosts discretely on hand, devoted to making your stay completely memorable. Resident horse called 'Bear'.

~

Paihia - Opua *5 km S of Paihia*

Rose Cottage *B&B Separate Suite*

Pat & Don Jansen

37A Oromahoe Road, Opua 0200, Bay of Islands

Tel (09) 402 8099 Fax (09) 402 8096
rosecottageopua@paradise.net.nz
www.bnb.co.nz/rosecottageopua.html

Double $100-$120 (Full breakfast)
Pet free home
Not suitable for children
1 Queen 1 Double (2 bdrm)
Bathrooms: 1 Private

Our home overlooks a bush garden and picturesque upper harbour and rural views. The guest wing is separate from host accommodation with private entrance, fridge, microwave, tea/coffee facilities and TV. Private bathroom / separate toilet for exclusive guest use with the option of one party or shared facilities. Comfortable rooms enjoy sea views. We are both retired and have been hosting guests since 1987. Our interests include local history, gardening fishing, sailing and walking. We look forward to helping you enjoy your stay. Inspections welcome.

Paihia - Opua *5 km S of Paihia*

Seascape *B&B Homestay Self-contained Flat*
Vanessa & Frank Leadley
17 English Bay Road, Opua, Bay of Islands

Tel (09) 402 7650 or 027 475 6793
Fax (09) 402 7650
frankandvanessa@leadley.co.nz

Double $140-$160 Single $80 (Special breakfast)
Self-contained flat $140-$160
Visa MC accepted
1 Queen (1 bdrm)
Bathrooms: 1 Ensuite

Photo Taken From House

Seascape is on a tranquil bush-clad ridge. Enjoy spectacular views, stroll through bush to the coastal walk-way, enjoy our beautifully landscaped garden, experience the many activities in the Bay, or relax on your own deck. We are keen NZ and international travellers. Other interests include music, art, gardening, fishing, boating, and Rotary. Our fully self-contained flat has queen-size bed, TV, laundry, kitchen, BBQ, own entrance and deck. You are welcome to join us for breakfast or to look after yourselves.

Paihia - Opua *5 km S of Paihia*

Pt Veronica Lodge *B&B Homestay*
Audrey & John McKiernan
39 Point Veronica Drive, Opua, Bay of Islands

Tel (09) 402 5579 Fax (09) 402 5579
stay@ptveronicalodge.co.nz
www.ptveronicalodge.co.nz

Double $160-$190 Single $100-$160 (Full breakfast)
Visa MC accepted
1 King/Twin 1 Queen (2 bdrm)
Bathrooms: 2 Ensuite

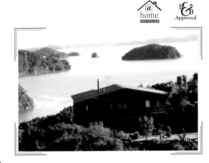

On the coast between Paihia and Opua located above the coastal track with views towards Paihia and Russell. A special place, peaceful, romantic, restful, with bush and coastal walks. We invite you to soak in the spa or rest on the decks. Bedrooms are air conditioned with views over an inlet. Shops, cafés and resturants are within ten minutes drive. An ideal base to explore the Bay of Islands and Northland. Audrey, John and our friendly dogs, Bonnie & Clyde, welcome you.

Paihia - Opua *5 km S of Paihia*

Waterview Lodge *B&B Apartment with Kitchen Cottage with Kitchen*
Antionette & Jess Cherrington
14 Franklin Street, Opua, Bay of Islands 0290

Tel (09) 402 7595 Fax (09) 402 7596
info@waterviewlodge.co.nz
www.waterviewlodge.com

Double $140-$230 Single $100-$140 (Full breakfast)
Children $20 Dinner $40-$50 Studio $150
Garden Unit $150-$200 Cottage $180-$300
Visa MC Amex Eftpos accepted
Children welcome
3 King 3 Queen 1 Double 1 Twin 5 Single (8 bdrm)
Bathrooms: 3 Ensuite 2 Private bath in cottage

Overlooking the picturesque Port of Opua, Waterview Lodge is a quality accommodation establishment. The Harbour and River Suites have expansive sea views of Opua. quality linen, ensuite, TV, CD, telephone, fridge and tea making facilities. Breakfasts are complimentary with the suites. The three bedroom cottage is a charming residence capturing sun and sea views. The two bedroom Garden unit is located next to the garden suite. We enjoy living at Waterview Lodge with our two sons, Ben 20 and Oliver 13, and our little dog Amy.

Northland

Russell *0.1 km W of Russell Central*

Te Manaaki *Apartment with Kitchen*

Sharyn & Dudley Smith
2 Robertson Road, PO Box 203, Russell 0242

Tel (09) 403 7200 or 021 972 171
Fax (09) 403 7537
triple.b@xtra.co.nz
www.bay-of-islands.co.nz/accomm/tmanaaki.html

Double $150-$280 Single $150-$280 (Full breakfast)
Children $20
Visa MC accepted
Children welcome
2 King (2 bdrm)
Bathrooms: 2 Ensuite

Te Manaaki overlooks the picturesque harbour and village of historic Russell with its delightful seaside restaurants, shops and wharf a gentle stroll away. Magnificent harbour, bush and village views are a feature of guests private accommodation. The Villa is an attractively appointed sunny spacious deluxe unit set in its own grounds (with garden spa) adjacent to the main house. The Studio is a self-contained suite-styled apartment on the ground floor of our new modern home. Both units have mini-kitchen facilities, Sky TV & off-street parking.

Russell *1 km NW of Russell Central*

Arapohue House *B&B*

Bradley & Vivienne Morrison
9 Wellington Street, Russell, Bay of Islands

Tel 09 403 8109 or 027 272 8881
021 943 484
Fax (09) 203 8107
arapohuehouse@xtra.co.nz
www.bay-of-islands.co.nz/accomm/arapohue

Double $160-$220 Single $140-$165 (Full breakfast)
Visa MC Eftpos accepted
Pet free home Not suitable for children
2 Queen (2 bdrm)
Bathrooms: 2 Ensuite all ensuite

This beautiful old bungalow has been rebuilt recently. Only 200 metres from Russell Beach, it is an easy leisurely, level walk to all the fine restaurants and coffee houses. Historic Russell, with it's museum and craft shops, offers natural history with nature walks, and beautiful beaches. We can organise any trips you wish, or alternately, you are welcome to spend time in our beautiful garden with a great book. All bedrooms have tea & coffee facilities, digital radio clocks, hair dryers & colour TV.

Russell - Okiato *9 km S of Russell*

Aimeo Cottage *B&B Cottage with Kitchen*

Annie & Helmuth Hormann
26 Okiato Point Road, Russell

Tel (09) 403 7494 or 027 272 2393
aimeo@xtra.co.nz
www.bay-of-islands.co.nz/aimeo

Double up to $175 Single $125-$155
(Special breakfast) Children $25
3 double bedroom holiday home with superb view
Visa MC accepted
Children welcome
2 King/Twin 1 King 1 Single (2 bdrm)
Bathrooms: 1 Ensuite 1 Private

A quiet place to relax. We have sailed half way around the world to find this beautiful quiet place in the heart of the Bay of Islands and would be happy to share this with you for a while. Aimeo Cottage is built on the hill of Okiato Point, overlooking the bay. In ten minutes you are in NZ's first capital, Russell, the site of many historic buildings, an interesting museum and art galleries For golfers, a complimentary set of clubs available (men's and women's).

Russell - Matauwhi Bay *1 km E of Russell*

Ounuwhao B&B *B&B Separate Suite Cottage with Kitchen Seperate Suite*

Marilyn Nicklin
16 Hope Avenue, Matauwhi Bay, Russell
The Heart of the Bay of Islands

Tel (09) 403 7310 or 027 414 1310
Fax (09) 403 8310   thenicklins@xtra.co.nz
www.bedandbreakfastbayofislands.co.nz

Double $250-$350 Single $160-$200 (Full breakfast)
Children under 12 $45
Self-contained & garden suite double $280-$350
Visa MC accepted
2 King 4 Queen 3 Twin 2 Single (7 bdrm)
Bathrooms: 5 Ensuite 2 Private

Welcome to historic Russell, the Heart of the Bay of Islands and the first settled area of NZ. Take a step back into a bygone era and spend some time with us in our delightful, nostalgic, immaculately restored Victorian villa (Circa 1894).

Enjoy your own large guest lounge; tea/coffee and biscuits always available, with open fire in the cooler months, and wrap-around verandahs for you to relax and take in the warm sea breezes. Each of our four queen rooms have traditional wallpapers and paintwork, with hand-made patchwork quilts and fresh flowers to create a lovingly detailed, traditional romantic interior.

Breakfast is served in our farmhouse kitchen around the large kauri dining table or alfresco on the verandah if you wish. It is an all home-made affair; from the freshly baked fruit and nut bread, to the yummy daily special and the jam conserves.

Our self-contained cottage is set in park-like grounds for your privacy and enjoyment: with two double bedrooms, it is ideal for a family or two couples travelling together. It has

a large lounge overlooking the reserve and out into the bay, a sunroom and fully self-contained kitchen. Wonderful for people looking for that special place for peace and time-out. Maximum four persons. Breakfast is available if required. Complimentary afternoon tea on arrival. Laundry service available.

We look forward to meeting you soon. Our homes are SMOKE-FREE. We are closed June and July.
EXPERIENCE OUR HISTORIC B&B. ENJOY A WORLD OF DIFFERENCE.

Russell - Te Wahapu *7 km S of Russell*

Bay of Island Cottages *B&B Cottage with Kitchen*
Jenny & Peter Sharpe
92B Te Wahapu Road, RD 1, Russell

Approved

Tel (09) 403 7757 or 0800 274 727
Fax (09) 403 7758
enquires@bayofislandscottages.co.nz
www.bayofislandscottages.co.nz/

Double $200-$250 Single $170-$200 (Special breakfast)
Dinner $45pp by arrangement
Visa MC accepted
Not suitable for children
1 King/Twin 3 Queen 1 Single (4 bdrm)
Bathrooms: 4 Ensuite

At the end of a little road which winds down to the water are four charming and stylish cottages. Their position makes them ideal for a summer holiday in the north, a romantic honeymoon or weekend. Here you can spend time in peace and privacy enjoying the sun, fresh air and views over the bay just below.

Each cottage is secluded within the garden and has a wide sunny terrace to make the most of the outdoors. The artistically furnished interiors include a spacious lounge/ bedroom, a well equipped kitchenette and ensuite. For your comfort there are top quality beds and bedding, cotton sheets, soft robes and towels. For your enjoyment there are books, magazines, TV , fresh flowers and home baking.

Breakfast is a special event with fine china, linen and silver. Each morning guests gather around our big table to share experiences, good food and conversation. Where possible the café style fare is from our own organic garden with free range eggs and local specialities.

Historic Russell is just seven minutes away by car and we can help you with maps and suggestions for local walks and sightseeing trips. For a quiet day at home our dinghy is on the beach ready for fishing or a leisurely paddle out in the bay.

Russell *1 km E of Russell*

Lesley's *B&B*

B&B
Approved

Lesley Coleman
1 Pomare Road, Russell, Northland

Tel (09) 403 7099 or 021 108 0369
three.gs@xtra.co.nz
www.bay-of-islands.co.nz/accomm/lesley.html

Double $140-$160 Single $105-$120
(Special breakfast) Children $30
Dinner $25
Visa MC accepted
Children welcome
1 Queen 2 Single (2 bdrm)
Bathrooms: 1 Private clawfoot bath, shower and toilet

Walk beside a palm cluster to our secluded home inspired by living in Greece. See Matauwhi Bay and overseas yachts from the deck. Enjoy breakfast (with organic emphasis) and eggs from our hens in the cosy guest conservatory. Our guest room has its own entrance and tea/coffee making facilities. Lesley's original artwork is on the walls and the private bathroom features a clawfoot bath. Guestbook comments: " We came exhausted and left refreshed!" "Awesome waffles." Billy the terrier lives here too. Welcome.

Russell *0.5 km N of Russell*

La Veduta *Homestay*

B&B
Approved

Danielle & Dino Fossi
11 Gould Street, Russell, Bay of Islands

Tel (09) 403 8299 Fax (09) 403 8299
laveduta@xtra.co.nz
www.laveduta.co.nz

Double $180-$200 Single $150-$180 (Full breakfast)
King-size room $220
Visa MC accepted
1 King 1 Queen 2 Double 1 Single (5 bdrm)
Bathrooms: 3 Ensuite 2 Private

La Veduta. Enjoy our mix of traditional European culture in the midst of the beautiful Bay of Islands. Historic heartland of New Zealand. La Veduta is the perfect pied a terre for your Northland holiday. We offer our guests a warm welcome and personalised service. All our bedrooms are individually styled, offering full sea view. A delicious cooked breakfast is served on the balcony. We can arrange tours and activities. Restaurants, beach, ferries handy. French and Italian spoken. Complimentary afternoon tea.

Russell *0.4 km N of Russell Central*

A Place in the Sun *B&B Separate Suite Apartment with Kitchen*

B&B
Approved

Pip & Oliver Campbell
57 Upper Wellington Street,
Russell 0202, Bay of Islands

Tel (09) 403 7615 Fax (09) 403 7610
sailing@paradise.net.nz
www.aplaceinthesun.co.nz

Double $130-$170 Single $100-$140
(Breakfast by arrangement)
Children by arrangement
Group of 4 $250-$280
Visa MC accepted Pet free home
2 Queen 1 Double (3 bdrm)
Bathrooms: 2 Ensuite

Welcome to our special place, 'Romantic Russell', this retired Kiwi sailing couple's perfect anchorage. Choose the Fern or Bay View, (combined for four guests) two private, queen bedroom ensuite apartments. TVs, barbecues. Great views overlooking Russell village and the Bay. Ranchsliders open to patio and garden(no stairs). Sunny, peaceful setting bordering bush reserve (kiwi habitat). Uncrowded beaches, heritage trails, brilliant night sky, cleaner air! Ideal for relaxing holidays or honeymoons. All cruises depart Russell. Cruise, sail or simply unwind. A different world. It's Paradise.

Northland

Russell *0.2 km N of Russell Central*

Villa Russell *Luxury B&B*

Sue & Steve Western
2 Little Queen Street, Russell, Bay of Islands

Tel (09) 403 8845 or 027 492 8912
Fax (09) 403 8845
info@villarussell.co.nz
www.kingfishercharters.co.nz

Double $165-$320 (Full breakfast)
Rollaway bed available for children up to 6
Visa MC accepted
1 King/Twin 2 Queen (3 bdrm)
Bathrooms: 3 Ensuite

Enjoy a welcoming visit to Villa Russell, two minutes from the beach and Russell's restaurants. Relax with magnificent views of the bay and wharf from the deck of our beautifully restored 1910 Villa, or from one of two spacious suites in the new guest cottage. A short walk takes you to a surf beach or up the historic Flagstaff Hill. Off-street parking provided. Charters on our 11.6 metre yacht Kingfisher may also be arranged to sail the Bay of Islands. Friendly family dog.

Russell *0.5 km SE of Russell*

Arcadia Lodge *Luxury B&B*

Brad Mercer & David McKenzie
10 Florance Avenue, Russell, 0255

Tel (09) 403 7756
Fax (09) 403 7721
arcadia@arcadialodge.co.nz
www.arcadialodge.co.nz

Double $175-$295 Single $100-$195 (Full breakfast)
Visa MC Eftpos accepted
Not suitable for children
2 King 2 Queen 3 Double (6 bdrm)
Bathrooms: 4 Ensuite 1 Private 1 Guest share

History, charm, good food and glorious view - Arcadia overlooks Russell's stunning Matauwhi Bay. Breakfast on the deck with fresh Kerikeri orange juice, northland fruit, our own home made muesli and jams, organic coffee and teas, followed by a delicious, daily café-style cooked special. All served with 180 degree views of water, bush and yachts. The house is furnished with a blend of the traditional and contemporary on original honey-coloured kauri floorboards, creating a warm, comfortable space in which to unwind. Come relax with us.

Russell - Te Wahapu *7 km W of Russell*

360 View *B&B*

Silvia & Peter
89B Te Wahahpu Road, Russell, 0272

Tel (09) 403 7573 or 027 454 3315
360view@tewahapu.co.nz
www.tewahapu.co.nz

Double $150-$195 (Special breakfast)
Dinner by arrangement
2 night minimum
2 King (2 bdrm)
Bathrooms: 2 Ensuite

Welcome to our century old villa in its tranquil surrounding. Relax in your private, spacious studio with 360 degree view over scenic reserve, inner bays, to Waitangi - Paihia. You will wake to the songs of tuis and fantails, a stunning sunrise and breakfast is served on the sunny front verandah. We are of Dutch-Swiss-Italian origin, and after owning a local restaurant for ten years, we are looking forward to host you and tantalize your tastebuds with fresh produce. Pets on the property.

Russell - Te Wahapu *7 km S of Russell*

A Tranquil Place *B&B*

Susanne & Uwe
14 Major Bridge Drive, off Te Wahapu Road,
Russell, 0242

Tel (09) 403 7588
Fax (09) 403 7588
TranquilPlace@xtra.co.nz
www.atranquilplace.co.nz

Double $150-$180 Single $120-$150
(Special breakfast)
Dinner by arrangement
Visa MC accepted
1 Queen (1 bdrm)
Bathrooms: 1 Ensuite

Our cosy home is nestled in native bush on Te Wahapu peninsula opposite historic Russell. You can access the secluded beach via a footpath next to the house and may use our rowing dinghy. Otherwise just relax on our spacious deck, go for a walk, enjoy romantic Russell or join a coach or boat trip to explore the further environment. We speak German and we love sailing, golfing & travelling, have been living in Asia for more than ten years.

Russell - Okiato *9 km SW of Russell*

Pipiroa Bay Homestay and Garden *B&B Apartment with Kitchen*

Paula & Gary Franklin
348 Aucks Road, Russell, 0272

Tel (09) 403 8856 or 027 295 3640
Fax (09) 403 8856   gpfranklin@xtra.co.nz
www.bay-islands.co.nz/accomm/pipiroa.html

Double $120-$150 Single $80-$120 (Full breakfast)
Children $20
Dinner $30pp includes glass of wine
Waterbased activities from $20pp
Visa MC accepted
Pet free home Children and pets welcome
2 Queen 1 Double 2 Single (4 bdrm)
Bathrooms: 2 Ensuite 1 Guest share

Nestled in the hillside, overlooking historically significant Pipiroa Bay, at Okiato Point, handy to Russell, Opua and Paihia, our warm north facing purpose built homestay bed and breakfast will delight you. As Kiwis, with years of sailing experience in the Bay of Islands, we will ensure you enjoy the best the Bay can offer. Choose from our self contained apartment and bed and breakfast suite and savour our delicious breakfast using fresh produce from the garden. Other meals by arrangement.

Russell *0.4 km N of Russell Centre*

Russell Bay Lodge *Luxury B&B*

Aom & Dave Metcalfe
71 Wellington Street, Russell, 0202

Tel (09) 403 7376 Fax (09) 403 7376
info@russellbay.co.nz
www.russellbay.co.nz

Double $150-$320 (Continental breakfast provisions)
Visa MC accepted
Pet free home
Not suitable for children
2 King (2 bdrm)
Bathrooms: 2 Ensuite

Romantic Russell, luxury accommodation, fabulous bay views ... our contemporary Russell Bay Lodge has an idyllic location on the slopes of Flagstaff Hill overlooking the township and its beautiful harbour. It is just a short walk to waterfront cafés, shops and al fresco dining. The purpose designed accommodation offers king suites with mini kitchen, TV/DVD/HiFi, own entrance and own patio area. We provide a sumptuous breakfast basket each day of your stay. Perfect for a honeymoon, or that special holiday treat. Select from a wide range of local activities, then later relax on the main balcony soaking up possibly the best sea views in Russell, and relect on another memorable day in the Bay !

Northland

Russell *0.1 km E of Information Centre*

The White House *Luxury B&B*
Emma & Steve Jury
7 Church Street, Russell, 0202

Tel (09) 403 7676 or 021 241 1010
info@thewhitehouserussell.com
www.thewhitehouserussell.com

Double $195-$320 Single $175.50-$288
(Full breakfast provisions)
Visa MC Eftpos accepted
Not suitable for children under 12
3 Super king (3 bdrm)
Bathrooms: 3 Ensuite

Come and have a truly unique stay with us in one of Russell's oldest houses (circa 1840). A beautifully restored villa with plenty of character. She features three well appointed rooms with super-king size beds and fresh new ensuites along with guest lounge and full kitchen. Indulge in absolute luxury ideally situated in the heart of Russell with 12:00 midday check-out. Enjoy a dip in the spa pool, read a book on the shaded sundeck or wander to the waterfront.

Russell *5 km S of Russell*

Hardings'-Aotearoa Lodge *B&B*
Dulcie, Kate & Lindsay Hyland
39 Aucks Road, Russell, 0272

Tel (09) 403 7277 or 027 473 8170
info@the-lodge.co.nz
www.the-lodge.co.nz

Double $195-$285 Single $185-$250 (Full breakfast)
Visa MC accepted
Pet free home
Not suitable for children
2 King/Twin 2 Queen (4 bdrm)
Bathrooms: 4 Ensuite

Welcome! Set in seven acres, overlooking Orongo Bay, we are just minutes from "Romantic Russell". We have two suites in Brook Barn and two in the main Lodge. All suites are well equipped with refrigerator, tea/coffee making facilities, hair dryer, toiletries, bathrobes and irons. Our spa and sauna will help you relax. We are happy to assist with the planning of your excursions during your time in the Bay. Or you may simply choose to take things easy, and soak up the wonderful surroundings!

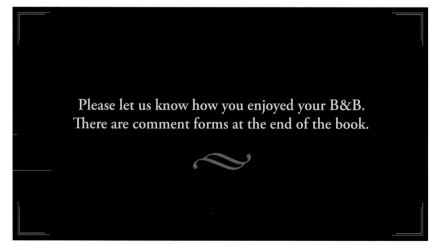

Please let us know how you enjoyed your B&B.
There are comment forms at the end of the book.

Pakaraka *15 km NW of Pahia*

Jarvis Family Farmstay & Equestrian Centre *B&B Farmstay*

Frederika & Douglas Jarvis
State Highway 1, Pakaraka, RD 2,
Ohaeawai, Bay of Islands

Tel (09) 405 9606 or 021 259 1120
Fax (09) 405 9607 baystay@igrin.co.nz
www.nzbaystay.com

Double $120-$130 Single $60-$70
(Continental breakfast)
Children under 9 half price Dinner $30 by arrangement
Discount for longer stays Visa MC accepted
2 Queen 2 Double 1 Twin (3 bdrm)
Bathrooms: 3 Private spa bathroom

The middle of everywhere en route SH1. A gateway for touring North & West Coasts and the Bay of Islands. Giant Kauri tree forest, swim with the dolphins, diving & fishing, Ngawha hot springs and pools, golf and Culture North Night Theatre.

Share the sunset at our homely, pet friendly Farmstay, with Winnie the Pooh sign at our gate. There's Winston our Great Dane and Piglet (they live with us) and outside Tigger n' Eeyore too.

Book a ride at Charlies Stables or stroll on the (30 acre) parkland to visit the horses and ponies. While the Patron can prepare a dinner party in his kitchen. Breakfast includes home made conserves, an orchard bowl of fruitfullness (parsley scrambled eggs a speciality). Al fresco dining on the deck with local wine and a crackling log chiminea.

Our fabulous subtropical palm and water garden is a bird lovers 'Bay of Islands' haven. Queensize honeymoon 4 poster bed suite and Scottish room. "Les Routiers" (UK) recommended.

Holiday bach and swimming pool planned for summer seasonclick on www.nzbaystay.com for Northland weather reports.

Northland

Opononi *50 km W of Kaikohe*

Koutu Lodge *B&B Homestay*
Tony and Sylvia Stockman
Koutu Loop Road, Opononi, RD 3, Kaikohe

Tel (09) 405 8882
Fax (09) 405 8893
koutulodgebnb@xtra.co.nz
www.wairereboulders.co.nz/koutulodge

Double $80-$100 Single $65 (Full breakfast)
Visa MC accepted
1 King 1 Queen 1 Double (3 bdrm)
Bathrooms: 2 Ensuite 1 Private

Situated on Koutu Point overlooking the beautiful
Hokianga Harbour, our home has views both rural
and sea. Two rooms have private entrances, decks, and ensuites, and are very comfortable. We are a
friendly, relaxed Kiwi couple, and our aim is to provide a memorable stay in the true B&B tradition.
Stay a while and enjoy everything the historic Hokianga has to offer. Koutu Loop Road is 4.3 km north
of Opononi then left 2.3 km on tar seal to Lodge on right.

Opononi *57 km W of Kaikohe*

Opononi Dolphin Lodge *B&B Separate Suite*
Sue & John Reynard
Corner of SH12 & Fairlie Crescent, Opononi

Tel (09) 405 8451
Fax (09) 405 8451
opononidolphinlodge@xtra.co.nz

Double $75-$105 Single $65-$95
(Continental breakfast)
Visa MC accepted
1 Queen 1 Double 1 Twin 1 Single (3 bdrm)
Bathrooms: 2 Ensuite 1 Private

Situated on the corner of Fairlie Crescent and SH12,
opposite a beach reserve on the edge of the pristine
Hokianga Harbour. Our sunsets are breathtaking. 20 minutes from "Tane Mahuta" the largest kauri tree
in the world. Step outside for picture postcard views of beautiful blue beconing waters and huge sand
dunes. Visit the boulders, sand board, walking tracks, boating, great fishing, local crafts. Come, enjoy the
friendly hospitality. The West Coast Diamond in the North awaits you.

Omapere *55 km W of Kaikohe*

Harbourside Bed & Breakfast *B&B*
Joy & Garth Coulter
State Highway 12, 1 Pioneer Walk, Omapere

Tel (09) 405 8246
harboursidebnb@xtra.co.nz

Double $95-$105 Single $70-$80
(Continental breakfast)
Visa MC accepted
1 Queen 2 Single (2 bdrm)
Bathrooms: 2 Ensuite

Our beachfront home on corner State Highway
12 and Pioneer Walk overlooking the Hokianga
Harbour is within walking distance of restaurants and
bars. Both rooms have ensuites, tea making facilities, refrigerators and TV with separate entrances onto
private decks to relax and enjoy superb views. We're close to the Waipoua Forest, West Coast beaches,
sand hills and historic Rawene. We have an interest in farming, forestry and education. Stay and share
our home and cat. Also available self catering flat.

Omapere *60 km W of Kaikohe*
Hokianga Haven Omapere Beachfront *B&B Separate Suite*

Heather Randerson
226 State Highway 12, Omapere, Hokianga

Tel (09) 405 8285 or 021 393 973
Fax (09) 405 8285
tikanga2000@xtra.co.nz
www.hokiangahaven.co.nz

Double $150-$180 Single $120-$150
(Continental breakfast)
2 night minimum stay October to March
1 Queen (1 bdrm)
Bathrooms: 1 Private

Snuggled into this peaceful private, beachfront location, our comfortable home embraces the continuously inspiring seascape of the dramatic harbour entrance and magnificent dune. Simply relaxing in this harbourside haven is revitalizing. Local artists, forest walks, horse riding, harbour cruising, fishing, river and coastal swimming are some of the natural delights to be enjoyed in this historic area. Enjoy light filled, spacious self contained facility with direct beach access. Our dog Saab is a willing walking companion. Range of healing therapies available.

Dargaville *2 km E of Dargaville*
Awakino Point Boutique Motel *Separate Suite*

June & Mick
State Highway 14, Dargaville
PO Box 168, Dargaville

Tel (09) 439 7870 or 027 451 9474
027 479 2126   Fax (09) 439 7580
awakinopoint@xtra.co.nz
www.awakinopoint.co.nz

Double $100-$125 (Continental breakfast)
Extra person $25 each
Visa MC Amex accepted
3 Queen 4 Twin (5 bdrm)
Bathrooms: 3 Ensuite private bathrooms

Unique property set on its own acreage surrounded by attractive gardens. Just two minutes drive from Dargaville on SH14 (The Whangarei Road) The best features of a NZ motel and a B&B have been amalgamated to give our guests the best of both worlds. You will enjoy your own one or two bedroom self-contained suite with private bathroom, friendly service and an attractive breakfast each morning. Guest laundry & BBQ available. Smoke-free Indoors.

Dargaville - Bayly's Beach *12 km W of Dargaville*
Ocean View *Cottage No Kitchen*

Paula & John Powell
7 Ocean View Terrace, Bayly's Beach, RD 7, Dargaville

Tel (09) 439 6256 or 021 040 0511
baylys@win.co.nz
www.bnb.co.nz/oceanview.html

Double $120 Single $80
(Continental breakfast provisions)
Children under 12 $10
Extra adult $20
Visa MC accepted Children welcome
1 Double 1 Single (1 bdrm)
Bathrooms: 1 Ensuite

Just off the trail, this expansive west coast beach is a wonderful place to relax. With a glimpse of the beach, your cottage is one minute walk to the beach and clifftop walkways. Locally enjoy the Funky Fish Café, 18-hole golf, astronomy adventures and more. Kai Iwi Lakes and Waipoua Forests are an easy day trip. Enjoy your sunny, comfortable cottage and breakfast at your leisure (provided in cottage). Internet and laundry available. With our two children, sleepy cat and delightful Jack Russell, we welcome you.

Dargaville *1.5 km S of Dargaville*

Kauri House Lodge *Luxury B&B*
Doug Blaxall
PO Box 382, Bowen Street, Dargaville

Tel (09) 439 8082 or 027 454 7769
Fax (09) 439 8082
kaurihouselodge@orcon.net.nz

Double $200-$275 Single $200 (Full breakfast)
Visa MC accepted
1 King/Twin 2 King (3 bdrm)
Bathrooms: 3 Ensuite

Kauri House Lodge sits high above Dargaville amongst mature trees. The 1880's villa retains all it's unique charm, style and grace with original kauri panelling and period antiques in all rooms.

Start your day woken by native birds, walk through extensive landscaped grounds or read in our library. In summer enjoy a dip in the large swimming pool. In winter our billiard room log fire is a cosy spot to relax for the evening.

Join Doug to explore beautiful mature native bush on the nearby farm overlooking the Wairoa River and Kaipara Harbour. The area offers many activities including deserted white sand beaches, fresh water lakes, river tours, horse treks, bush walks and restaurants.

THE MOST COMMON COMMENT IN OUR
VISITOR BOOK: "SAVE THE BEST TO LAST".

I have been hosting Bed & Breakfast for over 30 years,

"Perfect Accommodation, good host, these things make holidays worthwhile" - Frank & Annie, Holland

"Fantastic house and timber furniture, best we've seen" - Gary & Trish, Australia

Dargaville *2 km S of Dargaville*

Turiwiri B&B *B&B*

Bruce & Jennifer Crawford
Turiwiri RAPID 6775, State Highway 12, Dargaville

Tel (09) 439 6003
Fax (09) 439 6003
crawford@igrin.co.nz

Double $80 Single $40 (Continental breakfast)
2 Queen (2 bdrm)
Bathrooms: 1 Guest share Seperate Toilet

We enjoy sharing our local knowledge with guests in our modern, one level home. Excellent parking for vehicles and an expansive garden in the midst of our 37 acre working farmlet. Tarrif includes Continental Breakfast. Our family of three grown children all live away from home. Interests include family, farming, Rotary International, gardening (especially Heritage Roses) and Big Game fishing. We have Meg, a Jack Russell house dog, that loves everyone.

Dargaville - Tangowahine *25 km N of Dargaville*

Tangowahine Farmstay *Farmstay Separate Suite Cottage with Kitchen*

Pauline & Hugh Rose
1078 Tangowahine Valley Rd, RD 2 Dargaville

Tel (09) 439 1570 or 027 439 1570
027 439 1572
Fax (09) 439 5253
holiday@tangowahine.co.nz
www.tangowahine.co.nz

Double $135-$210 Single $120-$180 (Full breakfast)
Dinner $45 by arrangement
Visa MC accepted
1 King/Twin 1 King 3 Queen 4 Twin 1 Single (4 bdrm)
Bathrooms: 2 Ensuite 1 Private 1 Guest share

Tangowahine is a peaceful, private retreat on a working beef/sheep farm. Purpose built facility includes self-contained Taraire Cottage and studio en-suite, and features kauri walks, waterfalls and abundant bird life. Bush spas adjacent to cottage and garden spa near studio ensuite are chemical free, filled fresh each time. Northland's mild climate means Tangowahine is an all season destination and its central location provides proximity to kauri forests, New Zealand's longest driveable beach and many more. Numerous farm pets. Friendly assistance with Northland directions and attractions.

Matakohe *9 km S of Matakohe*

Petite Provence *B&B Homestay*

Linda & Guy Bucchi
703C Tinopai Road, RD 1 Matakohe

Tel (09) 431 7552
Fax (09) 431 7552
petite-provence@clear.net.nz
www.petiteprovence.co.nz

Double $145 Single $100 (Continental breakfast)
Dinner $40 by arrangement
Visa MC accepted
2 King/Twin 1 King 2 Queen (3 bdrm)
Bathrooms: 2 Ensuite 1 Private

Ten minutes from Matakohe Kauri museum, Petite Provence is set on seven hectares of rolling farmland. All rooms (insect screens) open onto a covered deck with panoramic and distant water views. Relaxing and peaceful atmosphere. Delicious evening meals, mediterranean, vegetarian, local cuisine. Guy is French, Linda a New Zealander. Our home in France was also a Bed & Breakfast. Loopy is our outside dog. Directions: From Matakohe museum drive 2 km towards Tinopai, turn left into Tinopai road, drive 7 km. Roadside sign on left.

Northland

Paparoa *1 km S of Paparoa*

Pioneer B&B *B&B Separate Suite Separate Luxury Cottage*

Rowie & Pete Panhuis
The Pines Road, Paparoa

Tel (09) 431 6033
pioneerbnb@xtra.co.nz
www.pioneerbnb.co.nz

Double $130 Single $100 (Special breakfast)
Children in twin room $50 each
Dinner $30 by arrangement
Children welcome
1 Queen 1 Twin (2 bdrm)
Bathrooms: 1 Ensuite 1 Guest share

Our historic kauri homestead echoes with the whispers of yesterday. Experience the ambience of the past in the self-contained comfort of 'Miss Pharaoh's Cottage'. In our unique home stay environment you may enjoy a continental breakfast, or perhaps a fresh flounder filet from the cool waters of the Kaipara Harbor. By arrangement, join us to hear Miss Pharaoh's story over a convivial glass, oysters perhaps, and a sizzling roast dinner from the Pines' original wood-fired stove. Perhaps some blackberry pie...? Pets on property.

Paparoa *7 km W of Paparoa*

Palm House *B&B Cottage with Kitchen*

Jenny & Hector MacKinnon
Pahi, RD 1, Paparoa

Tel (09) 431 6689
palmhouse@paradise.net.nz

Double $110 Single $75 (Full breakfast)
Children $55
Dinner $35
Garden cottage $110
Visa MC accepted
Children welcome
2 King/Twin 2 Queen (3 bdrm)
Bathrooms: 1 Ensuite 1 Guest share

Hector & Jenny are reknowned for their relaxed, friendly hospitality, candlelit meals of fine local produce and NZ wines. Enjoy staying at peaceful Pahi. Stroll along the tideline or stand on the wharf and watch the fish jump. Visit the largest Morton Bay Fig Tree in the Southern Hemisphere. Just 13 km from Matakohe Museum and en route to the spectacular Kauri Forest. Signposted on the main State Highway 12, travel 7 km down Pahi Road and reach Palm House.

Paparoa *1 km E of Paparoa*

The Old Post Office Guesthouse *B&B Guest House*

Janice Booth
Corner of State Highway 12 & Oakleigh Road
PO Box 79, Paparoa

Tel (09) 431 6444   Fax (09) 431 6444
paparoa.jan@xtra.co.nz

Double $95-$110 Single $50-$50
(Continental breakfast) Dinner $25
2 bedroom suite from $200 (sleeps 5)
Visa MC accepted
Children welcome
2 Queen 1 Double 2 Twin 4 Single (6 bdrm)
Bathrooms: 1 Ensuite 4 Private

From the moment you step inside you will succumb to the character and charm of this lovely old historic building (circa 1903), with delightful cottage garden and rural backdrop. Enjoy our true Kiwi hospitality, cuisine and homely atmosphere with separate guests lounges and free tea/coffee. Dinner by prior arrangement. Local restaurants Th/Fri/Sat/Sun only. Spend a day at the world famous Matakohe Kauri Museum only 8 km away or if, like us, you enjoy the outdoors, our kayaks are available to explore the nearby Kaipara Harbour.

Tutukaka Coast *29 km E of Whangarei*
Oturu Bed & Breakfast *B&B*

Hawthorne Family
31 Oturu Place, Tutukaka

Tel (09) 4343 678 or 021 216 2125
Fax (09) 4343 789
markbowen66@xtra.co.nz
http://oturu.bravehost.com/index.html

Double $120 Single $95 (Full breakfast)
Visa MC Eftpos accepted
Children welcome
1 Queen 2 Single (2 bdrm)
Bathrooms: 2 Ensuite

Overlooking Oturu Bay, we extend a warm welcome for you to join us and enjoy superior comfort and privacy in a relaxing environment. Accommodation is in new rooms, double or twin, each with separate entrances. The dining area on the deck looks out onto a stunning seascape. Just one minute away is the Tutukaka marina, which offers restaurants, shops, diving, fishing and kayaking. We are also close to several beautiful beaches and walkways. Explore the beautiful coast and enjoy the peace this location offers.

Whangarei Heads *31 km SE of Whangarei*
Manaia Gardens *Cottage with Kitchen*

Audrey & Colin Arnold
2487 Whangarei Heads Road, Taurikura, Whangarei

Tel (09) 434 0797
arnoldac@igrin.co.nz

Double $60-$80 Single $50-$60
(Accommodation only)
Children under 6 free
Extra person $10
Visa MC accepted Children welcome
2 Queen 1 Double (3 bdrm)
Bathrooms: 2 Private showers

We have a small farm with two quaint old self-contained cabins in the garden. They have comfortable beds and basic cooking facilities, (2-burner gas cooker or electric frypan), microwave, toaster, fridge, etc. There are nearby shops and galleries. Freezer space, laundry, barbecue available. This is a beautiful area with rocky bush clad hills, harbour and ocean beaches, lots of conservation land for walks. Or just relax in private. One cat. We are the only buildings in the bay. Mailbox 2487 on the Whangarei Heads Road.

Whangarei *12 km SW of Whangarei*
Owaitokamotu *B&B Homestay*

Minnie & George Whitehead
727 Otaika Valley Road, Otaika, Whangarei

Tel (09) 434 7554
Fax (09) 434 7554
minniegeorge@xtra.co.nz

Double $85-$100 Single $65 (Full breakfast)
Dinner $25 by arrangement
Children and pets welcome
2 King/Twin 2 Queen (3 bdrm)
Bathrooms: 2 Guest share

Come, enjoy the tranquility of Owaitokamotu, place of water. Magnificent rocks of all shapes and sizes, pristine bush, rambling walks, set in ten acres, easy contour. Created gardens, featuring ponds, bridges, archways, windmill, 1850s style shanty and more. Home wheelchair friendly. All bedrooms private access from exterior. TV, tea/coffee facilities. Join us for three course evening meal, $25 by arrangement. Restaurants nearby. Interests: travel, wood carving, our garden. Smoke-free indoors. Laundry facilities available. Warm welcome awaits you.

Whangarei *17 km E of Whangarei*

Parua House *B&B Homestay Farmstay*

Pat & Peter Heaslip
1113 Whangarei Heads Road,
Parua Bay RD 4, Whangarei 0174

Tel (09) 436 5855 or 021 186 5002
paruahomestay@clear.net.nz
www.paruahomestay.homestead.com

Double $150-$175 Single $90-$110 (Full breakfast)
Children half price Dinner $35
Visa MC accepted Children welcome
2 Queen 1 Twin (3 bdrm)
Bathrooms: 2 Ensuite 1 Private

Parua House is a classical colonial house, built in 1883, comfortably restored and occupying an elevated site with panoramic views of Parua Bay and the Whangarei Harbour.

The property covers 29 hectares of farmland including two protected reserves, which are rich in native trees (including kauri) and birds. Guests are welcome to explore the farm and bush, milk the jersey cow, explore the olive grove and sub-tropical orchard, or just relax in the spa pool on the veranda. (Cats and outside corgi) A safe swimming beach adjoins the farm, with a short walk to the fishing jetty; two marinas and an excellent golf course are are two minutes away.

Our wide interests include photography, patchwork quilting and horticulture.. The house is attractively appointed with antique furniture and a rare collection of spinning wheels. We have cats and an outside corgi

Awake to home-baked bread and freshly squeezed orange juice. Dine in elegant surroundings with generous helpings of home produce with our own eggs, home grown vegetables, olives and sub-tropical fruit (home-made ice cream a speciality). Pre-meal drinks and wine are provided to add to the bonhomie of an evening around a large French oak refectory table. As featured on TV's "Ansett NZ Time of Your Life" and "Corban's Taste NZ".

Whangarei *25 km SE of Whangarei*
Vealbrook B&B *B&B Homestay*

Bob & Pre Sturge
2013 McLeod Bay, Whangarei Heads, RD 4,
Whangarei Heads Road, Whangarei

Tel (09) 434 0098 Fax (09) 434 0098
pretoria@clear.net.nz
www.vealbrook.co.nz

Double $100 **Single** $85 (Full breakfast)
Children $15 Dinner $25
Self-contained unit $130 Children welcome
1 Queen 1 Double 1 Twin 3 Single (3 bdrm)
Bathrooms: 1 Guest share 1 bath, 2 showers & toilets

Stunning harbour views. Coastal scenic walks. Mountains to climb. 20 metres to the beach. Safe swimming, snorkelling, kayaking, good fishing at jetty. Local dairy nearby. Pine Golf Course 15 minutes away. Surfing ocean beach. Pleasant drive round beautiful ocean bays. The house is arranged with antique furniture. Antique lace garments on display. For breakfast enjoy Bob's home-made marmalades jellies. Freshly picked fruit and fruit juice. Vegetables, subtropical fruits. Dinner supplied on request. Pre-meal drinks. Enjoy warmth and friendliness of your hosts.

Whangarei *20 km W of Whangarei*
Juniper House *B&B Homestay*

Diane & Mike James
49 Proctor Road, Maungatapere, Whangarei

Tel (09) 434 6399 or 027 422 4498
Fax (09) 434 6399 diane.james@xtra.co.nz

Double $120-$135 **Single** $60-$70 (Full breakfast)
1 Queen 1 Double 2 Single (3 bdrm)
Bathrooms: 1 Ensuite 1 Guest share

Juniper House is a comfortable welcoming home set in a young avocado orchard. Relax in our extensive grounds, enjoy a game of tennis or swim in our saltwater pool. For the snooker enthusiast we have a full-size billiard table. We are an easy 15 minute drive from the Museum & Kiwi House, golf courses, cafés, galleries and Whangarei yacht basin. We offer full breakfast, dinner and drinks by arrangement. Our interests include sailing, fishing, classic cars and decorative art.

Whangarei - Taiharuru *25 km E of Whangarei*
Tidesong *B&B Homestay Apartment with Kitchen*

Ros & Hugh Cole-Baker
Beasley Road, Taiharuru Estuary, Whangarei

Tel (09) 436 1959 or 027 636 5888
stay@tidesong.co.nz
www.stay@tidesong.co.nz

Double $100-$120 **Single** $80-$80 (Full breakfast)
Dinner $30-$35 Children welcome
3 Queen 1 Single (3 bdrm)
Bathrooms: 2 Ensuite

From Whangarei drive east for 25 minutes to Taiharuru Estuary. Comfortable secluded accommodation in a separate upstairs flat. Full breakfast with extra home-cooked meals available. Safe kayaking and other boating from our jetty. Large garden with bush tracks and outdoor games. Close to fishing, shellfish, varied birdlife, and great walks on surf beaches and spectacular ridges. Relax afterwards in the gas-fired outdoor garden bath. Members of Northland Sustainable Tourism Charter Project. We look forward to showing you warm and friendly Northland hospitality.

Whangarei *7 km N of Whangarei City*
Lotus Lodge *B&B Farmstay*

Keith & Jill Clarke
58 Great North Road, Springs Flat, Kamo, Whangarei

Tel (09) 435 2294
Fax (09) 435 2294
lotuslodge@clear.net.nz

Double $100-$140 Single $65-$80
(Continental breakfast)
Dinner By arrangement
2 Double 1 Twin (3 bdrm)
Bathrooms: 1 Guest share

We invite you to share in our 200 acres of paradise. Two minutes from Kamo, five minutes to golf course. Experience moving cattle/sheep with farm dog Del, view native bush, find amazing limestone rocks, laze in the quietness of the garden, or read in the lounge. Make this your stop for seeing the north - beaches, fishing, diving, kauri forests, shopping, all in a day's outing. Our interests: gardening, classic cars, travel, art and people.

Whangarei Falls *6 km N of Whangarei City Center*
Totara Inn *B&B*

Chieko Osugi
56A Boundary Road, Tikipunga, Whangarei

Tel (09) 459 1818 or 021 0232 9540
Fax (09) 459 1818
chieko011003@msn.com
www.bnb.co.nz/TotaraInn.html

Double $90-$110 Single $45-$80
(Continental breakfast provisions)
Dinner $25pp on request
Pet free home
Not suitable for children
1 Double 1 Twin (2 bdrm)
Bathrooms: 1 Private 1 Guest share with/ a big bath tub

Nice cozy home in the bush in Tikipunga, Whangarei located in an outstanding landscape area. Tall Totara trees and a beautiful stream welcome you. Only five minute walk from the Whangarei Falls. Suitable for quiet retreat. Everybody is welcome, especially a single traveller!

Whangarei - Mount Tiger *18 km E of Whangarei*
Eden House *B&B Homestay*

Mike & Jane D'Alton
510 Owhiwa Road, Parua Bay, RD 1 Onerahi, Whangarei

Tel (09) 436 1938 or 027 366 4272
eden@igrin.co.nz
www.edenhomestay.co.nz

Double $120 Single $90 (Full breakfast)
Children $60, no charge for a baby sharing the room
Dinner $35/$30/$25pp - three/two/one course
Wine and drinks list available
Complimentary beverages
Visa MC accepted
1 King/Twin 2 Queen (3 bdrm)
Bathrooms: 1 Ensuite 1 Private 1 Family share

Wake to a spectacular sunrise! Relax in a spacious luxury bedroom with a deck overlooking stunning views to the distant Pacific Ocean. Nighttime tranquillity is broken only by the cry of an occasional owl. Amenities include, petanque, swimming pool, two lounges, TV/DVD/library, laundry and email. Enjoy a lovely rural setting with 11 acres of private native bush down to a creek and peaceful glade. Handy to scenic beaches, walks, sports, and only twenty minutes to charming Whangarei. Pets and children welcome by arrangement.

Whangarei - Kokopu *18 km W of Whangarei*
Riverdale Farm Bed & Breakfast *Luxury B&B Self Contained*

Samantha & Richard Taylor
Knight Road, Kokopu

Tel (09) 434 6808 or 021 262 1723
Fax (09) 434 6801 riverdalefarm@orcon.net.nz
www.riverdalefarm.co.nz

Double $60-$185 Single $40-$150 (Special breakfast)
Not suitable for pets or children
Dinner $40pp for Riverview Room guests only
Winter specials & gift vouchers available - see website
Visa MC accepted
1 Queen 1 Double (2 bdrm)
Bathrooms: 2 Private

Charming French style country farmhouse set on 35 acres, oozing peace and tranquillity. Choose from lavish accommodation - the Riverview Room in a private guest wing within the farmhouse with optional dinners available, or the budget priced self-catering accommodation of the Cabbage Tree Room off the garage. Farm walks to nearby Mangere Falls and award winning chapel. Several golf courses nearby. Just off the twin coast highway to the famous Matakohe Kauri Museum, and magnificent Kauri trees. A warm welcome assured. Resident cat & dog.

Whangarei - Kauri *5 km N of Whangarei*
Brantome Villa *B&B Homestay*

Valerie & Roger
454 Crane Road, RD 1, Kauri, Whangarei

Tel (09) 435 2088
Fax (09) 435 2089
relax@brantomevilla.co.nz
www.brantomevilla.co.nz

Double $190-$245 Single $190 (Special breakfast)
Dinner by arrangement $50pp
Visa MC accepted
Pet free home
(2 bdrm)
Bathrooms: 1 Ensuite

Brantome Villa has been completely refurbished in an upmarket contemporary style by Roger & Valerie. We want our guests to feel relaxed and pampered! For your comfort we have two fab rooms with ensuite. Both are fully air-conditioned. Brantome Villa has a beautiful country setting and is only two hours north of Auckland or ten minutes north of Whangarei, perfect for a Romantic Hideaway or Honeymoon. Please visit our website for full details.

Whangarei - Glenbervie *9 km NE of Whangarei*
Totara lodge Homestay *Luxury B&B Homestay*

John & Sue Hobden
252 Ngunguru Road Glenbervie,
RD 3 Whangarei, 0173

Tel (09) 437 6269   Fax (09) 437 6249
info@totaralodgehomestay.co.nz
www.totaralodgehomestay.co.nz

Double $185 Single $160 (Full breakfast)
Dinner $40 by prior arrangement
Visa MC accepted
Pet free home
Not suitable for children under 15
2 Queen (2 bdrm)
Bathrooms: 2 Ensuite

A warm welcome awaits you at Totara lodge where you can relax in the peaceful Glenbervie countryside. We feature tastefully decorated rooms throughout with luxurious queen size bedrooms for guests, which include tea/coffee making facilites, TV/DVDs, ensuites and private patios. A delicious breakfast is served offering fresh seasonal produce. Join is for dinner which is available by prior arrangement. Take some time out to explore the surrounding area which offers numerous recreational facilities set in scenic locations around Whangarei and the Tutukaka coast.

Whangarei Heads *28 km SE of Whangarei*

Bantry *Homestay*
Karel & Robin Lieffering
Little Munro Bay, RD 4, Whangarei Heads

Tel (09) 434 0751
Fax (09) 434 0754
robinl@igrin.co.nz

Double $110 **Single** $55 (Full breakfast)
Children under 12 half price
Dinner $35
Children and pets welcome
1 Queen 2 Single (2 bdrm)
Bathrooms: 1 Private 1 Guest share

We are a semi-retired couple with dog. We speak Dutch, French, German, Japanese and we like to laugh. Our unusual home with some natural rock interior walls is on the edge of a safe swimming beach, and bush reserve with walking tracks and several good fishing spots. A photographically fascinating area with wonderful views of coastal mountains. Guests have own entrance and sitting room all with sea views. Enjoyable food and NZ wine. Phone, fax, email us for reservations and directions. One party bookings only.

Whangarei Heads *23 km E of Whangarei*

Arches Lodge - Ridgeland Farm Estate *B&B Apartment with Kitchen*
Evan & Ada Davis
396-398 Owhiwa Road, Parua Bay, Whangarei, 0192

Tel (09) 436 1103 or 027 449 2475
chillout@arches.co.nz   www.arches.co.nz

Double $150-$180 **Single** $100-$140
(Continental breakfast provisions)
Children $50   Dinner available
Apartment includes full kitchen & laundry
Visa MC Amex accepted   Pet free home
4 King/Twin (4 bdrm)
Bathrooms: 1 Ensuite 1 Private Wheelchair friendly
ensuite & private bath in apartment

B&B with a difference! Enjoy the comforts of a lovely home, all to yourself. 23 minutes to CBD, 17 minutes to Airport. Tame & touchable sheep characters and nice people too! Snuggle into sumptuous superking/twin beds, soft feather pillows. Relax with a DVD or overlook 100 peaceful acres & private native forest from your covered deck. Gateway to spectacular Whangarei Heads - centrally located on the scenic route between Ocean Beach & Tutukaka. Two apartments sleep 1-6 each (one is wheelchair friendly). Be as interactive or independent as you wish. Inspection Welcome.

Ruakaka - Bream Bay *30 km S of Whangarei*

Island View Lodge *Luxury B&B Farmstay Separate Suite Apartment with Kitchen*
Joyce & Vince Roberts
34/27 Doctors Hill Road, Waipu, Ruakaka

Tel (09) 432 7842 or 027 441 9585
021 419 515 Fax (09) 432 7842
robertsb.b@xtra.co.nz
www.breambayfarmstay.co.nz

Double $100-$120 **Single** $60-$80 (Full breakfast)
Children $20 Dinner $30
Visa MC accepted
Children and pets welcome
2 Queen 2 Double (3 bdrm)
Bathrooms: 3 Ensuite 3 Private

Spectacular is the only words to describe the sea views from this brand new home built especially for the discerning travelers. Your own kitchen & laundry. Beautiful beaches, golf course, racetrack where Vince trains our racehorses and good restaurants are a short drive from our home. Meals include our home-grown lamb. As ex-dairy farmers with grown up family of four, we have enjoyed hosting B&B for 14 years, other interests include travel, golf and gardening.

Ruakaka *30 km S of Whangarei*

Waterview Bream Bay *B&B Farmstay Cottage with Kitchen*

Gayle & Rodney McPhee
34 Doctors Hill Road, Waipu, Ruakaka

Tel (09) 433 0050
Fax (09) 433 0050
rodneyandgaylesb.b@xtra.co.nz

Double $80 Single $50 (Full breakfast provisions)
Children $20
Dinner $25
Children and pets welcome
2 Queen 2 Single (3 bdrm)
Bathrooms: 1 Private 1 Family share

Waterview B&B offers a self-contained unit with panoramic sea and rural views. Our property has large gardens and children are welcome. Cot available. Large area for parking boats and wash down facility availble. Boat ramps are within ten minutes away at Marsden Cove. Beautiful beaches, golf course, race track and restaurants are only a few minutes away. We look forward to meeting with you.

Ruakaka *25 km S of Whangarei*

Edgewater B&B *Separate Suite*

Penny Britton
225 One Tree Point Road, Ruakaka, Northland

Tel (09) 432 7174 or 021 115 0918
penez@xtra.co.nz

Double $100-$115 Single $60-$75
(Continental breakfast provisions)
Not suitable for children
1 Double (1 bdrm)
Bathrooms: 1 Ensuite

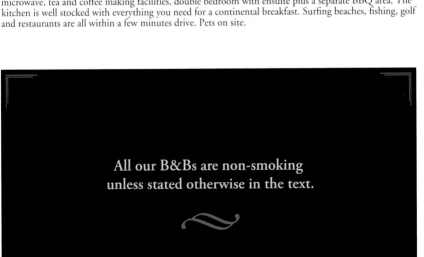

A warm and friendly welcome awaits you at my new beachfront retreat. Enjoy beach walks and magnificent uninterrupted views of Whangarei harbour and Mt. Manaia. Feel at home in a spacious modern self contained unit that includes Sky TV, microwave, tea and coffee making facilities, double bedroom with ensuite plus a separate BBQ area. The kitchen is well stocked with everything you need for a continental breakfast. Surfing beaches, fishing, golf and restaurants are all within a few minutes drive. Pets on site.

All our B&Bs are non-smoking
unless stated otherwise in the text.

Waipu Cove *10 km S of Waipu*

labonte@xtra.co.nz *Homestay Farmstay Apartment with Kitchen*

Andre & Robin La Bonte
PO Box 60, Waipu, Northland

Tel (09) 432 0645
Fax (09) 432 0645
labonte@xtra.co.nz

Double $100 Single $50 (Continental breakfast)
Dinner $20 by arrangement
Visa MC accepted
1 King 1 Queen 2 Double 2 Single (3 bdrm)
Bathrooms: 2 Private

Sleep to the sound of the ocean in a separate studio apartment or in guest bedrooms on our 36 acre seaside property. Explore our limestone rock formations or just sit and relax under the mature trees that grace our shoreline. The beach at Waipu Cove is a ten minute walk along the sea. We are a licensed fish farm, graze cattle, have flea-free cats and an outside dog. We are ocean and coastal engineers who enjoy hosting guests from around the world. American spoken.

Waipu Cove *8 km SE of Waipu*

Flower Haven *B&B Self-contained Downstairs Flat*
Shirley & Brian Flower
53 St Anne Road, Waipu Cove, RD 2, Waipu 0582

Tel (09) 432 0421
bnb@flowerhaven.com
www.flowerhaven.com

Double $116-$136 (Continental breakfast)
Visa MC accepted
Pet free home
Not suitable for children
2 Double (2 bdrm)
Bathrooms: 1 Private

Flower Haven is elevated with awesome coastal views, being developed as a garden retreat. The accommodation has separate access. Kitchen includes stove, microwave, fridge/freezer, washing machine, TV, radio. Linen, duvets, blankets and bath towels provided. Reduced tariff if continental breakfast not required. Our interests are gardening, genealogy and meeting people. Near bird sanctuary, museums, golf, horse treks, fishing, caving, walking tracks, oil refinery. Five minutes walk to restaurant, shop, surf beach, rocks. Whangarei 35 minutes, Auckland 1 1/2 hours. Visit our website for more details.

Waipu Cove *9 km SE of Waipu*

Melody Lodge *B&B Homestay*
Melody Gard
996 Cove Road, Waipu, Northland

Tel (09) 432 0939
Fax (09) 432 0939
melody@melodylodge.co.nz
www.melodylodge.co.nz

Double $90-$120 Single $75-$100
(Continental breakfast)
Not suitable for children
1 Queen 1 Double 2 Single (3 bdrm)
Bathrooms: 1 Ensuite 1 Guest share

Situated between the popular beaches of Waipu Cove and Langs Beach, Melody Lodge overlooks the whole of Bream Bay. Stunning sea views from all rooms. New cedar house with garden and spectacular stand of native bush adjacent. Resident artist and cat. Attached Art Gallery features local artworks, exclusive screenprinted souvenirs and cards. Swim at Waipu, stroll Langs Beach, study birdlife, experience the bush, a round of golf, horseriding, kayaking, fishing. Bush, sea, music, art and good conversation... relax and enjoy it all from Melody Lodge.

Waipu Cove *6.5 km SE of Waipu*

The Stonehouse *Apartment with Kitchen Cottage with Kitchen Backpackers Welcome*

Bob & Silvia Schmid
641 Cove Road, Waipu

Tel (09) 432 0432 or 021 207 9044
Fax (09) 432 0432
stonehousewaipu@xtra.co.nz
www.stonehousewaipu.co.nz

Double $90-$120 Single $80-$110
(Breakfast by arrangement)
Children $20
Visa MC accepted
Children and pets welcome
3 Queen 4 Single (4 bdrm)
Bathrooms: 2 Ensuite 1 Private

Get off the beaten track and relax in the selfcontained romantic Stonecottage or enjoy the privacy of the self-contained cabin. Green pastures, giant Pohutukawa trees, Maori Pa site and the lagoon with distant Mt Manaia are your views. Explore the adjacent lagoon with its bird sanctuary in our canoes or dinghies. Take a stroll through the dunes, watch and listen to the waves breaking on the shore, have a swim in summer, light your log fire in winter. German and French spoken. Ideal for families.

Kaiwaka *19 km N of Wellsford*

Landfall Lodge *Homestay*

Adrienne & Arnold Atkinson
306 Oneriri Road, RD 2, Kaiwaka, 0573

Tel (09) 431 2706 or 021 036 8929
Fax (09) 431 2706   landfall-lodge@clear.net.nz
www.landfall-lodge.co.nz

Double $120 Single $85 (Continental breakfast)
Children by arrangement   Dinner by arrangement
Single party (2-4 persons) $205
Visa MC accepted
Pet free home   Children welcome
1 King/Twin 1 Queen (2 bdrm)
Bathrooms: 1 Guest share ensuite

Welcome to our modern home at the beginning of the Kauri Coast and almost half way between Auckland and the Bay of Islands. We offer excellent beds,comfortable rooms, great showers, sunny lounge/dining room. Enjoy the sunsets over a glass of wine before a superb dinner. The West Coast beaches, world famous Kauri Museum, Kauri forests, golf courses and charming Mangawhai beach and walks are within easy reach. Your hosts have completed an extensive circumnavigation, and have a keen interest in travel and people.

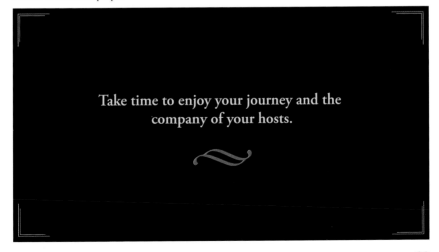

Take time to enjoy your journey and the
company of your hosts.

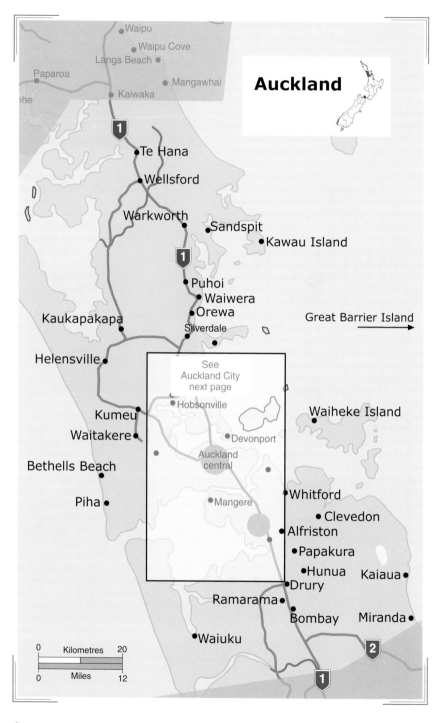

Auckland

Mangawhai Heads *1 km SE of Mangawhai Heads*

Mangawhai Lodge - A Room With a View Boutique B&B Inn
B&B Apartment with Kitchen self contained apartment
Jeannette Forde
4 Heather Street, Mangawhai Heads 0505

Tel (09) 431 5311 Fax (09) 431 5312
info@seaviewlodge.co.nz
www.seaviewlodge.co.nz

Double $155-$175 Single $135-$155
(Special breakfast) Visa MC accepted
Children 10 and over welcome
Mid winter xmas dinner for groups
2 King/Twin 2 Queen 8 Single (4 bdrm)
Bathrooms: 3 Ensuite 1 Private

Midway between Auckland Airport and the Bay of Islands, we offer the perfect beach and holiday destination for couples, groups, golfers & singles alike. Three stylish guest rooms and one self contained apartment open to wide verandahs. We offer a stylish, relaxing atmosphere with spectacular sea, island and beach views from most rooms. Golf course adjacent, off-street parking. Enjoy beaches/walkways, bird sanctuary. Walk to cafés and shops. A sumptuous cooked or continental breakfast for all tastes and dietary needs. For winter specials visit www.seaviewlodge.co.nz

Wellsford *6 km E of Wellsford*

Wisdome Cottage *Homestay Farmstay*
Peter and Sally Usher
196 Tomarata Valley Road, Tomarata, RD 4 Wellsford

Tel (09) 423 9558
wisdome-cottage@paradise.net.nz

Double $130 Single $115 (Full breakfast)
Children negotiable
Dinner by arrangement
Visa MC accepted
Children welcome
2 Queen (2 bdrm)
Bathrooms: 1 Ensuite 1 Private

Wisdome Cottage welcomes you for a relaxing and refreshing break in a deeply rural setting. Nestled amidst country gardens the cottage faithfully replicates a 17th century farmhouse, featuring beamed ceilings, open fires and hand crafted joinery. Barely an hour from Auckland, close to sensational beaches, bush walks and the Matakana wine country, the cottage is an ideal place to start or conclude Northland tours. Delicious dinners and local tours are also offered. Bicycles and kayaks available. Two children, one working dog, one idle cat!

Wellsford - Te Hana *6 km N of Wellsford*

The Retreat Historic Farmhouse *Farmstay*
Colleen & Tony Moore
Te Hana, RD 5, Wellsford 0975

Tel (09) 423 8547
enquiry@sheepfarmstay.com
www.sheepfarmstay.com

Double $100-$120 Single $65-$80 (Full breakfast)
Dinner $30pp by arrangement
Self-contained cottage $100
Visa MC Diners accepted
2 Queen 1 Double 1 Single (3 bdrm)
Bathrooms: 1 Ensuite 1 Private

Tony and Colleen welcome you to The Retreat, a spacious 1860s farmhouse built for a family with 12 children. Set well back from the road, the house is surrounded by an extensive landscaped garden, including a productive vegetable garden and orchard. Fresh produce from the garden is a feature in our home cooking.

Colleen is a spinner and weaver and our flock of sheep provides the raw material for the woollen goods that are hand-made and for sale from the studio. If you haven't got close up to a sheep this is your chance, as we always have friendly sheep to hand feed. We have hosted guests at The Retreat since 1988 and appreciate what you require.

We know New Zealand well, our families have lived in NZ for several generations and we have visited most places in our beautiful country, so if you have any questions on what to see or do, we are well equipped to provide the answers.

Also available is a self-contained cottage, close to the house, with the option of having meals with us, or self-catering.

The Retreat is very easy to find. Travelling North on SH1, we are 6 km north of Wellsford, look for the Weaving Studio sign on your left. You will pass through Te Hana before arriving at The Retreat. Kaiwaka is 13 km north of The Retreat.

Warkworth - Sandspit *7 km E of Warkworth*

Belvedere Homestay *Homestay*
M & R Everett
38 Kanuka Road, RD 2, Warkworth

Tel (09) 425 7201 or 027 2844 771
Fax (09) 425 7201
belvederehomestay@xtra.co.nz
www.belvederehomestay.co.nz

Double $160 Single $100 (Special breakfast)
Dinner $45pp
Visa MC accepted
2 Queen 1 Twin (3 bdrm)
Bathrooms: 1 Ensuite 2 Private

Sandspit the perfect stop to and from The Bay of Islands. Belvedere has 360 degree views, sea to countryside; it's awesome.

Relaxing decks, barbecue, garden, orchards, native birds and bush, peace and tranquillity with good parking. Air-conditioned, spa, games room, comfortable beds are all here for your comfort.

Many attractions are within 7 km and Margaret's flair with cooking is a great way to relax after an adventurous day with pre-drinks, two course meal and wine. Have a warm and relaxing stay with Margaret & Ron.

Warkworth *0.5 km N of Warkworth*
Homewood Cottage *B&B Separate Suite*

Ina & Trevor Shaw
17 View Road, Warkworth

Tel (09) 425 8667 or 021 114 8760
Fax (09) 425 9610
ina.homewoodcottage@xtra.co.nz

Double $100-$100 (Special breakfast)
Visa MC accepted
1 Queen 1 Twin (2 bdrm)
Bathrooms: 2 Ensuite

Welcome to our home in a peaceful garden with views of Warkworth and the hills. The spacious rooms ensure privacy and quiet. The new beds are comfortable with electric blankets and quilts. Each room has TV, teamaking, own entrance, and car park. No cooking. Afternoon tea and substantial continental breakfast served. Ina is an artist who also enjoys walking, music and her guests. Restaurants are two minutes away, beaches vineyards and crafts close by. A smoke free home. View Road is off Hill Street.

Warkworth *13 km E of Warkworth*
Maltby Homestay *B&B Self-contained unit*

Barbara & John Maltby
Omaha Orchards, 282 Point Wells Road,
RD 6, Warkworth

Tel (09) 422 7415
Fax (09) 422 7419
jandbmaltby@value.net.nz

Double $70-$90 **Single** $60-$75
(Continental breakfast) Extra guest $12
Dinner $15-$25 by arrangement
In-house accommodation also available
1 Queen 1 Double (1 bdrm)
Bathrooms: 1 Ensuite

Our home and self-contained unit (built 1999) is set on five acres nestled beside the Whangateau Harbour. Relax in the extensive gardens and swim in the beautifully appointed pool. Nearby is Omaha Beach, golf course, tennis courts, restaurants, art and craft studios, pottery works, museum, Sheep World, Honey Centre and Kawau Island. This is some of the prettiest coastline in New Zealand. John and Barbara look forward to sharing their little slice of paradise with you.

Warkworth - Sandspit *10 km E of Warkworth*
Sea Breeze *Apartment with Kitchen*

Di & Robin Grant
14 Puriri Place, RD 2, Sandspit Heights, Warkworth

Tel (09) 425 7220 or 021 657 220
Fax (09) 425 7220
robindi.grant@xtra.co.nz
www.bnb.co.nz/seabreeze.html

Double $150 **Single** $120 (Continental breakfast)
Visa MC accepted
Not suitable for children
1 Queen (1 bdrm)
Bathrooms: 1 Ensuite

Sea Breeze is a self-contained luxury apartment with magnificent sea views and surrounding bush. Breakfast is provided in the kitchenette to be enjoyed at your leisure and a bed-settee in the lounge doubles for extra guests. There are easy bush walks to the beaches immediately below the property. Take a cruise to Kawau Island or visit the many vineyards, galleries and cafés. Your hosts have travelled extensively and now enjoy gardening and boating in their spare time. Phone/fax for directions.

Warkworth *4.5 km W of Warkworth*

Willow Lodge *B&B Homestay*
Colin Hilditch & Vicki Webster
541 Woodcocks Road, RD 1, Warkworth 0981

Tel (09) 425 7676 or 021 104 1807
021 064 5567
Fax (09) 425 7676
willow_lodge@xtra.co.nz

Double $110-$130 Single $80-$100 (Full breakfast)
Children $30
Dinner by arrangement
1 Queen 1 Double 2 Twin (4 bdrm)
Bathrooms: 1 Ensuite 2 Private

You've just found what you were looking for - peace and old world charm, five minutes drive from picturesque Warkworth (45 minutes from Auckland). Willow Lodge is nestled amid two acres of landscaped gardens. We offer in-house or semi-detached accommodation. Enjoy guest TV lounge, tea/coffee, BBQ all of which opens onto a private courtyard. Colin, Vicki and their dog Boss look forward to warmly welcoming you to their home. Much to explore, plenty to enjoy and treasured memories to be created.

Warkworth *70 km N of Auckland*

Warkworth Country House *B&B*
Perry & Jan Bathgate
18 Wilson Road, RD 1 Warkworth, 0981

Tel (09) 422 2485 or 027 600 1510
Fax (09) 422 2485   p-jbathgate@xtra.co.nz
www.warkworthcountryhouse.co.nz

Double $120-$145 Single $95-$110 (Full breakfast)
Visa MC accepted   Children welcome
1 Queen 1 Twin (2 bdrm)
Bathrooms: 2 Ensuite

Warkworth Country House is 45 minutes north of Harbour bridge and situated in two acres of gardens and bush, surrounded by farmland. Each unit has ensuite with private entrance and patio, TV, tea/coffee, heater, electric blankets, radio and toiletries. Enjoy a full or continental breakfast in our dining room then visit one of the local places of interest. Warkworth township with its shops and restaurants is only three minutes drive away. You will always receive a warm and friendly welcome whenever you arrive. New owners with a wealth of travel and people experience. We will be happy to assist you in planning your travels around New Zealand over a glass of wine, tea or coffee in the comfort of our home.

Warkworth *1.8 km SE of Warkworth Information Centre*

RibbonWood B&B Apartment *B&B Apartment with Kitchen*
Berris & Alan Spicer
7 Thompson Road, Warkworth, 0981

Tel (09) 422 2685 or 027 241 9986
Fax (09) 422 2684
berris@ribbonwoodwarkworth.co.nz
www.ribbonwoodwarkworth.co.nz

Double $120-$160 (Special breakfast)
Dinner from $15pp   Extra person $30-60
Discount for 3+ night stay   Visa MC accepted
Pet free home   Children welcome
1 Queen 2 Twin (2 bdrm)
Bathrooms: 1 Private Bath & shower

Where true NZ hospitality and special experience await! Enjoy every home comfort - your own entrance, patio, light and airy lounge dining kitchen, luxury bathroom, wifi internet access. Your choice to self-cater, enjoy quality home cooking or cafés within three minutes. Our delightful country setting offers peace, privacy, views. We're 45 minutes north of Auckland, next to the famous Parry Kauri Forest in historic Warkworth Village, on the door step to Matakana Wine Country. Modern, boutique, warm, welcoming ... we cater for one group only.

Warkworth - Sandspit *10 km E of Warkworth*

Kotare Lodge *Apartment with Kitchen*

Judy & Graeme Maker
5 Kotare Place, RD 2, Sandspit Heights,
Warkworth, 0982

Tel (09) 425 7331 or 021 279 8116
Fax (09) 425 0311
makers@ihug.co.nz

Double $130-$160 Single $120-$150
(Continental breakfast)
Visa MC accepted
1 Queen 1 Twin (2 bdrm)
Bathrooms: 1 Private

Kotare Lodge has arguably the best views at Sandspit from Kawau Bay, Hauraki Gulf, Great Barrier, Little Barrier, the rural areas of Matakana and the inner harbour of Sandspit. Relax in your luxury self-contained apartment including swimming pool, Sky TV and spacious viewing decks. Enjoy bush walks to beaches, visit the many vineyards, galleries, cafés, restaurants, golf courses, Kawau Island ferry, all within a few minutes drive. Spend time cruising Kawau Bay and islands aboard our 54' Riviera launch (extra cost). The perfect stay.

Puhoi *9 km N of Orewa*

Westwell Ho *B&B*

Fae & David England
34 Saleyards Road, Puhoi, 0951

Tel (09) 422 0064 or 027 280 5795
Fax (09) 422 0064
dhengland@xtra.co.nz

Double $115 Single $95 (Full breakfast)
Children $35
Visa MC Amex accepted
Children welcome
1 Queen 1 Double 1 Single (2 bdrm)
Bathrooms: 1 Ensuite 1 Private

We welcome you to our sunny colonial-style home in the lovely Puhoi Valley. We are only two minutes by car west of Main North Highway up a small road behind the old pub in this historic Puhoi Village. The homestead has wide verandahs around three sides where you can relax as you view the gardens and beautiful trees. Nearby are the fantastic Waiwera Thermal Pools, or you could hire a canoe and paddle down the Puhoi River to Wenderholm Beach and Park. Sky TV available.

Waiwera *6 km N of Orewa*

Estuary Cottage *B&B*

Jenny & Bob Kelly
15 Weranui Road (PO Box 92), Waiwera, 0950

Tel (09) 426 2621 or 021 426 262
021 0247 0170
Fax (09) 426 2614
rj.kelly@ihug.co.nz

Double $110-$130 Single $80-$100 (Full breakfast)
Visa MC accepted
1 Queen 1 Single (1 bdrm)
Bathrooms: 1 Ensuite

A comfortable, centrally located B&B in the village of Waiwera - the beautiful Hibiscus Coast thermal area, with a safe scenic ocean beach, native bush covered hills, and world famous hot pools. Estuary Cottage - 'Owaimaru', is located on the tidal waters' edge, and offers quality accommodation with a stunning bedroom view, satellite television, tea & coffee making facilities, refrigerator, and a private ensuite. Our guests receive a generous discount to the nearby thermal pools.

Auckland

Villa Orewa *B&B Homestay*

Sandra & Ian Burrow
264 Hibiscus Coast Highway, Orewa, Auckland

Tel (09) 426 3073 or 021 626 760 (Ian)
021 556 960 (Sandra)
Fax (09) 426 3053
rooms@villaorewa.co.nz
www.villaorewa.co.nz

Double $150-$225 (Special breakfast)
Dinner by arrangement
Visa MC accepted
1 King/Twin 2 Queen (3 bdrm)
Bathrooms: 3 Ensuite

Welcome to our beautifully appointed Mediterranean style home, with white-washed walls and blue vaulted roofs. A taste of the Greek Isles on beautiful Orewa Beach. Stay in one of our self-contained rooms, each with private balcony, and enjoy the panoramic beach and sea views, or socialise with us in our spacious living areas. Orewa offers a great range of activities and amenities; with cafés, restaurants, and shopping all within a short level walk. We are sure your stay will be enjoyable and memorable.

Orewa - Red Beach *5 km S of Orewa*

Hibiscus House *B&B*

Judy & Brian Marsden
13A Marellen Drive, Red Beach, Whangaparaoa,
Hibiscus Coast, New Zealand

Tel (09) 427 6303 or 027 449 2 025
027 447 2056 Fax (09) 427 6303
jb.marsden@clear.net.nz

Double $100 Single $80 (Full breakfast)
Children 12 years or over
Dinner $25 by prior arrangement. Pet free home
2 Queen 2 Twin (3 bdrm)
Bathrooms: 2 Ensuite 1 Private
Modern tile and glass with exellent showers

We offer quality bed & breakfast, opposite a beach for the relaxing break you deserve, on route to Northland. Judy and Brian give friendly, personal hospitality in a very convenient location. Handy to shops, markets, cinema, beaches, golf courses and a leisure centre complex with heated swimming pool. Easy walks to surf, tennis and squash clubs. RSA five minutes away. Gulf Harbour Marina for ferries, fishing and sailing. Restaurants/bars/cafés for all tastes and occasions 5-15 minutes away. Sorry no pets. Children over 12 welcome.

Orewa - Puawai Bay *40 km N of Auckland*

Puawai Bay *B&B Apartment with Kitchen*

Audrey & Robert
31 Glenelg Road, Red Beach, Hibiscus Coast

Tel (09) 426 1165   Fax (09) 426 1165
bookings@puawaibay.co.nz
www.puawaibay.co.nz

Double $150-$300 Single $100-$250
(Continental breakfast)
Dinner and picnic baskets prepared on request
Visa MC Diners Eftpos accepted
Not suitable for children
5 King (5 bdrm)
Bathrooms: 5 Ensuite

Enjoy panoramic views from this spacious cliff edge location or kick back in our own picturesque vineyard. We offer a one bedroom luxury apartment, a spacious two bedroom apartment and three king-size rooms with ensuites. Facilities include a heated swimming pool, a sauna and a gym. Puawai Bay is 25 minutes from Auckland and is an ideal first or last night in NZ. Or stay for a few days and enjoy our beach, our wine and our local attractions.

Orewa - Red Beach *4 km S of Orewa*
Waiari B&B *B&B Homestay*

Bill Edwards & Bruce Watson
85 Whangaparaoa Road, Hadley Park,
Red Beach, Auckland 0932

Tel (09) 427 5914 or 027 485 0170
waiari@xtra.co.nz
www.waiari.co.nz

Double $120-$140 Single $100-$120
(Continental breakfast)
Not suitable for children
2 Queen 1 Double (3 bdrm)
Bathrooms: 2 Ensuite 1 Private

Waiari is a quality purpose built homestay set on two acres of garden & lifestyle block running down to the Weiti River. Enjoy the abundant bird-life, the peace and seclusion, an ideal stopover away from the city. Only 20 minutes north of the Bridge, the perfect place to relax. Visit fabulous beaches, international golf course, Waiwera thermal pools, the vineyards and potteries at Matakana. Spend the day visiting Tiritiri Matangi Island Bird Sanctuary.

Silverdale - Wainui *8 km SW of Silverdale*
Whitehills Country Stay *B&B Apartment with Kitchen*

Maureen & Dennis Evans
224 Whitehills Road, Wainui, RD 1 Kaukapakapa

Tel (09) 420 5666 or 027 448 9503
Fax (09) 420 5666
d-m.evans@clear.net.nz
www.bnbauckland.co.nz

Double $120 Single $75 (Continental breakfast)
Children negotiable
Dinner $30 by arrangement
Self-contained double $120, $130 with breakfast provisions
Visa MC accepted Children welcome
1 Queen 5 Single (3 bdrm)
Bathrooms: 2 Private

Relax and unwind at Whitehills situated 25 minutes from Auckland Harbour Bridge, seven minutes from Silverdale Motorway exit. Convenient for shops, beaches and golf courses. B&B is available in the main house or enjoy a comfortable, self-contained studio with its own kitchen, entrance and deck. Breakfast provisions can be provided. You are most welcome to wander around our garden, walk in the six acres of native bush or simply relax on the verandah. We look forward to meeting you.

Silverdale - Wainui *10.4 km W of Silverdale*
Ormond House *Luxury B&B*

Martin & Bridie Butler
470 Waitoki Road, RD 1 Wainui, Kaukapakapa

Tel 09 420 3317 or 021 048 5522
Fax 09 420 3318
info@ormondhousenz.com
www.ormondhousenz.com

Double $130-$175 Single $90-$110 (Full breakfast)
Children under 5 free, 5-13 $40
Visa MC Eftpos accepted
Pet free home
2 King 2 Queen 1 Single (4 bdrm)
Bathrooms: 4 Ensuite

Welcome to our large American style house on 4 acres with two hole 75 metre fairway with bunkers and pond. Set in the beautiful rolling hills of the Wainui Valley we are only 35 minutes from Auckland and are within easy reach of all major attractions in the Rodney District including beautiful Orewa Beach. Guests have access to the whole house including large conservatory, broadband is available. Your hosts Martin and Bridie are Irish, have travelled extensively and lived in Australia and Florida.

Whangaparaoa *8 km E of Orewa*

Verdelais *Luxury B&B Homestay Boutique Wedding Venue*
Glenys and David Ferguson
36 Tindalls Bay Road, Tindalls Bay, Whangaparaoa

Tel (09) 424 7031 or 021 041 4322
Fax 09 424 7031   glenys@verdelais.co.nz
www.verdelais.co.nz

Double $160-$180 **Single** $100-$120 (Full breakfast)
Visa MC accepted
1 King/Twin 2 Queen (3 bdrm)
Bathrooms: 2 Ensuite 1 Private

Verdelais is a luxury beachfront Bed and Breakfast and Boutique Wedding venue. It offers beauty, peace and comfort with genuine hospitality.

It is ideal for a weekend rest, a small wedding, local event, mini conference or a break in your journey. We have three rooms:- the Verdelais Suite is a garden suite with king size beds or twin beds, full bathroom with spa bath, private entrance and patio. The Coral and Aquarius Rooms have queen-size beds, ensuites and spectacular views of the bay. All rooms have TV/DVDs, tea and coffee making facilities, home-made cookies and reverse-cycle air-con. Sky and internet facilities are available in the comfort of our two lounge areas. We have ample and secure off-street parking.

Breakfast is a signature meal with seasonal vegetables and fruit home grown and freshly picked. Fresh eggs are laid daily by our four chooks. Enjoy a drink before dinner from our well stocked bar. Dinner is served by request at our dining table or on the veranda taking in the view of the bay. Alternatively there are a variety of international restaurants at nearby Manly Village.

Take a walk through our garden and down to the beach for a swim, there are three other safe beaches within easy walking distance. If you are lucky you may see dolphins swimming in the bay. Verdelais is ideally situated near Gulf Harbour International Golf Course and Marina, Waiwera Thermal Pools, Ferry to city and islands and the wineries. There are so many other attractions in the locality too numerous to list. Timmy our tabby and Monty our golden lab are happy and friendly members of our family. We look forward to your stay with us.

Whangaparaoa *4 km E of Orewa*
Duncansby by the Sea *B&B*

Kathy & Ken Grieve
72 Duncansby Road, Whale Cove,
Stanmore Bay, Whangaparaoa

Tel (09) 424 0025 or 027 200 9688
027 4422 278
Fax (09) 424 3607
duncansby@xtra.co.nz
www.duncansbybnb.co.nz

Double $120 Single $95 (Full breakfast)
Visa MC accepted
2 Queen (2 bdrm)
Bathrooms: 1 Ensuite 1 Private

Duncansby, our new home, offers relaxing panoramic sea views of the Hibiscus Coast. Located at Whale Cove between Red Beach and Stanmore Bay, our modern sunny well appointed rooms have own entrances, TV, decks, white linen, tea/coffee facilities. Paradise for golfers with 3 local courses including International Gulf Harbour Course with its boating marina. Bird watchers visit Tiritiri Island Bird Sanctuary, walk Shakespeare Park. Enjoy petanque, nine superb beaches, excellent local restaurants and cafés. Only 35 minutes north of Auckland City, we welcome you.

~

Whangaparaoa *5 km E of Orewa*
Peone Place *B&B Homestay Apartment with Kitchen*

Parke & Elizabeth Horne
35 Surf Road, Whangaparaoa, 0932

Tel (09) 424 1455 Fax (09) 424 1455
info@peone.co.nz
www.peone.co.nz

Double $110-$150 Single $30-$80
(Continental breakfast)   Children negotiable
Dinner by arrangement
Visa MC Eftpos accepted   Children welcome
2 King/Twin 1 Queen 3 Single (4 bdrm)
Bathrooms: 1 Private 1 Guest share

Welcome to our large, comfortable home, enjoy genuine, warm hospitality, wide sea views, & relax in our peaceful private garden with resident tuis. We have two double bedrooms and self-contained apartment.(Sleeps five) Extended stay/group rates. Attractions include beaches, thermal pools, golf courses, indoor snowslope, walks & quality restaurants. Peone Place is an ideal base for trips to boutique wineries, colourful markets, distinctive galleries and potteries, & nearby beautiful islands, including Tiritiri Matangi Bird Sanctuary. Enquire for guest discounts,Tiritiri lunches & maps. Be at ease at Peones!

~

Helensville *4 km SW of Helensville*
Rose Cottage *B&B Cottage with Kitchen*

Dianne & Richard Kidd
2191 State Highway 16, RD 2, Helensville

Tel (09) 420 8007 or 027 459 9135
Fax (09) 420 7966
kidds@xtra.co.nz
www.babs.co.nz/whenuanui

Double $110 Single $90
(Full breakfast provisions)
Visa MC accepted
1 Queen (1 bdrm)
Bathrooms: 1 Ensuite

Rose Cottage offers comfort and privacy set within peaceful gardens. Whenuanui is a 400 hectare Helensville sheep and beef farm providing magnificent farm walks. The family homestead and gardens have panoramic views over Helensville and the Kaipara Valley. Tasteful accommodation includes ensuite, TV and kitchenette. All-weather tennis court available for guests to use. Just 35 minutes from downtown Auckland on State Highway 16. A base to explore the Kaipara region or a great start or end to your Northland tour. Smoking outdoors appreciated.

Calico Lodge *B&B Homestay Countrystay B & B*
Kay & Kerry Hamilton
250 Matua Road, RD 1, Kumeu

Tel (09) 412 8167 or 0800 501 850
027 286 6064
bed@calicolodge.co.nz
www.calicolodge.co.nz

Double $150-$195 Single $110-$160 (Full breakfast)
Visa MC accepted
Pets welcome
2 King/Twin 2 Queen (4 bdrm)
Bathrooms: 2 Ensuite 2 Private

Kerry and Kay, Zippy our little dog, three cats and tame sheep welcome you to Calico Lodge. Amidst the wineries, wedding venues, and cafés of Kumeu and Waimauku, near west coast beaches, 25 minutes NW of Auckland our modern home on four acres has beautiful trees and gardens.

Under an hour from Auckland Airport, Calico Lodge is an ideal base to start or end your New Zealand holiday.

Hand made teddy bears and patchwork quilting (for sale) adorn the bedrooms and lounge in a separate guest wing.

Two minutes SH16, peace and stunning bush views complete the picture. We love to share our little piece of paradise.

At Calico Lodge we have free wireless broadband and a computer is available to check your email.

Hobsonville *20 km NW of Auckland*

Eastview *B&B Homestay Separate Suite*

Joane & Don Clarke
2 Parkside Road, Hobsonville, Auckland

Tel (09) 4169254 or 027 437 3400
eastview@xtra.co.nz
www.eastview.co.nz

Double $120-$135 Single $85-$100 (Full breakfast)
Children $30 (cot available) Dinner by arrangement
Extra adult discount in the Marina Suite
Visa MC accepted Children welcome
2 Queen 2 Single (3 bdrm)
Bathrooms: 2 Private

Situated at the western end of Auckland's beautiful harbour. Eastview is easy to find from the airport or travel routes north and south. Well located for exploring Auckland. Panoramic water/city views. Near to Kumeu wine country (popular for weddings), superb beaches, rainforest clad hills, gannet colony. We offer many personal homely touches. Two sunny accommodation areas. A two bedroomed suite, and a queen bedroom with private bathroom. A great place to relax after your trip or a day's sightseeing. Friendly small dog and cat.

Bethells Beach *15 km W of Swanson*

Bethell's Beach Cottages & Health Sanctuary and Rejuvenation
Apartment with Kitchen Cottage with Kitchen
Self-contained Cottages & 100 Seater Summer Pavilion
Trude & John Bethell-Paice
PO Box 95057, Swanson, Auckland

Tel (09) 810 9581   Fax (09) 810 8677
info@bethellsbeach.com
www.bethellsbeach.com

Double $250-$350 (Special breakfast $30pp)
Children under 12 half price
Dinner 2 course $40pp 3 course $50pp
Visa MC accepted   Children welcome
3 Queen 2 Double 3 Single (4 bdrm)
Bathrooms: 3 Private

Love dances in the beauty of Nature. When you stay at Bethells Beach Cottages you become one with the elements. The sights and sounds of nature will awaken your passionate spirit and time will cease to exist. Whether walking the beach, relaxing in your cottage, or sitting in the Scandinavian hot tub watching the sun set you will know that love is everywhere but here it flows a little more easily.

Waitakere Ranges - Swanson *4 km W of Swanson*

Panorama Heights *B&B*
Allison & Paul Ingram
42 Kitewaho Road, Swanson,
Waitakere City, Auckland

Tel (09) 832 4777 or 0800 692 624
Fax (09) 833 7773
nzbnb4u@clear.net.nz
www.panoramaheights.co.nz

Double $150 Single $110 (Full breakfast)
Dinner by request
Visa MC accepted
2 Queen 1 Twin (3 bdrm)
Bathrooms: 3 Ensuite 1 Private

Paul & Allison invite you to vist and share our extremely special location high in the Waitakere Ranges with tranquility, privacy and magnificent panoramic views across native rainforest to Auckland City and Rangitoto Island beyond. Explore 250 km walking/hiking trails in surrounding Regional Park, West Coast beaches (Piha, Karekare, Bethells, Muriwai) Wineries, two scenic golf courses. Train to city is nearby. Excellent quality accommodation is here for you to enjoy. Your hosts who reside next door encourage relaxation while we spoil you. Please Phone/Email for Bookings/Directions.

Auckland

Waitakere Ranges *15 km NW of Henderson*
Wairere Lodge *B&B Homestay*
Bob and Heather Harmes
351 Wairere Road, Waitakere, Auckland 0782

Tel (09) 8109 467
info@wairerelodge.co.nz
www.wairerelodge.co.nz

Double $130-$150 Single $95-$105 (Full breakfast)
Dinner 3 courses $40, 2 courses $30, 1 course $20,
Wine and beer available to purchase
Visa MC accepted
2 Queen (2 bdrm)
Bathrooms: 1 Guest share

Heading north on northwestern motorway, take Lincoln Road turn off; second set of lights turn right into Universal Drive, 2 km to roundabout, straight through on to Swanson Road; 4 km; turn right into Waitakere Road; 3 km, over the railway overbridge, turn left into Bethells Road; half km right into Wairere Road.

Ranui *15 km W of Auckland*
The Garrett *B&B Homestay*
Alma & Rod Mackay
295 Swanson Road, Waitakere City,
Auckland 0612

Tel (09) 833 6018
Fax (09) 833 6018
rodalmamacka@paradise.net.nz

Double $90 Single $60 (Continental breakfast)
2 King/Twin 1 King 2 Single (2 bdrm)
Bathrooms: 1 Ensuite

Just 15 minutes from Auckland City, five minutes from Henderson. The Garrett offers villa style accommodation with ensuite. Twin beds or king-size available. Accommodation for extra guests with folding beds on request; suitable for business people. High ceilings, period furniture and decor create a charming atmosphere in this delightful homestay, just minutes from Waitakere City. Attractions include wine trails, Art Out West - including Lopdell House Gallery, Waitakere Ranges, bush walks, Aratiki Centre, and golf courses. Westcity Shopping Centre, Lynn Mall and St Lukes.

Ranui *15 km W of Auckland*
The Brushmakers Cottage *B&B Apartment with Kitchen*
Jeanette & Roger Brown
20 Clearview Heights, Ranui,
Waitakere City, Auckland 0612

Tel (09) 833 8476 or 021 725 627
Fax 09 833 8476   r.g.brown@xtra.co.nz

Double $90-$150 Single $75-$110
(Continental breakfast)
Dinner by arrangement
Extra guests $20
Not suitable for children
3 Queen 1 Twin (4 bdrm)
Bathrooms: 1 Ensuite 2 Private 1 Family share

Choose between luxury self-contained apartment, featuring full kitchen, dishwasher, dining/lounge, TV/DVD, laundry, or traditional B&B. Backing onto a vineyard this peaceful location has views of both the Waitakere ranges and central Auckland. Ten minutes walk from train and bus stations and only 20 minutes drive from downtown Auckland. Close to both east and west coast beaches, gannet colony, golf courses, winery, cafés, restaurants and shopping malls. A great base for exploring Auckland. Ask about discounts. Some gluten-free food available.

Piha *20 km NW of Titirangi*

Piha Cottage *Cottage with Kitchen*

Tracey & Steve Skidmore
PO Box 48, Piha, Waitakere City, Auckland

Tel (09) 812 8514
info@pihacottage.co.nz
www.pihacottage.co.nz

Double $120-$140 Single $110-130
(Full breakfast provisions)
Children $30
Visa MC accepted
Pet free home Children welcome
1 Double 1 Single (1 bdrm)
Bathrooms: 1 Private

Leave the city behind. Beautiful Piha Cottage is hidden on a sunny, quiet bush setting, within easy walking distance of the surf beach and walking tracks. This spacious open plan home includes a kitchen, dining, living and sleeping areas. After a delicious self-serve breakfast (including waffles and maple syrup) go surfing, swimming or choose from one of Piha's outstanding walking tracks, through lush rainforest or along spectacular coastline. We, and our daughters, welcome you warmly and then allow you to enjoy the tranquility.

Piha *25 km W of Henderson*

Westwood Cottage *Cottage with Kitchen*

Dianne & Don Sparrow
95 Glenesk Road, Piha, Auckland

Tel (09) 812 8203
Fax (09) 812 8203
westwoodcottage.piha@xtra.co.nz

Double $120-$140
(Continental breakfast provisions)
Children $20
Visa MC accepted
Children welcome
1 Queen 1 Double (2 bdrm)
Bathrooms: 1 Private

Westwood Cottage offers a unique experience. Nestled in a secluded corner of our property, amongst beautiful bush overlooking Piha Valley. The Cottage is self-contained, open plan design, flowing on to a private deck. Full kitchen facilities with continental breakfast supplied. A cozy log fire for your enjoyment on cooler evenings. Off-road parking provided. Children five and over welcome. A short walk leads to Piha Surf Beach and bush walks include Kitekite Waterfall and Black Rock Dam. Forward book to avoid dissapointment.

Dairy Flat *4 km N of Albany*

Cottage Pukeko *Cottage with Kitchen*

Barry & Trish Vince
987 Highway 17, RD 2, Albany, Auckland

Tel (09) 415 8817
Fax (09) 415 8817
cottagepukeko@dairyflat.co.nz
www.dairyflat.co.nz

Double $130 Single $90
(Full breakfast provisions)
Children and pets welcome
1 King (1 bdrm)
Bathrooms: 1 Ensuite

A warm welcome awaits you at Cottage Pukeko. It is positioned only six minutes from the Albany Mega Centre on Highway 17. It offers self-contained accommodation set on six acres of park-like grounds. All furniture in the cottage is custom made by Barry and if you like any piece it can be made for you using native timbers. The cottage sleeps four adults (king and sofabed), own ensuite, TV and a fully stocked kitchen for breakfasts. Close to golf courses, beaches and restaurants

Auckland

Okura *20 km N of Auckland Central*

Okura B&B *B&B Separate Suite*
Judie & Ian Greig
20 Valerie Crescent, Okura,
North Shore City, Auckland

Tel (09) 473 0792
Fax (09) 473 1072
ibgreig@paradise.net.nz

Double $110 Single $85 (Full breakfast)
Visa MC accepted
1 Queen 1 Single (2 bdrm)
Bathrooms: 1 Private Own shower

Situated on Auckland's North Shore, Okura is a small settlement bounded by farmland and the Okura River, an estuary edged with native forest. If you like peace, quiet, with only bird song nearby, estuary and forest views, then this is for you. Accommodation includes your own, not shared, TV lounge, tea-making facilities, fridge, shower and toilet. Nearby is a wide variety of cafés, shops, beaches, walks, North Shore Stadium, Massey University and golf courses. Okura - one of Auckland's best kept secrets.

Coatesville - Albany *7 km N of Albany*

Camperdown *Farmstay*
Chris & David Hempleman
455 Coatesville/Riverhead Highway,
RD 3, Albany, Auckland

Tel (09) 415 9009
Fax (09) 415 9023
chris@camperdown.co.nz
www.camperdown.co.nz

Double $140 Single $95 (Full breakfast)
Children $50
Dinner $40
Children welcome
1 King/Twin 1 King 2 Queen 2 Single (4 bdrm)
Bathrooms: 2 Private 1 Guest share

We are only 20 minutes from Auckland City, relax in secluded tranquillity. Our home opens into beautiful gardens, native bush and stream offering the best of hospitality in a friendly relaxed atmosphere. On the farm we have sheep, cattle and pet lambs Our spacious guest areas consist of the entire upstairs. Guests may use our games room, play tennis on our new court, row a boat on the lake, or just stroll by the stream. Camperdown is easy travelling to the main tourist route north.

Albany - Coatesville *3 km N of Albany*

Te Harinui Countrystay *B&B*

Mike & Sue Blanchard
102 Coatesville/Riverhead Highway,
RD 3, Albany, Auckland

Tel (09) 415 9295
sue@teharinui.co.nz
www.teharinui.co.nz

Double $120 Single $85 (Full breakfast)
Children welcome by arrangement
Dinner $30 by arrangement
1 Queen 1 Twin 1 Single (3 bdrm)
Bathrooms: 1 Guest share
Bath with shower over and 2 toilets

Country hospitality as it used to be. A home from home in the country only 20 minutes from the city. Relax in the large garden, feed our pet coloured sheep and old horse, our dog and cat are friendly. Learn to spin and browse our craft shop. We can arrange outings to local attractions including gardens, orchards and beaches. Close to Albany stadium and Massey University, buses to the city. Generous breakfasts; coffee and teas are always available. Sue speaks French and is learning Mandarin.

Coatesville - Riverhead *30 km N of Auckland City*

Coatesville Lavender Hill *Luxury B&B Farmstay Bedroom/Ensuite/Dining/Lounge*

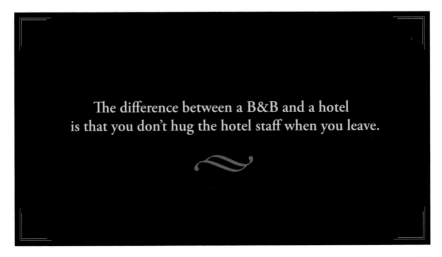

Tricia Henderson
11A Beacon Road, Coatesville, Auckland 0793

Tel (09) 412 5275 or (09) 412 5270
021 728 051 Fax (09) 412 5276
tricia@lavenderhill.co.nz
http://coatesville-lavenderhill.co.nz

Double $150-$200 Single $100 (Full breakfast)
Dinner by arrangement to suit
BBQ facilities available
Visa MC Amex Eftpos accepted
Not suitable for children
4 King/Twin (4 bdrm)
Bathrooms: 4 Ensuite Showers & mobility facilities

Luxury B&B farmstay accommodation in Coatesville/Riverhead; near Albany, Kumeu, Westgate. Superior Sealy beds, three rooms with ensuite, one room with separate mobility bathroom and ramp to outside. Set amongst the lavender beds, olive and lemon groves. Views to City and Riverhead Forest.

Mahoenui Lodge *Luxury B&B Cottage with Kitchen*

Margaret Wallace & Roy Richardson
344 Coatesville Riverhead Highway, Albany, Auckland

Tel (09) 415 8950 or 021 253 4582
Fax (09) 415 8956
margaret@mahoenuilodge.co.nz
www.mahoenuilodge.co.nz

Double $295-$395 (Full breakfast)
Dinner catered by arrangement
Visa MC Diners Amex Eftpos accepted
Pets welcome
1 King 1 Queen (2 bdrm)
Bathrooms: 1 Ensuite 1 Guest share
Cottage exclusive use to one party

A short drive across our harbour bridge (approx. 20 minutes) brings you to the village of Coatesville, acclaimed for its beautiful rural atmosphere, horses and some of Auckland's finest private gardens.

Mahoenui Lodge is boutique accommodation at its best and set in five acres of mature English garden. The accommodation is secluded and fully self contained providing peaceful relaxation or an opportunity to entertain a small group of friends by arrangement.

Breakfasts are included (free range eggs and local market produce). For lunch and evening dinner most prefer to enjoy the many and varied cafés and restaurants of the district, although professional catering is available by arrangement.

Margaret's two English Pointers together with the resident ducks, chooks, sheep and farm cat complete a peaceful, rural landscape. Stroll through the garden, relax, dine around the open outdoor fireplace or settle in to the lodge and enjoy the ambiance of antique oak and the warmth of a traditional English Inglenook.

Greenhithe *15 km N of Auckland*

Waiata Tui Lodge (The Song of the Tui) *B&B Homestay*
Therese & Ned Jujnovich
177 Upper Harbour Drive, Greenhithe, North Shore, Auckland, New Zealand

Tel (09) 413 9270 therese.jujnovich@gmail.com
www.bnb.co.nz/waiata.html

Double $100-$115 Single $70 (Special breakfast)
Children negotiable, cot available
Dinner $30 - two course with wine
Visa MC Amex accepted
Pet free home Children welcome
2 Queen 1 Twin 2 Single (3 bdrm)
Bathrooms: 2 Private 1 Guest share

A warm welcome to our haven. Eight acres of native forest and pasture only 15 minutes from NZ's largest city, yet so peaceful you could be in the heart of the countryside. A handy relaxing stay before your journey north.Spectacular views from over the kauri trees to the tranquil water below, with the distant Waitakere Ranges beyond.

Waken to tui song and the smell of freshly baked bread. A delicious healthy breakfast will be served: home-grown or local in-season fruit, various cereals, home-made yoghurt and spreads as well as a cooked breakfast, fruit juice, tea or coffee. From our large kauri breakfast table you can look out to the west and see the changing patterns of trees, water and tide. Perhaps a tui or a kereru (NZ's largest colourful pigeon) will stop for a drink at the birdbath on the adjoining deck.

You may like to walk in our lush rain forest with tree ferns and massive trees down to the waters edge or you can relax in the bush hammock. Do some bird watching or wander around our large garden usually bright with seasonal flowers. Swim in the pool during summer. Meet Harry, our friendly goat.

We have both travelled extensively overseas and within NZ and will be pleased to help you with your travel plans.

A Lockwood (solid-timber) home built for our family 30 years ago has been a homestay since 1987. Only minutes to North Harbour Stadium, North Shore Events Centre and east coast beaches. Five minutes to Greenhithe Village & its quality restaurants.

Karin's Garden Villa *B&B Cottage with Kitchen Apartment*
Karin Loesch & Family
14 Sinclair Street, Devonport, Auckland 0624

Tel (09) 445 8689 Fax (09) 445 8689
stay@karinsvilla.com
www.karinsvilla.com

Double $145-$175 Single $90-$135
(Continental breakfast) Children $25
Dinner by arrangement Self-contained cottage $185
Visa MC accepted
1 King/Twin 2 Double 3 Single (4 bdrm)
Bathrooms: 1 Ensuite 1 Private 1 Guest share

B&B
Approved

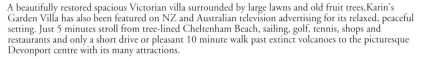

Tucked away at the end of a quiet cul-de-sac, Karin's Garden Villa - a Devonport dream - offers real home comfort with its light cosy rooms, easy relaxed atmosphere and the warmest of welcome from Karin and her family.

A beautifully restored spacious Victorian villa surrounded by large lawns and old fruit trees.Karin's Garden Villa has also been featured on NZ and Australian television advertising for its relaxed, peaceful setting. Just 5 minutes stroll from tree-lined Cheltenham Beach, sailing, golf, tennis, shops and restaurants and only a short drive or pleasant 10 minute walk past extinct volcanoes to the picturesque Devonport centre with its many attractions.

Your comfortable room offers separate private access through french doors, opening onto wide verandahs and cottage garden. And for those visitors wanting ultimate comfort and privacy, there is even a self-contained studio cottage with balcony and full kitchen facilities to rent (minimum 3 days). Sit down to a nutritious breakfast in the sunny dining room with its large bay windows overlooking everflowering purple lavender and native gardens. Guests are welcome to join the family barbecue and relax on our large lawn. We welcome longer stays and can arrange favourable discounts accordingly.

Help yourself to tea and German-style coffee and biscuits anytime, check your email and feel free to use the kitchen and laundry. For longer stays enquire about our new open-plan private Garden Apartment (sleeps 2-4) in the heart of Devonport. Karin comes from Germany and she and her family have lived in Indonesia for a number of years. We have seen a lot of the world and enjoy meeting other travellers. Always happy to help you arrange island cruises, rental cars, bikes and tours.

From the airport take a shuttle bus to our doorstep or to downtown ferry terminal. Courtesy pick up from Devonport Wharf. By car: after crossing Harbour Bridge, take Takapuna-Devonport turnoff. Right at T-junction, follow Lake Road to end, left into Albert, Vauxhall Road and then first left into Sinclair Street.Come as guests - leave as friends.

Devonport *1.5 km N of Devonport*
Ducks Crossing Cottage *B&B Homestay*
Gwenda & Peter Mark-Woods
58 Seabreeze Road, Devonport, Auckland

Tel (09) 445 8102
Fax (09) 445 8102
duckxing@splurge.net.nz

Double $90-$130 Single $65-$85 (Special breakfast)
Children $30
Pet free home
Children welcome
1 King/Twin 1 Queen 1 Single (3 bdrm)
Bathrooms: 1 Ensuite 2 Private

Welcome to our charming modern home in a garden setting. Peaceful, spacious, sunny bedrooms with television and clock radios. Tea, coffee and home-cooking available. We overlook Waitemata Golf Course and are five minutes from Narrow Neck Beach. Devonport Village, with cafés, restaurants and antique shops is two minutes by car or 15 minutes walk. Hosts are well travelled,informative and enjoy hospitality. Directions: airport door to door shuttle, or drive Route 26, Seabreeze Road, first house on left. Good off-street parking, courtesy ferry pick up on request.

All our B&Bs are non-smoking unless stated otherwise in the text.

Devonport *01 km E of Devonport*
Rainbow Villa *B&B*
Judy McGrath
17 Rattray Street, Devonport, Auckland

Tel (09) 445 3597
Fax (09) 445 4597
rainbowvilla@xtra.co.nz
www.rainbowvilla.co.nz

Double $150-$160 Single $100-$130 (Full breakfast)
Visa MC accepted
Pet free home
Not suitable for children
1 King 1 Queen 2 Single (3 bdrm)
Bathrooms: 3 Ensuite

Welcome to our Victorian villa (1885) nestled in a quiet cul-de-sac on the lower slopes of Mt Victoria. three elegant spacious rooms with ensuites, Sky TV. Spa pool in the garden. We serve a delicious full breakfast, coffee and tea available at all times. Situated just 100 metres from historic Devonport Village, five minute walk to ferry, only ten minute 'cruise' to downtown Auckland. Directions: Rattray Street is first on left past Picture theatre. Shuttles available at airport. Not suitable for children or pets.

Devonport *7.5 km S of Ferry Terminal*

The Jasmine Cottage *B&B Cottage with kitchenette*

Joan & John Lewis
20 Buchanan Street, Devonport, Auckland

Tel (09) 445 8825
Fax (09) 445 8605
joanjohnlewis@xtra.co.nz
www.photoalbum.co.nz/jasmine/

Double $100 (Full breakfast)
$110 for one night
1 Queen (1 bdrm)
Bathrooms: 1 Ensuite

Welcome to our cosy smoke-free quiet and private guest cottage. We are right in the heart of historic Devonport Village with all its attractions, cafés, beaches, golf course, scenic walks. The ferry to Auckland City and the Hauraki Gulf is three minutes walk away. A breakfast basket is delivered to your door and provides fruit juice, cereals, home made muesli and yoghurt, a platter of seasonal fruits, breads, jams, spreads, free-range eggs, breakfast teas and freshly brewed coffee. TV, fax.

Devonport *0.5 km N of Devonport*

Mahoe *B&B Apartment with Kitchen*

Judith & David Bern
15B King Edward Parade, Devonport, 0624

Tel (09) 445 1515 or 027 291 3727
Fax (09) 445 1515
info@mahoe.co.nz
www.mahoe.co.nz

Double $160-$200 (Breakfast by arrangement)
Children by arrangement
Visa MC accepted
2 Queen 1 Double (3 bdrm)
Bathrooms: 1 Ensuite 1 Private

Mahoe is an old school house transported from Huntly in 1985. Situated on the Devonport waterfront up a driveway in a peaceful setting. The upstairs B&B has queen room with deck and double room with lounge. The bathroom is separate. Our B&B is suitable for one couple or three or four people who are family or friends. We can accommodate three couples by including the apartment, which has a separate entrance and is fully equipped.

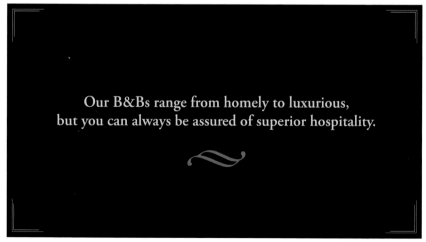

Our B&Bs range from homely to luxurious,
but you can always be assured of superior hospitality.

Auckland

Northcote Point *5 km N of Auckland CBD*

Auckland No 1 House *B&B*
Brian Holloway
1 Princes Street, Northcote Point, 0627

Tel (09) 480 7659
Fax (09) 480 7657
briankh@xtra.co.nz
www.nz-homestay.co.nz

Double $185-$220 Single $120-$160
(Full breakfast)
Children 3 in apartment
Visa MC accepted
Children and pets welcome
2 Queen 1 Double (3 bdrm)
Bathrooms: 1 Ensuite 3 Private

There is a bed and breakfast that really has the WOW factor. Auckland Number One House has its own swimming beach, a real Hobbit house in the garden, they breed Monarch butterflies, yet all this is only eight minutes from city centre.

Brian and Jay can have you personally met at the airport, and Jay's full cooked breakfasts are world famous. The harbour views by day and might are truly stunning - and they will even take you sailing on their 12 metre charter yacht.

See your country flag flying at the front door! The self contained Apartment on the waters edge is very suitable for travelling families We don't have any pets- except for a 14 year old grandaughter

Waiheke Island *1 km NE of Oneroa*

Watermark Studio Apartments *Separate Suite studio apartments*

Jo Underwood
17 Tawa Street, Little Oneroa,
Waiheke Island, Auckland 1081

Tel (09) 372 2762 or 027 346 6117
Fax (09) 372 2862   info@watermarkwaiheke.com
http://watermarkwaiheke.com

Double $175-$260 Single $175-$260
(Continental breakfast provisions available on request)
Dinner in village   Visa MC Diners accepted
Not suitable for children
6 King/Twin 3 King (3 bdrm)
Bathrooms: 3 Ensuite

Jo, (and her two burmese cats), is your host at Watermark. Quiet location 300 meters above beautiful beach. three private, self-contained studios face north. Floor to ceiling windows open onto private terraces maximising the lovely sea views from bed, living and terraces. TV/DVD/CD, wiresless internet, kingsize bed/kingtwin, radio, fridge, microwave/convection oven/grill, ensuite, linen, robes, slippers, iron/ironing board. BBQs, beach chairs, beach towels, penanque also available. Ten minute scenic walk to more beaches, kayaking, village, shops, cafés, galleries etc. Stunning walks. Vineyards closeby.

Auckland - Herne Bay *2.5 km W of Auckland central*

Moana Vista *Luxury B&B Homestay Guest House*

Tim Kennedy & Matthew Moran
60 Hamilton Road, Herne Bay, Auckland

Tel (09) 376 5028 or 0800 213 761
Fax (09) 376 5025
info@moanavista.co.nz
www.moanavista.co.nz

Double $180-$240 Single $140-$180
(Continental breakfast)
Visa MC Amex Eftpos accepted
Children welcome
2 Queen 1 Twin (3 bdrm)
Bathrooms: 2 Ensuite 1 Private

Just minutes stroll from the Waitmata Harbour, nestled in the exclusive enclave of Herne Bay. This charming, renovated two storey villa is owned and operated by your friendly hosts, Tim and Matthew. Two of the upper rooms have lovely harbour views. All rooms have LCD TVs with sky digital, DVD players and complimentary wireless internet access. In the evening you can wander up the road to visit any one of the award winning Ponsonby restaurants.

Auckland - Ponsonby *3 km W of Auckland Central*

The Big Blue House *B&B Homestay*

Kate Prebble & Lynne Giddings
103 Garnet Road, Westmere, Auckland

Tel (09) 360 6384 or 0800 360 6384
021 884 662
kate-lynne@xtra.co.nz
www.thebigbluehouse.co.nz

Double $130-$160 Single $80-$140
(Continental breakfast) Children $10
Dinner $50 by arrangment
Visa MC Eftpos accepted
Children welcome
2 King 3 Single (3 bdrm)
Bathrooms: 1 Ensuite 2 Family share

Kate and Lynne warmly invite you to enjoy our unique homestay environment close to Auckland's central city and harbour. Be greeted by our friendly cat and dog. Enjoy the luxury of spacious rooms with sea/hill views, TV, tea/coffee facilities, writing desk, electric blankets,heated towels and bathrobes. Generous continental breakfast. Luxuriate in our spa, splash in the pool. Take an easy stroll to the Auckland Zoo, Western Springs Stadium, cafés or seashore. Children welcome. Make yourself at home!

Auckland - Ponsonby *1 km NW of Auckland Central*

The Great Ponsonby *B&B Hotel*
Sally James & Gerard Hill
30 Ponsonby Terrace, Ponsonby, Auckland 1011

Tel (09) 376 5989 or 0800 766 792
Fax (09) 376 5527
info@greatpons.co.nz
www.greatpons.co.nz

Double $220-$350 Single $210-$275
(Special breakfast)   Pets welcome
Visa MC Diners Amex Eftpos accepted
6 King/Twin 4 Queen (11 bdrm)
Bathrooms: 111 Ensuite

B&B
Approved

Delightful small hotel providing bed & breakfast. Stay in a heritage 1890's villa restored with charm and flair providing you with quiet and peace. Your hotel is just two minutes stroll to Ponsonby's vibrant cafés, bistros, restaurants, art and craft galleries and just five minutes by taxi to the waterfront and central Auckland.

11 individually designed guestrooms with Pacific and New Zealand artworks. Accommodation choices include courtyard and palm garden studios, villa rooms and upstairs penthouse suite. Leisurely breakfast in the dining room or alfresco on the balcony. Freshly prepared cooked selection plus juices, fresh fruits and plunger coffee or tea choices. Free wirless internet. Socialise or read in the large comfortable lounge, balconies and courtyards. Friendly dog and cat - part of the family.

Auckland

Auckland - Ponsonby *1.5 km W of Auckland Central*

Colonial Cottage *B&B Homestay*
Grae Glieu
35 Clarence Street, Ponsonby, Auckland 1034

Tel (09) 360 2820
Fax (09) 360 3436
bnb@colonial-cottage.com

Double $100-$120 Single $80-$100
(Special breakfast)
Dinner $25 by arrangement
Pet free home
1 King 1 Queen 1 Single (3 bdrm)
Bathrooms: 1 Guest share

Delightful olde-world charm with modern amenities to assure your comfort - accent on quality. Hospitable and relaxing. Quiet with green outlook. Close to Herne Bay and Ponsonby Road cafés and quality restaurants. Airport shuttle service door-to-door. Handy to public transport, city attractions and motorways. Smoke-free indoors. Alternative health therapies and massage available. Special dietary requirements catered for. Organic emphasis. Single party bookings available.

Auckland - Ponsonby *2 km W of Information Centre*

Ponsonby Studio Loft *B&B Separate Suite Apartment with Kitchen*
Chrissy & Reg Price
9 Picton Street, Ponsonby, Auckland

Tel (09) 361 2461 or 021 637 908
021 336 640
info@ponsonbystudioloft.co.nz
www.ponsonbystudioloft.co.nz

Double $160 Single $160 (Tariff is for bed only,
breakfast by arrangement, popular option is local cafés)
Children $30
Visa MC Amex accepted
Pet free home   Children welcome
1 King 1 Double (1 bdrm)
Bathrooms: 1 Ensuite Separate shower

We are 100 meters from the cafés and shops of Ponsonby, yet nestled in a tree lined street of early 1900's wooden villas. The modern studio is completely separate and self-contained with kitchen, but local cafés are the Ponsonby experience. There's a great outlook, but still a cosy, warm and private feeling. Subtropical gardens. King-sized bed and luxury linen. Sky TV and broadband connection. Private balcony with views. Special long stay and winter prices.

Auckland CBD *0.5 km E of Auckland CBD*

Braemar on Parliament Street *B&B*
Susan Sweetman
7 Parliament Street, Auckland City Central, 1010

Tel (09) 377 5463 or 021 640 688
Fax (09) 377 3056
braemar@aucklandbedandbreakfast.com
www.aucklandbedandbreakfast.com

Double $205-$295 (Full breakfast)
Visa MC Diners Amex Eftpos accepted
Children and pets welcome
2 Queen 2 Double (4 bdrm)
Bathrooms: 1 Ensuite 1 Private 1 Guest share

A lovingly restored Edwardian townhouse in the Auckland CBD, Braemar provides comfortable, elegant accommodation to the discerning traveller. All upstairs bedrooms have posturepedic beds. All bathrooms have showers and claw foot baths. Complimentary toiletries, tea & coffee. Children welcome. Pets by prior arrangement. Toy poodles and cat live on site.

66

Auckland - Parnell *1.5 km E of Auckland Central*

Ascot Parnell 'a small b&b hotel' *Luxury B&B Homestay Hotel Guest House*

Therese & Bart Blommaert
St Stephens Avenue, Parnell, Auckland 1
Tel (09) 309 9012 Fax (09) 309 3729
info@ascotparnell.com   www.ascotparnell.com
Double $245-$385 Single $225-$325 (Full breakfast)
Dinner 50 restaurants in walking distance
Ask us about our winter packages
Visa MC Diners Amex accepted
1 King/Twin 2 Queen 3 Twin 2 Single (3 bdrm)
Bathrooms: 3 Ensuite in all rooms

Welcome to Ascot Parnell. Tranquil B&B accommodation. *A charming small b&b hotel *Your home away from home in Auckland *Spacious rooms *Walk to all city attractions *a Top Central location yet so quiet *garden surroundings *Spectacular sea-views *private secure car-parking *friendly hosts *Free wireless broadband internet *helpful travel advice .... Inquire direct with your hosts who look forward to welcoming you.

Auckland's most popular bed and breakfast since 1984. You will recommend it! Superbly equipped centrally located B&B hidden from the main street in tranquil garden surroundings. Uniquely located at a moment's stroll from Parnell Village. Walk to numerous cafés, restaurants, art galleries and boutiques and only 1.5 km (1 mile) to downtown Auckland city. The Rose Gardens and Auckland Museum is an easy five minute walk. The Airport Shuttle-Bus brings you to the door and if you come by car, there is secure underground parking.

Bedrooms are bright and spacious, with large windows that open, some with balconies and have either garden or harbour views. Rooms are all non-smoking with air-conditioning, phone and internet connection.

Every practical detail has been minutely considered from your point of view and only the highest quality has been sought in all things. There is much solid wood, pebbles in pot plants, marble in bathrooms, thick glass showers, mirrors, modern art, warm simple colours, perfect white linen on new beds. Mod cons include an open-plan kitchen with a coffee-maker, free juice & cookies. There's a Mac for guest use, security-swiper for the lift, a piano, CD player, laundry, the list goes on...

Breakfast is a five-course feast with freshly squeezed juice, seasonal or tropical fruits, yoghurt, cereals and homemade muesli, gourmet omelettes, bacon and eggs, Belgian pancakes, French toast etc.

Your hosts, Bart and Therese could not care more enthusiastically about their guests. They will help you book tours, rental cars and accommodations for your onward journey. Reservations are essential. A "meet and greet pick up" from the airport, railway or bus station can be arranged. Please ask when you book.

Auckland - Remuera *7 km N of Auckland Central*
Woodlands *B&B Homestay*

Jude & Roger Harwood
18 Waiatarua Road, Remuera, Auckland 1050

Tel (09) 524 6990
jude.harwood@xtra.co.nz
www.travelwise.co.nz

Double $135-$155 Single $110 (Special breakfast)
Visa MC accepted
Pet free home
Not suitable for children
1 King 1 Double 1 Twin 1 Single (3 bdrm)
Bathrooms: 1 Ensuite 1 Private

Guest book comments: "Absolutely purr-fect." "Very comfortable with stunning food." "A lovely oasis of calm with wonderful breakfasts." "Peaceful retreat with excellent breakfasts." Our breakfasts ARE special using seasonal fruit and produce. Relax by our heated swimming pool. Woodlands is very quiet, surrounded by native trees and palms and central to many places of interest. The three guest bedrooms have tea/coffee facilities, heated towel rails, swimming towels and colour TVs. Fridge. Safe off-street carparking. Arrive a guest - leave a friend.

Auckland - Remuera *1.5 km E of Newmarket*
Green Oasis *B&B Homestay Apartment with Kitchen*

James & Joy Foote
25A Portland Road, Remuera, Auckland 1050

Tel (09) 520 1921   Fax (09) 522 9004
footes1@xtra.co.nz
www.babs.co.nz/greenoasis

Double $120 Single $80 (Full breakfast)
Children $65
Laundry, ironing by arrangement with small charge
Visa MC accepted
Children welcome
1 Queen 1 Single (2 bdrm)
Bathrooms: 1 Private

Green Oasis, a secluded, tranquil location in a much loved garden of native trees and ferns, ten minutes to city centre. Close to the museum, antique and specialty shops, restaurants & cafés. An informal home of natural timbers, sunny decks where you will find us relaxed, welcoming and sensitive to your needs. Your accommodation, entered from a private garden, is self-contained with kitchen/dining room, tea/coffee making facilities, washing machine, TV. Special breakfast of seasonal and home-made taste sensations!

Auckland - Remuera *3 km E of Auckland Central*
Omahu Lodge *Luxury B&B*

Robyn & Ken Booth
33 Omahu Road, Remuera, Auckland 1050

Tel (09) 524 5648 or 021 954 333
Fax (09) 524 5108   info@omahulodge.co.nz
www.omahulodge.co.nz

Double up to $275 Single $160-$200 (Full breakfast)
Dinner by arrangement
Visa MC accepted
Pet free home Not suitable for children
1 King 2 Queen 1 Double 1 Twin 1 Single (4 bdrm)
Bathrooms: 4 Ensuite 1 Private plus luxurious separate
bath suite

Omahu Lodge is a spacious home with total privacy in a peaceful, residential setting. Choose from four spacious and beautifully appointed bedrooms all with ensuites, heated towels, bath robes and tea/coffee facilities. Rooms having views of Cornwall Park, Mt Hobson and Auckland's eastern/southern suburbs. Enjoy a sauna, spa or swim in the solar heated pool. Restaurants, parks, Epsom Showgrounds and public transport are easy walking distance. The city centre and Auckland's renowned harbour just ten minutes away by car. Dinner available by arrangement.

Auckland - Newmarket/Remuera

0.5 km N of Newmarket

Amerissit *B&B*
Barbara McKain
20 Buttle Street, Remuera/Newmarket, Auckland

Tel (09) 522 9297 or 027 284 4883
Fax (09) 522 9298
barbara@amerissit.co.nz
www.amerissit.co.nz

Double $185-$260 (Full breakfast)
Visa MC Diners Amex accepted
Pet free home Children welcome
2 King 1 Queen (3 bdrm)
Bathrooms: 3 Ensuite One Spa Bath

Kia ora - welcome. Amerissit is an architecturally designed bed & breakfast offering luxury accommodation close to Newmarket in Remuera, Auckland, New Zealand. Located among prestigious streets in a quiet cul-de-sac, the emphasis is on privacy, peace and tranquility. This convenient location, close to central Auckland, is only minutes by car to the popular restaurants, bars, cafés, shopping, art galleries and museums of Auckland City plus the Viaduct Harbour, Parnell, Newmarket and Remuera.

Auckland - Grey Lynn *5 km W of Auckland Central*

Henry's *Luxury B&B*
Henry Boller & Anne Sadler
33 Peel Street, Grey Lynn, 1002

Tel (09) 360 2700 or 027 210 2964
Fax (09) 360 2705
henrysonpeel@xtra.co.nz
www.henrysonpeel.co.nz

Double $200-$250 (Continental breakfast)
Visa MC accepted
Not suitable for children
1 King 1 Queen (2 bdrm)
Bathrooms: 2 Ensuite

Welcome to Henry's Boutique Accommodation. Our extensively renovated villa provides excellent facilities for the tourist, business person or simply a retreat for those wishing for some time out. Centrally situated, close to the heart of Auckland, Henry's is within short distances of all the most important sights and activities. The CBD and Ponsonby Road are just 2-5 km away. West Lynn shops with award winning bars and restaurants are within walking distance, Henry's overlooks Auckland harbour.

Auckland - Mt Eden *4 km N of Auckland Central*

811 Bed & Breakfast *B&B*
Bryan Condon & David Fitchew
811 Dominion Road, Mt Eden, Auckland 1003

Tel (09) 620 4284
Fax (09) 620 4286
811bnb@quicksilver.net.nz

Double $85 Single $55 (Full breakfast)
Children welcome
2 Double 1 Twin (3 bdrm)
Bathrooms: 2 Guest share

All are welcome at 811 Bed & Breakfast. Your hosts and their Irish water spaniels welcome you to their turn of the century home. Our home reflects years of collecting and living overseas. Located on Dominion Road (which is an extension of Queen Street city centre). The bus stop at the door, only ten minutes to city and 20 minutes to airport, shuttle bus from airport. Easy walking to Balmoral shopping area (excellent restaurants). Our breakfast gives you a beaut start to your day.

Auckland

Auckland - Mt Eden *2 km S of Auckland Central*

Bavaria B&B Hotel *B&B*

Ulrike & Rudolf
83 Valley Road, Mt Eden, Auckland 1024

Tel (09) 638 9641   Fax (09) 638 9665
bavaria@xtra.co.nz
www.bavariabandbhotel.co.nz

Double $139-$145 **Single** $95-$99 (Full breakfast)
Children over 2 $15
Extra adult $50
Please inquire about our reduced rates from May-Sept
Visa MC Amex accepted
1 King/Twin 4 Queen 2 Double 2 Twin 2 Single (11 bdrm)
Bathrooms: 11 Ensuite

Charming small hotel in quiet, historic, residential surroundings, close to city with excellent connections to town, Mt. Eden summit with panoramic views easily accessible, immaculate quality rooms with ensuites, phones; wireless internet access available, guest computer in lounge, healthy breakfast buffet-style, complimentary tea/coffee/biscuits, sunny lounge and peaceful garden, good shopping, fine restaurants & cafés nearby, off-street parking, friendly and welcoming atmosphere. Ask us for advice on rental cars, tours etc.

Auckland - Western Springs *5 km W of Town*

Hastings Hall *B&B Hotel*

Malcolm Martel
99 Western Springs Road, Western Springs

Tel (09) 845 8550 or 021 300 006
Fax (09) 845 8554
unique@hastingshall.co.nz
www.hastingshall.co.nz

Double $165-$375 **Single** $145-$295 (Full breakfast)
Visa MC Amex Eftpos accepted
Children and pets welcome
1 King 8 Queen (9 bdrm)
Bathrooms: 7 Ensuite 2 Private

Magnificently restored 1878 mansion, extensive grounds five minutes to city centre. Ideal for tourists, businesspersons or a retreat away to unwind. Enjoy gourmet breakfasts. There are nine themed guest rooms all with marble ensuites. The Grand Williams suite with private lounge to the Moulin Rouge loft suite in the Stables. Tropically landscaped grounds, formal lounge and large pool lounge with library, home theatre, computer, email & fax facilities. Furnished with antiques from the period, fine linen and warm fluffy towels. Ideal for small conferences, functions, meetings or seminars.

**Please let your hosts know if you have to cancel
they will have spent time preparing for you.**

Auckland - Epsom *5 km S of Auckland City Centre*

Millars Epsom Homestay *B&B*
Janet & Jim Millar
10 Ngaroma Road, Epsom, Auckland 1023

Tel (09) 625 7336
jmillar@xtra.co.nz
www.millarshomestay.co.nz

Double $110-$120 Single $70-$80 (Full breakfast)
Children $10-$20 Dinner $50
Visa MC accepted
Pet free home
Children welcome
1 King 1 Queen 2 Twin 1 Single (3 bdrm)
Bathrooms: 1 Ensuite 2 Private 2 showers,1 bath

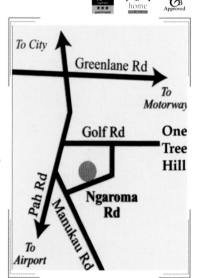

Our home, a spacious 1919 wooden bungalow, is surprisingly quiet and restful, set in a garden suburb in a tree-lined street, 200 metres from Greenwoods Corner Village with its bank, post office, reasonably priced non-tourist restaurants, and bus stop on direct route (15 minutes to the CBD).

There is a short walk to One Tree Hill, one of Auckland's loveliest parks with a playground, farm animals, groves of trees, the observatory, and a magnificent panorama of Auckland from the summit. A 15 minute walk through the park leads to the Expo Centre and Greenlane Hospital.

There are two accommodation areas - either the Garden Suite with its queen-sized double bedroom, large lounge with three single beds, patio, desk and TV, own bathroom, and which is the area we find really suitable for families; or the upstairs bedroom (king-size, can be converted to twin beds) with own ensuite, desk and TV.

We have travelled widely both in NZ and overseas (our son lives in Finland) and very much like conversing with guests and assisting in making their stay as pleasant as possible in our country and especially in this attractive suburb of Auckland. We are a smoke-free family. Jim and I were both born in NZ, and we belong to @Home NZ.

Auckland - Ellerslie *5 km SE of Auckland*

Ellerslie Bed & Breakfast Inn *B&B*
AnnaBella & Brian Gillies
6 Walpole Street, Ellerslie, Auckland

Tel (09) 589 1997 or 021 582 522
0800 589 199
Fax (09) 589 1994
info@ellersliebbi.co.nz
www.ellersliebbi.co.nz

Double $150-$180 Single $100-$150 (Full breakfast)
Visa MC accepted
Not suitable for children
2 Queen 1 Twin 2 Single (3 bdrm)
Bathrooms: 3 Ensuite

Nestled in a quiet section of Ellerslie, midway between city and airport guests can enjoy easy access to many of Auckland city's landmarks and attractions, as well as spoil themselves in our new custom designed home which offers up-to-the-minute facilities - ensuites, wireless internet and computer, guest only lounge, café style breakfasts, off-street parking - and all this at a very affordable price. Guest comments, "Wonderful hospitality, facilities and breakfast. Up there with the best". We do look forward to welcoming you soon. AnnaBella

Auckland - Orakei/Okahu Bay *4.8 km E of Auckland Central*

Nautical Nook/Free Sailing *B&B Homestay*
Trish & Keith Janes & Irish Setter
23B Watene Crescent, Orakei, Auckland

Tel (09) 521 2544 or 0800 360 544
027 439 7116
nauticalnook@bigfoot.com
www.nauticalnook.com

Double $110-$150 Single $90-$120 (Full breakfast)
Visa MC accepted
Children welcome
1 King/Twin 1 King 2 Queen (3 bdrm)
Bathrooms: 1 Ensuite 2 Private

Friendly, relaxed beachside hospitality overlooking park/harbour, 4.8km from downtown. 100 metres from Okahu Bay. Gourmet breakfast. Stroll along picturesque promenade to Kelly Tarlton's Underwater World, Mission Bay beach and cafés. Bus at door to downtown, ferry terminal, museums and Vector Arena. Unwind for 2-3 day stopover. Complimentary sailing on the harbour on our 34' yacht. We have a wealth of local knowledge and international travel experience and can assist with sightseeing, travel planning. Welcome! Pay cash and deduct 10% off listed rates. Excellent website! Free Wireless Internet.

Auckland - Mission Bay *6 km E of Auckland Central*

Cockell Homestay *Homestay*
Jean & Bryan Cockell
41 Nihill Cresent, Mission Bay, Auckland

Tel (09) 528 3809
cockells@xtra.co.nz

Double $100 Single $80 (Full breakfast)
Dinner $25 by arrangement
Visa MC accepted
Pet free home
Not suitable for children
1 Double (1 bdrm)
Bathrooms: 1 Private

We warmly welcome you to our comfortable split level home. The upper level is for your exclusive use including a private lounge. Five minutes walk to Mission Bay beach, cafés and restaurants and ten minutes scenic car or bus ride to down town Auckland and ferry terminal for harbour and islands in the Gulf. We are retired and look forward to sharing our special part of Auckland with you. Please phone for directions or airport shuttle bus to our door. Please no smoking.

Auckland - St Heliers *10 km E of Auckland*
McPherson B&B *B&B*

Jill & Ron McPherson
102 Maskell Street, St Heliers, Auckland

Tel (09) 575 9738
Fax (09) 575 0051
ron&jill_mcpherson@xtra.co.nz

Double $120 **Single** $85
(Continental breakfast)
1 Queen 1 Twin (2 bdrm)
Bathrooms: 1 Private

Welcome to our modern home with off-street parking in a smoke-free environment. One group of guests is accommodated at a time. Having travelled extensively ourselves we are fully aware of tourists' needs. eight minutes walk to St Heliers Bay beach, shops, restaurants, cafés, banks and post office. Picturesque 12 minutes drive along the Auckland waterfront past Kelly Tarlton's Antarctic and Underwater Encounter to downtown Auckland. Interests including all sports, gardening and Jill is a keen cross-stitch embroiderer. Not suitable for children/pets.

Auckland - St Heliers *12 km E of Auckland Central*
The Munro's *B&B Homestay*

Margaret and Don Munro
12 Emerson Street, St Heliers, Auckland 1071

Tel (09) 528 0459
Fax (09) 528 0459
dmlmunro@xtra.co.nz

Double $98-$120 **Single** $80-$90 (Full breakfast)
Dinner by arrangement
Pet free home
Not suitable for children
1 King/Twin 1 King (1 bdrm)
Bathrooms: 1 Ensuite

Our spacious guestroom has a king or twin comfortable bed(s), ensuite, private entry and patio area. There are tea/coffee facilities. Off-street parking. Located only 2 km from St Heliers Bay with a 10 km scenic waterfront drive to central Auckland. The airport is a 45 minute drive, or a taxi/shuttle bus will bring you to our door. Dinner is available by prior arrangement. We are a retired Scottish couple who have lived in the tropics, enjoy travel and conversation. No smoking please.

Auckland - Howick *3 km S of Howick*
Martini House *Luxury B&B Homestay*

Mark and Tina
183 Whitford Road, Howick, Auckland

Tel (09) 534 8585 or 027 496 1987
martinico@xtra.co.nz

Double $185-$215 **Single** $135-$165 (Full breakfast)
Visa MC accepted
Pet free home
Not suitable for children
1 King 2 Queen (3 bdrm)
Bathrooms: 1 Ensuite 1 Guest share

Martini House is located just 25 km from both Auckland Central and the Airport. It is ideally positioned as a staging post for touring the Coromandel or for accessing tourist attractions in greater Auckland. Features include swimming pool and spacious guest lounge with home theatre. We offer a revitalising stay with easy access to local attractions including restaurants, shopping, golf and parks.

Auckland - Howick *4 km E of Botany*

Lilian Gladys Cottage & Nellie Rose Retreat *Cottage with Kitchen*
Lorraine & Ivan Cox
288 Whitford Road, RD 1, Howick

Tel (09) 530 8854 or 021 906 072
Fax (09) 530 8854
li_cox@xtra.co.nz

B&B
Approved

Double $120-$140 (Breakfast by arrangement)
Children $10 - cot & highchair available on request
Minimum stay two nights
Weekly rate on request   Children welcome
1 Queen (1 bdrm)
Bathrooms: 1 Private

Scenic Whitford Bed & Breakfast or Short Term Accommodation.

The one bedroom Lilian Gladys & two bedroom
Nellie Rose Cottages are part of a nine acre country
estate. They are completely separate and self-contained
with their own entrances, private gardens & TV/DVD
players. These uniquely positioned cottages have all the
advantages of a rural setting and are minutes from major
shopping centres, theatres, beaches, parks, golf courses,
boutique wineries and local crafts. 30 minutes from
Auckland International Airport. Northern & southern
motorways, passenger ferry service to Auckland and
Waiheke Island are nearby.

Lilian Gladys Cottage ($120 - $140): Facing northeast
the cottage enjoys all day sun. The queen size bedroom
has a private reading/relaxation area; the settee in the
lounge converts into a double bed.

Nellie Rose Retreat ($150-$160): The Retreat is an all
timber cottage with its own grounds and double garage.
It sleeps 6; queen bed in main room, twin beds in second
room, settee in lounge converts to double bed.

Tea, coffee & biscuits to welcome you. Lorraine & Ivan
aim for your stay to be relaxing and carefree. Transport
to/from airport can be arranged. Bookings essential.

Auckland - Howick *2 km N of Howick*

French Lavender *B&B*

Michael & Barbara Davis
40 McCahill Views, Howick, Auckland

Tel (09) 535 4910
Fax (09) 535 4920
enquiries@frenchlavender.co.nz
www.frenchlavender.co.nz

Double $100 Single $80 (Continental breakfast)
Family Rates Available
Visa MC accepted
Children welcome
1 Queen 2 Single (2 bdrm)
Bathrooms: 1 Guest share

Set in a quiet cul-de-sac, French Lavender is a modern two storey home with the guest rooms on the upper level, sharing a private balcony overlooking the garden and 180-degree views. The guest lounge provides a separate spot for relaxation, peace and quiet. Your hosts have travelled extensively, enjoy meeting people, visiting local restaurants as well as gardening and an occasional round of golf. Stroll in the garden; watch the birds and fish or make friends with our two cats.

Auckland - Howick *1.5 km E of Botany*

No 44 *Apartment with Kitchen*

Rosemarie & Graham
44 Burnaston Court, Dannemora/Howick, 2016

Tel (09) 274 0406 or 027 444 7290
rosemariemorgan@xtra.co.nz

Double $100-$110 Single $95-$100
(Continental breakfast provisions)
Children welcome
Extra person $10 per day
1 Double 1 Single (2 bdrm)
Bathrooms: 1 Private 1 Guest share

Rosemarie and Graham invite you to relax in a quiet location with own private courtyard. Handy to Botany Town Centre, Meadowlands shops, Howick Village, beaches and ferry to the city. Gateway to Whitford, Beachlands and Clevedon. easily accessible to restaurants, cinemas and Golf Courses. Off season and longer term rates on request.

Auckland - Avondale *10 km W of Auckland Central*

Kodesh Community *B&B Apartment with Kitchen*

Kodesh Trust
31B Cradock Street, Avondale, Auckland

Tel (09) 828 5672 or 027 482 8643
027 601 3611   Fax (09) 828 5684
Kodeshtrust@xtra.co.nz
www.kodeshcommunity.org.nz

Double $70 Single $40 (Breakfast by arrangement)
Dinner $10   Flat $10 per person extra
Eftpos accepted
Pet free home   Children welcome
1 Queen 1 Double 1 Twin 1 Single (6 bdrm)
Bathrooms: 1 Private 2 Family share

Kodesh is an ecumenical, cross-cultural Christian community of around 25 residents, eight minutes by car from downtown Auckland. Single or double room available and a self-contained flat sleeps two to seven people. Large table tennis/meeting room available. Group rates available. An evening meal may be available in the community dining room Monday-Friday. Bookings essential. The atmosphere is relaxed and guests can amalgamate into the life of the community as much or little as desired. No pets, children under 12 welcome.

Auckland - Titirangi *15 km W of Auckland Central*

Kaurigrove *B&B*
Gaby & Peter Wunderlich
120 Konini Road, Titirangi, Auckland 7

Tel (09) 817 5608 or 027 275 0574
Fax (09) 817 5608
kaurigrove@yahoo.co.nz

Double $100-$110 Single $60 (Continental breakfast)
Visa MC accepted Children welcome
1 Queen 1 Single (2 bdrm)
Bathrooms: 1 Private

Welcome to our home! Kaurigrove offers a tranquil location amidst kauri trees in a park-like setting yet close to shops, cafés and restaurants. Situated at Titirangi, we are near Auckland's historic west coast with its magnificent beaches and vast native bush with a wonder-world of walking tracks. Gaby and Peter, your hosts of German background, are keen travellers themselves and are happy to introduce you to the highlights of Auckland and its surrounding areas. Non-smoking inside residence.

Auckland - Hillsborough *12 km S of city*

Mamreoak bnb *B&B*
Joyce Tan
78 Oakdale Road, Hillsborough, Auckland 1041

Tel (09) 624 0220 or (09) 624 6966
027 276 8398
Fax (09) 624 0227
info@mamreoak.co.nz
www.mamreoak.co.nz

Double $160-$225 Single $115-$150
(Continental breakfast)
Eftpos accepted
Pet free home
3 Queen 2 Double 2 Single (6 bdrm)
Bathrooms: 3 Ensuite 1 Guest share

Your hosts welcome you to their private haven- it's home but better. Mamre Oak Bed & Breakfast offers 6 queen, double and single bedrooms, including one very luxurious master bedroom with steam and massage bathroom facilities. Be mesmerized by the magnificent view of One Tree Hill while relaxing on the spacious balcony. All rooms are comfortably spacious and the solar-heated floor system keep your feet warm just like home, especially during those cold winter nights.

Auckland Airport - Mangere Bridge *14 km S of Auckland* Central

Mangere Bridge Homestay *Homestay*
Carol & Brian
1 Boyd Avenue, Mangere Bridge, Auckland

Tel (09) 636 6346
Fax (09) 636 6345
mangerebridgehomestay@xtra.co.nz

Double $95-$115 Single $75-$90 (Full breakfast)
Children 12 and under $20
Dinner $30 by prior arrangement
2 King/Twin 1 Double (3 bdrm)
Bathrooms: 3 Ensuite

We invite you to share our home, which is within ten minutes of Auckland Airport, an ideal location for your arrival or departure of New Zealand. We enjoy meeting people and look forward to making your stay an enjoyable one. We welcome you to join us for dinner by prior arrangement. Courtesy car to or from airport, bus and rail. Off street parking available. Handy to public transport. Short stroll to the waterfront. Please no smoking indoors. Our cat requests no pets. Inspection welcome.

Auckland Airport - Mangere *2 km N of Mangere*

Airport Homestay/B&B *B&B Homestay*

May Pepperell
288 Kirkbride Road, Mangere, Auckland

Tel (09) 275 6777 or 027 289 8200
Fax (09) 275 6728
marcia@venture.co.nz

Double $70 Single $45 (Continental breakfast)
Children $20
3 Single (2 bdrm)
Bathrooms: 1 Guest share

Clean comfortable home five minutes from airport but not on flight path. Easy walk to shops and restaurants. Ten minutes from shopping centres and Telstra Events Centre at Manukau. Aviation Golf Course near airport, also Villa Maria Winery. My interests are people, travel, Ladies' Probus and voluntary work. Beds have woollen underlays and electric blankets. There is a sunny terrace and fenced swimming pool. Courtesy car to/from airport at reasonable hour. Vehicles minded while you're away from $1 day. Bus stop very close.

Auckland - Mangere *4 km N of Airport*

Airport Bed & Breakfast *B&B*

Laurel Blakey
1 Westney Road, Corner of Kirkbride Road, Mangere

Tel (09) 275 0533
Fax (09) 275 0968
airportbnb@xtra.co.nz
www.airportbnb.co.nz

Double $90-$120 Single $75-$105
(Continental breakfast)
Visa MC Diners Amex Eftpos accepted
1 King 3 Queen 5 Double 1 Twin 7 Single (10 bdrm)
Bathrooms: 4 Ensuite 3 Guest share

Just five minutes drive from Auckland Airport a friendly welcome and great value accommodation awaits. Ten quality rooms, four ensuites, central heating, large TV/Sky/dining room. Internet access. Two minutes walk to city bus stop - see Auckland by bus and ferry on the $11 day pass. Restaurants/takeaways nearby. Car, cycle and luggage storage. Rental cars and NZ wide sightseeing tours booked. Courtesy airport transfer (6.30am -8.45pm), free phone at airport, dial 28. Buffet breakfast, complimentary tea/coffee.

Auckland - Manukau *6.5 km NE of Manukau City*

Tanglewood *B&B Homestay*

Roseanne & Ian Devereux
5 Inchinnam Road, Flat Bush,
Manukau City, Auckland

Tel (09) 274 8280
Fax (09) 634 6896
tanglewood@clear.net.nz

Double $110 Single $70 (Full breakfast)
Children $15
Visa MC accepted
Children and pets welcome
1 King 1 Queen 1 Double (3 bdrm)
Bathrooms: 1 Ensuite 1 Private

Our homely cottage, set in two acres is 20 minutes from the International Airport. Wake up to birdsong in our garden loft which is separate from the house, with deck overlooking large peaceful gardens and ponds. There are two cosy rooms inside the house. We are 30 minutes from downtown Auckland, close to Botany Shopping Centre and good restaurants. Delicious home-cooked breakfast includes eggs from our free-range hens. We have a swimming pool and friendly dog, Daisy. We offer you warm and relaxed hospitality.

Auckland - Manukau *6.5 km NE of Manukau*

Calico Cottage *B&B*

Patty & Murray Glenie
7 Inchinnam Road, Flat Bush, Auckland

Tel (09) 274 8527
Fax (09) 274 8528
MG-PT@xtra.co.nz

Double $100 Single $70 (Full breakfast)
Children $15
Visa MC accepted
Children and pets welcome
1 Queen 1 Single (2 bdrm)
Bathrooms: 1 Ensuite

Welcome to Calico Cottage. We are on two acres with garden, paddocks, sheep, chickens - free range eggs, and one dog who lives outdoors. Peaceful and yet only ten minutes from both Manukau City Centre and Botany Town Centre and 20 minutes from Auckland Airport. Transport to and from airport arranged if required. We have a double bedroom with new ensuite and a TV room adjoining for your own use. We look forward to your visit.

Auckland - Manurewa *2 km S of Manukau City*

Hillpark Homestay *B&B Homestay*

Katrine & Graham Paton
16 Collie Street, Manurewa, Auckland 2102

Tel (09) 267 6847 or 021 207 2559
Fax (09) 267 8718   stay@hillpark.co.nz
www.hillpark.co.nz

Double $100 Single $60 (Full breakfast)
Children $20
Dinner $20 by arrangement
Visa MC accepted
1 Double 4 Single (3 bdrm)
Bathrooms: 1 Ensuite 1 Guest share

Welcome to our sunny, spacious home and meet our friendly tonkinese cat. We are 15 minutes from Auckland Airport, 20 minutes from Auckland City centre, on the route south and the Pacific Coast Highway. Nearby are restaurants, Regional Botanic Gardens (Ellerslie Flower Show), TelstraClear Pacific Events Centre, Tipapa Events Centre, Manukau City Shopping Centre, Manukau Superclinic and Surgery Centre. Our interests include teaching, classical music, painting, gardening, photography, Christian activities, reading and travel. We are a smoke-free home. Directions: please phone or visit our website.

Auckland - Alfriston *10 km SE of Manukau City*

Top of the Hill Country Homestay *Luxury B&B Country Homestay*

Pat & Trevor Simpson
183 Fitzpatrick Road, Brookby RD 1,
Manurewa, Auckland

Tel (09) 530 8576
Fax (09) 530 8576
topofthehill@wc.net.nz
www.topofthehill.co.nz

Double $120-$140 Single $80-$80 (Full breakfast)
Not suitable for children under 12 years
Visa MC accepted
1 King/Twin 2 King (3 bdrm)
Bathrooms: 3 Ensuite

Be first to see the sunrise from our spacious well appointed home. High on the hill with breathtaking spectacular,landscape views to Auckland's sparking harbours and volcanoes. The guest wing has luxuriously large bedrooms,each with ensuite, plus floor to ceiling windows. Visit our friendly animals or just relax in the large lounge. We have a guest utility with cooking and laundry facilites. 25 minutes to Auckland Airport and city, close to Clevedon, Tipapa Events Centre, Botanical Gardens, beaches & vineyard tours. Discounted three day stays.

Whitford *25 km SE of Auckland*

Springhill Country Homestay *Farmstay*
Judy & Derek Stubbs
Polo Lane, Whitford, RD, Manurewa, Auckland

Tel (09) 530 8674
Fax (09) 530 8274
djstubbs@ihug.co.nz

Double $120 Single $80 (Full breakfast)
Children $40, one room suitable
Visa MC accepted
Children and pets welcome
1 Queen (1 bdrm)
Bathrooms: 1 Ensuite

Springhill is an eight hectare farm in Whitford, an attractive rural area approximately 25 km south-east of Auckland. We are close to a beautiful golf course, beaches and Auckland Airport. We farm angora goats and sheep, pets include a cat and a dog. Guest accommodation is one detached double room with ensuite, but children can be accommodated. TV, tea/coffee making facilities, and a private spa pool are available. Directions: left off Whitford Park Road. 1 km past golf course.

Clevedon *3 km S of Clevedon*

Karinya B & B *B&B Cottage with Kitchen*
Kevin & Judy Hanley
290 Clevedon Road, RD2 Papakura, Auckland

Tel (09) 292 9024 or 027 4759 317
Fax (09) 292 9025
hanley@xtra.co.nz
www.karinya.co.nz

Double $130-$160 Single $110-$110
(Continental breakfast provisions)
Lunch and dinner on request
Visa MC Diners Amex accepted
Pet free home Children welcome
2 King 1 Single (2 bdrm)
Bathrooms: 2 Ensuite

Kevin and Judy invite you to stay in their guesthouse set in 30 acres in the Clevedon Valley. Separate from the main homestead giving total privacy. Relax and enjoy the peace and quiet of the rural lifestyle. A variety of wineries, cafés, beaches, bush walks, and golf courses nearby.

Kaiaua *4 km N of Kaiaua*

Kaiaua Seaside Lodge *B&B Lodge*
Fran Joseph & Denis Martinovich
1336 Pacific Coast Highway, Kaiaua

Tel (09) 232 2696 or 027 274 0534
Fax (09) 232 2699
kaiaua_lodge@xtra.co.nz
http://bnb.co.nz/kaiauaseasidelodge.html

Double $110-$130 Single $75 (Continental breakfast)
Children welcome
3 Queen 2 Single (5 bdrm)
Bathrooms: 2 Ensuite 1 Guest share

The Lodge is situated on the water's edge of The Seabird Coast, famous for its birdlife, Miranda Hot Springs, regional parks and fish 'n chips. Four km north of Kaiaua township, the Lodge features attractive beach gardens and panoramic views of the Coromandel. It is ideally positioned for leisurely seashore strolls or more active tramps in the Hunua Ranges. Boating and fishing facilities are available. En suite rooms are spacious and the separate guest lounge has a refrigerator and television.

Miranda *30 km SE of Bombay Hills Freeway*

Miranda Views B&B *B&B Cottage with Kitchen*

Millie & Wayne Taylor
1213 Miranda Road, Miranda, 1872

Tel (09) 232 7800 or 027 494 2780
Fax (09) 232 7811
mill@xtra.co.nz

Double $145 **Single** $100 (Full breakfast provisions)
Children $30
Visa MC Eftpos accepted
Children welcome
1 Queen 3 Single (2 bdrm)
Bathrooms: 2 Guest share

O ur lifestyle farm is situated in the beautiful Miranda Valley; less than an hours drive south from Auckland Airport. Enjoy the panoramic views of our lush valley, the Firth of Thames and Coromandel Ranges in the background. Relax and unwind in your own private chalet, take in views on your own balcony, stroll around our farm, visit some of our local attractions, or just watch abit of TV. We along with our daughter Ashley and our two spoilt cats and one friendly dog welcome you.

Papakura *1.5 km W of Papakura*

Campbell Clan House *B&B*

Colin & Anna Mieke Campbell
57 Rushgreen Avenue, Pahurehure, Papakura

Tel (09) 298 8231 or 027 496 7754
Fax (09) 298 7792   colam@pl.net
www.campbellclan.co.nz

Double $125 **Single** $80 (Full breakfast)
Children negotiable
Dinner $30-$40 by arrangement
Discount for 3+ nights   Visa MC accepted
Pet free home   Children welcome
2 Queen 2 Single (3 bdrm)
Bathrooms: 2 Ensuite 1 Private

O ur peaceful location is within walking distance of trains and buses, shopping centre and restaurants. We are two minutes from motorway north/south, 15 minutes from airport and enroute to Firth of Thames and the Coromandel. Our separate upstairs guest accommodation includes three double bedrooms, large comfortable lounge with tea/coffee, tourist information, TV and private balcony with lovely view. We are happy to assist with any holiday arrangements, car hire, transfers and offer internet and laundry facilities. Discount for three or more nights.

Hunua - Paparimu *18 km S of Papakura*

Erathcree Countrystay *B&B Cottage with Kitchen*

Rob & Gillian Wakelin
10 Wilson Road, Paparimu, RD 3,
Papakura, 2583, Auckland

Tel (09) 292 5062 or 021 128 1547
Fax (09) 292 5064   gillrob@xtra.co.nz

Double $130 **Single** $100 (Breakfast by arrangement)
Children under 12 reduced rate, cot available
Dinner $40pp by arrangement
Additional person $30pp
Visa MC accepted
Children and pets welcome
1 Queen 1 Double (1 bdrm)
Bathrooms: 1 Private with shower, vanity & WC

A n easy drive to Auckland Airport/City (40-45 minutes approx), quick access to State Highway 2 for travel south ... but in its own tranquil world of green countryside, tree filled garden and Hunua Ranges backdrop. Well travelled hosts offer a warm, helpful welcome, the pets are friendly and the atmosphere relaxed. The cottage is a short garden stroll away from the house, with comfortable beds, fresh fruit and flowers, and country atmosphere. Wheelchairs: ground floor access only.

Drury *3 km E of Drury*

The Drury Homestead *B&B*

Carolyn & Ron Booker
349 Drury Hills Road, Drury, South Auckland

Tel (09) 294 9030 or 021 158 5061
Fax (09) 294 9035
druryhome@paradise.net.nz

Double $120 Single $70-$90 (Full breakfast)
Children negotiable
3 Queen 1 Twin (4 bdrm)
Bathrooms: 3 Ensuite 1 Private

Hosts Carolyn and Ron, have undertaken a labour of love in restoring an early colonial home to its former glory. The Drury Homestead was originally built circa 1879 and is set in majestic rolling farmland, bordered by native bush and a glorious tumbling stream. Choose from four character filled rooms, all with their own special views. Refurbished with an emphasis on comfort and style. Restaurants nearby. Situated five minutes from the main highway and 20 minutes from the airport. Family cat and dog.

Ramarama *7 km S of Drury*

Thistledown Lodge *B&B Homestay*

Sue & Archie McPherson
42 Coulston Road, Ramarama, Pukekohe RD 2

Tel (09) 238 1912 or 027 473 6313
inquiries@thistledownlodge.co.nz
www.thistledownlodge.co.nz

Double $130 Single $80 (Special breakfast)
Children negotiable
Dinner by arrangement
Visa MC accepted
Children welcome
1 King 2 Queen (3 bdrm)
Bathrooms: 3 Private

This peaceful country setting will be the perfect start or end to your holiday. Discover the secret of Archie's breakfasts which delight and surprise guests. The English-style country house has an idyllic setting down a leafy lane. Relax in quiet and spacious second floor bedrooms or unwind in the spa (jacuzzi) . Easy to find from Ramarama motorway exit, secure off-street parking and just 25 minutes from Auckland Airport.

Waiuku *5 km E of Waiuku*

Totara Downs *B&B Homestay*

Janet & Christopher de Tracy-Gould
355 Baldhill Road, RD 1, Waiuku,
Franklin Dristrict, Auckland 1852

Tel (09) 235 8505
Fax (09) 235 8504
totaradw@ihug.co.nz
www.totaradowns.co.nz

Double $150 Single $100 (Full breakfast)
Visa MC accepted
1 King/Twin 1 Queen (2 bdrm)
Bathrooms: 1 Ensuite 1 Private

Just 50 minutes drive south from Auckland International Airport and city, Totara Downs is found on a quiet country road. Set in large country house gardens with breath taking rural views. We offer feather and downs pillows and duvets, sitting room with open fire, swimming pool, lawn croquet. Historic Waiuku boasts wonderful peninsula beaches and country garden tours. With "Vita" our Dalmatian and two cats we look forward to meeting you. Not suitable for children under 12. Smoke-free home.

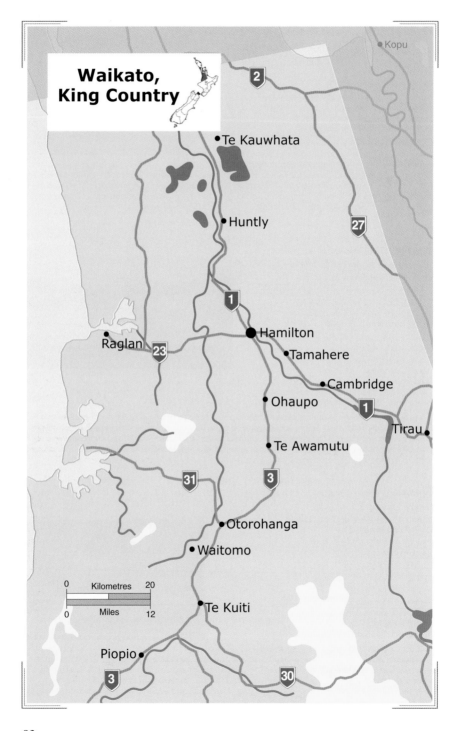

Waikato, King Country

Kopu

2

Te Kauwhata

Huntly

27

1

Raglan

23

Hamilton

Tamahere

Cambridge

Ohaupo

1

Tirau

Te Awamutu

31

3

Otorohanga

Waitomo

| 0 | Kilometres | 20 |
| 0 | Miles | 12 |

Te Kuiti

Piopio

3

30

Te Kauwhata *7 km E of Te Kauwhata*

Herons Ridge *B&B Farmstay Cottage with Kitchen*

Ruth & Craig Chamberlain
1131 Lake Waikare Scenic Drive, RD 1, Te Kauwhata

Tel (07) 826 4646
Fax (07) 826 4171
herons.ridge@xtra.co.nz
www.huntly.net.nz/herons.html

Double $120-$140 **Single** $60-$80 (Full breakfast)
Dinner by arrangement
Self-contained studio $140
Not suitable for children
1 Queen (1 bdrm)
Bathrooms: 1 Private

Welcome to your home in the Waikato. Our quality Garden Studio overlooking the pool and garden is the perfect setting for your stay. The farm, set amongst ponds and pinewoods, enhance our rural location close to Lake Waikare. Meet our cats Tabby and Mars, our two farm dogs and Fleur our pony. Meals are served inhouse by arrangement. Country walks, golf and hot springs - the choice is yours. From SH1 go through Te Kauwhata village, 6 km east along Waerenga Road, 1 km on right - Welcome.

~

Huntly *4 km NW of Huntly*

Parnassus Farm & Garden *B&B Farmstay Cottage with Kitchen*

Sharon & David Payne
Te Ohaki Road, RD 1, Huntly

Tel (07) 828 8781 or 021 458 525
Fax (07) 828 8781
parnassus@xtra.co.nz
www.parnassus.co.nz

Double $120-$140 **Single** $70-$100 (Full breakfast)
Children according to age
Dinner by arrangement
Visa MC accepted Children welcome
2 King/Twin 2 Double 2 Single (3 bdrm)
Bathrooms: 3 Private 1 Guest share

Experience farm life or simply relax on a working farm 1 hour south of Auckland and only 4 km off SH1. All bedrooms beautifully appointed with private facilities. Our home gardens supply produce & preserves for the Farm to Fork dining experience we are renowned for, and showcase a diverse range of trees & shrubs, fruits & vegetables. Farm, bush & wetland walks all easily accessible. Leave SH1 at traffic lights by Huntly KFC. Cross river, right, Harris Street 2 km, right, Te Ohaki Road, number 191.

~

Raglan *20 km S of Raglan*

Matawha *Farmstay*

Jenny & Peter Thomson
61 Matawha Road, RD 2, Raglan

Tel (07) 825 6709
Fax (07) 825 6715
jennyt@wave.co.nz

Double $130-$150 **Single** $60-$60 (Full breakfast)
Dinner $20
Cash or cheque only please
Not suitable for children
1 King 1 Double 4 Single (3 bdrm)
Bathrooms: 1 Private 1 Guest share 1 Family share

We live on the west coast and our family has farmed this land for 100 years. Come and enjoy our private beach, expansive garden, home-grown vegetables, spa, two cats and the peace of no other buildings or people for miles. Take bush or mountain walks, a scenic drive, go surfing or fishing, or maybe find the hot-water beach! Auckland 2.5 hours, Hamilton 1 hour, Raglan 30 minutes. Directions: Take Hamilton/Raglan route 23, turn left at Bridal Veil Falls sign, right at Te Mata onto Ruapuke Road, left onto Tuturimu Road and follow to T-junction, straight ahead across to cattlestop - 61 Matawha Road.

Raglan *0.8 km N of Raglan Central*

Journey's End Raglan Bed & Breakfast *Luxury B&B Separate Suite*

Tricia & Barry Ashby
49 Lily Street, Raglan, 3225

Tel (07) 825 6727 or 027 234 5184
tricia.barry@raglanaccommodation.co.nz
www.raglanaccommodation.co.nz

Double $120-$180 **Single** $90-$180 (Special breakfast)
Children by arrangement
Dinner by arrangement
Not suitable for children
2 Queen (2 bdrm)
Bathrooms: 2 Ensuite

Enjoy our panoramic views from your deck. Two luxury suites each purpose built with own ensuites, TV, DVD and lounge chairs. Beautiful guest lounge, dining room and kitchenette. Walk to wharf and enjoy fishing and sightseeing trips. Take a stroll to Raglan shopping centre with it many restaurants, cafés, bars, arts & crafts. Ten minute drive to world-famous surfing beaches, all this or just relax in comfort of your suite.

Hamilton *3 km N of Hamilton*

Kantara *Homestay*

Mrs Esther Kelly
7 Delamare Road, Bryant Park, Hamilton

Tel (07) 849 2070 or 027 263 9442
esther@slingshot.co.nz

Double $100-$125 **Single** $65 (Full breakfast)
Dinner $25
Pet free home
Not suitable for children
1 Double 1 Twin (2 bdrm)
Bathrooms: 1 Ensuite 1 Private

I have travelled extensively throughout New Zealand and overseas and welcome tourists to my comfortable home. I live close to the Waikato River with its tranquil river walks and St Andrews Golf Course. My interests are travel, golf, Mah Jong. Tea/coffee making facilities are available. I look forward to offering you friendly hospitality. Directions: from Auckland - leave main Highway north of Hamilton at round intersection into Bryant Road (large Blue sign-St Andrews. Turn left into Sandwich Road and second street on right.

Hamilton *1.5 km E of Hamilton Central*

Matthews B&B *B&B Homestay*

Maureen & Graeme Matthews
24 Pearson Avenue, Claudelands, Hamilton

Tel (07) 855 4269 or 027 474 7758
Fax (07) 855 4269
mgm@xtra.co.nz
www.matthewsbnb.co.nz

Double $100-$110 **Single** $50-$60 (Full breakfast)
Children half price
Dinner $25
1 Double 1 Twin (2 bdrm)
Bathrooms: 1 Guest share 1 Family share

Welcome to our home two seconds off the city bypass on Routes 7 & 9 at Five Crossroads. We are adjacent to the Waikato Events Centre, Ruakura Research Station, handy to the university and only three minutes from central city. Our home is a lived-in comfortable home, warm in winter and cool in summer, with a pool available. We enjoy spending time with visitors from NZ and overseas. We have travelled extensively and enjoy helping to plan your holiday. Dinner by arrangement.

Hamilton *3 km N of Hamilton Central*

Ebbett Homestay *B&B Homestay*
Glenys & John Ebbett
162 Beerescourt Road, Hamilton

Tel (07) 849 2005
johnebbett@xtra.co.nz

Double $105 Single $75 (Full breakfast)
Dinner $25
Pet free home
Not suitable for children
2 Single (1 bdrm)
Bathrooms: 1 Private

Only minutes from town centre, our 16 year old home has a spectacular view of the Waikato River (New Zealand's longest) and easy access to Hamilton's popular river walk. We enjoy sharing travel anecdotes, but also respect our guests' wish for privacy. Your room has its own tea/coffee facility and private bathroom. Only 85 minutes from Auckland International Airport, we appeal to tourists arriving or departing New Zealand. Our interests include people, music, sport, travel, gardening and community. 14 years of happy hosting.

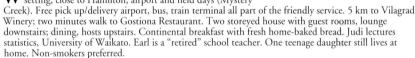

Hamilton - Ohaupo *4 km SW of Hamilton*

Green Gables of Rukuhia *B&B*
Earl & Judi McWhirter
35 Rukuhia Road, RD 2, Ohaupo

Tel (07) 843 8511 or 021 583 462
Fax (07) 843 8514
judi.earl@clear.net.nz

Double $90-$120 Single $50-$60 (Continental breakfast)
Visa MC accepted
Children welcome
2 Double 3 Single (3 bdrm)
Bathrooms: 1 Guest share

Warm, comfortable smoke-free family home in a quiet rural setting, close to Hamilton, airport and field days (Mystery Creek). Free pick up/delivery airport, bus, train terminal all part of the friendly service. 5 km to Vilagrad Winery; two minutes walk to Gostiona Restaurant. Two storeyed house with guest rooms, lounge downstairs; dining, hosts upstairs. Continental breakfast with fresh home-baked bread. Judi lectures statistics, University of Waikato. Earl is a "retired" school teacher. One teenage daughter still lives at home. Non-smokers preferred.

Hamilton *28 km S of Hamilton*

Country Quarters Homestay *B&B Homestay*
Ngaere & Jack Waite
11 Corcoran Road, Te Pahu, Hamilton

Tel (07) 825 9727
graeme.waite@xtra.co.nz

Double $80-$100 Single $40-$50
(Full breakfast)
Children $10
Dinner $25
Children and pets welcome
1 Queen 1 Twin 3 Single (5 bdrm)
Bathrooms: 2 Guest share
Bathroom & shower room

We welcome you to the peace and tranquillity of country life. Our place is central from Te Awamutu and Hamilton, located in the little farming community of Te Pahu, right under Mount Pirongia. We are in the middle of a block of chestnut trees and are quite secluded. Our home is very large and roomy and we have special facilities for the elderly person. Comfort and nice meals is what we offer you.

Waikato

Hamilton - Tamahere *10 km S of Hamilton*
Lenvor B&B *B&B Homestay*
Lenora & Trevor Shelley
540E Oaklea Lane, RD 3, Tamahere, Hamilton

Tel (07) 856 2027
Fax (07) 856 4173
lenvor@clear.net.nz

Double $110 Single $65 (Full breakfast)
Children $10-$25
Dinner by arrangement
Children welcome
3 Queen 3 Single (4 bdrm)
Bathrooms: 1 Ensuite 2 Guest share 1 Family share

Lenora and Trevor warmly invite you to relax and to share the comfort of our home Lenvor, which is set in a rural area, down a country lane. Our two storeyed home has guest rooms and small lounge upstairs; dining, lounge and hosts downstairs. Ten minutes to Hamilton or Cambridge, five minutes to Mystery Creek or airport. Lenora's interests are floral art and cake icing. Trevor enjoys vintage cars. Centrally situated for day trips to Coromandel, Tauranga, Rotorua, Taupo and Waitomo Caves.

Hamilton *10 km E of Hamilton*
A&A Country Stay *Farmstay Cottage with Kitchen*
Ann & Alan Marsh
275 Vaile Road, RD 4, Hamilton 3284

Tel (07) 824 1908 or (07) 824 1909
027 476 3014
aacountrystay@bordernet.co.nz

Double $140 Single $80 (Continental breakfast)
Children $20
Weekly rates for long-term stays
Visa MC accepted
Children and pets welcome
1 Queen 2 Single (2 bdrm)
Bathrooms: 1 Private

The Cottage is fully self-contained, 2 bedrooms, including laundry and Sky digital. Peaceful surroundings set in two acres of garden with a large pond. Sit, relax in privacy out on the veranda, have our ducks and doves visit you for that bit of bread while overlooking our 47 acres with sheep and cattle. Have a talk to our clydesdale (Sarah) and our miniature (Sha) who love people staying especially when they have apples in their hand. Two Jack Russells will also welcome you.

Hamilton - Ohaupo *15 km S of Hamilton*
Ridge House *B&B*
Margaret Birtles & Matthew Harris
15 Main Road, Ohaupo

Tel (07) 823 6555
Fax (07) 823 6550
m.a.birtles@xtra.co.nz

Double $80-$90 Single $65 (Continental breakfast)
Children $15
Dinner $20 by arrangement
Visa MC accepted
Children and pets welcome
2 Queen 1 Single (2 bdrm)
Bathrooms: 1 Ensuite 1 Guest share

We welcome you to come and visit our home with its wonderful lake and pastoral views. Our home is shared with our dog, Zoe, who loves to welcome visitors. We are just six minutes to Hamilton International Airport and can arrange pick up from there and car storage ($10). This is an ideal base for trips to Hamilton, Te Awamutu, Waitomo Caves, Cambridge, Rotorua and Tauranga. Mystery Creek (home of the Field Days) and popular golf courses are close by. Travel well.

Hamilton *12 km SW of Hamilton*

Uliveto Countrystay *Homestay Countrystay B&B*

Peter & Daphne Searle
164 Finlayson Road, RD 10, Ngahinapouri, Hamilton

Tel (07) 825 2116 or 027 200 5320
peedee@wave.co.nz
www.uliveto.co.nz

Double up to $120 Single $90 (Full breakfast)
Dinner by arrangement
Children welcome
2 Queen (2 bdrm)
Bathrooms: 2 Ensuite Private ensuite

Come and enjoy the peace and tranquility of the beautiful countryside. Wander in our olive grove and gardens or relax on your private deck. Hamilton City, airport and fieldays are 20 minutes away, or local restaurants 12 minutes. Nearby attractions include - Waitomo Caves, lavender farm, golf course, award winning winery, horse treks/tramping tracks on Mt Pirongia, Raglan beaches and cafés. To complete your day, share dinner and wine with us or relax in the guest lounge or our therapeutic spa.

Hamilton CBD *0.2 km N of Hamilton*

Home Hospitality *B&B Homestay*

Diana & Fred Houtman
7A Hamilton Parade, Hamilton,

Tel (07) 838 1538 or 021 170 3210 text only
frediana@ihug.co.nz
www.accommodationinnewzealand.co.nz//
homehospitality

Double $120 Single $60 (Full breakfast)
Cash or NZ cheques only
Dinner $25 - advance notice required
Reduction for multiple nights
Pet free home Not suitable for children
1 King/Twin 1 Queen (2 bdrm)
Bathrooms: 1 Guest share

Comfortable self-contained accommodation in a quiet riverside cul-de-sac in the centre of Hamilton. Private sitting room for guests, with tea/coffee making facilities. Leave your car in our secure off-road parking area and walk to restaurants, shops, theatres, sports venues, conference centres - no parking hassles. A handy point from which to explore a large area of central NZ. Hosts are well travelled & enjoy meeting new people. Dutch spoken.

Hamilton *10 km W of Hamilton*

Beaumere Lodge *B&B*

Isobel & Peter Wiren
10 Genevieve Way, Highbrook, RD 9,
Whatawhata, Hamilton

Tel (07) 829 8652 or 027 232 9149
Fax (07) 829 8652
beaumere@wave.co.nz

Double $100-$130 Single $60-$80 (Full breakfast)
Children by negotiation
Dinner and light meals by arrangement
Children and pets welcome
1 Queen 1 Twin (2 bdrm)
Bathrooms: 1 Private Seperate Spa-Bath & toilet

Wonderful country setting, magic views and sunsets over the Hakaramatas. Romantic fairy-lit gardens. Guest wing, own patio, spa. One-group bookings. Close to Golf, Zoo, Tree Arboratum, Bridal Veil Falls, Raglan seaside resort 25 minutes. Glowworm Caves one hour. En route Auckland-Waitomo-Taupo. Semi-retirees with a small dog & cat, enjoy golf, bowls, gardening, travel, and Isobel sings in a choir. Peter has lived in Japan and Korea so we are always delighted to help with language and travel plans. You are assured of a memorable stay.

Hamilton - Te Pahu *20 km W of Hamilton*

Harmony Hours Retreat and B&B *B&B Retreat*

Chrystene Hansen and Bill Bailey
1385 Te Pahu Road RD 5, Hamilton, 3285

Tel (07) 825 9877 or 021 128 6083
relax@harmonyhours.co.nz
www.harmonyhours.co.nz

Double $120-$150 Single $100-$100
(Special breakfast) Children under 12 $50
Dinner by arrangement $25pp
24 hour stay, all meals
Healing therapies available
1 Queen 1 Single (1 bdrm)
Bathrooms: 1 Ensuite

Relax in this beautiful, spacious, upstairs room with lovely views of rural waikato including Mount Pirongia. Soak in the spa pool on your very own balcony under a night sky. Bill and Chrystene offer a relaxing experience and are negotiable with meal times. Meals are homegrown, sprayfree or organic. Enjoy our two acre block, which also has gardens an orchard and sheep. Muffy is our resident cat. Enquire with Chrystene for a massage/healing. 20 minutes to Hamilton, 30 to Raglan, 90 to Auckland Airport.

Cambridge *0.3 km N of Cambridge Central*

Park House *B&B*

Pat & Bill Hargreaves
70 Queen Street, Cambridge

Tel (07) 827 6368   Fax (07) 827 4094
Park.House@xtra.co.nz
www.parkhouse.co.nz

Double up to $160 Single up to $130 (Full breakfast)
Visa MC Amex accepted
Not suitable for children
1 King/Twin 1 Queen (2 bdrm)
Bathrooms: 1 Ensuite 1 Private

Park House, circa 1920, is for guests of discernment who appreciate quality and comfort. For 20 years we have offered this superb setting for guests. Throughout this large home are antiques, traditional furniture, patchworks and stained glass windows creating an elegant and restful ambience. The guest lounge features an elaborately carved fireplace, fine art, library, TV and complimentary sherry. Bedrooms in separate wing upstairs ensues privacy. Unbeatable quiet location overlooking village green, two minute walk to restaurants, antique and craft shops.

Cambridge *5 km SW of Cambridge*

Birches *B&B Farmstay Cottage with Kitchen*

Sheri Mitchell & Hugh Jellie
263 Maungatautari Road, PO Box 194, Cambridge

Tel (07) 827 6556 or 021 882 216
Fax (07) 827 3552
birchesbandb@xtra.co.nz
www.birches.co.nz

Double $110 Single $75 (Special breakfast)
Children by arrangement
Dinner by arrangement
Visa MC accepted
Children and pets welcome
1 Queen 1 Double 1 Single (2 bdrm)
Bathrooms: 1 Ensuite 1 Private

Our character farmhouse offers open fires, tennis, swimming pool and hottub in country garden amongst renown horse studs. Proximity to Lake Karapiro makes Birches an ideal base for lake users. Hugh, a veterinarian, and I are widely travelled. Olivia, 15, attends St Peter's Cambridge. We have farm pets and a cat. Cherry Tree Cottage is ideal for couples wanting privacy. The twin room in farmhouse has private bathroom with spa bath. We serve delicious farmhouse breakfasts alfresco or in dining room.

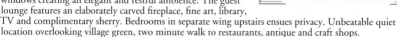

Cambridge *2 km S of Cambridge*
Glenelg *B&B Homestay*
Shirley & Ken Geary
6 Curnow Place, Cambridge

Tel (07) 823 0084   Fax (07) 823 4279
glenelgbnb@ihug.co.nz
www.cambridge.co.nz

Double $100 Single $65 (Full breakfast)
Children $25
Dinner $20 by arrangement
Visa MC accepted
Children and pets welcome
3 Queen 1 Twin (4 bdrm)
Bathrooms: 3 Ensuite 1 Private

Glenelg welcomes you to Cambridge to a new home with quality spacious accommodation - warm quiet and private overlooking Waikato farmland, with plenty of off-street parking. Beds have electric blankets and woolrests. 200 rose bushes in the garden. Five minutes to Lake Karapiro. Mystery Creek, where NZ National Field Days and many other functions are held is only 15 minutes away. Laundry facilities available. No smoking indoors please. Home away from home. For a brochure and directions please phone.

Cambridge *10 km N of Cambridge*
Dunfarmin *B&B Countrystay*
Jackie & Bob Clarke
46 Oaklea Lane, RD 3, Hamilton

Tel (07) 856 6643 or 027 611 5247
Fax (07) 856 6032
dunfarmin@wave.co.nz

Double $110 Single $60 (Full breakfast)
Children under 12 $25
Dinner $25 by arrangement
Visa MC accepted
Children welcome
2 Queen 2 Single (3 bdrm)
Bathrooms: 1 Ensuite 1 Guest share

Welcome to our home built among chestnut trees in a rural area, We are situated mid-way between Cambridge and Hamilton, two minutes off Highway 1. Five minutes away are the Hamilton Airport and Mystery Creek. Close by is the Waikato River with its lovely river walks and the paddle steamer and Hamilton Gardens. Cambridge has many cafés, restaurants, antique and craft shops. We are ex-farmers with alpacas, and Possum the cat.

Tirau *10 km S of Matamata*
Oraka Deer Park *Luxury B&B Farmstay Separate Suite Cottage with Kitchen*
Linda & Ian Scott
71 Bayly Road, RD1, Tirau

Tel (07) 883 1382
Fax (07) 883 1384
oraka@xtra.co.nz
www.oraka-deer.co.nz

Double $90-$245 Single $90-$200
(Breakfast by arrangement)
Dinner by arrangement
Visa MC Amex accepted
Children and pets welcome
2 King 1 Double 1 Single (3 bdrm)
Bathrooms: 2 Ensuite Showers

Scott Family, Ian & Linda and twins Lani & Travis, Labrador Tilly and two burmese. This is a working deer farm, restaurant and tourist business. Lovely garden with mature trees & flower borders, swimming pool & spa, tennis & petanque. Private & peaceful green Waikato countryside.

Te Awamutu *2 km S of Te Awamutu*

Leger Farm *B&B Farmstay*
Beverley & Peter Bryant
114 St Leger Road, Te Awamutu

Tel (07) 871 6676
Fax (07) 871 6679

Double $125-$140 Single $85-$100
(Full breakfast)
Dinner $35
1 Queen 1 Double 1 Twin 3 Single (4 bdr)
Bathrooms: 1 Ensuite 1 Private 1 Guest share

L eger Farm is a private residence with country living at its finest. The discerning leisure traveller seeking quality accommodation, in peaceful, relaxing surroundings, will find warm hospitality and every comfort here. Spacious bedrooms share stunning views of surrounding countryside. Each bedroom has its own balcony with garden vistas. We farm cattle and sheep, and are centrally based for visiting Waitomo Caves and black water rafting, Rotorua with its thermal activity and NZ's dramatic West Coast and ironstone sands. Golf course nearby for relaxation. Smoke-free home.

Otorohanga - Waitomo District *10 km S of Otorohanga*

Redwood Lodge *Luxury B&B Homestay*
John & Georgina Owen
222 Puketawai Road, RD 6, Otorohanga

Tel (07) 873 6685 or 027 541 1905
Fax (07) 873 6694
welcome@redwood-lodge.co.nz
www.redwood-lodge.co.nz

Double $140-$170 Single $110-$130 (Full breakfast)
Children by arrangement
Visa MC accepted
Children welcome
1 King/Twin 3 Queen 2 Single (4 bdrm)
Bathrooms: 4 Ensuite

O nly ten minutes from Waitomo Caves, Redwood Lodge offers travellers affordable luxury in a tranquil setting. John & Georgina welcome you to their well-appointed and comfortable home offering four good-sized heated/air conditioned ensuite rooms, each provided with tea/coffee making facilties. Enjoy our 12 acres of park-like grounds (for company take our Irish Terrier with you) our guest lounge and games room with TV and pool table. A hot spa, sauna and in-ground swimming pool are all available to our guests.

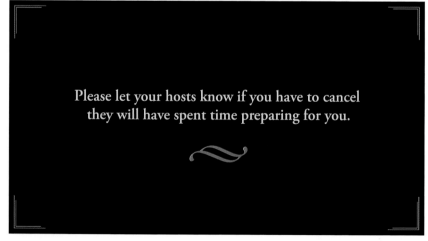

Please let your hosts know if you have to cancel
they will have spent time preparing for you.

Waitomo Caves *9.7 km W of Waitomo Village*
Te Tiro *B&B Farmstay Cottage with Kitchen*
Rachel & Angus Stubbs
970 Caves Te Anga Road, RD 8 Te Kuiti

Tel (07) 878 6328   Fax (07) 878 6328
tetiro@waitomocavesnz.com
www.waitomocavesnz.com

Double $100 **Single** $70
(Continental breakfast provisions)
Children $15per person
Dinner by prior arrangment
Familys of 5 welcome, we add extra mattress to loft
Visa MC accepted   Children and pets welcome
2 Queen 4 Single (2 bdrm)
Bathrooms: 2 Private with shower, toilet and washbasin.

Te Tiro (The View) welcomes you. Enjoy fantastic panoramic views of the central North Island and mountains. At night enjoy glowworms nestled in lush NZ bush only metres from your cottage. Situated on an established sheep farm with 350 acres of reserve bush. Our self-contained pioneer style cottages can accommodate up to five people in a cosy open plan room. Hosts Rachel and Angus have 30 years of tourism experience between them and would be happy to advise you on the wonders of Waitomo.

Waitomo Caves *16 km S of Otorohanga*
Waitomo Caves Guest Lodge *B&B Separate Suite*
Janet & Colin Beeston
7 Waitomo Caves Village, Waitomo Caves

Tel (07) 878 7641 or 0800 465 762
Fax (07) 878 7466
waitomocavesguestlodge@xtra.co.nz
www.waitomocavesguestlodge.co.nz

Double $90 **Single** $65 (Continental breakfast)
Children 0-5 years $5, 5-10 years $10, 10-15 years $15
Extra adult $20
Visa MC Eftpos accepted   Children welcome
7 Queen 7 Single (8 bdrm)
Bathrooms: 8 Ensuite

We are right in Waitomo Caves village, next door to the shop and café/bar, opposite a new café/restaurant and an easy walking distance to the Museum/i-SITE, Glowworm Caves, adventure caving offices and other eating places. Our quality ensuite studio units are in a beautiful peaceful garden setting, with lovely views over the surrounding countryside. You can expect a warm welcome from Colin, Janet and Gypsy the family dog. We can give you knowledgeable advice, make bookings for local activities and help you with your itinerary.

Te Kuiti - Waitomo District *20 km NW of Te Kuiti*
Tapanui Country Home *Luxury B&B Farmstay Cottage with Kitchen*
Sue & Mark Perry
1714 Oparure Road, Te Kuiti 3985

Tel (07) 877 8549 or 027 494 9873
Fax (07) 877 8541   info@tapanui.co.nz
www.tapanui.co.nz

Double $180-$250 **Single** $170-$200 (Continental breakfast provisions, full breakfast in Homestead)
Dinner by arrangement
Cottage $200-$320, max 4 guests
Visa MC Diners Eftpos accepted
Not suitable for children
3 King/Twin 1 Queen 1 Single (4 bdrm)
Bathrooms: 1 Ensuite 2 Private

Elegant 4 star plus country retreat located near the renowned Waitomo Caves. Magnificent homestead and spacious self-contained cottage set in quiet rolling hills amidst spectacular rock formations on a 1900 acre working sheep and cattle farm, with Boots the cat. Views from the spacious guest rooms induce a pure sense of tranquillity, ideal for romantic getaways! Enjoy delicious home cooking with world famous NZ wines. The cottage is fully equipped for self-catering. Experience NZ hospitality at its best. 2.5 hours to Auckland airport.

Waikato

Te Kuiti - Waitomo District *2 km N of Te Kuiti*

Simply the Best B&B *B&B Farmstay*
Margaret & Graeme Churstain
129 Gadsby Road, RD 5, Te Kuiti

Tel (07) 878 8191 or 027 666 9343
Fax (07) 878 5949
enquiry@simplythebestbnb.co.nz
www.simplythebestbnb.co.nz

Double $90 **Single** $45 (Continental breakfast)
Children negotiable
Dinner $20pp by arrangement
Pet cats on property
Children welcome
1 Queen 1 Double 1 Twin (3 bdrm)
Bathrooms: 1 Ensuite 1 Private 1 Guest share

Just 2.5 hours from Auckland Airport is our peaceful farmlet, signposted off SH3, northern end of Te Kuiti. We welcome you to 'Simply the Best' way to break a journey or to begin or end your New Zealand adventure. Happy to share our knowledge of the local area, Waitomo Caves, Blackwater rafting ten minutes away. Our comfortable one level home is unique for easy access from all rooms to decks overlooking stunning rural views. We offer secure parking, restaurants nearby, and 'above all' a place to remember.

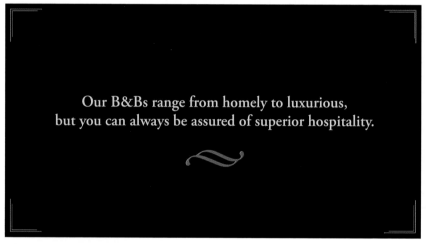

Our B&Bs range from homely to luxurious,
but you can always be assured of superior hospitality.

Te Kuiti - Waitomo District *2 km N of Te Kuiti*

Gadsby Heights *B&B Homestay Farmstay*
Janis & Ross MacDonald
137 Gadsby Road, RD 5, Te Kuiti

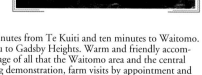

Tel (07) 878 3361 or 027 696 7122
Fax (07) 878 3361
info@gadsbyheights.co.nz
www.gadsbyheights.co.nz

Double $85-$100 **Single** $50-$60
(Continental breakfast) Children $15
Dinner $25   Extra adult $20
Visa MC accepted
Children and pets welcome
1 Queen 1 Double 2 Single (2 bdrm)
Bathrooms: 1 Ensuite 1 Private

Fantastic views, farm animals, lovely gardens, two minutes from Te Kuiti and ten minutes to Waitomo. Ross, Janis, Sophie (8) and Sox the cat welcome you to Gadsby Heights. Warm and friendly accommodation, conveniently located for you to take advantage of all that the Waitomo area and the central North Island have to offer. We have sheepshearing, dog demonstration, farm visits by appointment and a tour service available to take you to out of the way places and beyond. We look forward to meeting you.

Pio Pio - Waitomo District *19 km S of Te Kuiti*

Carmel Farm *B&B Homestay Farmstay*
Barbara & Leo Anselmi
1832 SH3, PO Box 93, Pio Pio

Tel (07) 877 8130 or 0800 877 813
Fax (07) 877 8130
Carmelfarms@xtra.co.nz

Double $100 **Single** $50 (Continental breakfast)
Dinner $25pp
Children and pets welcome
2 King/Twin 4 Single (4 bdrm)
Bathrooms: 1 Ensuite 1 Guest share

B&B
Approved

Barbara and Leo Anselmi operate a 2000 acre sheep, beef and dairy farm. You will be welcomed into an established homestead set in a picturesque limestone valley.

You will be treated to delicious home-cooked meals and the warmth of our friendship.

Whether mustering mobs of cattle and sheep, viewing the milking of 550 Friesian cows, driving around the rolling hills on the 4 wheeled farm-bike, basking in the sun by the pool or enjoying the gardens, you will feel relaxed and rejuvenated. Whether you seek excitement or tranquility, Carmel Farm is the perfect retreat.

We are ideally located for you to explore many other attractions. We are adjacent to a beautiful 18 hole golf course which welcomes visitors. The property is a short distance from black water rafting and canoeing activities, The Lost World Cavern, and the famous Waitomo Caves. Nearby are bush walks, waterfalls, and the home of the rare kokako bird. The Mangaotaki stream is a mecca for the trout enthusiast. We can help to arrange activities for people of all ages and interests; from garden visits to horse riding. (P.S. In the TV lounge there is Sky for those all-important rugby matches.) Please let us know your preference.

We are 140 km from Rotorua/Taupo. Directions: Travel 19 km south of Te Kuiti on SH3 towards Piopio. Carmel Farm is on the right. We can arrange to pick up from Otorohanga, Te Kuiti or Waitomo, if required.

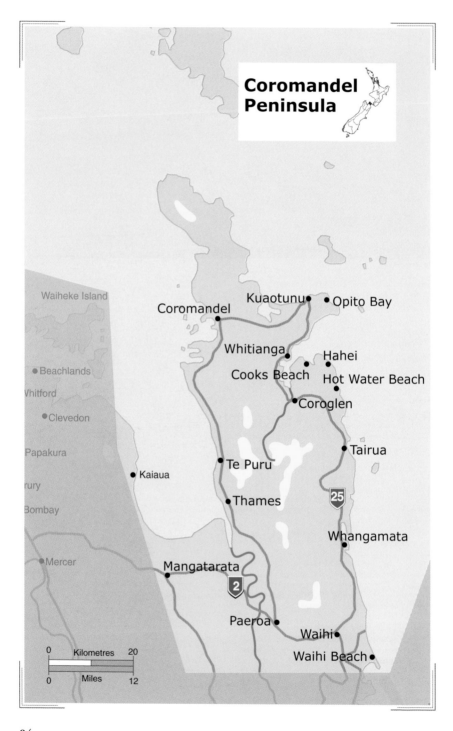

Coromandel Peninsula

Waiheke Island

Coromandel

Kuaotunu

Opito Bay

Whitianga

Hahei

Cooks Beach

Hot Water Beach

Coroglen

Beachlands

Whitford

Clevedon

Tairua

Papakura

Te Puru

Kaiaua

rury

Thames

25

Bombay

Whangamata

Mercer

Mangatarata

2

Paeroa

Waihi

Waihi Beach

0 Kilometres 20

0 Miles 12

Paeroa - Karangahake *7 km S of Paeroa*
Gold 'n Views Bed and Breakfast *Homestay Cottage with Kitchen*

Pamela and Nigel Blaikie
21 John Cotter Road, Karangahake, RD 4, Paeroa 3674

Tel 0800 023 259 or 021 902 780
Fax (07) 862 6905 goldnviews@orcon.net.nz
www.goldnviewsbnb.co.nz

Double $120-$190 Single $70-$85 (Full breakfast)
Children under 12 $25
Dinner $25 by arrangement
Cottage breakfast provisions available
Visa MC accepted   Pet free home   Children welcome
1 Queen 1 Double 2 Single (3 bdrm)
Cottage - shower Home - bath and shower

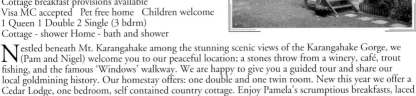

Nestled beneath Mt. Karangahake among the stunning scenic views of the Karangahake Gorge, we (Pam and Nigel) welcome you to our peaceful location; a stones throw from a winery, café, trout fishing, and the famous 'Windows' walkway. We are happy to give you a guided tour and share our local goldmining history. Our homestay offers: one double and one twin room. New this year we offer a Cedar Lodge, one bedroom, self contained country cottage. Enjoy Pamela's scrumptious breakfasts, laced with warm hospitality

Thames *8 km SE of Thames*
Wharfedale Farmstay *Homestay Farmstay Apartment with Kitchen*

Rosemary Burks
RD 1, Kopu, Thames

Tel (07) 868 8929
Fax (07) 868 8926
wharfedale@xtra.co.nz

Single $100 (Full breakfast)
Visa MC accepted
Not suitable for children
1 Double 2 Single (2 bdrm)
Bathrooms: 2 Private

For 17 years our guests have enjoyed the beauty of Wharfedale which has featured in Air NZ's "Airwaves" and Japan's "My Country" magazines. We invite you to share our idyllic lifestyle set in nine acres of park-like paddocks and gardens, surrounded by native bush. Delight in private river swimming, abundant bird life. We enjoy wholefood and organically grown produce. There are cooking facilities in the studio apartment. Cool shade in summer and cozy log fires and electric blankets in winter. Golf club nearby.

Thames *3 km SE of Thames*
Corolight B&B *B&B Homestay*

Julia & Bob Bissett
108 Whitehead Way, Parawai, Thames 3500

Tel (07) 868 5538 or 021 184 8334
Fax (07) 868 5537
juliabissett@clear.net.nz
www.corolight.co.nz

Double $115-$120 Single $80 (Full breakfast)
Visa MC accepted
1 King/Twin 1 Queen (2 bdrm)
Bathrooms: 1 Guest share

From the upstairs guest lounge, conservatory and deck, guests can enjoy expansive sea views and beautiful sunsets. Other guest facilities include a kitchenette, TV, DVD and stereo. Thames was historically a gold and timber town but is today regarded as the "gateway" to the Coromandel. Spectacular beaches, golf courses, cafés and restaurants; this quaint town provides a unique experience. Why not pamper yourself during your stay! Also available at Corolight are therapy sessions tailored to suit your needs. View website.

Coromandel

Coromandel

Thames *6.4 km E of Thames*
Mountain Top B&B *Homestay*
Elizabeth McCracken & Allan Berry
452 Kauaeranga Valley Road, RD 2, Thames

Tel (07) 868 9662
Fax (07) 868 9662
nzh_mountain.top@xtra.co.nz

Double $115-$120 Single $80 (Full breakfast)
Children half price
Dinner $30-$35
Visa MC Diners Amex accepted
Children and pets welcome
1 Queen 2 Twin (2 bdrm)
Bathrooms: 1 Guest share

Allan and I grow mandarins, native trees and raise coloured sheep on a small organic farm. Our private, peaceful, guest wing with lounge, TV and extensive library has bedrooms and decks with superb views overlooking river, forest swimming pools and mountains. Nearby Forest Park has wonderful walking tracks. We have a productive, rambly garden, Jack Russell Roly, cat Priscilla. No cell phone coverage - best to phone mornings or evenings. We love entertaining and cooking for people, mostly from farm produce. Let's look after you.

Thames *3 km S of Thames*
Totara Valley Barns *B&B*
Shona & Bruz MacGregor
65 Totara Valley Road, RD 1, Thames

Tel (07) 868 9730 or 027 310 3644
Fax (07) 868 9730
info@totarabarns.co.nz
www.totarabarns.co.nz

Double $135 Single $100 (Continental breakfast)
Dinner $35 Visa MC accepted
Not suitable for children
2 Queen (2 bdrm)
Bathrooms: 2 Ensuite

Unique, quality accommodation in a tranquil rural garden setting. 90 minutes south of Auckland Airport, Totara Barns is perfect as a relaxing getaway or as a base to explore the Coromandels exciting attractions. Separate guest accommodation with ensuites and spacious guest lounge. Enjoy the quiet surroundings, safe off-road parking, a generous continental breakfast and beautiful garden to unwind in at days end. Evening meal available using home-grown produce. Your local hosts, Shona and Bruz, assure you of true Kiwi hospitality.

Thames *8 km E of Thames*
Huia Lodge *B&B*
Celia & Murray Newby
589 Kauaeranga Valley Road, Thames

Tel (07) 868 6557
Fax (07) 868 6557
celian@wave.co.nz
www.thames-info.co.nz/HuiaLodge

Double $100 Single $65 (Full breakfast)
Children $20
Visa MC accepted
Children welcome
2 Queen 2 Single (2 bdrm)
Bathrooms: 2 Ensuite

Each unit has an ensuite and tea/coffee facilities. Relax and enjoy the tranquility of the valley, hike in the nearby Forest Park or circle the Peninsula to view the famous Coromandel scenery. We enjoy meeting travellers, love the rural lifestyle, grow fruit/vegetables, and enjoy the peace with our pet dog on our three acre paradise. Turn at BP corner (south end of township)into Banks Street then follow Parawai Road into the valley. We're 8 km from BP. Just 1 1/2 hours from Auckland.

Thames *2.5 km SE of Post Office*

The Heights *Luxury B&B*
Vicky & Phil English
300 Grafton Road, Thames, 3500

Tel (07) 868 9925 or 0800 68 9925 (NZ)
0808 337 7020 (UK)
1800 557 671 (AUS)
info@theheights.co.nz
www.theheights.co.nz

Double $195-$225 **Single** $185-$210 (Full breakfast)
Dinner $50-$60pp
Ariel premium non-alcoholic wines $25
Visa MC Diners Amex accepted
Not suitable for children
2 King (2 bdrm)
Bathrooms: 2 Ensuite

Set high on the mountain overlooking Thames, with panoramic views of mountains and sea, The Heights offers spacious, luxury B&B accommodation in a tranquil, private setting.

Relax with your own private deck or patio, private entrance, ensuite, tea making, fridge, Sky TV, DVD, Internet, and all the special touches for a memorable stay. Hosts Vicky and Phil love sharing with you all the best spots to visit, and our friendly cats add to the welcome.

The 100 km of views from the deck from Te Moana are worth the short climb of stairs, while garden-view Te Koru features its own fireplace.

Only 1.5 hours from Auckland International Airport, take time to pamper yourself at The Heights at the beginning or end of your stay in NZ.

Thames *6 km E of Thames*

Kauaeranga Country Bed and Breakfast *B&B Cottage with Kitchen*

Dave & Lyn Lee
446 Kauaeranga Valley Road, Thames, 2801
Tel (07) 868 6895   Fax (07) 868 6895
kauaeranga.country@xtra.co.nz
www.thames-info.co.nz

Double $120-$140 Single $80 (Special breakfast)
Children under 5 $20, over $30
Dinner $40pp with home-grown vegetables, local wines,
and delicious deserts
Visa MC accepted
Children and pets welcome
1 Queen 2 Twin 1 Single (2 bdrm)
Bathrooms: 1 Private Shub with shower above.

Set in a peaceful bush garden by the river this is a home away from home. The accommodation is spacious and comfortable with its own private entrance. The kitchen for self- catering, laundry facilities, living area with TV and video and private bathroom all adds to your comfort and privacy. Breakfast can be self served or join Dave and I for a special start to the day with hot home-made muffins. The stoney bottomed river is great for swimming and trout fishing.

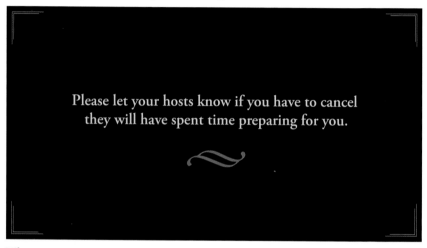

Please let your hosts know if you have to cancel
they will have spent time preparing for you.

Thames *1 km N of Information Centre*

Ocean View on Thames *Homestay Apartment with Kitchen*

Julie & Steve McLellan
509 Upper Albert Street, Thames, 3500
Tel (07) 868 3588
sjmclellan@xtra.co.nz
http://retreat4u.co.nz

Double $100-$150 Single $90 (Full breakfast)
Extra persons in apartment $25pp
Visa MC Eftpos accepted
Children welcome
3 Queen 1 Twin (4 bdrm)
Bathrooms: 2 Guest share
Guest share in homestay, one bathroom in apartment

Peace, tranquility, wonderful views and a very warm welcome await you at our attractive two-storey colonial style house, which has panoramic views over the Firth of Thames and only a ten-minute walk to the town centre and restaurants. Ocean View is a haven in its setting of beautifully landscaped gardens and with its array of native New Zealand birds. Thames is the perfect location from which to explore the stunning and varied scenery of the Coromandel Peninsula.

Thames *5 km S of Thames*

Thorold Country House *Luxury Homestay Self-contained Garden Apartment*

Wendy & Gary
36 Ngati Maru Highway, Kopu Thames, 3578

Tel (07) 868 8480 or 021 253 6746
thorold@xtra.co.nz
http://thames-info.co.nz/accommodation/thorold

Double $160-$240 Single $100 (Full breakfast)
Not suitable for children under 10
Dinner by prior arrangement
Garden apartment $220 self catering, $260 with breakfast
2 Queen 2 Twin (4 bdrm)
Bathrooms: 2 Guest share in homestay
1 Private in garden apartment.

Our private, peaceful, quality country home is ideally situated on six acres at the gateway to the Coromandel Peninsula. Views extend over the Coromandel Hills and Firth of Thames. Luxury guest rooms open onto wide verandas with private seating areas. Secluded swimming pool is set in subtropical garden. You are welcome to relax in the lounge or poolside or explore the property and meet our sheep. Dinner by arrangement. Approaching Thames on SH25, at Kopu turn right onto SH26, we are 100 metres on left.

Thames Coast - Te Puru *12 km N of Thames*

Te Puru Coast Bed & Breakfast *B&B Homestay Cottage with Kitchen*

Bill & Paula Olsen
2A Tatahi Street, Te Puru, Thames Coast, Thames

Tel (07) 868 2866   Fax (07) 868 2866
tepurucoastbnb@xtra.co.nz
www.tepurucoastbnb.co.nz

Double $110-$130 Single $80 Twin $105
(Full breakfast)   Children under 12 $25
Dinner $35pp, includes New Zealand wine or beer.
Self-contained unit $130 double, extra persons $25
Pet free home
1 Queen 1 Double 1 Twin 2 Single (3 bdrm)
Bathrooms: 1 Ensuite 2 Private

Welcome to the beautiful Thames Coast. Our modern comfortable home is 80 metres off the main coast road with off-street parking. Guest lounge has TV, books and tea & coffee facilities. You may choose a continental or cooked breakfast and evening meals are on request ($35.00pp) with complimentary New Zealand wine or beer. Our large deck is yours to enjoy or take a 2 minute walk to the beach. Fishermen welcome. The seperate self-contained unit where you do own cooking, has its own laundry, kitchen/dining, bathroom, BBQ area.

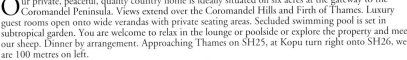

Coromandel *0.5 km E of Coromandel*

Country Touch *B&B Cottage No Kitchen*

Colleen & Geoff Innis
39 Whangapoua Road, Coromandel

Tel (07) 866 8310   Fax (07) 866 8310
countrytouch@xtra.co.nz
www.country-touch.com.nz

Double $100-$115 Single $75 (Full breakfast)
Children $10
Visa MC accepted
Children welcome
2 Queen 2 Twin (4 bdrm)
Bathrooms: 4 Ensuite

Geoff and I are a retired couple who enjoy meeting people, and invite you to a restful holiday in a country setting. With newly established trees and gardens, roses a speciality. You have the independence of four units situated apart from our home, all with fold out sofas, TV, fridge, tea and coffee making facilities. You have a country touch feeling with only a ten minute stroll to Coromandel township, where you can enjoy our local arts, crafts and restaurants. Come and enjoy.

Coromandel

Coromandel *10 km S of Coromandel*

AJ's Homestay *B&B Homestay*

Annette & Ray Hintz
24 Kowhai Drive, Te Kouma, RD, Coromandel

Tel (07) 866 7057 or 027 458 1624
Fax (07) 866 7057
rm.aj.hintz@actrix.co.nz

Double $110-$135 Single $85-$95
(Continental breakfast)
Dinner $35-$40
Visa MC accepted
Children welcome
1 King/Twin 2 Queen 1 Single (3 bdrm)
Bathrooms: 1 Ensuite 1 Family share

AJ's Homestay with panoramic sea views overlooking the Coromandel Harbour, spectacular sunsets. five minute walk to a safe swimming beach. Most mornings breakfast is served on the terrace. Our games room has a billiard and table tennis table. Dinner can be arranged. Directions: Thames coast main road (SH25) approximately 50 minutes. At the bottom of the last hill overlooking the Coromandel Harbour. Turn sharp left, at the Te Kouma Road sign. Travel past the boat ramp, next turn left. Kowhai Drive, we are number 24.

Coromandel *0.5 km S of Coromandel*

The Green House *B&B*

Barb & Tony
505 Tiki Road, Coromandel

Tel (07) 866 7303 or 0800 473 364
greeenhouse@orcon.net.nz
www.greenhousebandb.co.nz

Double $140-$165 Single $95-$120 (Special breakfast)
Visa MC accepted
Not suitable for children
1 King 1 Queen (2 bdrm)
Bathrooms: 2 Ensuite New ensuite bathrooms

This relaxed home has very comfortable facilities, lovely views over hills and sea, and is minutes walk to the excellent restaurants of Coromandel Town. Upstairs, the dedicated guest area has a lovely lounge with tea/coffee, fridge, TV, computer, videos, etc. The bedrooms, one with private deck, the other sea views, are separated by the guest lounge. Generous hospitality is offered. Freephone in NZ for this great place to stay.

Coromandel *3 km S of Coromandel*

Jacaranda Lodge *B&B*

Robin Münch
3195 Tiki Road, Coromandel, RD 1

Tel (07) 866 8002 or 021 252 6892
Fax (07) 866 8002
info@jacarandalodge.co.nz
www.jacarandalodge.co.nz

Double $120-$160 Single $65-$130 (Special breakfast)
Visa MC accepted Pet free home
Not suitable for children
4 Queen 1 Twin 1 Single (6 bdrm)
Bathrooms: 2 Ensuite 1 Private 1 Guest share

Robin invites you to share her spacious home set on six acres of tranquil country paradise. Located 3km south of Coromandel Town, Jacaranda Lodge provides the perfect escape: relax in one of the guest lounges; stroll around the delightful gardens; experience Coromandel's walks, unique attractions and spectacular coastline. Delicious continental breakfasts include fresh organic produce from Jacaranda's orchard. Large, comfortable bedrooms. Ensuite, private, shared bathrooms. Fully equipped guest kitchen (additional charge may apply). Special dietary needs can be catered for, including kosher. Sleep, eat, enjoy.

Coromandel - Te Kouma *10 km S of Coromandel*

Te Kouma B&B *B&B*

Kurt & Jo Muller
50 Puriri Road, Te Kouma, Coromandel

Tel (07) 866 7971
Fax (07) 866 7971
ko_jm_muller@xtra.co.nz

Double $120 Single $95 (Continental breakfast)
Children welcome
2 Queen 2 Twin (3 bdrm)
Bathrooms: 2 Ensuite 1 Family share
Sorry Showers only - no bath

Our well appointed home has, we think, the best views in the area. Kurt speaks German and makes delicious wholemeal breads, served for your breakfast with home preserved fruits and jams. Jo collects pacific seashells and old china. We live in a very tranquil place, abounding with bellbirds, tuis and pigeons, over looking Coromandel Harbour. Fishing trips can be arranged, Coromandel town 10 minutes north. Thames 45 minutes south.

Kuaotunu *17 km N of Whitianga*

Kaeppeli's *B&B Coastal Country*

Jill & Robert Kaeppeli
40 Gray Ave, Kuaotunu, RD 2, Whitianga

Tel (07) 866 2445 or 027 656 3442
Fax (07) 866 2445   paradise@kaeppelis.co.nz
www.kaeppelis.co.nz

Double $120-$180 Single $85-$120 (Full breakfast)
Children negotiable
Dinner $38 by arrangement
Visa MC Eftpos accepted
Children and pets welcome
2 King 4 Single (4 bdrm)
Bathrooms: 4 Ensuite

Country living in Style. A unique, secluded, peaceful haven. Relax, unwind, enjoy the natural beauty that surrounds you. Comfortable sunny rooms with magnificent sea views, private entrances & decks. Our Swiss Chef prepares sumptuous evening meals, using top quality local produce. Wood fired oven. Panoramic gazebo dining room. Kuaotunu has clean, safe, white, sandy beaches, kayaking, tennis, bush walks, horse trekking, fishing, golf, arts and crafts. Ideal for exploring the Coromandel. Children welcome. Pets to pamper. Our view? Simply the best.

Kuaotunu *16 km N of Whitianga*

@ The Peacheys *B&B Homestay*

Yvonne & Dale Peachey
15 Kawhero Drive, Kuaotunu RD 2, Whitianga

Tel (07) 866 5290
Fax (07) 866 4592
DYPeachey@xtra.co.nz
www.thepeacheys.co.nz

Double $140 Single $110 (Continental breakfast)
Dinner $35pp
Visa MC accepted
Not suitable for children
1 King 1 Queen 3 Single (2 bdrm)
Bathrooms: 2 Ensuite

Come and stay awhile to enjoy Kuaotunu, our piece of paradise. We have seven beaches to explore, and ours is only 100 metres from your spacious and comfortable room. We have coastal and forest walks close to Coromandel and Whitianga attractions. Experience our incredible night sky and amazing sunsets. Resturants and cafés are available in Whitianga and Matarangi, or arrange to have dinner with us. (Prior notice essential). Bathrobes, beach towels, refrigerator, tea & coffee available. Barley & Chelsea (the cats) also live here.

Kuaotunu *17 km N of Whitianga*

Blue Penguin *B&B Homestay Guest House*

Glenda Mawhinney & Barbara Meredith
11 Cuvier Crescent, Kuaotunu, RD 2, Whitianga 3592

Tel (07) 866 2222   Fax (07) 866 0228
holidayhomes@bluepenguin.co.nz
www.bluepenguin.co.nz

Double $110-$130 Single $75 (Accommodation only)
Children $35
Full house available Dec-Feb, 3 brm, 2 bath
Visa MC accepted
Children and pets welcome
1 King/Twin 2 Double 2 Single (2 bdrm)
Bathrooms: 1 Guest share

We welcome you to our architecturally designed home with spectacular views over the beach and pohutukawa trees to the Mercury Islands and Great Barrier. The master guestroom has king bed, window seats and small private balcony. Children love the family guestroom, 2 doubles, 2 singles, cot, TV/video, toys & games. We have a little foxy x. We are two professional women who manage 300 private beach houses available for holiday rental - see our website for full descriptions, colour photographs, seasonal rates and availability calendars.

Kuaotunu *17 km N of Whitianga*

Drift In B&B *B&B Homestay*

Yvonne & Peppe Thompson
16 Grays Avenue, Kuaotunu, RD 2, Whitianga

Tel (07) 866 4321 or 027 245 3632
Fax (07) 866 4321
driftin@paradise.net.nz
www.coromandelfun.co.nz/driftin

Double $125-$125 Single $70-$70 (Full breakfast)
Children negotiable
Visa MC accepted
Children welcome
1 Queen 2 Single (2 bdrm)
Bathrooms: 1 Guest share with bath and shower

Welcome is assured. This tranquil comfortable modern cedar home is designed to take full advantage of the sun and breathtaking island views by day and moonlit night. An unique beach theme pervades house and garden, small dog in residence. Just a minute stroll to white sand beaches for safe swimming and fossicking. Breakfast is a memorable occasion with sight and sounds of birds and sea complementing an excellent range of home cooking. Drift in, relax and enjoy this unique and special part of New Zealand.

Opito Bay *27 km NE of Whitianga*

At Opito *B&B*

Max & Bev
13 Stewart Place, Opito Bay, RD 2, Whitianga

Tel (07) 866 0317 or 027 418 5588
max-bev@xtra.co.nz

Double $130 Single $110 (Full breakfast)
Children $20
Dinner $25 by arrangement
Visa MC accepted
Pet free home Children welcome
1 Queen (1 bdrm)
Bathrooms: 1 Private Shower over 'shub' (mini-bath)

A warm kiwi welcome awaits you with complimentary tea & coffee and home baking on the deck. Our clean comfortable B&B offers you your own entrance, bathroom, guest area with sofa-bed, fridge, toaster, electric jug etc. Enjoy soaking in our spa after a swim or walk along Opito's beautiful, safe, white sandy beach, just 2 minutes stroll away. Restaurants at Whitianga or Matarangi or join us for a home cooked dinner or you may choose to self-cater on the BBQ. Laundry facilities available.

Whitianga *1 km S of Whitianga*
Cosy Cat Cottage *B&B Cottage with Kitchen*
Gordon Pearce
41 South Highway (town end), Whitianga

Tel (07) 866 4488
Fax (07) 866 4488
cosycat@xtra.co.nz
www.cosycat.co.nz

Double $90-$110 Single $65-$75 (Full breakfast)
Cottage $90-$160
Visa MC accepted
Children welcome
2 Queen 1 Double 1 Single (3 bdrm)
Bathrooms: 2 Ensuite 1 Private

Welcome to our picturesque two storied cottage filled with feline memorabilia! Relax with complimentary tea or coffee served on the veranda or in the guest lounge. Enjoy a good nights rest in comfortable beds and choose a variety of treats from our breakfast blackboard menu. You will probably like to meet Sylvie the cat or perhaps visit the cat hotel in the garden. A separate cottage is available with queen beds, bathrooms and kitchen. Friendly helpful service is assured - hope to see you soon!

Whitianga - Cooks Beach *17 km N of Tairua*
Mercury Orchard *B&B Cottage with Kitchen*
Heather and Barry Scott
141 Purangi Road, Cooks Beach, Whitianga

Tel (07) 866 3119
Fax (07) 866 3115
relax@mercuryorchard.co.nz
www.mercuryorchard.co.nz

Double $130-$175 Single $120-$140 (Full breakfast)
Children $20
Fig Tree Cottage $175 Paua Bach $175
Visa MC accepted Children welcome
1 King 2 Queen 2 Single (4 bdrm)
Bathrooms: 3 Ensuite

Paua Bach and Fig Tree Cottage are nestled amongst five acres of peaceful country gardens and orchard. Self- contained country style luxury with french doors opening onto your private deck. Crisp cotton bed linen, bathrobes, fresh fruit, flowers and candles. Special to the Bach, an old fashioned outdoor bath. Enjoy a Mercury Orchard full breakfast while listening to the birdsong.Barbeque your evening meal Kiwi style.Hot Water Beach and Cathedral Cove are 7-8 minutes drive. We share our home with two small dogs and a cat.

Whitianga *4 km N of Whitianga*
At Parkland Place *Luxury B&B*
Maria & Guy Clark
14 Parkland Place, Brophys Beach, Whitianga

Tel (07) 866 4987 or 021 404 923
Fax (07) 866 4946
parklandplace@wave.co.nz
www.atparklandplace.co.nz

Double $165-$200 (Full breakfast)
Children negotiable   Dinner by arrangement
Visa MC Eftpos accepted
Pet free home Children welcome
1 King/Twin 3 King 2 Queen 3 Single (5 bdrm)
Bathrooms: 5 Ensuite

Enjoy European hospitality in Whitianga's most luxurious hotel style accommodation. Maria, a ship's chef from Poland and New Zealand husband Guy, a master mariner, will make your stay a memorable experience. Large luxuriously appointed rooms. Magnificent breakfasts. Superb candle-lit dinners or BBQ by arrangement. Sunny picturesque outdoor area with spa pool. Large guest lounge with TV, library, music and refreshments. Situated near the beach and next to reserves and farmland ensures absolute peace and quiet. Privacy and discretion assured. You will not regret coming.

Coromandel

Whitianga - Coroglen *14 km S of Whitianga*
Coroglen Lodge *B&B Farmstay Separate Suite*
Wendy & Nigel Davidson
2221 State Highway 25, RD 1, Whitianga 3591

Tel (07) 866 3225
Fax (07) 866 3235
clover@wave.co.nz
www.mercurybay.co.nz/coroglen.html

Double $85-$100 Single $60-$80 (Continental breakfast)
Visa MC accepted
Children welcome
2 Queen 2 Single (3 bdrm)
Bathrooms: 2 Guest share

Coroglen Lodge is situated on 17 acres of farmland with cattle, sheep and alpacas. Nestled in the hills with views of the Coromandel Ranges, this is rural tranquillity. Halfway between Whitianga township and Hot Water Beach there is easy access to both areas and all attractions. Guest area is separate, relaxed, and spacious with a large sunny lounge area for your comfort. Wendy spins and knits with wool from her sheep and alpacas, and Nigel has a collection of vintage tractors.

Whitianga *4.5 km N of Hot Water Beach Turn -off*

Coppers Creek Farmstay *B&B Farmstay Cottage with Kitchen*
Graham & Pamela Caddy
1587 State Highway 25, Coroglen,
RD 1, Whitianga 3591

Tel (07) 866 3960   Fax (07) 866 3960
caddy.copperscreek@xtra.co.nz
www.copperscreekfarmstay.co.nz

Double $100 Single $90 (Full breakfast)
Children $20, no charge for pre-schoolers
Visa MC accepted
Children welcome
1 Queen 3 Single (2 bdrm)
Bathrooms: 1 Ensuite 1 Private

Coppers Creek is a small working beef breeding farm comprising of 120 acres of pasture, bush and streams. We have the usual assortment of farm animals including the odd teenager. Enjoy the freedom of our self-contained studio apartment and adjacent childrens bedroom, with private entrance and BBQ area, with fresh produce available from the farm garden in season. We are only 15 minutes drive from Hot Water Beach, Hahei, Cooks Beach and Whitianga. We enjoy boating, kayaking, fishing, diving and bush walks.

Whitianga *6 km N of Whitianga*
On The Beach *B&B*
Gordon and Diana Barnaby
66 State Highway 25, Simpson's Beach
RD 2 Whitianga, 3592

Tel (07) 866 2433 or 027 245 7496
gordon.diana@xtra.co.nz
www.onthebeachwhitianga.co.nz

Double $110-$150 Single $90-$120
(Continental breakfast)
Dinner by request
Visa MC accepted
Children welcome
1 Queen 1 Double 1 Single (2 bdrm)
Bathrooms: 2 Ensuite

Diana and Gordon look forward to exceeding your expectations when you choose to stay with them. They have travelled extensively and are aware of what their guests would expect when they are away from home. They look forward to making you welcome and to fulfil you needs.

Hahei *38 km S of Whitianga*

The Church *B&B Cottage No Kitchen Cottage with Kitchen*

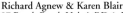

Richard Agnew & Karen Blair
87 Beach Road, Hahei, RD 1, Whitianga

Tel (07) 866 3533 or 027 459 6877
Fax (07) 866 3055   info@thechurchhahei.co.nz
www.thechurchhahei.co.nz

Double $100-$165 Single $100-$165
(Continental breakfast)   Children $10-$15
Dinner menu a la carte   Extra adult $20-$25
Visa MC Eftpos accepted   Children welcome
11 Queen 1 Double 11 Twin 13 Single (11 bdrm)
Bathrooms: 11 Ensuite

The Church is Hahei's unique boutique accom-
modation and dining experience. The Church building provides a character dining room/licensed restaurant for delicious evening meals. Wholesome breakfasts in purpose built breakfast room. 11 cosy wooden cottages scattered through delightful bush and gardens offer a range of accommodation and tariffs, with ensuites, fridges, tea and coffee facilities. Some cottages fully self-contained with woodstoves for winter.Small conference facilities. Enjoy the wonders of Cathedral Cove, Hot Water Beach, and the Coromandel Peninsula. Seasonal rates. Smoking outside.

Hahei Beach *0.5 km NE of Hahei shops and cafés*

Hawleys Bed and Breakfast Hahei *B&B*

Peter & Rhonda Hawley
19 Hahei Beach Road, RD 1, Whitianga

Tel (07) 866 3272 or 027 497 1090
Fax (07) 866 3273
hawleys@haheibeach.co.nz
www.haheibeach.co.nz

Double $160 Single $140 (Full breakfast)
Visa MC accepted
Children and pets welcome
1 Queen 2 Single (2 bdrm)
Bathrooms: 1 Private

Situated on the flat, half-way (200m) between the
beach and the shops and cafés. Ideal for those who enjoy extra space, privacy and comfort. The purpose built 2 double bedrooms and spacious bathroom, take up all of the second storey at the rear of the house. The larger room has a balcony and a queen size bed and the smaller room 2 single beds. A cot is available. There is secure garaging. No children at home and no pets.

Hahei *.8 km W of Hahei Beach*

Hahei Horizon *B&B Homestay*

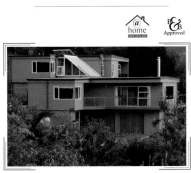

Peter & Kay Harrison
20 Grierson Close, Hahei, RD 1, Whitianga

Tel (07) 866 3281 or 021 160 7213
027 480 9273   Fax (07) 866 3281
pkharrison@xtra.co.nz
www.haheihorizon.co.nz

Double $140-$220 Single $120-$200 (Full breakfast)
Children welcome by arrangement
Studio by arrangement:, sleeps 4 - 1 queen 1 bunk
Visa MC accepted
1 King/Twin 1 King 1 Queen (3 bdrm)
Bathrooms: 3 Ensuite
Clean and white with all ammenities

Peter & Kay invite you to share our little piece of this special part of New Zealand. Hahei Horizon is
our home on the hill overlooking the beautiful bay at Hahei. Every room has stunning views of the coast and its surroundings. With down to earth Kiwi hospitality, relaxation is hard to avoid. All rooms are large with quality linen, tea/coffee, fridge, ensuites. Internet available. Easy walk to beach, cafés, close to Cathedral Cove and Hot Water Beach - A wonderful stay!!

Coromandel

Hahei *0.4 km SW of Hahei*
Hahei B&B *B&B*

Mark Cederman
6 Jackson Place, Hahei, RD 1 Whitianga

Tel (07) 866 3730 or 027 499 8879
Fax (07) 866 3750
info@haheibandb.co.nz
www.haheibandb.co.nz

Double $140-$200 (Full breakfast)
Visa MC Eftpos accepted
Children welcome
1 King 3 Queen 3 Single (4 bdrm)
Bathrooms: 2 Ensuite 2 Guest share

A warm welcome awaits you at Hahei Bed & Breakfast. This is a modern, purpose built home with a large swimming pool, beautiful gardens and sun drenched decks. Continental or cooked breakfast served in the privacy of your own rooms, or alfresco on the deck overlooking Hahei and the gardens. Local features and attractions include bush walks, diving and snorkelling in close proximity to digging your own hot pool at Hot Water Beach or walking to picturesque Catherdral Cove.

Hot Water Beach *28 km N of Tairua*
Auntie Dawns Place *Apartment with Kitchen*

Dawn & Joe Nelmes
15 Radar Road, Hot Water Beach, Whitianga RD 1

Tel (07) 866 3707 or 021 215 6300
dawn@auntiedawn.co.nz
www.auntiedawn.co.nz

Double $100-$130 Single $30-$60 (Continental breakfast)
Visa MC accepted
2 Queen 1 Double 1 Single (2 bdrm)
Bathrooms: 2 Private

H ot Water Beach is a surfbeach. At low tide hotwater bubbles up in the sand and you dig yourself a "hotpool". Our house is surrounded by huge Pohutukawa trees, three minutes walk from hotsprings. We have a terrier and Joe makes home-brew beer. Each apartment is comfortably furnished with a queen bedroom & spare bed in the living room. Tea, coffee, bread, butter, jam, milk, cereals provided, guests prepare breakfast at preferred time. Directions: turn right into Radar Road before café.

Tairua *45 km E of Thames*
Harbour View Lodge *B&B*

Linda & Wayne Jury
179 Main Road, Tairua

Tel (07) 864 7040 or 021 357 437
Fax (07) 864 7042
info@harbourviewlodge.co.nz
www.harbourviewlodge.co.nz

Double $190-$220 Single $160-$190 (Full breakfast)
Visa MC accepted
Not suitable for children
1 King/Twin 2 Queen (3 bdrm)
Bathrooms: 3 Ensuite

P eace & tranquility is yours when you stay in one of our luxury rooms with ensuite. Enjoy the swimming pool and tropical gardens. Start your day with a sumptuous breakfast while you enjoy the breathtaking views of the Tairua Harbour & Paku Mountain. A short stroll each evening to the local restaurants. We can help you plan each day as you experience Hot Water Beach, Cathedral Cove or one of the many other attractions. Our cats Jill & Daisy look forward to meeting you.

Tairua *45 km E of Thames*

Colonial Homestay *Luxury B&B Homestay*
Jenny & Bob Geddes
202 Paku Drive, Tairua, 3508

Tel (07) 864 7743   Fax (07) 864 7743
colonialhomestay@paradise.net.nz
www.colonialhomestay.co.nz

Double $180-$225 Single $170-$210 (Full breakfast)
Dinner by arrangement
Visa MC Eftpos accepted
Pet free home   Not suitable for children
2 Queen 1 Single (2 bdrm)
Bathrooms: 1 Ensuite 1 Private

Jenny & Bob offer you the cosy comforts of home in a quiet location near the top of Mount Paku, the volcanic peak which dominates the Tairua skyline.

After less than a two-hour drive from the Auckland airport, guests can relax on the surrounding decks to sample complimentary refreshments. An elevator with access to all floors is installed for the convenience of guests & their luggage. The Tui suite has queen size bed, balcony with seats overlooking the ocean & islands, ensuite bathroom & adjacent small lounge with library, fridge & tea/coffee making facilities. The elegant Kiwi room has queen size bed, private bathroom with bathrobes, French doors opening out onto the decks, tea/coffee making facilities with use of large lounge. Some of the special delights guests remark upon are the home-made muffins Jenny bakes daily. The smell of Bob's bread baking entices guests from their bedrooms with breakfasts so plentiful that lunches are sometimes not required!

Features & Attractions:* Visit Cathedral Cove, Hot Water Beach, Sailor's Grave* Library; free book exchange* Internet connection* Safe facility for valuables* Secure off-street parking* Bush walks* Restaurants within walking distance* Assistance with on-going travel arrangements

Coromandel

Whangamata *.2 km N of Town Centre*

Sandy Rose Bed & Breakfast *B&B*
Shirley & Murray Calman
Corner Hetherington & Rutherford Roads,
Whangamata

Tel (07) 865 6911
sandyrose@whangamata.co.nz
http://sandyrose.whangamata.co.nz

Double $130 Single $95 (Special breakfast)
Visa MC accepted
Pet free home
Not suitable for children
2 King/Twin 1 Queen 1 Double (3 bdrm)
Bathrooms: 3 Ensuite

A charming B&B in the Coromandel Peninsula's popular holiday destination, we have three tastefully decorated guest bedrooms, all with ensuite bathrooms, comfortable beds and in-room TVs. Complimentary tea & coffee is available in the guest lounge. We are ideally located, close to Whangamata's shops, cafés and restaurants, and an easy stroll to the surf beach, harbour and wharf. Enjoy our extensive continental breakfast and use our home as a base to relax and enjoy the natural attractions that Whangamata and area has to offer.

Whangamata *2 km S of Town Centre*

Kotuku *B&B Homestay Self-contained Studio Unit*
Linda & Peter Bigge
422 Otahu Road, Whangamata

Tel (07) 865 6128 or 027 358 1227
Fax (07) 865 6128
lindapeter@slingshot.co.nz
www.kotukuhomestay.co.nz

Double $108-$120 (Full breakfast)
Studio Unit $80
Visa MC Diners accepted
Children welcome
3 Queen (3 bdrm)
Bathrooms: 3 Ensuite

We offer comfortable homestay accommodation in a purpose built home. Rosie, our friendly dog and Elizabeth, the cat, will give you a warm welcome too! Relax in the spacious lounge or private patio; enjoy the Coromandel sunset from our outdoor spa. Kotuku is situated at the quieter end of Whangamata, just a two minute stroll to the lovely Otahu Estuary Reserve; ideal for walking, swimming, kayaking or just take a picnic lunch and watch the fascinating shorebirds. Bikes and kayaks are available for your use.

Waihi *1 km S of Waihi*

West Wind Gardens *B&B Homestay*
Josie & Merv Scott
58 Adams Street, Waihi

Tel (07) 863 7208
westwindgarden@xtra.co.nz
www.athomenz.org.nz

Double $85 Single $45 (Continental breakfast)
Children $20
Dinner $20
Visa MC accepted
Children welcome
1 Double 2 Single (2 bdrm)
Bathrooms: 1 Guest share

We offer a friendly restful smoke-free stay in our modern home and garden. Waihi is the gate way to both the Coromandel and the Bay of Plenty with its beautiful beaches. Waihi is a historic town with a vintage railway and a working gold mine discovered 1878 closed 1952. Reopened in 1989 as a open-cast mine. Beach ten minutes away, beautiful walks, golf courses, trout fishing. Enjoy a home cooked meal or sample our restaurants. Our interests are gardening, dancing and travel.

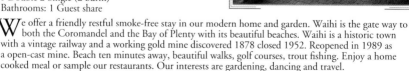

Waihi *2 km W of Waihi*
Ashtree House *B&B*
Anne & Bill Ashdown
20 Riflerange Road, Waihi

Tel (07) 863 6448 or 027 492 8915
Fax (07) 863 6443
ash.tree@clear.net.nz

Double $80 Single $50 (Full breakfast)
Children under 10 $10
Dinner $20pp
Garden Unit $35pp
Children welcome
1 Queen 1 Double 2 Single (3 bdrm)
Bathrooms: 2 Private 1 Guest share

Modern brick home set on the side of a hill with extensive views and access to trout river. Private guest wing comprising two double bedrooms, large private bathroom with shower and bath. Guest lounge with TV, stereo and large selection of New Zealand books. Laundry and separate toilet. Eight acres, large attractive garden and pond area. One house dog. Situated two minutes to centre of Waihi, complete privacy and quiet guaranteed. Self-contained unit with wheelchair facilities. Five minutes to beautiful Karangahake Gorge.

Waihi *0.5 km W of Waihi*
Chez Nous *B&B Homestay*
Sara Parish
41 Seddon Avenue, Waihi

Tel (07) 863 7538 or 027 644 5562
sarap@slingshot.co.nz

Double $65 Single $45 (Continental breakfast)
Children $20
Dinner $20pp by arrangement
Visa MC accepted
Children welcome
1 Queen 1 Twin (2 bdrm)
Bathrooms: 1 Guest share

Enjoy a relaxed and friendly atmosphere in a spacious, modern home in an attractive garden setting. Shops and restaurants are within easy walking distance. Discover past and present gold mining activities (tours available), sandy surf beaches, bush walks, 18 hole golf course, art, craft and wine trails. Waihi is an ideal stopover for the traveller who wants to explore the Coromandel Peninsula, Bay of Plenty and Waikato.

Waihi *1 km NW of Waihi*
Dragonfly Garden Bed and Breakfast *B&B*
Bert and Kathy
11 Parry Palm Avenue, Waihi, 2981

Tel (07) 863 9034 or 027 236 1997
wattsdue@paradise.net.nz
www.dragonflygardenbnb.co.nz

Double $130-$150 Single $90 (Full breakfast)
Dinner BBQ, outside garden oven
Not suitable for children
Pets welcome
1 Queen 1 Twin (2 bdrm)
Bathrooms: 2 Ensuite

Enjoy these charming and comfortable detached bedrooms with ensuites which are ideally situated amongst 1½ acres of mature trees and gardens with fishponds. We offer laundry facilities, outdoor garden oven, fireplace and BBQ area. Situated 1 minute from Waihi Centre, eight minutes from Karangahake george and 15 minutes from the beach. This area offers something for everyone. Your friendly hosts Bert and Kathy and Roco (the Tibetan Terrier) look forward to looking after you.

Waihi *6 km W of Waihi*

Waihi Waterlily Gardens *Luxury Cottage with Kitchen*
Self catered, B&B or Fully Catered Stays
Sam Gamble & Olivia Thorn
441 Pukekauri Road, RD 2, Waihi, 3682

Tel (07) 863 8267 or 021 369 671
Fax (07) 863 8231   info@waterlily.co.nz
www.waterlily.co.nz

Double $250-$290 (Full breakfast)
Children POA All meals available by arrangement
Base rate $250 double, extra guests $40pp
Visa MC Eftpos accepted   Pets welcome
2 King 1 Double (2 bdrm)
Bathrooms: 2 Ensuite

Architectural cottages 'Lily Pad' and 'Lotus' are privately located at the Waihi Waterlily Gardens, within fifteen enchanting acres of gardens, ponds and established grounds. Fully self-contained, your hosts Olivia and Sam also offer B&B or fully catered stays to make your experience even more memorable. Evening stars like youíve never seen before. The breathtaking silence of nature. Giant chess, enormous specimen trees, thousands of summer waterlilies, a cosy fire, an expansive deck. Make our place yours.

Waihi Beach *11 km E of Waihi*

Waterfront Homestay *Apartment with Kitchen*
Kay & John Morgan
17 The Esplanade (off Hinemoa Street), Waihi Beach

Tel (07) 863 4342 or 021 170 5058
Fax (07) 863 4342
k.morgan@xtra.co.nz

Double $110 (Continental breakfast)
Self catering breakfast option
Visa MC accepted
Pet free home
Children welcome
1 Queen 3 Single (2 bdrm)
Bathrooms: 1 Private

Waterfront Homestay. Fully self-contained, two double bedrooms. Suitable for two couples or small family group. Unit is lower floor of family home on waterfront of beautiful uncrowded ocean beach. Walk from front door directly onto sandy beach. Safe ocean swimming, surfcasting, surfing and coastal walks. Restaurant within walking distance or use facilities provided with accommodation. Waterfront Homestay is situated close to popular scenic coastal walks to Orokawa and Homunga Bays. Tariff $100 per couple, bed and continental breakfast. Hosts John & Kay Morgan.

Waihi Beach *15 km S of Waihi*

Paradiso *B&B Cottage with Kitchen*
Theo & Gerda Blok
101 Athenree Road, RD 1, Waihi Beach

Tel (07) 863 5350
Fax (07) 863 5678
paradijs@xtra.co.nz
www.paradisobb.co.nz

Double $100-$120 Single $60-$80
(Continental breakfast)
Children under 5 $10
Visa MC accepted
Children welcome
1 King 2 Single (1 bdrm)
Bathrooms: 1 Private

Paradiso, five acres of park-like gardens, with children's playground, nestled on the edge of Tauranga Harbour. A double-seated kayak is available to explore the harbour, native bush walks nearby. 5 km from Waihi Beach. We offer friendly B&B in clean, comfortable studio-style accommodation, or you can self-cater, be as private as you wish. Garden also used for Weddings and/or Wedding photographs. Very peaceful and only 3 km off SH2.

Waihi Beach *11 km E of Waihi*
Seagulls Bed & Breakfast *B&B Separate Suite*
Marie & Steve Quinlan
8 West Street (off Pacific Road), Waihi Beach

Tel (07) 863 4633 or 027 492 0033
Fax (07) 863 4634
seagullsquinlan@clear.net.nz

Double $100-$125 Single $95-$100
(Full breakfast)
Children welcome
2 Queen 1 Single (2 bdrm)
Bathrooms: 1 Guest share
Large and modern with bath and shower

Relax, unwind at beautiful Waihi Beach - gateway to Coromandel Peninsular, historic Karangahake Gorge walkways and Bay of Plenty. Enjoy spectacular panoramic views of main beach (three minutes walk) and Mayor Island. Watch the sunrise, listen to tuis sing in bush on boundary.Modern spacious luxury home with your own bedrooms, TV lounge, tea/coffee facilities with sea views. Excellent outdoor areas, cafés/restaurants closeby, swimming, surfing, fishing, beach and bush walks. Breakfasts include fresh seasonal fruits, homemade preserves, organic produce. Our foxy Jackie will greet you.

Waihi Beach *12 km N of Katikati*
The Candy's B&B *B&B Cottage with Kitchen*
Gloria & Neil Candy
43 Athenree Road, Athenree, Waihi Beach

Tel (07) 863 1159
Fax (07) 863 1196
neilcandy@ihug.co.nz

Double $110-$135 Single $80-$90
(Continental breakfast)
Dinner $32pp
Pet free home
2 King 2 Twin (3 bdrm)
Bathrooms: 1 Ensuite 1 Private 1 Guest share

Take time out: relax. Our near new home is on three acres, with beautiful harbour views: each room has a patio. Walk to Athenree Hotpools, drive three minutes to Waihi Surf Beach, ten minutes south to Katikati, two Local Golf Courses, Morton Winery, Lavender Farm. Ten minutes north to Waihi Goldmine, walks and excellent restaurants. Neil loves fishing, and Gloria loves crafts. Meals on request. This is paradise and our city pets agree. New one bedroom cottage

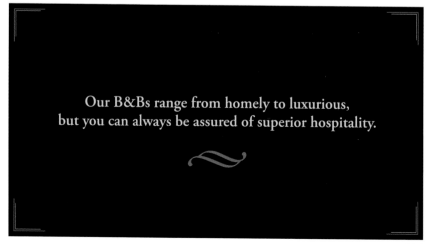

Our B&Bs range from homely to luxurious, but you can always be assured of superior hospitality.

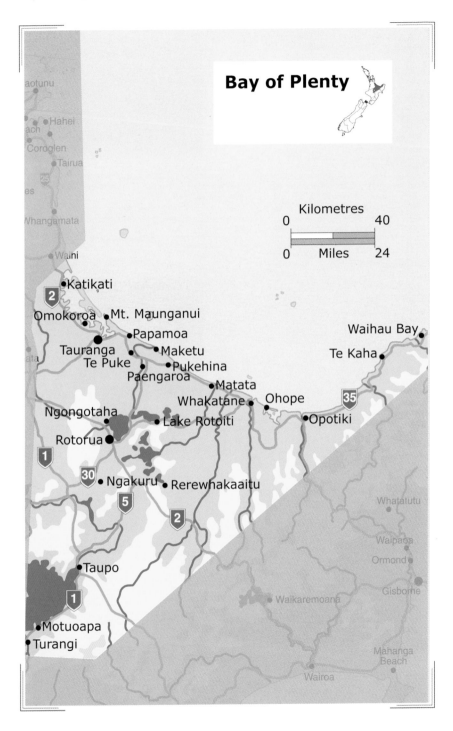

Bay of Plenty

Kilometres
0   40
0   Miles   24

aotunu

Hahei
ach

Coroglen

Tairua

es

Whangamata

Waini

•Katikati

2

Omokoroa   •Mt. Maunganui

•Papamoa

Tauranga   •Maketu
Te Puke   •Pukehina
Paengaroa
•Matata
Whakatane   •Ohope

Ngongotaha

•Lake Rotoiti   •Opotiki

Rotorua

Waihau Bay

Te Kaha•

35

1

30   •Ngakuru   •Rerewhakaaitu

5

2

Whatatutu

Waipaoa

Ormond•

•Taupo

1

Waikaremoana

Gisborne

•Motuoapa
•Turangi

Mahanga
Beach

Wairoa

Katikati *20 km S of Katikati*

Jones Lifestyle *Apartment with Kitchen*

Thora & Trevor Jones
Pahoia Road, RD 2, Tauranga

Tel (07) 548 0661   Fax (07) 548 0661
joneslifestyle@clear.net.nz
www.bnb.co.nz/joneslifestyle.html

Double $100 Single $70
(Continental breakfast provisions)
Children $20
Discounts for longer stays
Visa MC Diners accepted Pet free home
1 Queen (1 bdrm)
Bathrooms: 1 Private

Situated on Pahoia Peninsula and within easy reach of Tauranga and Katikati, our self-contained apartment is a very peaceful place to stay, with spectacular views of Tauranga Harbour and sunset over the Kaimai Ranges. It is a short walk to the beach. Our large garden is alive with birdsong. Amenities include fully equipped kitchen, bathroom, laundry, lounge with convertible sofa, games rooms (billiards, table tennis etc.). Extra bedrooms and private bathroom are available in main house. Deluxe continental breakfast (optional) provided for self service.

Katikati *3 km N of Katikati*

Aberfeldy *B&B Farmstay*

Mary Anne & Rod Calver
164 Lindemann Road, RD 1, Katikati

Tel (07) 549 0363 or 0800 309 064
027 590 9710   Fax (07) 549 0363
aberfeldy@xtra.co.nz
www.aberfeldy.co.nz

Double $120 Single $75 (Full breakfast)
Children $40   Dinner by arrangement
Visa MC accepted
Children and pets welcome
1 Queen 1 Twin 1 Single (2 bdrm)
Bathrooms: 1 Private We take one party only at a time.

Large home set in extensive gardens with private sunny accommodation. The private lounge opens onto a patio, and has TV and coffee making facilities. 1 party at a time . We farm sheep and cattle. Rod's associated with Kiwifruit and is a Rotarian. Panoramic views of bush-clad hills, farmland and harbour. Activities include bush and farm walks, meeting tame animals, especially Piglet & Lucy the Kune Kune pigs. Golf course, horse riding, and beaches nearby. Our old sheep and cattle dog "Boy" will welcome you .

Katikati *8 km N of Katikati*

Cotswold Lodge Countrystay *B&B*

Alison & Des Belsham
183 Ongare Point Road, RD 1, Katikati

Tel (07) 549 2110
Fax (07) 549 2109
cotswold@ihug.co.nz
www.cotswold.co.nz

Double $140-$165 Single $110 (Special breakfast)
Dinner by prior arrangement
Visa MC accepted
2 Queen 1 Double 1 Single (3 bdrm)
Bathrooms: 3 Ensuite Ensuite

Expect warm hospitality, a little luxury and a peaceful environment in our rural home situated between Katikati (Mural Town) and Waihi Beach and two hours from Auckland. Quality accommodation overlooking garden, kiwifruit and avocado orchards, with views to the Kaimai Ranges. All rooms with ensuite bathrooms and quality furnishings and linen. Yummy breakfast. Evening Meals by prior arrangement. Undercover hot tub on deck and petanque court in garden. Laundry Service available. Our Labrador is friendly.

Katikati *9 km N of Katikati*

Panorama Country Lodge *Luxury B&B Private Suites*
Barbara & Phil McKernon
901 Pacific Coast Highway (SH2), RD 1, Katikati

Tel (07) 549 1882 or 0211 655875
Fax (07) 549 1882
mckernon@xtra.co.nz
www.panoramalodge.co.nz

Double $160-$190 Single $120-$130 (Special breakfast)
Visa MC accepted
1 King 1 Queen 1 Twin (3 bdrm)
Bathrooms: 1 Ensuite 1 Private

Perfectly situated between beautiful Waihi Beach and Katikati. Nestling in the foothills of the Kaimai Ranges, magnificent ocean views from every room! Relax in spacious and peaceful guest suites, quality furnishings, french doors to swimming pool and terrace, TV, CD, DVD, slippers & robes, coffee & tea, delicious breakfasts, served: in-suite, terrace or dining room. Explore the grounds, orchards, paddocks and meet 'our boys' the alpacas, not forgetting our very friendly dog, Kaimai. Nearby: cafés, wineries, beaches, golf, bushwalks... 'We love it here...so will you!'

Katikati *2.5 km W of Katikati*

Busby Lodge *Luxury Homestay*
Elaine & Guy Robertson
251 Busby Road, RD 1, Katikati

Tel (07) 549 0189 or 027 490 8199
Fax (07) 549 0184
busbylodge@xtra.co.nz

Double $200 Single $120 (Full breakfast)
Visa MC accepted
1 King 1 Twin (2 bdrm)
Bathrooms: 2 Ensuite

Enjoy breathtaking, panoramic views from our new, friendly, warm homestay. Situated 2.5 km from Katikati and close to many attractions, including golf courses, walking tracks, wineries and beaches. We will share our wonderful lifestyle with you. Our spaniel Bess, with tail wagging, will guide you through our home, which offers ensuite bedrooms, large comfortable lounge, laundry facilities and wheelchair access. we are relaxed retired couple, with interests in aviation, boating, fishing, world affairs and good conversation. Home away from home.

Katikati *5 km SE of Katikati*

Tranquility Lodge *B&B Homestay*
Gayle & Capt Reynold Alvins
325 Rea Road, RD 2, Katikati, 3063

Tel (07) 549 3581 or 027 452 2960
Fax (07) 549 3582
tranquilitylodge@xtra.co.nz
www.tranquilitylodge.co.nz

Double $150 Single $120 (Special breakfast)
Visa MC accepted
2 King (2 bdrm)
Bathrooms: 2 Ensuite

Nestled in a peaceful valley, warm kiwi hospitality and our friendly Maremma dogs, cats, farmyard pets await you. Take a seat on our large freestanding deck, relax to the tune of birdsong and stream while viewing the Kaimai Ranges, or play a game of Petanque beside our patio area. Each king suite is sumptuously furnished, has its own private entry and deck from which you can enjoy the view of our lifestyle farm and gardens. Bathrobes, slippers, toiletries and hairdryers are supplied in each ensuite.

Katikati *9 km S of Katikati*

Burr-wood Countrystay *B&B Homestay*
Maureen and Alan Cook
449 Lund Road RD 2, Katikati, 3871

Tel (07) 549 2060
Fax (07) 549 2061
nzjewellery@clear.net.nz

Double $110-$115 Single $80-$90 (Full breakfast)
Not suitable for small children
Dinner $30 per head, two courses plus wine
Visa MC accepted
1 Queen 1 Twin (2 bdrm)
Bathrooms: 1 Private

Burr-wood is set in a two and a half acre garden and surrounded by native bush. An elevated situation, we overlook to a panorama of land and harbour and islands. Enjoy breakfast which includes homemade bread and jams; complimentary pre-dinner drinks, Dinner is available by arrangement. We are five minutes from SH2 and within easy reach of Bay of Plenty attractions We make unique jewellery from NZ Native Timbers. Only one party at a time. Home-baking, tea/coffee on arrival. Laundry available

Omokoroa *15 km N of Tauranga*

Walnut Cottage *B&B Self Contained Cottage with kitchenette*
Ken & Betty Curreen
309 Plummers Point Road,
Omokoroa, RD 2, Tauranga

Tel (07) 548 0692   Fax (07) 548 1764
walnuthomestay@actrix.co.nz
www.cybersurf.co.nz/curreen

Double $90-$100 Single $60-$90
(Continental breakfast)
Dinner $25
Pet free home
1 Queen 1 Double (2 bdrm)
Bathrooms: 1 Ensuite 1 Private

Situated on scenic Plummers Point Peninsula overlooking Tauranga Harbour we invite our guests to enjoy the tranquility our little corner of the world has to offer. Stroll along the Peninsula with its superb views, boat jetty and reserve. In the vicinity we have mineral hot pools, golf course, quarry gardens, tramping tracks, wineries and eating houses. Walnut Cottage is self-contained. Kowhai Suite has own entrance and conservatory with tea/coffee, T.V. Directions: Plummers Point Road is opposite Caltex Service Station on SH2.

Omokoroa *13 km N of Tauranga*

Serendipity *B&B Homestay*
Sarath & Linda Vidanage
77 Harbour View Road, Omokoroa, Tauranga

Tel (07) 548 2044 or 021 999 815
sarathv@yahoo.com
www.serendipitybnb.co.nz

Double $125 Single $85 (Full breakfast)
Children $30
Dinner $40
Visa MC accepted
Children welcome
2 Queen 2 Double (2 bdrm)
Bathrooms: 2 Private

Welcome to our home and garden nestled above spectacular Omokoroa Beach. The beach is a short walk down the steps. Leisurely walking treks take you through the groves and gardens of the peninsula. A beautiful golf course and local hot pools are minutes away. We are a well-traveled couple who have found our paradise. We love to cook and offer a varied cuisine from traditional to exotic. The best of Tauranga and The Bay of Plenty. Free telephone to U.S /Canada, U.K high speed internet

Omokoroa *17 km N of Tauranga*

Seascape *B&B*
Sue & Geoff Gripton
5 Waterview Terrace, Omokoroa

Tel (07) 548 1027 or 021 171 1936
grippos@xtra.co.nz
www.seascapenz.com

Double $110-$120 Single $90 (Full breakfast)
Visa MC accepted
1 Double 2 Single (2 bdrm)
Bathrooms: 1 Ensuite

Come share our stunning views of Tauranga Harbour and Kaimais. On our doorstep are beaches, walkways, golf, hot pools, boat ramps etc. Just halfway between Tauranga and Katikati, we offer a double room with ensuite and TV, twin room with shared bathroom, both with tea/coffee. Enjoy a cooked or continental breakfast with homemade bread and jams while gazing at view. Only three and a half kilometres from SH2, left at roundabout, first right, first left into Waterview Terrace. Geoff, Sue and our cat will welcome you.

Tauranga *3 km N of Tauranga Central*

Harbinger House *B&B Homestay*
Helen & Doug Fisher
209 Fraser Street, Tauranga

Tel (07) 578 8801 or 027 458 3049
Fax (07) 579 4101
d-h.fisher@xtra.co.nz
www.harbinger.co.nz

Double $80-$95 Single $60-$75 (Special breakfast)
Children half price
Dinner $25
Visa MC accepted
2 Queen 2 Single (3 bdrm)
Bathrooms: 1 Guest share

Harbinger House provides affordable luxury in the heart of Tauranga, being close to hospital, conference facilities, downtown and a new shopping mall 100 metres away. Our upstairs has been renovated with your comfort in mind, using quality furnishings, linen, bathrobes, fresh flowers, tea and coffee. A guest phone and laundry facilities are available. The queen rooms have separate vanities and private balconies. Breakfast is a gourmet event. We offer complimentary pick up from public transport depots and off-street parking is available.

Tauranga *8 km NW of Tauranga*

Oakridge Views *B&B*
Diane & Trevor Hinton
557 Cambridge Road, Tauriko, Tauranga

Tel (07) 543 0292 or 027 285 2189
Fax (07) 543 0294
oakridge.views@xtra.co.nz
www.oakridgeviews.co.nz

Double $100-$125 Single $70-$85
(Full breakfast $10.00 extra)
Children under 12 $30
Pet free home
Children and pets welcome
1 Queen 1 Twin (2 bdrm)
Bathrooms: 1 Ensuite 1 Private

Welcome to Oakridge Views, where your comfort is our concern. Enjoy our panoramic views of gardens and rolling hills. Relax in our comfortable one level home away from home with an acre of gardens. Handy to some of the top restaurants in the bay. Only ten minutes to downtown Tauranga and over the harbour bridge to Mt Maunganui. Attractions include garden walks, tramping, parks, wineries, beaches, golf courses. Spa pool available.

Tauranga - Matua *3 km S of Tauranga*

Aramoana *B&B*

Doreen Anderson

9 Seaway Terrace, Matua, Tauranga

Tel (07) 576 3058 or 027 320 0203
Fax (07) 576 3758
andersondem@xtra.co.nz
www.aramoanabnb.co.nz

Double $100 Single $80 (Full breakfast)
Children $35
Eftpos accepted
Children welcome
1 Queen 1 Twin (2 bdrm)
Bathrooms: 1 Guest share

Relax in comfort by the sea with fabulous views of the harbour and Mt Maunganui. Watch the ships coming and going to the port. Enjoy the lights at night and the moonlight sparkling on the water. Walk along the beach to parks. Dine or shop in nearby Cherrywood village or drive to golf, the nearest course only four minutes away. Use Aramoana as your base to explore the bay. Your host has extensive knowledge of the area and will make you very welcome.

Tauranga - Welcome Bay *15 km S of Tauranga City*

Villa Collini *Luxury B&B Homestay*

Margrit Collini & Andy Wurm
36 Kaiate Falls Road, RD 5,
Tauranga - Welcome Bay, 3175

Tel (07) 544 8322 or 021 047 8394
Fax (07) 544 8322   margrit@naturetours-nz.com
www.villacollini.co.nz

Double $130-$170 Single $105-$140
(Special breakfast)   Children negotiable
Dinner $45pp
Visa MC accepted
Pet free home   Children welcome
1 King/Twin 1 Queen (2 bdrm)
Bathrooms: 1 Ensuite 1 Guest share 2nd sep. toilet

Villa Collini means paradise ! Enjoy spectacular panoramic views of Mount Maunganui and the sea in a very quiet hilltop location. Get spoiled with great hospitality, generous superb cont. breakfast ("simply the best" - guests comments) gourmet dinners, comfortable beds and complimentary drinks. Relax in our park-like garden, walk the endless beaches or make a trip to Rotorua or White Island. We are well travelled and speak German as well. Come as a stranger and leave as a friend.

Tauranga *18 km S of Tauranga*

Tau Tau Lodge *B&B*

Barry & Lorraine
1133 Pyes Pa Road, RD 3, Tauranga 3021

Tel (07) 543 1600   Fax (07) 543 5089
tautaulodge@ihug.co.nz
www.tautaulodge.co.nz

Double $170-$200 Single $140-$160
(Special breakfast)
Dinner $35-$50
Visa MC Amex accepted
Not suitable for children
3 Queen 1 Double (4 bdrm)
Bathrooms: 3 Ensuite

Located between Tauranga and Rotorua - 35 minutes to Rotorua (with no sulphur smells) and 20 minutes to central Tauranga. On two acres of lovely gardens and lawns, stunning views of Tauranga, Mount Maunganui, Kaimai Ranges offering total peace, privacy and tranquility. Large private guest lounge with balcony, library, TV and antique furniture. Tea and coffee facilities, cotton robes, chocolates, hairdryers in each room. Cooked farmhouse or continental breakfast.Upon arrival complimentary drinks and nibbles. Two cats come with the Lodge.

Tauranga - Te Puna *12 km N of Tauranga*

Brookside Rest *B&B Separate Suite*
Monica & John Willis
13 I'Anson Road, Tauranga RD 6, 3002

Tel (07) 552 6786 or 021 420 478
Fax (07) 552 6784
jcmcwillis@clear.net.nz

Double $95-$115 Single $45-$65
(Continental breakfast provisions)
Children welcome
1 Queen 1 Double (2 bdrm)
Bathrooms: 1 Private 1 Guest share

Set in park-like gardens on a three acre farmlet only ten minutes to the city, our self-contained unit with undercover parking and patio area offers a restful yet convenient location close to walks, hot pools, beaches, golf course, cafés, pub & shops. A homely yet private atmosphere to enjoy with your hosts & their two cats, chooks & various farm animals. Continental breakfast provided, cooked dinners by arrangement. A definite for that "Home Away From Home" experience.

Tauranga - Whakamarama *15 km N of Tauranga*

Wildhaven Farm *Luxury B&B*
Robert & Bryony Cross
257 Whakamarama Road, RD 6, Tauranga

Tel (07) 552 5484 or 021 053 1043
Fax (07) 552 5484
roberthhcross@eol.co.nz
http://wildhaven.co.nz

Double $125-$145 Single $110-$125 (Full breakfast)
Children $15
Dinner by arrangement, 3 course $35pp
Payment by cash/cheque/internet
1 Double (1 bdrm)
Bathrooms: 1 Ensuite Large shower room with heated towel rail and hair dryer

We warmly welcome guests to our little slice of paradise. Our 77 acre working farm has uninterrupted coastal views of Mount Manganui, north to the Alderman Islands, which you can enjoy from the extensive landscaped gardens and heated swimming pool. We have one large air-conditioned double bedroom, a fold down sofa bed and a cot provides sleeping accommodation for children. Your hosts are, Robert & Bryony and their two children Emma (9) and Freddie (7) and their one year old friendly dog.

Mt Maunganui *9 km S of Mt Maunganui*

Pembroke House *B&B*
Cathy & Graham Burgess
12 Santa Fe Key, Royal Palm Beach,
Papamoa/ Mt Maunganui

Tel (07) 572 1000
PembrokeHouse@xtra.co.nz
www.pembrokehouse.co.nz

Double $90-$100 Single $70-$80
(Full breakfast)
Children $35
Visa MC accepted
2 Queen 1 Twin (3 bdrm)
Bathrooms: 2 Ensuite 1 Private

A modern home. Cross the road to the Ocean Beach, where you can enjoy swimming, surfing and beach walks. Enjoy stunning sea views while dining at breakfast. Near Fashion Island and Palm Beach Shopping Plaza, restaurants and golf courses. Near Mount Maunganui, Tauranga, Rotorua and Whakatane. Separate guest lounge with TV and tea making facilities. Cathy, a schoolteacher, and Graham, semi-retired - your hosts. We are widely travelled and enjoy meeting people. Our home is shared with our Persian cat, Crystal. Unsuitable for pre-schoolers.

Mt Maunganui - Papamoa *9 km SE of Mt Maunganui*

Hesford House *B&B Homestay*

Sally & Derek Hesford
45 Gravatt Road, Royal Palm Beach, Papamoa 3118

Tel (07) 572 2825
derek.sally@clear.net.nz
www.hesfordhouse.co.nz

Double $90-$140 Single $70-$80 (Full breakfast)
Children Negotiable
Visa MC accepted
Pet free home
Children welcome
2 Queen 1 Twin (3 bdrm)
Bathrooms: 1 Ensuite 1 Guest share

We invite you to stay in our tastefully decorated character home. Enjoy panoramic views of the Papamoa Hills together with exquisite sunsets. Opposite is the fabulous Fashion Island with various shops, cafés, popular restaurants, internet café and English Pub. Relax in a beautiful garden setting. Complimentary tea/coffee facilities, fridge and TVs in each room. Our location offers you blokarts (land yachts), a short stroll to our magnificent beach and only 50 minutes drive to Rotorua, Whakatane and Whangamata (Coromandel). Courtesy pickup from public transport.

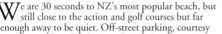

Mt. Maunganui *3 km S of Mt Maunganui*

Beachside *B&B*

Lorraine & Jim Robertson
21B Oceanbeach Road, Mt Maunganui

Tel (07) 574 0960 or 021 238 0598
beachside@ihug.co.nz
www.beachsidebnb.co.nz

Double $90-$140 Single $75-$90 (Full breakfast)
Visa MC accepted
1 King/Twin 2 Queen (3 bdrm)
Bathrooms: 2 Ensuite 1 Private

We are 30 seconds to NZ's most popular beach, but still close to the action and golf courses but far enough away to be quiet. Off-street parking, courtesy transport to/from local airport/buses. Enjoy stunning sea views from our guest lounge while indulging in a generous cooked breakfast plus seasonal fresh fruit salad, home-baked bread & real expresso coffee. We are widely travelled, enjoy meeting and helping our guests. Use our B&B as a base to explore White Island, Rotorua & Coromandel Peninsula.

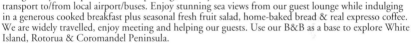

Te Puke *1.3 km W of Te Puke township*

Lazy Daze Cottage *Cottage with Kitchen*

Mel & Sharron Yeates
144 Boucher Avenue, Te Puke, Bay of Plenty

Tel (07) 573 8188 or 027 271 2188
027 626 2926
Fax (07) 573 8188
sharron.yeates@clear.net.nz
www.home.clear.net.nz/pages/sharron.yeates

Double $120 Single $90 (Full breakfast provisions)
Extra guest $35
Children welcome
1 Queen (1 bdrm)
Bathrooms: 1 Private no bath

Te Puke: Kiwifruit capital central to many tourist attractions with a temperate climate. 40 minutes to Rotorua's famous attractions and only 15 minutes to Mt Maunganui, popular with tourists for many reasons. Golf, fishing and white sandy beaches are but a few of the attractions that make this a great place to visit. We are keen golfers and equipment is available for your use. We have regular visits from grandchildren but your area will be private and quiet. We have two cats and an old dog.

119

Bay of Plenty

Te Puke *3.5 km S of Te Puke*

Aotea Villa *B&B Self Contained Bungalow*
Peter & Nanette Miller
246 Te Matai Road, Te Puke 3188

Tel (07) 573 9433 or 021 626 795
Fax (07) 573 9463
Millerph@xtra.co.nz
www.aoteavilla.co.nz

Double $110-$115 Single $85-$90 (Full breakfast)
Children under 13 $30
Visa MC accepted
Children and pets welcome
1 Queen 1 Double 4 Single (3 bdrm)
Bathrooms: 1 Ensuite 1 Guest share

Welcome to our relaxing and comfortable 1910 character villa situated in the heart of the vibrant Bay of Plenty in picturesque kiwifruit and avocado countryside. We are only minutes from Te Puke, 45 minutes from Whakatane and Rotorua and 20 minutes from Tauranga and Mount Maunganui. Enjoy our spa and swimming pool or relax on our wisteria covered verandahs and view our beautiful sunsets. Laundry and internet facilities available. Guest lounge and games room. Stunning local restaurants, excellent golf course close by. Visit our website.

~

Te Puke *1 km NW of Te Puke*

Princess Street Apartment. *B&B Apartment with Kitchen*
The Wilson Family
7 Princess Street, Te Puke, 3071

Tel (07) 573 9345
Fax (07) 573 9354
ruth_wilson@xtra.co.nz

Double $80-$90 Single $50-$60
(Continental breakfast provisions)
Children $15
1 King/Twin 2 Twin (2 bdrm)
Bathrooms: 1 Ensuite 1 Private

Fully self contained apartment situated in a quiet cul-de-sac in central Te Puke within walking distance to the township. Enjoy the many restaurants, cafés and shops. The modern apartment, with a full kitchen, laundry facilities, Sky TV. overlooks a solar heated swimming pool and a tranquil garden setting for your enjoyment. View the many amenities Te Puke has to offer - Kiwifruit Capital of the World, lovely beaches, numerous excellent golf courses nearby, and a 30-40 minute drive from Tauranga, Mount Maunganui, Whakatane and Rotorua.

~

Maketu Beach - Te Puke *60 km N of Rotorua (on the Coast)*

Blue Tides Beachfront Sea View Unit and B&B
B&B Apartment with Kitchen
Patricia Haine
7 Te Awhe Road, Maketu Beach, 10 km from Te Puke

Tel (07) 533 2023 or 025 2613077
0800 359 191   Fax (07) 533 2023
seaview@bluetides.co.nz
www.bluetides.co.nz

Double $130-$165 Single $130-$145 (Full breakfast)
Sea View Unit $130 double self-catering
Wonderful local café for dinners
Visa MC accepted
2 King/Twin 1 Queen (3 bdrm)
Bathrooms: 3 Ensuite 2 Private

Star rate 3+. The perfect place to end your busy days. Seasonal B&B and self-catering Sea View Unit year round, King bedroom with day bed, full kitchen, separate entrance and garage. Awesome coastal views, romantic sunsets and stunning starry night skies. Stay in an historic seaside village, white beaches with café on the surf. Delicious full breakfasts home-made with local produce. Easy drive to Rotorua, Tauranga, Whakatane & the Junction. Home of kiwifruit. Recommended minimum two night stay.

Pukehina Beach *21 km E of Te Puke*
Homestay on the Beach *Homestay*
Alison & Paul Carter
217 Pukehina Parade, Pukehina Beach, RD 9, Te Puke

Tel (07) 533 3988 or 027 276 7305
027 372 2886   Fax (07) 533 3988
p.a.carter@pukehina-beach.co.nz
www.homestays.net.nz/pukehina.htm

Double $110-$120 Single $70 (Full breakfast)
Children half price   Dinner $30   Unit $150
Visa MC accepted
Pet free home   Children welcome
2 Double (2 bdrm)
Bathrooms: 1 Guest share

Welcome to our absolute beachfront home situated on the Pacific Ocean. Your accommodation situated downstairs, allowing complete privacy if you so wish, includes, TV lounge with coffee/tea, fridge, microwave and laundry facilities, also available at separate rate. Enjoy magnificent views from your own sundeck, including White Island volcano and occasional visits from Dolphins and Orcas. Te Puke Golf course 13 km away. 30-40 minute drive from Tauranga, Mount Maunganui, Whakatane and Rotorua. Licensed restaurant/café 2 km, surf casting, swimming, walks or relax and enjoy our unique paradise.

Matata *34 km W of Whakatane*
Pohutukawa Beach B&B & Cottage
B&B Farmstay Cottage with Kitchen
Charlotte & Jorg Prinz
693 State Highway 2, RD 4, Whakatane

Tel (07) 322 2182
Fax (07) 322 2186
joe@prinztours.co.nz
www.beach.co.nz

Double $120 Single $100 (Continental breakfast)
Self-contained cottage (sleeps 4) $150-$180
Dinner $40
Visa MC accepted
Children welcome
1 King/Twin 3 Queen 1 Double 1 Twin (4 bdrm)
Bathrooms: 2 Ensuite 1 Private

Awesome Views. Beautiful setting. Interesting hosts. Rural and cosy. Organic farming and gardening. Two ensuite rooms. Self-contained or fully serviced guest house for six people. Relaxing at the pool, sauna and garden. Guided tours on demand. Dinners on request. English and German spoken. You are welcome!

Matata - Pikowai *30 km NW of Whakatane*
Fothergills on Mimiha *Self Contained B&B Suite*
Separate 2 Bedroom Cottage.
Bev & Hilton Fothergill
84 Mimiha Road, Pikowai/Matata, Whakatane

Tel (07) 322 2224 or 021 131 5171
027 460 5958   Fax (07) 322 2224
bev@fothergills.co.nz   www.fothergills.co.nz

Double $110-$170 Single $90-$125 (Special breakfast)
Children $20   Dinner $50pp by arrangement
Cottage double $320, 2 nights minimum, $750pw
Visa MC accepted   Children and pets welcome
2 Queen 1 Double 1 Twin 1 Single (4 bdrm)
Bathrooms: 1 Ensuite 2 Private 1 bathroom per venue

Here you will find stylish, comfortable accommodation, peace and quiet, friendly hospitable hosts and two outside dogs. Breakfasts, served in house or garden, are garden-fresh, home-made and delicious. Mimiha Cottage, Qualmark 4 stars, is a home-away-from home, fully equipped, everything you need for weekend or longer.Stroll in our idyllic garden, play petanque, walk along the unspoilt beach, up the country road or climb the wonderful hills. After a busy day, soak in the outdoor spa.Come and enjoy this slice of heaven

Whakatane *7 km W of Whakatane*

Whakatane Homestay- Leaburn Farm *Homestay*
Kathleen & Jim Law
237 Thornton Road, RD 4, Whakatane 3194

Tel (07) 308 7487 or 021 21 21 196
Fax (07) 308 7437
kath.law@xtra.co.nz
www.whakatanehomestay.co.nz

Double $85-$95 Single $55-$65 (Full breakfast)
Dinner $25-$35
Visa MC accepted
Pet free home
Pets welcome
1 Queen 2 Single (2 bdrm)
Bathrooms: 1 Guest share Spa

Looking for peace and quiet, or do you want to explore this sunshine coast? If stimulating conversation or a browse in an extensive library is something you enjoy, you are welcome here.

Other guests comments over the 24 years we have been home-hosting, include:
"Thanks for your warm hospitality, sharing your lovely home. We especially enjoyed talking with you and creating a new friendship." Ron & Dorothy, USA
"Our first experience of B&B has left a wonderful impression." David & Terri. NZ
"Wished we could have stayed longer." Dave & Margaret, UK

As young oldies, we enjoy company, farming tales, travel, business interests, and your choice of topic.

We are handy to the golf course, 7 km to thriving Whakatane Township. Special interests of genealogy, Lions Club, bowls and crafts. We have a café/restaurant on the property.

Our queen-bedded guest room is adjacent to a spa bathroom, separate shower and toilet, and is shared only with other guests if the twin bedroom is occupied. Be as busy as you like or enjoy restful country atmosphere. Pamper yourselves at our place.

Whakatane *18 km S of Whakatane*

Omataroa Deer Farm *Farmstay*
Jill & John Needham
Paul Road, RD 2, Whakatane 3192

Tel (07) 322 8399
Fax (07) 322 8399
jill-needham@xtra.co.nz

Double $105 Single $80 (Full breakfast)
Children $40 Dinner $25
1 King 1 Queen (2 bdrm)
Bathrooms: 1 Ensuite 1 Private

We invite you to stay with us in our contemporary home which sits high on a hill commanding panoramic views. We farm deer organically and grow hydrangeas for export. You will be the only guest so you have sole use of a quiet private wing. Your evening meal will be venison, lamb or fresh seafood with home-grown vegetables. We dive, fish, tramp, ski, golf and love to travel. Laundry available.

Whakatane *10 km S of Whakatane*

Baker's *B&B Homestay Cottage with Kitchen*
Lynne & Bruce Baker
40 Butler Road, RD 2, Whakatane

Tel (07) 307 0368 or 027 284 6996
Fax (07) 307 0368 bakers@world-net.co.nz
www.bakershomestay.co.nz

Double $120-$130 Single $90-$100
(Continental breakfast)   Children $20
Dinner $40 by arrangement
Self-contained private cottage available
Visa MC accepted Children and pets welcome
1 King/Twin 2 Queen 2 Single (4 bdrm)
Bathrooms: 2 Ensuite 1 Private

A friendly welcome to our lovely country home nestled amongst mature gardens croquet lawn and Avocado orchard. Enjoy our Swimming or spa pool Choose between our delightful fully self-contained two bedroom cottage or be pampered with bed & breakfast in our warm spacious home. Cosy guest lounge with comfortable sofas to relax on. Lynne and Bruce are keen outdoor hosts enjoying fishing, surfing, gardening and travel. White Island tours, dolphin watching, deep-sea fishing and diving activities can be arranged for your memorable stay.

Whakatane *1.5 km SE of Whakatane Central*

Crestwood Homestay *Luxury B&B*
Janet & Peter McKechnie
2 Crestwood Rise, Whakatane, Bay of Plenty

Tel (07) 308 7554 or 0800 111 449
027 624 6248   Fax (07) 308 7551
pandjmckechnie@xtra.co.nz
www.crestwood-homestay.co.nz

Double $120-$140 Single $90-$110
(Continental breakfast)
Dinner $35 (wine included)   Visa MC accepted
1 Queen 2 Single (2 bdrm)
Bathrooms: 1 Private 1 Guest share
Separate rate for guest sharing facilities

Style, comfort, warmth, stunning sea views and five minutes drive to town. Private, quiet self contained upstairs accommodation with spacious rooms, guest lounge, tea/coffee/fridge area and balcony to capture lovely views. Free internet, phone, TV, toiletries, hairdryer and all home comforts. Breakfasts include Janet's homemade jams and muesli. Wharf nearby for White Island volcano trips, dolphin watching and fishing charters. Helpful friendly hosts enjoy rugby, fly fishing, coastguard activities, chats around the table and family life.

123

Ohope Beach *8 km N of Whakatane*

The Rafters *Apartment with Kitchen*
Pat Rafter
261A Pohutukawa Avenue, Ohope Beach

Tel (07) 312 4856
Fax (07) 312 4856
The_Rafters_Ohope@xtra.co.nz
www.wave.co.nz/pages/macaulay/The_Rafters.htm

Double $80 Single $75 (Accommodation only)
Children $10
Extra adult $20, limit 1
Children and pets welcome
1 King 1 Single (2 bdrm)
Bathrooms: 1 Ensuite

Rafter

Breakfast is not supplied, Unit is self-contained. Minimum two night stay. Maximum 3 guests. Sea views: White, Whale islands, East Coast. Safe swimming. Many interesting walks. Golf, tennis, bowls, all within minutes.

Licensed Chartered Club Restaurant opposite. Trips to volcanic White Island, fishing, jet boating, diving, swimming with dolphins arranged.

Full cooking facilities; private entrance, sunken garden, BBQ. Complimentary: tea, coffee, biscuits, fruit, newspaper, personal laundry service. Pat's interests are: philosophy, theology, history, English literature, the making of grape wines and all spirits, golf, bowls, music and tramping. I have a friendly weimaraner dog.

Courtesy car available. House trained animals welcomed. Four restaurants and oyster farm within five minutes drive. I look forward to your company and assure you unique hospitality.

Directions: on reaching Ohope Beach turn right, proceed 2 km to 261A (beach-side) name "Rafters" on a brick letterbox with illuminated B&B sign.

Ohope Beach *6 km E of Whakatane*
Shiloah *B&B Homestay Cottage with Kitchen*
Pat & Brian Tolley
27 Westend, Ohope Beach

Tel (07) 312 4401
Fax (07) 312 4401

Double $90-$100 Single $50-$60 (Full breakfast)
Children half price
Dinner $18-$25 by arrangement
Self-contained unit available
1 Queen 1 Twin 4 Single (2 bdrm)
Bathrooms: 2 Private 1 Guest share
(2 Private bathrooms in house, 1 Guest share in cottage)

Homestay: paradise on the beach - view White Island and enjoy our hospitality. Facilities available for disabled guests - 5% discount. Well travelled. Also available is a self-catered unit, separate from our B&B, with one twin bedroom, one single bed and bed settee if required, complete with shower and kitchenette. Tariff; $60 own bedding, extra if supplied. Access to beach across road. Fishing, swimming, surfing, and bush walks.

Ohope Beach *8 km SE of Whakatane*
Oceanspray Homestay *Homestay Cottage with Kitchen*
Frances & John Galbraith
283A Pohutukawa Avenue, Ohope, Bay of Plenty

Tel (07) 312 4112 or 027 286 6824
Fax (07) 312 4192   frances@oceanspray.co.nz
www.oceanspray.co.nz

Double $150-$190 Single $80-$100
(Full breakfast provisions)
Children negotiable
Visa MC accepted
Children welcome
3 Queen 2 Twin (5 bdrm)
Bathrooms: 1 Ensuite 2 Private

Welcome to our beachfront home. Wonderful sea views from our upstairs decks. Our modern downstairs three bedroom apartment is self-contained with own kitchen, lounge, two bathrooms (one ensuite). Adjacent to our house is a two bedroom, modern, self-contained cottage. Families welcome. Home comforts - Sky TV, books, videos/toys for children. Continental breakfast provisions are supplied into your unit. John's pursuits are kayaking and longline fishing. Frances enjoys entertaining and providing excellent cuisine. Our very sociable cat,Barnaby,will greet you with a warm welcome.

Ohope *10 km SE of Whakatane*
Moanarua Beach Cottage *Cottage with Kitchen*
Miria & Taroi Black
2 Hoterini Street, Ohope

Tel (07) 312 5924 or 021 255 6192
info@moanarua.co.nz
www.moanarua.co.nz

Double $110-$140 Single $90-$130
(Continental breakfast)
1 baby or small child negotiable
Dinner by arrangement
1 King (1 bdrm)
Bathrooms: 1 Ensuite

Naumai, haere mai Miria and Taroi welcome you to a unique cultural experience in a romantic hideaway, a restful retreat nestled between the ocean and the harbour in sunny Ohope. Feel free to use BBQ, luxury spa and expansive decks with views of ocean and harbour. Chat with us about local history and Maori art works that adorn our home, cottage and garden. Kick back, relax in your private fully self-contained cottage or enjoy many local activities. Boat tours and kayaks available for hire.

Bay of Plenty

Ohope Beach *7.5 km E of Whakatane*
Seaview Bed and Breakfast *B&B Homestay*
Lynnette and Ross Nicholson
33 Waterford Avenue, Waterford Estate, Ohope

Tel (07) 312 6005 or 021 207 3838
Fax (07) 312 6005
r.lnicholson@xtra.co.nz
www.seaviewbb.co.nz

Double $110-$130 Single $90-$100
(Continental breakfast) Children negotiable
Dinner $30pp by arrangement
Visa MC accepted   Children welcome
1 Queen 1 Double 1 Twin (3 bdrm)
Bathrooms: 1 Guest share 1 Extra WC

Relax and enjoy the quiet gated location of Seaview with the lovely Ohope Beach just metres away. From the upstairs deck, guests can view White Island and Cape Runaway on clear days.Guests have their own lounge - TV/Video, Tea/Coffee facilities, BBQ, Microwave. Laundry available.Golf Club, Restaurants, Playground are close by. Lynnette and Ross, who are former farmers, have many interests including Sea/Lake fishing, Reading, Sports, Cooking.We, and a spoilt cat,"Two Bob", will ensure you enjoy your stay at Ohope.

Opotiki *18 km E of Opotiki*
Coral's B&B *B&B Farmstay Cottage with Kitchen*
Coral Parkinson
Morice's Bay, Highway 35, RD 1, Opotiki

Tel (07) 315 8052 or 021 299 9757
Fax (07) 315 8052
coralsb.b@wxc.net.nz

Double $90-$125 Single $70-$90
(Continental breakfast $15pp by arrangement)
Children $15
Dinner $25
Children and pets welcome
1 Queen 1 Double 2 Single (3 bdrm)
Bathrooms: 1 Private

We provide self-contained accommodation located on our hobby farm. As well as pets and farm animals we collect varied memorabilia. Enjoy the beach and bird life; swim at nearby sandy surf beach. fish, ramble over the rocks, explore caves. Our two storied cottage features lead-light windows, native timbers, large decks look out across the bay and native bush. three golf courses within an hours drive; covered parking, home-made bread and preserves. We have a clasic English Daimler car. Visit our local Marae.

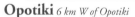

Opotiki *6 km W of Opotiki*
Coast View *Apartment with Kitchen*
Margaret Green
28 Paerata Ridge Road, RD 2, Opotiki

Tel (07) 315 5895
margg@xtra.co.nz

Double $90-$120 Single $60-$90 (Full breakfast)
Children $40-$60
Children welcome
1 King/Twin (1 bdrm)
Bathrooms: 1 Private

Relax in my bright, comfortable, fully self-contained ground floor unit with separate bedroom. Superb view of the Bay coast and five minutes from the beach. Base yourself here while you enjoy the attractions of this interesting area. I work part time, but I will enjoy meeting you and sharing my attractive home and warm hospitality. I have been an active tramper in this area and now enjoy biking, reading, talking and relaxing. All breakfast ingredients are provided. There are restaurants and take-aways available in Opotiki.

Opotiki - Waihau Bay *112 km N of Opotiki*
Waihau Bay Homestay *B&B Homestay Apartment with Kitchen*
Noelene & Merv Topia
10942 State Highway 35 Waihau Bay, RD 3, Opotiki

Tel (07) 325 3674 or 0800 240 170
n.topia@clear.net.nz
www.waihaubayhomestay.co.nz

Double $85-$100 Single $55-$75
(Continental breakfast) Children half price
Dinner $30 Visa MC Eftpos accepted
Children and pets welcome
2 King 1 Queen 2 Twin 2 Single (4 bdrm)
Bathrooms: 3 Ensuite 1 Private
All bathrooms are suitable for disabled

Surrounded by unspoiled beauty we invite you to come and enjoy magnificent views, stunning sunsets, swim, go diving, kayaking (we have kayaks) or just walk along the sandy beach. You are most welcome to join Merv when he checks his craypots each morning and his catches are our cuisine specialty. Fishing trips, horse treks and guided cultural walks are also available. We have two self-contained units with disabled facilities, and a double room with ensuite. Our cat Tosca enjoys making new friends.

Rotorua - Ngakuru *32 km S of Rotorua*
Te Ana Farmstay *Farmstay Cottage No Kitchen*
The Oberer Residence: Heather Oberer
Poutakataka Road, Ngakuru, RD 1, Rotorua

Tel (07) 333 2720 or 021 828 151
Fax (07) 333 2720
teanafarmstay@xtra.co.nz
www.teanafarmstay.co.nz

Double $100-$150 Single $90 (Special breakfast)
Children negotiable
Dinner by prior arrangement
2 Queen 4 Single (4 bdrm)
Bathrooms: 2 Ensuite 1 Family share

Te Ana, The Oberer family sanctuary since 1936, offers peace and tranquility in a spacious rural garden setting affording magnificent views of lake, volcanically-formed hills and lush farmland. Enjoy a leisurely stroll before joining host for a very generous country breakfast. Ideal base from which to explore the Rotorua and Taupo attractions, Waiotapu and Waimungu Thermal Reserves, Waikite Thermal mineral swimming pool and Tamaki Tours Hangi. Families welcomed by Sam, our loyal Jack Russell. Farm tour, canoe and fishing rod available.

Rotorua *4 km S of Rotorua*
Serendipity Homestay *B&B Homestay*
Kate & Brian Gore
3 Kerswell Terrace, Tihi-o-Tonga, Rotorua

Tel (07) 347 9385 or 027 609 3268
b.gore@clear.net.nz
www.serendipityhomestay.co.nz

Double $130-$140 Single $80 (Special breakfast)
Children under 12 $35
Dinner $35 by arrangement
Visa MC accepted
Pet free home
Children welcome
1 Queen 2 Single (2 bdrm)
Bathrooms: 1 Private spa bath plus shower

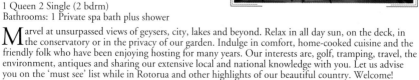

Marvel at unsurpassed views of geysers, city, lakes and beyond. Relax in all day sun, on the deck, in the conservatory or in the privacy of our garden. Indulge in comfort, home-cooked cuisine and the friendly folk who have been enjoying hosting for many years. Our interests are, golf, tramping, travel, the environment, antiques and sharing our extensive local and national knowledge with you. Let us advise you on the 'must see' list while in Rotorua and other highlights of our beautiful country. Welcome!

Bay of Plenty

Rotorua *4 km SW of Rotorua*

Hunts Farm *Farmstay*
Maureen & John Hunt
363 Pukehangi Road, 359 Pukehangi Road, Rotorua

B&B
Approved

Tel (07) 348 1352 or 027 486 3477
(07) 348 2874
sonyahunt@xtra.co.nz

Double $100 **Single** $70 (Full breakfast)
Children $30
Children welcome
1 King/Twin 2 Queen 2 Twin 2 Single (4 bdrm)
Bathrooms: 2 Ensuite 1 Guest share

Come relax in our neighbouring new homes as we help you plan your itinerary and book your local tours.

Explore our 150 acre scenic farm running beef and deer. Views of farm, lake, island, forest and city are magical. Guest areas have private entrances, lounges with tea/coffee facilities, TV, fridge.

First home child/pet free. Two triple rooms, each with ensuite lead to private terraces. Second home, two gorgeous children, two outdoor dogs and cat. Twin room and Queen room with ensuite, ideal for family groups.

Rotorua *14 km NE of Rotorua*

Brunswick *Homestay*
Joy & Lin Cathcart
99 Brunswick Drive, RD 4, Rotorua 3221

Tel (07) 350 1472 or 021 256 5355
Fax (07) 350 1472
joylin@clear.net.nz

Double $120 Single $70 (Full breakfast)
Visa MC accepted
Pet free home
Not suitable for children
1 King (1 bdrm)
Bathrooms: 1 Private adjacent to the bedroom

With peaceful surroundings and beautiful views over Lake Rotorua "Brunswick" is 15 minutes from Rotorua City centre and five minutes from Rotorua Airport. Having retired from dairy farming Lin now enjoys his golf; Joy plays bridge and gardening is a shared hobby. Our guest room has TV, hot drink facilities, refrigerator and balcony. We are smoke-free and have no pets. After 17 years of hosting and many return guests, a cuppa, Joy's homebaking and a warm welcome await you! Please phone or e-mail for directions.

Rotorua *5 km SE of Rotorua*

Walker Homestay & B&B *B&B Homestay Cottage with Kitchen*
Colleen & Isaac Walker
13 Glenfield Road, Owhata, Rotorua

Tel (07) 345 3882 or 021 050 9633
Fax (07) 345 3856   colleen.walker@clear.net.nz

Double $98-$120 Single $55-$65
(Continental breakfast)   Children half price
Dinner $25 by arrangement
Extra guest $15
Visa MC accepted
1 Queen 1 Double 1 Twin 1 Single (3 bdrm)
Bathrooms: 1 Ensuite 1 Private Cottage has own
bathroom. Room in house - ensuite

Two bedroom cottage in own garden area has lounge, kitchen, bathroom, and laundry. Room in house has ensuite; tea/coffee facilities; microwave; separate entrance and access to hosts living area. Have complete privacy or be one of the family. BBQ available. Colleen is a business administration tutor and Ike is a NZ Maori. He is a coach driver with a background of farming and paper industry, a keen fisherman and golfer. Two friendly dachshund dogs will welcome you. 24 hours notice for evening meal. Off-road parking.

Rotorua *3 km W of Rotorua*

West Brook *B&B Homestay*
Judy & Brian Bain
378 Malfroy Road, Rotorua

Tel (07) 347 8073 Fax (07) 347 8073

Double $90 Single $50 (Continental breakfast)
Children under 12 half price
Dinner $25
Visa MC accepted
Children welcome
4 Single (2 bdrm)
Bathrooms: 1 Family share

Retired farmers with years of hospitality involvement, live 3 km from city on western outskirts. Interests include meeting people, farming, international current affairs. Brian a Rotorua Host Lions member, Judy's interest extend to all aspects of homemaking and gardening. Both well appointed comfy guest rooms are equipped with electric blankets. The friendly front door welcome and chatter over the meal table add up to our motto: home away from home. Assistance with sightseeing planning and transport to and from tourist centre available.

Rotorua - Ngongotaha *17 km N of Rotorua*

Clover Downs Estate *B&B Homestay Farmstay*
Lyn & Lloyd Ferris
175 Jackson Road, RD 2, Ngongotaha, Rotorua

Tel (07) 332 2366 or 021 712 866
Fax (07) 332 2367
Reservations@cloverdowns.co.nz
www.accommodationinrotorua.co.nz

Double $225-$335 Single $205-$310 (Special breakfast)
Children negotiable
Visa MC Diners Amex accepted
Children welcome
3 King/Twin 1 King (4 bdrm)
Bathrooms: 4 Ensuite

Welcome to our fine country Bed & Breakfast accommodation on a deer and ostrich farm, nestled in a peaceful country setting just 15 minutes drive north of Rotorua city.

We can offer a choice of four individually decorated spacious king-size suites each comprising ensuite bathroom, tea/coffee making facilities, refrigerator, telephone, ironing facilities, hairdryer, TV, VCR, stereo & individual outdoor decks. We serve a leisurely breakfast each morning which, if you desire, is followed by our popular free deer and ostrich farm tour.

Visit our awesome cultural and scenic attractions. Minutes drive from our property you will discover a myriad of things to do and see: stand on active volcanoes, peer into craters, see boiling mud or just soak in a mineral pool. We can advise you on trout fishing at one of the many lakes and rivers in the area, walk cool forest glades or maybe play a round of golf. With days as busy as this you'll be glad to come home to our gracious haven of relaxation. If you wish to go out, Rotorua has some wonderful restaurants and cafés. or you may like to enjoy a Maori hangi and concert. We strive to exceed our guests' expectations through an ineffable blend of warmth, generosity and detail.

Directions: Take State Highway 5 to roundabout. Travel thru Ngongotaha village on Hamurana Road - go over railway line then take third left into Central Road. Turn first right into Jackson Road - Clover Downs Estate is number 175 on left hand side.

Rotorua *12 km NE of Rotorua*
Eucalyptus Tree Country Homestay *B&B Homestay Farmstay*
Manfred & Is Fischer
66 State Highway 33, RD 4, Rotorua

Tel (07) 345 5325
Fax (07) 345 5325
euc.countryhome@ihug.co.nz
http://homepages.ihug.co.nz/~euc.countryhome

Double $90 Single $60 (Full breakfast)
Dinner $30
1 King/Twin 2 Queen 1 Double (3 bdrm)
Bathrooms: 1 Private 1 Guest share

Welcome to our quiet, smoke-free, high quality country home. On our small farm near Lake Rotorua, close to Lake Rotoiti and Okataina, we have calves, sheep, chickens, ducks, rabbits, organic vegetables and fruit trees. Native bush drive to clear trophy trout fishing lakes and bush walks, thermal area, Maori culture, hot pools, skydiving, whitewater rafting. Our hobbies are trout fishing from boat, and fly fishing, hunting and shooting. We lived in the USA, Canada, Indonesia, Mexico and Germany and speak their languages.

All our B&Bs are non-smoking
unless stated otherwise in the text.

Rotorua *4 km E of Rotorua*
Aroden B&B Homestay *B&B Homestay*
Leonie & Paul Kibblewhite
2 Hilton Road, Lynmore, Rotorua

Tel (07) 345 6303 or 027 696 4211
Fax (07) 345 6353
aroden@xtra.co.nz

Double $130-$145 Single $90 (Full breakfast)
Children negotiable
Visa MC Diners accepted
2 Queen (2 bdrm)
Bathrooms: 1 Ensuite 1 Private

A great central location: city five minutes, Whakarewarewa Forest adjacent (glow-worms at night!), lakes and thermal nearby. Enjoy Aroden's style, peace and character: two lounge areas, well-appointed rooms, comfortable beds and fine linen, modern bathrooms (excellent showers), central heating/open fire, patio, spa and luxuriant garden with native tree collection. Leonie, background in teaching, and Paul, scientist, are fifth generation Kiwi with real knowledge of this remarkable area. And meet Taupo, Paul's delightful guide dog. Breakfast is special - this couple enjoys food! Leonie parlé français.

Rotorua - Lake Tarawera *15 km SE of Rotorua*

Boatshed Bay Lodge *B&B Apartment with Kitchen*

Lorraine & Graeme van Praagh
93 Spencer Road, Lake Tarawera, RD 5, Rotorua

Tel (07) 362 8080
Fax (07) 362 8060
laketarawera@xtra.co.nz
http://wwww.ltaketaraweraescape.co.nz

Double $90 Single $75 (Breakfast by arrangement)
Children $15
Self-contained $90
Visa MC accepted
Children and pets welcome
2 Queen 2 Single (2 bdrm)
Bathrooms: 2 Ensuite

Absolute lake edge with lawn to private jetty and sandy beach in a small rural community. 15 minutes from Rotorua's attractions and central to the surrounding region. Famous for trophy-sized trout, crystal clear water and pristine native bush. Bathe at Hotwater Beach, only accessible by boat or walk to The Tarawera Falls, described as one of the best short walks in NZ. Use a complimentary kayak or just relax. Dominated by Mt Tarawera, the lake & environs are dramatic in all seasons.

Rotorua - Lake Tarawera *20 km SE of Rotorua*

Lake Tarawera Rheinland Lodge *B&B Homestay*

Gunter & Maria
484 Spencer Road, RD 5, Rotorua

Tel (07) 362 8838
Fax (07) 362 8838
tarawera@ihug.co.nz

Double $120-$150 Single $85-$100 (Special breakfast)
Children half price
Dinner $45
1 King/Twin 1 Queen (2 bdrm)
Bathrooms: 1 Private 1 Family share

Located at the magic Lake Tarawera renowned for its scenery and history we offer warm hospitality with a personal touch. Expect total privacy, magnificent lake views, luxurious and relaxing outdoor whirlpool, spacious bathroom with shower and bath, fitness area, stereo, TV, internet connection, lake beach five minutes on foot, sea 45 minutes by car, bush walks, fishing and hunting trips by arrangement, home-made bread, German cuisine on request, organic garden, German/English spoken.

Rotorua *3 km N of Rotorua*

Ferntree Cottage *B&B Homestay Separate Suite*

Val & Geoff Brannan
1 Tatai Street, Rotorua

Tel (07) 348 0000 or 021 049 1910
0800 398 633 or 021 104 7203
ferntreecottage@yahoo.co.nz
www.ferntreecottage.co.nz

Double $110-$140 Single $100-$120 (Full breakfast)
Children negotiable
Dinner by arrangement
Free bottle of NZ wine three nights or more stay
Visa MC accepted   Children welcome
1 Queen 1 Double (2 bdrm)
Bathrooms: 1 Ensuite 1 Family share
Tiled, heated bathrooms, invigorating showers

After many years as hosts, we are continuing to offer friendly, helpful hospitality and knowledge of our wonderful country to guests. Lake Rotorua is almost on the doorstep and many attractions are nearby. Enjoy a tranquil garden, off street parking and ground floor accommodation. Secluded whirlpool (summer only), private garden deck and a comfortable bed allow you to recharge, ready for another day experiencing Rotorua. Enjoy a three course breakfast if you choose. Meet Snappercat and Josiedog.

Rotorua *10 km E of Rotorua*

Peppertree Farm *B&B Farmstay*
Robyn Panther & Barry Morris
25 Cookson Road, RD 4, Rotorua

Tel (07) 345 3718
Fax (07) 345 3718
peppertree.farm@xtra.co.nz

Double $105-$115 Single $70 (Full breakfast)
Children half price
Visa MC accepted
Children welcome
1 Double 2 Twin (3 bdrm)
Bathrooms: 1 Ensuite 1 Guest share

Handy to the airport our quiet rural retreat overlooking Lake Rotorua provides a picturesque and homely welcome. Farm animals are horses, cows, sheep, a young donkey and chickens. Lucy, our Cavalier King Charles spaniel, is a house pet, and Ben, our very friendly labrador lives outside. We are knowledgable locals who enjoy horse racing, rugby, most sports and meeting interesting people! If you wish to attend a Maori concert and hangi, we can arrange pick up and delivery back to the farm.

Rotorua Central *1 km S of Rotorua Central*

Innes Cottage *B&B Homestay*
Chris & Gill Innes
18A Wylie Street, Rotorua Central

Tel 0800 243 030 or (07) 349 1839
Fax (07) 349 1890
chris@clican.com
www.innescottage.co.nz

Double $100-$140 Single $95-$110
(Continental breakfast)   Children POA
Dinner by arrangement
Visa MC Diners Amex accepted
2 Queen 2 Single (3 bdrm)
Bathrooms: 2 Ensuite 1 Private

Centrally situated, within flat walking distance to restaurants and the city, set in a treelined quiet neighborhood only 100 metres from the main road. Close to Te Puia Thermal area and major tourist attractions are easily accessible. After 130 years heritage in the beverage industry we have travelled extensively, have collected a wealth of knowledge and many valuable contacts. Let us assist and advise you on the most popular and "must see" attractions and other highlights of our beautiful country. Free airport/bus pick up.

Rotorua *10 km N of Rotorua*

Ngongotaha Lakeside Lodge *Luxury B&B Lake Stay*
Lyndsay & Graham Butcher
41 Operiana Street, Ngongotaha, Rotorua

Tel (07) 357 4020 or 0800 144 020
027 385 2807
Fax (07) 357 4020
lake.edge@xtra.co.nz
www.rotorualakesidelodge.co.nz

Double $170-$230 Single $150-$200 (Full breakfast)
Children over 12 negotiable
Visa MC accepted
1 King 1 Queen 2 Single (3 bdrm)
Bathrooms: 3 Ensuite

Absolute lake edge, stunning panaramic views, fishing, bird watching, great food and warm hospitality are what you will find at our spacious comfortable home. The upper level is exclusively for guests with fully equipped lounge/conservatory overlooking the lake. All bedrooms have ensuite facilities with everything provided. The famous Waiteti Stream is only metres away, with Rainbow and Brown Trout waiting to be caught. Free use of fishing gear and canoe.... You catch and we'll cook. Safe parking and sulphur free. Multiple night rates.

Rotorua *10 km SE of Rotorua centre*

Lake Okareka B&B *B&B Homestay Apartment with Kitchen*

Patricia & Ken Scott
10 Okareka Loop Road, RD 5, Rotorua

Tel (07) 362 8245 or 0800 652 735
patricia.scott@xtra.co.nz
www.lakeokarekabnb.co.nz

Double $120-$150 Single $80-$100
(Special breakfast)
Dinner by arrangement
Children welcome
2 Queen 1 Double 1 Single (3 bdrm)
Bathrooms: 3 Ensuite

A very warm welcome awaits you at tranquil Lake Okareka, one of the most beautiful Lakes in the area. Our modern home captures magnificent Lake views and beyond to Mt Tarawera. Stroll along the waters edge, enjoy the native bush, ferns and birdlife. Use our local knowledge on all nearby hot pools, fishing, scenic, thermal, adventure and cultural activities. Excellent swimming, complimentary kayaks available. Our environment is quiet and peaceful yet only ten minutes from Rotorua. The perfect retreat with space, privacy and home comforts.

Rotorua *1 km N of rotorua*

Robertson House *B&B*

John Ballard
70 Pererika Street, Rotorua

Tel (07) 343 7559
Fax (07) 343 7559
info@robertsonhouse.co.nz

Double $110-$170 Single $80-$140
(Continental breakfast)
Extra person $50
1 King/Twin 2 Queen 2 Double 2 Single (5 bdrm)
Bathrooms: 3 Ensuite

Our historic home, only two minutes drive from city centre, was built by one of Rotoruas forefathers, in 1905. Under the auspices of the Historic Places Trust it has been carefully renovated, retaining its colonial charm. Relax in its warm comfortable atmosphere, or take time out on the verandah and enjoy our old English cottage garden resplendent with colour and fragrance, citrus trees and grape vines. Our friendly hosts are happy to assist with information and bookings for Rotorua's Maori cultural and sightseeing attractions.

Rotorua - Okere Falls - Lake Rotoiti *20 km N of Rotorua*

At The Ferns Bed & Breakfast *B&B Homestay Cottage with Kitchen*

Carol & Bernie Mason
48 Taheke Road, RD 4, Okere Falls, Rotorua

Tel (07) 362 4087 or 027 251 7932
027 446 7121   Fax (07) 362 4087
bcmason@xtra.co.nz
www.attheferns.co.nz

Double $145-$165 Single $145-$165 (Full breakfast)
Dinner $45 by arrangement
Extra person $20
Breakfast in self-contained $15 by request
Visa MC accepted   Children welcome
1 King 1 Queen 1 Single (2 bdrm)
Bathrooms: 1 Ensuite 1 Private

Secluded Okere Falls Lake Rotoiti accommodation, surrounded by tree ferns, bird song,close to shady walks and great trout fishing. If you enjoy peace, quiet and relish the chance to relax and enjoy nature, At The Ferns is the ideal place. Walk to the Lake, Okere Falls, kayak, white water raft or watch the fun. Choose from your own self-contained cottage in the lower garden or have bed & breakfast where the guest room gives you privacy with all the comforts of home.

Rotorua - Lake Rotoiti *20 km NE of Rotorua*

Lakestay Rotoiti *B&B*

Graeme & Raewyn Natusch
173 Tumoana Road, Lake Rotoiti, RD 4 Rotorua

Tel (07) 345 4089 or 027 418 8404
Fax (07) 345 4089
lakestayrotoiti@xtra.co.nz

Double $120-$150 Single $100-$120 (Full breakfast)
Dinner $30
Self-contained studio $120-$150
Off season rates May-Oct
Visa MC accepted
2 Queen (2 bdrm)
Bathrooms: 2 Ensuite

Lakestay Rotoiti, a very special destination for the discerning couple or individual travellers both summer and winter with friendly informative hosts and siamese cat. One of just three lakefront properties in a beautiful secluded sandy bay surrounded by native bush, forest and stunning lake views from all living and guest bedrooms. Excellent swimming, trout fishing, walking tracks and natural rejuvinating hot baths nearby. Guests enjoy complimentary use of kyaks, dingy, windsurfer and bicycles. Wonderful evening dinner by arrangement. Directions are essential. A truely unique experience.

Rotorua - Ngongotaha *8 km N of Rotorua*

Suncrest Ngongotaha B&B *B&B*

Amanda & Gary Gower
74 Hall Road, Ngongotaha, Rotorua

Tel (07) 357 4336 or 0800 357 4336
027 481 1458   Fax (07) 357 4356
gandagower@xtra.co.nz
www.suncrest.co.nz

Double $130-$150 Single $110-$120 (Full breakfast)
Dinner by arrangement
Visa MC accepted
1 Queen 1 Twin (2 bdrm)
Bathrooms: 1 Guest share with double spa bath, shower,
separate toilet & vanity.

Come stay where you are welcome to relax in our modern, comfortable, one level home, enjoying our facilities and sunny courtyard garden. Beautiful views of lake, mountains, sunsets. Close to tourist attractions and activities, fishing streams,walks, and two restaurants. We have lived many years in Rotorua and can assist you on what to see & do, bookings etc. Our interests are travel (NZ and abroad), gardening, music, Gary: trains big and small, Amanda: musician, card making, watercolour painting,needlework. Off street parking, tea/coffee, laundry.

Rotorua *3 km NE of Rotorua Airport*

Rotokawa Lodge *B&B Homestay*

Deborah Young
1135C Te Ngae Road, RD 4, Rotorua

Tel (07) 345 5911 or 027 447 6533
021 956 407
Fax (07) 345 5910
rotokawalodge@xtra.co.nz
www.rotokawa-lodge.co.nz

Double $160-$195 (Full breakfast)
Visa MC Eftpos accepted
3 King/Twin 2 Queen (5 bdrm)
Bathrooms: 3 Ensuite 2 Guest share

Welcome to the highlight of your holiday Our Cedarwood Lodge nestled on the shores of Lake Rotorua overlooking Mokoia Island on the fringe of the city, central to Rotorua's tourist attractions ie: Thermal Geysers, Maori villages, trout fishing etc. Offering spacious Super King/Queen ensuite rooms containing tea/coffee, TV/DVD's available. Our Japanese spa bathhouse is a must for weary travelling bodies. Our hearty cooked or continental breakfasts will sustain you for your day's adventures.

Rotorua's Legend on the Lake Homestay *B&B Homestay Apartment with Kitchen*

Murray & Heather Watson
33 Haumoana Street, Koutu, Rotorua

Tel (07) 347 1123 or 027 492 7122
Fax (07) 347 1313
muzzandheb@kol.co.nz
www.troutnz.co.nz

Double $135 Single $100 (Full breakfast)
Children $20
Dinner $45pp by arrangement
Additional adults $30pp per night
Visa MC accepted
Pet free home
2 Queen 1 Double 1 Single (3 bdrm)
Bathrooms: 1 Ensuite 1 Private

On arrival you will be greeted with our magnificent, quiet and secluded lakes-edge view and a genuine Kiwi welcome. Please join us on the lawn beside the lake for refreshments as we would love to help you plan your stay by sharing our local knowledge of the area and its many attractions.

Hearing the tranquil lapping of the lake you will find it hard to believe you are only 5 minutes drive from the city centre. You will find your self-contained apartment to have all the comforts of home (washing machine, TV, DVD, video, stereo, oven, microwave and dishwasher). Separate bedroom (queen) and living area/kitchen with ensuite access from both rooms. Free email access.

Our smoke-free apartment ensures a freshness you will enjoy. Breakfast includes fruit, yoghurt, cereal, juice and tea/coffee followed by a cooked breakfast - all this you can choose the time you would like to have it served. Breakfast is a great time to get to know us and for us to help you make the most of your time in this volcanic thermal paradise.

We are more than happy to assist with local bookings and recommend you sample some of the strong local Maori culture. Murray operates a trout fishing charter business on Lake Rotorua and Heather runs a gourmet food business, we have both travelled extensively, internationally and throughout New Zealand and enjoy meeting people from all over the world. We have been running homestays for the last 12 years and really know how to make your time here enjoyable and comfortable.

Feel free to sit on the lawn or in the conservatory and watch the spectacular sunsets we are lucky enough to enjoy almost every night. We hope you will arrive as our guests and leave as our friends.

Rotorua - The Redwoods *4 km E of Rotorua*

B&B @ The Redwoods *B&B Homestay*
Vivien & Peter Cooper
3 Awatea Terrace, Lynmore - Rotorua

Tel (07) 345 4499 or 027 270 3594
Fax (07) 345 4499   b&b@theredwoods.co.nz
www.theredwoods.co.nz

Double $130-$160 Single $130-$160 (Full breakfast)
Single bed available for child to share room
Dinner $35, silver service
Visa MC accepted   Pet free home
2 Queen 1 Single (2 bdrm)
Bathrooms: 2 Ensuite Unlimited hot shower

Secluded yet central! Two new luxurious ensuite guestrooms with private entrance, guest-only lounge, dining and outdoor living. Decor is simple and stylish, lounge opens onto courtyard and garden. We live upstairs in a split level home in quiet cul-de-sac; enjoy our company or the privacy of your own space. We combine interaction with discretion. Redwood Forest on your doorstep, city and lakes five minutes away with Rotorua's many attractions very accessible. Safe off-street parking. All our guests have enjoyed our personal service and quality recommendations.

Rotorua - Ngongotaha *12 km N of Rotorua*

Country Villa Luxury B&B *Luxury B&B Loft with kitchen*
Anneke & John Van der Maat
351 Dalbeth Road, RD 2, Ngongotaha

Tel (07) 3575 893
Fax (07) 357 5893
countryvilla@xtra.co.nz
www.countryvilla.biz

Double $175-$245 Single $175-$225 (Full breakfast)
Children up to 10 $40
Extra adult $85
Visa MC accepted
4 Queen 2 Twin 3 Single (6 bdrm)
Bathrooms: 4 Ensuite 1 Private
2 bedroom suite shares a private bathroom

So close to Rotorua and all its attractions and yet away from sulphur fumes and traffic. Enter this beautiful villa, which was originally built in Auckland in 1906 and shifted to this idyllic site in Rotorua, 90 years later, and you feel "at home". The restoration project took two years and John and Anneke now enjoy sharing it with travellers from around the world. The large gardens around the villa are home to many native birds. Views over green pasture towards lake Rotorua, Mt Ngongotaha and Tarawera.

Rotorua *5 km SW of Rotorua*

Hillside Homestead B.&B *B&B Homestay*
Lorraine & Jeff Nowland
99 Tihi Road, Springfield, Rotorua

Tel (07) 347 9337 or 027 441 1535
Fax (07) 347 9337
hillside.homestead@xtra.co.nz
www.hillsidehomestead.co.nz

Double $100-$130 Single $95-$110 (Full breakfast)
Visa MC Amex accepted
Pet free home
Not suitable for children
1 King 1 Queen (2 bdrm)
Bathrooms: 2 Private

You will feel welcome the moment you arrive. Boutique rooms with tea/coffee-making facilities. Refrigerator, telephone, mini-bar available. We have had 17 years as owner-operators of a major tourist attraction, specialising in fragrances, herbs for cooking, restaurant etc. We now enjoy being hosts in our unique homestead, making new friends and sharing our love for music. If in Rotorua for a special occasion we can organize your event . An ideal place to stay where hospitality is guaranteed.

Bay of Plenty

Rotorua *6 km NW of City*

Affordable Westminster Lodge and Cottage
B&B Farmstay Cottage with Kitchen
Gillian & Barry Gillette
58A Mountain Road, Rotorua, 3201

Tel (07) 348 4273 or 0800 937 864
Fax (07) 348 4205   westminster@slingshot.co.nz
www.westminsterlodge.co.nz

Double $100-$150 Single $70-$100 (Special breakfast)
Children under 14 $20
Fully cooked breakfast for extra $12pp
Visa MC Eftpos accepted   Children welcome
5 Queen 6 Twin 2 Single (8 bdrm)
Bathrooms: 3 Ensuite 3 Private 1 Guest share

Affordable Westminster Lodge and Cottage are English Tudor style homes nestled on the slopes of Mt Ngongotaha overlooking the city of Rotorua.

So country, yet only six minutes to the city centre. Panoramic views in the day and fairy land at night. We offer superior Bed and Breakfast accommodation in semi self contained units or lodge rooms at affordable prices or you can choose the self catering cottage Children are welcome in our large family rooms. The Lodge is Qualmark 3Star Plus and the Cottage a 4Star.

All rooms have tea and coffee making facilities fridge and microwaveEnjoy our delicious special breakfast with fresh fruit salad yoghurt and cereal, hot apple muffins (baked daily) and a freshly laid egg or a scrumptious fully cooked breakfast at a small extra cost.

Experience all the comforts of home in a warm and friendly atmosphere, ensuring your stay in our family home will always be remembered. Breathe in the fresh mountain air and relax in our spa pool that overlooks the city at the end of your busy day. We are a family of eight with five adopted children two still living at home. We have miniature cows and horses, sheep, chickens, and Mrs Pig. Our house pets are a cockatoo Paulie, the cat Socks and Holly and Benji our little dogs. All the animals are friendly and can be hand fed.

Rotorua *11 km N of Rotorua*
Te Ngae Lodge *B&B*
Anne & Sandy Cooper
54 SH33, RD 4, Rotorua

Tel (07) 345 4153
Fax (07) 345 4153
enquire@tengae.co.nz
www.tengae.co.nz

Double $100-$200 Single $80-$180 (Full breakfast)
Visa MC accepted
Children welcome
3 Queen 1 Twin (4 bdrm)
Bathrooms: 1 Ensuite 2 Private

Te Ngae Lodge, hosts Sandy, Anne and cat Furball, country but only 12 minutes from Rotorua City. Experience hospitality and superior accommodation in a relaxed garden atmosphere where tuis and bellbirds sing. Stay in the main house or separately in the Mokoia Suite with views to the lake and Mokoia Island. Share a sumptuous cooked breakfast and meet other guests during complimentary evening wine sampling. We can help plan itineraries to take in geothermal areas, Maori culture or walks in our beautiful lake areas. Welcome.

Rotorua - Rerewhakaaitu *45 km SE of Rotorua*
Ashpit Place *B&B Homestay*
Alison & Scott Marshall
815 Ashpit Road, Rerewhakaaitu, Rotorua 3073

Tel (07) 366 6709 or 021 117 0317
Fax (07) 366 6710
samarshall@clear.net.nz
www.ashpitplace.co.nz

Double up to $180 (Full breakfast)
1 Queen (1 bdrm)
Bathrooms: 1 Ensuite

Ashpit Place is a private home where you are hosted by the owners. An intimate, peaceful atmosphere is preserved for those seeking contemplation and relaxation. The house is set in a Dairy Farm overlooking Lake Rerewhakaaitu with breathtaking sunsets and Mt Tarawera standing a kilometre away. Use our local knowledge of nearby scenic, thermal, walking, fishing, hot pools, adventure, cultural or shopping. We are a short distance to both Rotorua and Taupo and close to Whirinaki National Park for recreational walking.

Rotorua *5 km N of Rotorua*
Tirohanga-nui (Big View) *B&B Homestay*
Angela & Tony Thompson
21 Grand vue Road, Kawaha Point, Rotorua

Tel 07 349 4810 or 021 170 3477
Fax 07 349 4811
a_thompson@clear.net.nz
www.bigview.co.nz

Double $140-$160 Single $90 (Full breakfast)
Children negotiable
2 Queen (2 bdrm)
Bathrooms: 1 Ensuite 1 Private

Your hosts Angela & Tony invite you to share in the experience, the peace and serenity of Tirohanga-nui (Big View) with its magnificent panoramic lake and city views, only five minutes from the city centre and local attractions. We recommend a minimum two night stay to allow enough time to discover Rotorua its maori culture, geothermal activity, and beautiful lake and bush walks. Accommodation is offered either self-contained with own entrance and private deck area or in the upstairs bedroom with own private bathroom.

Rotorua - Ngongotaha *12 km N of Rotorua*

Panorama Country Homestay *Luxury B&B Homestay Farmstay*

David Perry & Christine King
144 Fryer Road, Hamurana, RD 2, Rotorua

Tel (07) 332 2618 or 021 610 949
Fax (07) 332 2618   panoramahomestay@xtra.co.nz
http://panoramahomestay.co.nz

Double $160-$230 Single $110-$135 (Special breakfast)
Dinner by arrangement   Discount for over two nights stay
Visa MC accepted
1 King 1 Queen (3 bdrm)
Bathrooms: 2 Ensuite 1 Private

Aptly named Panorama is your ideal base to stay near Rotorua's many attractions. Take in the magnificent views overlooking Lake Rotorua and legendary Mokoia Island, Mt Tarawera and surrounding country side.

Feel the peace and tranquility as you relax under the stars in the outdoor heated massage spa pool, then curl up in front of the log fire in winter to stay cosy and warm. You may prefer to enjoy an energetic game of tennis on the championship sized court or take in many of the fantastic walks then come home and stretch out on the extra large beds in Panorama's peaceful surrounds for a perfect nights sleep.

The three spacious, luxury bedrooms have private bathrooms/ensuites containing, toiletries, heated towel rails, hairdryers, shaving points and heaters. The large comfortable inner spring beds are warmed with electric blankets, woollen underlays and feather quilts in winter. In the living area, the formal lounge has a native timber, cathedral ceiling, and an open fire where you can relax with a book and listen to soft music.

The large house is centrally heated and wheelchair accessible. Only 15 minutes from Rotorua, Panorama is situated on the northern side of the lake away from the sulphur smells. There is ample room for safe off street parking and helicopter access. Pet lambs and sheep can be fed by hand.

Dave and Chris welcome you to spend a few days at Panorama where hospitality is ensured in their country home. They have lived in Rotorua for many years and have a wealth of knowledge to assist you in enjoying your stay and the local attractions. They would be happy to help you with any bookings you may require.

Rotorua *5 km SW of Post Office*

Aria's Farm B&B *B&B Homestay Farmstay Separate Suite*

Kerris & Chris
396 Clayton Road, Rotorua

Tel 021 753 691 or (07) 348 0790
Fax (07) 348 0863 ariasfarm@xtra.co.nz
www.ariasfarm.com

Double $99-$130 Single $60-$110 (Full breakfast)
Children 0-3 $20 with cot, 4-12 $25
Dinner 3 course $30pp, main only $15pp
Laundry full load and dry $10
Visa MC accepted
Pet free home Children welcome
1 King 3 Queen 1 Twin 3 Single (5 bdrm)
Bathrooms: 1 Ensuite 2 Private 2 Guest share

Paradise near town - brand new modern lodge on three acres with secluded bush and stream, but with city bus right at the front gate! King & queen beds, ensuite/private bathrooms. Air con & central heating. Unlimited tea/coffee. Laundry, internet, off-street parking. Full breakfast with fresh eggs, luxury spa after a busy day. Join our fun-loving family with two kids, or enjoy your own privacy. Special winter rates, incl semi self-contained two bedroom unit.

Rotorua *4 km S of Rotorua*

Chef Homestay *B&B Homestay*

Trev & Phyl Hawkins
31 Exeter Place, Rotorua, 3015

Tel (07) 349 2450 or 027 292 6009
Fax (07) 349 2457
thchef@free.net.nz
www.chefhomestay.co.nz

Double $140-$150 Single $85-$120 (Special breakfast)
Dinner $45 by arrangement
Cash prefered
Pet free home
Not suitable for children
1 Queen 2 Single (2 bdrm)
Bathrooms: 1 Ensuite 1 Private

Enjoy spectacular city and lake views of Rotorua in peaceful surroundings. Close to Te Puia and city centre. Receive a warm welcome from Trev and Phyl who are happy to advise you on Rotorua's interesting district. Wander through the garden to access the Tree Trust Reserve and Park.

Rotorua Central *0.3 km SE of i-Site Centre*

Eaton Hall *B&B Guest House*

Ginni & Alan
1255 Hinemaru Street, Rotorua, 3010

Tel (07) 347 0366 or (07) 348 1839
Fax (07) 347 0366
eatonhallbnb@xtra.co.nz
www.eatonhallbnb.co.nz

Double $85-$110 Single $65-$80 (Full breakfast)
Children under 6 free, 6-14 $10
Visa MC Eftpos accepted
Pet free home Children welcome
5 Queen 1 Double 1 Twin 2 Single (9 bdrm)
Bathrooms: 6 Ensuite 1 Guest share

Eaton Hall is an 83 year old charming historic home right in the very centre of Rotorua Township. We offer a warm, secure, comfortable, quiet & smoke-free accommodation to all discerning travellers. Only a few minutes easy walk to the Polynesian Spa Pools, Museum, Government Gardens, the lovely Lakefront, Restaurants and Cafés, Trading Banks, the Central Rotorua Bus Terminals and Tourism & Information Centre. Enjoy a full and yummy breakfast every morning. We would love you to stay with us during your visit to Rotorua.

Taupo *3 km E of Central Taupo*

Yeoman's Hill Top Park Homestay *B&B Homestay*
Colleen & Bob Yeoman
61 Puriri Street, Taupo 3330

Tel (07) 377 0283
Fax (07) 377 4683

Double $120 Single $60 (Full breakfast)
Children $30
Dinner $30 by arrangement
Children welcome
1 Queen 1 Twin (2 bdrm)
Bathrooms: 1 Ensuite 1 Private

Bob and I have enjoyed hosting for many years, our lovely new home in Hill Top Park with beautiful mountains views makes our guests' stay in Taupo very special. All attractions are nearby, golf courses, thermal pools, Huka Falls and fishing. We are retired sheep and cattle farmers, who enjoy travelling and meeting other travellers. Bob excels at golf and is in charge of cooked breakfasts. Home-made jams and marmalade are my specialty. Please phone for directions. Good off street parking

Taupo - Acacia Bay *6 km W of Taupo*

Leece's Homestay *Homestay*
Marlene & Bob Leece
98 Wakeman Road, Acacia Bay, Taupo 3330

Tel (07) 378 6099 or 021 0243 9190
Fax (07) 378 6092

Double $90 Single $60 (Continental breakfast)
Visa MC accepted
1 King 1 Queen 2 Single (2 bdrm)
Bathrooms: 1 Guest share

Your hosts Bob, Marlene & Jaspa (our Birman cat) extend a warm welcome to our large wood interior home with woodfire for winter and north facing sunny deck from guest bedroom. Also magnificent view of Lake Taupo from lounge and front deck. There are bush walks and steps down to lake to swim in summer. We are awaiting your arrival with anticipation of making friends. Please phone for directions.

Taupo *3 km S of Taupo*

Hawai Homestay *Homestay*
Jeanette Jones
18 Hawai Street, 2 Mile Bay, Taupo

Tel (07) 377 3242 or 027 374 8425
jeanettej@xtra.co.nz

Double $110 Single $70 (Full breakfast)
Children $20
Dinner $20
Visa MC accepted
Children welcome
1 Queen (1 bdrm)
Bathrooms: 1 Private

Come relax and unwind in our comfortable, warm modern home. Befriend our adorable Shitzu who loves visitors. Enjoy delicious homemade cooking for a hearty breakfast. Sunny queen bedroom beside private bathroom and lounge with sofa bed for extra guest. Close to thermal pools, good walking paths, beautiful lake and restaurants. Our interests include travel, roses and church.

Taupo *1 km S of Taupo*

Pataka House *B&B Homestay Separate Suite*
Raewyn & Neil Alexander
8 Pataka Road, Taupo

Tel (07) 378 5481 Fax (07) 378 5461
pataka-homestay@xtra.co.nz
www.patakahouse.co.nz

Double $120 (Full breakfast)
Children $30
Separate suite $130
Visa MC accepted
Children welcome
2 Queen 4 Twin (4 bdrm)
Bathrooms: 1 Ensuite 1 Private 1 Guest share

Pataka House is highly recommended for its hospitality. We assure guests that their stay lives up to New Zealand's reputation as being a home away from home. We are easily located just one turn off the lake front and up a tree-lined driveway. Our garden room is privately situated, has an appealing decor and extremely popular to young and old alike. Stay for one night or stay for more as Lake Taupo will truly be the highlight of your holiday. Mika, a burmese, loves visitors.

Taupo *1 km N of Taupo Central*

Lakeland Homestay *Homestay*
Lesley, Chris & Pussycats
11 Williams Street, Taupo

Tel (07) 378 1952 or 027 487 7971
Fax (07) 378 1912
lakeland.bb@xtra.co.nz

Double $130-$140 Single $70 (Continental breakfast)
Visa MC accepted
1 Queen 2 Twin (2 bdrm)
Bathrooms: 1 Ensuite 1 Family share

Nestled in a restful tree-lined street, a mere five minutes stroll from the lake's edge and shopping centre Lakeland Homestay is a cheerful and cosy home that enjoys views of the lake and mountains. Keen gardeners, anglers and golfers Chris and Lesley work and play in an adventure oasis. For extra warmth on winter nights all beds have electric blankets, and laundry facilities are available. A courtesy car is available for coach travellers and there is off-street parking. Please phone for directions.

Taupo *15 km W of Taupo*

Ben Lomond *Cottage with Kitchen*
Mary & Jack Weston
1434 Poihipi Road, RD 1, Taupo

Tel (07) 377 6033 or 027 477 4080
Fax (07) 377 6033
benlomond@xtra.co.nz

Double $100 (Continental breakfast provisions)
Cottage $100 per night
Visa MC accepted
Children and pets welcome
1 Queen 2 Single (2 bdrm)
Bathrooms: 1 Guest share

Welcome to Ben Lomond. Jack and I have farmed here for 40 years and our comfortable family home is set in a mature garden. There is a self-contained cottage in the garden where you can do your own thing. Continental breakfast provisions supplied. We have interests in fishing, golf and the equestrian world and are familiar with the attractions on the Central Plateau. Our pets include dogs and cats who wander in and out. Taupo restaurants are 15 minutes away.

Taupo Countryside *35 km NW of Taupo*
South Claragh & Bird Cottage *B&B Homestay Cottage with Kitchen*

Lesley & Paul Hill
South Claragh, 3245 Poihipi Road, Taupo Region

Tel (07) 372 8848 Fax (07) 372 8047
welcome@countryaccommodation.co.nz
www.countryaccommodation.co.nz

Double $120-$150 Single $90-$120 (Full breakfast)
Children $20 (cottage) $45 (B&B)
Dinner $50pp
Bird Cottage $120 double
Visa MC accepted   Children welcome
1 Queen 1 Double 2 Single (3 bdrm)
Bathrooms: 2 Private

Turn into our leafy driveway and relax in tranquil, rambling gardens with two donkeys and a cat. Accommodation options: 1. Enjoy bed & breakfast in our comfortable, centrally heated farmhouse with delicious farm breakfasts. The freshest home-grown produce and excellent cooking make dining recommended. OR 2. Settle into Bird Cottage - cosy, with delightful views. Perfect for two, but will sleep 3-4. Firewood and linen provided. No meals are included in cottage tariff, but happily prepared by arrangement. Details and pictures on web site.

Taupo *14 km NW of Taupo*
Minarapa *B&B Country Stay*

Barbara & Dermot Grainger
620 Oruanui Road, RD 1, Taupo

Tel (07) 378 1931
info@minarapa.co.nz
www.minarapa.co.nz

Double $125-$150 Single $95-$120 (Full breakfast)
Children POA
Dinner by arrangement
Visa MC accepted
1 King/Twin 2 Queen 2 Twin (4 bdrm)
Bathrooms: 2 Ensuite 1 Private large rooms

Wend your way along a wonderful tree-lined drive into rural tranquillity. Minarapa, our extensive country retreat, 12 minutes from Taupo, is within easy reach of Orakei Korako, Huka Falls and other tourist attractions including Waitomo Caves, Here you may wander among colourful tree-sheltered gardens, play tennis, billiards, or ball with Toby the dog, visit friendly farm animals or relax in our guest lounge. Retire to spacious, comfortably appointed guest rooms, two with balcony and TV. All offer individual character and tea/coffee facilties.

Taupo *3 km S of Taupo*
Above Average Homestay *B&B Homestay*

Judi Thomson
59A Shepherd Road, Taupo

Tel (07) 378 4558 or 027 555 3123
Fax (07) 378 4558
judi.thomson@orcon.net.nz
www.bnb.co.nz

Double $120 Single $90 (Special breakfast)
Children by arrangement
Tea and coffee on arrival
Visa MC accepted
Children and pets welcome
2 Queen (3 bdrm)
Bathrooms: 1 Ensuite 1 Family share

Welcome to our completely private guest area, close to Taupo City and all amenities, restaurants, good shopping etc. plus three restaurants within walking distance. Accommodation includes queen-size bed, television, ensuite and private spa adjacent to your bedroom,in a very quiet and private location with abundant bird-life. Georgia, our social labrador, looks forward to your company. We are happy to suggest 'what's hot and what's not' for local activities and eateries. Airport pick-up if you

Taupo *2 km S of Info Centre*
Gillies of Taupo - Gillies Lodge *B&B*
Margi Martin & Alan Malpas
77 Gillies Avenue, Taupo, Box 1924, Taupo

Tel (07) 377 2377
Fax (07) 377 2373
info@gilliesoftaupo.co.nz
www.gilliesoftaupo.co.nz

Double $115-$125 Single $75-$95 (Full breakfast)
Not suitable for children
5 Double 8 Single (9 bdrm)
Bathrooms: 9 Ensuite

Taupo's original licensed guest house. Nine rooms all ensuited. A perfect base to explore Taupo's many attractions and make day trips to Rotorua, Napier, Waitomo Caves and National Parks. Peaceful, sunny, central and quiet with off-street parking. Relax and enjoy the views or sunsets from the lounge with log fire and library. Breakfast with your hosts and share their intimate local knowledge and sense of history. A true B&B experience. Good old fashioned values, genteel decor and ambience. Ideal venue for small groups. Reservations essential.

Taupo *2.5 km S of Taupo*
Fairviews *B&B Homestay*
Brenda Watson-Hughes & Mike Hughes
8 Fairview Terrace, Taupo 3330

Tel (07) 377 0773
fairviews@reap.org.nz
www.reap.org.nz/-fairviews

Double $135-$155 Single $115-$135 (Full breakfast)
Visa MC accepted
Pet free home
1 Queen 1 Twin (2 bdrm)
Bathrooms: 1 Ensuite 1 Private

You are invited to stay at our modern homestay situated in a tranquil neighbourhood within walking distance of hot pools, Botanical Gardens and lake. Relax and enjoy Fairviews' gardens. Be as private as you wish or socialise with hosts. Rooms are tastefully decorated and comfortable. Double room is large with private entrance, TV, fridge, tea/coffee facilities, robe and hairdryer. Generous breakfasts provided. Email and laundry are available at small charge. Our regional knowledge is extensive. Interests include theatre, travel, cycling, tramping, antiques/collectables.

Taupo *16 km N of Taupo*
Brackenhurst *B&B Homestay Farmstay Cottage with Kitchen*
Barbara & Ray Graham
801 Oruanui Road, RD 1, Taupo

Tel (07) 377 6451 or 027 445 6217
Fax (07) 377 6451
rgbg@xtra.co.nz

Double $100 Single $60 (Full breakfast)
Children $30   Dinner $45
Visa MC accepted
Pet free home
Children and pets welcome
2 Queen 1 Double 4 Single (4 bdrm)
Bathrooms: 2 Ensuite 2 Private

Brackenhurst is a modern Lockwood home on 14 acres of peaceful countryside with fantails, tuis and bellbirds in the large garden. highland cattle and lovely donkey. A warm welcome with peace and tranquility. . We are half a kilometre from SH1 and close to Huka Falls, geothermal activities, golf courses a days outing to Rotorua, Waitomo Caves or Napier. Private guests wing in the house or separate annex offer away from home comforts. Breakfast to suit, continental style or full English. Dinner available by arrangement.

Taupo - Acacia Bay *5 km W of Taupo*

The Loft *B&B*
Grace Andrews & Peter Rosieur
3 Wakeman Road, Acacia Bay, Taupo

Tel (07) 377 1040 or 027 485 1347
Fax (07) 377 1049   book@theloftnz.com
www.theloftnz.com

Double $145-$185 **Single** $100-$120 (Full breakfast)
Children $50-$75   Dinner $30-$45pp
Washing/internet available - price on application
Visa MC accepted   Pet free home   Children welcome
3 Queen 3 Single (3 bdrm)   Bathrooms: 3 Ensuite

Situated five minutes from Taupo township and a few minutes walk to Lake Taupo, The Loft is set in a small cottage garden adjacent to a native bush reserve.

Your hosts, Peter & Grace, are friendly people who delight in the best things in life. Both have travelled extensively throughout New Zealand and the rest of the world. Their passions vary from food and fine wine to tramping and gardening. Enjoy their scrumptious breakfast of fresh fruit salad, orange juice, freshly baked muffins and croissants; wonderful scrambled eggs with mushrooms, bacon and home grown tomatoes (seasonal), an experience not to be missed. Arrange an evening meal at The Loft and be treated to a pleasurable three-course dinner that will leave you with a lasting memory of New Zealand hospitality. After dinner, join your hosts for a complimentary port before retiring for a good nights sleep.

The upstairs guest accommodation comprises three private bedrooms with queen-size beds and ensuite bathrooms. Their style is rustic, romantic and warm where attention to detail shows that your comfort takes top priority. The lounge, with an open fire welcomes you to relax and chat about the Taupo region and your sight seeing plans. Trout fishing trips and adventure treks can be arranged by your hosts along with a myriad of other more relaxing activities.

Grace & Peter look forward to sharing their home and their company with you, assuring you of a warm welcome and a luxurious stay. Directions:www.theloftnz.com

Taupo *15 km N of Taupo*

Maimoa House *B&B Farmstay Apartment with Kitchen*
New apartment opening soon ask for details
Margaret & Godfrey Ellis
41 Oak Drive, off Palmer Mill Road, Taupo

Tel (07) 376 9000   mewestview@xtra.co.nz
www.maimoahomestay.co.nz

Double $105-$125 Single $75 (Special breakfast)
Children $30
Dinner $30 by arrangement
10% discount for 3 nights or more
Visa MC accepted
Children and pets welcome
1 Queen 1 Double 1 Twin (3 bdrm)
Bathrooms: 1 Ensuite 1 Guest share with large spa bath, seperate shower, toilet

Hello and welcome to our peaceful home with spectacular views over the mountains to the lake. Our spacious new apartment is now available, including our special breakfast. Join us in for a three course dinner (allergies catered for) with wine. Borrow our tandem or single bikes. We are very happy to arrange on-going recommended B&Bs, local trips & excursions. We have a friendly lab dog, a cat and a few cows. Our interests include church activities travelling and chatting over a glass of wine.

Taupo *1 km N of Town Centre*

Magnifique *B&B Homestay*
Gay & Rex Eden
52 Woodward Street, Taupo

Tel (07) 378 4915
Fax (07) 378 4915
info@magnifique.co.nz
www.magnifique.co.nz

Double $130-$150 Single $100-$120
(Special breakfast)
Visa MC accepted
Pet free home
2 Queen 2 Single (3 bdrm)
Bathrooms: 2 Private

We welcome you with refreshments and home-baking while you take in the magnificent sweeping views of town, lake and mountains. You may leave your car and walk just six minutes to Taupo's lovely restaurants and shops. Our focus in life is people, so be assured of a warm welcome and the highest standards of comfort and hospitality. Each room has tea making facilities, fridge, TV. We will treat you with our special breakfasts which have not yet failed to delight our guests.

Taupo *1 km N of Taupo*

Fourwinds Bed & Breakfast *B&B Homestay*
Catherine Culling
57 Woodward Street, Taupo, 3330

Tel (07) 376 5350
Fax (07) 376 5360
bnb@fourwindsbedandbreakfast.co.nz
www.fourwindsbedandbreakfast.co.nz

Double $110-$125 Single $85-$95 (Full breakfast)
Dinner by arrangement
Visa MC accepted
Not suitable for children
1 Double 2 Single (2 bdrm)
Bathrooms: 1 Guest share with separate toilet

A warm welcome and a refreshing cup of tea awaits your arrival at Fourwinds. Close to all Taupo attractions and town, with panoramic views of the Lake, Kaimanawa Ranges and mountains. The generous breakfast is served in dining room overlooking the wonderful view. Taupo is an excellent base for day trips to Rotorua, Waitomo, Hawkes Bay and Tongariro National Park. Catherine and Ambee (Cat) enjoy meeting guests from all corners of the world and look forward to you staying with us.

Taupo *3 km S of Taupo*

Moorhill *B&B Boutique Accommodation*
Liz & Peter Sharland
27 Korimako Road, Taupo

Tel (07) 377 1069 or 021 300 455
petenlizr@xtra.co.nz
www.moorhill.co.nz

Double $150-$185 (Full breakfast)
Dinner by prior arrangement
Laundry and internet at small charge
Visa MC accepted
No Pets Not suitable for children
1 King/Twin 1 King 1 Queen (2 bdrm)
Bathrooms: 2 Ensuite

Be assured of a warm welcome at Moorhill, boutique bed and breakfast accommodation at an affordable price. Relax and enjoy our delicious cooked breakfasts, spacious rooms and comfortable beds. Our smoke-free home is set in a large mature garden, a short walk to the Lake, the Botanical Gardens and a few minutes drive to town, excellent restaurants and thermal pools.

The downstairs Magnolia room has a queen sized bed, walk through wardrobe to large luxury ensuite and a sitting area opening onto the garden. Upstairs the spacious Cherry room has super king double or twin bed options, ensuite and views of Lake Taupo. Both well appointed rooms have quality cotton bed linen, duvets, tea making facilities, fridges, heated towel rails, hairdryers and electric blankets. The guest lounge opens onto sunny decks,the perfect place to share travel experiences over a glass of wine. There is ample off-street parking.

Take your time in Taupo, it is an ideal base from which to explore the many attractions including sparkling Huka Falls. World class trout fishing, boating, golf courses, adrenalin pumping activities are all available. The National Park volcanoes provide skiing, mountain walks, including the famous Tongariro Crossing, and are within easy reach. Rotorua and many thermal fields are less than one hours drive whilst Napier and Hawkes Bay vineyards are under two hours. We would be pleased to share our local knowledge, help arrange trips or onward bookings. Peter is a sports fan(atic) whilst Liz dabbles in flower painting and photography. We both enjoy meeting people, gardening, reading, music, good food and wine. We look forward to welcoming you to our home.

Taupo *3 km S of Taupo*

Moselle *B&B Apartment with Kitchen Self Contained*
Grahame & Anne Velvin
3 Te Hepera Street, Taupo, 3330

Tel (07) 377 2922 or 021 254 4511
Fax (07) 377 2290
ragevelvin@xtra.co.nz
www.moselletaupo.com

Double $170 (Full breakfast provisions)
Visa MC Amex accepted
Children and pets welcome
1 King/Twin (1 bdrm)
Bathrooms: 1 Ensuite

Moselle has had a major make over with quality furnishings in a French theme. Brand new super king bed and top quality linen. New modern ensuite and fully self-contained. Sky TV video and fresh breakfast food supplied daily to your requirements. A four minute drive to the Taupo Golf Club two minutes drive to de Brett's Thermal Hot Pools & five minutes drive to the Taupo Township, walking distance to the Lake. Private parking. 90 minutes to ski field.

Taupo *2 km S of Taupo*

Above the Lake at Windsor Charters *B&B*
Angela & Bruce Christoffersen
46 Rokino Road, Taupo, 3330

Tel (07) 378 8738 or 0800 788 738
027 272 9856
windsor-charters@xtra.co.nz
www.taupostay.com

Double $150-$180 Single $140-$170 (Full breakfast)
Visa MC accepted
1 King 2 Queen (3 bdrm)
Bathrooms: 1 Ensuite 1 Private 1 Guest share

On arrival, relax and enjoy magical lake, mountain and Taupo town views. Your supremely comfortable accommodation is centrally located in the heart of Taupo. Easy to find, and just a short stroll to the lake and Taupo's own, hot water beach. Walking distance to award winning restaurants. Join your hosts, Bruce, Angela & golden retriever named Koda for coffee or a glass of wine. Make use of our extensive local knowledge to plan your Taupo experience.

Taupo - Acacia Bay *5 km W of Taupo*

Te Moenga Lodge *B&B Separate Suite*
Brent & Jacque McClellan
60 Te Moenga Park, Reeves Road, Taupo, 3330

Tel (07) 378 0437 or 027 452 1459
Fax (07) 378 0438   info@temoenga.com
www.temoenga.com

Double $150-$295 Single $120-$220
(Special breakfast)
Children over 2 $50
Visa MC Amex Eftpos accepted
Children welcome
2 King/Twin 1 King 1 Queen (4 bdrm)
Bathrooms: 4 Ensuite Chalets have double spa bath

A comfortable retreat just a few minutes from the centre of Taupo providing the best views of Lake Taupo guaranteed! We have two private chalets, very spacious, well equipped with true attention to detail. Relax on your own deck with a breakfast hamper enjoying your magnificent views. Our two studio rooms have garden outlook, Ensuite bathrooms and comfortable Guest lounge and decks with outstanding views to relax and enjoy your stay. Pet boxer dog Scout in residence. We guarantee you an exceptional stay here at Te Moenga Lodge.

/ of Turangi Central
/B Homestay Cottage with Kitchen
rson
ngi
2
72
ra.co.nz
ww. .co.nz/accommodation/andersons

Double $120 Single $90 (Full breakfast)
Self-contained cottage sleeps 2-6 from $90-$95 double
Children in cottage only
Visa MC accepted
2 Queen 1 Twin (3 bdrm)
Bathrooms: 3 Ensuite

Welcome to our home, in quiet street, beside Tongariro River walkway, handy to restaurants and town and fishing. Arranged transport to Tongariro Crossing and National Park at your door. Lake Taupo and thermal baths five minutes drive. Upstairs rooms with balconies, queen beds, ensuites, fridge/tea/coffee, separated for privacy by landing. Downstairs twin suite, own entry, bathroom, fridge/tea/coffee, laundry and lounge to share maps of our volcanic area,or book activities and restaurants. Guest-shy cat. Cottage suitable for families.

~

Turangi *1 km S of Turangi Information Centre*
Brown Trout House *B&B Homestay*
Bruce & Nita Wilde
11 Kokopu Street, Turangi, 3334

Tel (07) 386 0308 or 027 253 3415
Fax (07) 386 0308 kohinoor@xtra.co.nz
www.browntrouthouse.co.nz

Double $120 Single $70 (Full breakfast)
Lunch & dinner by prior arrangement
Visa MC accepted
Not suitable for children
1 King/Twin 1 Queen 1 Single (3 bdrm)
Bathrooms: 1 Private 1 Family share

Welcome to Brown Trout house overlooking the Tongariro River in Turangi, halfway between Auckland and Wellington. Your comfortable bedroom with TV opens on to the deck. Have refreshments or step out our gate on to the Tongariro River Walkway or in to world famous fishing pools. Bruce is a passionate fisherman willing to share his knowledge. Shuttle pickup for the Tongariro Crossing arranged. Choose walks, golf, skiing or a hot swim 5 minutes drive away. Friendly experienced hosts willing to give genuine kiwi hospitality.

~

Turangi *15 km W of Turangi*
Omori Lake House *Luxury Lodge*
Niel & Raewyn Groombridge
31 Omori Road, Omori

Tel (07) 386 0420 or 021 667 092
stay@omorilakehouse.co.nz
www.omorilakehouse.co.nz

Double $135-$150 Single $120-$150
(Special breakfast)
Dinner by arrangement
Visa MC accepted
2 King (2 bdrm)
Bathrooms: 2 Ensuite

We offer new boutique accommodation high above Omori with stunning views across to Taupo. There are two ensuite guest rooms with king beds, tea/coffee facilities and private deck. One room suits disabled guests, with wide access, handrails and wet floor shower, while the other has its own bath. Raewyn loves to cook and eating well is part of the experience. Omori on the south west of the lake is close to a variety of activities including fly-fishing, bush walks, thermal pools and ski slopes.

Turangi - Motuoapa *10 km N of Turangi*

Meredith House *B&B Self-contained*

Frances & Ian Meredith
45 Kahotea Drive, Motuoapa, RD 2, Turangi

Tel (07) 386 5266 or 027 440 6135
Fax (07) 386 5270
meredith.house@xtra.co.nz

Double $100 Single $70 (Breakfast by arrangement)
Self-contained $120-140
Visa MC accepted
Children welcome
1 Queen 3 Single (2 bdrm)
Bathrooms: 2 Ensuite

Stop and enjoy this outdoor Paradise. Just off SH1 (B&B Sign). Overlooking Lake Taupo, our two storey home offers ground-floor self-contained accommodation with own entrance. Full breakfast on request. Fully equipped kitchen, dining room, lounge. two cosy bedrooms (each with TV). Vehicle/boat off-street parking. Minutes to marina and world-renowned lake/river fishing. Beautiful bush walks. 45 minutes to ski fields and Tongariro National Park. Our association with Tongariro/Taupo area spans over 30 years, through work and outdoor pursuits. Welcome to our retreat.

Turangi *54 km S of Taupo*

Founders at Turangi *B&B Homestay*

Peter & Chris Stewart
253 Taupahi Road, Turangi

Tel (07) 386 8539
Fax (07) 386 8534
chris@founders.co.nz
www.founders.co.nz

Double $170 Single $120 (Special breakfast)
Visa MC Eftpos accepted
Pet free home
Not suitable for children
1 King/Twin 1 King 3 Queen (4 bdrm)
Bathrooms: 4 Ensuite

Welcome to Turangi and to our New Zealand colonial-style home. Relax and enjoy the unique beauty of the trout fishing capital of the world. Many outdoor activities are available at this place for all seasons, with the Tongariro River, mountains of Tongariro National Park and magnificent Lake Taupo on our doorstep. four ensuite bedrooms open on to the veranda. Enjoy breakfast in our sunny dining room or pre-dinner drinks by the fire apres ski in the winter!

Turangi *16 km NW of Turangi*

Wills' Place *B&B*

Jill & Brian Wills
145 Omori Road, Omori

Tel (07) 386 7339 or 027 228 8960
Fax (07) 386 7339
willsplace@wave.co.nz
www.willsplace.co.nz

Double $135 Single $100 (Full breakfast)
Children negotiable
Dinner by arrangement
Visa MC accepted
2 Queen 2 Single (2 bdrm)
Bathrooms: 1 Private Bath with shower over

A lakeside home and superior guest suite with wonderful views. Fishing, boating, swimming, walks. Off the beaten track, yet only 10-15 minutes to shops, restaurants, thermal pools, Tongariro River, rafting, etc. 40 minutes to Tongariro National Park. Private suite with two bedrooms, full size bathroom with bath and shower, living area, tea-making facilities, fridge, microwave, television, laundry, email access. Private patio overlooking the lake. Exclusively yours with separate entry and safe parking. Very spacious for couple, ideal for family or small group.

Bay of Plenty

Bay of Plenty

At the Tongariro Riverside B&B and Homestay *B&B Homestay*

Leslie & Maryke Wilson
72 Herekiekie Street, Turangi

Tel (07) 386 7447 or 021 074 0749
leslie@bytheriver.co.nz
www.bytheriver.co.nz

Double $110 Single $90 (Special breakfast)
Dinner with wine $40pp by arrangement
1 King (1 bdrm)
Bathrooms: 1 Ensuite

Welcome to a peaceful and tranquil setting with abundant bird-life. Experience real Kiwi hospitality. Halfway between Auckland and Wellington with secure off-street parking. Make us your headquarters for the Tongariro Crossing. Shuttles arranged!!!! The world famous trout fishing river - the Tongariro is just metres from your king bed ensuite room with air-conditioning, fridge, TV, tea/coffee making facilities. Private entrance. Generous breakfast provided. Lunch and dinner by arrangement. Sauna, mountain bikes and fishing equipment are available for hire. Payment by cash or cheque.

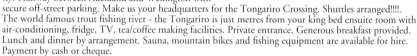

Ika Lodge *B&B Cottage with Kitchen*

Bob & Dianne Fussell and Mary Cronin
155 Taupahi Road, Turangi, 2751

Tel (07) 386 5538 or (07) 386 0538
Fax (07) 386 5356
ikalodge@xtra.co.nz
http://ika.co.nz

Double $120-$150 Single $120 (Full breakfast)
Picnic lunch or 3 course dinner by arrangement
Cottage $120
Visa MC Diners Amex Eftpos accepted
Children welcome
2 Queen 2 Double 1 Single (2 bdrm)
Bathrooms: 2 Ensuite 1 Private

Established in 1955 and operated as a superior bed and breakfast homestay, Ika Lodge is situated right along side the Tongariro River and the famous Tongariro Walkway. A walk out our back gate will have you fishing in seconds. We have a beautiful tranquil garden setting where many varieties of native birds come to visit. The Central Plateau has a great many sightseeing destinations, something for everybody. We serve lunch and evening meals by arrangement.

Dyden Cottage *B&B Cottage with Kitchen*

Debbie & John Davidson
Old Mill Lane, 134 Grace Road RD 2, Turangi

Tel (07) 386 6926 or 021 894 223
haydendavidson@xtra.co.nz

Double $100 Single $70
(Full breakfast provisions)
Children $10
Visa MC accepted
Children welcome
1 Queen 1 Single (1 bdrm)
Bathrooms: 1 Ensuite

Dyden Cottage offers self-contained accommodation set in five acres of lovely mature gardens and farmland. It has a separate entrance and private outdoor area. The cottage sleeps three, has an ensuite bathroom and living/kitchen area with television. The kitchen is stocked with everything you need for breakfast. Enjoy the peace and tranquility or take advantage of the world class fly fishing, hiking in nearby Tongariro National Park, local walks, golf, river rafting and skiing all within easy reach of Turangi.

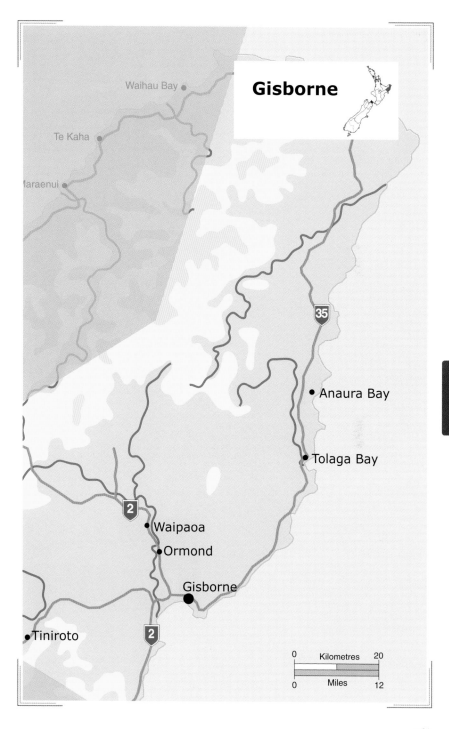

Gisborne

Waihau Bay

Te Kaha

Maraenui

35

Anaura Bay

Tolaga Bay

2

Waipaoa

Ormond

Gisborne

Tiniroto

2

Gisborne

| 0 | Kilometres | 20 |
| 0 | Miles | 12 |

Anaura Bay *23 km N of Tolaga Bay*

Anaura Beachstay or Willowflat Farmstay B&B *B&B Farmstay*
Self-contained Beachfront Cottage with Kitchen
June & Allan Hall
Anaura Bay, Tolaga Bay East Cape 3854, Gisborne

Tel (06) 862 6341 or 021 039 1136
Fax (06) 862 6371   willowflat@xtra.co.nz
www.anaurabeachstay.com

Double $120 Single $70 (Full breakfast)
Children half price Dinner $25
Rental $120-$200 per night
Children welcome
1 Queen 1 Double (2 bdrm)
Bathrooms: 1 Family share

Paradise: the best of both worlds. Relax in tranquility on our deck in picturesque Anaura Bay, glorious sunrises, white sand and backdrop of beautiful native bush, fishing, walkways..... OR soak in the spa at our spacious home Willowflat, our sheep, cattle and cropping farm. Tolaga Bay Village, medical centre, takeaways, restaurant, Cashmere Company, hunting, golf, within 12 km of Willowflat or 23 km of Beachstay. Self-contained option available both venues $120-$200 per night for two couples, minimum two nights.

Tolaga Bay *3 km N of Tolaga Bay*

Papatahi *Homestay Separate Suite*
Nicki & Bruce Jefferd
427 Main Road North, Tolaga Bay

Tel (06) 862 6623 or 021 283 7178
Fax (06) 862 6623
nickibrucej@xtra.co.nz

Double $110 Single $70 (Full breakfast)
Children half price
Dinner $35pp
Children welcome
1 Queen 1 Double 2 Single (3 bdrm)
Bathrooms: 1 Ensuite 1 Guest share

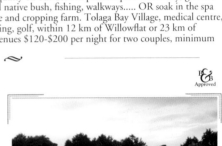

Papatahi Homestay... easy to find being just 3 km north of the Tolaga Bay township, on the Pacific Coast Highway. We have a comfortable, modern, sunny home set in a wonderful garden. Papatahi offers separate accommodation with ensuite. A golf course, fishing charters, the Tolaga Bay Cashmere Co. and several magnificent beaches are all just minutes away. Daily farm activities are often of interest to our guests. Friendly farm pets add to the experience! Great country meals and good wine are a speciality. Inspection will impress!

Waipaoa *20 km N of Gisborne*

The Willows *Farmstay*
Rosemary & Graham Johnson
Waipaoa, RD 1, Gisborne

Tel (06) 862 5605 or 027 483 7365
Fax (06) 862 5601

Double $85 Single $50 (Full breakfast)
Children 10% discount
Dinner $30 by arrangement
2 Queen 2 Single (3 bdrm)
Bathrooms: 1 Private 1 Guest share

Our home is situated on a hill amid a park-like garden with some wonderful trees planted by our forefathers. We enjoy the amenities available in the city and also the country life on our 440 acre property involving cattle, sheep, grapes and cropping. We now offer a double bedroom with a private bathroom. The bedroom has its own access so you can enjoy privacy if you so desire. We are situated 20 km north of Gisborne on SH2 through the scenic Waioeka Gorge.

Gisborne *5 km NE of Gisborne*
Beach Stay *B&B*

Peter & Dorothy Rouse
111 Wairere Road, Wainui Beach, Gisborne

Tel (06) 868 8111
Fax (06) 868 8162
pete.dot@xtra.co.nz

Double $90-$110 Single $60 (Full breakfast)
Children $10
Dinner $25pp
Pets welcome
1 Queen 2 Single (2 bdrm)
Bathrooms: 1 Ensuite 1 Private

We welcome you to our home which is situated right on the beach front at Wainui. The steps from the lawn lead down to the beach, which is renowned for its lovely clean sand, surf, pleasant walking and good swimming. Gisborne can also offer a host of entertainment, including golf on one of the finest golf courses, charter fishing trips, wine trails, Eastwood Hill Arboretum etc, or you may wish to relax on the beach for the day.

Gisborne *60 km SW of Gisborne*
Rongoio Farm Stay *B&B Farmstay Separate Suite*
Cottage with Kitchen Guest House

Philippa & Willie Purvis
1055 Ruakaka Road, Tiniroto, Gisborne

Tel (06) 867 4065   rongoio@paradise.net.nz
www.rongoiofarmstay.co.nz

Double $125 Single $90 (Full breakfast)
Children $40
3 course dinner available by arrangement
Rental tariff $120-$250
Visa MC accepted
2 Queen 1 Twin (3 bdrm)
Bathrooms: 1 Guest share separate bath/shower room

Come to our hill country sheep and cattle farm and enjoy rural NZ life. Close to the homestead is a secluded, 3 bedroom self-contained cottage. From this cosy home enjoy birdsong along with views of the trout filled Hangaroa River and waterfall. We encourage guests to participate in rural activities including fishing, kayaking, farm and garden walks and rides (Hackfalls arboretum is closeby). We have two daughters, two cats, a labrador, jack russell, chooks, pigs, pet goat, calf, lambs, farm dogs and horses.

Gisborne *40 km W of Gisborne*
Awawhenua *Farmstay*
Sally & Andrew Jefferd
RD 2, Ngatapa, Gisborne

Tel (06) 867 1313
Fax (06) 867 6311
jefferd@xtra.co.nz
www.bnb.co.nz/gisborne/results.html?town=gisborne

Double $150 Single $90 (Full breakfast)
Children half price
Dinner $30
Children and pets welcome
1 Queen 1 Double (2 bdrm)
Bathrooms: 1 Ensuite 1 Private 1 Family share

Five minutes drive from the famous Eastwoodhill, an internationally recognised arboretum, comprising 65 hectares of a variety of trees and shrubs. We live on a 1400 acre hill country property, farming sheep, cattle and deer. Set in a tranquil setting, we offer separate ensuite accommodation, a few metres from the main house. Tea, coffee making facilities provided. A complimentary Gisborne chardonnay or drinks, together with farm fresh food makes for a memorable experience. Reservations: free phone 0800 469 440 1313. Phone for directions.

Gisborne

Gisborne *14 km S of Gisborne*

Fairlight *B&B*
Kay & Don Orchiston
52 Saddler Road, RD 2, Gisborne 4072

Tel (06) 862 8499 or 027 440 9556
orchiston@clear.net.nz

Double $120 **Single** $70 (Full breakfast)
Children 6 and under free, others by arrangement
Dinner by arrangement
Children and pets welcome
1 King 1 Queen 1 Double 1 Single (4 bdrm)
Bathrooms: 1 Private 1 shower as well

Our home is situated on a hill with expansive views overlooking the sea, city and rural wine and citrus region. three bedrooms have a sea view. We can actually accommodate five people if they are in the same group. We are 14 km south of the city. Gisborne has beautiful beaches, scenic walks, restaurants, cafés, excellent sport facilities and many other local attractions. We have two friendly sheepdogs and two elusive bengal cats.

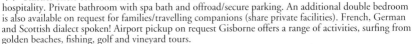

Gisborne *2.5 km NE of Gisborne*

Thistles *Homestay*
Barrie & Lesley Munday
137 Riverside Road, Gisborne

Tel (06) 868 8900 or 021 127 9841
thistles137@gmail.com

Double $120 **Single** $90 (Full breakfast)
Children half price
Pet free home
Children welcome
1 Queen 1 Double (2 bdrm)
Bathrooms: 1 Private

Within a short distance of Gisborne city centre, Thistles offers comfortable home from home hospitality. Private bathroom with spa bath and offroad/secure parking. An additional double bedroom is also available on request for families/travelling companions (share private facilities). French, German and Scottish dialect spoken! Airport pickup on request Gisborne offers a range of activities, surfing from golden beaches, fishing, golf and vineyard tours.

**All our B&Bs are non-smoking
unless stated otherwise in the text.**

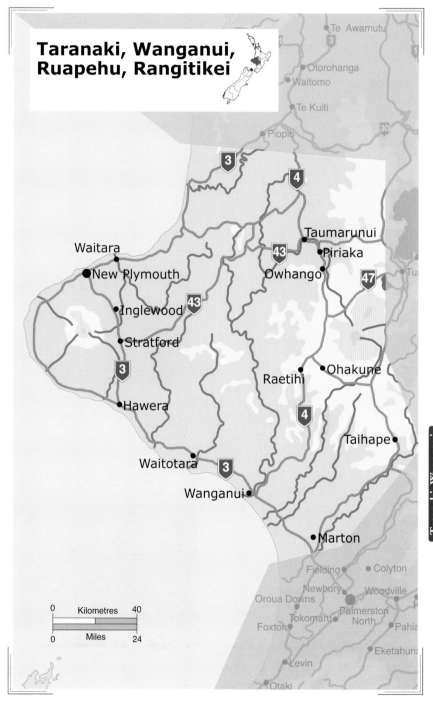

Taranaki, Wanganui, Ruapehu, Rangitikei

Te Awamutu

Otorohanga

Waitomo

Te Kuiti

Piopio

3

4

Taumarunui

Waitara

43 Piriaka

New Plymouth

Owhango

47 Tu

Inglewood **43**

Stratford

3

Raetihi

Ohakune

Hawera

4

Taihape

Waitotara **3**

Wanganui

Marton

Fielding Colyton

Newbury Woodville

Oroua Downs Palmerston North

Tokomaru

Foxton North Pahia

Eketahun

| 0 | Kilometres | 40 |
| 0 | Miles | 24 |

Levin

Otaki

New Plymouth *3 km S of New Plymouth*

Oak Valley Manor *B&B Farmstay*
Pat & Paul Ekdahl
248 Junction Road, RD 1, New Plymouth

Tel (06) 758 1501 or 027 442 0325
Fax (06) 758 1052
kauri.holdings@xtra.co.nz

Double $125-$150 Single $125
(Continental breakfast)
Children $1 per year up to 15 years
Visa MC accepted
Children and pets welcome
2 Queen 1 Single (2 bdrm)
Bathrooms: 2 Ensuite

Your hosts, Pat and Paul, two friendly people with experience in the hospitality industry, invite you to a unique bed & breakfast in their beautiful home with views of Mt Taranaki from all rooms. These beautiful views make an everlasting impression. Guests can choose their own privacy or socialise with us. We have a variety of animals, donkey, peacocks, pigs, ducks, geese and an ex-guide dog. Golf course five minute drive. Tariff reduces $150-$125 pending nights stayed.

New Plymouth *25 km N of New Plymouth*

Cottage by the Sea *Boutique Cottages with Kitchens*
Nancy & Hugh Mills
66 Lower Turangi Road, RD 43, Waitara

Tel (06) 754 4548 or (06) 754 7915
cottagebythesea@clear.net.nz
www.cottagebythesea.co.nz

Double $155-$185 Single $145-$175
(Breakfast by arrangement)
Restaurant nearby for dinner
Extra adults $2pp
Visa MC accepted   Not suitable for children
1 King 1 Queen 2 Double (4 bdrm)
Bathrooms: 4 Ensuite 1 ensuite per cottage

Find yourself, lose yourself - the choice is yours. Peacefulness and privacy are our specialty - a perfect atmosphere to unwind or spend that special weekend. Enjoy the everchanging seaviews, discover our tranquil sunken garden, wander down 100 handcrafted steps to the secluded black sandbeach. Two 1-bedroom cottages nestled in their own gardens, each sleeping four; and two new boutique, open-plan style, each sleeping two. All have kitchens, ensuites. Minutes from cafés, coastal walks, gardens and Mt Taranaki. See our website for photos and details.

New Plymouth *3 km W of New Plymouth CBD*

Vineyard Holiday Flat *B&B Separate Suite*
Shirley & Trevor Knuckey
12 Scott Street, Moturoa, New Plymouth

Tel (06) 751 2992 or 027 310 3669
Fax (06) 751 2995
shirley12vineyard@xtra.co.nz

Double $85 Single $55 (Full breakfast)
Children $20
2 adults, 2 children $120
Visa MC accepted
Children welcome
1 King/Twin 1 Double 2 Single (1 bdrm)
Bathrooms: 1 Ensuite

Situated in New Plymouth's port-view Moturoa suburb. Enter through hobby vines to the spacious upstairs open-plan studio penthouse; 360 degree views of harbour, mountains, city; coast north and south. Shoreline pleasures nearby including eateries. Guests may be as self-contained as wished; lock-up garage, separate entrance, mini-kitchen. Private balcony, dining-table, full AV options, phone. Extra bed(s) by arrangement. Ideally situated for exploring Taranaki's attractions, or the perfect R&R retreat. There is a pet cat.

New Plymouth *0.5 km W of New Plymouth*
Airlie House *B&B Apartment with Kitchen*
Gabrielle Masters
161 Powderham Street, New Pymouth

Tel (06) 757 8866 or 021 472 072
Fax (06) 757 8866   email@airliehouse.co.nz
www.airliehouse.co.nz

Double $110-$145 (Full breakfast)
Children negotiable
Studio $145 double
Visa MC Amex accepted
Children welcome
1 King/Twin 3 Queen 1 Twin 4 Single (5 bdrm)
Bathrooms: 1 Ensuite 3 Private 1 claw bath

Airlie House is a 110 year old character home nestled among mature trees and garden. This beautiful home provides three guest bedrooms with ensuites or private bathrooms, plus a studio apartment with its own kitchen and private bathroom. Located in central New Plymouth Airlie House is an easy five minute walk from shops, restaurants, the sea front, parks and many other local attractions. All rooms have many amenities available for your comfort, including Sky Digital TV, broadband and wireless internet access.

New Plymouth *5 km W of New Plymouth Centre*
Whaler's Rest *B&B*
Maureen & Denis Whiting
86A Barrett Road, New Plymouth

Tel (06) 751 4272 or 027 328 0268
whalersrest@clear.net.nz
www.whalersrest.co.nz

Double $100 Single $80 (Full breakfast)
Children $20
Children and pets welcome
1 Double 1 Twin (2 bdrm)
Bathrooms: 1 Ensuite 1 Private

Large double bedroom with ensuite, and your own deck for drinks, plus twin room with private bathroom. Breakfast, continental or cooked. We are on the gateway to Surf Highway, ten minutes to Oakura beach and five minutes to New Plymouth City featuring the Wind Wand, coastal walkway, Puke Ariki Museum and Pukekura Park. Your hosts Maureen and Denis who love their tennis and garden welcome you. We have a very sociable labrador Stella, and two cats, Tuffy and Biscuit. Please phone for bookings and directions.

New Plymouth *1 km N of New Plymouth*
City Lights *B&B*
Carol & John Donaldson
4 Nadine Stanton Drive, Bell Block,
Kingsdown, New Plymouth

Tel (06) 755 0149 or 025 221 9267
Fax (06) 755 0149
carol.sharpe@clear.net.nz

Double $80-$120 Single $75 (Full breakfast)
Children $20
Children and pets welcome
2 Queen 1 Twin (3 bdrm)
Bathrooms: 1 Ensuite 1 Guest share

Spectacular sunsets, peaceful relax country, city and sea views. Modern architecturally designed home, comfortable big bedrooms. Ten minutes to New Plymouth; five minutes to airport; drop-off or pick-up by arrangement. A guest lounge is available to make tea/coffee and has a microwave. Hop, skip, and jump to New Plymouth Golf course. John and I are happy and comfortable here with Barnie and Flash, our cats & Spencer our poodle.

New Plymouth *0.2 km N of New Plymouth*

Issey Manor *B&B Guest House*
Jan & Brian Mason
32 Carrington Street, New Plymouth

Tel (06) 758 2375
Fax (06) 758 2375
issey.manor@actrix.co.nz
www.isseymanor.co.nz

Double $135-$175 **Single** $110-$150 (Full breakfast)
Corporate and special rates available
Visa MC Amex Eftpos accepted
1 King/Twin 3 Queen (4 bdrm)
Bathrooms: 4 Ensuite

A stylish blend of old architecture and modern living. Issey offers four contemporary suites all with designer bathrooms. Well appointed for business or pleasure with separate guest lounge and kitchen, Sky TV, and just a minutes stroll to the city centre, wonderful restaurants, cafés, parks, Pukeariki, art gallery and coastal walkway. If you enjoy comfort, stylish decor, privacy and awesome service - try Issey. Jan, Brian, Louie the Bichon and Wattie the cat welcome you.

New Plymouth *0.01 km N of New Plymouth City*

Timata Ora *Luxury B&B*
Carol & Rodney Hall
55 Gover Street, New Plymouth, Taranaki

Tel (06) 757 9917 or 027 452 3885
Fax (06) 759 1654
carol_rodney@iconz.co.nz
www.timataora.com

Double $120-$130 **Single** $100-$120 (Full breakfast)
Family suite when both bedrooms used $200
Visa MC Eftpos accepted   Children welcome
4 Queen 1 Twin (5 bdrm)
Bathrooms: 3 Ensuite 1 Family share
All suites have own bathrooms

We warmly welcome guests to our fully refurbished central city home. A 1920's heritage home, Timata Ora offers three luxurious queen suites (one with 4 Poster) each with own bathroom, TV, fridge, hair drier, iron/ironing board, heated towel rails, complimentary beverages and in room treats. The famiy suite has two bedrooms with private bathroom and same amenities as other suites. Gregarious cat Murphy (the Butler) shares Timata Ora. Breakfast in your suite, dining room, in the conservatory or on the terrace.

New Plymouth - Waitara *12 km N of New Plymouth*

Loggers Retreat *B&B Cottage with Kitchen*
John & Brenda Reumers
42 Richmond Road, Waitara, 4373

Tel (06) 754 3131 or (06) 754 7668
Fax (06) 754 7668
loggersretreat@xtra.co.nz
www.windwand.co.nz/loggersretreat.htm

Double $130 (Full breakfast provisions)
Pet free home
Not suitable for children
1 Double (1 bdrm)
Bathrooms: 1 Private Private outside bath

A rustic character-filled private board and battened two storyed cottage. Situated on six acres of beautiful rural land, which hosts a hand-built double storyed log house and surrounded by native gardens. Enjoy a wine on the deck or on the bridge over the lake outside your door. This is a family with three adult children and a variety of farm animals. All under the watchful gaze of the majestic Mt Taranaki.

New Plymouth - Brixton *10 km N of New Plymouth*
Blue Heaven Villas Bed & Breakfast *B&B Self-Contained Villa*

Kaz Bruce
137 Raleigh Street, Brixton, RD 42 Waitara 4382

Tel (06) 7547513 or 027 216 9725
Fax (06) 754 7512
accommodation@blueheaven.co.nz
www.blueheaven.co.nz

Double $135-$145 **Single** $115-$125 (Full breakfast)
Visa MC accepted
Not suitable for children
2 King (2 bdrm)
Bathrooms: 1 Ensuite 1 Private

Peaceful, private and comfortable, guests have exclusive use of the 1908 Villa. Enjoy a swim in the indoor Solar heated pool(in season), or relax in the spa. Watch a video, DVD or Sky TV. Blue Heaven Villas is ideally situated to use as a base to explore Taranaki. Plenty of private and secure parking. Kaz would like to host your next visit to Taranaki. 10 km north of New Plymouth, Blue Heaven is 500 metres off SH3, five minutes from New Plymouth Airport, 3 km from Waitara

New Plymouth *1 km W of Post Office*
Arcadia Lodge *B&B*

Joanne & Mark Long
52 Young Street, New Plymouth, 4601

Tel (06) 769 9100 or 0800 ARCADE
Fax (06) 769 9120
arcadialodge@ihug.co.nz
www.arcadialodge.net

Double $75-$80 (Continental breakfast)
Extra Guest $15 per night
Visa MC Diners Amex Eftpos accepted
Pet free home
8 Queen 8 Double 16 Single (18 bdrm)
Bathrooms: 4 Ensuite 6 Guest share

Arcadia Lodge has a mix of 18 double, multi-bed and bunk rooms. Each room has a telephone, television, refrigerator and tea and coffee making facilities. Four rooms have ensuites and the rest share modern bathrooms.There are two lounges, with free broadband connection. A continental breakfast is included. Off-street parking is provided for 12 cars. Arcadia Lodge is wheelchair friendly. Arcadia Lodge is centrally located within easy walking distance of most of New Plymouth's amenities and the inter-city bus stop.

New Plymouth *1 km NE of Post Office*
The Grange *B&B*

Rachael Nielsen and Alan Clarke
44B Victoria Road, Brooklands, New Plymouth

Tel (06) 759 8004 or 027 434 5680
grangebandb@xtra.co.nz

Double $120-$130 **Single** $80-$90 (Full breakfast)
Visa MC Diners Amex accepted
Pets welcome
1 King/Twin 2 Queen (3 bdrm)
Bathrooms: 3 Ensuite

Come and stay in our modern architecturally designed award-winning home built with the privacy and comfort of our guests in mind. With unique bush views and a house designed to take full advantage of the sun, our guests can enjoy relaxing in the lounge or the extensive tiled courtyards and listen to the sounds of the native birds. The Grange is centrally heated, security controlled and located adjacent to the renowned Pukekura Park and Bowl of Brooklands. The city is within a short five minute walk. Rachael, Alan, your hosts Pablo, Beau the cats and Grace the dog will welcome you.

Taranaki, Wanganui, Ruapehu, Rangitikei

New Plymouth - Bell Block *9 km SE of New Plymouth*

Hideaway Cottage *Luxury B&B Cottage with Kitchen*

Donald & Robyn Johnson
231 Henwood Road, New Plymouth, RD 2

Tel (06) 755 1360 or 027 212 7099
donrobyn@xtra.co.nz
www.hideawaycottage.co.nz

Double $275 Single $250 (Special breakfast)
Visa MC accepted
Not suitable for children
1 Queen (1 bdrm)
Bathrooms: 1 Ensuite

We look forward to welcomimg youto our little bit of paridise, close to New Plymouth but a world away. Free airport pickup and complimentary wine each night to enjoy by the pool, spa or roaring log fire. A sumptuous breakfast delivered to the cottage with late checkout. Set on 22 acres but handy to the city many golf courses, moutain walks and the sea.

New Plymouth - Waitara *20 km N of New Plymouth*

Qahal *B&B Separate Suite Apartment with Kitchen*

Jill & Russell Fleet
20 Calgher Avenue, Waitara, 4320

Tel (06) 754 3236 or 021 754 325
fleet@slingshot.co.nz

Double $80-$100 Single $45-$60
(Breakfast by arrangement)
Families, double rate + $15 per child, max 3
Dinner $15pp, two course by arrangement only
Pet free home
3 Queen 1 Single (3 bdrm)
Bathrooms: 1 Guest share
Sleepout has family share shower

Jill & Russell live in a round house that was featured on TV3's "My house my Castle" winning the best converted category. We are situated five minutes from the beach, 15 minutes from New Plymouth and 35 minutes from Mt. Taranaki. We share the house with our grandaughter Chenoah, our cats, Saka and Pango, our dog Banjo.The property is two acres set in a 'green belt' at the end of a quiet culdesac with state highway 3 as one of it's boundaries.

Inglewood *20 km N of New Plymouth*

The Bank *Luxury B&B*

Allan & Vicki Wright
33 Rimu Street, Inglewood, 4651

Tel Freephone 0800 566 187 or (06) 756 6187
enquries@thebankinglewood.co.nz
www.thebankinglewood.co.nz

Double $130-$170 Single $95-$120 (Full breakfast)
Not suitable for children
Dinner by arrangement
Corporate rates available
Visa MC accepted
3 Queen (3 bdrm)
Bathrooms: 1 Ensuite 2 Private

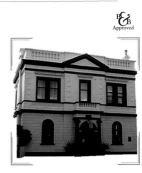

Situated 15 minutes from New Plymouth and 30 minutes from Mt Taranaki is The Bank. You are invited to share with us our heritage building built in 1898 and enjoy the luxury of the bedrooms, private bathrooms, guest lounge, kitchen and relax in our peaceful gardens. We will greet you with a hot drink and home baking or even a special glass of New Zealand wine. We live in the top story of The Bank along with our two elderly dogs Max and Sam.

Stratford *0.5 km N of Stratford*

Stratford Lodge (Stallards) *B&B Homestay Farmstay*
Billieanne & Corb Stallard
3514 State Highway 3, Stratford Northern Boundary

Tel (06) 765 8324   Fax (06) 765 8325
stallardbb@infogen.net.nz
www.stratfordlodge.co.nz

Double $90 Single $50 (Full breakfast)
Children $20   Dinner by arrangement
Double is 2 people   Visa MC Amex accepted
Pet free home Children welcome
2 Double 2 Twin 2 Single (4 bdrm)
Bathrooms: 4 Ensuite 1 Guest share

Quality "Upstairs Downstairs" comfort. Cooked or continental breakfast included. Free self-catering kitchen, tea, coffee, biscuits. Homely or private. Own key. Optional separate lounge. Restaurants, taverns, shops nearby. Rooms are antique, romantic with TV, heaters, electric blankets, serviced daily. Gardens, BBQ, row boat, bush bath, river walks. 15 minutes to Mt Egmont ski fields, climbing, tramping. Centrally located on edge of Stratford, easy distance to New Plymouth, museums, famous gardens, tourist attractions. Interests include gemstones travel, art. Welcome.

Egmont National Park *9 km W of Stratford*

Anderson's Alpine Lodge *Homestay Farmstay*
Berta Anderson
PO Box 303, Stratford, Taranaki

Tel (06) 765 6620 Fax (06) 765 6100
mountainhouse@xtra.co.nz
www.mountainhouse.co.nz

Double $175-$215 Single $175 (Full breakfast)
Dinner a la carte at the Mountain House Mountain
House tariff - double/single from $130
Visa MC Diners Eftpos accepted   Pets welcome
1 King/Twin 1 Queen 1 Double 2 Single (3 bdrm)
Bathrooms: 3 Ensuite

Swiss style lodge surrounded with native bush. Luxury accommodation with special alpine ambiance. Spectacular views of Mount Egmont/Taranaki. Egmont National Park opposite front gate. Five kilometres to Mountain House Motor Lodge and its famed restaurant (accommodation tariff from $130). 3 km to Stratford Plateau and skifield. Tramping, summit climbs, trout streams, gardens and museums nearby. Helicopter summit flights. Pet sheep, pig, ducks etc. Swiss Berta Anderson owned mountain lodges since 1976, winning many awards. Beautiful paintings from Keith, her husband (died Feb 03) are displayed.

Stratford *15 km NE of Stratford*

Te Popo Gardens *B&B Apartment with Kitchen Country Garden Retreat*
Bruce & Lorri Ellis
636 Stanley Road, RD 24, Stratford

Tel (06) 762 8775   Fax (06) 765 7182
tepopo@clear.net.nz
www.tepopo.co.nz

Double $145-$180 Single $105-$125
(Special breakfast)
Dinner $35-$45 by arrangement
Free access to separate kitchen for self catering
Visa MC Diners Amex accepted
2 King/Twin 1 King 1 Queen 2 Single (4 bdrm)
Bathrooms: 4 Ensuite Outside bath under the stars

Te Popo Gardens is a Garden of National Significance. We love to share this special place - expansive (34 acres) and beautiful woodland and perennial garden encircled by deep river gorges and native forest. Each of the spacious suites opens to the garden with private access, ensuite, woodfire, TV, sound system, and superior bed and linen. Special breakfast is served in the sunny conservatory or beside the fire. Wonderful dogs. Excellent access from/to the popular Forgotten World Highway (SH43) - to/from the Central North Island.

Taranaki, Wanganui, Ruapehu, Rangitikei

Hawera

Linden Park B&B *B&B*

Douglas & Merilyn Tippett
69 Waihi Road, Hawera

Tel (06) 278 5421
Fax (06) 278 5421
lindenpark@inspire.net.nz

Double $90 **Single** $65 (Continental breakfast)
Visa MC accepted
2 Queen 1 Double 1 Twin (4 bdrm)
Bathrooms: 1 Guest share

Welcome to our home, set in established grounds among Linden trees, centrally located on State Highway 3, opposite Hawera's aquatic centre and King Edward Park, and within a few minutes walk to cafés, restaurants and the town centre. The guest lounge with TV and tea/coffee facilities is where breakfast is served. Local attractions such as the mountain, trout streams (a trout fishing guide is available), gardens, beaches, golf courses, museums and local industry offer a variety of activities. We trust ours will be a home away from home as you enjoy the loveliness of South Taranaki.

Waitotara - Wanganui *29 km W of Wanganui*

Ashley Park *Farmstay Cottage with Kitchen*

Wendy Pearce
State Highway 3, Box 36, Waitotara, Wanganui

Tel (06) 346 5917
Fax (06) 346 5861
ashley_park@xtra.co.nz
www.ashleypark.co.nz

Double $95-$130 **Single** $80 (Full breakfast)
Dinner $30
Visa MC Diners Eftpos accepted
1 Queen 4 Single (3 bdrm)
Bathrooms: 1 Ensuite 1 Guest share

We have a 500 acre sheep and cattle farm and live in a comfortable home, set in an attractive garden with a swimming pool and tennis court. Also in the garden is an antique shop selling Devonshire teas. 100 metres from the house is a four acre park and lake, aviaries and a collection of hand fed pet farm animals. We welcome guests to have dinner with us. Self-contained accommodation is available in the park.

Wanganui *2 km NW of Wanganui City Centre*

Kembali *B&B Homestay*

Marylyn & Wes Palmer
26 Taranaki Street, St Johns Hill, Wanganui

Tel (06) 347 1727 or 027 244 4347
wespalmer@xtra.co.nz

Double $100-$115 **Single** $70-$85 (Full breakfast)
Small charge for laundry facilities
Visa MC accepted
Pet free home
Not suitable for children
1 Queen 1 Twin (2 bdrm)
Bathrooms: 1 Private

Kembali is a modern, centrally heated, sunny home in a quiet street overlooking trees and wetlands. Upstairs guest bedrooms, bathroom and lounge (with TV, fridge, tea/coffee) are for one party/groups exclusive use. Retired, no pets, children married, we offer a restful stay. We enjoy meeting people, gardening, travel, reading and have Christian interests. Off-street parking and laundry available. Five minutes drive to city, heritage buildings, restored paddle steamer, restaurants, museum, art gallery and walks. We look forward to welcoming you.

Wanganui *20 km NE of Wanganui*
Misty Valley Farmstay *Farmstay*
Linda & Garry Wadsworth
RD 5, 97 Parihauhau Road, Wanganui

Tel (06) 342 5767
linda.garry.wadsworth@xtra.co.nz

Double $100 Single $60 (Full breakfast)
Children $20-$30
Dinner $40 by arrangement
Visa MC accepted
Children welcome
2 Double 2 Twin (2 bdrm)
Bathrooms: 1 Guest share

Misty Valley is a small organic farm at 3.7 hectares. We prefer to use our own produce whenever possible. There are farm animals for you to meet including our brittany, George and cats, Alice and Calico, who all live outside. Our two grandchildren visit us regularly and children will be made very welcome. We are non-smoking, but have pleasant deck areas for those who do. Our famous river and historical city offer plenty of activities for the whole family to enjoy.

Wanganui *0.5 km N of Wanganui Centre*
Braemar House *B&B Guest House*
Clive Rivers
2 Plymouth Street, Wanganui

Tel (06) 348 2301   **Fax** (06) 348 2301
contact@braemarhouse.co.nz
www.braemarhouse.co.nz

Double $75-$95 Single $65-$75
(Continental breakfast)   Children $10
Dinner $25 by arrangement
Visa MC Eftpos accepted   Children welcome
3 Queen 2 Double 3 Twin (8 bdrm)
Bathrooms: 4 Guest share deluxe sized bath.

Welcome to 'Olde Worlde Charm'. This restored historic Homestead circa 1895, nestled alongside the Wanganui River, has a homely ambience making your stay restful and enjoyable. The graceful entrance leads to eight comfortable, centrally heated, period-designed bedrooms, guest drawing room and dining room. Laundry facilities, wireless internet, fully equipped kitchen available. Off-street parking set in beautiful gardens. The Homestead is close to the city and tourist attractions. The paddle steamer Waimarie passes daily in front of the Homestead. We look forward to you visiting Braemar House.

Wanganui *6 km N of Wanganui*
Arles B&B *B&B Apartment with Kitchen*
Sue & Tom Day
50 Riverbank Road, RD 3, Wanganui, 4573

Tel (06) 343 6557 or 021 257 8257
Fax (06) 343 6557
sue@arles.co.nz
www.arles.co.nz

Double $140-$180 Single $120-$150 (Full breakfast)
Children $30-35
1 King 2 Queen 1 Double 2 Twin (6 bdrm)
Bathrooms: 2 Ensuite, 1 Private in B&B
1 Private in apartment

Arles is a charming Edwardian homestead built in the 1880s adjacent to the Whanganui River. We offer affordable luxury to couples and families in the centrally-heated house or two bedroom separate modern apartment. All facilities are complimentary and include a fully-equipped kitchen, laundry, broadband/wireless internet, saltwater pool, barbecue and off-road parking. A sumptuous breakfast full of home-made delights starts the day for house guests. Along with our elderly cat we look forward to meeting you.

Taranaki, Wanganui, Ruapehu, Rangitikei

Taumarunui *5 km NE of Taumarunui*

Matawa Country Home *Farmstay*
Shirley & Allan Jones
213 Taringamotu Road, Taumarunui

Tel (07) 896 7722
Fax (07) 895 6927
costleyj@farmside.co.nz

Double $120 **Single** $70 (Full breakfast)
Children half price
Dinner by arrangement
Children welcome
1 King 1 Twin (2 bdrm)
Bathrooms: 1 Private

Our spacious home is situated 5 km from the centre of Taumarunui surrounded by a peaceful one acre garden with a native bush backdrop filled with NZ native birds. The bedrooms open on to a large verandah. Laundry available. A stream runs along one boundary of the 80 acre property suitable for walks and summertime swimming. A golf course is located within 2 km, along with guided mountain walks, canoeing, hot pools, scenic flights, skiing, trout fishing and white-water rafting are all within an hours drive.

Taumarunui - Piriaka *10 km S of Taumarunui*

Awarua Lodge *B&B Separate Suite*
Raewyn & Jack Vernon
1063 State Highway 4, Piriaka, Taumarunui

Tel (07) 896 8100 or 021 031 5151
Fax (07) 896 8102
info@awarualodge.co.nz
www.awarualodge.co.nz

Double $180 (Full breakfast)
Suite $350
Visa MC accepted
1 King/Twin 1 King (2 bdrm)
Bathrooms: 1 Private

Awarua Lodge, set in parkland grounds overlooking the Whanganui River, is self-contained guest accommodation offering a suite that sleeps four. The decor simply commands you to relax. Visit the Whanganui and Tongariro National Parks. Try your hand golfing on Taumarunui's premiere golf course, rated in the top NZ 50. Plan your adventures; tramping, fishing, canoeing, skiing, mountain biking. Watch sheep shearing and the milking of a large NZ dairy herd.

Taumarunui - Owhango *15 km S of Taumarunui*

Fernleaf *B&B Farmstay Cottage No Kitchen*
Carolyn & Melvin Forlong
58 Tunanui Road, RD 1, Owhango

Tel (07) 895 4847 or 0800 FERNLEAF
021 0275 3847 or 021 0275 3848
Fax (07) 895 4837
fernleaf.farm@xtra.co.nz

Double $80-$120 **Single** $85 (Full breakfast)
Dinner $25 Cottage $85
Visa MC Diners Amex accepted
Children welcome
2 Queen 1 Double 3 Single (4 bdrm)
Bathrooms: 2 Ensuite 1 Private

Relax in the tranquil Tunanui Valley just 500 metres from SH4. Close for convenience, far enough away for peace and quiet. We are the third generation to farm Fernleaf and our Romney sheep flock has been recorded every year for ninety years . The views from various vantage point on the farm are awesome, taking in the mountains: Ruapehu, Ngaruahoe, Tongariro and Taranaki. Enjoy our generous country hospitality, wonderful breakfast, a beautiful dalmatian Sally, and friendly cats. Other meals by arrangement.

Raetihi *0.5 km N of Raetihi*
Log Lodge *Luxury B&B*
Jan & Bob Lamb
5 Ranfurly Terrace, Raetihi

Tel (06) 385 4135
Fax (06) 385 4835
Lamb.Log-Lodge@Xtra.co.nz

Double $115 Single $60 (Full breakfast)
Children under 14 $40
Spa $5 per person
Visa MC accepted
1 Queen 1 Double 4 Single
Bathrooms: 2 Private
We only accept one booking at a time.

A unique opportunity to stay in a modern authentic log home sited high on seven acres on the edge of town. Completely private accommodation, with own bathroom. All sleeping on mezzanine, your own lounge with wood fire, snooker table, TV/video, stereo and dining area, opening onto large verandah, with swimming pool and spa available. Panoramic views of Mts Ruapehu, Ngauruhoe and Tongariro. Tongariro National Park and Turoa Skifield are a half hour scenic drive.

Ohakune *6 km W of Ohakune*
Mitredale *Homestay Farmstay*
Audrey & Diane Pritt
Smiths Road, RD, Ohakune

Tel (06) 385 8016 or 027 453 1916
Fax (06) 385 8016
mitredale@ihug.co.nz

Double $100 Single $60 (Continental breakfast)
Dinner $30pp by arrangement
Visa MC accepted Pets welcome
1 Double 2 Single (2 bdrm)
Bathrooms: 1 Family share

We farm sheep, bull beef and run a boarding kennel in a beautiful peaceful valley with magnificent views of Mt Ruapehu. Tongariro National Park for skiing, walking, photography. Excellent 18 hole golf course, great fishing locally. We are members of Ducks Unlimited (a conservation group)and our local wine club. We have two labradors. We offer dinner traditional farmhouse (Diane, a cook book author), or breakfast with excellent home-made jams. Take Raetihi Road, at Hotel/BP Service Station corner. 4 km to Smiths Road. Last house 2 km.

Ohakune *0.9 km SE of Ohakune Junction*
Dakune Lodge *B&B Ski Lodge*
Nicolas & Tasha Cowell
42 Park Avenue, Ohakune, 4625

Tel (06) 385 8448
Fax (06) 385 8448
info@dakunelodge.co.nz
www.dakunelodge.co.nz

Double $100-$125 Single $100
(Continental breakfast)
Summer rate $30pp
Visa MC Amex Eftpos accepted
2 Queen 5 Double 11 Single (9 bdrm)
Bathrooms: 3 Guest share

A beautiful wooden Lodge with mountain views in a quiet location, yet near the Junction. warm comfortable accommodation for singles, couples, families or groups with shared bathrooms. Facilities include sauna, games and drying rooms, sunbed and in-house massage clinic. Socialise by the log fire in our large friendly lounge. Meals by request. Open all year round - wonderful memories are made here!

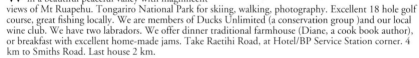

Taihape *1 km N of Taihape*

Korirata Homestay *B&B Homestay*
Patricia & Noel Gilbert
25 Pukeko Street, Taihape

Tel (06) 388 0315
Fax (06) 388 0315
korirata@xtra.co.nz

Double $90 Single $55 (Special breakfast)
Children under 10 half price
Dinner by arrangement
Visa MC accepted
4 Single (2 bdrm)
Bathrooms: 1 Guest share

A warm welcome awaits you at the top of the hill in Taihape, where panoramic views of mountains, ranges and countryside add to the tranquil surroundings. Three quarters of an acre is landscaped with shrubs, hydroponics, home-grown vegetables and chrysanthemums in season. Meals, are with hosts, using produce from the garden where possible. Comfortable beds with electric blankets. Rafting, bungy jumping and farm visits can be arranged. One hour to Ruapehu, Lake Taupo and two and a half hours to Wellington and Rotorua.

Taihape *6 km S of Taihape*

Grandvue *Homestay*
John & Dianne McKinnon
Wairanu Road, RD 4, Taihape

Tel (06) 388 1308 or 027 244 1309
Fax (06) 388 1308
grandvue@xtra.co.nz

Double $90 Single $55 (Continental breakfast)
Children 12 and under $25
Dinner by arrangement
Visa MC accepted
Children and pets welcome
1 Queen 2 Twin (2 bdrm)
Bathrooms: 1 Guest share Tiled shower/Spa bath

R elax in comfort in our cosy modern home situated in the heart of the Rangitikei on 90 acres of farmland. Only six minutes south of Taihape, two minutes off State Highway 1. Our home situated in spacious grounds boasts magnificent views of mountains and ranges. One hour to Mt Ruapehu, two hours to Taupo and three to Wellington with many local activity options available.Comfortable beds with electric blankets. Paddock facilities available for travelling animals. Basil a Burmese cat loves visitors.

Taihape *1 km S of Taihape*

Llanerchymedd *Luxury B&B Apartment with Kitchen*
Alan & Jan Thomas
10 Dixon Way, Taihape

Tel (06) 388 0283 or (06) 388 0666
021 127 6211
Fax (06) 388 0683
alajan@xtra.co.nz

Double $90 (Continental breakfast provisions)
Children $20 per head additional charge
Children welcome
2 Double 2 Single (1 bdrm)
Bathrooms: 1 Ensuite

W e are a married couple with two children and two cats. Llanerchymedd is a quiet residence, with established gardens. We are two minutes from Taihape and are easily located, 1 km south of the town with panoramic views of Mt Ruapehu. A tranquil walk up into the gardens is well rewarded with fantastic views. Take a glass of wine with you and relax in the top gazebo - you will feel on top of the world.

Taihape - Rangitikei *26 km NE of Taihape*

Tarata Fishaway *Luxury B&B Homestay Farmstay*
Stephen & Trudi Mattock
Mokai Road, RD 3, Taihape

Tel (06) 388 0354 or 027 279 7037
027 227 4986 Fax (06) 388 0954
fishaway@xtra.co.nz   www.tarata.co.nz

Double $120-$180 Single $60-$90
(Continental breakfast provisions)
Children under 12 half price Dinner $35pp by arrangement
Visa MC accepted Children and pets welcome
4 King/Twin 5 Queen 1 Double 3 Single (9 bdrm)
Bathrooms: 4 Ensuite 1 Guest share spa bath

We are very lucky to have a piece of New Zealand's natural beauty. Tarata is nestled in bush in the remote Mokai Valley where the picturesque Rangitikei River meets the rugged Ruahine Ranges. With the wilderness and unique trout fishing right at our doorstep, it is the perfect environment to bring up our three children.

Stephen offers guided fishing and rafting trips for all ages. Raft through the gentle crystal clear waters of the magnificent Rangitikei River, visit Middle Earth and a secret waterfall, stunning scenery you will never forget. Our spacious home and our large garden allow guests private space to relax and unwind. Whether it is by the pool on a hot summers day with a good book, soaking in the spa pool after a day on the river or enjoying a cosy winters night in front of our open fire with a glass of wine.

Come on a farm tour meeting our many friendly farm pets, experience our nightlife on our free spotlight safari and Tarata is only 6km past the new flying fox and bungy jump. Stay in our Homestead or in Tarata's fully self-contained River Retreats where you can enjoy a spa bath with million dollar views of the river and relax on the large decking amidst native birds and trees. Peace, privacy and tranquillity at its best! We will even deliver a candle light dinner to your door. We think Tarata is truly a magic place and we would love sharing it with you. Directions: Tarata Fishaway is 26 scenic kilometres from Taihape. Turn off SH1, 6 km south of Taihape at the Gravity Canyon Bungy and Ohotu signs. Follow the signs (14km) to the bungy bridge. We are 6 km past here on Mokai Road. Features & Attractions Trout Fishing and Scenic Rafting Visit LOTR, Anduin, Middle Earth 6 km past Bungy & Flying Fox Mini golf (with a difference) Swimming & Spa pool Bush walks/spotlight safaris Camp outs Clay Bird shooting

Taihape *32 km E of Taihape*

River Valley Lodge *Adventure Lodge*
Brian & Nicola Megaw
Mangahoata Road, Pukeokahu, Taihape, 4792

Tel (06) 388 1444 or 0800 248 666
Fax (06) 388 1859   thelodge@rivervalley.co.nz
www.rivervalley.co.nz

Double $169-$169 Single $158-$158 (Full breakfast)
Children please refer to our website
Dinner please refer to our website
Visa MC Amex Eftpos accepted   Children welcome
6 King/Twin 2 King (8 bdrm)
Bathrooms: 8 Ensuite with showers and toilets

River Valley, an Adventure Lodge, a special place that brings together people from different backgrounds, to share adventures, and enjoy beautiful surroundings. A place where the adventure activities are a core part of the operation, and are integral to the very culture of who we are. River Valley is pioneering the Adventure Lodge concept in New Zealand. An Adventure Lodge sits in the market between a backpackers and a luxury lodge. What makes an adventure lodge special is location, culture, and the adventures on offer.

Marton *45 km N of Palmerston North*

Rea's Inn *B&B Homestay*
Keith & Lorraine Rea
12 Dunallen Avenue, Marton

Tel (06) 327 4442 or 027 479 9589
Fax (06) 327 4442
keithandlorraine@xtra.co.nz

Double $85 Single $50 (Continental breakfast)
Children half price
Dinner $20
Visa MC accepted
Children welcome
1 Queen 1 Twin (2 bdrm)
Bathrooms: 1 Guest share

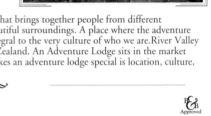

We have a warm comfortable home offering hospitality, peace and tranquility. Situated in quiet cul-de-sac with a private garden setting. Guests stay in separate wing of home. Close to Nga Tawa and Huntley Schools. Ideal for weekend retreat or stopover. (Only two hours from Wellington Ferry). Your comfort and pleasure are important to us. Clients enjoy our homemade hot bread served at breakfast. Our birman cat likes people too, and we all welcome you to come, relax and enjoy the friendly atmosphere at Rea's Inn.

All our B&Bs are non-smoking
unless stated otherwise in the text.

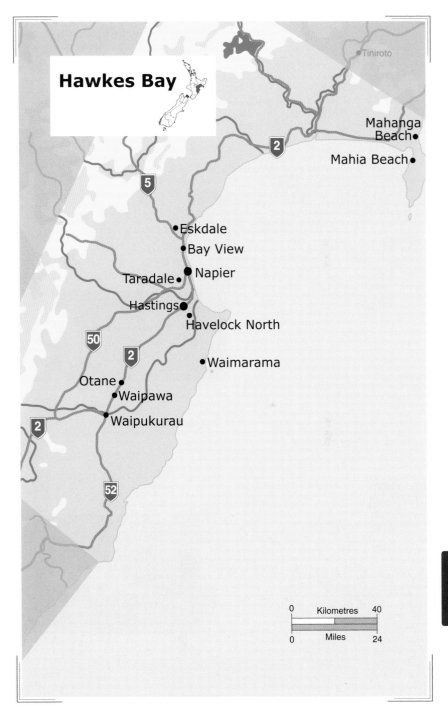

Hawkes Bay

Tiniroto

Mahanga Beach

Mahia Beach

Eskdale
Bay View
Taradale • Napier
Hastings
Havelock North

Waimarama

Otane
Waipawa
Waipukurau

0 Kilometres 40
0 Miles 24

Mahia Peninsula - Mahanga Beach *50 km N of Wairoa*

Reomoana *B&B Apartment with Kitchen*
Louise Schick
629 Mahanga Road, RD 8 Mahanga Beach,
Mahia, Hawkes Bay 4198

Tel (06) 837 5898   Fax (06) 837 5990
reomoana@paradise.net.nz
www.reomoana.co.nz

Double $120-$150 **Single** $60 (Continental breakfast)
Children $20   Dinner $35
Visa MC accepted
Children and pets welcome
2 Queen 1 Twin 1 Single (4 bdrm)
Bathrooms: 1 Ensuite 1 Private

Reomoana - The voice of the sea. Overlooking the Pacific with breathtaking views this rustic home with handcrafted features combines New Zealand and Hungarian creativity. Situated on a hillside the property is grazed by sheep and cattle, where walks may be enjoyed through QE 2 convenanted native bush. 5 minutes. walk to 8 km. of white sandy beach, a recreational paradise for swimming, surfing and fishing. Attractions:- Morere Hot Springs, Paua farm, Marae visits, Golf-course and fishing charters. 6 km. to Café Mahia and Sunset Point Restaurants.

~

Eskdale *10 km N of Napier*

Cornucopia Lodge *Luxury B&B Cottage with Kitchen*
Melanie Held
361 State Highway 5, Eskdale, Napier

Tel (06) 836 6508 or 021 921 211
stay@cornucopia-lodge.com
www.cornucopia-lodge.com

Double $120-$165 **Single** $80-$120
(Continental breakfast)
Dinner on request
Visa MC Diners Amex accepted
Children and pets welcome
1 Queen 1 Double (2 bdrm)
Bathrooms: 2 Ensuite

You will receive a warm welcome from Melanie and the friendly border collies at Cornucopia Lodge. The fully self contained Lodge is situated on three acres of gardens, is tastefully furnished and has two lovely bedrooms each with ensuite. The warm and cosy lounge has an open fireplace and the kitchen is fully equipped.

~

Bay View - Napier *12 km N of Napier*

Beachfront Homestay *B&B Homestay Separate Suite*
Christine & Jim Howard
20A Le Quesne Road, Bay View, Napier

Tel (06) 836 6530 or 027 44 7 7959
Fax (06) 836 6531   j-howard@clear.net.nz
www.beachfronthb.co.nz

Double $120 **Single** $60 (Full breakfast)
Children $25   Dinner $30
4 person apartment $200
Visa MC accepted
Children welcome
1 Queen 1 Double 1 Single (2 bdrm)
Bathrooms: 1 Private

Jim, Christine and Sarcha (Jack Russell) will welcome you to their beachfront home with breathtaking views of Hawkes Bay and local wineries. Guests are offered B&B or self-contained accommodation,own entrance on ground floor. Jim's a local transport operator and Christine works at a local café both enjoy meeting people and their interests are fishing and the outdoor life. Surfcasting fishing available. Beachfront homestay is just five minutes from the Napier Taupo turn off and 12 minutes from Napiers Marine Parade and cafés.

Bay View - Napier *12 km N of Napier*

Kilbirnie *Homestay*
Jill & John Grant
84 Le Quesne Road, Bay View, Napier

Tel (06) 836 6929 or 027 234 7363
jill.johng@xtra.co.nz
www.bnb.co.nz/kilbirnie.html

Double $85-$95 (Special breakfast)
Dinner $35pp by arrangement
Visa MC accepted
Not suitable for children
2 Queen (2 bdrm)
Bathrooms: 1 Ensuite 1 Private

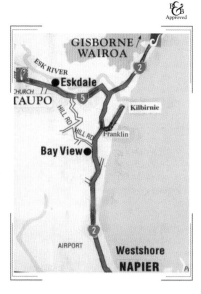

We moved with our dog in 1996 to the quiet end of an unspoiled fishing beach by the Esk River, attracted by the beauty and position away from the traffic, while only 15 minutes of a full range of harbourside restaurants north of Napier.

Kilbirnie is near the Taupo Road intersection with the Pacific Highway to Gisborne, with off-road parking. Upstairs, air-conditioned guest rooms have restful views of the Pacific Ocean one side or vineyards on the other, private bathrooms, excellent showers, abundant hot water, comfortable firm beds and guest lounge with TV tea making and ironing facilities, guests also welcome in family room.

Special breakfast overlooking the ocean is an experience which makes lunch seem superfluous. We are retired farmers with time to share good company, fresh imaginative food and juice, real coffee, an eclectic range of books, who invite you to enjoy our hospitality in modern surroundings. We have 17 years home hosting experience and are non-smokers.

Directions: from Taupo first left after intersection Highways 2 & 5. Franklin Road to Le Quesne, proceed to far end beachfront. From Napier first right after Mobil Station (0.7 km). Prior contact appreciated.

Bay View - Napier *12 km N of Napier*

The Grange *B&B Farmstay Self-contained Lodge*
Roslyn & Don Bird
263 Hill Road, Eskdale, Hawkes Bay
PO Box 136 Bay View, Hawkes Bay

Tel (06) 836 6666 or 027 281 5738
Fax (06) 836 6456   thefarmstay@xtra.co.nz
www.thefarmstay.com

Double $100-$120 Single $85 (Full breakfast)
Dinner $45pp, 3 course with wine
Self-contained lodge $140, extra person $25pp, opt breakfast
Visa MC accepted   Children welcome
1 King/Twin 1 King 1 Double 2 Single (3 bdrm)
Bathrooms: 2 Private

In the heart of a thriving WINE REGION overlooking
the picturesque Esk Valley nestles "THE GRANGE" our delightfully
modern "FARMSTAY" and superior SELF-CONTAINED "LODGE".
Private, spacious accommodation in relaxing peaceful surrounds with
spectacular rural, coastal and city VIEWS.

Feel the comforts of home as we tempt you with our farm produce,
baking, and preserves. We're an outgoing family who really enjoy the
company of guests. Hospitality is guaranteed! Experience our FARM life
with Roslyn, Zac (our weimaraner farm dog), and Sparkie(our resident
cat). Feed the sheep(Lisa, Lilley and Rose etc), cows (especially Snowy),
pigs (Bubble and Squeek), chickens and dairy goats (try milking Betsy)
or bottle-feeding a lamb (seasonal). Its a winelovers paradise! Don a third
generation WINEMAKER with more than 30 years experience is passionate about the wine industry and is happy to share his knowledge over
dinner or to help you plan your HAWKES BAY WINE ADVENTURE.

Explore the world's ART DECO Capital NAPIER 12 MINUTES drive
away and Hawke's Bay's many regional attractions within 30 minutes. Discover part of Cultural New
Zealand along the nearby rivers with Te Awa Maiden, our very talented local fishing guide or visit this
areas 3 wineries and rural cafés within 5 minutes of us. We are always happy to advise on any tours or
special requests as our knowledge, information and contacts throughout Hawkes Bay are invaluable.

Unwind on the Deck to the soothing chorus of native birds in the surrounding gardens and trees and
at day's end spend time romancing over our wonderful night sky. Email access available. We also offer
our Taupo (Kinloch) holiday home to those wishing to stay in that area. Share our home or retreat in
the Lodge. "Our Place Is Your Place." 1km off SH5 at Eskdale or 3km off SH2 at Bay View.

Bay View - Napier *10 km N of Napier*
Bev's on the Bay *B&B*
Beverley White
32 Ferguson Street North, Bay View, Napier

Tel (06) 836 7637
bevann@paradise.net.nz
www.bnb.co.nz/hosts/bevs.html

Double $115-$150 Single $90 (Full breakfast)
Visa MC Amex accepted
Pets welcome
1 King 1 Queen (2 bdrm)
Bathrooms: 1 Ensuite 1 Private

The rooms at Bev's on the Bay are large, modern, have quality beds & linen, own bathrooms, TVs, tea & coffee facilities, sitting areas, and private entrances. The king room has a balcony and panoramic sea views, the queen room opens to a courtyard. Paths through a fascinating cacti and succulent garden lead to the beach. Undercover parking provided. Close to the airport, restaurants and Napier's art deco, there is a winery in walking distance. Host Beverley White is a former businesswoman.

Bay View - Napier *10 km N of Napier*
Bay Bach *B&B Homestay*
Jill and Iain Angus
117 Rogers Road, Napier, 4104

Tel 06 836 5141 or 021 105 7512
Fax 06 836 5141   jill-iain@xtra.co.nz
www.baybach.co.nz

Double $140 Single $100 (Special breakfast)
Children by arrangement
Dinner $40pp by arrangement Lunches by arrangement
Visa MC Diners Amex accepted
Children and pets welcome
1 King/Twin 1 King (2 bdrm)
Bathrooms: 2 Ensuite

A warm friendly welcome awaits you at Bay Bach. Our architectural award winning uniquely stylish home has been built with your comfort and relaxation as it's primary goal. The beds and linen are of the highest quality and comfort. You have your own patio, entrance and car park with a two minute stroll to the sea. A ten minute drive will take you into our beautiful Art Deco city, Napier. Wineries abound as do cafés and restaurants. Hear the sea and look down the grapes to the Bay View hills and enjoy a delicious breakfast made to your requirements.

Napier *1 km N of Napier*
Spence Bed & Breakfast *B&B Homestay*
Kay & Stewart Spence
17 Cobden Road, Napier

Tel (06) 835 9454 or 0800 117 890
Fax (06) 835 9454
ksspence@actrix.gen.nz

Double $150 Single $100 (Full breakfast)
Visa MC accepted
Children welcome
1 Queen 1 Single (1 bdrm)
Bathrooms: 1 Ensuite

Welcome to our comfortable near new home. Quiet area, 10-15 minutes walk from Art Deco City centre. Guest suite opens outside to patio, petanque court and colourful garden. Lounge includes double bed settee, TV, kitchenette with tea making facilities, fridge and microwave. Bedroom has queen and single beds, ensuite bathroom. We have hosted for over ten years and enjoy overseas travel. Able to meet public transport. Directions: port end Marine Parade, Coote Road, right into Thompson Road, left into Cobden Road opposite water tower.

Napier *1.5 km N of Post Office*

A Room with a View *B&B Homestay*

Robert McGregor
9 Milton Terrace, Napier

Tel (06) 835 7434
Fax (06) 835 1912
roomwithview@xtra.co.nz

Double $100 **Single** $70
(Continental breakfast)
Visa MC accepted
1 Queen (1 bdrm)
Bathrooms: 1 Private with bath & shower,
directly oppposite bedroom

Having hosted for ten years with my late wife, I'm continuing to enjoy companionship, conversation and laughter with guests. Spacious room with sea view. Fourth generation property with 100 year old garden. 15 minute walk to restaurants at historic Port Ahuriri or our world famous Art Deco city centre. Private bathroom (bath and shower). Laundry facilities available. Free pick-up service. Off-street parking. Smoke-free inside please. I'm interested in travel, gardening, the arts, and especially local history, as I'm Executive Director of the Art Deco Trust.

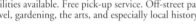

Napier *1.2 km N of Napier Central*

Hillcrest *B&B Homestay*

Nancy & Noel Lyons
4 George Street, Hospital Hill, Napier

Tel (06) 835 1812
lyons@inhb.co.nz
www.hillcrestnapier.co.nz

Double $100-$110 **Single** $75-$80
(Continental breakfast)
Visa MC accepted
Pet free home Not suitable for children
1 Double 2 Single (2 bdrm)
Bathrooms: 1 Guest share

If you require quiet accommodation just minutes from the city centre, our comfortable home provides peace in restful surroundings. Relax on wide decks overlooking our garden, or enjoy the spectacular sea views. Explore nearby historic places and the botanical gardens. Your own lounge with tea/coffee making; laundry and off-street parking available. We have travelled extensively and welcome the opportunity of meeting visitors. Our interests are travel, music, bowls and embroidery. We will happily meet you at the travel depots. Holiday home at Mahia Beach available.

Napier *5 km S of Napier*

Snug Harbour *Homestay*

Ruth & Don McLeod
147 Harold Holt Avenue, Napier

Tel (06) 843 2521
Fax (06) 843 2520
donmcld@clear.net.nz
www.snugharbour.co.nz

Double $95-$110 **Single** $70 (Full breakfast)
Dinner $35 by arrangement
Visa MC accepted
Pet free home
1 Queen 1 Twin (2 bdrm)
Bathrooms: 1 Ensuite 1 Family share

Ruth & Don welcome you to their comfortable home with its rural outlook and sunny attractive patio. The garden studio with ensuite and tea making facilities has its own entrance. We are situated on the outskirts of Napier City, the art deco city of the World, and in close proximity to wineries and many other tourist attractions. We both have a background in teaching, with interests in travel, gardening and photography.

Napier *1 km N of Napier (On Hill Above City)*
The Coach House *Cottage with Kitchen*
Jan Chalmers
9 Gladstone Road, Napier

Tel (06) 835 6126 or 021 251 5847
janchalmers@paradise.net.nz
www.thecoachhouse.co.nz

Double $100 Single $80 (Full breakfast provisions)
Children $25, babies free
4 people $160
Visa MC accepted
Children and pets welcome
1 Queen 2 Single (2 bdrm)
Bathrooms: 1 Private

On the hill over-looking a gorgeous Mediterranean garden and sea views, the historic Coach-house is tastefully renovated and totally self-contained. It contains two bedrooms, open plan kitchen, dining, living rooms, bathroom and separate toilet. The fridge will be full of a variety of breakfast supplies. TV and radio included and fresh flowers in all rooms. The sunny deck has a table and chairs and gas barbecue. Off-street parking and easy access plus peace and privacy complete the picture.

Napier - Taradale *7.5 km SW of Napier*
279 Church Road *B&B Homestay*
Sandy Edginton
279 Church Road, Taradale, Napier

Tel (06) 844 7814 or 021 447 814
Fax (06) 844 7814
sandy.279@homestaynapier.co.nz
www.homestaynapier.co.nz

Double $120-$150 Single $90-$100 (Full breakfast)
Dinner by arrangement
Smoking area available
Visa MC accepted
1 Queen 1 Double 1 Single (2 bdrm)
Bathrooms: 1 Guest share Separate toilet

279, an elegant and spacious home set amongst mature trees and gardens, offers excellent hospitality in a relaxed, friendly atmosphere to domestic and international visitors. Located adjacent to Mission Estate and Church Road Wineries, restaurants and craft galleries, 279 is within a short drive of Art Deco Napier, Hastings, golf courses, and tourist activities. I welcome you to 279 and will help make your visit the highlight of your travels.

Napier - Taradale *10 km W of Napier*
Otatara Heights *B&B Apartment with Kitchen*
Sandra & Roy Holderness
57 Churchill Drive, Taradale, Napier

Tel (06) 844 8855
Fax (06) 844 8855
sandroy@xtra.co.nz

Double $90 Single $70 (Continental breakfast)
Extra guest $35
1 Queen 1 Double (1 bdrm)
Bathrooms: 1 Private

Comfortable, quiet apartment in the heart of our foremost wine producing area. Superb day and night views over Napier and local rural scenes. Ten minutes drive to the art deco capital of the world. 2 km to Taradale Village. Safe off-street parking. Top quality restaurants and wineries nearby. We are a friendly couple who have enjoyed B&B overseas and like meeting people. Our interests are travel, theatre, good food and wine. Bella, our cat, keeps to herself. Handy to EIT and golf course.

Napier - Marine Parade *0.5 km N of Napier*
Mon Logis *B&B*

Gerard Averous
415 Marine Parade, Napier
PO Box 871, Napier

Tel (06) 835 2125 or 027 472 5332
Fax (06) 835 8811
monlogis@xtra.co.nz
www.babs.co.nz/monlogis

Double $160-$220 Single $120-$160 (Full breakfast)
Visa MC Diners Amex accepted
Not suitable for children
2 King/Twin 1 King 1 Queen (4 bdrm)
Bathrooms: 3 Ensuite 1 Private

A little piece of France nestled in the heart of the beautiful wine-growing region of Hawkes Bay. Built as private hotel in 1915, this grand colonial building is a few minutes walk from the city. Now lovingly renovated Mon Logis will cater to a maximum of eight guests. Downstairs, an informal guest lounge invites relaxation, television viewing or a quiet time reading. Guests can help themselves to coffee/tea and home-made biscuits at any time.

Napier *1 km N of Napier*
Cobden Garden Homestay *Luxury B&B Homestay*

Rayma and Phillip Jenkins
1 Cobden Crescent, Bluff Hill, Napier

Tel (06) 834 2090 or 0800 426 233
027 695 1240
Fax (06) 834 1977
info@cobden.co.nz
www.cobden.co.nz

Double $160-$200 Single $140-$180 (Full breakfast)
Children negotiable
Visa MC Diners Amex Eftpos accepted
2 King/Twin 1 King 1 Single (3 bdrm)
Bathrooms: 3 Ensuite

We invite you to share our sunny, colonial villa on Bluff Hill. Enjoy spacious bedrooms furnished for your comfort with; quality bedding, lounge furniture, TV with DVD player, refreshments, robes, hairdryer. Relax in the garden, on the veranda or in a guest lounge. Check emails on the guest computer with wireless access. Join us for complimentary tasting of local wine and hors d'oeuvres each evening. Choose breakfast from a selection of homemade and local foods. Your stay will be memorable. Two unobtrusive cats in residence.

Napier Hill *1 km N of Napier*
Maison Béarnaise *B&B Homestay*

Christine Grouden & Graham Storer
25 France Road, Bluff Hill, Napier 4110

Tel (06) 835 4693 or 0800 624 766
Fax (06) 835 4694
chrisgraham@xtra.co.nz
www.maisonbearnaise.co.nz

Double $155 Single $110 (Full breakfast)
Visa MC accepted
Not suitable for children
2 Queen (2 bdrm)
Bathrooms: 2 Ensuite

Christine, Graham & Brewster (shy cat), welcome you to our attractive, peaceful oasis. Walk to city centre, restaurants, Bluff lookout. Off-street parking, email access, laundry service available. Large bedrooms have views, comfortable beds, electric blankets, and DVD-television. Relax with tea / coffee in your room or guest lounge where newspapers, magazines, books are at your disposal. Delicious breakfasts including home grown and local produce served in dining room or colourful courtyard. Friendly adult retreat. Christine, Napier born, happily shares her wealth of local knowledge.

Napier *0.5 km N of Napier Central*
Seaview Lodge *B&B Homestay*
Catherine & Evert Van Florenstein
5 Seaview Terrace, Napier

Tel (06) 835 0202 or 021 180 2101
cvulodge@xtra.co.nz
www.aseaviewlodge.co.nz

Double $140-$160 Single $100-$120
(Continental breakfast)
Visa MC accepted
1 King/Twin 1 King 1 Single (3 bdrm)
Bathrooms: 1 Ensuite 2 Private

Seaview Lodge is a lovingly renovated, spacious late Victorian home. This inner city, beachside bed and breakfast offers a warm welcome and spectacular views. Enjoy breakfast on the lower verandah while watching the waves break on the shore. In the evening relax in the spacious guest lounge or on the upstairs balcony. Situated across the road from the beach, hot pools and conference complex and a three minute stroll to the city centre makes Seaview Lodge an ideal place to explore Napier from.

Napier *1 km N of Napier*
East Towers *Homestay*
Dale & Alan East
121 Thompson Road, Napier

Tel (06) 834 0821 or 027 661 2806
Fax (06) 834 0824
alandales.easttowers@xtra.co.nz

Double $130 Single $75-$100 (Full breakfast)
Pet free home
1 Queen 2 Single (2 bdrm)
Bathrooms: 1 Private

Dale & Alan welcome you to East Towers. Quality accommodation for a couple or group of up to four people. Two bedrooms with queen, double or two king singles. Own lounge, tea making facilities, TV. Quiet area, stunning views, native birds, rambling gardens. Off-street parking. 15 minutes walk to Napier City. Ten minutes walk to Bluff Hill lookout. Arrive as guests, leave as friends.

Napier *1 km N of Napier Central*
Villa Vista B&B *B&B*
Tina Roulston & Tim Barker
22A France Road, Bluff Hill, Napier

Tel (06) 835 8770 or 027 435 7179
Fax (06) 835 8770
accommodation@villavista.net
www.villavista.net

Double $145-$160 Single $110-$125
(Special breakfast)
Children negotiable
Visa MC accepted
Children welcome
3 Queen 1 Single (3 bdrm)
Bathrooms: 3 Ensuite

A grand Edwardian villa blessed with fantastic views over the sea to Cape kidnappers from every large and private bedroom. Ensuite, air-conditioning, television, tea/coffee making facilities in each bedroom. Selection of continental and cooked breakfasts are served in the spacious dining room. Amicable children and pets residing. Welcome to Napier.

Hawkes Bay

Napier *3 km S of Napier*
Art Deco Te Awa *B&B*
Kay & Rod Goodspeed
19 Te Awa Avenue, Napier

Tel (06) 835 1618 or 027 211 0023
Fax (06) 835 3689
kaypat1@xtra.co.nz

Double $130-$150 (Full breakfast)
Pet free home
1 Queen 1 Double 1 Twin (3 bdrm)
Bathrooms: 1 Ensuite 1 Private

Art Deco Te Awa is spacious, executive quality accommodation. Ideal for visiting NZ's Art Deco City. Breakfast includes locally grown fresh fruit, home made muesli and preserves. Quality beds with fine linen. Our guest rooms include one spacious double room with ensuite bathroom, and one queen and one twin bedroom with private bathroom, all with heated towelrail, hairdryer and complimentary toiletries. Five minutes to city centre. Ten minutes to airport. Walking distance to the beach and 18 hole golf course. Easy access to Hawke's Bay's wineries.

Napier - Puketapu *25 km W of Napier*
Te Puna Farmstay *Farmstay*
Sarah & Tony
301 Apley Road, Puketapu RD 6, Napier 4021

Tel (06) 844 8753 or 021 165 8306
Fax (06) 844 8753
tonykeele@clear.net.nz
www.farmstaynapier.co.nz

Double $95-$125 **Single** $65-$75 (Full breakfast)
Dinner $25 by prior arrangement
Children and pets welcome
1 King/Twin 1 Queen 1 Single (3 bdrm)
Bathrooms: 1 Private 1 Guest share

Welcome to our small farm with sheep, cattle, various poultry and treecrops, dogs and friendly indoor cat. Set in lovely countryside yet only 20 minutes from Napier. Try dinner with our chemical free seasonal produce and our keen interest in local wines.

Napier *6 km SW of Napier*
Greenswood on the park *B&B Homestay*
Joan & Ted Skudder
395 Westminster Ave, Greenmeadows, Napier

Tel 0(6) 844 5354 or 027 420 9663
Fax (06) 844 5354
ejskud@xtra.co.nz

Double $100-$130 **Single** $75-$80 (Full breakfast)
Visa MC accepted
Pet free home
2 Queen 1 Twin (3 bdrm)
Bathrooms: 1 Ensuite 1 Guest share

We extend to you a warm welcome to our modern home and offer comfortable accommodation in a delightful setting, opposite Anderson park and within an easy ten minute drive to the Napier CBD. We are in a handy situation for wineries, tourist activities and shops. The bedrooms open out into our garden and swimming pool area for privacy and relaxation and all rooms have tea-making facilities. We enjoy meeting with our guests and helping to make your holiday memorable. Good off-street parking.

Napier *0.5 km N of Town Centre*
The Green House On The Hill *B&B*
Ruth Buss & Jeremy Hutt
18B Milton Oaks, Milton Road, Napier

Tel (06) 835 4475 or 021 187 3827
Fax (06) 835 4475
ruth@the-green-house.co.nz
www.the-green-house.co.nz

Double $120-$130 Single $90-$100 (Special breakfast)
Children negotiable
10% discount for 3 or more nights
Visa MC Eftpos accepted
Pet free home Children welcome
3 Queen (3 bdrm)
Bathrooms: 1 Ensuite 1 Guest share

The Green House on the Hill is a Vegetarian owned B&B, five minutes walk from the heart of Art Deco Napier, set in quiet woodland, with plenty of native birds and sea views! We offer a friendly, smokefree environment to our guests. Happy to cater for special diets, please ask when booking! Home made breads and preserves for breakfast. Our hillside home is built on several levels, unsuitable for wheelchairs. We have ample parking or can pick up from airport, buses etc. Email access available.

~

Napier - Hastings *11 km S of Napier - midway Napier/Hastings*
Copperfields *Cottage with Kitchen Apartment with Kitchen*
Pam & Richard Marshall
Pakowhai Road, Napier

Tel (06) 876 9710 or 021 212 9631
Fax (06) 876 9710   copperfields@copperfields.co.nz
www.copperfields.co.nz

Double $100-$130 Single $100-$110
(Continental breakfast provisions) Children under 12 $15
Extra guest $25pp   Dinner $35pp by arrangement
Separate self-contained flat, weekly rates negotiable
Visa MC accepted   Pets welcome
1 King/Twin 1 Double 3 Single (3 bdrm)
Bathrooms: 2 Private

Welcome to Copperfields lifestyle orchard within ten minutes of Napier, Hastings, Havelock North and Taradale - central for all tourist attractions. Guests stay in Glen Cottage, spacious two bedroom self-contained cottage attached to our house with private entrance. Large lounge with log fire, fully equipped kitchen/dining. Also private "Church Flat"-unique self-contained accommodation in a historic church and antiques, furniture, craft & art gallery. Family rates negotiable. Dogs welcome (conditions apply). Special three course dinner available by prior arrangement.

~

Hastings City *1 km N of Hastings Central*
McConchie Homestay *Homestay*
Barbara & Keila McConchie
115A Frederick Street, Hastings

Tel (06) 878 4576 or 021 078 5328
barbaramcconchie@xtra.co.nz
www.bnb.co.nz

Double $95 Single $60 (Full breakfast)
Children $25
Dinner $25 by arrangement
Visa MC accepted
Children welcome
1 Queen 2 Single (2 bdrm)
Bathrooms: 1 Guest share

Enjoy our peaceful garden back section, no traffic noises, yet central to Hastings City. My Siamese cat says 'Hi'. Nearby are parks, golf courses, wineries, orchards and the best icecream ever. Short trips take you to spectacular views, Cape Kidnapper's gannet colony, or Napier's art deco, hot pools, or just relaxing and enjoying great hospitality. Directions: from Wellington, arriving Hastings City, turn left into Eastbourne Street, right into Nelson Street, right into Frederick Street, cross Caroline Road. Driveway on right. 115A first house off driveway.

Hawkes Bay

Hastings *14 km NW of Hastings*

Grandvue Country Stay *B&B Homestay*
Dianne & Keith Taylor
Grandvue, 2596 State Highway 50, RD 5, Hastings

Tel (06) 879 6141 or 027 668 0252
Fax (06) 879 6988   homestays@xtra.co.nz
www.bnb.co.nz/grandvuehomestay.html

Double $95-$120 Single $65 (Full breakfast)
Children negotiable   Dinner $25   Visa MC accepted
Pet free home   Children welcome
1 King/Twin 1 Queen (2 bdrm)
Bathrooms: 1 Ensuite 1 Family share

Recently retired and moved from our farm but still the same genuine and caring hospitality. Enjoy with us in a relaxed atmosphere in our extensive private garden the wonderful views over vineyards in the Gimlett Gravels and Ngatarawa area, and to Havelock North hills in the distance.

Comfortable beds with firm mattresses make for a good nights sleep (electric blankets for winter warmth). Sit and chat when time allows over a generous breakfast cooked or continental with homemade preserves and goodies - inside or alfresco. Dinner available on request.

Our interests include tramping, bushwalks, gardening, travel and genealogy. Having travelled extensively we do enjoy meeting local and overseas visitors. Let us advise you on all the wonderful things to see and do while in our lovely Hawkes Bay. There are many wineries close by with restaurants, Safari trips to the gannets, Orchard tours, Trout fishing, Golf courses, Panoramic views from Te Mata Peak, Havelock North with boutique shops and cafés and Napier the Art Deco City of the world are just a few. We can arrange tours for you too, and also advise you on your travel through

NZ. After nearly 20 years of hosting we have an ever increasing circle of friends with many returning. Please read our guests comments on our B&B Book website. Guests are welcome to use the swimming pool in summer and the tennis court. Dianne is one of a few in NZ who has a certificate in Homestay Management. We look forward to meeting you, and our aim is to make your stay memorable. Arrive as a guest and leave as our friends. Easy access and plenty of parking.

Hastings *2 km NW of Hastings*
Woodbine Cottage *B&B Homestay*
Ngaire & Jim Shand
Woodbine Cottage, 1279 Louie Street, Hastings

Tel (06) 876 9388 or 029 876 9388
nshand@xtra.co.nz

Double $100 Single $80 (Continental breakfast)
Dinner $25pp by arrangement
Visa MC accepted
Not suitable for children
1 Queen 1 Twin (2 bdrm)
Bathrooms: 1 Guest share shower,spa bath,

Our home is set in half an acre of cottage garden on the Hastings boundary close to Havelock North. A tennis court for the energetic, and a spa bath to relax in at night. Hastings City centre is five minutes by car and Havelock North two minutes. Splash Planet, with its many water features and hot pools is only two minutes away. We look forward to your company and can assure you of a comfortable and relaxing stay. Not suitable for small children or pets.

Hastings *3 km S of Hastings*
Raureka *B&B Separate Suite*
Rosemary & Tim Ormond
26 Wellwood Road, RD 5, Hastings

Tel (06) 878 9715 or 021 104 5124
029 627 5887   Fax (06) 878 9728
r.t.ormond@xtra.co.nz

Double $100 Single $80
(Continental breakfast provisions)
Visa MC Amex accepted
Pet free home
Not suitable for children
1 Queen (1 bdrm)
Bathrooms: 1 Ensuite

Quietness and privacy are the main ingredients of staying at Raureka. The accommodation is situated separately from the house but close enough for visitors to feel welcome and cared for. Hosts Rosemary and Tim will provide help and advice for planning a successful day around this beautiful region. Fresh flowers, home-baking and complimetary wine are among the many treats ensuring your stay here is a home away from home. Relax by our pool or enjoy a walk amongst our unique 100 year old oak trees.

Hastings *12 km W of Hastings & Taradale*
Stitch-Hill Farm *B&B Homestay Farmstay*
Charles Trask
170 Taihape Road, RD 9, Hastings

Tel (06) 879 9456
Fax (06) 879 9806
cjtrask@xtra.co.nz

Double $110 Single $65 (Continental breakfast)
Dinner $35 by arrangement
Payments cash or NZ Cheque
2 King/Twin 2 King (2 bdrm)
Bathrooms: 2 Ensuite Bath available

Welcome to Hawkes Bay, the premier food and wine region of New Zealand. Stitch-Hill invites you to relax in the quiet countryside surrounded with panoramic views. Our prime location is just minutes from the city centres, wineries, attractions, fishing and tramping. In our comfortable smoke-free home we offer the very best hospitality. Your requirements our challenge. Your choice of two rooms, twin or super king in each, with ensuite. Stroll in our gardens,our acres, talk to Alpacas. Unsuitable for children and pets.

Hastings *11 km S of Hastings*

Imperial Orchards *B&B Homestay*
Vivian & Robert Dickson
68 Montana Road, Bridge Pa, Hastings

Tel (06) 879 4533 or 021 034 7424
Fax (06) 879 4337
homestay_bb@yahoo.co.nz

Double $100-$140 Single up to $80
(Special breakfast)
Visa MC accepted
Pets welcome
1 King/Twin 1 Queen 1 Single (3 bdrm)
Bathrooms: 1 Guest share

Welcome to a haven set in the heart of the Hawkes
Bay wine district, We offer superking/twin and double rooms, a guest living room with TV, fridge and
tea and coffee facilities. Enjoy a special breakfast including home-made preserves and fresh baking. Relax
with a glass of wine around the pool or on the terrace and enjoy the garden and rural views. We back onto
Hawkes Bay Golf Course with the Equestrian Centre, Hawkes Bay Car Club and aerodrome nearby.

Havelock North - Hastings *16 km S of Havelock North*

Wharehau *Homestay Farmstay*
Ros Phillips
1604 Middle Road, Havelock North,
RD 11, Hastings 4178

Tel (06) 877 4111 or 021 0271 9215
Fax (06) 877 4115
ros.phillips@xtra.co.nz
www.wharehau.co.nz

Double $120 Single $60 (Full breakfast)
Children half price   Dinner $30
Beach bach $130-$150
Visa MC accepted
2 Queen 2 Twin 1 Single (4 bdrm)
Bathrooms: 1 Guest share 1 Family share

Wharehau is in the beautiful Tuki Tuki valley -a great base for Hawkes Bay experience. Quarter of an
hour travel from Hastings or Havelock North in the midst of Wine Country. Close to golf courses,
Splash Planet, gannets and art deco. Or enjoy the peace and space on the farm. Weather permitting
a farm 4WD tour is available. Walks available locally. Trout fishing (local guide can be hired) in the
Tuki Tuki River. Comfortable beach bach at Kairakau Beach is available for rent.

Havelock North *1 km N of Havelock North*

Weldon Boutique Bed & Breakfast *Luxury B&B Homestay Boutique*
Pracilla Hay
98 Te Mata Road, Havelock North, Hawkes Bay

Tel (06) 877 7551 or 021 146 2495
Fax (06) 877 7051
pracilla@weldon.co.nz
www.weldon.co.nz

Double $150-$165 Single $110-$130
(Special breakfast)   Dinner $55
Visa MC accepted   Children welcome
2 Queen 1 Double 1 Twin (4 bdrm)
Bathrooms: 2 Private 2 Guest share
Upstairs shower/toilet. Downstairs bath/shower

Weldon is 100 years old and offers quality, comfort and peace with a romantic old world charm
and a French Provincial ambience. Accommodation is in spacious, elegantly appointed bedrooms,
furnished with period and antique furniture. TV & refreshments are provided and a lounge is available.
Fresh flowers, fine linen and fluffy towels reflect the luxury of fine accommodation. Breakfastis served
alfresco throughout summer and in a warm cosy dinning room in winter. 2 toy poodles (James and
Thomas) will greet you enthusiastically!

Havelock North *5 km N of Havelock North*
Totara Stables *B&B Homestay*
Sharon A. Bellaart & John W. Hayes
324 Te Mata - Mangateretere Road,
Havelock North, RD 2, Hastings

Tel (06) 877 8882 or 027 486 3910
Fax (06) 877 8891
bookings@totarastables.co.nz
www.totarastables.co.nz

Double $130-$150 Single $100 (Continental breakfast)
Visa MC accepted
Not suitable for children
1 King/Twin 1 Queen 1 Twin (3 bdrm)
Bathrooms: 1 Ensuite 1 Private

Offering a unique Bed & Breakfast experience in a lovingly restored 1910 villa. Take a peek into the museum of early pioneer farming displayed in the century old stables or marvel at the simplicity of early stationary motors. Feed the hand reared deer or arrange a ride in a classic 1951 Sunbeam Talbot motor car. We are located in the heart of the Te Mata wine region only minutes from the pictureque village of Havelock North. Non-smoking and not suitable for children under 12 years.

~

Havelock North *4 km E of Havelock North*
Borak Orchard B&B *B&B Homestay*
Doris & Mike Curkovic
433 Te Matamangateretere Road,
RD 12, Havelock North

Tel (06) 877 6699 or 027 408 2575
Fax (06) 877 6615
dcurkovic@clear.net.nz
www.borakbed-breakfast.co.nz

Double $130-$140 Single $100
(Continental breakfast)
Visa MC accepted
2 Queen 1 Single (2 bdrm)
Bathrooms: 1 Private

Welcome, and experience relaxing hospitality on our apple orchard five minutes from the centre of Havelock North. Minutes away from seven wineries, restaurants and boutique cheese factory. Activities include petanque on site, trout fishing over the fence, golf courses, beaches and bushwalks, Te Mata Peak and gannets at Cape Kidnappers. Special continental breakfast included. English, German & Croatian spoken. Our guest wing accommodates 1 to 5 people, one party bookings only. 10 minutes drive to Hastings 15 minutes to Napier.

~

Havelock North *3 km S of Havelock North*
Endsleigh Cottages/Muritai *Luxury Cottage with Kitchen*
3 Self Contained Cottages
Denis & Margie Hardy
22 Endsleigh Road, Havelock North

Tel (06) 877 7588 or 027 444 3800
Fax (06) 876 0275
endsleigh.cottages@xtra.co.nz
www.endsleigh.cottages.co.nz; www.muritai.co.nz

Double $100-$350 Single $100-$250
(Breakfast provisions first night)
Muritai Villa $1,300 per night - Sleeps 13 comfortably
Visa MC Amex accepted
Pet free home
Children welcome
4 Queen
Bathrooms: 3 Ensuite Cottages 3 baths Muritai 5 bathrooms

From Havelock North take Middle Road south for 3 km. Cross intersection with Gilpin & Iona Roads, then left into Endsleigh Road. Cottages on right.Muritai - 68 Duart Road Havelock North

Havelock North *0.5 km S of Havelock North*
The Loft Art Studio and Bed and Breakfast *B&B Homestay*

Iris & John
10 Woodford Heights, Havelock North, 4130

Tel (06) 877 5938 or 021 474 729
027 276 1238
Fax (06) 877 5938
theloft@hawkesbayaccommodation.com
www.hawkesbayaccommodation.com

Double $120-$240 (Special breakfast)
Dinner by arrangement in romantic setting $40pp
Visa MC Eftpos accepted
1 King 1 Queen (2 bdrm)
Bathrooms: 1 Ensuite 1 Private 1 Guest share
Bathroom is shared with 4 guests

Come and be pampered in our paradise. We, Iris and John, fourth generation New Zealanders will greet you with complimentary refreshments. Our architectural home has many unique features and superb views of Hawke's Bay. Use the courtyard and /or deck and enjoy your stay.. We will serve you a delicious breakfast. Have a luxurious soak in the spa bath, luxury linen.John is an artist with a house studio to visit. We are close to our best attractions and can advise you on excursions.

Havelock North *2 km NE of Havelock North*

Options *B&B Homestay*

Rosemary & Graham Duff
92 Simla Ave, Havelock North, 4130

Tel (06) 877 0257 or 027 653 7270
Fax (06) 877 0257
gr.duff@xtra.co.nz

Double $125-$125 Single $100-$100 (Full breakfast)
Children negotiable
Dinner by arrangement
Visa MC accepted
Pet free home
1 King 1 Queen 1 Twin 1 Single (3 bdrm)
Bathrooms: 1 Ensuite 1 Private

Options offers: Near Te Mata Peak; Views; five minutes to Havelock North village; Wine, gannets and Art Deco all within 30 minutes; Swimming pool and spa; Private sheltered patios; Pet free home; Wireless internet connection; Breakfast inside or outside depending on the weather; Optional evening meal at an additional cost; A home away from home.

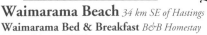

Waimarama Beach *34 km SE of Hastings*

Waimarama Bed & Breakfast *B&B Homestay*

Rita & Murray Webb
68 Harper Road, Waimarama, Hawkes Bay

Tel (06) 874 6795
Fax (06) 8746 795
rwebb@kol.co.nz

Double $110 Single $65 (Full breakfast)
Dinner $25pp
Visa MC accepted
2 Double (2 bdrm)
Bathrooms: 1 Guest share

Lovely beach for surfing, swimming, diving, boating, fishing etc. Bushwalks and golf course nearby. Situated only five minutes walk from beach with lovely views of sea, local park and farmland. Nearest town is Havelock North - 20 minutes drive, with Napier 40 minutes. We have two double rooms available and separate toilet and bathroom for guests. Cooked breakfast is offered and dinner is available if required. Please phone for reservations phone (06) 874 6795. No smoking inside please. Pets: one cat, one dog.

Otane *8 km N of Waipawa*
Ludlow Farmstay *B&B Farmstay Cottage with Kitchen*
Gwen & Neil White
53 Drumpeel Road, RD 1, Otane

Tel (06) 856 8348 or 027 441 8354
Fax (06) 856 8348
ludlow.white@xtra.co.nz
www. ludlowfarmstay.co.nz

Double $150 Single $90 (Full breakfast provisions)
Children $20-$30
Dinner $30 by arrangement
Children welcome
1 King/Twin 1 Queen 1 Double (3 bdrm)
Bathrooms: 1 Private

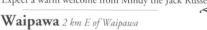

Ludlow is a 560 hectare extensive cropping farm, growing mainly wheat and barley, squash pumpkins, sweetcorn and peas with lamb and beef finishing. Our recently renovated shearers' cottage is situated in private surroundings, 50 metres from main homestead, with full kitchen facilities, BBQ, laundry, open fire and views over the Drumpeel Valley Farmland, with stock grazing alongside the cottage. Swimming pool and Astrograss tennis court available for guests' use. Farm tour available on request. Expect a warm welcome from Mindy the Jack Russell terrier.

Waipawa *2 km E of Waipawa*

Haowhenua *Farmstay*
Caroline & David Jefferd
77 Pourerere Road, RD 1, Waipawa 4170

Tel (06) 857 8241 or 027 268 4854
Fax (06) 857 8261
d.jefferd@xtra.co.nz

Double $120 Single $90 (Full breakfast)
Children half price
Dinner $30pp
Visa MC accepted
Children welcome
1 Queen 1 Twin (2 bdrm)
Bathrooms: 1 Ensuite 1 Family share

Welcome to Haowhenua. Country hospitality at its best in our spacious comfortable colonial home in a peaceful park-like setting with attractive gardens and swimming pool. Dinner is available on request. We are just 2 km from SH2 and within 30 minutes of Hawkes Bay's major attractions. Please phone for directions.

Waipawa *1 km NE of Waipawa*
Abbot Heights *B&B*

Jacqui & Charlie Hutchison
6 Parkland Drive, Waipawa

Tel 027 4330146 or (06) 857 8585
Fax (06) 857 8580
chipper@paradise.net.nz

Double $150 Single $100
(Continental breakfast)
Not suitable for children
2 Queen (2 bdrm)
Bathrooms: 1 Ensuite 1 Private

Welcome to Parkland Drive! Your relaxed, easy going hosts (and their cat Myrtle) enjoy meeting all new guests at their stunning modern manor set in 12 acres of private gardens. Facilities include a splendid private lounge, luxury goose down duvets, plush bathrobes, top quality linen, spa bath and electric blankets. New gym, indoor heated pool, golf, vineyard, hot-air ballooning, art gallery, theatre, museum, cafés and antique shops are only five minutes away. Golden sandy beaches, tramping, hunting and fishing are within 30 minutes.

Waipukurau *2 km S of Waipukurau*

Woburn Homestead *Luxury B&B*

Heatha Edwards

216 Hatuma Road, RD 1, Waipukurau

Tel (06) 858 8880 or 027 452 9112
(06) 858 9668
heatha.harcourts@xtra.co.nz
www.woburnhomestead.co.nz

Double $250-$300 Single up to $150 (Special breakfast)
Dinner available by prior arrangement
Visa MC accepted
Not suitable for children
2 Queen 2 Twin (3 bdrm)
Bathrooms: 3 Ensuite

Welcome to Woburn Homestead, an exquisite seven bedroom home with six bathrooms, built in 1893 and listed Historic Places Trust.Heatha and Philip adore sharing their home, which also has 2 teenage boys who are usually out and about, and 3 tubby Labradors, who relentlessly patrol the grounds for any stray snacks or crumbs!

We are delighted to offer you a Colonial New Zealand experience, with antique china, bone handled cutlery and authentic furnishings to allow you to step back in time to enjoy Victorian country living on a grand scale.Each Suite has a new luxury ensuite (with Satin Jet showers and huge claw foot tubs) plus a fabulous bed with 600 thread count Egyptian cotton sheets in a generous room with country views.

You'll be warmly welcomed with fresh flowers, glossy magazines, bottled mineral water and gourmet tea or coffee served in the finest antique porcelain delivered to your room if required.

There are several private lounges , formal Victorian dining room, new in ground pool and croquet lawns at your disposal, a lavish feast for a breakfast menu, and for anything else, please just ask.We hope you enjoy being thoroughly spoiled in opulent surroundings.

Waipukurau *20 km S of Waipukurau*

Hinerangi Station *Farmstay Cottage with Kitchen*

Caroline & Dan von Dadelszen
615 Hinerangi Road, RD 1, Waipukurau

Tel (06) 855 8273 Fax (06) 855 8273
caroline@hinerangi.co.nz
www.hinerangi.co.nz

Double $150 Single $90 (Full breakfast)
Children $30 Dinner $35pp
Self-contained cottage $120 double, extra guests $40pp
Children and pets welcome
1 King/Twin 2 Queen 3 Single (4 bdrm)
Bathrooms: 2 Private
Homestead: shower & bath Cottage: shower & bath

Hinerangi Station is a 2500 acre sheep, cattle and deer station set in the rolling hills of Central Hawkes Bay. Our spacious 1920 homestead was designed by Louis Hay of Napier Art Deco fame. It has a full sized billiard table, and tennis court and swimming pool in the garden. Guests have their own entrance. We have a terrier and cat."The Cookhouse", a renovated 100 year old cottage offers self-contained accommodation for couples and families. Children free if staying more than one night.

~

Waipukurau *4.5 km S of Waipukurau*

Pukeora Vineyard Cottage *Cottage with Kitchen*

Kate Norman
Pukeora Estate, 208 Pukeora Scenic Road,
RD 1 Waipukurau (off SH2 south of Waipukurau)

Tel (06) 858 9339 or 021 205 1307
021 701 606   Fax (06) 858 6070
cottage@pukeora.com
www.pukeora.com

Double $110 Single $80 (Continental breakfast)
Children $25
Visa MC accepted
1 Queen 1 Double 2 Twin 1 Single (3 bdrm)
Bathrooms: 1 Private

Enjoy exclusive hire of our charming, hilltop cottage which boasts stunning views over the vineyard, river, plains and beyond. The spacious 1920's cottage, with rimu floors, sunny verandah, and open plan lounge/kitchen with log fire, is a private annex to our house. Pukeora Estate, set on 86 acres, is a five hectare vineyard, boutique winery and functions venue. Your hosts Kate and Max, with daughters Jessica (age five) and Marika (age four), and three cats, welcome you. Endless outside space for children. Wine tasting/sales available.

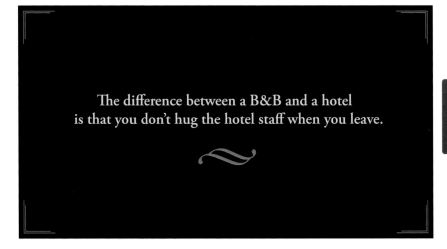
The difference between a B&B and a hotel
is that you don't hug the hotel staff when you leave.

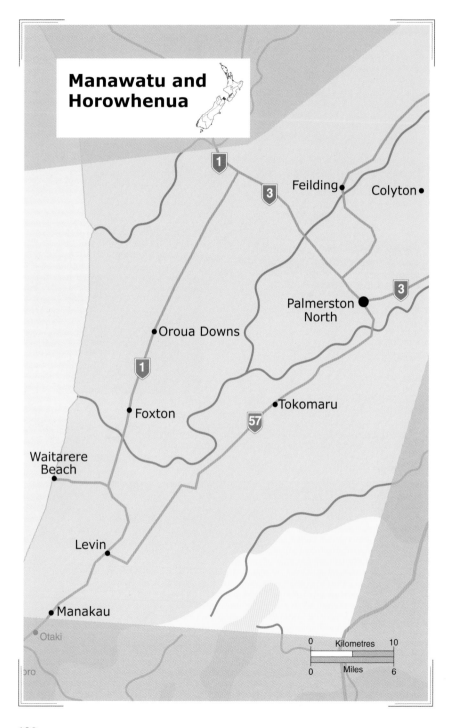

Manawatu and Horowhenua

Feilding *0.25 km N of Feilding Central*

Avoca Homestay *Homestay*
Margaret Hickmott
12 Freyberg Street, Feilding

Tel (06) 323 4699
margh-avoca@inspire.net.nz

Double $95 **Single** $70 (Full breakfast)
Dinner $25 by arrangement
1 Queen 2 Twin (2 bdrm)
Bathrooms: 1 Ensuite 1 Family share

Enjoy a break in friendly Feilding, 13 times winner of New Zealand's Most Beautiful Town Award. You are assured of a warm welcome and an enjoyable stay in a comfortable smoke-free home set in an attractive garden with mature trees and a colourful shrubbery. Off-street parking is provided for your vehicle. The main bedroom has a queen-size bed, ensuite and an outside entrance for your sole use. We are within easy walking distance of the town centre and well situated for the Manfield Park complex.

Palmerston North *3 km NW of Palmerston North Centre*

Bradgate *B&B Homestay*
Frances
3 Celtic Court, Roslyn

Tel (06) 355 5956
vige@value.net.nz

Double $80 **Single** $40-$50
(Full breakfast)
Dinner $25
1 Queen 1 Double 1 Twin (3 bdrm)
Bathrooms: 1 Guest share

Welcome to Bradgate, a four bedroomed brick townhouse located in a quiet cul-de-sac. 30 years ago my husband and I came to New Zealand. We owned a restaurant by Virginia Lake in Wanganui and after retiring we ran a bed & breakfast overlooking the river. Having recently shifted to Palmerston North it was time to open our home again as a bed & breakfast. I have an energetic labrador named Crunchy. I enjoy playing golf, gardening and meeting people. Non-smoking house, dinner by arrangement.

Palmerston North *3 km W of Palmerston North*

Andellen *Farmstay Separate Suite*
Kay & Warren Nitschke
580 Kairanga Bunnythorpe Road,
RD 8, Palmerston North

Tel (06) 355 4155 or 027 244 1393
021 900 226   Fax (06) 355 4155
kw@inspire.net.nz

Double $90-$120 **Single** $45-$70
(Continental breakfast) Children $20
Dinner $30pp by arrangement
Visa MC accepted
Children and pets welcome
1 King 2 Queen 2 Single (3 bdrm)
Bathrooms: 1 Ensuite 1 Private spa bath

Kay, Warren and Libby (11 years) welcome you to Andellen, a lovely spacious modern homestead set on 65 acres with extensive lawn and garden. We offer guests privacy and the opportunity to relax in an elegant, tranquil and private country setting. Own semi-detached accomodation incl. lounge, TV and spa bath. Seasonal farm activities available. Children very welcome. City 3km away. We have a pet cat and dog. Dinner by arrangement.

Palmerston North *5.5 km E of City Centre*

Clairemont *B&B*
Joy & Dick Archer
10 James Line, RD 10, Palmerston North

Tel (06) 357 5508
Fax (06) 357 5501
clairemont@inspire.net.nz

Double $80 Single $50 (Continental breakfast)
1 Double 1 Twin (2 bdrm)
Bathrooms: 1 Guest share

Welcome to Clairemont. We are a rural spot within the city boundary, plenty of trees and a quite extensive garden. On our 1 ¼ acres we keep a few sheep, silky bantams, and our little dog Toby. We are handy to river walks, golf course, and shops are a few minutes away. We have a cosy, spacious family home we would like to share with you. Our interests are walking, gardening, model engineering and barbershop singing. Good off-street parking. Supper provided.

Palmerston North *13 km E of Palmerston North*

Country Lane Homestay *B&B Homestay*
Fay & Allan Hutchinson
52 Orrs Road, RD 1 Aokautere, Palmerston North

Tel (06) 326 8529 or 027 448 5833
Fax (06) 326 9216
countrylane@xtra.co.nz

Double $100-$140 Single $75-$95 (Full breakfast)
Dinner $25-$30
Not suitable for children
1 King/Twin 1 King 1 Queen 1 Double 1 Single (3 bdrm)
Bathrooms: 1 Ensuite 2 Private 1 Family share

Luxury country living, short distance from Palmerston North, near Manawatu Gorge, below wind farm. 10 km from Pacific College and 2 km from Equestrian Centre. Excellent stop over en route to/from Wellington or East Coast. Our home is newly decorated, with antiques in a country traditional style surrounded by our garden. Sawmill on the property, coloured sheep, horses and calves. Manawatu River borders our property. It is our pleasure to provide home-cooked meals with some local produce. Directions: please phone. A brochure with map is available.

Palmerston North *5 km SW of Central Palmerston North*

Udys on Anders *B&B Apartment with Kitchen*
Glenda & Tim Udy
52 Anders Road, Palmerston North

Tel (06) 354 1722 or 027 440 9299
kiwitim@clear.net.nz
www.udysonanders.co.nz

Double $120 Single $100 (Full breakfast)
Children $20
Dinner negotiable
Visa MC accepted
Children welcome
1 Queen 1 Double (1 bdrm)
Bathrooms: 1 Ensuite

We offer superior accommodation. An elegantly furnished self-contained apartment, own lounge and full kitchen. Quiet country location, huge lawn, edge of town, seven minutes to CBD. Plexipave tennis court, beautiful mediterranean courtyard and large games room for our guests to make use of. Cleanliness, attention to detail and great hospitality are our priorities. We are well travelled and love meeting people. Enjoy your own space or get to know us. So... come, relax, enjoy. Tariff includes full breakfast. Apartment is smoke-free. Dinner by arrangement.

Tokomaru *19 km S of Palmerston North*
Hi-Da-Way Lodge *Cottage with Kitchen*
Sue & Trevor Palmer
21 Albert Road, RD 4, Palmerston North

Tel (06) 329 8731
Fax (06) 329 8732
hi-da-way-lodge@xtra.co.nz

Double $120-$195 Single $95
(Continental breakfast)
Dinner by arrangement
Cottage $95-$195
1 Double 2 Single (2 bdrm)
Bathrooms: 1 Private

Looking for something unique? Then Hi-Da-Way
Lodge extends a warm welcome. The fully self-contained rustic cabin is set in a peaceful garden setting surrounded by trees and has its own spa, TV, video and fridge/freezer. Guests may enjoy a shared swimming pool or BBQ, or just meander around our 6.5 hectare property. Situated just ten minutes from Massey University and 1.5 hours from Wellington off State Highway 57. We have two boys still at home and a pet dog who enjoys meeting people. Treat yourself.

Waitarere Beach *14 km NW of Levin*
Dunes *B&B Homestay*
Robyn & Grant Powell
10 Ngati Huia Place, Waitarere Beach 5500

Tel (06) 368 6246 or 027 285 3643
sand.dunes@xtra.co.nz
http://waitarere.dunes.googlepages.com

Double $115 Single $90
(Continental breakfast)
Dinner $30
Visa MC accepted
2 Queen (2 bdrm)
Bathrooms: 2 Ensuite

Robyn & Grant Powell welcome you to our new
absolute beachfront retreat. Enjoy beach walks and magnificent views of Kapiti and Mounts Taranaki and Ruapehu. We offer two queen-size bedrooms with own private entrance and deck areas, ensuites, own living areas with TV, tea/coffee making facilities - continental breakfast provided. Situated 14 km northwest of Levin, approximately one and a half hours from Wellington and 35 minutes from Palmerston North. Laundry facilities, off-street parking, non-smoking. Dinner by arrangement.

Levin *1 km NE of Levin*
Fantails *Self-contained B&B Cottages with Kitchen*
Heather Watson
40 MacArthur Street, Levin

Tel (06) 368 9011   Fax (06) 368 9279
fantails@xtra.co.nz
www.fantails.co.nz

Double $125-$150 Single $95-$125 (Special breakfast)
Children negotiable   Dinner by arrangement
Self-contained cottages $110-$150
Visa MC accepted
Children and pets welcome
1 King 2 Queen 1 Twin 4 Single (4 bdrm)
Bathrooms: 3 Ensuite 1 Private

Fantails is a lovely haven in a hectic world something different'beautiful themed gardens of two acres.
Very comfortable beds, quiet surroundings but beautiful native bird song in the morning. Organic food, home baking in a totally relaxing enviroment. Lovely self-contained cottages (home away from home) laundry facilities. Security. Simply the best value say returning guests plus the Golfers of course come back every year to play on our excellent local courses. End your day in the Sauna or Lavender Massage bath.

Levin *5 km S of Levin*

Ardo Highland Haven *B&B Farmstay*

Malcolm & Rachel Phillips
170 McLeavey Road, RD 20, Levin

Tel (06) 368 7080 or 021 506 990
Fax (06) 368 7080
info@ardohighlandhaven.co.nz
www.ardohighlandhaven.co.nz

Double $120 Single $90 (Full breakfast)
Dinner by arrangement
Visa MC accepted
1 Queen 1 Twin 1 Single (3 bdrm)
Bathrooms: 1 Private We take one booking only.

Travelling to or from Wellington? Our country home on ten acres is easy to find. A private, peaceful haven perfect for a good night's sleep, with highland cattle and coloured sheep to pamper. We offer refreshments on arrival and dinner by arrangement. Laundry facilities are available. After dairy farming for 25 years we are enjoying our change of lifestyle and look forward to meeting you. Our family have left home, just Mandy, our Australian Terrier, and Lola, our grey tabby cat, to greet you.

Levin *3 km NE of Levin*

Annandale Manor *B&B & Fejoa Orchard*

Malcolm & Rebecca
108 Arapaepae Road, SH 57, Levin, 5510

Tel 0800 201 712 or (06) 368 5476
Fax (06) 368 5473
annandalemanor@xtra.co.nz
www.annandalemanor.co.nz

Double $110-$135 Single $100-$120 (Full breakfast)
Children 12 years and under half price
Dinner - two course $35pp
Children and pets welcome by arrangement
1 Queen 1 Double 1 Twin (3 bdrm)
Bathrooms: 1 Guest share

Look no further you will find it here. Colonial elegance infused with peace, serenity and abundant hospitality. Prepare to be charmed by the grand old lady that is Annandale Manor. The gardens and orchard with bird song and ambience. You will find activities to energise or slumber to revitalise, with hunting and rafting to beaches and bush walks. The Horowhenua experience that you will not want to miss. Its all here now just waiting for you.

Please let us know
how you enjoyed your B&B experience.
Ask your host for a comment form
or leave a comment on www.bnb.co.nz

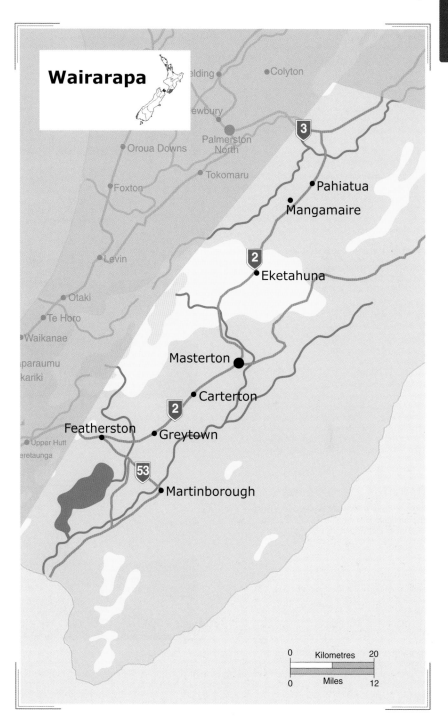

Pahiatua - Mangamaire *8 km S of Pahiatua*

Lizzie's Country Bed & Breakfast *B&B Countrystay Separate Suite Apartment with Kitchen*

Lizzie & Craig Udy
86 Mangamaire Road, Mangamaire, Pahiatua

Tel (06) 376 7367 or 027 204 2648
Fax (06) 376 7367
craigandlizudy@inspire.net.nz
www.bnb.co.nz/hosts/lizzies.html

Double $120 **Single** $120 (Full breakfast provisions)
Children $10 (Babies Free)   Extra adult $30
Visa MC accepted
Pet free home Children welcome
1 King 1 Twin (2 bdrm)
Bathrooms: 1 Private

Lizzie & Craig welcome you to our friendly home. Your tastefully decorated accommodation is totally private, self contained, spacious and even includes a private movie theatre. We have native gardens, outdoor settings and a book exchange. The award winning local café is a popular place to dine. By day enjoy the Manawatu and Wairarapa districts and by night enjoy the ambience of your wonderful accommodation. We are a convenient stopover halfway between Wellington and Hawkes Bay and only two minutes drive off State Highway 2.

~

Eketahuna *45 km N of Masterton*

Brookfields Lodge *B&B*

Terry & Corinna Carew
31 Alfredton Road, Eketahuna, 4900

Tel (06) 375 8686
terry@brookfieldslodge.co.nz
www.brookfieldslodge.co.nz

Double $100 **Single** $80 (Full breakfast)
Visa MC Eftpos accepted
Children welcome
3 Queen (3 bdrm)
Bathrooms: 3 Ensuite

Brookfields - more than just a restaurant. Welcome to our bed and breakfast where you're always treated as a new friend. With children of our own we know the rigors of traveling but let us make your stay more relaxed. Stay in our newly renovated en suite accommodation and try our licensed restaurant. Visit Mount Bruce, home of the Kiwi, the famous Tui Brewery or just enjoy fishing, hunting, tramping or a golfing weekend. You'll be surprised at how much there is to do around Eketahuna.

~

Masterton *3 km W of Masterton*

Harefield *B&B Farmstay Cottage with Kitchen*

Marion Ahearn
147 Upper Plain Road, Masterton

Tel (06) 377 4070
Fax (06) 377 4070

Double $80 **Single** $45-$50 (Full breakfast)
Children half price
Dinner $20 by arrangement
Self-contained flat for 2 $60
Children welcome
1 Double 1 Single (1 bdrm)
Bathrooms: 1 Private

A warm welcome awaits you at Harefield, a small farmlet on the edge of town. A quiet country garden surrounds the cedar house and self-contained flat. The flat has one bedroom with double and single beds. Two divan beds in living area. Self-cater or have breakfast in our warm dining room. Convenient for restaurants, showgrounds, vineyards, schools, tramping. 1.5 hour drive to Picton Ferry. We enjoy meeting people, aviation, travel, reading, art, farming and tramping. Baby facilities available. Smoke-free.

Masterton *10 km W of Masterton*
Tidsfordriv *B&B Homestay*
Glenys Hansen
54 Cootes Road, Matahiwi RD 8, Masterton

Tel (06) 378 9967
Fax (06) 378 9957
ghansen@contact.net.nz

Double $90-$95 Single $60 (Full breakfast)
Children half price
Dinner $25 by arrangement includes pre-dinner drink
Visa MC accepted
Children welcome
1 Queen 2 Single (2 bdrm)
Bathrooms: 1 Private

A warm welcome awaits you at Tidsfordriv - a 64 acre farmlet - seven kilometres off the main bypass route. Enjoy the comforts of a modern home set in parklike surroundings with large gardens & lakes. Bird watch with ease and enjoy the peaceful serenity of this 'Rural Retreat'. Glenys invites you to join her for dinner and enjoy good conversation about gardening, conservation and travel. Two friendly dogs are the outdoor pets. Enjoy visits to Pukaha Mount Bruce Wildlife Centre, and other Wairarapa attractions.

Masterton *1 km E of Masterton*
Mas des Saules *Homestay*
Mary & Steve Blakemore
9A Pokohiwi Road, Homebush, Masterton

Tel (06) 377 2577 or (027) 620 8728
Fax (06) 377 2578
mas-des-saules@wise.net.nz

Double $110 Single $75 (Full breakfast)
Children $40
Dinner $35
Visa MC accepted
Children and pets welcome
2 Queen (2 bdrm)
Bathrooms: 1 Guest share

H idden down a tranquil country lane, discover our authentic French Provencal farmhouse with its landscaped garden, stream, and courtyard. Swimming and trout fishing in nearby river. Our children have departed, leaving us with a cat, small dog, and cattle on our small farm. Guest lounge and bathroom with bath and shower. Open fire and central heating. Enjoy farmhouse cooking with fresh vegetables from our large country garden, barbecues and picnic lunches. We are a well-travelled couple who enjoy helping guests discover the unspoilt Wairarapa.

Masterton *1 km W of Masterton Urban Boundary*
Llandaff *B&B Farmstay*
Elizabeth & Robin Dunlop
161 Upper Plain Road Masterton

Tel (06) 378 6628 or 021 359 562
Fax (06) 378 6628
llandaff@xtra.co.nz
www.wairarapa.co.nz/llandaff

Double $110-$120 Single $70-$70 (Full breakfast)
Children $25   Dinner $30
Children welcome
1 King 2 Queen 1 Double 1 Twin (5 bdrm)
Bathrooms: 1 Ensuite with shower only 2 Guest share

E legantly restored, the homestead boasts beautiful native NZ timbers throughout, wood panelled rooms, polished floors, old pull-handle toilets, a 'coffin' bath, open fireplaces and cosy woodburning kitchen stove. Explore the historic hayloft and stables, washhouse, dunny, produce shed, gardener's shed, pavilion and dove cote. See the vintage farm machinery. Relax in the majestic garden beneath 120 year old trees, or wander the farm and feed the animals. Bike riding, croquet and petanque are available to guests. Enjoy a cooked breakfast with dinner available on request.

Masterton *8 km E of Masterton*

Vista Homestay *B&B Homestay*

Carol & Quenten Hansen

339B Te Ore Ore Settlement Road, RD 6, Masterton

Tel (06) 370 8919 or 027 360 6499
Fax (06) 370 8919
cqhansen@xtra.co.nz

Double $90-$95 Single $60 (Continental breakfast)
Children $25
Dinner $25pp includes pre-dinner drink
Visa MC accepted
Pet free home
Children welcome
1 Queen 2 Single (2 bdrm)
Bathrooms: 1 Private 1 party per booking

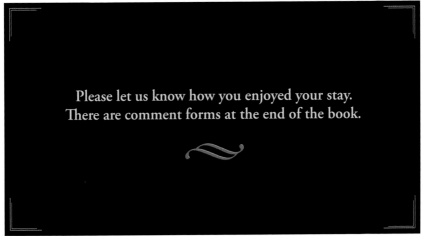

More than just stunning views, Vista Homestay is situated in a tranquil environment where you will be welcomed by the smell of fresh flowers home baking and good coffee. Our modern home and garden are for you to enjoy along with a private spa pool. To make your visit memorable we would love you to join us for dinner.

Please let us know how you enjoyed your stay.
There are comment forms at the end of the book.

Carterton *1 km N of Carterton*

Homecroft *B&B*

Christine & Neil Stewart
Somerset Road, RD 2, Carterton

Tel (06) 379 5959
homecroft@xtra.co.nz

Double $90-$105 Single $60 (Full breakfast)
Dinner $30pp by arrangement
1 Queen 1 Double 1 Twin (3 bdrm)
Bathrooms: 1 Ensuite 1 Private

Homecroft is surrounded by our country garden. Handy to the vineyards, crafts, antiques, and golf courses of the Wairarapa. Wellington and the inter-island ferry are 90 minutes away. Guest accommodation is in a separate wing of the house with small lounge, the bedrooms open onto a deck. The double room with ensuite, The Croft, is separate from the house. All bedrooms overlook the garden. A leisurely breakfast at Homecroft is an enjoyable experience. We look forward to making your stay with us happy and relaxing.

Martinborough *1 km SW of Martinborough*
Ross Glyn *Homestay*
Kenneth & Odette Trigg
1 Grey Street, Martinborough

Tel (06) 306 9967
Fax (06) 306 8267
rossglyn1@hotmail.com

Double $95 Single $65 (Full breakfast)
Dinner from $25 by arrangement
Children welcome
1 Double 2 Single (2 bdrm)
Bathrooms: 1 Private 1 Guest share

Our home nestles in over two acres of landscaped gardens which includes a rose garden, orchard, Japanese garden and we are surrounded by vineyards. Both our guestrooms have french doors opening onto a sunny deck with private access. Guests are welcome to relax with us and our spoilt cat in our large cosy (woodburner heated) lounge. Breakfast includes fresh croissants, home-made jams, jellies and preserved fruit. Cooked breakfast on request and dinner by arrangement.

Martinborough *0.5 km NW of Martinborough*
Oak House *B&B*
Polly & Chris Buring
45 Kitchener Street, Martinborough

Tel (06) 306 9198 Fax (06) 306 8198
chrispolly.oakhouse@xtra.co.nz
http://buringswines.co.nz

Double $120-$130 Single $60 (Special breakfast)
Children by arrangement
Dinner by arrangement
Visa MC accepted
Children welcome
2 Queen 2 Single (3 bdrm)
Bathrooms: 1 Ensuite 1 Guest share

Our characterful 80 year old Californian bungalow offers gracious accommodation. Our spacious lounge provides a relaxed setting for sampling winemaker Chris's wonderful products. Our guest wing has its own entrance, bathroom (large bath and shower) and separate toilet. Our new bedroom has ensuite facilities. Bedrooms enjoy afternoon sun and garden views. Breakfast features fresh croissants, home-preserved local fruits and conserves. Creative cook Polly matches delicious dishes (often local game) with Chris's great wines. Tour our onsite winery with Chris. Meet our multi-talented cats.

Martinborough *0.5 km N of Martinborough Central*
Beatson's of Martinborough *B&B Guest House*
Karin Beatson & John Cooper
9A Cologne Street, Martinborough, Wairarapa

Tel (06) 306 8242 or 027 449 9827
Fax (06) 306 8243
beatsons@wise.net.nz
www.beatsons.co.nz

Double $150 Single $120 (Full breakfast)
Dinner by arrangement
Visa MC accepted
4 King/Twin 4 Queen (8 bdrm)
Bathrooms: 8 Ensuite

Beatsons offer a friendly and relaxed stay. Harrington and Cologne are restored villas operated as hosted guest houses for your year round comfort. Individually decorated spacious bedrooms with ensuites feature. In the living rooms, french doors open onto verandahs overlooking the gardens. Full country breakfasts use local produce, home-made breads and preserves. Dinner and functions by arrangement. Beatson's are just five minutes walk from Martinborough Square with its cafés and restaurants. Close to great wineries.

Martinborough *1 km W of Martinborough*
The Old Manse *B&B Homestay*
Sandra & John Hargrave
Corner Grey & Roberts Streets, Martinborough

Tel (06) 306 8599 or 0800 399 229
Fax (06) 306 8540
info@oldmanse.co.nz
www.oldmanse.co.nz

Double $170-$190 (Full breakfast)
Visa MC Diners Amex Eftpos accepted
Not suitable for children
5 Queen 1 Twin (6 bdrm)
Bathrooms: 6 Ensuite

In the heart of the wine district, a beautifully restored Presbyterian Manse, built 1876, has been transformed into a boutique homestay. Spacious, relaxed accommodation in a quiet, peaceful setting. one twin, five queen-size bedrooms all with their own ensuites. All day sun. Off-street parking, open fireplace. Amenities include spa pool, petanque, billiards. Enjoy breakfast or wine overlooking vineyard. Walking distance to Martinborough Square with selection of excellent restaurants. Close to vineyards, antique and craft shops, adventure quad bikes and golf courses. Qualmark 4+

Martinborough *1 km S of Martinbrough Village Square*
The Martinborough Connection *B&B*
David & Lorraine Murray
80 Jellicoe Street, Martinborough, 5711

Tel (06) 306 9708 or 027 438 1581
Fax (06) 306 9706
martinboroughconnection@xtra.co.nz
www.martinboroughconnection.co.nz

Double $130-$130 Single $110-$110 (Full breakfast)
Children in room with extra bed $15
Additional adult in room with extra bed $30
Visa MC Eftpos accepted   Pet free home
4 Queen 1 Single (4 bdrm)
Bathrooms: 4 Ensuite

Bed & breakfast accommodation situated within the Martinborough wine village. Originally built in 1889 the property has been fully restored retaining its original character. Open your bedroom door to a sunny verandah and garden. Start the day with a scrumptious breakfast, before visiting Martinboroughs wineries,or Cape Palliser with its spectacular coastline, lighthouse & furseal colony. Relax at the end of the day in the guest lounge with its open fire or outside in the lovely gardens. We look forward to hosting you.

If you need any information ask your hosts,
they are your own personal travel agent and guide.

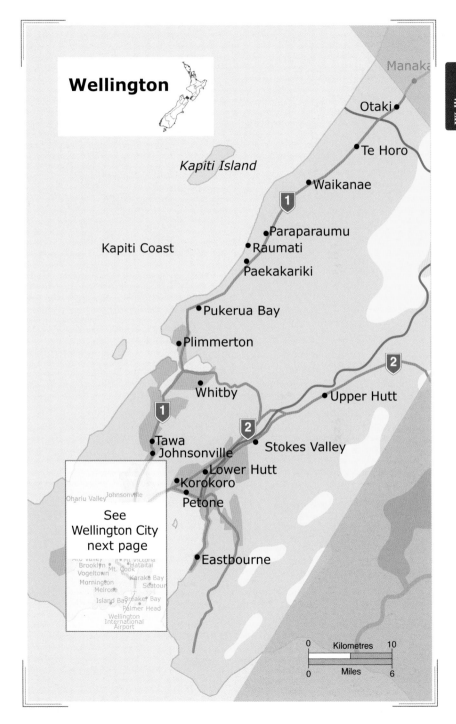

Wellington

Manak

Otaki

Te Horo

Kapiti Island

Waikanae

Kapiti Coast

Paraparaumu

Raumati

Paekakariki

Pukerua Bay

Plimmerton

Whitby

Upper Hutt

Tawa

Johnsonville

Stokes Valley

Lower Hutt

Korokoro

See Wellington City next page

Ohariu Valley   Johnsonville

Petone

 Aro Valley   Mt. Victoria
Brooklyn   Hataitai
Vogeltown   Mt. Cook
Mornington   Karaka Bay
Melrose   Seatoun
Island Bay Breaker Bay
Palmer Head
Wellington
International
Airport

Eastbourne

0   Kilometres   10

0   Miles   6

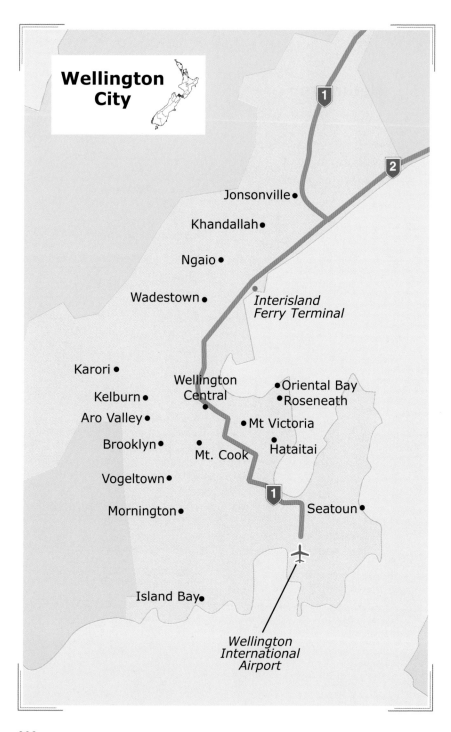

Wellington City

1

2

Jonsonville●

Khandallah●

Ngaio ●

Wadestown●

Interisland Ferry Terminal

Karori ●

Kelburn●

Wellington Central●

●Oriental Bay
●Roseneath

Aro Valley●

●Mt Victoria

Brooklyn●

●Mt. Cook

Hataitai●

Vogeltown●

1

Mornington●

Seatoun●

Island Bay●

Wellington International Airport

Te Horo *7 km N of Waikanae*

Pateke Lagoons Wetlands *B&B Farmstay*
Peter & Adrienne Dale
152 Te Hapua Road, Te Horo, RD 1, Kapiti Coast

Tel (06) 364 2222 or 027 543 9661
Fax (06) 364 2214
peter@pateke-lagoons.co.nz
www.pateke-lagoons.co.nz

Double $215 Single $195 (Special breakfast)
Dinner $65 including wine
Visa MC accepted
Not suitable for children
2 Queen 1 Single (2 bdrm)
Bathrooms: 2 Ensuite 1 Private wheelchair bathroom

Pateke Lagoons overlooks a private 50 acre wetland and waterfowl refuge on the Kapiti Coast. It offers peace and quiet in tranquil rural surroundings. Two guest rooms, each with ensuite and private courtyard. Large lounge with wildfowl and wetland ecology library. Beautiful views of farmland, sea and wetland. Easy 30 minute walking tracks through native bush and wetland. Fresh seafood is our specialty with garden fresh vegetables. Special breakfast using local products. Feed the horses and pet the cats. Open wetlands are unsuitable for children.

Waikanae Beach *5 km W of Waikanae*

Konini Cottage & Homestead *Homestay Cottage with Kitchen*
Maggie & Bob Smith
26 Konini Crescent, Waikanae Beach, Kapiti Coast

Tel (04) 904 6610 or 027 260 6492
Fax (04) 904 6610
konini@paradise.net.nz
www.konini.co.nz

Double $130-$150 (Breakfast by arrangement)
Children under 13 $10
Extra adult $20
Cafés/restaurants within walking distance
Visa MC Amex accepted   Children welcome
2 Queen 2 Single (3 bdrm)
Bathrooms: 2 Private

Escape to the Coast. Many say "If only we had known we would have stayed longer". Set in an acre of tranquil grounds, the Lockwood Cottage & Homestead offer a restful haven only 300 metres from the beach and border the Golf Links. Furnished and kept to the highest standard your stay will be memorable. Either self-cater or traditional B&B. Directions: Turn off SH1 at traffic lights to beach, 4 km to old service station, take right fork, then first right, 1 km to Konini Crescent.

Waikanae *1 km E of Waikanae*

Country Patch *Apartment with Kitchen Cottage with Kitchen*
Sue & Brian Wilson
18 Kea Street, Waikanae

Tel (04) 293 5165 or 027 457 8421
027 296 3716
Fax (04) 293 5164
stay@countrypatch.co.nz
www.countrypatch.co.nz

Double $150-$220 (Full breakfast provisions)
Children $25
Visa MC accepted
Children welcome
2 King/Twin 1 Queen 2 Single (3 bdrm)
Bathrooms: 3 Ensuite

Two delightful self-contained accommodation sites. Country patch studio with its own entrance and deck has a queen bed with ensuite and twin beds on the mezzanine floor of the kitchen lounge. Country patch villa has an open fire and a large verandah with magic views. It is wheelchair accessible and the two bedrooms (each with ensuite) have king beds that unzip to twin. We warmly invite you to share our patch of the country.

Wellington

Waikanae *6 km E of Waikanae*

RiverStone *B&B Cottage with Kitchen*

Paul & Eppie Murton
111 Ngatiawa Road, Waikanae

Tel (04) 293 1936
Fax (04) 293 1936
riverstone@paradise.net.nz
www.riverstone.co.nz

Double $100-$120 Single $70 (Full breakfast)
Children $45
Visa MC accepted
1 Queen 1 Twin (2 bdrm)
Bathrooms: 1 Private

Birdsong, the sound of the river and complete privacy. Peace and quiet with a scrumptious breakfast and comfortable accommodation. Riverstone has scenic views a garden with river walks and local pottery and café. Waikanae, five minutes by car, has cafés, shops, boutiques, Lindale Farm Park, the Southward Car Museum, Nga Manu Bird Sanctuary, golf courses and beautiful beaches. Pick up from train or bus. Laundry facilities. Smoke-free. Internet available.

Waikanae *45 km N of Wellington*

Waimoana *B&B Homestay*

Elizabeth and Bryan Couchman
63 Kakariki Grove, Waikanae 5036, Kapiti Coast

Tel (04) 293 2005 or 021 0222 0217
waimoana.waikanae@xtra.co.nz

Double $110 Single $80
(Continental breakfast)
1 Queen (1 bdrm)
Bathrooms: 1 Ensuite

Waimoana was purpose built as a quality homestay. Enjoy majestic sea views over Kapiti from the sundeck or pool. Living rooms radiate from a glass-roofed atrium featuring an indoor swimming pool, garden and waterfall. Our guest room has its own private entrance, parking and ensuite facilities. Refreshments are always available in the conservatory. Local activities include native bush walks, beach, first-class restaurants and cafés, craft and mosaic shops, bird sanctuaries and golf courses. A warm welcome awaits you from our three sons and cat Tabitha.

Paraparaumu Beach *5 km NW of Paraparaumu*

Beachstay *Homestay*

Ernie & Rhoda Stevenson
17 Takahe Drive, Kotuku Park,
Paraparaumu Beach 5032

Tel (04) 902 6466 or 027 353 2375
Fax (04) 902 6466
ernandrho@paradise.net.nz
http://bnb.co.nz/beachstayparaparaumu.html

Double $85 Single $60 (Continental breakfast)
Dinner $25 by arrangement
Visa MC accepted
Pet free home   Children welcome
1 Double 2 Single (2 bdrm)
Bathrooms: 1 Private

Enjoy warm friendly hospitality in the relaxing atmosphere of our modern new home. Peaceful surroundings next to river estuary and beach. Wonderful views of sea, lake and hills. Lovely coastal and river walks. Close to Paraparaumu Beach world ranking golf course and Southwards Car Museum. Trips to Kapiti Island Bird Sanctuary can be arranged with prior notice. South Island Ferry Terminal 45 minutes away. We enjoy meeting people and sharing our love of NZ scenery and bush walking. Ernie paints landscapes. Enquiries welcome.

Paraparaumu *43 km N of Wellington*
By the Sea Rosetta Boutique Bed & Breakfast *Luxury B&B*

Lorraine & Michael Sherlock
349 Rosetta Road, Paraparaumu, Kapiti Coast

Tel (04) 905 9055 or 021 122 0939
Fax (04) 905 9055
rosettahouse@paradise.net.nz
www.rosetta.co.nz

Double $120-$165 (Full breakfast)
Visa MC accepted
Children welcome
1 King/Twin 2 Queen 1 Double (4 bdrm)
Bathrooms: 2 Ensuite 1 Private

Generous gourmet/cooked breakfast included in our tariff. Delightful home set in gardens just a few footsteps to our magnificent beach and the Romantic Waterfront Restaurant. The Champagne Room with Ensuite is very spacious. The Gardens Suite has two double bedrooms opens out to our outdoor colourful gardens. Suitable two to four guests and families. Ideal stopover for the South Island Ferry. Afternoon tea on arrival,flowers and chocolates in your room. Fridge, laundry, internet, off street parking for cars, campervans, secure parking for moterbikes. Our guests rate us four stars.

Paraparaumu Beach *1 km W of Information Centre*
Tudor Manor *Luxury B&B*

Vince & Lisa Eggels
10 Tudor Court, Paraparaumu Beach

Tel (04) 298 3436 or 027 452 4419
Fax - lisa@tudormanor.co.nz   www.tudormanor.co.nz

Double $190-$220 (Full breakfast)
Children $15   Visa MC Eftpos accepted
3 Queen (3 bdrm)
Bathrooms: 3 Ensuite

Tudor Manor is a wonderful bed and breakfast just five minutes walk to Paraparaumu Beach, cafés, shops and the world famous Links golf course. You'll be spoilt with chocolates, complimentary drinks, fluffy bath robes to use while you stay. Large up to date DVD collection and flat screen TVs in every room. The rooms are themed, Safari suite (African), Regency (4 poster, English, fit for a queen) and Bordeaux (french country). We have a solar heated pool, spa pool and a gymnasium. Our three girls live at home, and our cat is not allowed in the guest rooms. Wellington Entertainment book is welcome, as is Bartercard. At the Paraparaumu lights, turn into Kapiti Road, drive three minutes and take the second road on the right after the airport. 10 Tudor Court. We look forward to meeting you.

Raumati Beach *3 km SW of Paraparaumu*
Sea Haven *B&B Homestay*

Jan & Laurie Bason
325 Rosetta Road, Raumati Beach

Tel (04) 902 0047 or 021 0279 8803
Fax (04) 902 0045
jan-laurie@paradise.net.nz

Double $110 Single $90
(Continental breakfast)
Visa MC accepted
Not suitable for children
1 Queen (1 bdrm)
Bathrooms: 1 Private

Welcome to our spacious smoke-free home. Our guest room opens to a small garden, with seating amongst native trees. Private access to the beach. 200-300 metres from village shops, restaurants, swimming pool, bowling green and Marine Gardens. Kapiti Miniature Railway is situated at Marine Gardens with various locomotives running on Sunday afternoons. Golf courses in the area. Laurie, a railway enthusiast, has a miniature locomotive and collection of railway memorabilia. We enjoy overseas travel, and throughout NZ in our Motorhome. One shy cat in residence.

Pukerua Bay *30 km N of Wellington*

Sheena's Homestay *Homestay*

Sheena Taylor
2 Gray Street, Pukerua Bay, Porirua City 5026

Tel (04) 239 9947   Fax (04) 239 9942
homestay@sheenas.co.nz
www.sheenas.co.nz

Double $90 Single $50 (Full breakfast)
Children $25
Dinner $15-$25pp by arrangement
Visa MC Amex Eftpos accepted
Children and pets welcome
1 Double 1 Twin 1 Single (2 bdrm)
Bathrooms: 1 Family share

Come share our warm, sunny smokefree home with two friendly cats - Tabitha & Sienna. Relax in the conservatory, enjoy the views. Sheena's a keen woolcrafter - stay two nights and have a go at spinning, felting or weave a scarf. Pukerua Bay, home of creative people, has an interesting beach about 15 minutes walk. Frequent trains to Wellington (good bus service) for day trips. Restaurants/cafés 5-15 minutes drive. Most special diets catered for, lunches arranged. Off-street parking; laundry facilities; bike storage; campervan powerpoint; cot/highchair.

Plimmerton *6 km N of Porirua*

Aquavilla Seaside Self-contained B&B *B&B Cottage with Kitchen*

Graham & Carolyn Wallace
16 Steyne Avenue, Plimmerton, Porirua

Tel (04) 233 1146 or 027 231 0141
aquavilla@paradise.net.nz
www.aquavilla.co.nz

Double $150-$180 Single $150 (Special breakfast)
Children negotiable
Dinner $50
Extra adults $50
Visa MC accepted
1 Queen 1 Single (1 bdrm)
Bathrooms: 1 Private

In the gorgeous garden of our seaside villa, your architecturally-designed accommodation features courtyard, kitchenette, barbeque and comfort-plus. Guests love the crisp cotton sheets, flowers, homemade biscuits and artistic touches. Explore Wellington easily by car or rail, or enjoy the forest and beach walks, cafés and restaurants, golfing, galleries, shopping and windsurfing close by. Scrumptious breakfast menu has light or full cooked options: homemade muesli or blueberry pancakes and sweetcorn fritters, etc. Warm and widely-travelled, we're art and nature lovers and very welcoming! Safe parking.

Plimmerton *2 km S of Plimmerton*

SeaStyle *Luxury Apartment with Kitchen*

Chrissy & Jack Lyons
10 Cluny Road, Plimmerton, Wellington

Tel (04) 233 9648 or 021 284 0461
Fax (04) 233 9645
bookings@seastyle.co.nz
www.seastyle.co.nz

Double $120-$150 (Continental breakfast provisions)
Children $30pp, maximum 2
Visa MC accepted
Pet free home   Children welcome
1 Queen 1 Double (1 bdrm)
Bathrooms: 1 Ensuite

Stay in style by the sea in a self contained apartment. One queen bed, one pull out double couch. Fully equipped kitchenette, ensuite, washer/dryer, TV, DVD, phone, off street parking. Just 25 minutes from Wellington City by road/rail. Close to beach, station, shops and restaurants. Directions: Off SH1 at Plimmerton, Steyne Avenue, cross railway to Plimmerton shops, turn left into Beach Road. Follow the beach until you reach Cluny Road. Turn right into Cluny Road, to Number 10, entrance is off Motuhara Road.

Plimmerton *23 km N of Wellington*

DreamWaters Self-Contained B&B *B&B Apartment with Kitchen*

B&B
Approved

Brent & Julie Smallbone
9A Gordon Road, Karehana Bay, Plimmerton 5026

Tel (04) 233 2042 or 027 688 8371
027 688 8375
relax@dreamwaters.co.nz
www.dreamwaters.co.nz

Double $150-$190 Single $150-$190
(Continental breakfast provisions)
Children $20 Sofabed in lounge
Visa MC accepted
1 King (1 bdrm)
Bathrooms: 1 Private

Enjoy spectacular sea, island and coastal views from this stunning accommodation attached to our new architecturally designed home.

Watch sailboats and windsurfers, sunsets and South Island from your lounge, bedroom and private decks. Swim and beach walk. Rocks and waves a stones throw from your seaside deck.

Skylights, floor to ceiling double glazed, tinted windows optimize the view. Heated floor tiles. Luxury. Your own entrance, offstreet parking. SKY, phone, computer jack-point. Private, safe.

Cafés and golf nearby, Interisland Ferry, Stadium and Te Papa 20 minutes away.

Wellington

Whitby *10 km NE of Porirua*

Oldfields *Homestay*

Elaine & John Oldfield
22 Musket Lane, Whitby, Wellington

Tel (04) 234 1002 or 021 254 0869
oldfields@ihug.co.nz
www.oldfieldshomestay.co.nz

Double $115 Single $95 (Full breakfast)
Dinner $25 by arrangement
Visa MC accepted
2 Queen (2 bdrm)
Bathrooms: 1 Guest share

Would you enjoy a stay in a tranquil home with bush views and overlooking a mature and well-tended garden? Oldfields is situated in a quiet cul-de-sac in the suburb of Whitby, ten minutes by car from Paremata Station and 25 minutes from central Wellington. Having travelled and lived overseas we are always interested in meeting people, whether they are from just up the road in New Zealand or further a field. We welcome you to stay with us and our cats Tinker & Roxy.

All our B&Bs are non-smoking
unless stated otherwise in the text.

Tawa *15 km N of Wellington*

Chaplin Homestay *B&B Homestay*

Joy & Bill Chaplin
3 Kiwi Place, Tawa, Wellington

Tel (04) 232 5547 or 021 146 5717
021 298 4569
Fax (04) 232 5547
chapta@xtra.co.nz

Double $90 Single $50 (Continental breakfast)
Dinner by arrangement
Visa MC accepted
Pet free home
Not suitable for children
1 King 1 Double 1 Single (3 bdrm)
Bathrooms: 1 Private 1 Guest share

You will find No 3 in a quiet cul-de-sac with safe off-street parking seven minutes by car and rail to Porirua City and 15 minutes to Wellington and the InterIsland Ferry Terminal. Relax in comfort and enjoy good restaurants, close proximity to beaches, tenpin bowling, swimming pool and fine walks. Phone for directions and notification for dinner if required. Laundry facilities available.

Tawa *15 km NW of Wellington CBD*

Perry Homestay *B&B Homestay*
Jocelyn & David Perry
5 Fyvie Avenue, Tawa, Wellington 5028

Tel (04) 232 7664
djperry@actrix.co.nz

Double $90 Single $60 (Special breakfast)
Children $20
Dinner by arrangement
Visa MC accepted
Children welcome
1 Double 1 Twin 1 Single (3 bdrm)
Bathrooms: 1 Guest share 1 Family share

We are a retired couple. Together with our cat Boots we welcome you to stay with us. There is a five minute walk to the suburban railway station with a half hourly service into the city (15 minutes) and north to the Kapiti Coast. Alternatively you can drive north to the coast, enjoying sea and rural views before sampling tourist attractions in this area. We are happy to provide transport to and from the Interisland ferry. Laundry facilities available.

Johnsonville *8 km N of Wellington*

Paparangi Homestay *B&B Homestay*
Joy & Autry Kawana
145 Helston Road, Johnsonville, Wellington

Tel (04) 478 1747 or 027 485 6432
autry.joy@xtra.co.nz

Double $95 Single $60 (Full breakfast)
Dinner with family $20
Children and pets welcome
1 Queen 1 Double 1 Twin 1 Single (2 bdrm)
Bathrooms: 1 Ensuite 1 Family share

Paparangi Homestay is a restored cottage, over 100 years old and set in over one acre of cottage gardens. We are situated 2 km from Johnsonville Railway station and shopping centre. We have a friendly dog, two cats and hens. We enjoy sharing a pre-dinner drink with our guests and you are welcome to have dinner with us with prior arrangement. Ample off-street parking available. Bedrooms have TV/radio and Sky TV is available in the lounge. Autry is a keen hunter and golfer and could arrange a game. We also enjoy watching rugby. We can accommodate a small dog by arrangement and have kennel. Children are welcome and smoking is okay on the verandah. Autry and Joy enjoy the company of other nationalities and our home is your home while you are with us.

Upper Hutt - Te Marua *7.4 km N of Upper Hutt*

Te Marua Homestay *Homestay*
Sheryl & Lloyd Homer
108A Plateau Road, Te Marua, Upper Hutt

Tel (04) 526 7851 or 0800 110 851
027 450 1679
Fax (04) 526 7866
sheryl.lloyd@clear.net.nz

Double $100 Single $70 (Continental breakfast)
Dinner $25pp by arrangement
Visa MC Diners Amex accepted
Not suitable for children
1 Queen 1 Double (2 bdrm)
Bathrooms: 1 Private

Our home is situated in a secluded bush setting. Guests may relax on one of our private decks or read books from our extensive library. For the more energetic there are bush walks, bike trails, trout fishing, swimming and a golf course within walking distance. The guest wing has a kitchenette and television. Lloyd is a landscape photographer with over 30 years experience photographing New Zealand. Sheryl is a teacher. Travel, tramping, skiing, photography, music and meeting people are interests we enjoy.

Upper Hutt *45 km N of Wellington*

Tranquility Homestay *B&B Homestay*

Elaine & Alan
136 Akatarawa Road, Birchville, Upper Hutt

Tel (04) 526 6948 or Free Phone 0800 270 787
027 675 8341   Fax (04) 526 6968
tranquility@xtra.co.nz
www.tranquilityhomestay.co.nz

Double $90-$120 Single $70-$120
(Continental breakfast)   Children negotiable
Dinner $25 by prior arrangement   Airport pick up
Visa MC Diners Amex accepted
Children and pets welcome
1 King/Twin 1 Queen 1 Double 1 Single (4 bdrm)
Bathrooms: 2 Ensuite 2 Family share Luxury queen ensuite with spa bath, double has ensuite

Tranquility Homestay. The name says it all. Escape from the stress of city life approx 30 minutes from Wellington off SH2. Close to Upper Hutt - restaurants, cinema, golf, racecourse, leisure centre (swimming), bush walks. We are near the confluence of the Hutt and Akatarawa Rivers which is noted for its fishing. 13 km to Staglands. Country setting, relax, listen to NZ tuis, watch the fantails or wood pigeons, or simply relax and read. Comfortable, warm and friendly hospitality.

Upper Hutt *3 km S of Upper Hutt*

Brentwood Manor *B&B and Self-contained Units*

Ron & Misty Vink
5 Brentwood Street, Trentham, Upper Hutt

Tel (04) 528 6727 or 027 527 0122
Fax (04) 528 6725   info@brentwoodmanor.co.nz
www.brentwoodmanor.co.nz

Double $125-$185 Single $110-$135
(Continental breakfast)   Children negotiable
Dinner By Arrangement
Visa MC accepted
3 Queen 2 Double 2 Twin (7 bdrm)
Bathrooms: 2 Ensuite 1 Guest share 1 Family share
Self-contained have ensuites.

Ron & Misty invite you to capture the essence of early 20th century New Zealand in one of only 80 Chapman-Taylor designed and handcrafted homes. Set in private, tree-fringed grounds, Brentwood Manor provides a welcome sanctuary from the hustle and bustle of life. Stay in the Manor itself in bed & breakfast style accommodation or spend the night in unique self-contained settler style cottages. Just minutes from Upper Hutt City Centre and around the corner from buses and trains. Romantic Getaway Packages and Airport Transfers available by arrangement.

Lower Hutt *1 km N of Lower Hutt Centre*

Judy & Bob's Place *Homestay*

Judy & Bob Vine
11 Ngaio Crescent, Woburn, Lower Hutt

Tel (04) 971 1192 or 021 510 682
027 450 0682   Fax (04) 971 6192
bob.vine@paradise.net.nz

Double $120 Single $60 (Full breakfast)
Dinner $35
Visa MC Diners Amex accepted
Pet free home
1 Queen 2 Single (2 bdrm)
Bathrooms: 1 Private Limit:
1 booking a time to obviate bathroom sharing

Located in Woburn, a picturesque and quiet central city suburb of Lower Hutt, known for its generous sized houses and beautiful gardens. Within walking distance of the Lower Hutt downtown, 15 minutes drive from central Wellington, its railway station and ferry terminals; airport 25 minutes; three minutes walk to Woburn Rail Station. Private lounge and TV. Love to entertain and share hearty Kiwi style cooking with good New Zealand wine. Laundry facilities. Transfer transport available. High speed internet connections.

Wellington

Lower Hutt *3 km E of Hutt City*

Casa Bianca *B&B Apartment with Kitchen*
Jo & Dave Comparini
10 Damian Grove, Lower Hutt. Wellington

Tel (04) 569 7859 or 027 357 4395
Fax (04) 569 7859
casabiancanz@xtra.co.nz
http://Casa Bianca NZ

Double $95-$120 Single $75-$100
(Continental breakfast provisions)
Longterm stays available
Visa MC accepted
Pet free home   Not suitable for children
1 King 1 Single (1 bdrm)
Bathrooms: 1 Private

Our B&B is close to Hutt City. A short hop to the Open Polytech, Hutt Hospital, and Waterloo station. Wellington is 20 minutes away. We have a lovely self-contained apartment with double bedroom. bathroom, large lounge, fully equipped kitchen, laundry and a single bed in the lounge. Breakfast provisions provided in apartment. Stays long or short term. If you are relocating call us first. Enjoy our special hospitality. Broadband, Safe off-street parking. Not suitable for children. Non smoking please.

Lower Hutt *2 km SE of Lower Hutt*

Dungarvin *B&B Homestay*
Beryl & Trevor Cudby
25 Hinau Street, Woburn, Lower Hutt

Tel (04) 569 2125 or 021 252 2933
t.b.cudby@clear.net.nz
www.bnb.co.nz/dungarvin.html

Double $105-$120 Single $80-$100 (Full breakfast)
Dinner by arrangement
Visa MC accepted
Pet free home
Not suitable for children
1 Queen (1 bdrm)
Bathrooms: 1 Private

Our fully refurbished 77 year old cottage retains its original charm. It is 15 minutes from the ferry terminal and the stadium, and 20 minutes from Te Papa - The Museum of New Zealand. Our home is centrally heated and the sunny guest bedroom looks over our secluded garden. The bed has an electric blanket and wool duvet. Vegetarians are catered for, laundry facilities are available and we have ample off-street parking. Our main interests are travel, music, gardening, shows and NZ wines.

Lower Hutt *0.5 km SE of Lower Hutt Central*

Rose Cottage *B&B Homestay*
Maureen & Gordon Gellen
70A Hautana Street, Lower Hutt, Wellington

Tel (04) 566 7755 or 021 481 732
Fax (04) 566 0777
gellen@xtra.co.nz

Double $110-$125 Single $95-$110 (Full breakfast)
Dinner $35 by arrangement
Visa MC accepted
Not suitable for children
1 King/Twin 1 Queen (2 bdrm)
Bathrooms: 1 Ensuite 1 Family share

Relax in the comfort of our cosy home which is just a five minute walk to the Hutt City Centre and 15 minutes to ferries. Originally built in 1910 the house has been fully renovated. Interests include travel, gardening, sports and live theatre. As well as TV in guest room there's coffee and tea-making facilities. Breakfast will be served in our dining room at your convenience. Unsuitable for children. We look forward to welcoming you into our smoke-free home which we share with Scuffin our cat.

Lower Hutt - Korokoro *12 km N of Wellington*

Devenport Estate *B&B Hobby Vineyard*
Alasdair & Christopher
1 Korokoro Road, Korokoro, Petone, Wellington 5012

Tel (04) 586 6868
Fax (04) 586 6869
devenport_estate@hotmail.com
http://homepages.paradise.net.nz/devenpor

Double $125-$150 Single $100-$125
(Continental breakfast)
Visa MC Diners accepted
Children welcome
3 Queen 2 Single (3 bdrm)
Bathrooms: 2 Ensuite 1 Private
Ensuite - Showers, Private - Shower over Bath

Stay at the closest hobby vineyard to the capital. Only 15 minutes to Ferry/City & Stadium yet with the privacy and quietness of a country retreat. Devenport Estate is an Edwardian-styled homestead overlooking Wellington Harbour, built at the turn of the century (2000!) based upon the MacDonald family home in Scotland.

Nestled amongst native bush we have carved out a colourful garden around the homestead and planted over 400 Pinot Gris/Pinot Noir grapevines in our hobby vineyard. Devenport was built for views, comfort and peacefulness.

Guests enjoy stunning sea, bush and garden views.
Bedrooms contain queen-sized bed, writing desk, chairs, TV, tea-making services, hair dryer, electric blanket with either an en suite or private bathroom. Relax in the guest living room or outside in the sun on the titanic deck chairs. Play petanque or deck quoits, admire the vines and water features or watch the yachts sail past on the harbour.

Avoid city stress and leave your car here, we are only a 15 minute train ride to central Wellington. Devenport provides; free WiFi broadband internet, free laundry service for stays of two or more nights. Some limits apply. We have plenty of off street parking. Breakfast in the formal Dining Room or alfresco, overlooking Somes Island. At night, enjoy the vast variety of restaurants of Petone's Jackson Street - only a five minute drive from Devenport. Alasdair, Chris and our two cocker spaniels, welcome you to a comfortable stay in Wellington on our vineyard estate.

Lower Hutt - Stokes Valley *8 km NE of Lower Hutt*

Kowhai B&B *B&B Homestay*
Glenys & Peter Lockett
88A Manuka Street, Stokes Valley, Lower Hutt

Tel (04) 563 6671 or 027 443 3341
p_g.lockett@xtra.co.nz

Double $110-$110 Single $80-$80
(Full breakfast)
Visa MC accepted
Pet free home
2 Queen 1 Double (3 bdrm)
Bathrooms: 1 Private

Awake to birdsong in our spacious, tasteful bedrooms with bath robes and hairdriers provided. Relax in the lovely guest lounge with balcony, Sky TV, CD player and tea & coffee facilities. We offer off-road parking at the door and delicious breakfast with seasonal fresh fruit. Sports, theatre and travel are our interests and we have a wide knowledge of the greater Wellington area.

Lower Hutt - Harbourview *1.5 km W of Lower Hutt*

Harbourcity View B & B *B&B Homestay*
Mary Quayle
14 City View Grove, Harbourview, Lower Hutt 5010

Tel (04) 586 0557 or 027 688 3306
harbourcityview@paradise.net.nz

Double $110-$150 Single $60-$80
(Full breakfast)
Dinner $35pp by arrangement
Visa MC accepted
Not suitable for children
2 King/Twin 1 Single (3 bdrm)
Bathrooms: 1 Ensuite 1 Family share

Situated on the edge of a bush reserve with panaramic views of Wellington harbour, Hutt river, and Eastern hills. Minutes from Melling Station and Lower Hutt CBD. 15 minutes drive or train to Wellington Central, Ferry Terminal, and Westpac Stadium. Hike in the Regional Parks, fish the Hutt River, golf on the nearby courses. Sightseeing tours can be arranged. Transfers available. Guest tea and coffee making facilities. I look forward to welcoming you into my home. Be part of the household or enjoy your independence.

Eastbourne - York Bay *3 km N of Eastbourne*

Bush House *Homestay*
Belinda Cattermole
12 Waitohu Road, York Bay, Eastbourne

Tel (04) 568 5250 or 027 408 9648
Fax (04) 568 5250
belindacat@paradise.net.nz

Double $100 Single $80
(Special breakfast)
Dinner by arrangement
1 Double 1 Single (2 bdrm)
Bathrooms: 1 Private 1 Family share

Come and enjoy the peace and tranquility of the Eastern Bays. You will be hosted in a restored 1920's settler cottage nestled amongst native bush and looking towards the Kaikoura mountains of the South Island. My love of cordon-bleu cooking and the pleasures of the table are satisfied through the use of my country kitchen and dining room. Other attractions: A Devon Rex cat. Eastbourne is a small seaside village across the harbour from Wellington City with a range of attractions.

Eastbourne - Days Bay *12 km E of Wellington*
Treetops Hideaway *B&B Apartment with Kitchen*

Robyn & Roger Cooper
7 Huia Road, Days Bay, Eastbourne

Tel (04) 562 7692 or 027 616 9826
Fax (04) 562 7690
bnb@treetops.net.nz
www.treetops.net.nz

Double $150-$170 Single $130-$140
(Continental breakfast provisions)
Children $30   Extra adults $42.50
Visa MC accepted
1 King (1 bdrm)
Bathrooms: 1 Private

Ride our private cable car through native bush to Treetops Hideaway, a secluded romantic retreat overlooking Wellington harbour. Sparkling sea views from bedroom and lounge; fully-equipped kitchenette, luxury bath/shower, phone, wireless broadband, separate entrance. Wake to bellbird song; breakfast on your garden patio; relax with books, TV, DVD. Beach, cafés, galleries, ferry to Central Wellington 200 metres (20 minute ride, berths near Te Papa and The Stadium). Inter-island ferry 20 minutes. 'This place is Dreamland - a Kiwi Shangri-la.' Self-catering $150 double.

~

Eastbourne - Lowry Bay *14 km N of Wellington*
Lowry Bay Homestay *B&B Homestay*

Pam & Forde Clarke
35 Cheviot Road, Lowry Bay, Eastbourne, Wellington

Tel (04) 568 4407 or 0508 266 546
Fax (04) 568 4408
homestay@lowrybay.co.nz
www.lowrybay.co.nz

Double $130-$160 Single $100-$130 (Full breakfast)
Children negotiable
Visa MC Diners Amex accepted
Pet free home
1 King/Twin 1 Queen 1 Single (2 bdrm)
Bathrooms: 1 Private

Warm, restful, peaceful, yet close to Wellington and Hutt Cities, transport, restaurants and art galleries. Play tennis on our court, stroll to the beach, walk in the bush, sail on our 28 foot yacht, or relax under a sun umbrella on the deck. Native birds abound. Our sunny, elegant bedrooms have garden views, TV, tea/coffee and central heating. We share with our two grown up daughters, Isabella and Kirsty, interests in sailing, skiing, tennis, ballet and theatre. Laundry. From SH2 follow Petone signs then Eastbourne.

~

Eastbourne *20 km E of Wellington*
The Anchorage *B&B Homestay*

Bet & Wal Louden
107 Marine Parade, Eastbourne, Wellington

Tel (04) 562 8310 or 021 049 5169
021 329 993
betandwal@paradise.net.nz

Double $130 Single $100
(Continental breakfast)
Extra guests $50
Visa MC accepted
Children welcome
1 Queen 1 Single (2 bdrm)
Bathrooms: 1 Private

Welcome to our waterfront property, wonderful views of Wellington Harbour and city. One minute walk to Eastbourne Village and wharf, supermarket, cafés, restaurants, pub, antique shops and art gallery. We offer for the more adventurous a choice of guided bush walks from an easy two hours to a demanding seven hours (bookings essential; Mon-Friday only), panoramic views of Wellington Harbour, outstanding beech, northern rata and podocarp forests. Coastal walks (mountain bike rides) to Pencarrow Lighthouse. Kayak trips also available. Labrador, Splash on property.

Eastbourne - Mahina Bay *3 km N of Eastbourne Village*

Kanuka Hill Homestead *B&B Homestay*
Charles & Baba
38 Mahina Rd, Mahina Bay, Eastbourne 5013

Tel (04) 562 6399 or 021 125 6162
charlesb@sunflower.co.nz
Fax (04) 562 6319
kanukahill@sunflower.co.nz
www.sunflower.co.nz

Double $120 (Full breakfast provisions)
Cooked breakfast or dinner by arrangement
Single/double rate same   Additional guests $30 per night
Visa MC accepted   Pet free home
1 Queen 1 Double (2 bdrm)
Bathrooms: 1 Private, we take one party only at a time

Nestled high on a Wellington harbour hillside, Kanuka Hill Homestead offers awesome, breathtaking views down a bush clad valley to the harbour.

The homestead is brand new - being completed as we type up this description - with purpose designed rooms for guests on the middle level of the home (up one storey with easy stairs). The guest suite has a separate entry from the main entry for the hosts.

Two rooms, one with a queen sized bed, table, TV, etc and the other a sitting room/sleeping room with sofa-bed, TV, DVD etc. Both rooms share a similar magnificent view as does the private bathroom with shub (shower over small bath), toilet, etc. The bed-sitting room also opens out onto a deck (with glass fronted safety wall to enable the view to be taken in from the room).

There is also a small kitchenette area with sink, microwave, toaster, kettle, cutlery, crockery etc.

The homestead is on a large property backing on to reserve land above, with bush walks and more harbour views. A high-level boundary track and public walkway takes one over the hill into Days Bay and the nearby cafés. A 3 km walk (or drive) to Eastbourne village brings you to a small shopping centre with cafés/restaurants.

A 90 person sea ferry plies regularly between Days Bay wharf and Wellington city on the other side of the harbour.

Wellington - Khandallah *7 km N of Wellington*

Clothier Homestay *Homestay*

Sue & Ted Clothier
22 Lohia Street, Khandallah, Wellington

Tel (04) 479 1180 or 027 246 6158
Fax (04) 479 2717
sclothier@xtra.co.nz

Double $110 Single $80
(Continental breakfast)
Not suitable for children
1 Twin (1 bdrm)
Bathrooms: 1 Ensuite

This is a lovely, sunny and warm open plan home with glorious harbour and city views. A quiet easily accessible street just ten minutes from the city and five minutes from the ferry. Close to Khandallah Village where you can make use of the excellent local restaurant, café or Monteiths pub. We are a non-smoking household. Another family member is an aristocratic white cat called Dali. We enjoy sharing our home with our guests.

Wellington - Khandallah *7 km N of Wellington*

The Loft in Wellington *B&B Separate Suite*

Phillippa & Simon Plimmer
6 Delhi Crescent, Khandallah, Wellington

Tel (04) 938 5015 or 021 448 491
plimmers@paradise.net.nz

Double $110 Single $90
(Continental breakfast provisions)
Visa MC accepted
Pet free home
Not suitable for children
1 Queen (1 bdrm)
Bathrooms: 1 Ensuite

The Loft in Wellington offers the discerning traveller comfort and style in a beautifully appointed self-contained studio (no cooking facilities). Enjoy complete privacy with your own entrance and new ensuite bathroom. Cable TV, off-street parking, laundry and internet access available. 10 minutes from downtown Wellington. Close to ferry terminal. 300 metres to local train and bus. 15 minutes train ride direct to Westpac Stadium. 500 metres from Khandallah Village and local restaurants. Studio not suitable for pets. We have three young children.

Wellington - Ngaio *7 km NW of Wellington*

Ngaio Homestay *B&B Homestay Apartment with Kitchen*
Jennifer & Christopher Timmings
56 Fox Street, Ngaio, Wellington

Tel (04) 479 5325
Fax (04) 479 4325
enquiries@ngaiohomestay.co.nz
www.ngaiohomestay.co.nz

Double $140-$180 Single $100-$140 (Continental breakfast)
Children negotiable
Dinner $35pp by arrangement
Self-contained $160-$180 double, extra person $45
Visa MC accepted
1 Queen 1 Double 2 Twin 3 Single (4 bdrm)
Bathrooms: 3 Ensuite 1 Private

Welcome to Wonderful Wellington! Share your visit with us and enjoy helpful personal hospitality! Our unusual multi-level open plan character home [built1960] is in the suburb of Ngaio. Guests may leave their car here and take the train to CBD [ten minutes] We are five minutes by car to InterIsland Ferry terminal.

Our double room has tea/coffee facilities, quality bedding, tiled ensuite and french doors opening onto a deck and private jungle garden. Breakfast is continental. Evening meals an optional extra.

Two self-contained apartments, 1 queen, 1 twin, adjacent to our property, are comfortable, convenient, tastefully furnished and recently re-decorated. Each apartment also has a couch with a fold-out bed in lounge, fully equipped kitchen, shower, bath, laundry facilities, cable TV, phone and internet [small fee] There is a large garden with trees, birds and views. Perfect for business, holiday or relocating.

Jennifer plays harp at home and live piano music daily in NZ's top department store.

Compliment from guest: "This is a home where there is beautiful music, art and love." Do come and share! Please phone before 11am or after 3pm or fax or email. Bookings essential.

Wellington - Wadestown *2.5 km NW of Wellington*

The Nikau Palms Bed & Breakfast *B&B*
Diane & Bill Boyd
95 Sar Street, Wadestown, Wellington 6012

Tel (04) 499 4513 or 027 674 0644
Fax (04) 499 4517
thenikaupalms@xtra.co.nz
www.thenikaupalms.co.nz

Double $160-$180 Single $115-$120
(Full breakfast)
Visa MC accepted
2 Queen 1 Single (2 bdrm)
Bathrooms: 2 Ensuite

You are invited to share our spectacular views of Wellington Harbour overlooking the city, Interisland ferry and Westpac Stadium, all within walking distance. Our home is a few minutes drive from Wellington's attractions, Historic Thorndon's restaurants, shops and Heritage Trail and Katherine Mansfield's birthplace. The bedrooms include ensuites, one with private sitting room. Full cooked or continental breakfast provided. Tea and coffee making facilities and refrigerator in bedrooms. Off-street parking provided.

Wellington - Wadestown *2 km N of Wellington*

Harbour Lodge Wellington *B&B*
Lou & Chris Bradshaw
200 Barnard Street, Wadestown, Wellington

Tel (04) 976 5677 or 021 032 6497
lou@harbourlodgewellington.com
www.harbourlodgewellington.com

Double $180-$260 (Continental breakfast)
Children negotiable
Visa MC Amex accepted
Children welcome
4 King (4 bdrm)
Bathrooms: 4 Ensuite

Let your stresses be gently lulled away in the luxurious comfort of this beautiful new lodge. Admire the fabulous views of Wellington Harbour from the large sunny deck. Swim in the 11 metre indoor heated pool or take a spa. Laze in the comfort of a large guest lounge with an open fire and stunning harbour views. All this is only a few minutes drive from central Wellington, ferry terminal or Wellington Stadium. Children of all ages welcome, no pets please.

Wellington - Wadestown *2.3 km N of Central Wellington*

Annaday Homestay *B&B Homestay*
Anne & David Denton
39 Wadestown Road, Wellington

Tel (04) 499 1827   Fax (04) 472 1190
annaday@tavis.co.nz
www.tavis.co.nz/annaday

Double $130-$200 Single $90-$150 (Full breakfast)
Children $20-$50
Dinner $20-$35
Sauna $5
Children and pets welcome
2 King/Twin 2 King 2 Queen 2 Twin (5 bdrm)
Bathrooms: 1 Ensuite 1 Private 1 Guest share
1 Family share

Superb views. Excellent facilities. Fast internet. Hospitality adapted to suit you. Start with courtesy pickup, enjoy our free orientation tour of the city, borrow a book, join us for dinner or try the local takeaways or cafés. On the bus route, close to the city, ferries, train & will take you to the airport. Near Wellington Stadium & Bowen Hospital. Our dog and grandson stay out of guest areas but make friends if you choose. Discounts/negotiable rates for longer stays and groups.

Wellington - Wadestown *2 km NW of Information Centre*
Ahu Mairangi *B&B*
James and Helen
128 Weld Street, Wadestown

Tel (04) 473 7157
Freephone 0800 678 031
james.quinn@xtra.co.nz

Double $120-$140 **Single** $100-$110
(Continental breakfast)
Pet free home
1 Queen 1 Double (2 bdrm)
Bathrooms: 1 Ensuite 1 Private

Welcome to "Ahu Mairangi"Located high up on the hills above Wellington City for awesome views and maximum sun. Our recently modernised home has a large guest bedroom with ensuite which has both bath and shower. Also a second double bedroom with adjoining bath room and separate WC. Both rooms have peaceful bush views so come and enjoy a relaxing stay in our beautiful city. As we adjoin the town belt there are some great walks for the fitter guests. Airport and ferry pickups available (surcharge).

Wellington - Karori *4 km W of Wellington CBD*
Bristow Place *B&B Apartment with Kitchen*
Helen & Tony Thomson
8 Bristow Place, Karori, Wellington

Tel (04) 476 6291 or 021 656 825
Fax (04) 476 6293
h.t.thomson@xtra.co.nz

Double $160-$200 **Single** $130-$160 (Full breakfast)
Dinner by arrangement
Long stay or self-catered by arrangement
Visa MC accepted
Children welcome
1 Queen 2 Double (2 bdrm)
Bathrooms: 2 Private

We offer a private apartment, able to sleep up to four, that can be enjoyed either as a regular B&B facility or on a self-catered, self-serviced basis. We also have another guestroom with double bed and private bathroom. Enjoy Sky TV, electric blankets, bathrobes, heated towel rails, etc. Share coffee and conversation with us. We enjoy music, theatre, travel, sports and bridge. German spoken. Inner suburb location with ample parking, good transport and local shops and restaurants. Internet, fax and laundry service at small charges.

Wellington - Karori *6 km W of Wellington*
Norlan Homestay *Homestay*
Dale Mansill
15 Cathie Place, Karori, Wellington

Tel (04) 476 4469 or 027 612 3605
Fax (04) 476 4472
dale.mansill@xtra.co.nz

Double $100 **Single** $70 (Continental breakfast)
Twin $100
Children and pets welcome
1 Queen 1 Twin 1 Single (2 bdrm)
Bathrooms: 1 Ensuite 1 Family share

Enjoy comfort and good company at Norlan Homestay in the suburb of Karori 15 minutes from the city centre. Close to transport, local shops, restaurants, and cable car. Relax in front of the log burner with Sox the cat or take advantage of Wellington's many sights and cultural activities. Continental breakfast provided. Laundry facilities, internet, Sky TV available. Plenty of parking. Happy to pick up from ferry terminals. Choice of queen with ensuite and single or twin share bathroom.

Wellington - Karori *5 km W of Wellington*

Campbell Homestay *Homestay*
Murray & Elaine Campbell
23 Parkvale Road, Karori 6012 Wellington

Tel (04) 476 6110 or 027 453 5080
Fax (04) 476 6593 ctool@ihug.co.nz

Double $110 Single $70 (Continental breakfast)
Children half price   Dinner $35 by arrangement
Visa MC accepted   Children and pets welcome
1 Queen 1 Twin 1 Single (2 bdrm)
Bathrooms: 1 Guest share Separate toilet, full bathroom/
shower next to bedrooms

Welcome to our home right in the village of Karori, but only ten minutes from the central city. Dine with us, or eat out at the local taverns, restaurants/cafés, enjoy our local village shopping centre, library, Post Office and other amenities all within a few minutes walking distance. As we are on the main bus route, guests, if they wish, can park their car off street and take the bus into the city. We are happy to pick you up from ferry, train, bus or airport terminals and of course make sure you do not miss your onward connection. We are situated close to the Karori Wildlife Sanctuary, Botanic Gardens and Otari-Wilton's Bush, Cable Car, historic Thorndon's boutique shopping centre and restaurants, Katherine Masefield's birthplace. and the Westpac Stadium.

"Absolutely Positively Wellington" is a dynamic ever changing compact city making it easy to walk from one place to the next and with simply the most friendly helpful people. Take advantage of Wellington's cultural events: orchestra, ballet, opera, galleries and theatres. Visit our fabulous modern museum Te Papa or take a shuttle ferry across the harbour.

We have two guest bedrooms, one queen and one twin which can also be a single. Guests have the sole use of a separate toilet and a full sized bathroom next door to the bedrooms. Relax and make yourself at home - use our laundry, garden, lounge, email/internet facilities. Meet Charlie our border collie dog Children of all ages welcome. Our home is perfect for business folk or families relocating as it is so close to all the village amenities including schools. Weekly rates on application Evening meals are an optional extra, $35 per person. From the motorway, when coming into Wellington from the north, take the Hawkestone Street/Karori exit off the motorway and follow the signs up past the Botanic gardens, through the tunnel, up the hill past the Marsden shops and down to the Karori village. Turn right at the lights into Parkvale Road (first turn past the Shopping Mall), then turn left down the drive to No 23 where a big welcome awaits you.

Wellington - Karori *5 km W of Wellington City*
Harbour Vista B&B *B&B Homestay*
Gina and Peter Sisson
24 Kilsyth Street, Wellington, 6012

Tel (04) 476 2477 or 021 139 0606
Fax (04) 476 2479
pgsisson@xtra.co.nz
www.harbourvista.co.nz

Double $140-$200 (Full breakfast)
Visa MC accepted
Pet free home
Not suitable for children
1 King 1 Queen (2 bdrm)
Bathrooms: 1 Ensuite 1 Private

Welcome to our home situated in a quiet cul-de-sac with awesome views of our suburb, hills and our beautiful harbour! We are five to ten minutes from the Cable Car, Botanical Garden, the Bird Sanctuary and the city. We are widely travelled and enjoy meeting and sharing our home with fellow travellers. Rooms have tea and coffee making facilities, electric blankets, hair dryer and bathrobes. Extremely comfortable beds and a warm welcome awaits you. Internet and laundry service available.

Wellington - Karori *2 km N of the Central City*
B&B and Homestay *B&B Separate Suite Apartment with Kitchen*
Judit & Julian Farquhar
15 Nottingham Street, Wellington, 6005

Tel (04) 976 8144
Fax (04) 976 8144
judit.farquhar@gmail.com

Double $130-$200 Single $90-$150
(Breakfast by arrangement)
Children welcome at discount rates
Dinner by arrangement $20-$35
Major currencies accepted
Children welcome
2 Double 2 Single (2 bdrm)
Bathrooms: 1 Ensuite 1 Private 1 Family share

Welcome to our 99 year old eco colonial home in the Wellington suburb of Karori with a beautiful mature organic garden, five minutes from the central city. We are a well-traveled Hungarian-Kiwi couple with our six year old daughter. There is music, art and technology inside. Good transport and local shops and restaurants. We offer a separated guestroom for two people with its own WC, cooking ability and also a sef-contained, private apartment with kitchen, able to sleep up to four people.

Wellington - Kelburn *1 km W of Wellington Central*
Rawhiti *B&B*
Annabel Leask
40 Rawhiti Terrace, Kelburn, Wellington

Tel (04) 934 4859
Fax (04) 972 4859
rawhiti@paradise.net.nz
www.rawhiti.co.nz

Double $240-$300 Single $200-$264 (Full breakfast)
Longer stay rates available
Visa MC accepted
Children over 12 welcome
1 King/Twin 1 King (2 bdrm)
Bathrooms: 2 Ensuite

Rawhiti is located in the prime suburb of Kelburn and within walking distance of the city centre. Magnificent views of harbour and city are seen from all rooms including the small private garden at the rear. A charming 1903 two storeyed Victorian home is furnished to create an elegant and tranquil ambience. It's historical features, wonderful outlook and quality chattels combine to offer guests a special stay in Wellington. A two minute walk to the cable car, botanic gardens and Victoria University.

Wellington - Kelburn *1 km W of City Centre*

Above Town Bed and Breakfast *B&B*

Maria & Michael Phelan
23 Rimu Road, Kelburn, Wellington 6012

Tel (04) 971 5737
abovetownbnb@paradise.net.nz

Double $140-$170 Single $120-$150
(Full breakfast)
Visa MC accepted
1 King/Twin 1 Double (1 bdrm)
Bathrooms: 1 Ensuite

Enjoy our spacious guest room in a quiet street above the city centre. Nearby Wellington's cable car to central city locations and the harbour. Walk to Victoria University and Botanic Gardens. Te Papa, downtown entertainments and Stadium are easily reached. Knowledgeable hosts, Maria and Michael, can provide information to help you explore Wellington. Then relax in your stylish room with sitting area, TV, coffee/tea making, airconditioning and fridge. Double futon for extra guests; quality linen; separate entrance and roadside parking. Friendly pet dog in residence.

Wellington - Aro Valley *2 km SW of Information Centre*

Millie's Bed & Breakfast *B&B Homestay*

Miriam Busby
33 Holloway Road, Aro Valley, Wellington 6021

Tel (04) 381 2968 or 021 254 7308
Fax (04) 381 2969
miriam.busby@paradise.net.nz
www.milliesbb.co.nz

Double $130 Single $80 (Full breakfast)
Children $40
Dinner $20 for Colonial cottage cuisine
1 Double 1 Single (2 bdrm)
Bathrooms: 1 Family share
1 bath available for guests to use

Named after Millie, the pet cat, at Millie's you awake to the sound of native birdsong. The house is nestled in a bushy valley near the Karori Sanctuary. Situated on a heritage trail, Millie's is close to a bus-stop, Aro Street cafés, restaurants and shops. 20 minutes walk to city. Free off-street parking available. Complimentary breakfast. 1 extra divan bed in kitchen. Deck with BBQ. Dinner, scenic drives, walks & therapeutic art sessions are extra services available. Milllie's does not have a credit card facility. Guests pay by cash or cheque.

Wellington - Oriental Bay *0.75 km N of Courtenay Place*

No 11 *B&B*

Virginia Barton-Chapple
11 Hay Street, Oriental Bay, Wellington

Tel (04) 801 9290 or 027 288 4461
Fax (04) 801 9295
v.barton-chapple@xtra.co.nz

Double $130-$150 Single $110-$125
(Special breakfast)
Visa MC accepted
1 King/Twin (1 bdrm)
Bathrooms: 1 Family share

Step up to a bed & breakfast with stunning views of Wellington Harbour and the inner city. No 11 is an easy stroll to Te Papa: the museum of New Zealand, the City Art Gallery, all the major theatres and cinemas, great restaurants and cafés. Virginia has extensive knowledge of what's going on, and where to go. The comfortable room has an adjacent bathroom, electric blankets, and tea & coffee facilities. Breakfast will be an occasion. Cat in residence.

Wellington - Mt Cook *2 km SE of Wellington*

Apartment One *B&B Homestay*
Jim & Colleen Bargh
2 King Street, Mt Cook, Wellington

Tel (04) 385 1112 or 027 247 8145
027 275 0913
apartmentone@yahoo.co.nz

Double $130-$140 Single $90-$100
(Full breakfast)
Visa MC accepted
Not suitable for children
2 Queen 1 Single (2 bdrm)
Bathrooms: 2 Ensuite

Experience apartment living in the city. We moved off the farm into our converted warehouse to try city life. We love its ever-changing beauty and the people are simply the best. Come try it for yourself. Two minutes walk to the Basin Reserve and 10-15 minutes walk to Courtenay Place (Wellington's restaurant, café and theatre district). Less than ten minutes drive to the ferry terminal and airport. We serve a deluxe breakfast to get you through your eventful day.

Please let us know
how you enjoyed your B&B experience.
Ask your host for a comment form
or leave a comment on www.bnb.co.nz

Wellington - Mt Victoria *0.5 km E of Courtenay Place*

Austinvilla *B&B Apartment with Kitchen*
Zarli & Mark
11 Austin Street, Mt Victoria, Wellington

Tel (04) 385 8334
info@austinvilla.co.nz
www.austinvilla.co.nz

Double $140-$180 (Continental breakfast)
Visa MC Eftpos accepted
Not suitable for children
2 Queen (2 bdrm)
Bathrooms: 2 Ensuite

Top location: Set amongst beautiful gardens in one of Mt Victoria's elegant turn-of-the-century villas, Austinvilla is within minutes walk of theatres, restaurants, Oriental Bay and Te Papa. Close to public transport and short drive to airport, ferries, and Westpac Stadium. Two self-contained apartments with individual entrances come equipped with queen bed, ensuite (bath and shower), kitchen, living/dining area, cable TV, phone and wireless internet access. Both offer privacy, sun and city views with one having its own patio/garden. Laundry facilities and off-street parking available.

Wellington - Mt Victoria *0.5 km E of Central Wellington*

Villa Vittorio *B&B Homestay*
Annette & Logan Russell
6 Hawker Street, Mt Victoria, Wellington

Tel (04) 801 5761 or 027 432 1267
Fax (04) 801 5762
villa@villavittorio.co.nz
www.villavittorio.co.nz

Double $185-$220 Single $125-$135 (Full breakfast)
Dinner from $50
Visa MC Diners Amex accepted
1 Double (1 bdrm)
Bathrooms: 1 Private

WELCOME TO VILLA VITTORIO. Centrally located close by Courtenay Place. Short walk to restaurants, theatres, shopping, conference centres, Te Papa Museum, Parliament & Stadium. Guest bedroom with TV, tea & coffee facilities. Adjoining sitting room with balcony overlooking city. Bathroom with shower and bath.

Breakfast served in Italian styled dining room or outside in courtyard. We enjoy having guests, having travelled extensively ourselves. Transport and gourmet dinner by arrangement. Garaging and laundry at small charge. No children or pets.

Directions: phone, fax, email or write.

Wellington - Roseneath *3 km E of Wellington Central*

Harbourview Homestay and B&B *B&B Homestay*

Hilda & Geoff Stedman
125 Te Anau Road, Roseneath, Wellington

Tel (04) 386 1043 or 021 0386 351
hildastedman@clear.net.nz
http://nzhomestay.co.nz/harbourview_homestay

Double $130-$170 Single $100-$150 (Full breakfast)
Dinner from $40
Visa MC accepted
Children welcome
1 Double 2 Single (2 bdrm)
Bathrooms: 2 Private

Five minutes drive from Wellington city, ten minutes drive from the airport and on the No. 14 bus route. The house offers comfortable hospitality and elegance. Each bedroom opens to a wide deck, offering expansive views of Wellington harbour. Pleasantly decorated rooms quality beds and linen, separate guest's bathroom with shower and spa bath. Harbourview is situated in a peaceful setting close to the city, catering for business people, tourists and honeymooners. A surcharge will be added if paying by credit card.

Wellington - Roseneath *2 km E of Central City*

Panorama *B&B*

Peg Mackay
1 Robieson Lane, Roseneath

Tel (04) 801 8691 or 021 801 869
pegmackay@hotmail.com
www.wellingtonpanorama.co.nz

Double $120-$150 (Continental breakfast)
Evening meals by arrangement
2 Queen (2 bdrm)
Bathrooms: 1 Private

Above Oriental Bay lie in bed enjoying the panorama of ships, ferries and tugs and the sun, peace and privacy of our warm modern home. You have your own deck and sitting room with TV, tea/coffee etc. Take the 5 minute walk to Mt Victoria or the 15-20 minute walk down to Oriental Bay and the city, galleries and Te Papa: the Museum of New Zealand. Taste NZ in the many nearby cafés and restaurants. Ferry/Airport ten minutes, city five minutes drive.

Wellington - Roseneath *1 km E of Wellington CBD*

Maida Vale *B&B*

Bessie Sutherland
6 Maida Vale Road, Roseneath, Wellington

Tel 027 332 1570 or (04) 970 5184
bess@woosh.co.nz
www.maidavalebnb.co.nz

Double $180 Single $60-$150 (Continental breakfast)
Children negotiable
Weekly rates negotiable
Visa MC accepted
Children welcome
1 King 1 Single (2 bdrm)
Bathrooms: 1 Ensuite

Our centrally located home has spectacular views across the harbour to the city centre. The larger room has an ensuite. Both rooms are on the ground floor and have their own entrance (our family lives above). The city centre, restaurants, theatres and museums are a five minute drive away or, alternatively, a 20 minute walk along the waterfront. The airport and ferry terminals are 10-15 minutes away. The family will greet you with a warm welcome as will Zoe, the Jack Russell terrier.

Wellington

Wellington - Roseneath *2 km N of Central City*

Crescent Point *B&B*

Bobbi & John Gibbons
18 The Crescent, Roseneath, Wellington 6011

Tel (04) 972 3464 or 027 485 0846
Fax (04) 972 3465
gibbonsjg@paradise.net.nz

Double $200-$250 Single $150 (Full breakfast)
Dinner by arrangement
Visa MC accepted
Children and pets welcome
2 Queen (2 bdrm)
Bathrooms: 1 Ensuite with spa bath 1 Private

We welcome you to sunny Crescent Point, a spacious modern home with panoramic views overlooking the harbour above Oriental Bay. We offer two bedrooms with cable TV, one with ensuite & spa bath, one with private bathroom, kitchenette, own entrance and carpark. Take a five minute bush walk to Oriental Bay beach, then a pleasant ten minute walk to the City entertainment area, with restaurants, theatres and Te Papa. 10-15 minute drive to Central City and Ferry. Ten minutes to Wellington Airport. There is a cat in residence.

Wellington - Hataitai *3 km E of Wellington CBD*

Top O' T'ill *B&B Homestay Apartment with Kitchen*

Cathryn & Dennis Riley
2 Waitoa Road, Hataitai, Wellington 6021

Tel (04) 976 2718 or 027 471 6482
Fax (04) 976 2719
top.o.hill@clear.net.nz
www.topotill-homestay.co.nz

Double $120-$130 Single $75-$95 (Full breakfast)
Self-contained $110-$140
Visa MC accepted
Pet free home
Not suitable for children
2 Queen 1 Twin 1 Single (4 bdrm)
Bathrooms: 2 Ensuite 1 Private 1 Guest share

Hataitai - 'breath of the ocean', is a popular eastern suburb midway between the airport and central Wellington. City attractions are 5-10 minutes by bus or car. Our comfortable family home of 60 years is a welcome retreat for guests. The quality studio/apartment is fully equipped - long and short term rates on application. We share a range of cultural interests, have travelled widely, and will help you make the most of your visit to Wellington. Directions: included in web site.

Wellington - Brooklyn (City End) *3 km SW of Wellington City Centre*

Karepa *Homestay*

Ann & Tom Hodgson
56 Karepa Street, Brooklyn, Wellington

Tel (04) 384 4193   Fax (04) 384 4180
golf@xtra.co.nz
www.holidayletting.co.nz/karepa

Double $130-$165 Single $95-$125 (Full breakfast)
Children by arrangement
Dinner $35 by arrangement
Extra guest $35pp
Visa MC accepted
Children welcome
2 King 1 Double 1 Single (3 bdrm)
Bathrooms: 2 Ensuite 1 Guest share

Stay at Karepa, our sunny, spacious home overlooking city, harbour and mountains. The secluded rear garden adjoins native bush. Private guest rooms have TV and tea/coffee facilities. City five minutes, ferry ten and airport 15. Residents of 23 years, ex-UK, we have travelled widely, play golf and tennis, and enjoy Wellington's many attractions. Ann gardens and Tom watches from his deckchair. On-site parking. Bus at door. Laundry facilities. Sorry, no smokers or pets. Please phone/fax for directions.

Wellington - Vogeltown (South Mt Cook) *3 km S of CBD*

Finnimore House *B&B Homestay*
Willie & Kathleen Ryan
2 Dransfield Street, Vogeltown, Wellington

Tel (04) 389 9894   Fax (04) 389 9894
w.f.ryan@xtra.co.nz
www.finnimorehouse.co.nz

Double $95-$120 Single $75-$90 (Full breakfast)
Children $20 Visa MC accepted
Children welcome
2 Queen 2 Single (2 bdrm)
Bathrooms: 1 Guest share

Welcome to our historical manor five minutes drive from downtown Wellington. Your hosts, Willie and Kathleen Ryan, offer warm hospitality, spacious victorian rooms, a hearty breakfast, and a traditional B&B experience in a welcoming family home with a genuine Irish flavour. Our great location is close to: airport, ferries, restaurants, Basin Reserve, hospital, zoo, Massey University, Hurricanes training ground, National School of Dance and Drama. Secure private parking on-site, convenient public transport. Laundry facilities (available if staying three nights). Wellington is yours at Finnimore House.

Wellington - Mornington *3 km S of Wellington Central*

Ngahere House *Homestay*
Hilary & David Capper
147 The Ridgeway, Mornington, Wellington

Tel (04) 389 4501
hilary.capper@gmail.com

Double $120 (Full breakfast)
Please note Agent's fee extra
Pet free home
Not suitable for children
1 Queen (1 bdrm)
Bathrooms: 1 Private

Relax in our private, sunny and contemporary home. Enjoy panoramic views of the city, harbour and mountains from our sunroom and deck or sit by our cosy fire. Five minutes drive from downtown Wellington and close to the airport and ferries. On bus route. Guest facilities - spacious double room, coffee table, lounge chairs, TV, desk and private balcony. Well appointed bathroom. Restaurants, art deco cinema nearby. We enjoy meeting people, travel, reading, films, walking, the Arts, and welcome conversation with our guests.

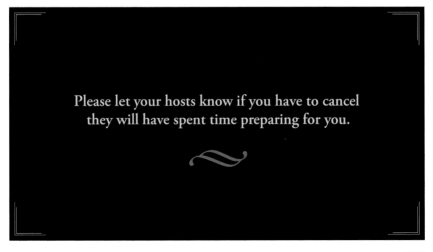

**Please let your hosts know if you have to cancel
they will have spent time preparing for you.**

Wellington - Seatoun *10 km SE of Courtenay Place*

The Admiral's Breakfast B&B Apartment
Luxury B&B Apartment with Kitchen

Karen Cronin & Wren Green
97 Inglis Street, Seatoun, Wellington

Tel (04) 934 5913 or 021 304 524
enquiries@admiralsbreakfast.co.nz
www.admiralsbreakfast.co.nz

Double $175 Single $155 (Full breakfast provisions)
Complimentary champagne gift basket on arrival
Visa MC accepted
Not suitable for children
1 Queen (1 bdrm)
Bathrooms: 1 Ensuite

Enjoy the luxury of a spacious apartment in Seatoun. Quiet location, yet only four minutes to the airport, twelve minutes to downtown. Start the day with a breakfast, fit for an admiral. The apartment is completely self-catering with all the makings for a fine breakfast provided. Check emails via free broadband in your apartment and enjoy breakfast at your leisure. Private courtyard with wonderful harbour views. Excellent restaurants and cafés close by. We welcome travellers for short or longer stays. We are both seasoned travellers.

Just as we have a variety of B&Bs
you will also be offered a variety of breakfasts,
and they will always be generous.

Wellington - Island Bay *4 km S of Courtenay Place*

Buckley Homestay *B&B Homestay Separate Suite*
Mrs Wilhelmina Muller
51 Buckley Road, Melrose, Island Bay, Wellington

Tel (04) 934 7151 or 021 112 3445
Fax (04) 934 7152
willy.muller@paradise.net.nz
www.buckleyhomestay.co.nz

Double $95-$140 Single $85-$110
(Continental breakfast)   Children negotiable
Dinner by arrangement   Visa MC accepted
Pet free home   Children and pets welcome
1 King/Twin 1 Queen 3 Single (3 bdrm)
Bathrooms: 2 Private 1 Family share

Large two storey sunny home with spectacular scenery and beautiful views over Wellington. New tastefully decorated, private entrance, one bedroom, self-contained suite with private balcony, TV, conservatory. Handy to hospitals. We are interested in food, wine, travel, relaxing and meeting people. Willy is a nurse, enjoys cooking, gardening and speaks Dutch. No pets or children at home. Off-street parking, complimentary refreshments, dinner by arrangement. On bus route. Handy to all tourist attractions, and airport.

Wellington - Island Bay *6 km S of Wellington City Central*

The Lighthouse & The Keep *Self-contained*
Bruce Stokell
326 The Esplanade & 116 The Esplanade,
Island Bay, Wellington

Tel (04) 472 4177 or 027 442 5555
bruce@thelighthouse.net.nz
www.thelighthouse.net.nz

Double $180-$200 (Full breakfast provisions)
Visa MC accepted
Not suitable for children
1 Double (1 bdrm)
Bathrooms: 1 Private

B&B
Approved

Island Bay - 10 minutes city centre, 10 minutes airport, 20 minutes ferry terminal.

The Lighthouse is on the south coast and has views of the island, fishing boats in the bay, the beach and rocks, the far coastline, the open sea, the shipping and, on a clear day, the South Island. There are local shops and restaurants.

The Lighthouse has a basic kitchen and bathroom on the first floor, the bedroom/sitting room on the middle floor and the lookout/bedroom on the top. Romantic.

The Keep is a stone tower just two minutes from The Lighthouse. It has a lounge/basic kitchen on one level and a bed with ensuite on the next level. Also a spa bath in the bedroom. It is very cosy and has excellent views of the sea, especially in a storm. Stairs from the bedroom lead to a hatch which opens on to the roof.

Wellington - Island Bay *3 km S of Courtenay Place*

Ma Maison *Boutique B&B*
Margo Frost
9 Tamar Street, Island Bay, Wellington
Tel (04) 383 4018 or 027 2429 827
Fax (04) 383 4018
bedandbreakfast@paradise.net.nz
www.nzwellingtonhomestay.co.nz
Double $130 Single $110 (Full breakfast)
Visa MC accepted
2 Queen (2 bdrm)
Bathrooms: 1 Ensuite 1 Private

Luxury in a warm, comfortable home at a realistic price, our 1920's home is decorated with a French flavour. Drive to door, lovely garden.

The brown guest room has it's own entrance and ensuite, the blue room has private bathroom. Both rooms have queen posturepedic beds and are equipped with everything to make your stay as comfortable as possible.

Island Bay is a popular seaside suburb with excellent local restaurants. We are eight minutes by car to the city and very handy to great bus service.

A full delicious breakfast is served at a time to suit you. Resident family cat.

Wellington - Island Bay *7 km S of Wellington City Central*

Nature's Touch Guest House *B&B*
Maarten & Natsuko Groeneveld
25A Happy Valley Road, Owhiro Bay, Wellington

Tel (04) 383 6977 or 027 559 0966
Fax (04) 383 6977
info@naturestouchguesthouse.com
http://naturestouchguesthouse.com

Double $110-$160 Single $90-$140 (Full breakfast)
Children $45
Japanese Dinner $35pp,
European Dinner $30pp
Visa MC accepted
Children welcome
2 King 2 Single (2 bdrm)
Bathrooms: 1 Ensuite 1 Family share
Lying bath with seaviews

"Thank you again for a wonderful visit to your home. Your meal was stupendously prepared and we often regret that our appetites were not up to the generous portions! We loved our seal hunt" Leslie, Mike, Zealand and Scotland from USA

"...thank you both for a wonderful stay. Your B&B is very beautiful and homely. The views are spectacular. The trip out to the seals was wonderful even though we didn't see a seal. The scenery is outstanding and different. Now about your wonderful breakfast. They are the best we have had in NZ and I must admit in the world" Margie & Joe From Australia

A warm welcome from us and our friendly dog, Lucky! We are just a short stroll to the beach and the reserve. Only ten minutes drive to the city, 15 minutes drive to the ferry terminal and the airport. Upper Boat Bedroom is for you to enjoy whole of upstairs and elevated views as well as privacy. We are building Lower Boat bedroom and a lying bathroom wtih seaviews. It will be completed around spring 2007. Enjoy tranquillity.

Wellington - Island Bay *In Wellington*

Island Bay Homestay *Homestay*

B&B
Approved

Theresa & Jack Stokes
52 High Street, Island Bay, Wellington 6023

Tel (04) 970 3353 or 0800 335 383
Fax (04) 970 3353
tandjstokes@paradise.net.nz
www.wellingtonhomestay.com

Double $90 Single $55 (Full breakfast)
Not suitable for children under 12 years of age
2 Double (2 bdrm)
Bathrooms: 2 Private

We live in a Lockwood house, at the end of High Street in a very private section. Our land goes three quarters of the way up the hill and above that is Town Belt. Wonderful views, overlooking the Cook Strait with its ferries, cargo and fishing boats on the move day and night. We see planes landing or taking off (depending on wind direction) but the airport is round a corner and we get no noise from it.

We only let two of our rooms and each has its own private bathroom, just outside the bedroom door. TV in rooms. A warm, comfortable smoke-free home with warm clean comfortable beds and two warm owners who enjoy meeting people. We do our best to provide good, old fashioned Homestay, without charging the earth! We have two lovely Moggies. Not suitable for children under

Directions:
From State Highway 1 or 2 take the Aotea Quay turn-off. (From the ferry take the city exit). Follow the main road which bears slightly to the left until you come to a T junction (Oriental Parade). Turn right in to Kent Terrace and get in the right hand lane before going round the Basin Reserve (cricket ground) and in to Adelaide Road. Keep going straight, up the hill and the road becomes The Parade. Keep going until you reach the sea and then turn SHARP right (new guests can easily miss this turn-off) into Beach Street. Left and left again in to High Street and up the private road at the end.

From Wellington Airport: take the rear exit (past the cargo warehouses) and turn right. Follow the coast road for 10 minutes and Beach Street is on the right. For the Navigator we live at - Lat. S.41.20.54 Long E.174.45.54. 14. Full breakfast 7.30am onwards. Regrets we cannot accept bookings from guests arriving from Australia on the midnight arrivals or guests leaving on the 6am departures.

For the Navigator we live at:
Lat. S.41.20.54.
Long. E.174.45.54 14

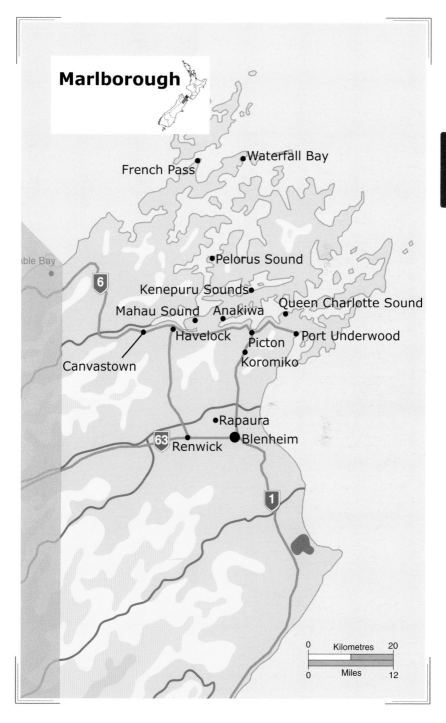

Marlborough

Waterfall Bay
French Pass
Pelorus Sound
Kenepuru Sounds
Queen Charlotte Sound
Mahau Sound Anakiwa
Havelock
Port Underwood
Picton
Canvastown
Koromiko

Rapaura
Renwick ● Blenheim

0 Kilometres 20
0 Miles 12

Marlborough

Picton *1 km E of Picton Central*

Retreat Inn *B&B Homestay*
Alison & Geoff
20 Lincoln Street, Picton

Tel (03) 573 8160 or 021 143 2224
Fax (03) 573 7799
elliott.orchard@xtra.co.nz
www.retreat-inn.co.nz

Double $100-$135 (Special breakfast)
Room rate $100-$135
Not suitable for children
2 Queen 2 Single (3 bdrm)
Bathrooms: 1 Ensuite 1 Private 1 Guest share

Set in peaceful bush surroundings, Retreat Inn Homestay/B&B offers you comfort & rest, with a yummy breakfast! Three guest bedrooms - One queen (ensuite, bath and shower) downstairs, with outside access to fern/seating area. Two upstairs rooms, queen and twin (private or guest share bathroom) Great for a group of four. Marlborough province is diverse, unforgettable - come stay two or three nights and explore what we have to offer. Flat off-street parking. A happy two person/two cat household!

Picton *0.5 km SE of Picton Central*

Grandvue *B&B Homestay Apartment with Kitchen*
Rosalie & Russell Mathews
19 Otago Street, Picton 7220

Tel (03) 573 8553 or 0800 49 1080
Fax (03) 573 8556
enquiries@grandvuepicton.co.nz
www.grandvuepicton.co.nz

Double $110-$125 Single $60-$75 (Full breakfast)
Children $35 Visa MC accepted
Pet free home Children welcome
2 Queen 1 Twin (3 bdrm)
Bathrooms: 1 Ensuite 1 Family share

On the hills above Picton, Grandvue is a quiet haven in a secluded garden with a grandview. It's a five minute walk to the shopping area, restaurants, the waterfront & bushwalks. Russell, retired, enjoys boating, fishing & gardening. Rosalie an enthusiastic patchworker, loves cooking & gardening. Both enjoy meeting people. The accommodation is spacious, warm, quality self-contained with kitchen and ensuite. Other rooms available in our home. Feast on magnificent views from our conservatory while enjoying a wholesome breakfast. Courtesy transport, parking & laundry facilities

Picton *0.25 km SE of Picton*

Rivenhall *B&B Homestay*
Nan & Malcolm Laurenson
118 Wellington Street, Picton, Marlborough 7220

Tel (03) 573 7692
Fax (03) 573 7692
rivenhall.picton@xtra.co.nz

Double $140 Single $100 (Full breakfast)
Visa MC accepted
Pet free home
Children welcome
1 Queen 1 Double (2 bdrm)
Bathrooms: 2 Private

Up the rise, on the left, at the top of Wellington Street, is Rivenhall. A gracious home with all the warmth, comfort and charm of days gone by, overlooking the town of Picton with its background of surrounding hills. Yet it is an easy walk to the centre of town or the ferry's beyond. Courtesy pick up from the ferry, bus or train. The Marlborough Sounds start at the bottom of our street.

Picton *0.5 km N of Picton*

Echo Lodge *B&B Homestay*

Lyn & Eddie Thoroughgood
5 Rutland Street, Picton

Tel (03) 573 6367
Fax (03) 573 6387
echolodge@xtra.co.nz

Double $100 Single $60 (Full breakfast)
Half hour foot massage $10
1 Double 1 Twin 1 Single (3 bdrm)
Bathrooms: 2 Ensuite 1 Private

Lyn, Eddie and our little dog Osca welcome you to home-style comfort at Echo Lodge. Starting your day with a smorgasbord breakfast of home-grown produce and freshly baked bread. A five minute stroll into Picton takes you to great restaurants. From our front gate there are lovely bush walks to Bob's Bay, The Snout or Marina. Tea and coffee in your room, ensuite or private facilities, a sunny patio and log fire for chilly nights ensures your comfort. Courtesy car and off-street parking

Picton - Kenepuru Sounds *80 km NE of Havelock*

The Nikaus *B&B Farmstay*

Alison & Robin Bowron
86 Manaroa Road, Waitaria Bay, RD 2, Picton

Tel (03) 573 4432 or 027 454 4712
Fax (03) 573 4432
info@thenikaus.co.nz
www.thenikaus.co.nz

Double $120 Single $60 (Full breakfast)
Dinner $30
Visa MC accepted
1 Queen 4 Single (3 bdrm)
Bathrooms: 1 Guest share

The Nikaus sheep & cattle farm is situated in Waitaria Bay, Kenepuru Sound, two hours drive from Blenheim or Picton. We offer friendly personal service in our comfortable spacious home. Large gardens contain rhododendrons, roses, Camellia, lilies and perennials, big sloping lawns and views out to sea. House pets Minny (Jack Russell-cross) Honey (Lab) and four cats, Other animals include the farm dogs, donkeys, pet wild pigs, turkeys, hens and peacocks. Country meals, home-grown produce. Operators available for fishing trips, launch charters, golf and various walks.

Picton - Ngakuta Bay *11 km W of Picton*

Bayswater *B&B Homestay Apartment with Kitchen*

Paul & Judy Mann
25 Manuka Drive, Ngakuta Bay,
Queen Charlotte Drive, RD 1, Picton

Tel (03) 573 5966
Fax (03) 573 5966

Double $85-$100 Single $65 (Continental breakfast)
2 people in self-contained unit $120
Each additional person $30
1 Queen 1 Twin (2 bdrm)
Bathrooms: 1 Ensuite 1 Private

Welcome to Bayswater B&B in Ngakuta Bay, situated 11 km from Picton and 24 km from Havelock off Queen Charlotte Drive in the beautiful Marlborough Sounds. Your accommodation consists of a self-contained apartment with two double bedrooms, two bathrooms, kitchen, dining and lounge. Spectacular views over Ngakuta Bay and the surrounding bush. The Bay has a picnic area and safe swimming; the Queen Charlotte Track is close by. Remember to bring food if self-catering. Suitable for longer stays. Come and relax in paradise. Complimentary transport available.

Picton - Queen Charlotte Sounds *16 km W of Picton*

Tanglewood *B&B Homestay Separate Suite Apartment with Kitchen*

Linda & Stephen Hearn
1744 Queen Charlotte Drive, The Grove, RD 1, Picton

Tel (03) 574 2080 or 027 481 4388
Fax (03) 574 2044
tanglewood.hearn@xtra.co.nz

Double $125-$145 Single $95 (Full breakfast)
Dinner $40
Self-contained $190
Visa MC accepted
2 King/Twin 1 Queen 2 Single (4 bdrm)
Bathrooms: 4 Ensuite

Modern architectural home nestled amongst the native ferns overlooking Queen Charlotte Sounds. Enjoy our luxury Super-king/twin ensuite rooms with balcony and views; or a self contained guest wing which includes queen and two single beds (with ensuites), lounge, kitchen and sunny balcony/BBQ area. Relax in our jacuzzi surrounded by beautiful native garden and birds or view the glow-worms. Substaial breakfast provided before your day's pursuits, swimming, fishing, kayaking, walking the Queen Charlotte Walkway or exploring Marlborough Wineries. Fifth generation Kiwi hospitality at its best.

Pelorus - Mahau Sound *33 km W of Picton*

Ramona *B&B Homestay*

Phyl & Ken Illes
460 Moetapu Bay Road, Mahau Sound, Marlborough

Tel (03) 574 2215 or 027 247 6668
Fax (03) 574 2915
illes@clear.net.nz

Double $120 Single $85 (Continental breakfast)
We can accomodate 3 children
3 course dinner served with local wine
Tea & coffee available in conservatory
Visa MC accepted
Pet free home Children welcome
2 Double 2 Twin (2 bdrm)
Bathrooms: 1 Private Hair dryer in bathroom

Our waterfront home on the beautiful Mahau Sound has been designed for you to share. Our guest floor has its own conservatory, here you can view the passing water traffic. Awake to the call of bellbirds and tuis, and after breakfast stroll around our rhododendron garden, or fossick on the beach. In the evening, see our glowworms. Phyl's interests include quilting, gardening and oilpainting. Ken is a retired builder. Visits to local craft studios can be arranged. We host only one party at a time.

Picton - Queen Charlotte Sounds *11 km W of Picton*

Waterfront Bed & Breakfast *B&B Homestay*

Vicki & David Bendell
Queen Charlotte Drive, 2383 Little Ngakuta Bay,
RD 1, Picton

Tel (03) 573 8584 or 021 216 5955
bendell@xtra.co.nz
www.picton.co.nz/waterfront

Double $165-$185 Single $165 (Full breakfast)
Children $40 under 5 free
Dinner $40pp with notice - freshly caught fish/mussels,
cheese platter Diners accepted Children welcome
1 Queen 1 Double 2 Single (2 bdrm)
Bathrooms: 1 Ensuite 1 Private 1 Family share

Our waterfront accommodation is as close to the waters edge as you can get. The aptly named "Boatshed" with ensuite and "Pacific" Room with private bathroom are separate from the cottage. A 180 metre jetty (pier) is right out front - ideal for fishing or evening stroll to see the water fluoresce. Kayak, fishing rods, loungers, petanque, sportscruiser available or row the clinker dinghy with picnic hamper. Handy to Queen Charlotte Track our young family and dog welcome you for a break from the ordinary.

Picton *3 km NE of Picton*

Michiru *B&B*
Rosemary & Paul Royer
247B Waikawa Road, Waikawa, Picton

Tel (03) 573 6793
Fax (03) 573 6793
royer@xtra.co.nz
www.picton.co.nz/for/michiru

Double $130 Single $75 (Special breakfast)
Dinner $50 by arrangement
Visa MC accepted
Children welcome
1 King 1 Queen 2 Single (3 bdrm)
Bathrooms: 1 Ensuite 2 Private

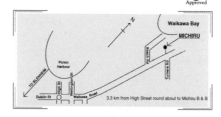

We only have one aim - to give you the finest and most memorable experience that we are able to provide. We overlook Waikawa Bay and the beautiful Queen Charlotte Sounds so you can watch the ferries and cruise ships pass while enjoying breakfast: and all of this is only 3 km from Picton town centre.

The bright and sunny rooms are all located on the ground floor with a lovely private guest lounge and garden patio. Guests have the use of laundry facilities, bikes and kayaks around the bay. We invite you to join us for Rosemary's delightful three course dinners with a glass of wine (by arrangement). We will of course meet or drop you at the ferry terminal, especially if you are walking the Queen Charlotte Track and don't have your own transport. There is a waterside restaurant and a café/bar within five minutes walk of the house. You'll love this location!

Walk the Queen Charlotte Track, kayak or sail the Queen Charlotte Sounds, take half or whole day winery tours, daily dolphin watch tours, re-live The Edwin Fox experience (she's the world's ninth oldest ship), visit the fascinating Seahorse World, and finally our favourite place Karaka Point historical site. Superb accommodation for the discerning guests!

237

Marlborough

Picton *0.5 km N of Picton Central*

The Gables *B&B Cottage No Kitchen*

Ian & Paula Allen
20 Waikawa Road, Picton

Tel (03) 573 6772
Fax (03) 573 6772
info@thegables.co.nz
www.thegables.co.nz

Double $120-$160 Single $90 (Full breakfast)
Children $15
Visa MC accepted
Children and pets welcome
4 Queen 1 Double 2 Single (5 bdrm)
Bathrooms: 4 Ensuite 1 Private

The Gables is a charming and historic homestead situated close to all of Picton's attractions and amenities. A leisurely amble takes you to the splendid foreshore area, or a selection of restaurants, pubs, shops and supermarkets. Breakfasts at The Gables are designed to give you a fulfilling and enjoyable start to an active day. Ian and Paula will make every effort to ensure that their lovely old residence will become your home away from home for the duration of your stay.

Picton *0.5 km E of Picton*

Glengary *B&B*

Glenys & Gary Riggs
5 Seaview Cresent, Picton

Tel (03) 573 8317 or 027 498 6388
g.riggs@xtra.co.nz
www.glengary.co.nz

Double $120-$140 Single $65
(Continental breakfast)
Not suitable for children
2 King/Twin 2 Queen (3 bdrm)
Bathrooms: 2 Ensuite 1 Private

Located a short drive from Picton Ferry Terminal and a few minutes walk to the town centre. Inner harbour across the road. Whether you are interested in visiting wineries, fishing, bush walking, cruising, sea kayaking or simply relaxing in idyllic surroundings Glengary Bed & Breakfast is ideally located to explore the Marlborough area. Your friendly hosts will provide you with the best service to ensure your stay in the beautiful Marlborough Sounds is relaxing and enjoyable. Ferry pick up. Family cat in residence.

Picton - Anakiwa *22 km W of Picton*

Tirimoana House *Luxury B&B Lodge*

John & Michelle Hotham
257 Anakiwa Road, RD 1, Picton

Tel (03) 574 2627 or 021 167 2342
Fax (03) 574 2647   bookings@tirimoanahouse.com
www.tirimoanahouse.com

Double $160-$260 Single $120-$180 (Full breakfast)
Children please enquire
Dinner by arrangement $45-$55pp 2-3 courses,
prepared by Qualifed Chef from local fare
Visa MC Eftpos accepted
4 Queen (4 bdrm)
Bathrooms: 4 Ensuite

Enjoying superb sea views of the Marlborough Sounds, Tirimoana House is located a convenient thirty minute drive from both Picton and the Marlborough wineries. Our two-storey home sits on an elevated waterfront site once occupied by the historic Tirimoana Hotel. Our four sumptuous bedrooms are all ensuite, all have antique French queen size beds (one has a 1789 four poster) antique bedside cabinets and chandeliers. One suite sleeps four.

Our home has antique furniture throughout and many works of art both local and international, collected by your hosts on their NZ & international travels (John and Michelle are both artists).
Close by is the renowned Queen Charlotte Track (walk out - water taxi back), kayaking, mountain biking and of course those famous wineries. Relax afterwards in our swimming pool or in front of the log fire in winter before enjoying a gourmet dinner of local fare and wines. Michelle is an international chef. The Blistered Foot Café is open from 11am-4pm for guests, those walking the Queen Charlotte Track or waiting for the water taxi.

Minimum two night stay from Dec 1 till Feb 28th
Winter rates May 1st -Sept30th less 20%
We have a poodle called Shug

Marlborough

Picton

Palm Haven *B&B*

Allan & Robyn Healey
15A Otago Street, Picton

Tel (03) 573 5644 or 021 173 2567
palmhaven@xtra.co.nz

Double $120 Single $85 (Continental breakfast)
Visa MC Eftpos accepted
Pet free home
Not suitable for children
3 Queen 1 Twin (4 bdrm)
Bathrooms: 3 Ensuite 1 Private

Palm Haven, a modern purpose-built home designed for your comfort and convenience. Just a few minutes walk to the town centre to cafés, restaurants and leisure activities. Guest rooms, three with queen beds and ensuites, one room with twin beds and private bathroom All rooms have tea and coffee making facilities TV and bar fridge. We provide courtesy pick up from the ferry terminal train and bus.

Picton - Anakiwa *22 km W of Picton*

Queensview BnB *B&B Separate Suite Apartment with Kitchen*

Ann & John McGuire
259G Anakiwa Road, Anakiwa - Picton, RD 1

Tel (03) 574 2363 or 021 0229 2864
queensview@xtra.co.nz
http://picton.co.nz/queensviewbnb

Double $120-$180 Single $90-$120 (Full breakfast)
Dinner by arrangement - BBQ facilities available
Local hotel 6 minutes drive
Pet free home Children welcome
1 Queen 1 Double 1 Twin (3 bdrm)
Bathrooms: 1 Ensuite 1 Private 1 Guest share
Shared bathroom can be booked as Private

Our elevated deck over the top of the Punga trees offers guests arguably some of the best views off the Queen Charltte Sound. The shoreline no more than a three minute walk. The Queen Charlotte Track (10 minutes walk), the holiday town of Picton (30 minutes), the marina & mussel town of Havelock (25 minutes) and the winery district of Blenheim (40 minutes). So if your holiday is walking, swimming, boating, fishing, kayaking or exploring the many wineries, then Queensview BnB is the ideal central location.

Picton *0.25 km SW of Post Office*

Marineland Heritage House B & B *B&B*

Rosemary Baxter & Peter Broad
28 Waikawa Road, Picton, 7250

Tel (03) 5736 429 or Freephone: 0800 616 429
Fax (03) 5737 634
marineland@xtra.co.nz
www.marinelandaccom.co.nz

Double $75-$110 Single $65-$110
(Continental breakfast)
Dinner By arrangement
Visa MC Diners Amex Eftpos accepted
Not suitable for children
1 King 1 Queen 5 Double 3 Twin 1 Single (11 bdrm)
Bathrooms: 5 Ensuite 6 Guest share

Enjoy Marineland Heritage House B & B, built in 1925 for the local doctor. All downstaris rooms have ensuites, upstairs rooms have shared bathrooms. Rooms have electric blankets and tea/coffee making facilities. A comfortable lounge with Broadband internet access & TV. Adjacent to the lounge is the breakfast room for our "Picton Breakfast", a wheat & gluten free option is available. We offer a laundry and off-street parking. We are a few minutes walk from town centre & water front.

Picton - Koromiko *5 km S of Picton*
Koromiko Valley Homestead *B&B*

Pat & Ian McKinnon
30 Freeths Road, Koromiko, Picton

Tel (03) 573 7518
Fax (03) 573 7538
koromikohomestead@ihug.co.nz
www.koromikohomestead.co.nz

Double $145-$185
(Full breakfast)
Not suitable for children
2 Queen (2 bdrm)
Bathrooms: 2 Private

Only 5 km south from Picton and a short distance off State Highway 1, we welcome you to stay in the self-contained wing of our rural homestead set on ten acres. The quality accomodation includes private guest lounge, kitchen and dining room. Have breakfast served in your suite or alfresco on the garden deck. Stroll though our large gardens, play golf at the nearby course, or hire one of our specialised two-seater classic-style sports cars. Complimentary transfers to Picton airport or ferry.

Blenheim *3 km S of Blenheim*
Hillsview *Homestay*

Adrienne & Rex Handley
Please phone for directions

Tel (03) 578 9562
Fax (03) 578 9562
aidrex@xtra.co.nz

Double $95-$110 Single $65-$85
(Full breakfast)
Less 10% if pre-booked by the night before
1 King/Twin 1 Double 2 Twin (3 bdrm)
Bathrooms: 2 Private

Welcome to our warm, spacious, non-smoking home in a quiet suburb with outdoor pool, off-street parking, and no pets. All beds have quality mattresses, electric blankets and wool underlays. Interests: Rex's (retired airline pilot) - are aviation oriented - models, microlights, homebuilts and gliding. Builds miniature steam locomotives, has 1930 Model A soft-top tourer vintage car and enjoys barbershop singing. Adrienne's - cooking, spinning, woolcraft. Let us share these hobbies, plus our caring personal attention, complimentary beverages and all the comforts of home with you.

Blenheim - Rapaura *12 km NW of Blenheim*
Thainstone *Homestay Cottage with Kitchen*
Vivienne & Jim Murray
120 Giffords Road, RD 3, Rapaura

Tel (03) 572 8823   Fax (03) 572 8623
thainstone@xtra.co.nz
www.thainstone.co.nz

Double $120 Single $70 (Full breakfast)
Dinner $35
Self-catering house (sleeps 2-4), no breakfast $120-$180
Visa MC Amex accepted
Not suitable for children
1 King 2 Queen 2 Twin (5 bdrm)
Bathrooms: 1 Ensuite 1 Private 1 Guest share

Our large home is surrounded by vineyards and within walking distance of the Wairau River and several wineries. In our home there are three upstairs bedrooms and a guest lounge which opens onto an enclosed, solar heated swimming pool. The self-catering house has two bedrooms and is fully equipped for longer stays. We are widely travelled and some interests are bird watching, trout fishing, woodworking and cards. Evening meals, by prior arrangement, are served with Marlborough wines. Unsuitable for children.

Marlborough

Blenheim *1 km W of Blenheim Central*

Beaver B&B *Homestay Cottage with Kitchen*

B&B Approved

Jen & Russell Hopkins
60 Beaver Road, Blenheim

Tel (03) 578 8401 or 021 626 151
Fax (03) 578 8401
rdhopkins@xtra.co.nz
http://marlborough.co.nz/beaver/

Double $100 **Single** $60
(Continental breakfast)
Visa MC accepted
Not suitable for children
1 Queen (1 bdrm)
Bathrooms: 1 Ensuite

Our self-contained unit has its own entrance and off-street parking. Five minutes drive from central Blenheim and ten minutes drive from the wineries and the Aviation Heritage Centre. The bed is queen-size. The mini-kitchen has a microwave, small sink and fridge containing items for a self-serve continental breakfast to have at your leisure. The bathroom has a large bath and a separate shower and toilet. Two cats live with us and we have bikes for hire.

Blenheim *2.5 km N of Blenheim*

Philmar *B&B Homestay*

B&B Approved

Wynnis & Lex Phillips
9 Maple Close, Springlands, Blenheim

Tel (03) 577 7788
Fax (03) 577 7788
philmar9@xtra.co.nz

Double $80-$100 **Single** $60
(Continental breakfast)
Dinner $20pp by arrangement
2 Queen 1 Twin (3 bdrm)
Bathrooms: 1 Ensuite 1 Guest share

Welcome to our home 2.5 km from the town centre. Guests can join us in our spacious sunny living areas. We both enjoy all sports on TV and our other interests include wood turning, handcrafts and the Lions organisation. Blenheim has many wineries, parks, craft shops, art galleries and golf courses. Not far from Picton, Nelson & Kaikoura whale watching. We share our home with our pets, Lucy-Lu and Louie. Smoking is not encouraged. Just phone to be picked up at airport, bus or train.

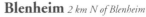

Blenheim *2 km N of Blenheim*

Baxter Homestay *B&B Homestay Luxury Unit with Kitchen/Dining*

B&B Approved

Kathy & Brian Baxter
28 Elisha Drive, Blenheim

Tel (03) 578 3753 or 021 129 2062
Fax (03) 578 3796
baxterart@xtra.co.nz
www.baxterhomestay.com

Double $140-$200 (Continental breakfast)
Pet free home
Children welcome
1 King/Twin 1 King 2 Queen 1 Single (4 bdrm)
Bathrooms: 2 Ensuite 1 Guest share
Bath & shower in king/twin ensuite

Brian, a well known New Zealand artist, and Kathy welcome you to their spacious, sunny, quiet modern home and art gallery. Original artwork throughout house. Guests can enjoy magnificent panoramic views over Blenheim and nearby vineyards, or explore their terraced gardens, chosen for Hunters Garden Marlborough tours 2006. We can arrange visits to wineries, gardens, ski-field, golf courses restaurants etc. Laundry facilities available. Our interests include gardening, music, travel, fishing, skiing, golf and other sports, art, video production, and meeting people. No single night bookings at peak times.

Blenheim *2 km N of Blenheim*
The Willows *B&B Homestay*
Millie Amos
6 The Willows, Springlands, Blenheim

Tel (03) 577 7853
Fax (03) 577 7853

Double $112 Single $70
(Continental breakfast)
1 Queen 2 Twin (2 bdrm)
Bathrooms: 1 Private

Only 2 km from the centre of town. The Willows is a spacious and modern home in close proximity to shops, restaurants and wineries. Peaceful location surrounded by lovely gardens. I welcome you to my home, so please phone first.

Blenheim *1 km N of Blenheim Central*
Maxwell House *Homestay*
John and Barbara Ryan
82 Maxwell Road, Blenheim

Tel (03) 577 7545
Fax (03) 577 7545
mt.olympus@xtra.co.nz

Double $135 Single $100
(Full breakfast)
Visa MC accepted
Children welcome
1 Queen 1 Twin (2 bdrm)
Bathrooms: 2 Ensuite

Welcome to Marlborough. We invite you to stay at Maxwell House, a grand old Victorian residence. Built in 1880 our home has been elegantly restored and is classified with the Historic Places Trust. Our large guest rooms are individually appointed with ensuite, lounge area, television and tea & coffee making facilities. Breakfast will be a memorable experience, served around the original 1880's kauri table. Set on a large established property Maxwell House is an easy ten minute walk to the town centre. Non-smoking.

Blenheim *30 km S of Picton*
ParkView B&B *B&B Homestay*
Geoff & Shirley Cant
30 Solway Drive, Blenheim, Marlborough

Tel (03) 578-4492 or 0800 784 492
021 299 1705 or 021 141 7660
Fax (03) 578-4492 parkviewbb@xtra.co.nz
www.parkviewbb.co.nz

Double $120-$130 Single $85-$95 (Cont. breakfast)
Children $35 Cooked breakfast by arrangement.
Visa MC accepted Pet free home Children welcome
3 Queen 1 Single (3 bdrm)
Bathrooms: 1 Ensuite 1 Private 1 Family share
Bath & shower in ensuite

Shirley & Geoff welcome you to ParkView, a modern residence set in a quiet Blenheim suburb. It is adjacent to Harling Park which incorporates a Japanese Garden and backs on to the Wither Hills Farm Park with walking and mountain bike tracks which allows complete freedom to wander the beautiful hills. That can be before or after touring the many wineries around Blenheim. Blenheim is 30 minutes south from Picton, the terminal for the inter-island ferry from the North Island. It is less than two hours to Kaikoura and four hours to Christchurch International Airport

Marlborough

Blenheim *0.1 km W of Central Blenheim*

Henry Maxwell's Central B&B *B&B*

Rae Woodman
28 Henry Street, Blenheim

Tel (03) 578 8086 or 0800 436 796
Fax (03) 578 8086
stay@henrymaxwells.co.nz
www.henrymaxwells.co.nz

Double $100-$150 Single $75-$80 (Full breakfast)
Children welcome tarriff depending on age
Visa MC accepted Children welcome
3 Queen 2 Twin 3 Single (4 bdrm)
Bathrooms: 2 Ensuite 1 Private 1 Guest share
Bath in the large bathroom

Welcome to Henrys, a gracious 75 year old home. Guests have spacious quiet rooms, two with ensuites, two share bathroom. TV, tea, coffee, cookies and complimentary port. Queen size beds and large comfortable arm chairs. All overlook gardens. Breakfast in the unique dining room (maps and charts) is something to remember. three minutes stroll to town, many excellent restaurants, shops, theatre, movies, etc. Henrys, corner of Henry and Munro Streets between High Street and Maxwell Road. Off-street parking. Relax and enjoy the garden and sun.

Blenheim *7 km N of Blenheim*

Blue Ridge Estate *B&B Homestay*

Lesley & Brian Avery
50 O'Dwyers Road, RD 3, Blenheim

Tel (03) 570 2198
Fax (03) 570 2199
stay@blueridge.co.nz
www.blueridge.co.nz

Double $175-$215 Single $160-$200 (Full breakfast)
Visa MC accepted
2 Queen 2 Twin (3 bdrm)
Bathrooms: 1 Ensuite 2 Private

Set on a 20 acre purpose-designed homestay property, Blue Ridge Estate, 2002 Marlborough Master Builders' "House of the Year", enjoys a rural setting with stunning views across vineyards to the Richmond Range and is close to many of Marlborough's fine wineries, restaurants and gardens. Our home has proven most popular with both international and New Zealand visitors. Come share our home with Bella our friendly young labrador, where comfort and privacy will ensure your Marlborough visit is indeed a memorable one.

Blenheim *9 km NW of Blenheim*

Stonehaven Vineyard Homestay *B&B Homestay*

Paulette & John Hansen
414 Rapaura Road, RD 3, Blenheim

Tel (03) 572 9730 or 027 682 1120
Fax (03) 572 9730
stay@stonehavenhomestay.co.nz
www.stonehavenhomestay.co.nz

Double $225-$250 Single $145 (Full breakfast)
Children suitable 10 years and over
Three course gourmet dinner $60pp wine available
Guest bike hire $30 per day Visa MC accepted
1 King 1 Queen 1 Twin (3 bdrm)
Bathrooms: 2 Ensuite 1 Private Twin room private bathroom is downstairs

Stonehaven is surrounded by beautiful gardens and 17 acres of Sauvignon Blanc vines in the premium grape growing area of Marlborough. Spacious and comfortable, our home commands exquisite views over the vineyards to the Richmond Ranges. Close by are some of NZ's most outstanding wineries. Our delicious breakfasts are often served in the summerhouse overlooking the pool. Dinner available by arrangement We have a cat and a labrador. We look forward to making your stay with us as relaxing or as active as you choose.

Blenheim *1.5 km S of Blenheim*

Green Gables *B&B*

Mike & Debbie Pepler
3011 State Highway 1, St Andrews, Blenheim 7274

Tel (03) 577 9205 Fax (03) 577 9205
relax@greengablesbedandbreakfast.co.nz
www.greengablesbedandbreakfast.co.nz

Double $180-$200 Single $120-$130 (Full breakfast)
Dinner by arrangement $60pp including glass of wine
Visa MC accepted
Children and pets welcome
1 King/Twin 3 Queen (3 bdrm)
Bathrooms: 3 Ensuite 1 Guest share

Green Gables is set back from the road, nestled on 3.5 acres. The Opawa River borders the northern garden boundary. Four spacious guest rooms, three with ensuite. All rooms have seating, TV, tea/coffee facilities, robes, hairdryers and toiletries. Guest lounge and balcony. Breakfast is served around the large table and boasts fresh or home made hot and cold combinations. We will customise a breakfast to suit you. Evening meals available by prior arrangement. Special diets catered for. Wireless connection, internet, computer and fax are available.

Blenheim *1 km W of Blenheim Central*

Artlee House *B&B Homestay*

Leona Dawson
76B Lakings Road, Blenheim

Tel (03) 579 2225 or 027 431 4117
Fax (03) 579 2225 leona@artleehouse.co.nz
www.artleehouse.co.nz

Double $150-$195 Single $100-$150 (Full breakfast)
Visa MC accepted Not suitable for children
1 King 3 Single (3 bdrm)
Bathrooms: 1 Private 1 Guest share
Bath & Shower, Toilet separate

Artlee House welcomes you. You will enjoy a central location minutes from the town centre and airport, just off SH6. Wineries, restaurants, Omaka Aviation Heritage centre and galleries are close by. Relax, feel at home in peaceful garden setting. featuring mature trees, natural spring fed creek. Enjoy pure NZ bodycare by Linden Leaves along with robes, CD radio/clock, hairdryers etc. A complimentary wine/beer on your arrival, including homemade treats, tea and coffee - 24 hours. Leona's hobbies include art, crafts, walking and meeting people.

Blenheim *3 km S of Blenheim*

Redwood Heights *Luxury B&B*

Kathy & Mike Besley
245 Redwood Street, Blenheim, 7201

Tel 0800 733 001 or (03) 578 0143
Fax (03) 578 0143
k.besley@xtra.co.nz
www.redwoodheights.co.nz

Double $110-$175 Single $80 (Full breakfast)
Children by arrangement
Visa MC accepted
Children welcome
1 King 1 Queen 1 Twin (3 bdrm)
Bathrooms: 1 Ensuite 2 Private

Relax in modern, private quality accommodation. Enjoy extensive views and a country atmosphere. Stream Reserve Room is spacious, with ensuite and refreshment making facilities. Separate guest lounge and balcony. Close to wineries, restaurants, 3 km to town centre. Adjacent to Wither Hills walkways and bike tracks. A perfect base for day trips to Picton, Marlborough Sounds, Kaikoura or Nelson. Two friendly cats, kept outside. Wireless internet available and free laundry. Room pictures and information on website.

Marlborough

Blenheim - Rapaura *14 km NW of Blenheim*

Harvest Fine Accommodation *B&B Homestay*
Janet & Brent Nicholson
90 Jeffries Road, RD3, Blenheim, 7273

Tel (03) 572 9010 or 021 907 280
queries@harvestfineaccommodation.co.nz
www.harvestfineaccommodation.co.nz

Double $160-$220 Single $140-$200 (Full breakfast)
Portacot, high chair & babysitting available
Visa MC accepted
Children welcome
1 Queen 1 Double (2 bdrm)
Bathrooms: 1 Ensuite 1 Private

Welcome to Harvest Fine Accommodation. Situated on our 20 acre working vineyard in the heart of Marlborough ten minutes drive to Blenheim township. Located directly opposite Herzog Winery and Luxury Restaurant and close to many other fine wineries. Janet and Brent and their family welcome you to stay and enjoy the beauty and ambience of their architect designed, newly renovated home. Please see our website for more pictures of our property and comments from our guestbook. Children welcome. We have a lovely cat named Grace.

Blenheim Central *1.5 km SW of Post Office*

Radfield House *Luxury B&B*
Jayne & Bill
126 Maxwell Road, Blenheim, 7201

Tel (03) 578 8671 or 021 357 038
jaynebill@xtra.co.nz
www.radfieldhouse.co.nz

Double $150-$180 (Full breakfast)
Children welcome by arrangement
Dinner $20-$35 by arrangment
House trained pets welcome by arrangement.
Visa MC Eftpos accepted
2 Queen (2 bdrm)
Bathrooms: 1 Guest share 2 Guest toilets

Enjoy luxury Bed and Breakfast accommodation at Radfield House, one of Blenheim's more gracious properties. We provide courtesy transfers to/from Picton ferry terminals or the local airports. Free tea, coffee and juice also free use of mountain bikes to tour the vineyards or kayaks to explore the local rivers. Our main aim is to make your stay as comfortable and memorable as possible. Bill and Jayne look forward to meeting you and BeeJay our baby Birman Seal Point loves lots of cuddles.

Renwick *10 km W of Blenheim*

Clovelly *B&B Homestay*
Don & Sue Clifford
2A Nelson Place, Renwick, Marlborough 7204

Tel (03) 572 9593 or 027 695 1614
Fax (03) 572 7293
clifford@actrix.co.nz
www.clovelly.co.nz

Double $130 Single $100 (Special breakfast)
Visa MC accepted
Children welcome
1 King/Twin 1 Queen (2 bdrm)
Bathrooms: 2 Private

Our colonial style home is set in lovely private grounds in the heart of vineyard country. We overlook organic orchards and out to the Richmond Range. Complimentary refreshments on arrival. Visit the quaint local English pub - dine in the village or vineyard restaurants. We are close to a number of prestigious vineyards. Complimentary bicycles (including a 1938 vintage tandem!) are available for guests to cycle the vineyards. Don, Sue and our Scottish terriers Chloe and Phoebe and cat Sophie, will welcome you most warmly.

Renwick *10 km W of Blenheim*
Olde Mill House B&B & Bike Hire *B&B Homestay*

Diane Sutton
9 Wilson Street, Renwick, Marlborough

Tel (03) 572 8458 or 0800 653 262
0800 OLD BNB   Fax (03) 572 8458
info@oldemillhouse.co.nz
www.oldemillhouse.co.nz

Double up to $130 (Continental breakfast)
Visa MC Amex accepted
Children welcome
1 King/Twin 1 Queen 1 Single (3 bdrm)
Bathrooms: 2 Ensuite 1 Private

Welcome to our elevated character bungalow, refurbished for your comfort whilst retaining its olde world charm. Our property consists of an extensive spa/BBQ, garden area for you to relax in and enjoy views to the Richmond Ranges. We provide complimentary cycles for you to enjoy the local wine trail, a complimentary transfer service to local vineyard restaurants for evening dining. We also provide a wireless broadband internet service. We both enjoy gardening, motorcycling and our Border Collie dogs Rosie & Vinnie.

Near French Pass - Pelorus Sounds *110 km NE of Nelson*
Ngaio Bay Eco-homestay and B&B *B&B Homestay*

Jude & Roger Sonneland
Ngaio Bay, French Pass Road, Pelorus Sounds

Tel (03) 576 5287   Fax (03) 576 5287
welcome@ngaiobay.co.nz   www.ngaiobay.co.nz

Double $160 Single $120 (Special breakfast)
Children 3-12 $80 under 2 $30 all inclusive
Dinner $40pp, children 3-12 years $15
Lunch $20pp, Picnic $15pp, $8 per child 3-12
Visa MC Eftpos accepted Children welcome
2 King 3 Single (2 bdrm)
Bathrooms: 2 Private Rose & Dolphin self-contained,
Garden Cottage bathroom in main house

Ngaio Bay, two hours scenic drive from Nelson or Blenheim, with private beach, is an authentic Kiwi experience. Near awesome waters of French Pass. The Garden Cottage and Rose & Dolphin are comfortable and private, overlooking beach, garden and bush. A honeymooners favourite. Guests linger at dinner enjoying scrumptious food and good conversation, open fire for cool evenings. Organic vegetable and flower garden and orchard, eco-composting toilets. Swim, walk, boat, relax; your choice.! Private fireheated bath on beach. special. Children welcome. Three loveable labradors.

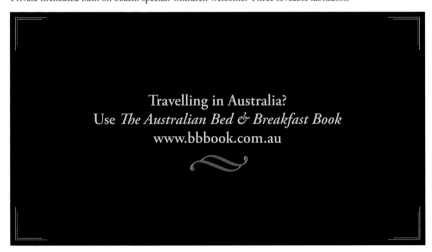

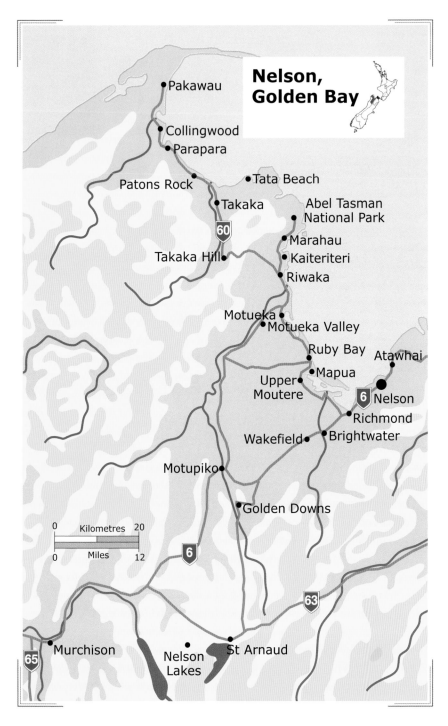

Nelson, Golden Bay

Pakawau

Collingwood

Parapara

Patons Rock

Tata Beach

Takaka

60

Abel Tasman
National Park

Marahau

Takaka Hill

Kaiteriteri

Riwaka

Motueka

Motueka Valley

Ruby Bay

Atawhai

Upper
Moutere

Mapua

6 Nelson

Richmond

Wakefield

Brightwater

Motupiko

Golden Downs

0   Kilometres   20

0   Miles   12

6

63

65 Murchison

Nelson
Lakes

St Arnaud

Nelson - Atawhai *6 km NE of Nelson*

Mike's B&B *B&B Homestay*

Mike Cooper & Lennane Cooper-Kent
4 Seaton Street, Nelson

Tel (03) 545 1671
mikecooper@actrix.co.nz
www.bnb.co.nz/hosts/kent

Double $75-$90 **Single** $75-$90 (Full breakfast)
Dinner $35pp with prior notice
Visa MC Diners accepted
2 Queen (2 bdrm)
Bathrooms: 2 Ensuite with showers

Five minutes NE of Nelson City we welcome you to our comfortable home in a quiet neighbourhood with extensive views out over Tasman Bay to the mountains beyond. Our guests accommodation is almost self contained and includes ensuite bedrooms a kitchenette with a fridge/freezer, microwave and complimentary tea and coffee making facilities, a small lounge with TV and some of our collection of books. Laundry facilities are available for your use. Our interests include travel, education, sea fishing and our aging schnauzer dog.

Nelson *2 km SW of Central Nelson*

Harbour View Homestay *B&B Homestay*

Judy Black
11 Fifeshire Crescent, Nelson

Harbour View Homestay Nelson NZ

Tel (03) 548 8567
Fax (03) 548 8667
harbourview-homestay@xtra.co.nz

Double $140-$155 **Single** $120-$140
(Continental breakfast)
Full breakfast extra $10pp
Visa MC accepted
2 Queen 2 Single (3 bdrm)
Bathrooms: 2 Ensuite 1 Private

Our home is above the harbour entrance. Huge windows capture spectacular views of beautiful Tasman Bay, Haulashore Island, Tahunanui Beach, across the sea to Abel Tasman National Park and mountains. Observe from the bedrooms, dining room and decks, ships and pleasure craft cruising by as they enter and leave the harbour. If you can tear yourself away from our magnificent view, within walking distance along the waterfront there are excellent cafés and restaurants. Judy, David and Possum the cat welcome you for a memorable stay.

Nelson *5 km SW of Nelson*

Arapiki *B&B Apartment with Kitchen Self-contained Homestay Units*

Kay & Geoff Gudsell
21 Arapiki Road, Stoke, Nelson

Tel (03) 547 3741
bnb@nelsonparadise.co.nz
www.nelsonparadise.co.nz

Double $85-$120 **Single** $70-$90
(Continental breakfast optional $7.50pp)
Visa MC accepted
1 Queen 1 Double 1 Single (2 bdrm)
Bathrooms: 2 Ensuite

Enjoy a relaxing holiday in the midst of your trip. The two quality smoke-free units in our large centrally located home offer comfort, privacy and offstreet parking. The larger Unit 1 is in a private garden setting. A ranchslider opens on to a deck with outdoor furniture. It has an electric stove, microwave, TV, auto washing machine and phone. Unit 2 has a balcony with seating to enjoy sea and mountain views. It has a microwave, hotplate, TV & phone. We have two tonkinese cats.

Nelson *2.5 km S of Nelson*

Sunset Waterfront B&B *B&B Separate Suite*
Bernie Kirk & Louis Balshaw
455 Rock Road, Nelson

Tel (03) 548 3431 or 027 436 3500
Fax (03) 548 3743
waterfrontnelson@xtra.co.nz

Double $140-$150 Single $110-$120 (Full breakfast)
Self-catering cottage $180
Visa MC accepted
2 Queen 1 Twin 1 Single (2 bdrm)
Bathrooms: 2 Ensuite

Sunset Waterfront B&B provides wonderful panoramic sea and mountain views of Tasman Bay. Ideally situated to walk to quality seafood restaurants. Stroll along the promenade to enjoy the sunset or take an evening walk along the beach. Ten minutes drive from the airport and bus station. Quiet and secluded location. Freshly brewed coffee and local fresh produce provided. Also freshly picked raspberries and strawberries when in season. No children under 12. Come enjoy our paradise! Parking right up to the house. Cottage available next door.

Nelson *3 km E of Nelson*

Brooklands *B&B Homestay*
Lorraine & Barry Signal
106 Brooklands Road, Atawhai, Nelson

Tel (03) 545 1423 Fax (03) 545 1423
barry.lori@xtra.co.nz

Double $100-$140 Single $75-$90 (Full breakfast)
Children by arrangement
Dinner $40
Visa MC accepted
Pet free home
Children welcome
1 King 1 Queen 1 Double 1 Twin (3 bdrm)
Bathrooms: 1 Ensuite 1 Guest share spa bath

Spacious, luxurious four level home with superb sea views. Spacious well furnished king room on top level. Next level has two bedrooms sharing large bathroom with spa bath for two. One bedroom has a private balcony. Spacious indoor/outdoor living areas. We enjoy sports, travel and outdoors. Lorraine makes dolls and bears and enjoys crafts, gardening and cooking. We are close to Nelson's attractions - beaches, crafts, wine trails, national parks, lakes and mountains. We enjoy making new friends. Smoke-free. Courtesy transport available.

Nelson *0.75 km SW of Nelson Central*

Peppertree B&B *B&B*
Richard Savill & Carolyn Sygrove
31 Seymour Avenue, Nelson

Tel (03) 546 9881   Fax (03) 546 9881
c.sygrove@clear.net.nz

Double $120 (Continental breakfast)
Children $20
Dinner $30-$40 by arrangement
Extra adult $35
Visa MC accepted
Children welcome
1 Queen 1 Double 1 Single (1 bdrm)
Bathrooms: 1 Ensuite

Enjoy space and privacy in our heritage villa, only ten minutes riverside walk from Nelson's city centre. The master bedroom has an ensuite bathroom and walk-in wardrobe. Your private adjoining rooms include a large lounge with double innersprung sofabed, single bed, heat pump, Sky TV, fridge, microwave, kettle etc. Also sunroom with cane setting and private entrance. Email/internet/fax facilities and off-street parking available. Children are welcome. We have two daughters aged 13 and 11, and a friendly cat called Chocolate.

Nelson *0.5 km N of Information Centre*

Grampian Villa *B&B*
John & Jo Fitzwater
209 Collingwood Street, 208 Collingwood Street, Nelson

Tel (03) 545 8209 or 021 459 736 (Jo)
021 969 071 (John)   Fax (03) 548 7888
Jo@GrampianVilla.co.nz
http://GrampianVilla.co.nz

Double $130-$350 Single $130-$350 (Special breakfast)
Children POA   Dinner POA
Visa MC Eftpos accepted
Not suitable for children or pets
2 King/Twin 2 King 3 Queen 1 Single (8 bdrm)
Bathrooms: 8 Ensuite

Located in the tree-lined streets below The Grampians overlooking Nelson City, historic Grampian Villa & Cottage are a pleasant 5 minute walk to Nelson's City Centre.

Grampian Villa offers 4 spacious ensuites (3 SuperKing, 1 Queen with clawfoot bath and shower) each have french doors opening onto the spacious verandahs with views of Nelson City and the sea. Grampian Cottage offers 4 great value-for-money rooms. (1 SuperKing, 2 Queen and 1 Single), all with ensuites.

Grampian Villa Facilities: spacious tiled showers with heated floors and large heated towel rails Wireless DSL internet access.

Writing desk in all rooms. TV, DVD, in-house movies etc. available in all bedrooms Complimentary tea/coffee, port, local chocolates, cookies. Enjoy a Latte/Expresso from our professional coffee machine.

Gourmet/Special breakfast changes every day. TV, VCR, CD, DVD, Stereo & SKY available in Lounge Central heating for your comfort We regret that we cannot accommodate children under the age of 12 years or pets.

We now have a friendly boxer (Bonnie) who loves all of our guests.

To check for availability and/or make a reservation please go online to:
http://art.globalavailability.com/guests/guest-main.php?pid=271

Nelson *2 km S of Nelson*
Beach Front B&B *B&B*
Oriel & Peter Phillips
581 Rocks Road, Nelson

Tel (03) 548 5299 or 021 063 9529
Fax (03) 548 5299
peterp@tasman.net
www.bnb.co.nz

Double $100-$135 Single $100 (Full breakfast)
Visa MC accepted
Not suitable for children
1 Queen 1 Double (2 bdrm)
Bathrooms: 1 Ensuite 1 Private

As recommended by The Rough Guide. Our home is situated overlooking Tahunanui Beach, Haulashore Island and Nelson waterfront-amazing daytime mountain views-magnificent sunsets. Enjoy a wine out on the deck with your hosts. Excellent restaurants and cafés within walking distance, stroll to beach or five minute drive to city. Golf course, tennis courts and airport nearby. One hour drive to Abel Tasman. Both rooms have ensuite/private facilities, quality beds, electric blankets, fridge, TV, tea & coffee making facilities, heaters, iron and hairdryers. Kiwi Host.

Nelson *0.1 km N of Nelson Information Centre*
Mikonui *B&B*
Elizabeth Osborne
7 Grove Street, Nelson

Tel (03) 548 3623
bess.osborne@xtra.co.nz

Double $100-$120 Single $80-$100 (Full breakfast)
Visa MC accepted
3 Queen (3 bdrm)
Bathrooms: 3 Ensuite

100 metres from the Visitor Information Centre in the heart of Nelson City is the Mikonui. This delightful house built in the 1920s, has been the Blair Family home for more than 50 years. The lovely rimu staircase leads to three tastefully appointed guest rooms all with ensuites. A delicious continental and cooked breakfast are served each morning. Just a short stroll to restaurants, cafés, the cinema and the beautiful Queens Gardens. Come and enjoy the hospitality at the Mikonui, you won't be disappointed. Off-street parking.

Nelson *2 km N of Nelson*
Lamont B&B *B&B*
Pam & Rex Lucas
167A Tahunanui Drive, Nelson, New Zealand

Tel (03) 548 5551 or 027 435 1678
Fax (03) 548 5501
rexpam@xtra.co.nz

Double $115 Single $75 (Full breakfast)
Children by arrangement
Dinner $30
Visa MC accepted
Children welcome
1 Queen 1 Double (2 bdrm)
Bathrooms: 1 Private 1 Guest share

We are in a position to offer high standard accommodation having two double bedrooms with own toilet and bathroom facilities. Our house is on a private property in Tahunanui Drive opposite the Nelson Surburban Club where it is possible to get an evening meal most nights. A two minute drive to Tahuna Beach and five minutes to a number of waterfront restaurants gives plenty of variety and choice. We are a few minutes from the airport. Pick-up from airport and bus. Two cats in residence

Nelson - Atawhai *7 km N of Nelson*

A Culinary Experience *Luxury B&B Homestay*
Kay & Joe Waller
71 Tresillian Avenue, Atawhai, Nelson

Tel (03) 545 1886 or 0800 891 886
Fax (03) 545 1869
kpastorius@xtra.co.nz
www.a-culinary-experience.com

Double $175-$225 Single $160-$210 (Special breakfast)
Not suitable for young children
Join your hosts for a 3-course gourmet dinner
Cooking Classes and Therapeutic Massage can be booked
Visa MC accepted Pets welcome
2 King/Twin 2 King (2 bdrm)
Bathrooms: 2 Ensuite

Welcome to our lovely home filled with original art, laughter and fabulous food. Your caring hosts have created a unique boutique accommodation. Joe, a Naturopath, provides therapeutic massage. Kay, cookbook author and former cooking school owner, provides delightful dinners or cooking classes. Let us pamper you.

Enjoy gourmet breakfasts: Blueberry Pancakes with glazed bananas, Eggs Benedict, French Crepes. After exploring Nelson's wineries, galleries, restaurants, golfing or hiking/kayaking in Able Tasman Park, indulge in a massage and a soak in the spa. Choose the quiet, sun-drenched garden or a peaceful patio, sipping a complimentary glass of wine served with yummy appetizers to celebrate sensational sunsets, exquisite bay & mountain views. Read in the sculpture garden and quaff the aroma of fresh herbs, fruit, and organic produce that we grow for our legendary meals. Or sit and chat about boats, art, Rotary, The Red Hat Society, travels and beautiful New Zealand.

Book one of our luxurious rooms: king-size beds, imported linens, heated tile ensuites (bathrooms). Homemade pastries, 24 hour tea facilities, laundry and broadband are next to the guest lounge. With so much to do in the region, a stay of three or more nights is recommended. Arrive as guests - leave as friends.

Nelson *1 km E of Nelson Cathedral*

Te Maunga - Historic House *B&B Homestay Self catered Unit*

Anne Kolless
15 Dorothy Annie Way @ 82 Cleveland, Nelson

Tel (03) 548 8605 or 021 201 2461
temaungahouse@xtra.co.nz
www.nelsoncityaccommodation.co.nz

Double $90-$130 Single $75-$90 (Special breakfast)
Children negotiable
Self-catered $140
Visa MC accepted
Pet free home Children welcome
1 Queen 2 Double 1 Twin (3 bdrm)
Bathrooms: 2 Private 1 Guest share showers

Anne welcomes you to her family's 1930's registered Historic House, a stunning and unique, native woods example. Still mainly as original with modern facilities, Te Maunga sits on a knoll, within a rambling garden, giving commanding views over Nelson City, sea and Valleys, with only five minutes to downtown. Enjoy your special continental style breakfast including local fruits, yoghurts, cheeses , home-made breads, and preserves, or maybe your aperitif, while taking in the amazing views. Self-catered unit is next door! NZQA Food safety Cert.

All our B&Bs are non-smoking
unless stated otherwise in the text.

Nelson - Atawhai *5 km N of Nelson on SH6*

Strathaven Lodge *B&B Homestay*

Julie & Hugh Briggs
42 Strathaven Place, Atawhai, Nelson

Tel (03) 545 1195 or 027 243 5301
Fax (03) 545 1195
strathavenlodge@xtra.co.nz
www.strathavenlodge.com

Double $125-$200 Single $100-$125 (Full breakfast)
Children $50
Dinner $40pp
Visa MC Diners accepted
Pet free home Children welcome
1 King 1 Queen 1 Single (3 bdrm)
Bathrooms: 2 Private

Imagine relaxing in the terrace spa, enjoying the beautiful sea and mountain views, the spectacular sunsets, listening to the melodious songs of the tuis and bellbirds. Sleep deeply in very comfortable beds, in suites each with private bathrooms, robes, TV's and hairdryers. Savour Hugh's generous breakfasts! Enjoy this slice of paradise and share your travel experiences with your well travelled hosts, over a complimentary glass of local wine or beer. "Luxury with a smile"

Nelson *1 km E of Nelson Central*

Sussex House Bed & Breakfast *B&B*
Victoria & David Los
238 Bridge Street, Nelson

Tel (03) 548 9972
Fax (03) 548 9975
reservations@sussex.co.nz
www.sussex.co.nz

Double $140-$170 Single $110-$140
(Full breakfast)
Visa MC Amex Eftpos accepted
Children welcome
5 Queen 3 Twin 3 Single (5 bdrm)
Bathrooms: 4 Ensuite 1 Private

Experience the peace and charm of the past in our fully restored circa 1880s B&B, one of Nelson's original family homes. Situated beside the beautiful Maitai River, Sussex House has retained all the original character and romantic ambience of the era. It is only minutes' walk from central Nelson's award-winning restaurants and cafés, the Queens Gardens, Suter Art Gallery and Botanical Hill (The Centre of NZ) and many fine river and bushwalks.

The five sunny bedrooms all have TVs and are spacious and charmingly furnished. All rooms have access to the verandahs and complimentary tea and coffee facilities are provided. Breakfast includes a variety of fresh and preserved fruits, hot croissants and pastries, home-made yoghurts, cheeses and a large variety of cereals, rolls, breads and crumpets. Cooked breakfasts are available.

Other facilities include: wheelchair suite; free email/internet station; fax; courtesy phone; laundry facilities; separate lounge for guest entertaining; complimentary port; tea & coffee facilities; very sociable cat (Riley). We have lived overseas and have travelled extensively. We speak French fluently.

Nelson *3 km N of Nelson*

Havenview Homestay *B&B Homestay*
Shirley & Bruce Lauchlan
10 Davies Drive, Nelson, 7010

Tel (03) 546 6045 or 027 420 0737
0800 546 604
havenview@paradise.net.nz
www.havenview.co.nz

Double $130-$155 (Full breakfast)
Two course dinner with a glass of wine $35pp
Visa MC accepted
Not suitable for children
2 Queen (2 bdrm)
Bathrooms: 1 Ensuite 1 Private

Welcome to our sunny modern home; three minutes from the centre of Nelson. Relax on our deck sipping a complimentary local wine while enjoying panoramic views across the sea to Able Tasman Park. We can organise your trip to the park; book wine tours; or recommend a golf course (we play golf). Enjoy dinner with us, or dine at a restaurant; then enjoy our moonlight spa before retiring for the night. Together with our two friendly ginger cats, we'll make your stay a pampered experience.

Richmond *0.5 km E of Richmond*

Hunterville *Homestay*
Cecile & Alan Strang
30 Hunter Avenue, Richmond, Nelson

Tel (03) 544 5852
Fax (03) 544 5852
strangsa@clear.net.nz

Double $100 Single $70 (Full breakfast)
Children half price
Dinner $30 by arrangement
Children and pets welcome
1 King 1 Twin 1 Single (3 bdrm)
Bathrooms: 1 Private 1 Family share

Experience a family welcome in a real Kiwi home with drinks poolside in summer, or a cuppa and home-made biscuits. Our home is up a short driveway where we enjoy birdsong from surrounding trees. We are enroute to Golden Bay and Able Tasman park but just 15 minutes from Nelson City. We travel frequently so appreciate travellers needs;comfortable beds, laundry, generous breakfasts, dinner with local food and wine. Our interests: music, reading, bridge, our friendly Dalmatian(Coco) and the company of guests.

Richmond *1 km E of Richmond*

Antiquarian Guest House *B&B*
Robert & Joanne Souch
12A Surrey Road, Richmond, Nelson

Tel (03) 544 0253 or (03) 544 0723
021 417 413   Fax (03) 544 0253
souchebys@clear.net.nz
http://souchebys@clear.net.nz

Double $95-$125 Single $80 (Full breakfast)
Children $10   Visa MC accepted
Children and pets welcome
1 King 1 Queen 1 Twin (3 bdrm)
Bathrooms: 1 Ensuite 1 Guest share

Bob & Joanne Souch welcome you to their peaceful home only two minutes from Richmond (15 minutes drive south of Nelson) - excellent base for exploring National Parks, beaches, arts/crafts, ski fields etc. Relax in the garden, beside the swimming pool or in our large TV/guest lounge. Tea/coffee facilities, home-baking and memorable breakfasts. Our family pet is Gemma (friendly border collie). As local antique shop owners we know the area well.

Richmond *12 km SW of Nelson*

Idesia *B&B*

Jenny & Barry McKee
14 Idesia Grove, Richmond, Nelson

Tel (03) 544 0409 or 0800 361 845
Fax (03) 544 0402
idesian@xtra.co.nz
www.idesia.co.nz

Double $100-$120 (Full breakfast)
Dinner $35 by arrangement
Visa MC accepted
Pet free home
1 King/Twin 1 Queen (2 bdrm)
Bathrooms: 1 Ensuite 1 Private

You are assured of a warm welcome and quality service at Idesia Bed & Breakfast. Our home, elevated for sun and views is in a quiet grove easily accessible from State Highway 6. Breakfast is served with fresh seasonal fruits and a sizzling cooked selection. Join us for dinner, however Richmond‚Äôs restaurants are close by. We offer broadband wireless network, off-road parking, information/booking Abel Tasman National Park. With our proven B&B experience we aim to give service and hospitality so you enjoy our regions attractions.

Brightwater *10 km NW of Richmond*

Westleigh *Homestay Farmstay*
John and Dell
Westleigh, Waimea West, Brightwater, Nelson, 7091

Tel (03) 542 3654
westleigh@paradise.net.nz

Double $125 Single $80-$100 (Full breakfast)
Dinner 3 course with wine
Visa MC accepted
Pet free home
Not suitable for children
2 Queen 1 Double (3 bdrm)
Bathrooms: 2 Ensuite 1 Guest share

Country home in 27 acres of privacy. House dates from c1860, now updated. Ten minutes to Richmond, golf and beach. Good local restaurants, but most guests eat with us,- more sociable and the food is ok too. A place for RnR, and central to all Nelson attractions. Directions: From Nelson, R6 past Richmond, turn off right at Brightwater, stay on that road c 5K. Westleigh sign prominent lhs. Or phone!

Wakefield *16 km S of Richmond*

Bushwalk B&B & Homestay *B&B Homestay*
Bruce & Sandra Monro
15 Hunt Terrace, Wakefield, Nelson 7025

Tel (03) 541 9615
s_bmonro@orcon.net.nz

Double $100-$140 Single $75-$90
(Full breakfast)
Children welcome by arrangement
1 King 1 Queen (2 bdrm)
Bathrooms: 1 Ensuite 1 Family share
Ensuite has shower, family share bath

Our home is in the trees adjacent to Faulkner's Bush Reserve surrounded by Totara, Beech, pungas and ferns. It is only a five minute stroll through the bush to the local shops and restaurants. Relax with Missy the cat on the elevated deck or in the courtyard with the native birds. With a pottery and workshop on site you can be taught how to make a pot on the wheel, with your host, Bruce. Our interests are travel, music, golf, pottery and furniture making.

Nelson, Golden Bay

Mapua Village *30 km W of Nelson*
Mapua Seaview B&B *B&B Homestay*
Murray & Diana Brown
40 Langford Drive, Mapua Village, Nelson

Tel (03) 540 2006
seaview@mapua.co.nz
www.mapua.co.nz

Double up to $145 (Full breakfast)
Visa MC accepted
2 Queen (2 bdrm)
Bathrooms: 2 Ensuite

Seaview B&B commands stunning views of both Waimea Estuary and Richmond Mountains. Local Mapua waterfront restaurants are just a few minutes stroll along our estuary pathway. Easy 25 minute drive to either Nelson City or the Abel Tasman National Park, which is very popular for its golden sands scenic forest treks and boat trips. Our modern home is nestled on elevated sunny garden setting being off-street, and very peaceful. Our guests often remark on our stunning estuary vista, especially while breakfasting on the deck.

Mapua - Nelson *30 km W of Nelson*
Hartridge *B&B*
Sue & Dennis Brillard
103 Aranui Road, Mapua, Nelson

Tel (03) 540 2079 or 021 189 7622
Fax (03) 540 2079 stay@hartridge.co.nz
www.hartridge.co.nz

Double $130-$185 Single $95-$150
(Continental breakfast) Dinner $45pp
Discounts for 2 nights or more Seasonal discounts
Visa MC accepted Not suitable for children
1 King/Twin 1 Queen 1 Double (3 bdrm)
Bathrooms: 2 Ensuite 1 Private

Delightful, Historic Places listed 1915 home. Midway between Nelson City and fabulous Abel Tasman National Park with its hiking, kayaking or simply cruising. Quiet elevated position in coastal Mapua Village. Antiques, fine arts, mature gardens. Recent upstairs accommodation private and sunny. Every effort made for that vital good night's sleep. Sue's beautifully presented gourmet breakfasts include daily baking, local fruit, great coffee/teas. Private parking, stroll to restaurants, shops, charming wharf area. Beach loop-walk one hour. Experienced hosts with local knowledge, complimentary extras. Internet broadband.

Mapua *30 km W of Nelson*
Accent House B&B *Luxury B&B*
Wayne & Jacqui Rowe
148 Aranui Road, Mapua Village, Nelson 7005

Tel (03) 540 3442 or 0800 540 3442
027 540 3442
Fax (03) 540 3442
info@accentbnb.co.nz
www.accentbnb.co.nz

Double $185-$225 Single $185-$225 (Full breakfast)
Visa MC Eftpos accepted
Pet free home
3 Queen (3 bdrm)
Bathrooms: 3 Ensuite

Welcome to our new luxury B&B set on 1.5 acres alongside our lagoon rich with local birdlife, beachwalks and drenched in Tasman Bay sunshine. Stroll to Mapua Village, experience the local shops, cafés, award winning restaurants, local arts and crafts studios. Check out the many local wineries all within a few minutes drive. Easy drive to Nelson City and Abel Tasman National Park. Private guest entrance, lounge with outdoor access & tea/coffee making facilities, laundry. TVs in all suites and access to outdoor sitting areas.

Mapua *4 km S of Mapua*

Kimeret Place Boutique B&B *Luxury B&B Apartment with Kitchen*
Cottage with Kitchen
Gill & Ian Knight
Bronte Road East (off SH60), Near Mapua, Nelson

Tel (03) 540 2727
Fax (03) 540 2726
stay@kimeretplace.co.nz
www.kimeretplace.co.nz

Double $190-$340 Single $150-$270
(Special breakfast)
2 bedroom cottage $275-$335
Visa MC Diners Eftpos accepted
4 King/Twin (4 bdrm)
Bathrooms: 4 Ensuite

A tranquil coastal setting in the heart of the wine & craft region with stunning views, heated swimming pool and spa. Just 4 km to restaurants and 30 minutes to Abel Tasman National Park. A range of accommodation all with ensuite facilities, (two with spa-baths), TV, Hi-fi, tea/coffee, fridge, sitting area and views from either balcony or deck. The two bedroom cottage also has a kitchenette and dining area. Light meals, laundry and internet are also available. Dog-lovers may wish to meet our two friendly labradors.

Ruby Bay *20 km W of Nelson*

Broadsea B&B *B&B*
Rae & John Robinson
42 Broadsea Avenue, Ruby Bay, Nelson

Tel (03) 540 3511
Fax (03) 540 3511
raer@clear.net.nz

Double $120 Single $100 (Full breakfast)
Children not suitable
1 Queen (1 bdrm)
Bathrooms: 1 Ensuite 1 Private

Beach front accommodation, with lovely walks on beach and reserve; cafés and tavern close by, as are wineries and restaurants. We are 15 minutes from Richmond and Motueka, 30 minutes from Nelson and the airport. Abel Tasman and Kaiteriteri are within 40 minutes drive. We want our guests to feel at home and have their privacy in a peaceful and private setting. Coffee, tea and old fashioned home-made biscuits available. Our Birman cat Bogart will greet you when you arrive.

Ruby Bay *32 km W of Nelson*

Sandstone House *B&B*
John & Jenny Marchbanks
30 Korepo Road, Ruby Bay, Nelson

Tel (03) 540 3251 or 027 514 0652
Fax (03) 540 3251
sandstone@rubybay.net.nz
www.rubybay.net.nz

Double $220 Single $200 (Full breakfast)
Visa MC accepted
Not suitable for children
2 Queen (2 bdrm)
Bathrooms: 2 Ensuite

Welcome to Sandstone House - the ideal place to relax, stay a few days and explore this delightful region. We enjoy a maritime and semi-rural situation, ideally situated midway between Nelson and Motueka. We are handy to all the fine attractions that this region has to offer - National Parks, wineries, award winning restaurants, beaches, arts and crafts, the famous Mapua Wharf and lots lots more. We have 35 years local knowledge and are happy to assist you to make the most of your holiday.

259

Upper Moutere *19 km SE of Motueka*

Lemonade Farm Apartment *Luxury B&B Apartment with Kitchen Self-contained*

Linda & Ian Morris
99 Roses Road, RD 2 Upper Moutere, Nelson 7175

Tel (03) 543 2686 or 021 059 0464
stay@lemonadefarm.co.nz
www.lemonadefarm.co.nz

Double $170-$200 Single $150-$180 (Full breakfast)
Children 0-3 free, 4-12 $20
Extra adult $40   Dinner by arrangement
Self-catering option available
Visa MC accepted   Children welcome
2 Queen 2 Single (2 bdrm)
Bathrooms: 1 Private

You are the only guests in this sunny self-contained apartment. Soak in the outdoor spa pool and watch the cows graze after a day of exploring the Abel Tasman or tasting Moutere wines. There's a substantial cook-your-own breakfast basket. Relax in modern décor with quality linens and air-conditioning. Broadband internet available. "What a wonderful peaceful place! We felt truly pampered with all the special touches. Hands down one of the finest B&Bs we've ever stayed in!" Stephanie and Marty, California. Directions: 1. SH6 (the inland Moutere Highway) 2. Neudorf Rd 3. Rosedale Rd 4. Roses Rd.

Motueka Valley *18 km S of Motueka*

Mountain View Cottage/Dexter Farmstay *Farmstay Cottage with Kitchen*

A & V Hall
Waiwhero Road, RD 1, Motueka

Tel (03) 526 8857
Fax (03) 526 8857
ajandvhall@xtra.co.nz

Double $95 Single $60 (Special breakfast)
Dinner $25
Cottage $95
Visa MC accepted
1 King/Twin 1 Queen (2 bdrm)
Bathrooms: 1 Ensuite 1 Private

Your hosts Alan & Veronica offer B&B, farmstay and separate cottage accommodation on our 35 acre organic property complete with unique dexter cows and native bush covenanted area. Perfectly situated for anglers, close to three National Parks and art/craft/garden trails. Mountain View Cottage is completely self-contained while our homestead offers spacious bedroom with own ensuite, tea/coffee & TV facilities. Meals are cooked on our wood-fired range and breakfast comprises choice of home-made muesli, bread, yoghurt, and organic eggs. A very warm welcome completes the picture.

Motueka Valley *16 km SW of Motueka*

Waitakiroa Farmstay B & B *B&B Farmstay*

Dianne & Errol Boyes
RD 1, Westbank Road, Motueka

Tel (03) 526 8003
waitakiroa@xtra.co.nz
www.riverfarmstay.co.nz

Double $120 Single $85 (Continental breakfast)
Children under 2 free
Extra person $25 per night
Dinner not provided
Guest BBQ facilities available
Children welcome
1 Queen 1 Double 1 Single (2 bdrm)
Bathrooms: 1 Ensuite

Dianne and Errol welcome you to Waitakiroa Farm-stay. Our 320 acre farm is situated on the banks of the Motueka river, famous for its trout fishing, and in the heart of the beautiful Motueka valley. We are close to Motueka township, stunning Kaiteriteri Beach, 3 national parks, (Nelson Lakes National Park, Abel Tasman National Park, known worldwide for its scenery, and Kahurangi National Park) Come and enjoy a tour of our farm with Errol and experience rural New Zealand life with our family!

Motueka Valley *25 km S of Motueka*

The Kahurangi Brown Trout *B&B Homestay Farmstay Apartment with Kitchen*

David Davies & Heather Lindsay
2292 Westbank Road, Pokororo, RD 1, Motueka

Tel (03) 526 8736 or 021 141 0717
Fax (03) 526 8736
enquiries@kbtrout.co.nz
www.kbtrout.co.nz

Double $130 Single $115 (Full breakfast)
Children $25 share room
Dinner $45pp, includes salad, fresh bread, wine, dessert
Our gardens are 100% organic
Visa MC accepted
Children and pets welcome
2 King/Twin 3 King 3 Single (3 bdrm)
Bathrooms: 3 Ensuite and an outdoor wood fired bath

Enjoy the sound of the beautiful Motueka River, which runs past our house. Step across the road for trout fishing, or a refreshing swim. Come "home" for a delicious meal made with our home grown organic fruit and vegies. Enjoy the garden with its pizza oven, fish pond, ducks and the wood fired bush bath.

Comments from last years visitors book say it all: This is by far our favourite B&B/homestay we've stayed at in NZ. Wonderful place and location. What more could a traveller ask for. Blissful spot! Thoroughly enjoyed our stay with very thoughtful hosts and the best bed we've met in NZ. A good laugh. Wonderful food, delightful company, and cosy ambience. There are places and there are PLACES and this is a GREAT PLACE! Scenic splendour, great hospitality and peaceful ambience are rich ingredients that match the stunning home cooking. Long live the Brown Trout! Exploring the area has been the highlight of our trip. Sand sea followed by a 360 degree view from mount Arthur. Such variety and warm hospitality! Wish some of our friends were with us. What an idyllic setting. Great food and conversation. Mt Arthur was a spectacular hike and a feast for the eyes (and soul). Food was outstanding. Hope we will return. Wonderful stay, luxurious rooms and delicious food. Until now we have been missing the best.

Motueka Valley *26 km S of Motueka*

Doone Cottage Country Homestay *B&B Homestay*

Approved

Glen & Stan Davenport
2281 Motueka Valley Highway, RD 1, Motueka 7196

Tel (03) 526 8740
Fax (03) 526 8740
doone-cottage@xtra.co.nz
www.doonecottage.co.nz

Double $110-$185 **Single** $110-$155 (Full breakfast)
Dinner by arrangement
Visa MC accepted
2 King/Twin 1 Queen (3 bdrm)
Bathrooms: 3 Ensuite

Charming 130 year old cottage welcoming guests for 25 years. Secluded native flora & flower gardens in mountain setting overlooking Motueka River Valley. Five Trout rivers - Guiding available. In-house Guestrooms plus Private Garden Chalet. Enjoy countrystyle B & B, homemade breads, preserves, organic vegetables. Sheep, chickens, ducks, donkeys. Weaving/Woolcraft Studio. Short distance Abel Tasman, Kahaurangi, Nelson Lakes. Or just relax & soak up the country atmosphere of yesteryear in this special place. Nelson 45 minutes, Picton 2.^{1}/2 hours, Westcoast 3 hours.

Motueka Valley *20 km SW of Motueka*

Vistara Bed and Breakfast *B&B Homestay*

Approved

Bruce & Guruvati Dyer
2035 Motueka River Valley, RD 1 Motueka, 7196

Tel (03) 526 8288 or 021 079 7919
Fax (03) 526 8288
info@vistara.co.nz
www.vistara.co.nz

Double $95 **Single** $75 (Continental breakfast)
Children $15   Dinner $25
Visa MC accepted
Children and pets welcome
1 Queen 1 Double 2 Single (3 bdrm)
Bathrooms: 2 Guest share

We welcome you to Vistara a relaxed peaceful haven situated on our seven acre property adjacent to the Motueka River. Attractions include great river swimming, native birds and bush, a beautiful garden, mountain scenery and Jess our Jack Russell dog. Bedrooms feature polished floors and charming décor. Guests have their own lounge, tea and coffee facilities and are welcome to use the meditation room. Enjoy a delicious breakfast of home-made preserves, yoghurt, muesli and fresh organic fruit. Meals are organic, vegetarian and lovingly prepared.

Motueka *1.4 km E of Motueka*

Williams B&B *B&B Homestay*

Approved

Rebecca & Ian Williams
186 Thorp Street, Motueka

Tel (03) 528 9385
Fax (03) 528 9385
B&B@motueka-homestay.co.nz
www.motueka-homestay.co.nz

Double $110-$120 **Single** $60 (Full breakfast)
Children $20
Dinner by arrangement
Continental Breakfast $110pn
Full Breakfast $120pn
1 Queen 1 Double 1 Single (2 bdrm)
Bathrooms: 2 Ensuite

We only look expensive. We are 1.4km to Motueka shopping centre and 1.2 km to 18 hole golf course. Each bedroom has own ensuite. The guest lounge has tea & coffee making facilities and fridge. Motueka is the stop-over place for visitors to explore Abel Tasman and Kahurangi National Parks. Golden Bay and Kaiteriteri golden sands beach is 10km away. We have a Jack Russell dog. Visa and Mastercard accepted.

Motueka *2 km S of Motueka*

Grey Heron - The Italian Organic Homestay *B&B Homestay*
Sandro Lionello & Laura Totis
110 Trewavas Street, Motueka 7161

Tel (03) 528 0472   Fax (03) 528 0472
sandro@greyheron.co.nz
www.greyheron.co.nz

Double $90-$120 Single $50-$80
(Continental breakfast)
Dinner $25-$35pp   Children welcome
3 Queen 1 Single (4 bdrm)
Bathrooms: 1 Ensuite 1 Guest share

We are a couple from Northern Italy, much travelled and keen on tramping, mountaineering and motorbiking. We welcome you to our private hideaway and birdwatchers' paradise on the tidal estuary.

Pleasant beach-walks at our door-steps, far enough from the noise of the main roads and yet only five minutes drive to shops and restaurants. Or you can relax here after your exploring day, join us for dinner and taste our italian organic cuisine overlooking a beautiful sunset behind the mountains and enjoying Sandro huge collection of Jazz records.

The Abel Tasman NP is 20 minutes drive; 45 minutes to the alpine, easy accessible, Kahurangi NP and to Nelson City. The Guest Accommodation includes both ensuite and shared-facilities with toilet room and bathroom each separate. The ensuite bedroom is small and cosy, no TV, ground-level entrance and private driveway. Basic tea-coffee facilities and secure off-street parking.

We serve a generous Continental breakfast with organic home-made breads and jams, fresh fruit and juice. As keen walkers and mountaineers we can give helpful hints to maximize your exploration of the area. We also offer guided walks thanks to Sandro's experience as geologist and to our interest in the local flora and fauna. Rock-climbing and Italian Language lessons by arrangements.

Water-Taxi ticketing service and Kayak Tours booking service available. We are conveniently located just around the corner from the reliable and well-known "Sea Kayak Company". Regrettably we don't accept Visitor Information Centres vouchers. "Benvenuti tutti gli amici italiani!"

Motueka *1 km E of Motueka*

Golf View Chalet *B&B Apartment with Kitchen*

Kathleen & Neil Holder
20A Teece Drive, Motueka

Tel (03) 528 8353
info@GolfViewChalet.co.nz
www.GolfViewChalet.co.nz

Double $105-$130 Single $80 (Special breakfast)
Children in B&B $20, in apartment $15
Self-contained apartment $110 double, extra adult $20
Visa MC accepted
Children welcome
3 Queen 1 Double 4 Single (4 bdrm)
Bathrooms: 1 Ensuite 2 Private

Welcome to our sunny home with mountain views, adjoining 18 hole golf course, beside the sea. Enjoy our lovely garden setting. Sleep well in comfortable beds. Close to restaurants, National Parks and golden beaches. Central in the Nelson region for day trips. Breakfast option available for self-cater apartment (extra). Carport with apartment. Complimentary laundry, tea/coffee making facilities, guest fridge, BBQ. Directions: from High Street (main street), State Highway 60, turn into Tudor Street, left Thorp Street, right Krammer Street, left into Teece Drive.

Motueka *10 km S of Motueka*

Motueka River Hills Bed & Breakfast *B&B*

Anthea Garmey & Andrew Claringbold
394 Westbank Road, RD1, Motueka

Tel (03) 528 8979 or 027 208 3106
Fax (03) 528 8979
stay@motuekariverhills.co.nz
www.motuekariverhills.co.nz

Double $130-$150 Single $120 (Full breakfast)
Portacot available for young children
Dinner available by arrangement
Children welcome
1 King/Twin (1 bdrm)
Bathrooms: 1 Ensuite

Motueka River Hills is nestled on the foothills of the Kahurangi National Park above the Motueka River. We have stunning views over rural Motueka, Tasman Bay and out to D'Urville Island. Listen to Morepork while you relax and unwind in the steaming hot outdoor bath. Awake to a gorgeous sunrise and the chorus of native birds. Enjoy a continental or cooked breakfast. Andrew is a keen fly fisherman and can provide a guiding service. We share our home with daughter Hannah and our cat, Basil.

Kaiteriteri *10 km N of Motueka*

Bracken Hill B&B *Luxury B&B*

Grace & Tom Turner
293 Kaiteriteri Road, RD 2, Motueka

Tel (03) 528 9629
Fax (03) 528 9629
graceturner@xtra.co.nz
www.bnb.co.nz/brackenhillbb.html

Double $130-$140 Single $100-$110
(Continental breakfast)
Visa MC accepted
Pet free home   Not suitable for children
2 Queen 1 Twin (3 bdrm)
Bathrooms: 3 Private

Coastal Luxury. Welcome to our tasteful, spacious modern home. Rooms all have sea views over Tasman Bay. Enjoy mountains, native bush, sunrises, sunsets & stars! A viewing sundeck leads to a unique natural rock garden. Guests' TV lounge, laundry facility. Experience Kaiteriteri Beach, Marahau, Kahurangi/Abel Tasman National Parks and Golden Bay.Kayaking,and water taxis. Restaurants close by. Interests: travel & guests will delight in a refreshing breakfast at our peaceful haven. Friendly hosts, Grace & Tom.

Kaiteriteri *12 km N of Motueka*

Bayview *B&B*
Tim Rich
2 Bayview Heights, Kaiteriteri, RD 2, Motueka 7197

Tel (03) 527 8090   Fax (03) 527 8090
book@kaiteriteribandb.co.nz
www.kaiteriteribandb.co.nz

Double $165-$195 (Full breakfast)
Visa MC accepted
Pet free home
Not suitable for children
1 King/Twin 1 King 1 Twin (2 bdrm)
Bathrooms: 2 Ensuite

Welcome to a piece of paradise. This modern house has huge windows with outstanding sea views overlooking Kaiteriteri Beach out to Abel Tasman National Park. Large, beautifully furnished guest rooms have every convenience you could want. Enjoy delicious home cooked breakfast in the dining room with your host who has an intimate knowledge of the Abel Tasman National Park. Laundry, email and booking facilities for boat trips, walking and kayaking are available. I am happy to share my home, extensive book collection and general lifestyle with you so I encourage you to stay a while and enjoy this unique area.

Kaiteriteri *13 km N of Motueka*

Everton B&B *B&B*
Martin & Diane Everton
25 Kotare Place, Little Kaiteriteri, RD 2 Motueka

Tel (03) 527 8301 or 021 527 830
Fax (03) 527 8301
everton@xtra.co.nz
www.evertonbandb.co.nz

Double $120-$150 Single $100
(Continental breakfast)
Wireless Internet
Visa MC accepted
Pet free home
1 King 1 Queen 1 Twin (3 bdrm)
Bathrooms: 1 Ensuite 1 Guest share

With wonderful sea views we are two minutes walk from the golden sands of Little Kaiteriteri Beach. Breakfast includes fresh bread or muffins and nearby are excellent restaurants. Our interests include Rotary, Toastmasters, golf, music, travel, and boating. The Abel Tasman National Park is right here where you can kayak, walk and take boat trips. Martin is licensed to take you on a personalised trip in our boat if you choose. We offer email access and wireless internet. We have no pets and are non-smokers.

Kaiteriteri *13 km N of Motueka*

The Haven *Cottage with Kitchen*
Tom & Alison Rowling
Rowling Heights, RD 2, Kaiteriteri, Motueka 7197

Tel (03) 527 8085
Fax (03) 527 8065
thehaven@internet.co.nz
www.thehaven.co.nz

Double $200
(Continental breakfast provisions)
Self-contained extra person $50
1 King 2 Twin (2 bdrm)
Bathrooms: 1 Ensuite 1 Private

The Haven - Paradise with a nautical theme. Self-contained two bedrooms, Captains Cabin with king-size bed and ensuite, Crews Quarters with two large twin beds and private bathroom. Galley kitchen with generous breakfast provisions. Two decks providing outdoor living. Enjoy relaxed family atmosphere, spectacular views, swimming pool, private bush track to beach. Minimum stay two nights, not suitable for small children.

Kaiteriteri *13 km N of Motueka*

Robyns Nest B&B *Separate Suite Apartment with Kitchen*
Robyn & Mike
1 Rowling Road, Kaiteriteri

Tel (03) 527 8466 or 021 431 735
Fax (03) 527 8466
robynod@ihug.co.nz
www.accommodationkaiteriteri.co.nz

Double $130-$180 Single $100-$120
(Continental breakfast)
Children negotiable
Visa MC accepted
2 Queen 1 Single (2 bdrm)
Bathrooms: 2 Ensuite

Take the track through our garden and walk 100 metres to the beautiful Kaiteriteri Beach with golden sand, clear water and safe swimming. Kaiteriteri is also the departure point for Launches, Water-Taxis and Kayaking into the Abel Tasman National Park. Private entry via your own terrace, television, hairdryer, refrigerator and tea, coffee & toast making facilities, off-street parking and guests BBQ area. Continental breakfast includes home-made muesli and preserves. We have a moggie called JJ.

Kaiteriteri - Tapu Bay *12 km N of Motueka*

Maison Luc *B&B Cottage with Kitchen*
Angie & Martin Lucas
Tapu Bay, 410 Riwaka-Kaiteriteri Road,
RD 2, Motueka

Tel (03) 527 8247 or 0800 468 815
027 221 6090   Fax (03) 527 8347
info@maisonluc.co.nz
www.maisonluc.co.nz

Double $100-$115 Single $95-$105
(Continental breakfast)
Cottage Single $110 Double $130 Extra guest $15
Visa MC accepted   Children welcome
3 Queen 1 Double 1 Twin (4 bdrm)
Bathrooms: 1 Ensuite 1 Private 1 Guest share

Maison Luc is centrally located to the Abel Tasman National Park and 1 km to the golden sands of beautiful Kaiteriteri beaches. Relax by our sun trapped pool or walk two minutes to local beaches. We have a fully self contained cottage set in peaceful garden surroundings. We offer a choice of three B&B rooms, two with seaviews or our ensuite room with own entrance. (Complementary tea, coffee & homebaking). Enjoy delicious breakfasts in a relaxed family atmosphere, Angie, Martin and Lu (dog).

Kaiteriteri *12 km N of Motueka*

Wall Street Accommodation *B&B Separate Suite Apartment with Kitchen*
Dr Hans Brutscher & Fiona Thornton
6 & 8 Wall Street, Kaiteriteri, RD 2, Motueka 7197

Tel (03) 527 8338 or 021 544 335
021 216 6440
Fax (03) 527 8338
stay@kaiteriteribnb.co.nz
www.kaiteriteribnb.co.nz

Double $115-$165 Single $105-$165
(Continental breakfast)   Visa MC accepted
Pet free home   Children welcome
1 King/Twin 3 Queen (4 bdrm)
Bathrooms: 2 Ensuite 1 Private

Two modern stylish homes in a peaceful bush setting, centrally located to explore Abel Tasman National Park, Golden Bay and Nelson environs. Minutes to golden-sanded Kaiteriteri beach, kayak companies and water taxis. Restaurants and store are just a short drive away. We offer three Queen rooms and 1 SuperKing/Twin room - choose from B&B, Self-contained or Accommodation only. All rooms have their own courtyard, separate entry, tea/coffee making facilities, TV or DVD. (Kitchenette & full kitchen options available). German, French spoken.

Kaiteriteri *13 km S of Motueka*

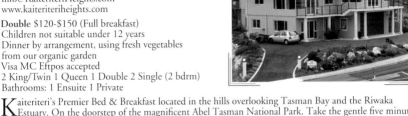

Kaiteriteri Heights *B&B Separate Suite Apartment with Kitchen*

Mary & Richard Shee
28 Cederman Drive, Kaiteriteri Heights, Motueka

Tel (03) 527 8662
info@KaiteriteriHeights.com
www.kaiteriteriheights.com

Double $120-$150 (Full breakfast)
Children not suitable under 12 years
Dinner by arrangement, using fresh vegetables
from our organic garden
Visa MC Eftpos accepted
2 King/Twin 1 Queen 1 Double 2 Single (2 bdrm)
Bathrooms: 1 Ensuite 1 Private

Kaiteriteri's Premier Bed & Breakfast located in the hills overlooking Tasman Bay and the Riwaka Estuary. On the doorstep of the magnificent Abel Tasman National Park. Take the gentle five minute stroll down to Little Kaiteriteri beach, with its golden sands and safe swimming. Full privacy, or interact as part of the family. Shared facilities include the outdoor deck with barbeque area, coffee/tea facilities, spa pool, the main lounge area with TV with Sky, Office facilities including Phone, Fax and Email.

Abel Tasman National Park - Marahau *18 km NW of Motueka*

Abel Tasman Bed & Breakfast *B&B Cottage with Kitchen Motels*

George Bloomfield
Abel Tasman National Park, Marahau

Tel (03) 527 8181   Fax (03) 527 8181
abel.tasman.stables.accom@xtra.co.nz
www.abeltasmanstables.co.nz

Double $110-$150 Single $80-$100
(Continental breakfast)
Dinner by prior arrangement
Cottage $150 (sleeps 4)
Visa MC accepted
Pet free home   Children welcome
3 Queen 2 Double 4 Single (6 bdrm)
Bathrooms: 5 Ensuite 1 Private 1 Family share Showers

Great views, hospitality, peaceful garden setting are yours at Abel Tasman Stables accommodation. Closest ensuite facility to Abel Tasman National park. Guests comments include: 'I know now that hospitality is not just a word', TH, Germany. 'Wonderful place, friendly hospitality. The best things for really special holidays. We leave a piece of our hearts', P&M, Italy. 'The creme-de-la-creme of our holiday. What a view', MN & JW, England. Homestay bed & breakfast or self-contained options. Café close by.

Abel Tasman National Park *17 km NW of Motueka*

Split Apple Rock Homestay *B&B Homestay*

Thelma & Rodger Boys
116 Tokongawa Drive, Split Apple Rock,
RD 2, Motueka

Tel (03) 527 8182
splitapplerock@hotmail.com
www.splitapplerock.com

Double $140-$165 Single $120-$150
(Full breakfast)
Dinner $35 by arrangement
Children welcome
1 Queen 1 Twin (2 bdrm)
Bathrooms: 2 Ensuite

Enjoy 180 degree panoramic sea views of Tasman Bay and Abel Tasman National Park. Our Eco-log home rooms have private entrances and decking. We are within walking distance of golden sand beaches, five minutes drive to Marahau and the start of Abel Tasman National Park where walking, kayaking, boating, swimming and more are available. Two cats in residence. Directions: on the Marahau/Kaiteriteri Road take the Tokongawa Drive turn-off, 1.2km up Tokongawa Drive the "Split Apple Rock Homestay" sign is on your right.

Able Tasman National Park *8 km N of Motueka*

Fraser Highlands *B&B or Cottage with Kitchen*
Sue & Jim Fraser
177 Riwaka-Sandy Bay Road, RD 2, Motueka 7160

Tel (03) 528 8702 or 027 283 8861
fraserhighlands_nz@hotmail.com
www.fraserhighlands.co.nz

Double $110-$160 Single $90-$140
(Continental breakfast)
Children $10   Dinner $30
Visa MC accepted
Children welcome
3 Queen (3 bdrm)
Bathrooms: 3 Ensuite Claw foot bathroom on request

Welcome to our unique Scottish home with spectacular panoramic views. The peaceful location has numerous native birds, walking tracks, and large gardens. To add to your comfort we have a spacious lounge with an open fire, and family room. A delicious continental breakfast includes freshly baked home-made breads, muffins, and a variety of fruit. Available on request are - evening meals, guided tours, and a beauty therapist. Within 15 minutes you could be enjoying beaches, restaurants, vineyards, flying, tramping, fishing or Abel Tasman National Park.

Takaka Hill *17 km NW of Motueka*

Kairuru Farmstay Cottages *Farmstay Cottage with Kitchen*
David and Wendy Henderson
Kairuru, Takaka Hill, Motueka, 7161

Tel (03) 528 8091 or Freephone 0800 524 787
Fax (03) 528 8091   kairuru@xtra.co.nz
www.kairurufarmstay.co.nz

Double $160-$220 Single $145-$160
(Breakfast by arrangement)
Children $30   Dinner $55 per adult
Extra person $30   Visa MC accepted
Pet free home   Children welcome
2 King/Twin 2 Queen 1 Double 1 Twin (6 bdrm)
Bathrooms: 3 Private 3 shower & 2 baths

We are third generation farmers and offer guests 3 cottages. Kea 3 bedrooms (sleeps 1-6), Pipit 2 bedrooms (sleeps 1-5) and Canaan 1 bedroom (Sleeps 1-2).The cottages are very comfortable with great views.We have two grown children - often helping out on the farm.There is a paddock nearby especially put aside for our tame animals. Feeding and handling our pet sheep, goats and calves are encouraged, a special delight for children.Our farm is on the Takaka Hill 25 minutes (or 17 km) from Motueka on State Highway 60

Takaka - Patons Rock Beach *10 km W of Takaka*

Patondale *Farmstay Cottage with Kitchen*
Vicki & David James
Patons Rock, RD 2, Takaka

Tel (03) 525 8262 or 0800 306 697 (NZ only)
027 493 6891
Fax (03) 525 8262
patondale@xtra.co.nz
www.patonsrockbeachvillas.co.nz

Double $125 Single $125
(Breakfast provisions first night)
Children $20
Visa MC accepted
Pet free home   Children welcome
4 King 8 Single (8 bdrm)
Bathrooms: 4 Private

Four sunny, spacious, deluxe self-contained units, own attached carports. Two bedrooms. Peaceful rural setting at the seaward end of our dairy farm yet only a few minutes walk to beautiful Patons Rock Beach. Central location, approx. Five minutes to Mussell Inn. Simply the Best. Your Kiwi hosts, David & Vicki invite you to be our guests.

Takaka - Tata Beach *15 km NE of Takaka*

The Devonshires *B&B Homestay*
Brian & Susan Devonshire
32 Tata Heights Drive, Tata Beach, RD 1, Takaka

Tel (03) 525 7987   Fax (03) 525 7987
devs.1@xtra.co.nz

Double $100 Single $70 (Full breakfast)
Children not suitable   Dinner $25-$30 by arrangement
Visa MC accepted
1 Queen (1 bdrm)
Bathrooms: 1 Ensuite

The Devonshires live at Tata Beach and invite you to enjoy their comfortable home and stroll to the nearby beautiful golden beach. A tranquil base for exploring the truly scenic Golden Bay, the Abel Tasman Walkway, Kahurangi National Park, Farewell Spit, amazing coastal scenery, fishing the rivers or visiting interesting craftspeople. Brian, an educator, wine and American Football buff is a keen fisherman. Susan enjoys crafts, painting, gardening and practising her culinary skills. Charlie Brown and Hermione are the resident cats. Longer visits welcomed.

Takaka *5 km S of Takaka*

Rose Cottage *B&B Cottage with Kitchen*
Margaret & Phil Baker
Hamama Road, RD 1, Takaka

Tel (03) 525 9048
Fax (03) 525 9043

Double $90-$110 Single $80
(Breakfast by arrangement)
Self-contained units $100-$135
Visa MC accepted
3 Queen 6 Single (6 bdrm)
Bathrooms: 4 Private

Rose cottage, much loved home of Phil & Margaret, is situated in the beautiful Takaka valley, in 2.5 acres of garden amongst 300 year old Totara trees, ideally situated to explore Golden Bay's many attractions. Our three self-contained units have full kitchens, private sun decks and quality furniture made by Phil in his craft workshop. The 12 metre indoor solar-heated swimming pool is available to our guests. Our interests are travel, photography, gardening, arts and crafts.

Takaka *10 km E of Takaka*

BenGar-Pohara *B&B*
Joan & John Garner
91 Selwyn Street, Pohara, Golden Bay, Takaka, RD

Tel (03) 525 9088
jjgarner@xnet.co.nz

Double $100-$100 (Continental breakfast)
Dinner by arrangement
Not suitable for children
2 Queen (2 bdrm)
Bathrooms: 1 Guest share separate toilet room

Joan & John built a new house by Pohara's beach and golf course. The house is just across the road from beach. Golf course is a five minute walk from the house.
Rooms have private deck & look out towards the mountains that surround Golden Bay. All guests will be welcomed by Jed the Jack Russell, who is ever ready to give a guided tour of his "beach". Tess, our Birman cat will make the occasional appearance.

Parapara *20 km NW of Takaka*
Hakea Hill House *B&B*
Vic & Liza Eastman
PO Box 35, Collingwood 7054

Tel (03) 524 8487
Fax (03) 524 8487
vic.eastman@clear.net.nz

Double $130 Single $90 (Full breakfast)
Children $50
Family dinner by arrangement
Visa MC accepted
Children and pets welcome
2 Queen 6 Single (3 bdrm)
Bathrooms: 2 Guest share bathtub and shower

H akea Hill House at Parapara has views from its hilltop of all Golden Bay. The two storey house is modern and spacious. Two guest rooms have large balconies; the third for children has bunk beds and a cot. American and New Zealand electric outlets are installed. Television, tea or coffee, telephone and broadband lines are available in rooms. Vic is a practising physician with an interest in astronomy. Liza is a quilter and cares for outdoor dogs. Please contact us for reservations and directions.

Collingwood *25 km N of Takaka*
Skara Brae Garden Motels & Bed and Breakfast
B&B Cottage with Kitchen
Joanne & Pax Northover
7 Elizabeth Street, Collingwood

Tel (03) 524 8464
Fax (03) 524 8474
skarabrae@xtra.co.nz
www.accommodationcollingwood.co.nz

Double $130 Single $100 (Continental breakfast)
2 self-contained units $95
Visa MC accepted
2 Queen 1 Double 1 Twin 2 Single (4 bdrm)
Bathrooms: 1 Ensuite 3 Private

S kara Brae, the original police residence in Collingwood built in 1908, has been tastefully renovated over the years. Our historic home is in a quiet, peaceful garden setting. Join us in the house for bed & breakfast, or our two self-contained motel units. Either way you will experience a warm welcoming atmosphere and individual attention. We are a minute away from the excellent Courthouse Café and local tavern bistro bar and it is a short stroll to the beach. Farewell Spit trips depart close by.

Collingwood *25 km N of Takaka*
Heron's Rest *B&B Cottage with Cooking Facilities*
Maureen & Angus Scotland
23 Gibbs Road, Collingwood Township, Golden Bay

Tel (03) 524 8987
Fax (03) 524 8987
stay@herons-rest.co.nz
www.herons-rest.co.nz

Double $90-$110 Single $65 (Special breakfast)
Children Negotiable
Visa MC accepted
1 Queen 1 Double 1 Twin 2 Single (3 bdrm)
Bathrooms: 2 Ensuite 1 Family share

T ravelling towards the tip of the South Island, your journey is rewarded by spectacular sea, mountain and estuary views, all visible from Heron's Rest. We're situated in between the Abel Tasman and Heaphy Tracks and surrounded by superb sandy beaches, being a short bush-walk (or drive) away from Farewell Spit Tours and Collingwood eateries. Welcoming hosts offer relaxation, comfort and lasting memories served up with home-made and locally-produced foods plus complimentary drinks. Potter's studio; internet, hairdryer, BBQ and laundry available. Directions: see website map.

Pakawau *9 km N of Collingwood*

Twin Waters Lodge *Luxury Lodge*
Trish & Mike Boland
PO Box 33, Collingwood

Tel (03) 524 8014
Fax (03) 524 8054
twin.waters@xtra.co.nz
www.twinwaters.co.nz

Double $200-$200 Single $180-$180 (Full breakfast)
Dinner by arrangement
Visa MC accepted
Not suitable for children
1 King/Twin 3 Queen (4 bdrm)
Bathrooms: 4 Ensuite

Nestled harmoniously beside a tidal estuary and just fifty metres from a sandy beach, Twin Waters features curved timber ceilings, panoramic windows and multilevel decks. The elegant interior has ample space for guests to enjoy its charm and tranquility. Waking to tuis singing, breakfasting in the sun, sipping wine on the decks overlooking the estuary, or savouring a delicious dinner, there's sure to be a special moment to remember. Trish and Mike and their feline companions look forward to welcoming you at Twin Waters.

Nelson Lakes - St Arnaud *85 km S of Nelson*

Nelson Lakes Homestay *Homestay*
Gay & Merv Patch
RD 2, State Highway 63, Nelson 7072

Tel (03) 521 1191
Fax (03) 521 1191
Home@Tasman.net
www.nelsonlakesaccommodation.co.nz

Double $125 Single $90 (Full breakfast)
Dinner $40pp by arrangement
Visa MC accepted
2 King/Twin 1 Queen (2 bdrm)
Bathrooms: 2 Ensuite

Nestled on the sunny slopes of the St Arnaud Mountain Range, Nelson Lakes National Park, our spacious modern home is designed for the comfort and convenience of our guests. Spacious ensuite rooms, with doors opening on to our garden, large comfortable lounge and terrace to relax on at the end of the day and admire the magnificent mountain views. Laundry facilities are available and three course meals by prior arrangement. We have a house cat. Directions: State Highway 63, 4 km east of St Arnaud.

Murchison *0.2 km N of Murchison*

Murchison Lodge *B&B*
Shirley & Merve Bigden
15 Grey Street, Murchison

Tel (03) 523 9196 or Freephone 0800 523 9196
info@murchisonlodge.co.nz
www.murchisonlodge.co.nz

Double $140-$180 Single $115-$160 (Full breakfast)
Children over 12 welcome
Dinner by arrangement
Free wireless broadband
Visa MC accepted
1 King/Twin 2 Queen 1 Twin (4 bdrm)
Bathrooms: 3 Ensuite 1 Private

Relax at this warm timber Lodge with its comfortable beds and hearty BBQ breakfasts. Set on four acres, we have various animals and a friendly puppy. The Buller River provides swimming holes and fishing access; trees and mountains surround us, yet Murchison's cafés are within five minutes walk. Unpack your bags for a while to explore three National Parks; fly-fish, raft or play golf before returning home to a cold beer on the sunny verandah or a wine in front of the log fire.

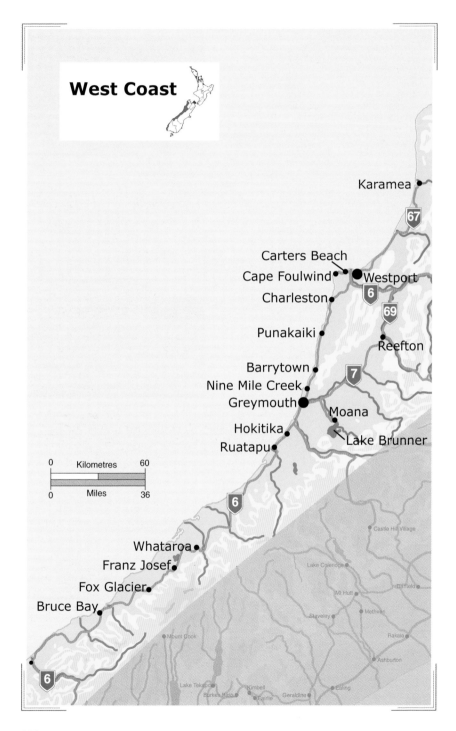

West Coast

Karamea

67

Carters Beach
Cape Foulwind
Charleston
Westport
6

69

Punakaiki

Reefton

Barrytown
Nine Mile Creek
Greymouth

7

Moana
Hokitika
Lake Brunner
Ruatapu

0   Kilometres   60

0   Miles   36

6

Whataroa
Franz Josef
Fox Glacier
Bruce Bay

Castle Hill Village
Lake Coleridge
Mt Hutt
Oxfield
Staveley
Methven
Mount Cook
Rakaia
Ashburton
Lake Tekapo
Kimbell
Burkes Pass
Fairlie
Geraldine
Ealing

6

Reefton *0.1 km S of Reefton Central*

Reef Cottage B&B and Café *B&B Cottage with Kitchen*

Susan & Ronnie Standfield
51-55 Broadway, Reefton

Tel (03) 732 8440 or 0800 770 440
Fax (03) 732 8440
info@reefcottage.co.nz
www.reefcottage.co.nz

Double $100-$150 Single $85-$125 (Full breakfast)
Children half price
Dinner by arrangement $10-$35
Visa MC Diners Amex Eftpos accepted
1 King/Twin 1 Queen 2 Double (4 bdrm)
Bathrooms: 2 Ensuite 2 Private Queen suite has bath

Built in 1887 from native timbers for a local barrister. This historical Edwardian home has been carefully renovated to add light and space without losing its olde world charm. Elegantly decorated the house features charming character rooms serviced daily. Centrally heated. Reefton is nestled in historic gold and coal mining country, between native beech forests and the Inangahua River. Reef Cottage is unrivalled as the finest accommodation in Reefton. Reef Café next door offers casual dining, specialist coffees and decadent desserts. Trout fishing, hiking, 4WD.

Reefton *.1 km N of Reefton Central*

Quartz Lodge *B&B*

Paddy & Alan Rainey
78 Shiel Street, Reefton, West Coast

Tel (03) 732 8383 or 0800 302 725
Fax (03) 732 8083
quartz-lodge@xtra.co.nz
www.quartzlodge.co.nz

Double $90-$130 Single $70-$95 (Full breakfast)
Children $25
Dinner $15-$30
Visa MC accepted
Children and pets welcome
1 King 1 Queen 1 Twin 1 Single (3 bdrm)
Bathrooms: 1 Ensuite 1 Private 1 Guest share

A friendly welcome awaits you when you arrive at Quartz Lodge superior accommodation in the heart of Reefton. Guests only entrance will take you upstairs to rooms with huge picture windows, luxurious beds, quality linen, robes and so much more. Complimentary coffee and a selection of teas are available in your spacious private lounge/dining area. Laundry service and Internet is also available upon request. We pride ourselves on making you feel at home. Quality and comfort says it all!

Karamea *84 km N of Westport*

Beachfront Farmstay B&B *B&B Farmstay*

Dianne & Russell Anderson
Karamea, SH 67, Karamea

Tel (03) 782 6762 or 027 249 8827
Fax (03) 782 6762
farmstay@xtra.co.nz
www.WestCoastBeachAccommodation.co.nz

Double $150-$170 Single $120 (Special breakfast)
Children negotiable
Dinner $50
Visa MC accepted
1 King 1 Queen 1 Twin (3 bdrm)
Bathrooms: 2 Ensuite 1 Family share

Our dairy farm has 2.5 km of coastline overlooking the wild Tasman Sea, a two minute walk and you will be on a sandy beach usually all to yourself. Relax in elegant rooms with every convenience and privacy. Special farmhouse breakfasts are generous, home preserving, tasty fish, bacon and egg dishes. Join us for delicious country cuisine, farm grown meat, fresh fish, organic vegetables, homemade desserts served with NZ wine. Our area offers day walks, unique limestone arches and caves, golf, trout fishing.

West Coast

West Coast

Karamea *0.5 km S of Karamea*

Bridge Farm *Farmstay*
Rosalie & Peter Sampson
Bridge Street, Karamea, RD 1, Westport

Tel (03) 782 6955 Fax (03) 782 6748
stay@karameamotels.co.nz
http://karameamotels.co.nz

Double $100-$140 (Continental breakfast)
Children $10
Extra adult $20
Visa MC Eftpos accepted
Children welcome
6 Queen 8 Single (10 bdrm)
Bathrooms: 8 Private

Since relinquishing their dairy farm to daughter Caroline and son-in-law Bevan, Rosalie and Peter have purpose-built on the property accommodation that neatly bridges the gap between motel and farm stay. Both are happy to share their extensive knowledge of their district, people and environment and introduce guests to the many short walks that Karamea offers. Each quality suite is self contained and has a private lounge that overlooks the farm to Kahurangi National Park beyond. A small mob of tame deer and alpaca graze nearby.

Westport - Cape Foulwind *11 km SW of Westport*

Steeples Cottage & B&B Homestay *B&B Homestay*
Separate Suite Cottage with Kitchen
Pauline & Bruce Cargill
48 Lighthouse Road, Cape Foulwind, Westport

Tel (03) 789 7876 or 0800 670 708
021 663 687   thesteeples@xtra.co.nz
www.baches.co.nz/bhh/listing/0/1005

Double $100 Single $60 (Full breakfast)
Children $20   Whitebait dinner by arrangement
Self-contained cottage $110   Studio B&B $100
Children welcome
4 Queen 1 Single (4 bdrm)
Bathrooms: 3 Ensuite 1 Private

Enjoy our peaceful rural accomodation, lovely gardens, magnificent sea views, rugged coastline, beautiful beaches & tranquil sunsets. Great swimming, surfing, fishing. Walk the popular seal colony walkway, dine at The Bay House Restaurant or friendly Star Tavern. Local attractions includes golf course, Coaltown Museum, jet boating, horse riding, underworld & white water rafting, bush walks & Punakaiki National Park. We have a Jack Russell and cat. Laundry and off-street parking. Self-contained cottage and queen ensuite studio also available. Whitebait meals by arrangment. Internet available.

Westport *2 km N of Westport Centre*

Chrystal Lodge *Separate Suite Apartment with Kitchen*
Ann & Bill Blythe
Corner of Craddock Drive & Derby Street, Westport

Tel (03) 789 8617 or 0800 259 953
Fax (03) 789 8617
blythea@xtra.co.nz

Double $95 Single $75
(Continental breakfast optional $10pp)
Visa MC accepted
Children welcome
2 Queen 1 Single (2 bdrm)
Bathrooms: 2 Ensuite

Ann and Bill would like to welcome you to Chrystal Lodge. We are situated on 20 acres beside a beach ideal for walking, surfing and fishing. Our separate self-contained units have a fully equipped kitchen/lounge with ensuite bedrooms. The garden setting has ample off-street parking. Free guest laundry. Pony available for children. We have one shy cat. Seasonal rates. Directions: turn right at the post office, continue down Brougham Street, turn left at Derby Street until at the beach.

Westport *1 km N of Westport*

Havenlee Homestay *B&B Homestay*

Jan & Ian Stevenson
76 Queen Street, Westport

Tel (03) 789 8543 or 0800 673 619
Fax (03) 789 8502
info@havenlee.co.nz
www.havenlee.co.nz

Double $100-$150 Single $90 (Continental breakfast)
Children negotiable
Visa MC accepted
Children welcome
2 Queen (2 bdrm)
Bathrooms: 1 Private 1 Guest share

Peace in Paradise - this is Havenlee: a welcoming, relaxed, spacious, quality homestay where you will feel at home right away. Centrally located, an idyllic base from which to explore the environmental wonderland, share local knowledge or just to take time out. Checkout the adventure experiences and local attractions. Soak up the nature, rest and restore body and soul in the peace and quiet of a garden oasis. Fantastic continental-plus breakfast. Laundry facilities available. Treat yourself - stay awhile and feel exhilerated.

Westport - Carters Beach *3 km S of Westport*

Bellaville *B&B*

Marlene & Ross Burrow
10 State Highway 67A, Carters Beach
PO Box 157, Westport

Tel (03) 789 8457 or 0800 789 845
bellaville@xtra.co.nz

Double $100 Single $70 (Full breakfast)
Children $15
Extra Adult $20
Pet free home
Children welcome
1 Queen 1 Single (1 bdrm)
Bathrooms: 1 Ensuite 1 Private Spa Bath

Wake to the sound of waves pounding on our safe walking and swimming beach. Off-street parking. Quiet sunny extra large, spacious studio room with private entrance, own patio, private bathroom with spa bath, shower and separate toilet. Ideal for a family. Electric blankets, TV, tea & coffee and home-baking. Close to all activities, coastal walks, seal colony. Short walk to friendly café/bar, golf course, beach, airport, play ground. We have travelled extensively overseas and in NZ, we look forward to meeting you.

Westport - Carters Beach *4 km S of Westport*

Carters Beach B&B *B&B*

Sue & John Bennett
Main Road Carters Beach,
On State Highway 67A, Westport

Tel (03) 789 8056 or 0800 783 566
027 589 8056
cartersbeachaccom@xtra.co.nz
www.bnb.co.nz/cartersbeachbb.html

Double $100 Single $70-$80 (Continental breakfast)
Pet free home
Children welcome
2 Queen 1 Twin (3 bdrm)
Bathrooms: 1 Ensuite 1 Private

Carters Beach - a lovely relaxed atmosphere, Situated only 4 km south of Westport. Three minute walk to our beach, with fully licenced resturant/café and bar. Golf links, world famous seal colony and Bay House Café within a few minutes drive. Our rooms are very spacious with TV and tea/coffee making facilities. Own private entrance-ways with sun decks. Laundry facilities available by arrangement. Ideal accommodation for couples travelling togeather. We look forward to meeting and sharing our local knowledge with you. Cheers, Sue and John Bennett.

Westport - Cape Foulwind *11 km S of Westport*

Cape House *B&B Homestay*
Dave Low & Mark Rapley
Tauranga Bay Road, Cape Foulwind, Westport 7892

Tel (03) 789 6358 or 027 481 8672
stay@capehouse.co.nz
www.capehouse.co.nz

Double $100-$120 Single $65-$75
(Continental breakfast)
Extra guest $20
2 Queen 2 Single (2 bdrm)
Bathrooms: 1 Ensuite 1 Private

Cape House is a large and warm open style house in a secluded environment with a funky and friendly atmosphere. Your hosts are Dave the surfer and fisherman and Mark the technical guy. Chill out or enjoy the outdoors. Very near by are the Cape Foulwind walkway, seal colony, beaches, surfing and fishing. Local options for eating are a stroll to the local tavern, or award winning The Bay House Café. Free internet access is available. Free wireless internet. We have an inside cat.

Westport - Ngakawau *25 km N of Westport*

Charming Creek B&B *B&B Beachside*
Gay Sweeney
24 Main Road, Ngakawau

Tel (03) 782 8007 or 027 481 6736
0800 TO RELAX (0800 867 3529)
info@bullerbeachstay.co.nz
www.bullerbeachstay.co.nz

Double $129.99-$149.99 Single $115-$135
(Full breakfast) Children under 5 free
Dinner $30pp advance booking required
Visa MC accepted Children welcome
1 King/Twin 2 Queen (3 bdrm)
Bathrooms: 2 Ensuite

Sleep to the sound of the sea behind, the bush-clad high plateau and the spectacular one-day Charming Creek Walk in front, the Tasman Sea. Try our driftwood-fired hot tub at sunset on the edge of the waves unforgettable! All suites with ensuites, massage showers and private sundecks 24 hour Swiss Espresso machine, broadband internet.Cafés and art closeby - easy day trips to Pancake Rocks, Denniston, and the Oparara Wetlands. Full breakfasts included. Dinner by arrangement. Non-smoking inside.

If you would like dinner
most hosts require 24 hours' notice.

Charleston *17 km S of Westport*

Birds Ferry Lodge and Luxury Cottages
Luxury Lodge & Self-contained Lakeside Cottages
Alison & Andre Gygax
Birds Ferry Road, 8 km North Charleston,
just off SHW 6, 17 km South Westport

Tel 0800 212 207 or 021 337 217
info@birdsferrylodge.co.nz
www.birdsferrylodge.co.nz

Double $200-$300 **Single** $200-$250 (Full breakfast)
Cottages suitable for children
Dinner our speciality - be sure to book
Ask about our off season special deals
Visa MC accepted
1 King/Twin 1 King 2 Queen 1 Double 1 Twin 2 Single
(3 bdrm)
Bathrooms: 3 Ensuite, 1 purpose built for wheelchair use

Take time out from your journey for a few days, to relax and unwind at Birds Ferry Lodge. We are located 4-5 hours driving time from The Glaciers, Nelson, Picton and Abel Tasman. You will enjoy a tranquil spot with views of Mountains, Ocean and native forest.

Guests are often astounded by the remote location yet we are only 15 minutes from "town". No landline, TV, or clock - just a wealth of peace seclusion and beauty. Lodge guests enjoy sunsets from the heated spa, privately accessed ensuite guest accommodation, refreshments, laundry service, internet, cooked breakfast. 2 friendly in-house Terriers. Dinners by arrangement, include Quality New Zealand Wines. Home produced vegetables and free-range eggs are used wherever possible. Holistic Massage Therapy also available.

Ferry Man's Cottage enjoys the same views as the Lodge and is situated at the very end of Birds Ferry Road. Complete privacy, garden bath and all the comforts of Birds Ferry Lodge with your own kitchen and laundry facility. Sleeps 2-6. Okari Lake Hideaway - Private Lakeside country cottage. Sleeps 2-4. Cottage tariffs include a quality breakfast hamper. Andre, a New Zealand tour guide with 15 year's experience can accompany you on a personal tailor made local tour.

Punakaiki - Barrytown *27 km N of Greymouth*
Golden Sands Homestay *Homestay*
Sue & Tom Costelloe
4 Golden Sands Road, Barrytown, Runanga

Tel (03) 731 1115
Fax (03) 731 1116
goldensands@paradise.net.nz

Double $95-$105 Single $55 (Continental breakfast)
Children by arrangement
Dinner by arrangement
Visa MC accepted
Children welcome
2 Queen 1 Twin (3 bdrm)
Bathrooms: 1 Ensuite 2 Private

Nestled between the Paparoa Range and Tasman Sea on the corner of Golden Sands Road Barrytown and the Greymouth-Westport Scenic Highway, Golden Sands Homestay offers a friendly atmosphere and comfortable rooms.Handy to Punakaiki, the Pancake Rocks and the Paparoa National Park to the north, with Greymouth a 25 minute drive to the south. As well as stunning views and wonderful sunsets We have internet facilities, a cosy fire in winter and a contented cat. Access and facilities for disabled people.

Punakaiki - Barrytown *20 km N of Greymouth*
Kallyhouse *B&B Homestay Apartment with Kitchen*
Kathleen & Alister Schroeder
13 Cargill Road, Barrytown, RD 1, Westland

Tel (03) 731 1006
Fax (03) 731 1106
kallyhouse@xtra.co.nz
www.bnb.co.nz/schroeder.html

Double $115-$130 Single $75 (Continental breakfast)
Visa MC accepted
Pet free home
3 Queen 1 Twin (4 bdrm)
Bathrooms: 1 Ensuite 1 Guest share 1 Spa Bath

We have a new spacious home on a quiet rear section, a garden setting, native bush backdrop and sea views. We offer a self-contained flat downstairs, with queen room and twin beds in spacious living area. Kitchen, bathroom, washing machine, parking and separate entrance. Also two queen rooms upstairs. Breakfast with host. Punakaiki Pancake Rocks and adventure activities in Paparoa National Park, ten minutes north. Greymouth 20 minutes south. Turn at Allnations Hotel, past three houses on left, up lane, house on left. Licensed Restaurant handy.

Nine Mile Creek *14 km N of Greymouth*
The Breakers *B&B*
Jan Macdonald
PO Box 188, Greymouth, Westland

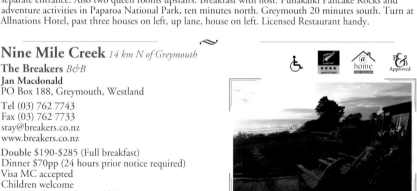

Tel (03) 762 7743
Fax (03) 762 7733
stay@breakers.co.nz
www.breakers.co.nz

Double $190-$285 (Full breakfast)
Dinner $70pp (24 hours prior notice required)
Visa MC accepted
Children welcome
2 King 2 Queen 2 Twin (4 bdrm)
Bathrooms: 4 Ensuite

Stunning views overlooking the Tasman Sea and two acres of native bush and gardens, Breakers is a great place to finish your day or base yourself while exploring the Coast. Walk on the beach or sit back and relax, enjoy the view with the sound of breaking waves rocking you to sleep. Private and peaceful, yet close enough to all the activities the Coast has to offer, Pancake Rocks, Paparoa National Park and the best stretch of coastline in NZ. Two friendly dogs on site.

Greymouth *0.5 km N of Greymouth Central*

Ardwyn House *Homestay*
Mary Owen
48 Chapel Street, Greymouth

Tel (03) 768 6107 Fax (03) 768 5177
ardwynhouse@hotmail.com

Double $85-$90 Single $55 (Full breakfast)
Children half price
Visa MC accepted
Children welcome
2 Queen 3 Single (3 bdrm)
Bathrooms: 1 Guest share

Ardwyn House is three minutes walk from the town centre in a quiet garden setting offering sea, river and town views. The house was built in the 1920s and is a fine example of an imposing residence with fine woodwork and leadlight windows, whilst being a comfortable and friendly home. Greymouth's ideally situated for travellers touring the West Coast being central with good choice of restaurants. We offer a courtesy car service to and from local travel centres and also provide off-street parking.

Greymouth *6 km S of Greymouth*

Paroa Homestay (formerly Pam's Homestay) *Homestay*
Pam Sutherland
345 Main South Road, Greymouth

Tel (03) 762 6769 or 027 323 3118
Fax (03) 762 6765
paroahomestay@xtra.co.nz
www.paroahomestay.co.nz

Double $110-$140 Single $100-$110
(Special breakfast)
Children negotiable
Visa MC accepted
1 King 1 Double (3 bdrm)
Bathrooms: 1 Ensuite 1 Private 1 Guest share

Relax on terraces overlooking the sea and watch incredible sunsets. Three minutes walk to the beach. Towering trees, native bush surrounds spacious classic home with luxurious guest lounge. Excellent restaurants nearby. Experience superb continental breakfast as baking and cooking is Pam's forte (previously owning Greymouth's busiest café/bar). Pam has NZQA Food Hygiene qualifications. West Coast born, Pam's local knowledge is invaluable. Pam enjoys hospitality, antiques, organic gardening and bush walking. Pam has welcomed guests for 13 years. Guest comments "Best breakfast in NZ" "incredible hospitaliy".

Greymouth *3 km S of Greymouth*

Maryglen Homestay *Homestay*
Allison & Glen Palmer
20 Weenink Road, Karoro, Greymouth

Tel 0800 627 945 or (03) 768 0706
Fax (03) 768 0599
mary@bandb.co.nz
www.bandb.co.nz

Double $110-$140 Single $90-$125
(Continental breakfast)   Children negotiable
Snack dinner $20 Full dinner (pre-notice) $40
Visa MC accepted   Children welcome
2 King/Twin 1 Queen 1 Single (3 bdrm)
Bathrooms: 3 Ensuite all private

Large Native ferns and bush surround our hillside home overlooking the sea. Our guests comment- amazing location. The sound of the surf will lull you to sleep. Off the main road, quiet location, two rooms have own deck entrance. Amazing sunsets, Complimentary transport available from bus/train. Let us share our wonderful coast with you as we help you plan your days-scenic tours, bush walks, Argo Bike tours, Trans-scenic train (a must), Shantytown History Village, Punakaiki Pancake Rocks. Your home away from home.

Greymouth *6 km S of Greymouth*

Sunsetview *B&B Homestay Apartment with Kitchen*

Russell & Jill Fairhall
335 Main South Road, Greymouth 7801, South Island

Tel (03) 762 6616
Fax (03) 762 6616
sunsetview@xtra.co.nz

Double $100-$140 Single $90-$120 (Full breakfast)
Children by arrangement
Dinner & lunch by arrangement
Visa MC accepted
Children and pets welcome
2 King/Twin 1 King 1 Queen (4 bdrm)
Bathrooms: 2 Ensuite 1 Private

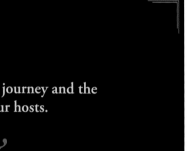

Jill & Russell welcome you to our sunny modern home with amazing sea and mountain views. We offer well-appointed superior bedrooms. Sky TV in rooms. Home-cooked meals available on request. Outdoor areas, pool and barbecue. Short walk to beach, shop approx. five to ten minutes walk Courtesy car available to local resturants, travel centres. Off-street parking. Downstairs apartment has two bedrooms (either can be king double or single beds) bathroom with wardrobe/dressing room. Kitchen with dining/lounge area. Own entrance with undercover parking.

Take time to enjoy your journey and the
company of your hosts.

Greymouth *0.2 km N of Tranz Alpine Terminal*

Golden Coast B&B *B&B*

Glad Roche
10 Smith Street, Greymouth, 7801

Tel (03) 768 7839
Fax (03) 768 7869
goldencoast@clear.net.nz

Double $90-$95 Single $70-$75 (Full breakfast)
Ensuite room $130 including a cooked breakfast
Visa MC accepted
Pet free home
Children welcome
2 Queen 1 Double 1 Twin (4 bdrm)
Bathrooms: 1 Ensuite 2 Guest share

Welcome to Golden Coast Bed & Breakfast established in 1967. The Roche family offers warm, friendly, affordable accommodation set in lovely gardens. Superb views of Grey River and only 200 metres above Tranz Alpine train/bus terminal. Excellent beds, own TV and electric blankets. Full cooked breakfast and complimentary tea/coffee in guest lounge. We are the closest B&B to town centre where you will find lovely restaurants. We can also arrange tours to Shantytown, Pancake Rocks and day tours to the Glaciers. Off-street parking available.

Greymouth - New River *12 km S of Greymouth*
New River Bluegums B&B *B&B Farmstay Cottage with Kitchen*

Sharon & Michael Pugh
985 Main South Road, New River, Greymouth

Tel (03) 762 6678 or 027 438 5324
027 664 4265
Fax (03) 762 6678
mail@bluegumsnz.com
www.bluegumsnz.com

Double $135-$180 Single $95-$125 (Full breakfast)
Children $25   Dinner by arrangement
Visa MC accepted
1 King 2 Queen 2 Double 1 Single (3 bdrm)
Bathrooms: 1 Ensuite 2 Private

The Pugh family welcome you to the warmth and comfort of their log and stone home on a small farm. The homestead offers a king room with balcony. Two luxurious self-contained cottages, superbly appointed, cosy, (double-glazing, heat pumps) secluded, overlooking the tennis court. Wake to morning birdlife, stroll around paddocks with cattle, feed the sheep or Piggy (Kunekune) and Coco (labrador). "Beautiful setting! Delightful home! Your relaxed and welcome manner made us feel like we were somewhere special, we certainly were, thank you!" G&K Guestbook.

Greymouth *5 km N of Greymouth*
Kia Ora Homestay *Homestay*

Ashley & Linda Morley
15 Keith Road, Paroa, Greymouth

Tel (03) 762 6770   Fax (03) 762 5850
stay@kiaora-homestay.co.nz
www.kiaora-homestay.co.nz

Double $95-$100 Single $65-$70
(Continental breakfast)
Children negotiable
Dinner $30 by arrangement
Visa MC accepted
1 Queen 1 Twin 1 Single (3 bdrm)
Bathrooms: 1 Guest share 1 Family share

Kia Ora ("Greetings, Welcome") Set in very quiet surrounds off the main road. The sound of the sea and birdsong predominate. A place to relax and unwind. Large lounge, opening onto the deck. Enjoy a complimentary beer, seaview and stunning sunsets. Five minutes from town centre & historic Shantytown. There are many attractions nearby. We've travelled extensively and are able to help with forward planning. We offer you a very warm welcome.Guest comments "Excellent accommodation - would like to have stayed longer"

Greymouth *15 km S of Greymouth*
Chapel Hill *B&B Homestay Farmstay*

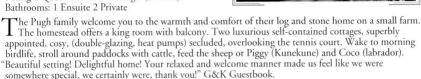

Joy & John Ruesink
783 Rutherglen Road, Paroa, Greymouth

Tel (03) 762 6662
info@chapelhill.co.nz
http://art.globalavailability.com/guests/guest-main.
php?pid=431

Double $90-$110 (Full breakfast)
Dinner $30 Complimentary wine and nibbles
Visa MC accepted
Children welcome
2 King/Twin 2 Queen 1 Single (3 bdrm)
Bathrooms: 1 Ensuite 1 Private 1 Guest share

Touch the ferns out your window! Spectacular architect-designed country stay in a rainforest setting, ONLY 15 minutes south of Greymouth on the Christchurch-Glaciers Highway. Huge logfire for those cooler evenings, free email, big comfy beds with electric blankets. Hearty country breakfasts included. Home-grown food. Dinner, wine, beer available. 40 minutes to Pancake Rocks & Hokitika Gorge, 60 minutes to Arthurs Pass. Non-smoking inside. Pets, farm and wildlife on the property. Unusual multi-level design is unsuitable for toddlers or disabled. Inquire about block or group bookings.

Greymouth *1 km S of Greymouth Post Office*

Jivana Retreat *Luxury B&B Private Chalet*

Approved

Sandie & Brent
8 Leith Crescent, Greymouth

Tel (03) 768 6102
Fax (03) 768 6108
sandie@jivanaretreat.co.nz
www.JivanaRetreat.co.nz

Double $130-$160 Single $110 (Special breakfast)
Children $20   Dinner $30
Private Chalet $160
Pet free home   Children welcome
1 King 2 Queen 1 Twin (3 bdrm)
Bathrooms: 1 Ensuite 1 Private 1 Guest share Outdoor bath

Jivana Retreat is a serene, affordable, quality haven. Sandie spoils you with a homemade organic breakfast menu of your choice, served indoors in the sunny conservatory, or lush outdoors. Special diets catered for. Dinners, and guided tours can be pre-arranged.Pamper yourself with a, massage, reflexology or relaxing yoga session while you stay. Purification/Detox Health programs on request. Beaches, lakes, and rivers are all nearby. *'A stunning location & tranquil oasis in this mad world! Beautiful hospitality, which refreshes the soul'* B Jones.

Lake Brunner - Moana *35 km E of Greymouth*

Lake View B&B *Cottage with Kitchen*

Brent & Madeline Beadle
18 Johns Road, Moana, Westland

Tel (03) 738 0886 or 027 431 8022
Fax (03) 738 0887   browntrout@minidata.co.nz
www.brentbeadle.com

Double $110-$130 Single $90-$100
(Continental breakfast provisions)
Children 12 and under $10   Extra adult $20
Award winning café in village Hotel does bar meals
Visa MC accepted
Pet free home   Children welcome
1 King 2 Single (2 bdrm)
Bathrooms: 1 Private

Lake View B&B offers guests fantastic views of Lake Brunner from the lounge, the decking or while lying in bed. Accommodation is a very private self-contained cottage adjacent to our house only five minutes walk to the village centre, café or hotel. The lake is famous for its trout fishing 365 days and Brent is a fishing guide. Lake tours, canoe hire, bush walks and a pottery are all close by. The Tranz Alpine stops at Moana. Christchurch is three hours away by road.

Moana - Lake Brunner *34 km E of Greymouth*

Lake Brunner B&B & Golf Course *B&B*

Pete & Deb Connor
2046 Arnold Valley Road, Moana., RD 1 Dobson

Tel (03) 738 0646
Fax (03) 738 0647
bnb-golf@lake-brunner.co.nz

Double $230 Single $180 (Full breakfast)
Visa MC Diners Amex Eftpos accepted
Not suitable for children
6 King (6 bdrm)
Bathrooms: 6 Ensuite

A warm welcome awaits you at our new purposely built B&B. Nestled along side beautiful native bush only minutes from the lake front. All our rooms have king-sized beds, fridge, TV and ensuite facilities. Complimentary tea and coffee are available in both your room and the guests lounge. Your room opens to a peaceful deck to enjoy the scenery and golf course. The attractions in the area are countless: fishing, bush walks, gold panning and the best little golf course in the area.

Hokitika *2 km N of Hokitika*

Hokitika Heritage Lodge *Luxury B&B Homestay Cottage with Kitchen*
Dianne & Chris Ward
46 Alpine View, Hokitika

Tel (03) 755 7357 or 0800 261 949
027 437 1254   Fax (03) 755 8760
hokitikaheritage@xtra.co.nz
www.hokitikaheritagelodge.co.nz

Double $210-$250 Single $210-$210 (Full breakfast)
Dinner by arrangement   Visa MC accepted
Not suitable for children
1 King/Twin 1 King 3 Queen 1 Single (5 bdrm)
Bathrooms: 3 Ensuites in Bank House; 1 Private in Gatehouse Cottage

Enjoy amazing NZ hospitality in our boutique Lodge, set on 1 1/2 acres, overlooking extensive views of the Tasman Sea, Hokitika Town and Southern Alps, including Mount Cook.

Incorporating 'Bank House' where full B&B is provided, along with spacious, beautifully decorated rooms, all with ensuites. Our 'Gatehouse Cottage', just completed in 2007, is self-catering, and provides two beautiful bedrooms with a private bathroom (breakfast available on request). Stylish decor, with attention to detail, reflects NZ, West Coast and family history, including Gold, Jade and Heritage themed rooms. Dianne (Literacy Teacher), and Chris (Property Consultant & Rotarian) are happy to help with your travel arrangements. They enjoy chatting with guests over a welcoming drink, homebaking or canapes.

Enjoy a bush setting spa or relax in one of the outside seating areas where you can enjoy the views or the quiet peaceful bush surroundings. Broadband internet, wireless network & television available. Stay a night or three (or more) so you can relax in our Heritage Lodge, as well as explore the beautiful West Coast.

2006-2007 comments read: "We envy you your beautiful home, and you allowed us to share it with you...A delightful stay with great NZ hospitality...Fun, laughter and superb accommodation...Wonderful hosts...Cherished memories of our too short a stay."

Directions: Find us by following Lodge signs from the main road to the airport, along Tudor Street, turning left into Airport Drive. Turn right at the top of the hill into Alpine View. Travel to the end of the street, turning left into our drive. Follow the road around the house to the parking area and main entrance.

Hokitika *3 km S of Hokitika*
Meadowbank *B&B Rural Homestay*

Alison & Tom Muir
Takutai Road, RD 3, Hokitika

Tel (03) 755 6723
Fax (03) 755 6723

Double $90 Single $60 (Full breakfast)
Children half price
Dinner by arrangement
Children welcome
1 Double 2 Single (2 bdrm)
Bathrooms: 1 Guest share

Tom and Alison welcome you to their lifestyle property, situated just minutes south of Hokitika. Our large home, which we share with two cats, is modern, sunny and warm, and has a large garden. Nearby we have the beach, excellent golf-links, Lake Mahinapua, paddleboat, river, and of course Hokitika, with all its attractions. Directions: travel south 2 km from south end of Hokitika Bridge on SH6, turn right - 200 metres on right. North-bound traffic - look for sign 1 km north of Golf-links and Paddleboat.

Hokitika - Upper Kokatahi *28 km E of Hokitika*
Sheridan Farmstay *Farmstay Cottage with Kitchen*

Trish & Terry Sheridan
Middle Branch Road, Upper Kokatahi RD 1, Hokitika

Tel (03) 755 7967
tpsheridan@xtra.co.nz

Double $120 Single $70 (Full breakfast)
Children negotiable
Dinner $30 by arrangement
Self-contained cottage from $75
Children welcome
1 Queen 2 Double 3 Twin (6 bdrm)
Bathrooms: 1 Ensuite 2 Guest share 1 Family share

Welcome to our 1000 acre dairy farm at the top of Kokatahi Valley 28 km east of Hokitika. Numerous day walks, three rivers with trout fishing and kayaking and Lake Kaniere are all minutes away. Share our home with our three lovely cats or stay in our self-contained unit. We enjoy meeting people and love travelling. Terry enjoys current affairs and all sports while Trish is happy in the kitchen or garden. Enjoy dining with us in peaceful surroundings.

Hokitika *7 km E of Hokitika*
Riverside Villa *B&B Homestay*

Margaret & Alan Stevens
185 Woodstock-Rimu Road, RD 3, Hokitika

Tel (03) 755 6466 or 027 437 1515
riversidevilla@actrix.co.nz

Double $110-$130 Single $75 (Full breakfast)
Children negotiable
Dinner $35 B/A, 3 courses with a glass of wine
Visa MC accepted
Pet free home
Children welcome
1 Queen 1 Twin (2 bdrm)
Bathrooms: 1 Ensuite 1 Private Robes provided

Set in extensive grounds with tranquil river and mountain views, Riverside Villa is a haven for relaxation a short drive away from Hokitika. We combine the elegance of a 100 year old villa with the warmth of large open plan lounge and sunny verandahs. An ideal place for peaceful stopover. With the Hokitika river on the boundary, it is a fisherman's paradise with our own glowworm grotto. We are keen travellers, have an extensive knowledge of NZ outdoors and enjoy meeting people. Warm hospitality assured.

Hokitika *2 km E of Hokitika*
Woodland Glen Lodge *Luxury B&B*
Janette & Laurie Anderson
Hau Hau Road, Blue Spur, Hokitika

Tel (03) 755 5063 or 0800 361 361 (NZ only)
027 201 6126
Fax (03) 755 5063
l.anderson@xtra.co.nz
www.hokitika.net

Double $140-$250 **Single** $130-$180 (Full breakfast)
Visa MC Diners Amex Eftpos accepted
Not suitable for children
5 Queen 2 Twin 2 Single (5 bdrm)
Bathrooms: 3 Ensuite 1 Guest share

Our 6500 square foot lodge is located on 21 acres and is surrounded in native kahikatea trees providing quiet and privacy. A great place for a retreat or time out. Most guests base themselves in Hokitika for visits to the glaciers and Punakaiki, allow two nights. We welcome you to Woodland Glen Lodge, we are widely travelled and have many experiences to share with you. Laurie is a retired police officer and commercial pilot, Janette is a health professional with a keen interest in quilting.

Hokitika *1 km N of Hokitika*
Top View Homestay/B&B *B&B*
Lin & Colin Jackson
24 Whitcombe Terrace, Hokitika,

Tel (03) 755 7060 or 027 381 7206
Fax (03) 755 7060 topview24@clear.net.nz
www.topview.co.nz

Double $110-$120 **Single** $80 (Full breakfast)
Children price depending age
Reduced rates for longer stays
Visa MC accepted
Pet free home Children welcome
2 Queen 2 Twin (3 bdrm)
Bathrooms: 1 Ensuite 1 Guest share
Bath and shower in guest share bathroom

We offer you a place to relax with a superb view of mountains, sea and sunsets. Colin and Lin are retired farmers with many interests including Lions and Diabetes Societies. For those with Alergies, this is a pet free home. We look forward to your company over a cup of tea or coffee. From the main road north, turn at the Airport sign on Tudor Street, take the next left into Bonar Drive to the top of the hill on to Whitcombe Terrace, turn left.

Hokitika *1 km E of Post Office*
Amberlea B & B *B&B*
Sharyn & Butch Symons
146 Gibson Quay, Hokitika, 7900

Tel (03) 755 7346
Fax (03) 755 7349
rpsmsymons@hotmail.com

Double $120-$140 **Single** $100-$120 (Full breakfast)
Children under 5 $10, under 12 $30
Children and pets welcome
3 Queen 1 Twin (4 bdrm)
Bathrooms: 2 Ensuite 1 Guest share
All bathrooms have showers

Sharyn and Butch along with their Bichons and cats invite you to their quiet friendly home situated beside the Hokitika River. Relax in the lovely gardens or watch the sunsets over the Tasman Sea and the Southern Alps. We are a five minute walk from the town centre and all of its tourist attractions, resturants and beach. Visit the Hokitika Gorge. Visit our great greenstone, paua, gold and ruby rock shops or relax at the beach or lakes enjoying the clean air.

Ruatapu *12 km S of Hokitika*
Berwick's Hill *B&B Homestay*
Eileen & Roger Berwick
Ruatapu, 106 Ruatapu-Ross Road,
State Highway 6, RD 3, Hokitika

Tel (03) 755 7876
Fax (03) 755 7870
berwicks@xtra.co.nz
www.berwicks.co.nz

Double $100-$130 Single $60-$80 (Full breakfast)
Dinner $40 by arrangement
Visa MC accepted
2 King/Twin 1 Queen (2 bdrm)
Bathrooms: 1 Ensuite 1 Private 1 bath in ensuite

Welcome to Berwick's Hill. We offer you a warm and relaxed stay in our comfortable home. Magnificent views of the Tasman Sea and the Southern Alps are seen from the main living areas. Experience the sunsets and sunrises. We are close to Lake Mahinapua, bush walks, the beach and golf course. On our hobby farm we have sheep, cattle, and one Farm Dog also hens. we share our home with our cat and our house dog.

Whataroa *35 km N of Franz Josef*
Matai Lodge *Farmstay*
Glenice & Jim Purcell
Whataroa, South Westland

Tel (03) 753 4156 or 0800 787 235
021 395 068
Fax (03) 753 4156
jpurcell@xtra.co.nz

Double $150-$180 Single $120 (Full breakfast)
Dinner $40pp
1 King/Twin 1 King 2 Single (3 bdrm)
Bathrooms: 1 Ensuite 1 Private

When your coming to the Glaciers, walk in the world heritage park or visit the White Heron Bird Sanctuary we warmly welcome you to share our spacious home, this tranquil rural valley retreat. 20 minutes from Franz Josef Glacier. Upstairs is a suite of two bedrooms, conservatory and private bathroom. Downstairs a king-size ensuite. You're welcome to join us for a home-cooked dinner with NZ wines. Our motto is: A stranger is a friend we have yet to meet. Glenice speaks Japanese, is a keen golfer, and has taught felting, weaving and spinning in Japan.

Whataroa - South Westland *13 km N of Whataroa*
Mt Adam Lodge *B&B Homestay Farmstay*
Elsa & Mac MacRae
State Highway 6, Tetaho, Whataroa, South Westland

Tel (03) 753 4030 or 0800 675 137 (NZ only)
mtadamlodge@paradise.net.nz
www.mountadamlodge.co.nz

Double $115-$140 Single $85-$90
(Continental breakfast)
Fold-away bed $20 extra
Visa MC Eftpos accepted
Children welcome
2 Queen 1 Double 2 Twin 2 Single (7 bdrm)
Bathrooms: 5 Ensuite 2 Guest share

If you're wanting to escape the crowds in the busy tourist centres then we are an ideal place for you to stay. Just a short 35 minute drive north of Franz Josef Glacier. We are situated on our farm at the foot of Mt Adam surrounded by farmlands and beautiful native bush. Our lodge offers comfortable accommodation and a fully licensed restaurant. You can stroll along the river bank and the farm tracks meeting our variety of animals along the way.

Whataroa *3.6 km NW of Whataroa*
Whataroa Country Home Stay *B&B Homestay*
Stellamaris & Bruce Graham
360 Whataroa Flat Road, RD 1,
Whataroa, South Westland. 7886

Tel (03) 753 4130 or 021 294 7358
bruceandstell@xtra.co.nz

Double $110-$120 Single $80-$85
(Continental breakfast)
Pet free home
Children welcome
1 Queen 2 Twin (3 bdrm)
Bathrooms: 1 Guest share 1 Family share

Stay in a truly rural environment on our 220 cow dairy farm, with a recently renovated homestead that features extensive use of native timber. Admire the stunning alpine views, the rose garden, visit the local native White Heron colony, or drive thirty minutes south to Franz Josef and view its magnificent glacier. Skiplane or helicopter up to a landing on the snow, or take one of the many walks. We have two cats and would would not mind children over ten, but no pets please.

Franz Josef *5 km N of Franz Josef Glacier*
Ribbonwood Retreat *Luxury B&B Cottage with Kitchen*
Julie Wolbers & Jo Crofton
26 Greens Road, Franz Josef Glacier

Tel (03) 752 0072
Fax (03) 752 0272
ribbon.wood@xtra.co.nz
www.ribbonwood.net.nz

Double $180-$275 (Full breakfast)
Visa MC accepted
Not suitable for children
1 King 2 Queen 1 Single (3 bdrm)
Bathrooms: 1 Ensuite 1 Private 1 Family share
Luxurious tiled bathrooms, private next to bedroom.

Guests commented: Superb hospitality, food, facilities and local advice. Thank you so much. Angela and Steve, Kent, UK. Ribbonwood has stunning views of the surrounding mountains, glaciers and forests. Hosts Julie is a local schoolteacher and Jo was a ranger in conservation for nearly 30 years. At Ribbonwood we pride ourselves on our friendly personalised advice, catering for just a few guests because we want you to feel completely at home.

Fox Glacier *20 km S of Franz Josef*
Roaring Billy Homestay *B&B Homestay*
Kathy & Billy
PO Box 16, 21 State Highway 6, Fox Glacier

Tel (03) 751 0815 or 027 668 9768
Fax (03) 751 0815
billy@xtra.co.nz

Double $90-$130 Single $85-$95
(Special breakfast)
Visa MC accepted
Not suitable for children
1 King/Twin 1 Double 1 Twin (2 bdrm)
Bathrooms: 1 Private 1 Guest share

Welcome to the comfort, warmth and hospitality of our two storey home. Our livingroom, kitchen, diningroom and veranda are upstairs and lined with local timbers, with 360 degree views of glacier valley, mountains, farms and the township. We're the closest homestay to the glacier and two minutes walk to all eating and tourist facilities. We are happy to book your local activities. The bus goes past our home. We offer a special cooked vegetarian breakfast. We have one cat, Koko the Tonkinese.

Fox Glacier *0.5 km W of Fox Glacier*

The Homestead *B&B Farmstay*
Noeleen & Kevin Williams
PO Box 25, Cook Flat Road, Fox Glacier

Tel (03) 751 0835
Fax (03) 751 0805
foxhomestead@slingshot.co.nz

Double $140-$180 (Full breakfast)
Cooked breakfast $7pp
Pet free home
Not suitable for children
1 King/Twin 1 King 1 Queen (3 bdrm)
Bathrooms: 2 Ensuite 1 Private

B&B Approved

Kevin and Noeleen, welcome you to our 2200 acre beef cattle and sheep farm. Beautiful native bush-clad mountains surround on three sides, and we enjoy a view of Mt Cook.

Our spacious 105 year old character home, built for Kevin's grandparents, has fine stained glass windows. The breakfast room overlooks peaceful pastures to the hills, and you are served home-made yoghurt, jams, marmalade, scones etc, with a cooked breakfast if desired.

The guest lounge, with its beautiful wooden panelled ceiling, has an open fire for cool autumn nights.

A rural retreat within walking distance of village facilities, with Matheson (Mirror Lake) and glacier nearby. It is our pleasure to help you with helihikes, helicopter scenic flights and glacier walks.

Unsuitable for small children. Bookings recommended. Smoke-free.

Directions: On Cook Flat Road, fifth house on right, 400 metres back off road before church.

Fox Glacier *3 km W of Fox Glacier*

Fox Glacier Mountain View B&B *B&B Homestay Cottage with Kitchen*
Karen Simpson

Approved

1 Williams Drive, Fox Glacier, West Coast, South Island

Tel (03) 751 0770   Fax (03) 751 0774
info@foxglaciermountainview.co.nz
www.foxglaciermountainview.co.nz

Double $155-$185 Single $150 (Full breakfast)
Children welcome, portacot available   TIANZ member
Internet facility available   TV in all rooms
Visa MC Eftpos accepted   Children welcome
3 King (3 bdrm)
Bathrooms: 3 Ensuite 1 Private

Welcome to my peaceful hideaway set on 8 acres of pure nature at its best. This eight year old country home has it all. With wide-open landscape, breathtaking views of Mt Cook and Mt Tasman, and surrounded by bush-clad hills with magnificent reflections on my own special pond.

I have a cosy self-contained cottage (for two) with basic kitchenette facility and en-suite. Inside my home, are en-suited super king/twin bedrooms, also super king/twin bedrooms with a private bathroom. Three bedrooms have private access. There are two bedrooms, with an adjoining bathroom between, ideal for a family of four.

The area is ecologically diverse, from the West Coast's sub-temperate rain forest, to one of the lowest flowing Glaciers in the Southern Hemisphere at Fox Glacier.

Situated near one of the most photographed mirror lakes in New Zealand (Lake Matheson), and just a short distance further, is access to the wild West Coast (Gillespie's Beach) with long tracks of rugged coastline, which is home to many New Zealand fur seal colonies. From walking adventures to adrenaline activities, I can happily assist enhancing your Glacier experience to the full.

It's truly "a piece of paradise" - I'd like to share the comfort and individual uniqueness with you.

I have travelled extensively in New Zealand as part of my career, gaining a wealth of tourism knowledge, and can help in your travel plans (where to go, or what to do and see) around the rest of our beautiful country. Please check on my website for booking availability, and driving directions.

West Coast

West Coast

Fox Glacier *1 km W of Fox Glacier*
Fox Glacier Homestay *Homestay*
Eunice & Michael Sullivan
64 Cook Flat Road, Fox Glacier

Tel (03) 751 0817
Fax (03) 751 0817
euni@xtra.co.nz

Double $90-$120 Single $80-$90
(Continental breakfast)
Children and pets welcome
1 Queen 1 Double 1 Twin 1 Single (3 bdrm)
Bathrooms: 1 Family share

Eunice and Michael are third generation farming and tourism family. We have three grown children, one dog (Ruff) and three cats (Bushy Tail, Sabrina & Tig). Our grandparents were founders of the Fox Glacier Hotel. We are a couple who enjoy meeting people and would like to share the joys of living in our little paradise (rain and all). Our home is surrounded by a large garden and has views of the mountains and Mt Cook. A five minute walk from township.

Fox Glacier *.2 km N of Fox Glacier*
The White Fox B&B *B&B Homestay*
Jane Wellard & Gary Scott
4 State Highway 6, PO Box 82, Fox Glacier

Tel (03) 751 0717 or 027 306 6759
Fax (03) 751 0717
thewhitefox@slingshot.co.nz
www.thewhitefoxbandb.co.nz

Double $140-$170 Single $120-$150
(Continental breakfast)
Children negotiable by age
Visa MC accepted
Children and pets welcome
1 Queen 1 Single (1 bdrm)
Bathrooms: 1 Ensuite

Relax and enjoy the warmth and hospitality of a genuine NZ family home. Gary is a fourth generation local and we have considerable knowledge to assist our guests. We offer an easy to find location. Your room has a superior comfort bed, quality linen, electric blankets, TV and modern ensuite. Wake to the aroma of freshly baked bread & enjoy a generous Continental breakfast. We share our sunny home with two young daughters Meghan & Isla & Jess the Border Collie.

Bruce Bay *50 km S of Fox Glacier*
Mulvaney Farmstay *Farmstay*
Malai Millar
PO Box 117, Bruce Bay, South Westland

Tel (03) 751 0865
Fax (03) 751 0865
malai.millar@xtra.co.nz

Double $170-$180 Single $110-$120
(Continental breakfast)
Dinner $40 per person
Not suitable for children
1 King 1 Queen (3 bdrm)
Bathrooms: 1 Ensuite 1 Family share

We run a beef farm. Our house was originally built by my Great Uncle Jack Mulvaney, who was of Irish descent and of hard character. He built this house for his Irish bride but she never arrived, sadly he lived here alone. We have lived here for over 20 years. Enjoy a pleasant and peaceful stay at our home. Situated 50 km south of Fox Glacier (40 minutes) and 60 km north of Haast (50 minutes). We are well sign posted from the main highway.

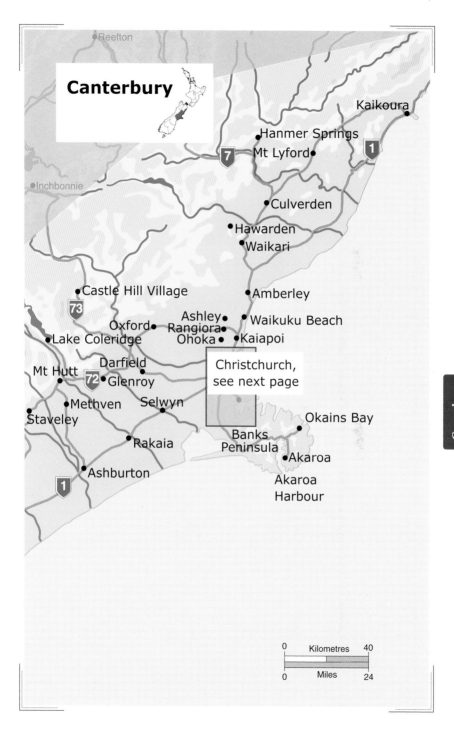

Canterbury

Reefton

Kaikoura

Hanmer Springs
Mt Lyford

7

1

Inchbonnie

Culverden

Hawarden
Waikari

Castle Hill Village

73

Amberley

Ashley
Oxford Rangiora
Lake Coleridge Ohoka

Waikuku Beach
Kaiapoi

Darfield
Mt Hutt Glenroy

72

Methven Selwyn
Staveley

Christchurch,
see next page

Okains Bay

Rakaia

Banks
Peninsula
Akaroa

Ashburton

1

Akaroa
Harbour

0   Kilometres   40

0   Miles   24

Canterbury

291

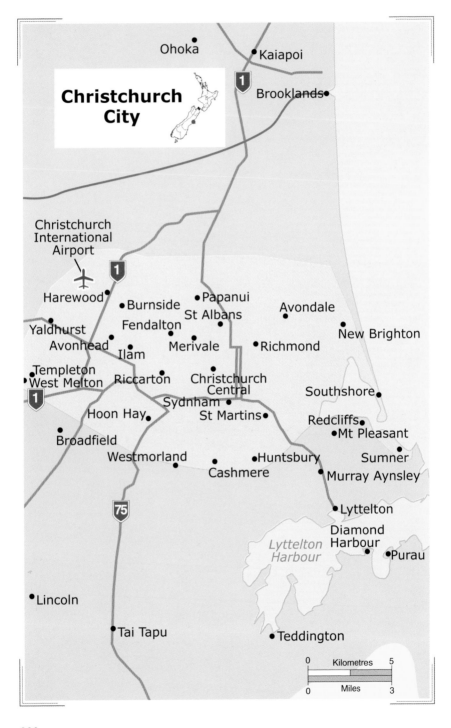

Christchurch
City

Ohoka
Kaiapoi
Brooklands

Christchurch
International
Airport

Harewood
Burnside
Papanui
St Albans
Avondale
Fendalton
New Brighton
Yaldhurst
Avonhead
Merivale
Richmond
Ilam
Templeton
West Melton
Riccarton
Christchurch
Central
Southshore
Hoon Hay
Sydnham
St Martins
Redcliffs
Broadfield
Mt Pleasant
Westmorland
Huntsbury
Sumner
Cashmere
Murray Aynsley
Lyttelton
Diamond
Harbour
Lyttelton
Harbour
Purau

Lincoln

Tai Tapu
Teddington

0   Kilometres   5
0   Miles   3

Kaikoura *130 km S of Blenheim*

Bay-View *Homestay*
Margaret Woodill
296 Scarborough Street, Kaikoura

B&B Approved

Tel (03) 319 5480   Fax (03) 319 7480
bayviewhomestay@xtra.co.nz
www.bnb.co.nz/bayviewkaikoura.html

Double $95-$100 Single $60 (Full breakfast)
Children under 14 $20   Dinner $30   Children and pets welcome
1 Queen 1 Twin 1 Single (3 bdrm)
Bathrooms: 1 Ensuite 1 Private 1 Guest share

Our spacious family home on Kaikoura Peninsula has splendid mountain and sea views and is exceptionally quiet. Only five minutes from the Kaikoura township, off the main highway south. The house nestles in an acre of colourful garden and there is plenty of off-street parking.

A guest lounge is available or you are more than welcome to socialise with the host. Laundry facilities and tea/coffee with home-made baking available. There is a solar heated swimming pool for guests use. Traditional breakfast with home-baked bread, muesli, home preserves, available early as required for whale/dolphin watching guests. Enjoy breakfast in the dining area or out on the sunny deck whilst taking in the magnificent mountain view.

We book local activities and happily meet bus or train. Margaret, your friendly host, has lived in the area for most of her life. She has a grown family of four, and seven grandchildren. Margaret enjoys gardening, bowls, sewing and choir. She especially enjoys warmly welcoming guests into her home.

"Let Our Home be Your Home". Guests comments: "This B&B is an unforgettable memory for me in NZ five weeks travel" (Japan). "Beautiful place, beautiful food, fabulous hospitality, Margaret. Thank you for opening up your home and welcoming us. Be back again" (Wellington). "Thank you for meeting the train and showing us the area. You were highly recommended and we absolutely endorse this" (UK). "Many thanks for your generous hospitality. You and your lovely home are a credit to B&B Homestays" (UK). "The most amazing breakfast in all of New Zealand. The views are amazing too and so is Margaret's hospitality" (Australia). "We felt like family! Thank you for such a lovely visit and wonderful, delicious meals. We thank you a million!" (USA).

Canterbury

293

Bendamere House *B&B Homestay*
Ellen & Peter Smith
37 Adelphi Terrace, Kaikoura

Tel (03) 319 5830 or 0800 107 770
Fax (03) 319 7337
bendamerehouse@xtra.co.nz
www.bendamere.co.nz

Double $140-$200 **Single** $120-$150
(Continental breakfast, full at extra cost) Children $20 extra
Visa MC Diners Eftpos accepted
5 Queen 3 Twin 3 Single (5 bdrm)
Bathrooms: 5 Ensuite

Kerry and Julie Howden along with their sons Kieran 16, Matthew 13 and Jeremy 10 welcome you to Bendamere House which boosts five luxury ensuite rooms all with private balconies where you can relax and enjoy the breathtaking views of the Pacific Ocean and Mountain Range and watch the dolphins perform for you at times of the year!

Relax and unwind in our expansive lawns and rose gardens with a bottle of wine on our garden furniture. We are situated within five minutes walk to the Kaikoura township and close to all sightseeing attractions.

All of our rooms have first class facilities with large ensuites, quality sleepyhead beds, TV, Tea and coffee facilities, silent fridges, bathrobes, heatpumps and electric blankets. Private, secure off-street parking directly behind your room and courtesy pick up/drop off to trains /buses.

A delicious continental breakfast served in our communual dining room includes fresh fruit salad, yoghurt, cereals, toast, spreads and homebaked muffins, tea and coffee. Homebaked cookies are supplied in your room.

Some of our guests comments-:
Robin Gaslan-USA- *"The most amazing place I've been in in NZ! Best views in the world and the greatest hosts!"*
Tania & Claudia-Germany- *"Wonderful Hosts! Exquisite views! Great Accommodation! Beautiful Garden! Thanks!"*

Kaikoura - Oaro *22 km S of Kaikoura*
Waitane Homestay *B&B Homestay Cottage with Kitchen*

Kathleen King
Oaro, RD 2, Kaikoura

Tel (03) 319 5494
Fax (03) 319 5524
kathleen.king@xtra.co.nz

Double $85-$95 Single $50 (Full breakfast)
Children $25
Dinner $25 by arrangement
Visa MC accepted
Children and pets welcome
1 Double 4 Single (3 bdrm)
Bathrooms: 2 Private

Waitane is 48 acres, close to the sea and looking north to the Kaikoura Peninsula. Enjoy coastal walks to the Haumuri Bluff with bird watching, fossil hunting etc, or drive to Kaikoura along our beautiful rocky coast. This is a mild climate and we grow citrus and sub-tropical fruits, mainly feijoas. Guest room in house has two single beds. Self-contained unit has two bedrooms, sleeps four. One friendly cat lives here. Join me for dinner - fresh vegies, home preserves and home-made ice cream.

Kaikoura *4 km NE of Kaikoura Town Centre*
The Point *B&B*

Peter & Gwenda Smith
Fyffe Quay, Kaikoura

Tel (03) 319 5422
Fax (03) 319 7422
pointsmith@xtra.co.nz
www.pointbnb.co.nz

Double $100-$120 Single $80-$90
(Continental breakfast)
Visa MC accepted
2 Queen (2 bdrm)
Bathrooms: 2 Ensuite

We offer a warm and friendly welcome to our home, which we share with our two daughters. Enjoy the quiet, unique location of this beautiful old farmhouse built in the late 1800's. Our 90 acres farmland is part of the Kaikoura Peninsula. Located on the waterfront gives spectacular views of the sea and mountains. Ideally situated for walks on and around Kaikoura Peninsula and the Seal Colony. Short walk to top Kaikoura restaurants. We run daily Sheep Shearing Shows, have farm dogs and a cat.

Kaikoura *183 km N of Christchurch*
Nikau Lodge & Cottage *B&B*

John & Lilla Fitzwater
53 Deal Street, Kaikoura (central), Kaikoura

Tel (03) 319 6973 or 021 682 076
Fax (03) 319 6973
stay@NikauLodge.com
www.NikauLodge.com

Double $110-$225 Single $110-$225 (Full breakfast)
Visa MC Eftpos accepted
Pet free home
Not suitable for children
1 King/Twin 6 Queen 1 Double 1 Twin (9 bdrm)
Bathrooms: 6 Ensuite 1 Private 1 Guest share

Conveniently located in the heart of Kaikoura close to SH1 with magnificent hilltop views of sea and mountains, Nikau Lodge & Cottage offer high quality affordable B&B accommodation. Five minutes walk takes you to Kaikoura's main street where you can enjoy local rock lobster. Relax in the hot-tub or garden with a glass of wine and gaze at the stars and snow-capped mountains. Internet access, Sky TV, complimentary tea/coffee, laundry, in-room TV/movies. John & Lilla welcome the opportunity to make your stay enjoyable and memorable.

Canterbury

Kaikoura *1 km NW of Kaikoura Central*
Driftwood Villa B&B *Deluxe B&B*

Suzy & Chris Valkhoff
166A Beach Road, Kaikoura

Tel (03) 319 7116 or 027 476 7000
Fax (03) 319 7116
stayatdriftwoodvilla@xtra.co.nz
www.driftwoodvilla.co.nz

Double $135-$180 Single $105-$125 (Full breakfast)
Children $20   Full use of kitchen
Visa MC accepted
Children welcome
1 King 3 Queen 1 Twin 4 Single (4 bdrm)
Bathrooms: 4 Ensuite

This one looks good! Many guests before you have found this the ideal place and atmosphere to relax. Guests enjoy the freedom of the whole house while the hosts are unobtrusive and have separate accommodation. Facilities include wireless internet and computer, spacious lounge, Jacuzzi, garden and fully equipped kitchen. Conveniently located opposite Kaikoura Day Spa (beauty and relaxation treatments) and a short walk to shops and supermarket. Needless to say that all our rooms are of a good standard and decorated with warmth and style.

Kaikoura *1 km N of Central Kaikoura*
Admiral Creighton B&B *Luxury B&B*

Yvonne & Tony Steadman
191 Beach Road, Kaikoura

Tel 0800 742 622 or (03) 319 7111
Fax (03) 319 7111
admiral.creighton.b2b@ihug.co.nz
www.admiral-creighton.com

Double $120-$160 Single $120-$160
(Full breakfast)
Visa MC Amex accepted
Not suitable for children
4 Queen 1 Twin (5 bdrm)
Bathrooms: 3 Ensuite 2 Private

Tops in Service. Best in Value. Superior in Comfort and style. You will love staying at this lovely B&B. On arrival enjoy a complimentary wine or beer as you soak up the magnificent vista of the Seaward Kaikoura Mountains. Select from the menu your favorite cooked or continental breakfast. Feed the trout, eels and ducks in our stream boundry. Spacious living. Pick up and drop off transport available.Level off street parking. Our Cockatoo Creighton will welcome you warmly. On line booking at www.admiral-creighton.com

Kaikoura *2 km S of Information Centre*
Pacific Allure Heights *B&B Apartment with Kitchen*

Judy & Alan Hickey
278 Scarborough Street, Kaikoura

Tel (03) 319 5669 or (03) 319 7402
021 319 735   Fax (03) 319 5669
accommodation@pacificallure.co.nz
www.pacificallure.co.nz

Double $160-$240 Single $120-$140
(Continental breakfast provisions)
Children Under 12 $15   Extra adult $20
Visa MC accepted   Children welcome
2 King 1 Double (2 bdrm)
Bathrooms: 2 Ensuite 2 Private

Relax in comfort in modern self-contained apartments which open onto private courtyards with sweeping veiws of the Pacific ocean and the Kaikoura ranges. Our apartments are located on the Kaikoura Penninsula nestled among beautiful gardens. We offer king size beds, kitchen facilities, TV, double-glazing & off-street parking. Tariff includes continental breakfast. We book for local tourist attractions. Your hosts Judy & Alan care about your comfort and are commited to making your stay memorable. Third house on right past the penninsula lookout.

Kaikoura *130 km S of Blenheim*

A Rest-n-Kai *B&B*

Carmel Tindall
5 Fyffe Ave, Kaikoura

Tel (03) 319 7330 or 021 182 7442
cartin@slingshot.co.nz
www.arestnkai.co.nz

Double $100-$120 **Single** $40-$65 (Full breakfast)
Children $20
Babies $10
Pet free home
Children welcome
1 Queen 1 Single (2 bdrm)
Bathrooms: 1 Ensuite 1 Family share

Welcome to my home where I offer a Rest-n-Kai. Kai meaning food in Maori. I am a retired nurse and still enjoy caring for people. The home is new and comfortable, with lovely mountain views from the main rooms and external access from the large bedroom. A short walk into the township and other attractions including Whalewatch and Dolphin Encounter. I am happy to assist guests with directions and bookings. Many complimentary comments in visitors book indicate satisfaction with A Rest-n-Kai.

Kaikoura - Mangamaunu *15 km N of Kaikoura*

SurfWatch *B&B Separate Suite Cottage with Kitchen*

Lynn & David Robinson
1137 State Hwy One, Kaikoura, 7340

Tel (03) 319 6611 or 027 616 2903
(03) 319 6658   **Fax** (03) 319 6658
bnb@ofu.co.nz
www.surfwatchbnb.com

Double $120-$225 **Single** $120-$225
(Continental breakfast provisions)
Visa MC accepted
Children and pets welcome
1 King 1 Queen 1 Single (2 bdrm)
Bathrooms: 1 Ensuite 1 Private 1 Ensuite, 1 Private

Kia Ora! The wow factor is here. Five acres of tranquil rural country setting with stunning views overlooking the Pacific Ocean. Quiet and relaxing, melt away the city hustle-bustle in our spacious lawn and gardens. From the OceanView Ensuite you can watch dolphins play while Sharkeys Cottage is nestled in the garden. Both have kitchenettes, private entrances, parking, and are uniquely decorated with local wood and stone. Breakfast at your leisure. Wireless broadband. Lynn, David, Jessica (15) and dogface Layla look forward to meeting you.

Kaikoura *5 km N of Kaikoura*

Titoki Lodge Country Stay *Luxury Country Stay & Cottage*

Sean & Charlotte
38A Titoki Drive, RD 1, Kaikoura, 7371

Tel (03) 319 6095 or 021 251 7780
charlottephoon@gmail.com
www.titokilodge.co.nz

Double $140-$180 **Single** $100-$140 (Full breakfast)
Children negotiable
Dinner $30
Lunch available by arrangement
Full board packages available
Children welcome
2 Queen 1 Double 1 Twin (3 bdrm)
Bathrooms: 1 Ensuite 1 Guest share

We invite you to stay with us our newly built, modern home and cottage. All rooms are clean and stylish and guests are welcome to make themselves at home in one of our two living rooms, the deck, or in the garden and paddocks enjoying a walk amongst the many tame animals that we have. Our home offers peace, quiet and magnificent views that will ensure you won't want to leave. Welcome to our piece of paradise!

Canterbury

Kaikoura *130 km S of Blenheim*

Churchill Park Lodge *B&B Separate Suite*
Gordon & Priscilla Wright
34 Churchill Street, Kaikoura, Marlborough

Tel (03) 319 5526 or 0800 363 690
cplodge@ihug.co.nz
www.churchillparklodge.co.nz

Double $120 Single $95 (Continental breakfast)
Children by arrangement   Visa MC accepted
1 Queen 1 Double 1 Twin (2 bdrm)
Bathrooms: 2 Ensuite

Churchill park lodge is conveniently located in central Kaikoura on SHWY1 (Churchill street) on the hill capturing the magnificent Kaikoura mountain and sea views.

We welcome you to our purpose built, self contained upstair units with ensuite bathrooms (the double ensuite is compact but well appointed). We get many guests comment on how comfy the beds are. The units have TV, fridge, lounge settee, dining suite, balcony table and chairs, heating and electric blankets with tea and coffee making facilities including plunger coffee. There is also off-street parking and a private guest entrance with laundry facilities available. We serve a continental breakfast to your room for

you to enjoy at your leisure. We believe the sea and mountain views from your room are unbeatable in Kaikoura.

Our B&B is only five minutes walk through Churchill park to the town centre. Where you will find shops, restaurants, cafés, the information centre and beach.

Cilla & Gordon are a down to earth "Kiwi" couple who are keen fishermen. You are welcome to join us on any trips we have planned, checking the lobster pots, catching a fish by boat or surfcasting from the beach. Also the local stream has many brown trout which are very challenging to catch.

We have two friendly dogs (who do not have access to the guest area) "Miss Spanky" a fun Bichon/Tibetan terrier X and "Xena" an aging pointer. We can book local activities or tours, and will happily meet you at the bus or train.

Kaikoura *5 km N of Kaikoura*

Ardara Lodge *B&B Cottage with Kitchen*
Winnie & Phil Hood
233 Schoolhouse Road, RD 1, Kaikoura

Tel (03) 319 5736 or 0800 226 164
ardara@xtra.co.nz
www.ardaralodge.com

Double $110-$150 Single $110-$140
(Continental breakfast)
Children by arrangement
Cottage $165-$250
Visa MC accepted
Children welcome
7 Queen 3 Twin 4 Single (7 bdrm)
Bathrooms: 5 Ensuite 1 Private

After and exhilarating day exploring the natural splendours of Kaikoura unwind in the tranquility of Ardara Lodge.

You will enjoy a relaxed and peaceful stay in a beautiful rural setting near the magnificent Kaikoura mountains. Relax on the decks and enjoy Winnie's colourful garden which complements the panoramic veiw. Enjoy the outdoor hot tub (spa), veiw the Kaikoura mountains by day and the stars by night or read a book in the guest lounge.

The cottage has an upstairs bedroom with a queen and two single beds. Downstairs there is a bedroom with a queen bed, a bathroom with a shower and a lounge, kitchen, dining room. The deck is private with a great veiw of the Mountains. It has been very poplular with groups, families and honeymoon couples. The house has ensuite bathrooms with queen beds, plus a two bedroom unit, all with TV, fridge, settee and coffee/tea facilities. You have you own private entrance and you are welcome to come and go as you please. We offer laundry facilities, off street parking and a courtesy car from the bus/train. There is an excellent restaurant, Donnegal House, within walking distance.

Phil owns a construction company based in Blenheim and Winnie was an office assistant before purchasing Ardara Lodge. Phil's hobbies are fishing, diving, motor racing, squash and harriers. Winnie's hobbies include gardening, lace making, embroidery and fishing. We like meeting people and look forward to your company.

Directions: Driving North, 4 km from Kaikoura on State Highway 1, turn left into Schoolhouse Road and continue 1.5 km until our sign.

Canterbury

Mt Lyford *21 km N of Waiau on SH70*
Bell Bird Haven *B&B Homestay*
Greg & Glenda Baker
20 Lulu's Lane, Mt Lyford, RD Waiau 8275

Tel (03) 315 6411
Fax (03) 315 6442
info@mt-lyford.com
www.mt-lyford.com

Double $225 Single $190 (Full breakfast)
Home cooked dinner available
Visa MC accepted
Not suitable for children
2 Queen (2 bdrm)
Bathrooms: 2 Ensuite

Imagine enjoying a glass of wine on the deck in one of the most spectacular locations in the country. You can relax or be as adventurous as you like, there are a wide range of things to do and see. Our guests tell us that the beds are so comfortable. Dinner (real home cooked kiwi style) is available, advance notice appreciated. You are assured of the warmest of welcomes by open and friendly hosts.

Hanmer Springs *5 km SW of Hanmer Springs*
Mira Monte *B&B Countryhomestay*
Anna & Theo van de Wiel
324 Woodbank Road, Hanmer Springs

Tel (03) 315 7604 or 021 129 9339
Fax (03) 315 7604
relax@miramonte.co.nz
www.miramonte.co.nz

Double $140-$150 Single $100-$110
(Special breakfast) Children negotiable
Visa MC accepted
Children welcome
2 King 1 Single (2 bdrm)
Bathrooms: 2 Ensuite

Close to the thrills of Hanmer Springs, at the foot of the mountains, lies our peaceful home. Our guest rooms have been tastefully decorated to make your stay special. Relax in your own sitting room or join us. We make a great espresso! We are here to pamper you. There is a grand piano and our large garden has a swimming pool. We speak Dutch and German. Mindy, our Jack Russell is part of the family. Come as a Stranger! Leave as a Friend!

Hanmer Springs *0.1 km E of in Hanmer village*
Cheltenham House *Luxury Boutique B&B Cottage No Kitchen*
Maree & Len Earl
13 Cheltenham Street, Hanmer Springs

Tel (03) 315 7545 Fax (03) 315 7645
enquiries@cheltenham.co.nz
www.cheltenham.co.nz

Double $190-$230 Single $160-$200
(Special breakfast)
Children by arrangement
Extra person $40
Visa MC Diners Eftpos accepted
Children and pets welcome
2 King/Twin 5 Queen 1 Single (6 bdrm)
Bathrooms: 5 Ensuite 1 Private

Located on a quiet street, 200 metres from the Thermal Pools, restaurants & forest walks, we renovated this gracious 1930's home with the guests' comfort paramount. The four spacious, sunny suites in the house and two cottage suites in the park-like garden, are centrally heated. Enjoy breakfast of your choice served in your own suite and complimentary wine in the billiard room in the evening. Star-gaze, while soaking in the garden spa. Together with our sociable siamese & labrador, we look forward to meeting you.

Hanmer Springs *1 km SW of Hanmer Springs*

Albergo Hanmer Lodge & Alpine Villa *Luxury B&B & Separate Suite & Apartment with kitchen & Cottage with kitchen & B&B & Self-contained Villas*

Bascha & Beat Blattner
88 Rippingale Road, Hanmer Springs

Toll-Free 0800 342 313 Ph/fax (03) 315 7428
albergo@paradise.net.nz www.albergohanmer.com
Check web for packages

Double $160-$250 Single $120 (Special breakfast)
Dinner by prior arrangement   Villa $260-$525
Visa MC Diners Amex Eftpos accepted
Pet free home Children Welcome
1 King 3 King/Twin 1 Queen 2 Single (4 bdrm)
Bathrooms: 4 Ensuite

BREAKFAST - WELLNESS - CUISINE

Arrive at Albergo to blitz your senses in the fresh n' fun eclectic interiors with whimsical touches. **Dramatic alpine views** from all windows. **Stretch out on super king beds**, with TV/fridge/tea & coffee, and spacious ensuites (great water pressure) - choose the spa one for that bubble bath delight! European comforts for all seasons: floor heat, double glaze, aircon. Relax in cosy corners or wander out to the sunken Feng Shui courtyard, with soothing waterfall & fragrant lavenders galore. **Privacy & all day sun**: 2 minutes from Hot Pools, shops & cafés, or via new scenic walkway. **Ask about pamper package delights, fishing & hunting.**

Your dedicated hosts have spent 7 years refining the Albergo experience by creating the stand alone Alpine Villa, with self-catering options. The awesome cinema & DVD library compliments the superb American king bedroom with large ensuite, boasting 'wow' views from the high panorama window, while you shower! Slip on a fluffy bathrobe, wander out to the split-level courtyard with private Jacuzzi and soak up Hanmer's starry night skies.

We are passionate about breakfasts! Served at a time to suit you, **Albergo's renowned 3-course breakfast** offers over 10 choices: Creative fruit platters or Swiss Birchermuesli, followed by the wafting smell of the famous **homemade bread, & fine Italian coffee**.This perfect fusion of NZ & Swiss cuisine features: Salmon Eggs Benedict, French fluffy omelets, wafer-thin crepes, 'Albergo Egg Nests' or 'Full NZ', with crispy bacon. Fondue dinners by prior arrangement.

'Best breakfasts ever and Gold award for porridge' Sheila Bennett, NYC. *'Loved the milk jug containing cow - the decor and food was divine'* Charlotte, UK. *'Your quirky decors are a feast for the eyes, what an accommodation experience'* Gavin & Kerrie, Brisbane

DIRECTIONS: At junction before main village, 300m past Caltex Garage, take **Argelins Rd** (Centre branch), take 2nd road left **Rippingale Rd**. Albergo Hanmer is 800m down on the left (Sign at drive entrance).

Canterbury

Canterbury

Hanmer Springs *130 km N of Christchurch*
Cheshire House *Luxury B&B*

Jan & Chris Ottley
164C Hanmer Springs Road,
Highway 7A, Hanmer Springs

Tel (03) 315 5100 or 0800 337 332
janandchris@xtra.co.nz

Double $140-$170 **Single** $110-$130 (Full breakfast)
Children over 10 years
Visa MC Eftpos accepted
Pet free home
Children welcome
2 Queen 1 Twin (3 bdrm)
Bathrooms: 3 Ensuite

Cheshire House is conveniently located two minutes drive from Hanmer Springs township. Come and be spoilt with our English hospitality, and then relax in one of our three beautifully furnished ensuite bedrooms, with your own private guest entrance and stunning mountain views. Jan & Chris will ensure that you have a memorable stay and breakfast in Hanmer Springs. There are many activities for you to enjoy if you wish. Then Experience Hanmer Springs delightful thermal pools and then relax, by indulging your health, body, and mind.

Hanmer Springs *130 km NW of Christchurch*
Oakview Hanmer Springs *B&B Separate Suite Apartment with Kitchen*

Michael & Jenny Malthus
46 Jacks Pass Road, Hanmer Springs

Tel (03) 315 7757 or 021 577 570
Fax (03) 315 7746
stay@oakview.co.nz
www.oakview.co.nz

Double $160-$200 **Single** $110-$130 (Full breakfast)
Visa MC Amex Eftpos accepted
Pet free home
1 King 2 Queen 1 Twin (3 bdrm)
Bathrooms: 2 Ensuite

Well appointed accommodation within a modern gracious home overlooking large gardens through a vista of oak trees onto the golf course. Only 250 metres easy walk to the Thermal Pools, shops and a great selection of restaurants. Your hosts Jenny and Michael will do everything possible to make your stay welcome and enjoyable. The choice of accommodation varies from two bedroom self contained apartments with kitchens, to one bedroom suites all with their own entrances, spa baths and showers.

Hanmer Springs *25 km N of Culverden*
Hanmer View *B&B*

Jane & Brendan Byrne
8 Oregon Heights, Hanmer Springs, 7334

Tel (03) 315 7947
hanmerview@xtra.co.nz
www.hanmerview.co.nz

Double $170-$175 **Single** $130-$150 (Full breakfast)
Visa MC accepted
Not suitable for children
1 King/Twin 2 Queen (3 bdrm)
Bathrooms: 3 Ensuite

Hanmer View, surrounded by beautiful forest and adjoining Conical Hill track. Stunning panoramic alpine views. Purpose built to ensure guests enjoy quiet, relaxing stay in warm, spacious quality ensuite rooms. A DVD is available for your pleasure and Wireless Internet is complimentary. Tea, coffee and homebaking always available and your hosts, Jane and Brendan delight in serving you a generous scrumptious cooked & continental breakfast. Short stroll to village, thermal pools and tourist attractions. See letterbox sign, on right, end Oregon Heights.

Culverden *3 km S of Culverden*

Ballindalloch *Farmstay*

Diane & Dougal Norrie
Longplantation Road, Culverden RD 2,
North Canterbury 8272

Tel (03) 315 8220 or 027 437 3184
Fax (03) 315 8220
dianedougal@xtra.co.nz

Double $130 Single $80 (Full breakfast)
Children $35
Dinner $35 by arrangement
Children welcome
1 Queen 2 Single (2 bdrm)
Bathrooms: 1 Guest share

Welcome to Ballindalloch, a family farming enterprise with 3 family members farming on their own behalf on 4,000 acre irrigated farms, now milking 2,500 cows. We are just over 1 hour north of Christchurch, half an hour to Hanmer Springs, 1 ½ hours to Kaikoura Whale Watch. Culverden is situated between two excellent fishing rivers. Having travelled extensively overseas we appreciate relaxing in a homely atmosphere - this we extend to our guests. Our cat is Thomas. We look forward to welcoming you.

Hawarden *2 km N of Hawarden*

The Dutch Station *Countrystay Luxury B&B and self-contained guesthouse*

Rein Bakker & Gertruud Steltenpool
135 Bentleys Road, RD 1, Hawarden 7385

Tel (03) 314 2200
info@thedutchstation.co.nz
www.thedutchstation.co.nz

Double $120-$200 Single $70-$85 (Full breakfast)
Dinner by arrangement
Children and pets welcome
See our website for further information and arrangements
1 King 1 Queen 2 Single (3 bdrm)
Bathrooms: 1 Ensuite with bath and bidet
1 Private with sliding showers

Perfectly situated in the middle of the Alpine-Pacific Triangle, surrounded by beautiful views of the Southern Alps. Our new premises offers luxury European style comfort in a quiet, rural setting. The self-contained guesthouse includes 2 bedrooms, bathroom, fully equipped kitchen and living with satellite TV. The B&B-room contains a cooler, coffee/tea facilities and TV. Guests can play a free game of 'Dutch Golf' on our course, which is the only 'Dutch Golf' course in New Zealand. Infrared sauna and Internet facilities. Our cat is Scuff.

Amberley *1 km S of Amberley*

Bredon Downs *B&B Homestay*

Bob & Veronica Lucy
Bredon Downs, Amberley, RD 1, North Canterbury

Tel (03) 314 9356
Fax (03) 314 9357
lucy.lucy@xtra.co.nz
www.bredondownshomestay.co.nz

Double $120-$140 Single $75 (Full breakfast)
Dinner $40 (including wine)
Visa MC accepted
Children welcome
1 Queen 1 Twin 1 Single (3 bdrm)
Bathrooms: 1 Ensuite 1 Private

Our drive goes off SH1 and so we are conveniently en route to and from the Interisland Ferry, just 48km north of Christchurch and 100 km south of the Kaikoura whales, and within easy reach of Hanmer Springs. The house is surrounded by an English style garden with swimming pool, and close to the Waipara wineries, beach and attractive golf course. We have travelled extensively and lived overseas, and now share our lives with a newfoundland, three geriatric donkeys and Barney the cat!

Amberley *1 km W of Amberley*

Kokiri B&B *B&B Apartment with Kitchen*

Pat & Graham Shaw
65 Douglas Road, Amberley 7410, North Canterbury

Tel (03) 314 9699 or 021 033 3173
021 132 2439   Fax (03) 314 9699
grahampat@actrix.co.nz
www.kokiribnb.co.nz

Double $110-$130 (Continental breakfast)
Children $15   Extra guest in apartment $15
Children and pets welcome
1 King 1 Queen 1 Single (2 bdrm)
Bathrooms: 1 Ensuite 1 Private
Spa bath in Private bathroom

Our Colonial home lies in the peaceful countryside, opposite Amberley Domain. Relax and enjoy strolling around our garden with our Labrador, doves and fish! Find comfort in your centrally heated accommodation and enjoy the abundance of home produce with your extensive continental breakfast. 1 km to excellent restaurants. Five minutes to the Waipara Valley vineyards, Amberley golf course, beaches and a variety of walking tracks. One hour to Hanmer Springs and Mt Lyford Skiing. 40 minutes to Christchurch and 100 km to marine interests at Kaikoura.

Amberley *45 km N of Christchurch*

Amber Cottage Bed & Breakfast *B&B Homestay*

Elizabeth Perkins
23 Teviot View Place, Amberley, 7410

Tel (03) 314 7077 Fax (03) 314 7030
ambercottage@xtra.co.nz

Double $110-$130 Single $80-$90 (Full breakfast)
Children under 12 half price
Dinner $30 by arrangement
Visa MC accepted
Pet free home
Children welcome
1 Queen 1 Twin (2 bdrm)
Bathrooms: 2 Ensuite

Enjoy a warm comfortable stay at Amber Cottage set on half an acre of gardens and orchard in a quiet street. I enjoy cooking, gardening and take pleasure in sharing home-grown produce. Having enjoyed friendly hospitality on travels overseas I look forward to returning it. Amberley is situated close to the beach, golf course the vineyards and wineries of Waipara. Turn into Amberley Beach Road, then right into Teviotview Place.

Waikuku Beach *30 km N of Christchurch*

Emmanuel House *B&B*

Graham & Mary Dacombe
20 Allin Drive, Waikuku Beach,
North Canterbury 7402

Tel (03) 312 7782
Fax (03) 312 7783
emmanuel.house@xtra.co.nz

Double $95 Single $55 (Continental breakfast)
Children under 5 free, under 12 half price
Dinner $20 by arrangement
Children welcome
1 Double 1 Twin 1 Single (3 bdrm)
Bathrooms: 1 Guest share

You are special to us, and we warmly invite you to our new one level purpose-built home in its park-like setting with wheelchair access throughout. Emmanuel House is 2 km from the main highway, within walking distance of the beach and 30km north of Christchurch. Close by is the thriving rural township of Rangiora. Amateur radio ZL3NZ and ZL3MD, music, correspondence, and people are our interests. Complimentary tea/coffee/home-baking always available.

Rangiora *30 km N of Christchurch*
Willow Glen *B&B*

Glenda & Malcolm Ross
419 High Street, Rangiora

Tel (03) 313 9940 or 027 498 4893
Fax (03) 313 9946
rosshighway@xtra.co.nz
www.willowglenrangiora.co.nz

Double $130 **Single** $90 (Continental breakfast)
Cooked breakfasts $10
Visa MC accepted
Not suitable for children
1 Queen 1 Double (2 bdrm)
Bathrooms: 1 Ensuite 1 Private

Nestled on the northern side of Rangiora township on Scenic Highway 72, 20 minutes from Christchurch International Airport, walking distance to great cafés, restaurants. We invite you to share our enchanting English style home for Kiwi hospitality. Off-street parking available. Comfortable beds, electric blankets, quality linen, continental breakfast or $10 for a hearty cooked breakfast per person. Bedrooms overlook garden and surrounding countryside. Relax in the spa with a glass of wine. Meet Lucy our foxy and our two spoilt cats.

Rangiora *14 km NW of Rangiora*
Sarolych Farm Homestay *B&B Homestay*

Lin & Chris Leppard
387 Stonyflat Road, North Loburn, RD 2 Rangiora

Tel (03) 312 8910 or 021 160 5087
leplin@hotmail.com

Double $120 **Single** $80 (Full breakfast)
Children by arrangement
Dinner $30pp by arrangement
Visa MC accepted
Children welcome
1 Double 1 Twin (2 bdrm)
Bathrooms: 1 Ensuite 1 Family share

Welcome to our small alpaca farm which we share with two lazy cats. Our home is warm and comfortable with wonderful mountain views. Our bedrooms have electric blankets, heaters, TVs and drink making facilities. The family bathroom has a spa bath. 40 minutes from Christchurch and the airport we are centrally located for many North Canterbury attractions; Hanmer Springs hotpools, the Canterbury wine growing regions, skifields and Kaikoura's whale watching. We can arrange local horse treks for you too. We look forward to meeting you.

Rangiora *2 km E of Rangiora*
Coldstream House *Luxury B&B Farmstay Cottage No Kitchen*

Willemina & Rupert Ward
11 Coldstream Road, Rangiora, 8254

Tel (03) 310 6006 or 021 039 6016
Fax (03) 310 6007
willeminaward@hotmail.com
www.coldstreamhouse.co.nz

Double $120-$140 **Single** $100-$120 (Continental breakfast)
Dinner not offered but cafés and restaurants nearby
Not suitable for children
1 Queen 1 Double (2 bdrm)
Bathrooms: 1 Ensuite, spacious with shower 1 Family share

Coldstream House is one of the original pioneer Homesteads of Canterbury. It offers an enchanting and delightful real New Zealand experience. The "Copper Cottage" guest cottage is 130 years old and has a pretty country bedroom with ensuite and private verandah with farm view. The Main House offers a luxurious bedroom overlooking 130 year old tranquil formal English gardens and grass tennis court surrounded by beautiful old trees and a wild flower garden.

Canterbury

Canterbury

Oxford *60 km W of Christchurch*
Country Life *B&B Apartment with Kitchen*
Helen Dunn
137 High Street, Oxford, North Canterbury 7430

Tel (03) 312 4167

Double $75-$80 Single $45-$50
(Full breakfast)
Dinner $20 by arrangement
Children and pets welcome
3 Double (2 bdrm)
Bathrooms: 1 Ensuite 1 Family share

Country life has been operating since 1987, the house is 80 years old and has a spacious garden, warm and sunny. Helen enjoys meeting people from far and wide - whether overseas visitors or those wanting a peaceful break away from Christchurch - all are welcomed at Country Life. High Street is left off the Main Road. Sign outside the gate.

Oxford *54 km W of Christchurch Airport*
Hielan' House *B&B Homestay Countrystay*
Shirley & John Farrell
74 Bush Road, Oxford, North Canterbury

Tel (03) 312 4382 or 0800 279 382 (freephone)
027 4359 4350   Fax (03) 312 4382
hielanhouse@ihug.co.nz
www.hielanhouse.co.nz

Double $130-$150 Single $110-$120 (Full breakfast)
Children POA   Dinner by arrangement
Visa MC accepted
Children and pets welcome
1 King/Twin 1 Queen 1 Twin 1 Single (2 bdrm)
Bathrooms: 2 Ensuite

Our quality upstairs guest rooms have their own relaxing areas, ensuites, separate entrance. TV, tea/coffee facilities, fridges, hairdryers, bathrobes. Complimentary laundry, internet facilities, Sauna, spa, outdoor swimming pool, golf clubs to use. Enjoy John's breakfasts, dinners with home-grown meat, vegetables in season. We enjoy meeting people and look forward to spoiling you. Relax, unwind on our six acres in peaceful, rural Oxford yet three minutes from Inland Scenic Route 72 via Bay Road and Bush Road. Farm animals. Easy drive to Christchurch.

Ohoka *6 km W of Kaiapoi*
Oakhampton Lodge *B&B*
Angus & Jackie Watson
24 Keetly Place, Ohoka, Kaiapoi RD 2, 8252

Tel (03) 312 6413 or 021 502 313
Fax (03) 312 6314
info@oakhampton.co.nz
www.oakhampton.co.nz

Double $130-$150 (Full breakfast)
Not suitable for young children
Dinner $30 available on request
Visa MC Eftpos accepted
1 King 1 Queen 1 Twin (3 bdrm)
Bathrooms: 2 Ensuite

Set amongst four acres of lawns, mature trees and herbaceous borders, Oakhampton Lodge is the perfect place to unwind and experience a slice of country life. Ideal for weekend stays or as a stopover while travelling around New Zealand. Heading north from Christchurch on the Northern Motorway (SH1) take second Kaiapoi/Ohoka turnoff over Waimakariri River, follow signs to Ohoka. Keetly Place is 6 km along Mill Road, on right, just before Ohoka Hall and Service Station. No 24 is on your right.

Kaiapoi *15 km N of Christchurch*
Morichele *B&B*
Helen & Richard Moore
25 Hilton Street, Kaiapoi

Tel (03) 327 5247 Fax (03) 327 5243
morichele@xtra.co.nz

Double $100 **Single** $70 (Full breakfast)
Children negotiable   Dinner by arrangement
1 Double 1 Twin (2 bdrm)
Bathrooms: 1 Guest share

Helen & Richard provide comfortable accommodation in a beautiful garden setting, close to rivers and beaches for fishing, golf course and walks. With off-street parking, your own entrance, sitting/dining area with fridge, tea and coffee making facilities, TV and video. Cafés and restaurants within walking distance alternatively, if you prefer, you are welcome to bring back takeaways or barbeque in the garden. A two hour drive will take you to ski fields, Hanmer Springs themal reserve, Akaroa (home of the Hector's Dolphin) and Kaikoura (whale watching).

Kaiapoi - Mandeville *20 km N of Christchurch*
Ohoka Meadows B&B / Gatehouse Cottage
B&B Farmstay Cottage with Kitchen
Mary & Graeme Chisnall
49 Ohoka Meadows Drive, RD 2 Kaiapoi, 7692

Tel (03) 313 1781   Fax (03) 313 1781
ohokameadows@xtra.co.nz
www.ohokameadows.co.nz

Double $120-$150 **Single** $100 (Full breakfast)
Children POA
Dinner by arrangement
Children welcome
1 King 1 Queen 1 Twin (3 bdrm)
Bathrooms: 3 Ensuite

The Chisnall family welcome you into their home. Stay in our large, modern rooms with your own facilities, our luxurious fully equipped cottage with kitchen or enquire about our apartment in the Christchurch city. Take the alpacas for a walk or feed the other animals.Try your skill putting on the golf greens. Enjoy four acres of landscaped grounds and admire the mountains. Only 22 km to Christchurch International Airport and Shopping Malls. Our interests include model engineers, jetboating, teaching and entertaining guests.

Christchurch - Brooklands *18 km N of Christchurch Centre*
Ataahua *B&B Cottage No Kitchen Wedding Venue, Honeymoon accomodation*
Julie & Mura Anderson
96 Harbour Road, Brooklands, Christchurch

Tel (03) 329 8382 or 021 022 62513
enquiries@ataahuachristchurch.co.nz
www.ataahuachristchurch.co.nz

Double $120-$180 **Single** $75-$120
(Breakfast by arrangement)   Children by arrangement
Café opposite, great restaurants handy or bring picnic
Weddings by arrangement
Visa MC Diners accepted   Pets welcome
2 Queen 1 Double (3 bdrm)
Bathrooms: 3 Ensuite
Spa in Te Moemoea - others able to enjoy

Kia ora from your friendly hosts Julie, Mura and Tane our newfoundland dog. We're proud New Zealanders and our enjoyment of Maori culture is reflected in our unique waterfront home with a collection of Maori art. We are happy to sing you a waiata or two!. Walk in the wildlife reserve or alongside the lagoon next to Ataahua. Also a beautiful wedding and honeymoon venue -we specialise in pacific weddings.

Canterbury

Christchurch - Harewood *7.5 km N of Christchurch Centre*

St James B&B *Luxury B&B*
Margaret & David Frankish
125 Waimakariri Road, Harewood, Christchurch 8005

Tel (03) 359 6259 or 025 224 4982
027 432 0996
Fax (03) 359 6299
dj.frankish@xtra.co.nz
www.stjamesbnb.com

Double $120-$160 Single $75-$90 (Full breakfast)
Children $40
Visa MC accepted
1 King 1 Queen 1 Single (2 bdrm)
Bathrooms: 1 Ensuite 1 Private

Located five minutes from Christchurch Airport, ten minutes from city. Begin/ end your South Island trip in our warm, modern home with its tranquil garden setting, and the horses who share our three acre property. Our lovely guest rooms include private lounges, ensuite bathroom and private spa/bathroom upstairs. Rooms have tea/coffee facilities and TV. Internet access is available. We have 2 teenage children and a spaniel. Close by are golf courses, excellent restaurants, shopping, Wildlife Reserve, McLeans Island Recreation Area and Antarctic Centre.

Christchurch - Harewood *7.5 km N of Christchurch City Centre*

Evansleigh *B&B Homestay*
Faye Forsyth
344 Gardiners Road, Harewood, Christchurch

Tel (03) 359 8872
Fax (03) 359 6683
bookings@Evansleigh.com
www.Evansleigh.com

Double $120-$140 Single $90-$110
(Full breakfast)
Children negotiable
Visa MC accepted
Children and pets welcome
2 Queen 2 Single (3 bdrm)
Bathrooms: 1 Ensuite 1 Private 1 Guest share

Welcome to Evansleigh. My home is an award winning Colonial Villa set in large English gardens on a small farmlet. Situated just minutes from the airport, city centre, International Golf Resort, wildlife reserves, award-winning restaurants and shops. Private entrance, guest sitting room and spacious well appointed bedrooms and bathrooms. A full cooked breakfast is served in the dining room or alfresco on the veranda. I share my property with my dog, cat, and horses. Well travelled host, warm reception.

Christchurch - Yaldhurst *8 km W of Christchurch Central*

Gladsome Lodge *B&B Homestay*
Stuart & Sue Barr
314 Yaldhurst Road, Russley, Christchurch 8042

Tel (03) 342 7414 or 0800 222 617
Fax (03) 342 3414   sue@gladsomelodge.com
www.gladsomelodge.com

Double $100-$130 Single $95-$110
(Continental breakfast)   Children 0-5 free, 5-12 $20
Dinner $25 by arrangement
Cooked breakfast available
Visa MC Diners Amex accepted
3 Queen 1 Double 1 Twin 2 Single (5 bdrm)
Bathrooms: 2 Ensuite 3 Guest share One

Located close to airport with easy access to key attractions. Be assured of professional, attentive hosting in a friendly environment. Enjoy our tennis court, swimming pool or sauna. Guest internet access available. We are able to accommodate couples travelling together. Have knowledge of Maori history and culture. Our house is centrally heated. On bus route to city. On route to ski fields and West Coast Highway.Outside friendly dog. Hosts Sue and Stuart, New Zealanders who have travelled and have a wide variety of interests.

Christchurch - Yaldhurst *12 km W of Christchurch*
Miners Arms Alpaca Farmstay B+B *B&B Farmstay Separate Suite*

Lorna & Steve Tanner
441 Old West Coast Road, RD 6, Christchurch

Tel (03) 342 5827 or 021 050 4060
Fax (03) 342 5826 l
orna@minersarms.co.nz
www.minersarms.co.nz

Double $120-$140 Single $80-$90
(Full breakfast)
Children over 7 welcome
Visa MC accepted
1 Queen 1 Single (2 bdrm)
Bathrooms: 1 Private

Share our idyllic country lifestyle, close to the city, ten minutes from the airport. Our comfortable upstairs guest suite, for the exclusive enjoyment of you and your traveling companions, has a well-equipped lounge, two bedrooms, bathroom, balcony and views of our ten acres of orchards, woodland, gardens and paddocks. Explore them at leisure, meet and feed our alpacas, sheep, chickens and gentle Maremma sheepdogs. We are close to restaurants/wineries, golf, raceways, zoo, river walks, fishing and on the mountain ski-fields route.

Christchurch - Avonhead *10 km W of Christchurch Central*
Russley 302 *B&B Homestay Farmstay*

Helen & Ron Duckworth
302 Russley Road, Avonhead, Christchurch 8042

Tel (03) 358 6510 or 021 662 016
Fax (03) 358 6470
haduck@ducksonrussley.co.nz
www.ducksonrussley.co.nz

Double $120-$140 Single $80-$120 (Full breakfast)
Dinner (with local wines) by arrangement
Complimentary airport transfers
Visa MC accepted
1 King 1 Queen 1 Twin 1 Single (4 bdrm)
Bathrooms: 1 Ensuite 2 Private 1 Guest share

Located on the main north/south highway near Christchurch airport Russley 302, is well placed for guests arriving and departing the "garden city". Guest rooms are attractive and well equipped with in room tea/coffee facilities, refrigerators, televisions, electric blankets, clock/radios and hair dryers. Laundry facilities and email/fax are part of our service. Dinner is available by prior arrangement. Stay awhile, we are proud of our city which has much to offer and is an ideal base for excursions to Canterbury's hinterland.

Christchurch - Burnside *8 km NW of Christchurch*
Burnside Bed & Breakfast *B&B*

Elaine & Neil Roberts
31 O'Connor Place, Burnside, Christchurch 8005

Tel (03) 358 7671
Fax (03) 358 7761
elaine.neil.roberts@xtra.co.nz

Double $90-$110 Single $65-$70
(Continental breakfast)
Pet free home
Children welcome
1 Queen 1 Twin (2 bdrm)
Bathrooms: 1 Guest share

Welcome to our comfortable, modern home in quiet street, five minutes from the airport and 15 minutes to the city centre. Relax in the garden with tea or coffee and freshly baked muffins. Enjoy a generous continental breakfast with home-baking and preserves. Free broadband internet, laundry facilities and off-street parking available. Private bathroom facilities arranged with prior booking at $110. Our interests include sport, gardening, reading, travel and local history. We enjoy sharing our home with guests and look forward to meeting you.

Canterbury

Christchurch - Burnside *7 km W of Christchurch*

Stableford Airport B&B *B&B*

Margaret & Tony Spowart
2 Stableford Green, Burnside, Christchurch 8053

Tel (03) 358 3264 or 027 415 034
stableford@xtra.co.nz
www.stableford.co.nz

Double $140 **Single** $130
(Full breakfast)
Visa MC accepted
2 Queen 1 Twin (3 bdrm)
Bathrooms: 2 Ensuite 1 Private

Welcome to Stableford, the closest B&B to the Christchurch Airport, making it ideal for arriving or departing visitors. City bus-stop at door. We are situated adjacent to the prestigious Russley Golf Club. Let us know if you require a tee booking at the Russley Golf Course. Stableford is new, clean and comfortable with a separate guest lounge. Good restaurants nearby or dinner by arrangement. Our interests are travel, sport, music, & antiques.

Christchurch - Burnside *8 km NW of City Centre*

Blossom Tree Homestay *B&B Homestay*

Lorna Watson
29 O'Connor Place, Burnside, Christchurch 8005

Tel (03) 358 2635
Fax (03) 358 2665
blossomtree@xtra.co.nz

Double $100-$120 **Single** $60-$80
(Continental breakfast)
Children $20
1 Queen 2 Double (3 bdrm)
Bathrooms: 2 Private 1 Guest share

Located 5 minutes from Christchurch Airport, free transfer to and from airport, car hire depots very close, 15 minutes from City Centre. Good bus services closeby. Russley Golf Course and a variety of excellent restaurants and cafés nearby. Modern seven year old home, along with it's owners, Lorna & Lyndsay and lovely cat Emma, welcomes bed & breakfast guests. Enjoy lovely surroundings and a generous continental breakfast. Off-street parking and laundry facilities available. We look forward to welcoming you.

Christchurch - Ilam *7.5 km NW of Christchurch*

Anne & Tony Fogarty Homestay *Homestay*

Anne & Tony Fogarty
7 Westmont Street, Ilam, Christchurch 8041

Tel (03) 358 2762
Fax (03) 358 2767
tony.fogarty@xtra.co.nz

Double $95 **Single** $50
(Continental breakfast)
Dinner $30 by arrangement
Visa MC accepted
4 Single (2 bdrm)
Bathrooms: 1 Guest share 1 Family share

Our home is in the beautiful suburb of Ilam, only minutes from Canterbury University and Canterbury University College of Education. Close to Christchurch Airport (seven minutes by car) and the railway station (ten minutes). A bus stop to the central city, with its many attractions is 50 metres from our home. Willing to arrange transport from airport or train. Excellent local information. Guests are welcome to use our laundry. Complimentary tea and coffee at any time. Stay with us and get value for money.

Christchurch - Papanui *5 km E of Christchurch Airport*
Heatherston Boutiqe Bed and Breakfast *Luxury B&B*
Jan & Murray Binnie
46 Searells Road, Christchurch, 8005

Tel (03) 355 3239 or 027 418 8961
Fax (03) 355 3259
enquiries@heatherston.co.nz
www.heatherston.co.nz

Double $120-$150 Single $120 (Full breakfast)
Not suitable for children
2 King/Twin 1 Queen 1 Single (3 bdrm)
Bathrooms: 3 Ensuite

Comfortable, convenient and quiet. A superbly situated, purpose-built, modern house with every convenience, only ten minutes from the Airport, and ten minutes from Central Christchurch. Heatherston has a sunny guests' kitchenette/lounge, bedrooms with comfortable beds, refreshment facilities, and television. Ensuites have heated towel rails, hairdryers and toiletries. Heatherston is close to shops and restaurants, and is conveniently located for sight-seeing in the city, or travelling to wineries, walking tracks, golf courses, and skifields. Heatherston is the perfect tranquil retreat!

Christchurch - Fendalton *3 km NW of Christchurch City Centre*
Glenveagh B&B *B&B*
Alison & Ian Boyd
230C Clyde Road, Fendalton, Christchurch

Tel (03) 351 4407 or 0800 000 107
Fax (03) 351 4406   boyd45@xtra.co.nz
www.glenveagh.co.nz

Double $100-$190
(Continental breakfast)
Children by arrangement
Visa MC Eftpos accepted
1 King/Twin 1 King 1 Queen 2 Double
1 Twin 2 Single (3 bdrm)
Bathrooms: 1 Ensuite 1 Private

Ian & Alison welcome you to our beautiful home in a quiet area of Fendalton, Christchurch. Just off airport,city road. We have three guest rooms, upstairs and downstairs a lounge, courtyard. Tralee: King/twin/triple with ensuite and TV. Erigal: Twin with private bathroom and TV. Galway: Queen with private bathroom and TV. Restaurants within walking distance. Off-street parking. Courtesy car from airport, bus, train. Five minutes by car to central city, bus at gate. Continental breakfast. No smoking inside. Look forward to your company.

Christchurch - Fendalton *3 km NW of Cathedral Square*
Anselm House *B&B*
Jan & Leigh Webber
34 Kahu Road, Fendalton, Christchurch

Tel (03) 343 4260 or 0800 267 356
Fax (03) 343 4261
anselm@paradise.net.nz
www.anselmhouse.co.nz

Double $150-$190 Single $130-$150
(Full breakfast)   Dinner $65pp
Visa MC accepted
Pet free home   Not suitable for children
2 Queen (2 bdrm)
Bathrooms: 2 Ensuite

Kia ora! Anselm House is a landmark home beside the Avon River. Guests are welcome to relax in our peaceful, riverside garden, or cross over the brick bridge to view historic Riccarton House and walk through Deans Forest. We provide free airport and TranzAlpine transfer and safe, off-street parking. Four minute walk to Riccarton Road for restaurants, shops and banks. Walk across Hagley Park to the Botanical Gardens, the Museum, Arts Centre, Art Gallery and Cathedral Square. On city centre bus route. Friendly, family atmosphere.

Canterbury

Canterbury

Christchurch - Riccarton *6 km E of Christchurch Central*
Sunrise *B&B Homestay Guest House*
Ella & Kamal
9 Main South Road, Upper Riccarton, Christchurch

Tel (03) 981 3807 or 0800 526 924
027 480 8955   Fax (03) 981 3809
stay@sunrisebnb.co.nz
www.sunrisebnb.co.nz

Double $60-$75 **Single** $45-$55
(Continental breakfast)
Children negotiable
Visa MC accepted
1 Queen 1 Double 4 Twin 1 Single (5 bdrm)
Bathrooms: 2 Guest share

Sunrise BnB welcomes you to the Garden City. We are a caring, comfortable and affordable accommodation with 'room only' options. Walking distance to University, shopping areas, 24x7 super market and internet café. Sunrise has a homely atmosphere and offers warm sunny rooms, independent kitchen, lounge, laundry, parking. We have courtesy pick up from airport, rail, and bus (by arrangement) and offer excellent weekly and long term rates. Your hosts: Ella, Kamal and family including Gypsy, our affectionate German Shepherd. We look forward to see you soon.

Christchurch - Riccarton *6 km W of City centre*
Thistle Guest House *B&B Guest House*
John & Alison Goodfellow
21 Main South Road, Christchurch, 8042

Tel (03) 348 1499 or 0800 932 121
Fax (03) 348 1577
stay@thistleguesthouse.co.nz
www.thistleguesthouse.co.nz

Double $75-$90 **Single** $53-$68
(Continental breakfast)
Visa MC Amex Eftpos accepted   Children welcome
1 King 4 Queen 3 Twin 4 Single (10 bdrm)
Bathrooms: 1 Ensuite 3 Guest share

A small friendly guest house offering quality homestyle accommodation. Ten private bedrooms with fridge, tea/coffee facilities and wireless internet access for laptops. Fully equipped guest kitchen, lounge, off-street parking and attractive garden. Laundry facilities and guest telephone also available. Handy to Canterbury University and College of Education and two minutes walk to shops, restaurants and 24 hour supermarket. On good bus route to city (15 minutes) and ten minutes drive from airport. Courtesy pick-up by arrangement. Weekly rates and tariffs excluding breakfast also available.

Christchurch - Riccarton *4 km NW of Christchurch*
No10 Bed & Breakfast *B&B*
Betty & Keith Grice
10 Bradshaw Terrace, Riccarton, Christchurch, 8011

Tel (03) 302 0709 or 027 496 6902
Fax (03) 302 0707
betty@no10.co.nz
www.no10.co.nz

Double $120-$150 **Single** $100-$130
(Continental breakfast)
Pet free home
Not suitable for children
2 Queen (2 bdrm)
Bathrooms: 1 Private 1 Guest share

Eight minutes from the airport and five minutes from Christchurch central city you will find friendly helpful hospitality in a comfortable, attractive and warm bungalow on a quiet cul-de-sac in the hub of vibrant Riccarton. Walking distance to all of Riccarton's many facilities and attractions. Walking distance to central city via Hagley Park. We offer a non-smoking environment, TV, refrigerator, electric blankets, heater. No children or animals. Bookings are essential although a phone call two hours prior is all that is required. We will be pleased to see you.

Christchurch - Riccarton *1 km N of Christchurch Central*

Greatstay Boutique Accommodation
Luxury B&B Boutique Accommodation
Lesley & John Ruske
33 Kilmarnock Street, Christchurch, 8011

Tel (03) 343 1377
ruske.greatstay@xtra.co.nz
http://greatstay.co.nz

Double $230-$250 Single $150-$180 (Full breakfast)
Children $50 by arrangement
Visa MC accepted
Pet free home
1 King/Twin 2 Queen 2 Twin (3 bdrm)
Bathrooms: 3 Ensuite

A wonderful home to begin your holiday. We are 60+ and enjoy meeting guests. We enjoy classic cars and sport. Luxury spacious,clean, quiet ensuited accommodation. Indulge yourselves with a cooked/continental breakfast. Guest lounge for a quiet social happy hour before going out for dinner to a variety of restaurants. Our home is quiet and restful, an easy picturesque walk to all attractions through Hagley Park and Botanic Gardens. A car is not necessary while staying with us, as public transport at gate. "Come as a guest, leave as a friend."

Christchurch - Merivale *2 km N of Christchurch*

Leinster B&B *B&B Homestay*
Kay & Brian Smith
34B Leinster Road, Merivale, Christchurch

Tel (03) 355 6176 or 027 433 0771
Fax (03) 355 6176
brian.kay@xtra.co.nz

Double $150-$175 Single $120
(Special breakfast)
Children negotiable
Visa MC accepted
Children welcome
1 Queen 1 Double 1 Single (2 bdrm)
Bathrooms: 1 Ensuite 1 Private

A t Leinster Bed & Breakfast we pride ourselves on creating a relaxed friendly atmosphere in our modern sunny home. Only five minutes to city centre (art gallery, museum, botanical gardens, Cathedral Square, casino, town hall etc), ten minutes from the airport. For evening dining convenience there are excellent restaurants just a leisurely stroll away at Merivale Village. Laundry, email, fax and off-street parking facilities makes us your home away from home. Bedrooms have TV, electric blankets, heaters, tea/coffee. Well behaved puss and pooch in residence.

Christchurch - Merivale *3 km N of Christchurch*

Melrose *B&B*
Elaine & David Baxter
39 Holly Road, Merivale, Christchurch

Tel (03) 355 1929 or 027 647 5564
Fax (03) 355 1927
BaxterMelrose@xtra.co.nz
www.melrose-bb.co.nz

Double $120 Single $75 (Full breakfast)
Children $30
Visa MC accepted
Children welcome
3 Queen (3 bdrm)
Bathrooms: 1 Ensuite 1 Private 2 Guest share

A warm welcome awaits you at Melrose, a charming character home (1910) located in a small quiet street, just off Papanui Road only minutes away from the city and all the shops, restaurants and cafés of Merivale. Our house is spacious, we offer large rooms with tea & coffee making facilities and a private dining room/lounge. We have many interests and having travelled extensively, are keen to accommodate your needs. Our family comprises two daughters and a boxer, Milly. Off-street parking. Children are welcome.

Christchurch - Merivale *3 km N of Cathedral Square*

Summers House B&B *B&B Homestay Apartment with Kitchen*

Jackie & Kieran
274 Papanui Road, Merivale, Christchurch 8005

Tel (03) 355 1145 or (03) 355 2500
Fax (03) 355 2501
stay@summers.net.nz
www.summers.net.nz

Double $80-$160 Single $60-$100 (Full breakfast)
Children in family unit, max 2
Long term negotiable
Visa MC accepted
2 King/Twin 2 King 3 Queen 3 Single (8 bdrm)
Bathrooms: 1 Ensuite 3 Private 1 Guest share
1 Family share Claw foot with shower over

Summers B&B at Knowles Court, a Christchurch listed Heritage Home of grand and regal proportions set on nearly half an acre surrounded by a high brick wall and mature trees in prestigious Merivale. Handy to the city centre, transport and airport. Easy walking distance to quality restaurants and shopping. Variety of accommodation available including self catering apartments - from $80 double, $90 single including tax and breakfast. Affordable, spacious, gracious and tranquil - A home away from home."

Christchurch - Merivale *1.5 km N of Cathedral Square*

Chestnuts on Holly *Luxury B&B*

Sue & Andre de Villiers
27 Holly Road, Merivale, Christchurch

Tel (03) 355 7977 or 021 519 382
Fax (03) 355 7977
enquiries@chestnutsonholly.co.nz
www.chestnutsonholly.co.nz

Double $200-$250 Single $150-$200
(Full breakfast)
Visa MC Amex Eftpos accepted
Children welcome
2 Queen 1 Double (3 bdrm)
Bathrooms: 3 Ensuite

Chestnuts on Holly was built in circa 1901 from native kauri timber and has been restored to reflect the charm and elegance of a bygone era. The tastefully furnished ensuite bedrooms are cosy in winter and lovely and cool during summer. Guests have their own private lounge and dining room where they can relax. Special gourmet breakfasts are served in the dining room or in summer, on the verandah. Cathedral Square is an easy stroll away with buses and restaurants within a few minutes walk.

Christchurch - Richmond *2 km E of CBD*

Avon Grove Villa Bed & Breakfast *B&B*

Janice & Ian Cundall
273 River Road, Christchurch, 8013

Tel (03) 381 7099 or 027 442 3076
enquiries@avongrovevilla.co.nz
www.avongrovevilla.co.nz

Double $140-$160
(Full breakfast)
Visa MC accepted
Children welcome
2 Queen (2 bdrm)
Bathrooms: 2 Ensuite

Situated beside the Avon River this 1900's Avon Grove Villa welcomes you to Christchurch City. There are several restaurants and shops within a ten minute walk. Two large, comfortably appointed, double guest rooms, each with the original fireplace and large bay windows, are available. Each room has an ensuite, TV, and tea and coffee facilities. A full cooked breakfast is served daily. Avon Grove Villa is owned by Janice and Ian Cundall. They have two adult children.

Christchurch - Avondale *8 km NE of Christchurch Central*

Hulverstone Lodge *B&B*
Diane & Ian Ross
18 Hulverstone Drive, Avondale, Christchurch

Tel (03) 388 6505 or 0800 388 650 (NZ only)
Fax (03) 388 6205
hulverstone@caverock.net.nz
www.hulverstonelodge.co.nz

Double $110-$140 Single $80-$110
Visa MC accepted
Pet free home
Not suitable for children
3 King/Twin 1 Queen 1 Single (4 bdrm)
Bathrooms: 2 Ensuite 1 Private 1 Guest share 1 Family share

Gracing the bank of the Avon River in a quiet suburb, yet only ten minutes from the city centre, stands picturesque Hulverstone Lodge. From our charming guest rooms watch the sun rise over the river, catch glimpses of the Southern Alps or enjoy views of the Port Hills. Delightful riverside walks pass the door. A pleasant stroll along the riverbank leads to New Brighton with its restaurants, sandy Pacific Ocean beach and pier. Numerous golf courses and the QEII Leisure Complex are close at hand.

Located just off Christchurch's Ring Road system, Hulverstone Lodge offers easy access to all major tourist attractions, while frequent buses provide convenient transport to the city. An ideal base for holidays year-round, Hulverstone Lodge is only a couple of hours from quaint Akaroa, Hanmer Springs' thermal pools, Kaikoura's Whalewatch, and several ski fields.

You are guaranteed warm hospitality and quality accommodation at Hulverstone Lodge. All our rooms are decorated with fresh flowers from our garden. A delicious breakfast, either cooked or continental, is included in the tariff. We also offer: - complimentary pick up; - king, queen or twin beds;- français parlé, Deutsch gesprochen.

Come and experience the ambience of Hulverstone Lodge.

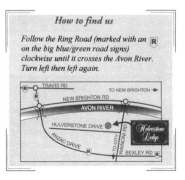

How to find us

Follow the Ring Road (marked with an R *on the big blue/green road signs) clockwise until it crosses the Avon River. Turn left then left again.*

Christchurch - Southshore *4 km S of New Brighton*
On The Shore Boutique Bed and Breakfast *Luxury B&B*

Peter Knight & Tamara Young
126B Rocking Horse Road, Southshore,
Christchurch, 8062

Tel Landline (03) 388 5505 or 021 202 2211
enquiries@ontheshore.co.nz   www.ontheshore.co.nz

Double up to $199 Single up to $175
(Special breakfast) Children under two free
Extension room extra cost
Dinner Vegetarian or BBQ by arrangement
Visa MC Diners Amex accepted
1 Queen 1 Double 2 Single (2 bdrm)
Bathrooms: 1 Ensuite

Experience Christchurch's most spectacularly located B&B. Relax in this absolute waterfront romantic retreat. Million dollar views, unspoilt beaches, spectacular sunsets await the discerning traveler. Sail our catamaran, kayak, surf, swim, walks, wind/kitesurf, golf or indulge in the waterfront spa. Birdwatchers paradise. Private entrance, TV, fridge, hairdryer, tea/coffee, Breakfast hamper, balcony with beautiful views of the estuary, port hills, over city to Southern Alps. Close to restaurants bars, 12 minutes city centre, bus at gate. Pickups by arrangement Kiwi, Brit, two children, dog, cat, 100 fish greet you!

Christchurch City *0.8 km N of Christchurch Cathedral Square*
Home Lea B&B *B&B Homestay*

Pauline & Gerald Oliver
195 Bealey Avenue, Christchurch

Tel (03) 379 9977 or 0800 355 321
Fax (03) 379 4099
homelea@xtra.co.nz
www.homelea.co.nz

Double $145-$190 Single $95-$135 (Special breakfast)
Children negotiable
Dinner by arrangement
Extra adult $35
Visa MC Amex accepted
1 King 2 Queen 4 Single (4 bdrm)
Bathrooms: 2 Ensuite 2 Private

Home Lea offers the traveller a comfortable and enjoyable stay. Built in the early 1900s, Home Lea has the charm and character of a large New Zealand home of that era: rimu panelling, leadlight windows, and a large lounge with a log fire. Off-street parking. Wireless/broadband internet available for guests. Special diets catered for. Pauline and Gerald are happy to share their knowledge of local attractions and their special interests are travel, sailing and music.

Christchurch City *1.2 km N of Christchurch Central*
Eliza's Manor on Bealey *B&B*

Ann Zwimpfer & Harold Williams
82 Bealey Avenue, City Central, Christchurch

Tel (03) 366 8584 or 0800 366 859
Fax (03) 366 4946
info@elizas.co.nz
www.elizas.co.nz

Double $185-$295 Single $165-$275
(Special breakfast)
Visa MC Diners Amex Eftpos accepted
Pet free home
Not suitable for children
4 King 4 Queen 1 Single (8 bdrm)
Bathrooms: 8 Ensuite with large tiled walk in showers

Eliza's is a beautifully restored Victorian mansion, built in 1861. The original architecture includes a magnificent staircase in the foyer, lead light windows and wood panelling. The tariff includes a full continental and cooked breakfast. It is a short drive from the airport and a 15 minute level walk to the Arts centre, botanical gardens, art gallery, museum, city centre, golf course and restaurants. Free parking and internet access is available to guests. We are a day trip to Hanmer Springs, Akaroa, and Kaikoura.

Christchurch City *.5 km NW of Christchurch CBD*

Windsor B&B Hotel *B&B Hotel*
Carol Healey & Don Evans
52 Armagh Street, Christchurch 1

Tel (03) 366 1503 or 0800 366 1503
Fax (03) 366 9796
reservations@windsorhotel.co.nz
www.windsorhotel.co.nz

Double $128 Single $89 (Full breakfast)
Triple $162 Quad/Family $180
Visa MC Diners Amex Eftpos accepted
12 Double 18 Twin 10 Single (40 bdrm)
Bathrooms: 24 Guest share

L ooking for Bed & Breakfast in Christchurch, then try The
Windsor. Built at the turn of the century this inner city
residence is located on the Tourist Tram Route and is within
5-10 minutes walk of the city centre, restaurants, convention
centre, casino, galleries, museum and botanical gardens. Guests
are greeted on arrival by our pet dachshund, Miss Winnie
and shown around our charming colonial style home. Often
described as traditional, this family operated bed & breakfast
hotel prides itself on the standard of accommodation that it
offers. The warm and comfortable bedrooms are all decorated
with a small posy of flowers and a watercolour by local artist
Denise McCulloch.

The shared bathroom facilities have been conveniently
appointed with bathrobes provided, giving warmth and comfort
in the bed & breakfast tradition. Such things as "hotties" and
"brollies" add charm to the style of accommodation offered, as
does our 1928 Studebaker sedan.

Our generous morning breakfast (included in the tariff) offers
fruit juice, fresh fruits, yogurt and cereals followed by bacon
and eggs, sausages, tomatoes, toast and marmalade, and is served in the dining room each morning
between 6.30 and 9.00. The 24 hour complimentary tea & coffee making facilities allow guests to use
them at their own convenience. "Supper" (tea, coffee and biscuits) is served each evening in the lounge
at 9.00. As part of our service the hotel offers "Free" broadband internet / wireless access, coin operated
laundry, luggage lift, off-street parking for the motorist and bicycle and baggage storage.

QUOTE THIS BOOK FOR 10% DISCOUNT

Christchurch City *1 km N of Christchurch Central*
The Devon B&B *B&B*

Sandra & Benjamin Humphrey
69 Armagh Street, Christchurch

Tel (03) 366 0398   Fax (03) 366 0392
stay@thedevon.co.nz
www.thedevon.co.nz

Double $128-$180 Single $89-$145 (Full breakfast)
Children under 15 $30
Extra adults $40
Visa MC Diners Amex Eftpos accepted
6 Queen 3 Twin 2 Single (11 bdrm)
Bathrooms: 6 Ensuite 1 Private 4 Guest share

The Devon is a personal guest house located in the heart of beautiful Christchurch City, which offers elegance and comfort in the style of an olde worlde English manor. Just five minutes walk to Christchurch Cathedral, Town Hall, and Convention Centre, casino, museum, art gallery, hospital and botanical gardens in Hagley Park. TV lounge, tea & coffee making facilities. Off-street parking. Free broadband internet/wireless access and luggage storage.

Christchurch City *0.5 km N of Cathedral Square*
Martina Bed & Breakfast *B&B*

Sunny Morley
302 Gloucester Street, Central City, Christchurch

Tel (03) 377 7150 F
ax (03) 377 7476
martinabedandbreakfast@ihug.co.nz

Double $120-$140 Single $100-$120
(Continental breakfast)
1 Queen (1 bdrm)
Bathrooms: 1 Ensuite ensuite

Martina is a charming, Victorian house with a peaceful garden, four blocks from Cathedral Square. A short walk takes you to all the city has to offer - restaurants, shopping, museum, arts centre, art galleries, botanical gardens, movies and theatre. Your downstairs room has a queen bed, bay window, TV, video, telephone and ensuite bathroom.We have off-street parking and a bus stop at the gate. Host and teenage children are well travelled, lived overseas and speak Spanish.

Christchurch City *1 km E of Centre*
The Chester *B&B*

Jennifer & Jan van den Berg
Suite 3, 173 Chester Street East, Christchurch City

Tel (03) 366 5777 or 021 365 495
Fax (03) 365 6314
thechester@clear.net.nz
www.thechester.com

Double $110-$135 Single $95-$110
(Continental breakfast)
Visa MC accepted
Pet free home
Not suitable for children
1 King/Twin 1 Single (2 bdrm)
Bathrooms: 2 Ensuite

The Chester B&B Apt 3,situated in the historic Old Wards Brewery Building, dates back to the 1850s. Now converted into elegant apartments, this unique suite offers all modern comforts and amenities in close walking distance of the city centre, restaurants, banks, town hall, arts centre, casino & convention centre. Perfect for holiday or business. Your hosts Jan & Jennifer van den Berg will ensure your stay is comfortable and memorable. Car Rentals,Theatre & concert bookings can be arranged on request.

Christchurch City *1.5 km SW of Information Centre*
Pomeroy's B&B *B&B Hotel*
Phil & Vikki
282 Kilmore Street, PO Box 7681, Christchurch

Tel (03) 374 3532 or 021 374 282
021 555 689 Fax (03) 337 8196
phil.hanrahan@xtra.co.nz
www.pomeroyspub.co.nz

Double $80-$200 Single $120-$130 (Full breakfast)
Dinner can be purchased at pub next door
Visa MC Diners Amex Eftpos accepted
Children and pets welcome
3 Queen (3 bdrm)
Bathrooms: 2 Ensuite in B&B 1 Guest share

An exquisite B&B attached to the historic Pomeroy's Olde Brewery Inn and just four blocks from the centre of town. Phil, Vikki and son Kingsley are your hosts. Our cooked breakfast consists of gourmet sausages, dry smoked bacon, field mushrooms, NZ tomatoes, home made hashbrowns and eggs cooked to your liking. The continental breakfast consists of organic toasted museli, weetbix, fresh fruit, bread for toast with homemade jams and a variety of other local treats. When available we chose to use only organic foods.

Christchurch City *0.5 km N of Christchurch Central*
Riverview Lodge *B&B Luxury Bed and Breakfast*
Andrea & Mark van Dooren
361 Cambridge Terrace, Christchurch

Tel (03) 365 2860   Fax (03) 365 2845
riverview.lodge@xtra.co.nz
www.riverview.net.nz

Double $170-$210 Single $100-$150
(Special breakfast)
Visa MC accepted
Children welcome
1 King/Twin 2 Queen 1 Single (4 bdrm)
Bathrooms: 3 Ensuite 1 Private

If you like quality accommodation in a relaxed and quiet atmosphere, just a few minutes srtoll along the picturesque Avon River to the city centre: this is the place to stay. Riverview Lodge is a restored Edwardian residence that reflects the grace and style of the period with some fine kauri carvings. Guest rooms are elegant combining modern facilities with colonial furnishings. Breakfast is a house specialty offering a varied choice of continental and cooked fare served in The Turret Dining Room. Beautifully restored Edwardian villa in wonderful quiet location. Just a ten minute river walk to Cathedral Square.

Christchurch City *0.5 km SW of Information Centre*
Slingerland Green Stay *B&B Apartment with Kitchen*
Catherine Slingerland
25 Cambridge Terrace, Christchurch, 8013

Tel (03) 379 7632
caseo@xtra.co.nz
http://sites.yellow.co.nz/site/slingerland

Double $120 Single $100
(Special vegeterian breakfast)
Children $20
Extra person $20
Visa MC Eftpos accepted
Children and pets welcome
1 Queen 2 Double 2 Single (3 bdrm)
Bathrooms: 1 Ensuite 1 Private 1 Family share

Relax in front of the picture window in the sunny and spacious lounge, watch the ducks swimming in the Avon River and people embarking on a punt ride through the Botanic Gardens. Many other attractions are within a short walk: The Canterbury Museum, The Arts Centre, the Tramway & Cathedral Square. Start your day with a healthy breakfast of fresh fruit & juices, bread, eggs and vegetarian sausages. We have off-street parking, a swimming pool & welcome children of all ages and well-behaved pets.

Christchurch - West Melton *12 km W of Christchurch*

Castle View Vineyard Retreat *Luxury Separate Suite Vineyard Retreat*

Michele Columbus & Leiv Bjerga
84 Johnson Road, West Melton,
RD 5, Christchurch, 7675

Tel (03) 3651 952 or 027 680 1005
Fax (03) 3477 337   michelec@slingshot.co.nz
www.castleview.co.nz

Double $195-$245 (Continental breakfast provisions)
Children $15pp over 4 occupants
Dinner by arrangement
Extra Adult $20pp over 4 occupants
Visa MC Diners Amex accepted   Pet free home
1 King 2 Double (1 bdrm)
Bathrooms: 1 Ensuite

Brand new (810sq ft) luxury vineyard retreat, close to Christchurch city and skifields. Gas fire, separate room for wet gear and changing plus washing facilities. Large luxury ensuite with double shower and spa bath. LCD TVs x2 and home theatre system. Outlook to secure heated swimming pool. Very quiet. View to the Southern Alps. Alpacas in the paddock. Porsche rental cars available to complete your memorable stay.

Christchurch - Templeton *3 km S of Hornby*

Cedarview Farm Homestay B&B *B&B Homestay Farmstay*

Carol & Terrance White
33 Barters Road, Templeton RD 5, Christchurch

Tel (03) 349 7491 or 027 433 5335
Fax (03) 349 7755
cedarviewfarm@xtra.co.nz
www.cedarviewhomestay.com

Double $125-$170 Single $100-$120 (Full breakfast)
Children POA
Visa MC accepted
Pet free home Children welcome
1 King 1 Queen 2 Single (3 bdrm)
Bathrooms: 1 Ensuite 1 Private

Cedarview Farm Homestay B&B is ideally situated for visitors to Christchurch. Our modern smoke free home is close to the Airport, main highways, local shopping center, bars & restaurants. We are an easy 15-20 minute drive into the central city. All our rooms are bright well appointed and have lovely views out over our small farm where we keep cattle, sheep, hens, a farm cat called Alfie and Labrador called Ruby. We enjoy a lifestyle that is quiet and relaxed. Enquiries are welcome. We look forward to meeting you soon.

Christchurch - Sydenham *2 km NW of Christchurch City Square*

The Designer Cottage *B&B Homestay Cottage with Kitchen*

Chet Wah
53 Hastings Street West, Sydenham, Christchurch City

Tel 0800 161 619 or (03) 377 8088
021 210 5282
Fax (03) 377 8099
stay@designercottage.co.nz
www.designercottage.co.nz

Double $80-$150 Single $45-$60
(Continental breakfast)
Whole house $100-$250 for six people
Visa MC accepted
Pet free home
4 Queen 1 Double 1 Twin 1 Single (7 bdrm)
Bathrooms: 1 Ensuite 1 Private 5 Guest share

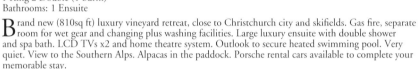

The Designer cottage B&B Homestay is a charming place to stay. Just off Colombo Street situated in peaceful surroundings, and within 20 minutes walk to the city centre or one minute walk to amenities. There is off-street parking and free pick up from city centre on arrival (by arrangement only). Once settled in you will be welcomed with a 'mean' cup of coffee or tea by the friendly host.

Christchurch - St Martins *3 km S of Christchurch City Centre*

Kleynbos B&B *B&B Separate Suite Apartment with Kitchen*

Gerda De Kleyne & Hans van den Bos
59 Ngaio Street, Christchurch

Tel (03) 332 2896
KLEYNBOS@xtra.co.nz
www.kleynbos.co.nz

Double $80-$100 Single $60-$75
(Continental breakfast)
Children welcome, cot available
Apartment $ 100-$130
Visa MC accepted
2 Queen 2 Double 2 Single (4 bdrm)
Bathrooms: 2 Ensuite 1 Private 1 Guest share

Quality accommodation with a personal touch, since 1991. 3 km to city centre, in an easy to find, friendly, tree-lined street. Your large ensuite rooms are $100 with microwave, fridge and jug. A computer is available to keep in contact with friends and family. A self-catering option is available in the apartment, sleeps five for $100-$130. The children are 18 and 15 years old. Directions; SH74 Barbadoes Street, Waltham Road, Wilsons Road, right into Gamblins Road, first left is Ngaio Street.

Christchurch - Westmorland *7 km SW of Christchurch*

Slippers *Luxury B&B*

Georgie & Ron McKie
66 Penruddock Rise, Westmorland 8002, Christchurch

Tel (03) 339 6170 or 021 022 97650
Fax (03) 339 6170
mckiepic@paradise.net.nz
www.slippersbnb.co.nz

Double $190 Single $120 (Full breakfast)
Dinner $50pp including fine wine
Visa MC accepted
Not suitable for children
1 King/Twin 1 Single (2 bdrm)
Bathrooms: 1 Private

Pure wool slippers await you when you arrive at Slippers. Enjoy stunning views of the Alps, Canterbury Plains and the city. Your suite of rooms includes two bedrooms, lounge, private bathroom, private entrances and secluded balcony area. Special diets catered for. Home baking, fruit bowl, tea and plunger coffee always available. Off street parking. City bus at gate. Photographers, use our darkroom and digital facilities. Allow us and our two cats to help you to get the most from your Christchurch stay. Check our website.

Christchurch - Westmorland *7 km SW of Cathedral Square*

Sportmans Lodge *B&B*
Phil & Pauline Wilson
6 Ennerdale Row, Westmortland, Christchurch 8025

Tel (03) 339 8633
Fax (03) 339 8632
sportsmanlodge@xtra.co.nz

Visa MC accepted
3 King/Twin (3 bdrm)

The Sportsman's Lodge was purpose built in 1997, for the outdoor sportsmen and women in mind, and is a private large modern home in a very quiet, well established area with off-street parking. The lodge offers three private super-king-twin guestrooms upstairs. The guest lounge provides panoramic views of the Southern Alps and Canterbury plains, while the living and dining rooms feature great city views at night. Town is only ten minutes away, five minutes to mall, ten minutes to train and 20 minutes to airport.

Christchurch - Cashmere *6 km S of City Centre*

B&B - 51A *B&B Private suite, own bathroom and separate entrance*

Malcolm & Judie Douglass
Edgehill, 51A Bowenvale Avenue,
Cashmere, Christchurch

Tel (03) 332 5504
Fax (03) 332 5506
douglass.edgehill@clear.net.nz
www.bnb.co.nz/douglass.edgehill.html

Double $140 (Continental breakfast provisions)
Single $120 plus $20pp
2 Double (2 bdrm)
Bathrooms: 1 Private

Edgehill a comfortable home in a quiet leafy location in south Christchurch, only ten minutes drive from city centre and 25 minutes to the airport. Private suite with bathroom, double bedroom, sitting room with pull out double bed. Relax in this secluded section with courtyard, sunny verandah, terraced gardens and trees. Parks, cafés, restaurants, river, hillside walks are all close by. Share your experiences with Malcolm (civil engineer and town planner) and Judie (professional actress).

Christchurch - Huntsbury *4 km S of Christchurch Central*

Andaview B&B *Luxury B&B*

Anne & Keith Clark
18 Woodlau Rise, Huntsbury, Christchurch 8022

Tel (03) 332 5522
Fax (03) 332 5592
andaview@xtra.co.nz
www.andaview.co.nz

Double $170-$230 Single $150-$175
(Full breakfast)
Visa MC Eftpos accepted
Pet free home
Not suitable for children
1 King/Twin 1 King (2 bdrm)
Bathrooms: 1 Ensuite 1 Private Double spabath

Experience genuine Kiwi hospitality only ten minutes from the city centre. Suites are designed with executives and the discerning traveller in mind. Our guest rooms have spectacular views and amenities to satisfy your every need. Relax in our guest lounge with a New Zealand wine and watch the sun set behind the mountains. We offer free Hi-speed internet access and complimentary airport/rail pick up or drop off.

Christchurch - Murray Aynsley *4 km SW of City Centre*

Pool House *B&B Separate Suite*

Jill & Richard Entwistle
57 Aynsley Terrace, Murray Aynsley,
Christchurch, 8022

Tel (03) 337 0380 or 021 131 6441
entwistle@slingshot.co.nz

Double $125 Single $90
(Continental breakfast)
Children welcome by arrangement
1 King/Twin (1 bdrm)
Bathrooms: 1 Ensuite

The Pool House offers quiet and comfortable, private self-contained accommodation with separate living and sleeping areas, bathroom ensuite. Ample self-serve continental breakfast provided. Children by arrangement, on a sofa-bed. Outdoor swimming pool. Hansen Park and the Heathcote River offering gentle riverside walks and a children's playground. Central Christchurch and the Port of Lyttelton are 10 minutes by bus or by car. Local sandy beaches are 10-15 minutes by car.

Christchurch - Redcliffs *110 km E of Cathedral Square*

Pegasus Bay View *B&B Separate Suite*
Denise & Bernie Lock
121A Moncks Spur Road, Redcliffs, Christchurch

Tel (03) 384 2923 or 021 254 2888
pegasusbay@slingshot.co.nz
www.pegasusbayview.co.nz

Double $120-$140 Single $115
(Continental breakfast)
Visa MC accepted
1 Queen 1 Double (2 bdrm)
Bathrooms: 1 Private

Enjoy spectacular views over the South Pacific and across the city to the Southern Alps from our modern home. Your private guest suite has its own entrance and is tastefully furnished, with spacious bedroom, TV lounge (which can converted to a second double bedroom for additional family/friends) and private bathroom. Relax over a delicious breakfast, served outside on warm days, while enjoying the stunning panorama. Close to beach and restaurants and just 15 minutes drive from Christchurch City centre. We offer wireless broadband access.

Christchurch - Mt Pleasant *9 km E of Cathedral Square*

A Nest on Mount Pleasant *B&B Apartment with Kitchen*
Kathryn & Kai Tovgaard
24 Toledo Place, Mount Pleasant, Christchurch 8081

Tel (03) 3849 485 or 027 203 0637
Fax (03) 3848 385
thenestonMP@xtra.co.nz
www.anestbnb.co.nz

Double $95-$120 Single $85-$110 (Full breakfast)
Children discounted   Dinner by arrangement
Visa MC Diners Amex accepted
Pet free home   Children welcome
2 Queen 2 Twin (3 bdrm)
Bathrooms: 1 Ensuite 1 Private

Unique fully self-contained home , yet with all the service and warm hospitality of a homestay. This is the promise of The Nest.The Nest is situated in one of Christchurch's most loved hill suburbs with views of our estuary, sea and mountains beyond. Tranquil and secure, with garage parking, TV, DVD, stereo, & BBQ. Very close to Christchurch's best beaches with excellent cafés and restaurants, Ferrymead Historic Park, Lyttelton Harbour, Tamaki Heritage Village and hillside walks with breathtaking views to the Southern Alps.

**If you need any information ask your hosts,
they are your own personal travel agent and guide.**

Canterbury

Christchurch - Mt Pleasant *8 km E of Christchurch*

Mt Pleasant Bed & Breakfast *B&B Separate Suite with full-size private kitchen*

Nicola & Paul Kristiansen
14 Hobday Lane, Mt Pleasant,
Christchurch

Tel (03) 384 9220
Fax (03) 384 9235
Kristiansen@xtra.co.nz
http://mtpleasantbandb.co.nz

Double $110 **Single** $90
(Continental breakfast)
Children $20 Big size lounge
Visa MC accepted
Pet free home
Children welcome
1 Queen (1 bdrm)
Bathrooms: 1 Ensuite
Private sauna holds six

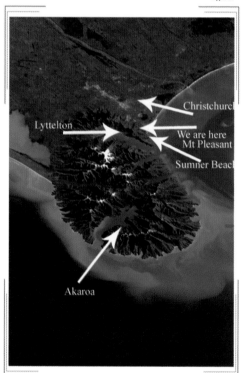

This unique home offers a friendly and relaxed stay in your private suite. Enjoy your spacious and comfortable queen bedroom, ensuite bathroom with vintage cast-iron bath (such bliss our guests tell us!)

Sitting room with private entrance leading to deck and sauna. Own kitchen facilities. Explore the huge rambling garden facinating with waterwheel, plentiful trees and abundant bird life.

Conveniently situated 15 minutes from city, ten minutes to popular Sumner Beach, five minutes to windsurfing, gondola, walking and bike tracks. You'll love it!

Christchurch - Sumner *12 km E of Cathedral Square*

Villa Alexandra *B&B Homestay Apartment with Kitchen*
Self Contained Beach Front Apartment.

Wendy & Bob Perry
1 Kinsey Terrace, Christchurch 8081

Tel (03) 326 6291 Fax (03) 326 6096
villa_alexandra@xtra.co.nz
www.villaalexandra.co.nz

Double $120 Single $90 (Full breakfast)
Children under 12 $15
Apartment $150 per night
Children and pets welcome
1 Queen 1 Double 1 Twin 1 Single (3 bdrm)
Bathrooms: 2 Ensuite 1 Private

Enjoy the warmest hospitality in our spacious turn of the century villa overlooking Sumner Bay. Our home retains the graciousness of a bygone era while offering all modern comforts. In winter enjoy open fires, cosy farmhouse kitchen and on sunny days the verandah and turret. Spectacular sea views from Sumner to the Kaikouras. We enjoy food, wine, music, gardening, tramping, travel. Five minutes walk to beach; off-street parking; laundry. Also self-contained beach front apartment, two double bedrooms, $150 per night, minimum three nights.

Christchurch - Sumner Beach *12 km E of Cathedral Square*

Cave Rock Bed & Breakfast *B&B*

Gayle & Norm Eade
16 Esplanade, Sumner, Christchurch

Tel (03) 326 6844 or 027 436 0212
Fax (03) 326 5600 eade@chch.planet.org.nz
www.caverockguesthouse.co.nz

Double $130-$140 Single $105-$115
(Continental breakfast provisions)
Children $20 Corporate Rates available
Visa MC Eftpos accepted Children welcome
4 Queen (4 bdrm)
Bathrooms: 4 Ensuite, 1 with spa bath

The Cave Rock B&B - Sumner's Beachfront accommodation opposite Sumner's Cave Rock. Hosts Gayle & Norm Eade enjoy meeting people from overseas and within NZ. Large spacious double rooms with sea views, TV, heating and ensuite bathrooms, can sleep up to four. Kitchen facilities adjacent. Sumner - the ideal holiday location, 15 minutes from Christchurch City, excellent bus service - café/bars, shops, cinema, within walking distance. Hill and cliff walks close by, safe sandy beach across the road. We have a friendly dalmatian dog.

Christchurch - Sumner *13 km E of Christchurch Cathedral Square*

Abbott House Sumner Bed & Breakfast
Self-contained suite with kitchen, & self-contained studio

Janet & Chris Abbott
104 Nayland Street, Sumner, Christchurch

Tel (03) 326 6111 or 0800 020 654
021 654 344 or (03) 326 7034
Fax (03) 326 7034
info@abbotthouse.co.nz
www.abbotthouse.co.nz

Double $120-$140 Single $100-$120 (Breakfast provisions first night)
Children $10 Weekly discounts
Visa MC accepted
3 King/Twin (3 bdrm)
Bathrooms: 1 Ensuite 1 Private

Your hosts, Chris and Janet Abbott welcome you to our historic restored 1870s villa in Christchurch's unique seaside village. Our home is one block from the beach, and an easy ten minute walk along the beach to Sumner's many cafés, restaurants, boutique shops and cinema. Both suite and studio have king-sized beds, own kitchen areas, TV, DVD and internet access. Off-street parking. Laundry facilities. Home-baked bread.

Canterbury

Canterbury

Christchurch - Sumner *15 km E of Cathedral Square*

Scarborough-Heights *Luxury B&B*

Barbara & Brian Hanlon
21 Godley Drive, Scarborough, Christchurch 8081

Tel (03) 326 7060 or 027 229 7312
Fax (03) 326 7061
stay@scarborough-heights.co.nz
www.scarborough-heights.co.nz

Double $180 Single $120 (Full breakfast)
Children 5-12 $50
Dinner $50 by arrangement
Visa MC accepted
1 King 1 Queen 3 Single (2 bdrm)
Bathrooms: 1 Ensuite 1 Private with bath and shower.

Scarborough-Heights is a striking, modern architecturally designed home set in an award winning garden, high on Scarborough Hill and offering luxurious bed & breakfast accommodation. All rooms offer spectacular views of the Southern Alps, Christchurch City and South Pacific Ocean. We provide friendly hospitality in peaceful, quiet surroundings yet are only 20 minutes from the city centre and five minutes from the trendy and popular seaside village of Sumner with its many cafés, speciality shops and cinema. We share our home with two cats.

Christchurch - Sumner *13 km E of Cathedral Square*

Tiromoana *B&B Guests' kitchen facilities*

Helen Mackay & Brian Lamb
89 Richmond Hill Road, Sumner, Christchurch

Tel (03) 326 6209 or 021 070 3777
Fax (03) 326 6208
relax@tiromoana.co.nz
www.tiromoana.co.nz

Double $130-$150 Single $95-$135 (Full breakfast)
Children $25
Visa MC accepted
1 King/Twin 1 Queen 1 Double (3 bdrm)
Bathrooms: 1 Ensuite 1 Private
Plus bath outside under the stars!

Sumner, only 15 minutes from the city, within easy walking of village cafés, movie theatres, specialty shops and the beach. Tiromoana was built in 1904 in a spectacular position overlooking the beach. A perfect spot to relax, wander the garden, have a bath outside under the stars and sleep to the sound of the sea. The atmosphere is friendly, relaxed and informal, providing guests' lounge and kitchen facilities, with a fresh and generous breakfast provided. Laundry facilities are available. We look forward to welcoming you.

Lincoln *20 km S of Christcurch*

Hazelview *Apartment with Kitchen*

Diane & Rick Fraser
1153/2 Springs Road, Lincoln, 7647

Tel (03)3253362
enquiry@hazelview.co.nz
www.hazelview.co.nz

Double $130 Single $110
(Continental breakfast provisions)
Children can use existing king-size bed in lounge
Full breakfast by arrangement
Visa MC accepted
1 King 1 Double (1 bdrm)
Bathrooms: 1 Ensuite

In a totally private rural setting Hazelview nut orchard is only a short drive from the city and airport. The upstairs apartment has one luxury bedroom with finest linen, ensuite bathroom (spa bath and separate shower), spacious lounge, TV & VCR, guest library, kitchen facilities and extra bed. Restaurants, wineries, golf, Lincoln Village and University are all nearby. Coffees, teas and nibbles included. Be assured of a warm welcome and memorable stay. Two cats and two young adults at home.

Tai Tapu *20 km SE of Christchurch*
Fantail Lodge on Greenpark *Country B&B*
Pamela & Doug Hueston
164 River Road, Tai Tapu-Lincoln,
Christchurch RD 2, 7672

Tel (03) 325 7572 or 027 433 7706
027 425 7007
Fax (03) 325 7572
riversidegpk@xtra.co.nz

Double $100-$130 Single $90
(Continental breakfast)
Visa MC accepted
1 King 1 Double (2 bdrm)
Bathrooms: 1 Ensuite 2 Family share

Located on River Road meandering along the Halswell River. Artist Pamela and Photographer Doug share the comfort of their elegant and spacious home, with guests separate lounge (with piano) for privacy. Ensuite, TV, electric blankets. Set in extensive landscaped grounds, in tranquil country surroundings, views of the Alps, sunsets, nestled in our ten acre farmlet, farming cattle and sheep. Native birds: Fantails and Pukekos often frequent our garden. Pick-up from Airport, (25 km.) buses or train by arrangement. Local award winning winery, restaurants within 12 km.

Lyttelton *9 km E of Christchurch*
Shonagh O'Hagan's Guest House *B&B*
Shonagh O'Hagan
Dalcroy House, 16 Godley Quay, Lyttelton

Tel (03) 328 8577 or 027 434 6351
shonagh.ohagan@xtra.co.nz
www.lytteltonharbour.co.nz

Double $125 Single $100 (Full breakfast)
Children $30 per child in same room as parents
Dinner $40 by arrangement
Visa MC accepted
Children welcome
1 King/Twin 2 Queen 1 Double (4 bdrm)
Bathrooms: 1 Guest share 2 Family share

Dalcory House built 1859, has been a boarding school, private residence, rental property, and hostel for naval ratings in WW2. Shonagh your hostess is a cook, nurse, educator, health manager and mother. Have a comfortable night's sleep in pleasant surroundings with a clear view of Lyttelton Port and Harbour, five minutes walk from the centre of Lyttelton and 15 minutes drive to the centre of Christchurch. Shonagh and her son will ensure your stay is comfortable and memorable.

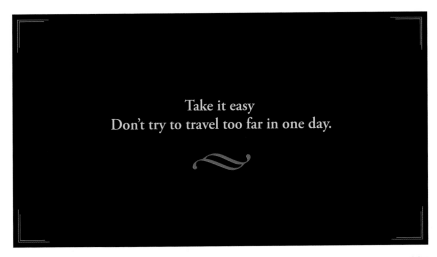

Take it easy
Don't try to travel too far in one day.

Lyttelton *9 km E of Christchurch*

The Rookery *B&B Homestay*

Angus & Rene Macpherson
9 Ross Terrace, Lyttelton, 8082

Tel (03) 328 8038
rooks@amma.co.nz
http://therookery.co.nz

Double $131-$148 Single $84 (Full breakfast)
2 Queen 1 Single (3 bdrm)
Bathrooms: 1 Ensuite 1 Family share

The Rookery is one of Lyttelton's oldest cottages with delightful panoramic views over the harbour. To capture the character of the Victorian era we as designers have paid particular attention to the colours and finishes that ensure our visitors' enjoyment during their stay. Rooms are double glazed with underfloor heating and electric blankets. Only 15 minutes from the Garden City we are ideally located for exploring the Banks Peninsula. Angus, Rene and our two cats Cleopatra and Ceasar offer you a warm and friendly welcome.

If you would like dinner most hosts require 24 hours' notice.

Governors Bay *13 km E of Christchurch*

Tintagel House *B&B*

Niare & Alister Scoble
22 Zephyr Terrace, Governors Bay, RD 1,
Lyttelton, Christchurch, Canterbury 8971

Tel (03) 329 9580 or 021 058 2075
tintagelhouse@xtra.co.nz
http://tintagelhouse.co.nz

Double $140-$180 Single $80-$90 (Full breakfast)
Children by arrangement
Not suitable for small children
Cash or cheque only
Pets welcome by arrangement
1 King 1 Queen 1 Twin (2 bdrm)
Bathrooms: 1 Ensuite 1 Private

Set in a tranquil garden' Tintagel House', which was built in 1964, over looks the top end of Lyttelton harbour. We came to live here in 2005 after spending six years in the UK, where Niare ran a B&B in our National Trust House, at Lanhydrock in Cornwall, supported by the animals Jolee (white retriever) Cinnamon and Dolly-Pepper, (cats). Our day begins and ends with the song of bellbirds. A ten minute walk down to the Jetty passes the local pub and café.

Akaroa - Barry's Bay *12 km W of Akaroa*

Rosslyn Estate *B&B Homestay Farmstay*
Ross, Lynette, Kirsty (15) & Matt (13) Curry
Barry's Bay, RD 2, Akaroa

Tel (03) 304 5804 or 027 237 8609
Fax (03) 304 5804
rosslyn@akaroanz.co.nz

Double $120-$140 Single $100 (Full breakfast)
Children negotiable
Dinner $35pp
1 night stay $140, 2 or more nights $120 per night
Visa MC accepted
2 Queen (2 bdrm)
Bathrooms: 2 Ensuite

Rosslyn is a large historic homestead built in the 1860's of native timbers milled on the property, set on a working dairy farm amid the rolling hills of Banks Peninsula over looking the serene Akaroa Harbour.

Our family home of four generations situated within informal gardens offers the tranquillity of farm life, while our entrance is conveniently situated on the main road between Christchurch and 12 km before Akaroa, allowing you to explore this intriguing volcanic peninsula with ease. While with us you will have a large ground floor bedroom, firm queen bed, ensuite bathroom, antiques, central heating and screened windows for your comfort. A spa room, pool and laundry are also available at no charge.

Breakfast ranges from fresh fruit to full cooked. We take pride in offering quality home grown and prepared produce and preserves, served at the family table in the farm style kitchen.

We have been privilaged to share our lifesyle with guests since 1987, in that time we have enjoyed some amazing experiences, fantastic dinner conversations and long breakfasts, we trust we can enhance your trip as well with local knowledge and a slice of a kiwi family, which includes our pets.

We look forward to welcoming you with a refreshing tea, coffee or cool drink served with home baking.

Directions: State Highway 75, Rosslyn Estate sign behind picket fence (left travelling to Akaroa) in Barry's Bay. The house is set 400m from the entrance.

329

Akaroa - Paua Bay *12 km E of Akaroa*

Paua Bay Farmstay *B&B Farmstay*
Murray & Sue Johns
Postal: C/- 113 Beach Road, Akaroa, Banks Peninsula

Tel (03) 304 8511 or 021 133 8194
Fax (03) 304 8511
info@pauabay.com
www.pauabay.com

Double $120-$140 (Full breakfast)
Children negotiable
Dinner $40
Children welcome
1 Queen 1 Twin (2 bdrm)
Bathrooms: 1 Ensuite 1 Guest share

Time spent at Paua Bay is a truely unique experience. Not only will you be able to enjoy the wonderful surroundings but also you will join a traditional NZ farming family sharing their daily endeavors.

Set in a private bay our 900 acre sheep, cattle & deer farm is surrounded by spectacular coastline, native bush & streams. You are spoilt for choice, walk to the beach, enjoy seals and extensive birdlife, join in seasonal farm activities.

The farmhouse is surrounded by a wonderful garden and around each corner in the path is a new surprise, a secluded moonlight bath.....a hammock....a sculpture. The guest room has wooden floors, a clawfoot bath, fresh flowers and from the queensize bed you can watch the sun rise out of the South Pacific.

In the evening take the opportunity to enjoy the company of our sixth generation farming family. Share a generous meal of fresh farm produce with relaxed conversation around the large kitchen table. New Zealand wines & beers are included.

The nearby historic French settlement of Akaroa offers guests world renouned harbour cruises and its Hector dolphins. Quiet wanderings exploring this village allows guests time to reflect on days gone by.

Banks Peninsula - Okains Bay *18 km N of Akaroa*

Kawatea *Farmstay*
Judy & Kerry Thacker
1048 Okains Bay Road, Okains Bay, Banks Peninsula

Tel (03) 304 8621   Fax (03) 304 8621   kawatea@xtra.co.nz

Double $120-$155 Single $80-$95 (Full breakfast)
Children by arrangement   Dinner $35   Visa MC accepted
3 Queen 2 Single (3 bdrm)
Bathrooms: 1 Ensuite 1 Private 1 Guest share
Bath, Shower, Seperate Toilet

Experience the grace and charm of yesteryear, while enjoying the fine food and wine of NZ today. Revel in the peace of countrylife, but still be close to sights and activities. Welcome to Kawatea, an historic Edwardian homestead set in spacious gardens, and surrounded by land farmed by our Irish ancestors since the 1850s. Built in 1900 from native timbers the house features stained glass windows and handcrafted furniture, and has been carefully renovated to add light and space without losing its original charm.

Linger over your choice of breakfast in the garden conservatory. Join us for summer barbeques on the expansive verandahs, savouring seafood from the Bay, and creative country fare from our garden and farm. On cooler evenings gather around the dining table by the fire, sharing experiences with fellow travellers.

Participate in seasonal farm activities, feed the pet sheep or wander our 1400 acre hillside farm, climbing to enjoy a panoramic view of Banks Peninsula. Enjoy Okains Bay's unspoilt swimming beach, observe the birdlife on the estuary, or walk along the scenic coastline to secluded bays and a seal colony with excellent photographic opportunities. Learn about Maori culture and the life of early settlers at the acclaimed Okains Bay Museum.

Explore Akaroa, with its strong French influence, visit art galleries and craft shops. Golf, kayak, take a harbour cruise, swim with the rare Hector's Dolphin, sample local wines and watch traditional cheeses being made.

We have been providing farmstays since 1988, and offer thoughtful personal attention and friendly hospitality in a relaxed atmosphere. Directions: Take Highway 75 from Christchurch through Duvauchelle. Turn left at signpost marked Okains Bay. Drive to the top of the Bay - we are 6km downhill on the right.

Canterbury

Canterbury

Akaroa

LeLievre Farmstay *Homestay Farmstay*
Hanne & Paul LeLievre
Box 4, Akaroa, Banks Peninsula

Tel (03) 304 7255
Fax (03) 304 7255
Double.L@Xtra.co.nz
www.sealtours.co.nz

Double $125 Single $70
(Full breakfast)
Dinner $30
Children welcome
1 Queen 1 Double 1 Single (2 bdrm)
Bathrooms: 2 Ensuite

Our home is situated 1.5 km up Takamatua Valley and 5 km from Akaroa. We farm sheep, cattle deer and usually have a menagerie of orphaned pets etc. Our interests include golf and bridge. We invite you to enjoy some good old fashioned country hospitality. A trip to the Akaroa Seal Colony, which featured on the TV programmes A Flying Visit, Totally Wild and The Great Outdoors, is a must do. Safari includes a scenic drive, through, a working farm, with the farmer.

Akaroa

The Maples *B&B*
Lesley & Peter Keppel
158 Rue Jolie, Akaroa

Tel (03) 304 8767
Fax (03) 304 8767
maplesakaroa@xtra.co.nz
www.themaplesakaroa.co.nz

Double $130-$150 Single $100
(Full breakfast)
Visa MC accepted
3 Queen 1 Single (3 bdrm)
Bathrooms: 3 Ensuite

The Maples is a charming historic two storey home built in 1877. It is situated in a delightful garden setting, three minutes walk from the cafés and waterfront. We offer two queen bedrooms with ensuites upstairs and a separate garden room with a queen and single bed also ensuite. You can relax in the separate guests' lounge where tea and coffee is available. Our delicious continental and cooked breakfasts include freshly baked croissants and home -made jams.

Akaroa

Onuku Heights B&B, Farmstay & Horse Treks *B&B Farmstay*
Eckhard Keppler
Onuku Heights, Akaroa

Tel (03) 304 7112
Fax (03) 304 7116
onuku.heights@paradise.net.nz
www.onuku-heights.co.nz

Double $240-$330 (Full breakfast)
Dinner $40-$60 by prior arrangement
Visa MC accepted
3 King (3 bdrm)
Bathrooms: 3 Ensuite

Onuku Heights is a charming, carefully restored 1860s homestead overlooking the Akaroa Harbour. Nestled in orchard and tranquil gardens with an abundance of bird life, surrounded by native bush reserves, streams and waterfalls on a 309 hectare working sheep farm. Spacious rooms furnished with antiques, comfortable firm king-size beds, exquisite ensuite bathrooms. The two guest rooms in the homestead have majestic sea views, the sunny cottage room is looking to the rose garden. Separate guest lounge with an open fire and verandah. Heated pool.

Akaroa *80 km SE of Christchurch*
Wilderness House *Luxury B&B*
Jim & Liz Coubrough
42 Rue Grehan, Akaroa

Tel (03) 304 7517 or 021 669 381
Fax (03) 304 7518
info@wildernesshouse.co.nz
www.wildernesshouse.co.nz

Double $260 Single $260 (Full breakfast)
Dinner by arrangement
Visa MC Eftpos accepted
Not suitable for children
1 King/Twin 3 Queen (4 bdrm)
Bathrooms: 3 Ensuite 1 Private

Treat yourself to a memorable experience in one of Akaroa's gracious historic homes. Built in 1878 our home is set in a one acre garden including a petite vineyard. Rooms have wireless internet, harbour/valley views and feature gorgeous linen, garden flowers, a selection of teas, coffee and home-baking. Linger over our special breakfasts. Secluded and private we are just a stroll to the village. Join us for a glass of our wine each evening. Unwind, relax and enjoy! Resident cats, Beethoven and George.

Akaroa Harbour - French Farm *70 km SE of Christchurch*
Bantry Lodge *B&B Cottage with Kitchen*
Dolina Barker
French Farm, RD 2, Akaroa

Tel (03) 304 5161 or 027 313 2406
Fax (03) 304 5162
barker.d@xtra.co.nz
www.bantrylodge.co.nz

Double $130-$150 (Full breakfast)
Dinner $40 by arrangement
Self-contained cottage sleeps 4
Visa MC Diners Amex accepted
Children and pets welcome
2 Queen 2 Double (3 bdrm)
Bathrooms: 2 Private 1 Guest share

This historic home has views across Akaroa Harbour 50 metres away. Ground floor queen room has french doors to verandah and sea views, private bath. Upstairs queen room with balcony overlooks harbour , private bath. Coffee, tea facilities provided with home-baking. The comfortable sitting room is for relaxing or joining me for a drink. Full breakfast is served in the elegant dining room. Tranquillity and space. A self-contained cottage sleeps four. Linen, breakfast ingredients supplied. One shy cat.

Akaroa *80 km SE of Christchurch*
La Belle Villa *B&B*
Alice & Paul Hewitson
113 Rue Jolie, Akaroa

Tel (03) 304 7084 or 021 0459 156
Fax (03) 304 7084
bookings@labellevilla.co.nz
www.labellevilla.co.nz

Double $140-$160 Single $120-$140
(Special breakfast)
Visa MC accepted
Children welcome
1 King 2 Queen 1 Twin (4 bdrm)
Bathrooms: 4 Ensuite

A warm welcome awaits you. Relax in the comfort of a bygone era, and appreciate the antiques in our picturesque historic villa with separate guest lounge. Built in the 1870s as the first doctor's surgery in Akaroa it is now established on beautiful, mature grounds. Enjoy the indoor/outdoor living, and gently trickling stream. We offer to make your stay with us special. Breakfast alfresco with real coffee. Being centrally situated, restaurants, cafés, wine bars and beach are all in walking distance.

Canterbury

Mulberry House *B&B Homestay*
Anne Craig & Jack Clark
9 William Street, Akaroa 8161

Tel (03) 304 7778 or (03) 304 7793
Fax (03) 304 7778
anneandjacknz@yahoo.com
www.mulberryhouse.co.nz

Double $125-$165 Single $90 (Special breakfast)
1 night stay $10 surcharge
Children welcome
1 King 1 Queen 1 Twin 1 Single (3 bdrm)
Bathrooms: 2 Ensuite 1 Private

B&B
Approved

Experience the very best in homestyle accommodation and delight in the setting of Mulberry House, which accommodates up to six guests. All rooms are beautifully decorated and feature quality beds and fine linen. There is a choice of double rooms, with or without ensuite, and a twin room which will delight children.

The romantic poolside summerhouse has its own kitchen, ensuite and garden to provide total privacy if desired.

Breakfasts are a specialty and feature a choice of American, European, English, and New Zealand styles. Champagne breakfasts and other meals by arrangement. Meals can be served outside in the summer months overlooking the pool.

Your hosts: Well travelled and semi retired Anne Craig and Jack Clark offer unparalleled hospitality. Fussy about food, both Anne and Jack love to cook: Anne preserves and bakes, and Jack adds his American expertise to breakfasts of pancakes, waffles, omelettes, fresh fruits, and delicious coffee from the espresso machine.

Guest Comments - Desmond Balmer (LondonGuardian/Observer Travel) recommends Mulberry House as amoungst New Zealand's Top Twenty. Featured on Sydney's channel 7 "Ernie Dingo's Getaway" as "the place to stay "in Akaroa. Featured in Autumn 2000 European "Wining and Dining.

Akaroa *75 km NE of Christchurch*

Garthowen B&B *Luxury B&B*
Sharon & Ian Moore
7 Beach Road, Akaroa, Banks Peninsula

Tel (03) 304 7419 or 027 437 1096
Fax (03) 304 7419
info@garthowen.co.nz
www.garthowen.co.nz

Double $260-$280 Single $240-$240 (Full breakfast)
Children $100
Visa MC Eftpos accepted
4 King/Twin (4 bdrm)
Bathrooms: 4 Ensuite 1 claw foot bath

Garthowen B&B is stunning, elegant, romantic and private. We will provide you with the perfect setting in which to relax, unwind and feel pampered.

Situated right on the waterfront of Akaroa's Main Street, purposely built to the original 1890's guest house, opened Dec 06, absolutely beautiful home with harbour views. Your own dining room and lounge to view the harbour or sit by the fire with a good book.

Enjoy a delicious breakfast from our scrumptious breakfast menu served either in the dining room or on the balcony overlooking the harbour.

A guest wireless broadband computer, mini bar, fridge. All rooms have sea views, tv, dvd, air conditioning, underfloor heating, personalised gowns, tea/coffee, biscuits, quality linen, fresh flowers, super-king beds and your own veranda with table and chairs.

Complimentary Port, mineral water and Chocolates. Dine out at one of our fine restaurants only a two minute stroll away. We will make your stay a memorable one!

Bonnie and Jessie our two Jack Russells love being spoiled by our guests. Our home is yours!
Guest comments: 'Wonderful caring and gracious hosts" - Jeremy & Wendy Lezin, USA

Canterbury

Canterbury

Akaroa *80 km SE of Christchurch*

Chez Fleurs *B&B*
Jan & Paul Wallace
15 Smith Street, Akaroa 7520

Tel (03) 304 8674 or 021 155 7727
Fax (03) 3048974
chezfleurs@xtra.co.nz
www.chezfleurs.co.nz

Double $160 Single $140 (Continental breakfast)
Visa MC accepted
Pet free home
Not suitable for children
2 Queen 1 Twin (3 bdrm)
Bathrooms: 2 Ensuite 1 Private

Bonjour! Chez Fleurs is ideally situated 150 metres up from the beach and 3 minutes walk to cafés, galleries, restaurants, shops and Information Centre. Enjoy our stunning waterfront views, beautiful garden and native birdlife, while relaxing on your own private balcony. We offer superior accommodation with private tea/coffee making facilities, fridge, TV, hairdryers and fresh flowers in suites. Guest laundry and BBQ. Secure off-street parking. Your delicious breakfast, using fresh home-grown produce is served alfresco, on your own balcony. 'A bientôt'. See you soon!

Akaroa *80 km SE of Christchurch*

Aka-View *B&B*
Lib & Ben Hutchinson
5 Langlois Lane, Akaroa, 7542

Tel (03) 304 8008 or 027 459 6042
Fax (03) 304 8008
aka-view@xtra.co.nz
www.aka-view.co.nz

Double $160-$170 Single $125-$135
(Full breakfast)
Visa MC accepted
Pet free home
3 Queen 1 Twin (4 bdrm)
Bathrooms: 2 Ensuite 1 Private

Aka-View is a puurpose built Mediterranean styled Bed & Breakfast. The upper level features two queen suites, one twin, private guest study, separate tea /coffee facilites, all with unsurpassed harbour views. In addition, guests may choose to use the formal lounge, with cosy fire, stylish but comfortable furnishings. A romantic option is our lower level garden studio-private coutyard, sunny, queen with ensuite, lounge, TV, full tea/coffee making facilities. Enjoy a continental or cooked breakfast in the kitchen or delivered to your garden studio.

Banks Peninsula - Okains Bay *20 km N of Akaroa*

Rowandale Homestead *Luxury B&B get-a-way retreat*
Angela Thacker
Rowandale Homestead, Okains Bay, Banks Peninsula

Tel (03) 304 8615   Fax (03) 304 8615
rowandalefarm@xtra.co.nz
www.rowandalehomestead.co.nz

Double $195-$250 Single $125-$195
(Special breakfast) Children under 5 free, over 5 $30
Dinner $45pp, 85% organic, gourmet with nz wines
Visa MC accepted
Children welcome
2 Queen 2 Single (3 bdrm)
Bathrooms: 1 Private with large bath and shower,
and separate toilets

Escape, relax and indulge in one of the Peninsula's largest historic homesteads of fifth generation farming. 3 km to beach (kayaks available). Treated to complimentary delights, meals to fit the stature, organic morning coffee delivered to your door, banquet breakfast where & whenever you wish. Enjoy siestas on our balcony beds, with a French tub to soak in the sunset. Linger in the magnificant billiards room with open fire. Original antiques, stunning craftsmanship, formal garden and bedroom fires! Stay for a truly memorable experience. Late checkout.

Highcountry Canterbury - Castle Hill *33 km W of Springfield*
The Burn Alpine B&B *B&B Homestay*
Bob Edge & Phil Stephenson
11 Torlesse Place, Castle Hill Village, Canterbury

Tel (03) 318 7559   Fax (03) 318 7558
theburn@xtra.co.nz   www.theburn.co.nz

Double $120-$140 Single $70-$80
(Continental breakfast) Children under 13 half price
Home cooked dinner $30pp
Dinner, Bed & Breakfast $100
Visa MC accepted   Children welcome
3 Queen 1 Twin (4 bdrm)
Bathrooms: 2 Guest share with showering facilites
and seperate toilets

One hour west of Christchurch, a carefree atmosphere prevails at The Burn. Nestled in the heart of the Southern Alps, it's arguably New Zealand's highest B&B. We designed and built our alpine lodge to maximise mountain vistas. Centered in the mystic Castlehill Basin, surrounded by native forest, this is a fantastic place to return after a days activity or just kick back and relax on the sunny deck. A host of outdoor sports include ski/snowboarding, hiking, mountain biking, and flyfishing. Professional flyfishing guiding available.

Darfield *4 km W of Darfield*
The Oaks Historic Homestead *B&B Homestay*
Madeleine de Jong
State Highway 73, Corner of Clintons Road, Darfield

Tel (03) 318 7232 or 027 241 3999
Fax (03) 318 7236
theoaks@quicksilver.net.nz
www.theoakshomestead.co.nz

Double $150-$275 Single $140 (Full breakfast)
Dinner $45pp on request
Visa MC Eftpos accepted
Children and pets welcome
3 Queen 1 Single (4 bdrm)
Bathrooms: 1 Ensuite 2 Private

One of Canterbury's oldest homesteads, restored to its former glory. Located amidst stunning scenery of the Southern Alps to the Westcoast, with ski fields, golf courses and tourist attractions on its doorstep. The Oaks features: guest rooms with ensuite/private bathrooms, a guest dining and living room featuring stunning open fires, a traditional large homestead kitchen, beautiful verandas for outdoor entertaining. Children welcome. Pets on request. Your Host Madeleine speaks five languages and is a keen cook. Wherever possible I try to use fresh organic produce.

Glenroy *24 km S of Darfield*
Glendowns *B&B Farmstay*
Hamish & Carol Lowe
24 Windwhistle Road, RD 2 Darfield, Canterbury 7572

Tel (03) 318 6509 Fax (03) 318 6904
corkycat@paradise.net.nz

Double $110 (Special breakfast)
Dinner pre-select from menu for a tailor made meal $35pp
Visa MC Eftpos accepted
Not suitable for children
1 Double (1 bdrm)
Bathrooms: 1 Family share

Enjoy tranquility on our farm nestled in 50 acres at the Canterbury Foothills with views of Mt Hutt. With our market garden you can help pick your own veggies, see them prepared and enjoy with your evening meal. See the working dogs moving sheep or simply relax in the mature gardens. Situated on Highway 72 we are close to the Mt Hutt ski field. You can also enjoy the local jet boat rides, golf, fishing, tramping, hot air ballooning and scenic helicopter flights. We also have one child and five cats.

Canterbury

Lake Coleridge *35 km NW of Methven*
Lake Coleridge Lodge *B&B Guest House Lodge*
Kerry & Joanne Munro
Hummock Road, Lake Coleridge Village, Canterbury

Tel (03) 318 5002 or 0800 525 326
Fax (03) 318 5004
lakecoleridge@paradise.net.nz
www.lakecoleridgelodge.co.nz

Double $210-$240 Single $120-$135 (Full breakfast)
Children 10 and over welcome.
Dinner included in Tariff
Visa MC Eftpos accepted
1 Queen 4 Double 4 Twin (9 bdrm)
Bathrooms: 2 Ensuite 4 Guest share

Nestled in a hidden alpine valley, surrounded by the majesty of the Southern Alps, Lake Coleridge Lodge welcomes travelers to a peaceful mountain village atmosphere. From the head of the valley, a 20 minute drive deep into the mountains provides breathtaking views of New Zealand's mountain region, with the main divide appearing directly ahead. Your hosts will delight in telling you about the rich history of the Coleridge Basin, from Glaciers to Maori greenstone trading, and New Zealand's oldest working power station.

Mt Hutt - Methven *6 km E of Methven*
Pagey's Farmstay *B&B Farmstay*
Shirley & Gene Pagey
663 Methven-Chertsey Road, RD 12 Rakaia

Tel (03) 302 1713
Fax (03) 302 1714
pageysfarmstay@wave.co.nz
www.tourism.net.nz

Double $110 Single $90 (Special breakfast)
Children under 12 half price
Dinner $30pp Spa pool
Pet free home Children welcome
1 King 1 Queen 4 Single (3 bdrm)
Bathrooms: 2 Private new - large showers

Enjoy hospitality and freedom in our lovely expansive home with new kitchen, bathrooms, large bedrooms with luxurious beds, set amidst aged oak trees and large rose garden. Watch our 47" TV and its many channels. Enjoy pre-dinner drinks, wine, crystal clear mountain water and home-grown cuisine. Star gaze in our luxurious massaging spa. Surrounding activities include breathtaking bush walks, two superior golf courses, ballooning and skiing. Short notice is our speciality. Directions from Methven town centre, turn down Methven Chertsey Road, signposted 6 km.

Take time to enjoy your journey and the
company of your hosts.

Mt Hutt - Methven *11 km W of Methven*

Glenview Farmstay *B&B Farmstay Cottage No Kitchen*
Helen & Mike Johnstone
142 Hart Road, Methven

Tel (03) 302 8620
Fax (03) 302 8620
helenmikejohnstone@yahoo.com

Double $110 Single $55 (Full breakfast)
Children $25
Dinner $25
2 Queen 2 Double 1 Twin 2 Single (5 bdrm)
Bathrooms: 1 Ensuite 1 Guest share Ensuite in unit

Glenview farmstay is situated at the base of Mt Hutt Ski Field, with the house designed to look at the mountains and down the Canterbury Plains to the Port Hills.

We farm cattle and sheep on our 1200 acre farm. We have a golden labrador and a cat.

There is a peaceful unit in the garden which is suitable for a couple or a family. It has two bedrooms, one with a queen bed and the other with one double and one single bed, ensuite, TV, tea & coffee making facilities and wonderful views. The rooms in the house have separate access, good heating and are non-smoking. Dinner by arrangement. Free farm tours on request.

Methven is only ten minutes away and we are very close to good fishing, golf, ballooning, bush walks and jet boating. Free transfers to local walkways. One hour from Christchurch and we are on the way to Queenstown along Highway 72.

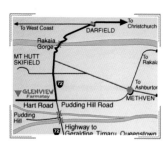

Mt Hutt - Methven *4 km NW of Methven - Mt Hutt Village*

Green Gables Deer Farm *B&B Farmstay*
Irene & Mike Harris
185 Waimarama Road, Methven-Mt Hutt Village, Postal No. 12, Rakaia

Tel (03) 302 8308 or New Zealand 0800 466 093
Fax (03) 302 8309
greengables@xtra.co.nz
www.nzfarmstay.com

Double $140-$180 Single $110-$140 (Special breakfast)
Child $55
Dinner $50pp by arrangement
Visa MC accepted
Children welcome
2 King 2 Twin (3 bdrm)
Bathrooms: 2 Ensuite 1 Private

Set in tranquil surroundings at the foot of Mt.Hutt, Green Gables Deer Farm is withing easy reach of Christchurch (1 hour), Kaikoura for Whale Watching and Dolphins (3 hours), Mt.Cook (3.5 hours) and Queenstown (approx 5.5 hours).

Our stylish rooms have all the comforts you will require with your own private entrance opening out onto the garden with a backdrop of graceful deer wandering in the paddocks and the ever changing colours of the mountain views. There is plenty of room to stroll, maybe feed the pet deer and meet our friendly dogs or just relax and unwind.

Start your evening meal with a complimentary pre-dinner drink and enjoy the fresh local produce used in our home cooked meals and desserts..

ACTIVITIES:- Try out the many summer and winter activities close by - Golf courses at Methven and Terrace Downs (club & cart hire available), Fishing, Hot Air ballooning, Jet Boating, Skiing, 4WD Scenic Tours (available by arrangement), Horse Trekking, Scenic Flights, Ecotours and Alpine Rhododrendon Walks to name but a few. There are even trips to "Eldoras" the Lord of the Rings film site at Mt.Sunday

LOCATION:- Situated on S/H77 4kms N/W Methven. From Inland Scenic-Route 72 turn into S/H77 travel 5 km Green Gables Deer Farm is on the right.

Staveley - Mt Somers *20 km SW of Methven*
Korobahn Lodge *B&B Homestay*
Caroline & John Lartice
Burgess Road, Staveley

Tel (03) 303 0828
carolinel@slingshot.co.nz
www.korobahnlodge.co.nz

Double $130-$160 **Single** $100-$120 (Full breakfast)
Dinner $45
Visa MC accepted
Children welcome
2 Queen 1 Twin (3 bdrm)
Bathrooms: 3 Ensuite

Welcome to our unique North American barn style homestead. Korobahn is tucked into the foot of Mt Somers and stands in several acres of gardens, surrounded by farmland. The property has been totally refurbished, and offers high quality accommodation and comfort. Korobahn Lodge is on Inland Scenic Highway 72, approximatly 110 kilometres southwest of Christchurch Airport and on the way to Mt Cook and Queenstown. Local activites include bush walking, horse treks,Lord of the Rings film site, jet boating, fishing, in season skating and skiing.

Rakaia *50 km S of Christchurch*
St Ita's Guesthouse *B&B Guest House*
Miriam & Ken Cutforth
11 Barrhill/Methven Road,
Rakaia Township, Canterbury

Tel (03) 302 7546 or 027 488 8673
Fax (03) 302 7564
stitas@xtra.co.nz
www.stitas.co.nz

Double $120 **Single** $70 (Full breakfast)
Children $30 Dinner $30pp
Visa MC accepted
2 Queen 1 Double 4 Single (4 bdrm)
Bathrooms: 3 Ensuite 1 Private with bath

Relax in our elegant and comfortable historic former convent, 600 metres from SH1 in small town New Zealand. Excellent base for exploring Ashburton District. Excellent first and last stop from Christchurch International Airport. Three bedrooms have ensuites and garden views. The fourth the Chapel has a private bathroom. Walking distance to local shops, great cafés, crafts and winery. Close to golf and salmon fishing, 30 minutes to skiing, jet boating. Dinner by arrangement. Full breakfasts. Share the open fire with our two moggies.

Canterbury

Ensuite or private bathroom is yours exclusively.
Guest share bathroom is shared with other guests.
Host share bathroom is shared with the family.

Ashburton *8 km W of Ashburton*

Carradale Farm *B&B Farmstay*
Karen & Jim McIntyre
Ferriman's Road (Rapid no. 200), RD 8, Ashburton

Tel (03) 308 6577 Fax (03) 308 6548
jkmcintyre@xtra.co.nz
www.ashburton.co.nz/carradale

Double $120-$140 Single $80 (Full breakfast)
Children under 12 half price   Dinner $40 by arrangement
Caravan powerpoint $25   Visa MC accepted
2 King/Twin 1 Queen (3 bdrm)
Bathrooms: 1 Ensuite 2 Private

We are 8 minutes from Ashburton and 1 hour from Christchurch airport. Our homestead, which captures the sun in all rooms, is cosy and inviting. It is situated in a sheltered garden where you can enjoy peace, tranquillity and fresh country air or indulge in a game of tennis.

All guest rooms have comfortable beds, electric blankets, reading lamps and tea/coffee making facilities. Laundry and ironing facilities available.

Dinner is by arrangement and features traditional New Zealand cuisine including home grown meat and vegetables. Breakfast is served with delicious home-made jams and preserves.

We have a 220 acre irrigated sheep and cattle farm. You may like to be taken on a farm tour or enjoy a walk on the farm. As we have both travelled extensively in New Zealand, Australia, United Kingdom, Europe, North America, Zimbabwe and South Africa. We would like to offer hospitality to fellow travellers. Our hobbies include meeting people, travel, reading, photography, gardening, sewing, cake decorating, rugby, cricket, Jim belongs to the Masonic Lodge and Karen is involved in Community Affairs.

For the weary traveller a spa pool is available. For young children we have a cot and high chair. Our resident cat 'Lady Jane' is on hand to comfort you. There is a power point for camper vans. We are one hour from Christchurch International Airport.
CARRADALE FARM "WHERE PEOPLE COME AS STRANGERS AND LEAVE AS FRIENDS."

Ashburton *90 km S of Christchurch*

Weir Homestay *B&B Homestay*
Pat & Dave Weir
35 Leeston Street, Ashburton Central

Tel (03) 308 3534
d&pweir@xtra.co.nz

Double $90 Single $45
(Breakfast by arrangement)
Dinner $20
Visa MC accepted
1 Double 3 Single (2 bdrm)
Bathrooms: 1 Ensuite 1 Guest share 1 Family share

Our comfortable home is situated in a quiet street with the added pleasure of looking onto a rural scene. We are 10-15 minutes walk from town.Guest rooms have comfortable beds with electric blankets. We welcome the opportunity to meet and greet visitors and wish to make your stay a happy one. Your hosts are retired but active, hobbies general/varied from meeting people to walking etc. Request visitors no smoking inside home. Off-street parking.

Ashburton *7 km SE of Ashburton*

Lake Hood Homestay B&B *B&B Homestay*
Eric & Eleanor Weir
14 Witney Lane, Lake Hood, Ashburton

Tel (03) 302 6914
Fax (03) 302 6914
enquiries@lakehoodhomestay.co.nz
www.lakehoodhomestay.co.nz

Double $120-$140 (Full breakfast)
Visa MC accepted
Pet free home
Not suitable for children
1 King/Twin 1 Queen (2 bdrm)
Bathrooms: 2 Ensuite

Lake Hood Homestay B&B is located on the canal network adjoining Lake Hood, 7 km from Ashburton. Lake Hood is home to a variety of water sports and popular for swimming, jogging, walking, fishing or just generally relaxing. Our homestay comprises two brand new studio suites each featuring: separate entrance, King or Queen bed (twin by arrangement), private en-suite, television, tea/coffee making, door to patio and canal-side garden. Delicious country-style breakfast included. Free use of kayaks, bicycles. Sailing, fishing by arrangement. See www.lakehoodhomestay.co.nz

Just as we have a variety of B&Bs
you will also be offered a variety of breakfasts,
and they will always be generous.

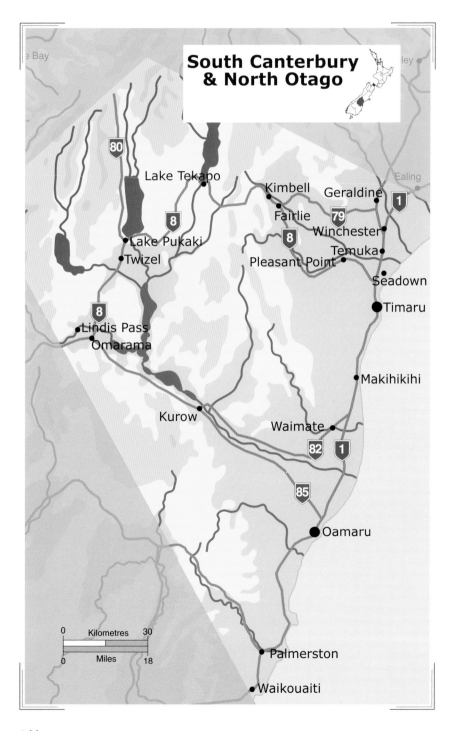

South Canterbury & North Otago

Geraldine *0.5 km S of Geraldine*

Victoria Villa *B&B Cottage with Kitchen*

Leigh & Jerry Basinger
55 Cox Street, Geraldine 7930

Tel (03) 693 8605 or 0800 537 533
027 482 1842   Fax (03) 693 8605
jbasinger@xtra.co.nz

Double $100-$125 Single $80-$100 (Full breakfast)
Children $10-$15
Dinner by arrangement
Detached studio unit
Visa MC Amex accepted
3 Queen 2 Double 2 Single (4 bdrm)
Bathrooms: 3 Ensuite 1 Private

Welcome to our historical villa, completely refurbished - spacious bedrooms with ensuites or private bathroom. Off-street parking, private entrance and lounge. Molded ceilings, native woods. Also, separate studio with ensuite and light cooking area; ideal for family. On Highway 79 to Mt Cook and Queenstown. Seven minutes walk to Geraldine Village which has boutique movie theatre, fine restaurants, sports pub, world class glass blower, boutique shops, two golf courses. Adjacent to domain. Personality pet dog and cat. Your hosts will assist to make your stay enjoyable.

Geraldine *0.2 km S of Geraldine*

Lilymay *B&B*

Lois & Les Gillum
29 Cox Street, Geraldine

Tel (03) 693 8838 or 0800 545 9629
lilymay@xtra.co.nz

Double $90-$95 Single $65-$70
(Full breakfast)
Children $20-$25
Visa MC accepted
Children welcome
2 Queen 1 Double 3 Twin 3 Single (3 bdrm)
Bathrooms: 2 Guest share

Closest B&B to village shops, restaurants & cafés. A charming character home set in a large colourful garden. A friendly, warm welcome is assurred with tea/coffee and Lois' home-baked cookies. Ample off-street parking and separate guest entrance. Teas, coffee, etc. available at all times in the guest lounge with cosy open fire. We are on the main road to Mt Cook, the Southern Lakes and mountains. The ideal stopover from Christchurch (137 km).

Geraldine *3 km N of Geraldine*

Rivendell *B&B Homestay Apartment with Kitchen*

Erica & Andrew Tedham
Woodbury Road, RD 21, Geraldine

Tel (03) 693 8559 or 021 264 1520
rivendellnz@xtra.co.nz
www.rivendellnz.co.uk

Double $85-$130 (Full breakfast)
Self-contained studio unit with kitchen $95
Not suitable for children
Pets welcome
1 Queen 1 Double 1 Single (3 bdrm)
Bathrooms: 2 Ensuite 1 Family share

Set in over three acres, Rivendell is a traditional New Zealand villa and has beautiful secluded gardens that can be enjoyed relaxing on the large verandah or in the heated spa pool. Our home provides all modern facilities including central heating, internet and laundry. The delightful village of Geraldine with its numerous cafés, restaurants, shops and cinema is only five minutes drive. We offer you a truly warm welcome together with our friendly dogs & animals.

South Canterbury
North Otago

Geraldine *1.5 km W of Geraldine Centre*

The Downs B&B *B&B*
Alycen & Myron Cournane
5 Ribbonwood Road, The Downs, RD 21, Geraldine

Tel (03) 693 7388 or 021 675 249
Fax (03) 693 7388
info@thedowns.co.nz
www.thedowns.co.nz

Double $150-$250 Single up to $150 (Full breakfast)
Visa MC Diners Amex accepted
Children welcome
3 Queen 1 Twin (4 bdrm)
Bathrooms: 3 Ensuite 1 Private
Bathrooms have heaters, hairdryers & quality toiletries.

Alycen, Myron & Max (the cat) opened this new business early in 2005. The house dates from the 70s but since then has undergone some major alterations. The upper level is now totally for guest use. There are three high quality ensuite guest rooms (one with extra bedroom if required). Free guest laundry. Guest lounge/breakfast room with open bar, tea, coffee etc. Step from the lounge onto the balcony and down to the large lawn and gardens. Enjoy the peace and quiet!

Geraldine *0.5 km S of Geraldine*

Forest View *B&B*
Denese Roy
128 Talbot Street, Geraldine

Tel (03) 693 9928 or 0800 572 740
Fax (03) 693 9928   forest.view@xtra.co.nz

Double up to $120 Single up to $80 (Full breakfast)
Children negotiable, roll way, crib, high chair available
Dinner $30 by arrangement, special 3-4 course with wine
Sleep-out $45-$65 with continental breakfast
Visa MC accepted
Pet free home   Children and pets welcome
1 King 1 Queen 1 Double 2 Twin 1 Single (5 bdrm)
Bathrooms: 1 Ensuite 1 Private 1 Guest share
Hair dryers, heaters, shampoo etc provided.

More than just a night's lodging, come experience elegant hospitality. Forest View's original owner is back from California and ready to pamper you. Enjoy complimenary afternoon tea in the gardens. Take a five minute stroll to the charming english like village, or short forest walks. A scrumptious three course gourmet breakfast with memorable entrees. Choose from french toast, pancakes, omelets and more. Common guest book comment: "Best breakfast in NZ." Internet, laundry & guest lounge.

Winchester *16 km N of Timaru*

Stonybanks *B&B*
Chris & Andrew Lush
Stonybanks 32 Harrisons Road,
Winchester, South Canterbury

Tel (03) 615 8385 or 027 661 5888
thegrange@ihug.co.nz

Double $110 Single $75 (Full breakfast)
Pet free home
Children welcome
2 Queen 2 Single (4 bdrm)
Bathrooms: 1 Ensuite 1 Private 1 Guest share

Stonybanks is a comfortable, well appointed home set in six acres of beautiful grounds. We are just off Highway 1 in the village of Winchester, moments from Highway 79 to Mt Cook, Queenstown and Southern Lakes. The area is renowned for its world class salmon and trout fishing. We are within easy driving distance of restaurants, pubs and cafés, and are happy to share our knowledge of the south island with you. We are 200 metres north of the Winchester Village on Harrison Road.

Timaru - Seadown *4.8 km N of Timaru*
Country Homestay *Homestay*
Margaret & Ross Paterson
491 Seadown Road, Seadown, RD 3, Timaru

Tel (03) 688 2468 or 021 213 7434
Fax (03) 688 2468

Double $90 Single $50 (Full breakfast)
Children half price
Dinner $25
Visa MC Diners Amex accepted
1 Double 2 Single (3 bdrm)
Bathrooms: 1 Guest share

Our homestay is approximately ten minutes north of Timaru, situated 4.8 km on Seadown Road off State Highway 1 at Washdyke - third house on left past Pharlap Statue. We have hosted on our farm for 11 years - now retired and have a country farmlet with some farm animals, with views of farmland and mountains. Day trips to Mt Cook, Hydro Lakes and ski fields, fishing, golf course few minutes away. Laundry facilities available. Interests are farming, gardening, spinning, embroidery and overseas travel.

≈

Timaru *1 km W of Timaru*
Jones Homestay *Homestay*
Margaret & Nevis Jones
16 Selwyn Street, Timaru

Tel (03) 688 1400
Fax (03) 688 1400
nevisjones@xtra.co.nz

Double $120 Single $70
(Full breakfast)
Children half price
Visa MC accepted
2 Double 1 Twin (3 bdrm)
Bathrooms: 2 Ensuite 1 Guest share

Welcome to our spacious character brick home built in the 1920s and situated in a beautiful garden with a grass tennis court. A secluded property with off-street parking and views of the surrounding sea and mountains. Centrally situated, only five minutes from the beach and town with an excellent choice of cafés and restaurants. On arrival tea is served on our sunny verandah. Hosts have lived and worked extensively overseas, namely South Africa, UK and the Middle East, and enjoy music, theatre, tennis and golf.

≈

Timaru *0.25 km N of Timaru Central*
Bidwill House *Homestay*
Dorothy & Ron White
15 Bidwill Street, Timaru

Tel (03) 688 5856 or 027 238 8122
Fax (03) 688 5870
bidwillhouse@xtra.co.nz

Double $120 Single $90 (Full breakfast)
Children half price
Visa MC accepted
Pet free home
Children and pets welcome
1 King/Twin 2 Single (2 bdrm)
Bathrooms: 1 Ensuite bath & shower

Bidwill House offers superior personalised homestay in a classic two storeyed centrally heated home with a delightful garden in a quiet street in central Timaru - five minutes walk to the town centre, restaurants and Caroline Bay. The guest bedroom has a super king/twin with a smaller bedroom with two single beds. The two rooms are only available to the one booking. Laundry facilities available. We look forward to welcoming guests to our home, and offer our hospitality to those who prefer a homestay.

South Canterbury
North Otago

Timaru *16 km N of Timaru*
Ashfield House B&B *B&B*
Ray & Wendy Pearson
71 Cass Street, Temuka

Tel (03) 615 6157
ashfield@paradise.net.nz
www.ashfield.co.nz

Double $100-$150 Single $85-$100
(Full breakfast)
Visa MC accepted
4 Queen (4 bdrm)
Bathrooms: 1 Ensuite 1 Guest share

Ashfield House, a Victorian villa built in 1883 is set in four acres of woodlands complete with stream, ducks and trout. The house features the original marble fireplaces, gilt mirrors, and a full size snooker table. Only 15 minutes walk from shops and restaurants, Ashfield House is close to skifields, salmon and trout fishing. Join us with our cats and Newfoundland dogs for a wonderful stay in a lovely setting. Guests welcome to use laundry.

Timaru *3 km S of Timaru*
Mountain View B&B *B&B Homestay Farmstay*
Marlene & Norman McIntosh
23 Talbot Road, RD 1 Kingsdown, Timaru

Tel (03) 688 1070 or 021 261 5653
Fax (03) 688 1069
mvhomestay@xtra.co.nz
www.bnb.co.nz/mtview.html

Double $95 Single $60 (Full breakfast)
Children under 13 $20
Dinner $25 by arrangement
Visa MC accepted   Children welcome
1 Queen 1 Double 1 Twin (3 bdrm)
Bathrooms: 2 Private 1 bath

Mountain View is a farmlet on Talbot Road, 200 metres from State Highway 1. Blue and white Bed & Breakfast signs on highway, 3 km from Timaru. Retired farmers with pet deer and sheep. House is situated in tranquil garden overlooking farmland with views of mountains. Private bathrooms - laundry facilities available. Tea & coffee. Nearby fishing, golf courses, walk to sea coast. Day trips comfortably taken to Mt Cook, hydro lakes and ski fields. We enjoy meeting people and look forward to offering our hospitality.

Timaru *8 km W of Timaru*
Berrillo *Luxury B&B Homestay*
Owen & Liz Berrill
32 Gladstone Road, RD 4, Timaru

Tel (03) 686 1688 or 021 295 2451
Fax 03 686 1678
oberrill@xtra.co.nz
www.berrillo.co.nz

Double $145 Single $100 (Full breakfast)
Children $45
Dinner $40pp by arrangement
Visa MC accepted
1 Queen 2 Twin (2 bdrm)
Bathrooms: 2 Ensuite
Power shower, hair driers, heated towel rails

A Touch of Tuscany in Timaru. A warm welcome awaits you and we offer a complimentary glass of wine on the terrace overlooking stunning views of Mt Cook. Our award winning Home of the Year 2000 is nestled in an olive grove. We have a purpose-built guest wing with separate antique furnished lounge, Sky TV, tea/coffee making facilities. Sit and chat with us or just relax and enjoy the peace. We enjoy golf, art and music. Golf courses nearby, ski fields one hour away. Resident labrador.

Timaru *0.1 km W of Central Timaru*

Sefton Homestay Bed & Breakfast *B&B Homestay*

Trish & John Blunden
32 Sefton Street, Seaview, Timaru

Tel (03) 688 0017 or 027 473 7366
027 470 0000
Fax (03) 688 0042
trish@seftonhomestay.co.nz
www.seftonhomestay.co.nz

Double $120 **Single** $100 (Full breakfast)
Children half Price
Visa MC accepted
Children welcome
1 King/Twin 1 Queen 1 Double (3 bdrm)
Bathrooms: 1 Ensuite 1 Private

Relax in our superbly appointed and spacious two storey character brick home with sweeping views from the mountains to the sea. Refurbished with the feel of yesteryear, but with ambience and style you will love. All our children have left home with the exception of our labrador Ollie who enjoys meeting people as we do. A genuine five minute walk to the nearest restaurants

Pleasant Point - Timaru *17 km W of Timaru*

Longview Bed & Breakfast *B&B Farmstay*

Anita & Alan Blakemore
86 Longview Road, Pleasant Point, Timaru 8772

Tel (03) 614 7766 or 027 308 5078
longview86@xtra.co.nz
www.longviewfarmstay.co.nz

Double $130-$140 **Single** $80-$100 (Full breakfast)
Children up to $40
Dinner by prior arrangement $35
Visa MC accepted Children welcome
2 Queen 1 Twin (3 bdrm)
Bathrooms: 1 Guest share

Combine tranquility and stunning panoramic mountain views with the convenience of being two hours drive from Christchurch and Mt Cook. Longview is situated on 25 acres, 2 km from Pleasant Point. Wander through the olive grove, relax in our private guest lounge, or join us and meet Becky our Cocker Spaniel. Attractions in the area include pre-European Maori rock art, steam train, 18-hole golf course and three major ski fields. A choice of cafés and restaurants can be found nearby.

Timaru *1 km S of Information Centre*

Blueberry Cottage *B&B Homestay*

Barbara & Rodger Baird
72A High Street, Timaru

Tel (03) 684 3115 or 027 636 4301
Fax (03) 684 3172
relax@blueberrycottage.co.nz
www.blueberrycottage.co.nz

Double $95-$100 **Single** $70-$75
(Continental breakfast)
Children negotiable
Visa MC accepted
1 King/Twin 1 Double (2 bdrm)
Bathrooms: 1 Guest share Bath and wet shower

Our delightfully upgraded 1950's brick home offers comfort and spectacular views of the ocean and inland to Mt Cook. The tastefully furnished rooms have television and separate patios. Handy to hospital, gardens & beach. Walking distance to shops, café/bars, or eating place of your choice. Day trips to lakes, skiing in winter, Mt Cook, fishing rivers, bush walks and towns nearby. Our interests can be detected by our nautical theme, the vintage car in the garage and our choice of music. "Relaxation at its best".

South Canterbury, North Otago

Timaru *1 km N of Post Office*
Nelson Heights B&B *B&B*

Claire & Lindsay
12 Nelson Terrace, Timaru, South Canterbury

Tel (03) 688 6646 or 027 274 3318
Fax (03) 688 6646
claire.lindsay@xtra.co.nz
www.nelsonheights.co.nz

Double $160-$170 Single $140 (Full breakfast)
Visa MC Diners Amex Eftpos accepted
1 King/Twin 3 King (4 bdrm)
Bathrooms: 4 Ensuite One with Spa Bath

A warm welcome to our 1920's villa. Nelson Heights is centrally situated to Caroline Bay, Restaurants, CBD and shopping. The guest lounge features SKY, DVD, Internet, Tea/Coffee facilities. Our balcony views the Bay and Port and a must to enjoy breakfast alfresco. Complimentary transport, golf on champion course, laundry facilities. Beautifully appointed bedrooms, flat screen TVs, internet and modern ensuites all designed to cater for your comfort, satisfaction and enjoyment. Our 20 years in the hospitality industry ensures that your needs are catered for.

Timaru *163 km SW of Christchurch*
Elizabeth Court Guest House *B&B Guest House*

Ginny Corry
39 Elizabeth Street, Timaru, 7910

Tel (03) 686 6091 or 027 692 1899
Fax (03) 684 7914
ginnys_lizzycourt@xtra.co.nz
www.elizabethcourtbnb.com

Double $80-$100 Single $60-$70 (Full breakfast)
Children up to 12 $10
Dinner by arrangement
Visa MC Eftpos accepted
Children and pets welcome
6 Queen 6 Double (12 bdrm)
Bathrooms: 2 Guest share 1 Family share

Elizabeth Court is a 17 bedroom former rest home which has been lovingly transformed into a B&B. Just a three minute or so walk to downtown Timaru, movies, restaurants, boutiques, supermarkets and nightlife. Enjoy our warm comfy beds and wake up to the smell of a cooked or continental breakfast. A home away from home. Come and stay a while with your host Ginny.

Fairlie *3 km W of Fairlie*
Fontmell *B&B Homestay Farmstay*

Anne & Norman McConnell
Nixons Road 169, RD 17, Fairlie

Tel (03) 685 8379
Fax (03) 685 8379

Double $100-$120 Single $65 (Full breakfast)
Children $35
Dinner $25
Cottage $190
2 King/Twin 1 Queen 1 Double
2 Twin 1 Single (4 bdrm)
Bathrooms: 1 Private 1 Guest share

Our farm consists of 400 acres producing lambs, cattle and deer. The house is situated in a large English style garden with many mature trees in a tranquil setting. In the area are two ski fields, golf courses, walkways and scenic drives. Informative farm tours available. Our interests include golf, gardening and music. New fully self-contained three bedroom cottage with panoramic views of the Fairlie Basin. Directions: Nixons Road 1 km West of Town Centre, Fontmell 2 km up Nixons Road.

Fairlie *1.5 km NW of Fairlie*
Ashgrove *B&B*

Maria & Stewart Evans
Mt Cook Road, Fairlie

Tel (03) 685 8797 or 027 289 5323
Fax (03) 685 8795
maria@ashgrove.co.nz
www.ashgrove.co.nz

Double $125 Single $85
(Continental breakfast provisions)
Children negotiable
Visa MC accepted
Pet free home   Children and pets welcome
1 King/Twin 1 Queen (2 bdrm)
Bathrooms: 1 Ensuite 1 Private

Enjoy a restful stopover on your South Island journey at our three acre farmlet. Our house is set amongst established trees and gardens. Guest facilities include a spacious private sunny sitting room, microwave, fridge, TV, tea & coffee are available. Cot available. We also offer refreshments for sale. Only ten minutes walk to award winning restaurants. We are happy to share our knowledge of the South Island, especially to trampers and those keen to fish the clear lakes & rivers of the region.

Fairlie - Kimbell *8 km W of Fairlie*
Rivendell Lodge *B&B Homestay Countrystay*

Joan Gill
15 Stanton Road, Kimbell, RD 17, Fairlie

Tel (03) 685 8833 or 027 4819 189
Fax (03) 685 8825
Rivendell.lodge@xtra.co.nz
www.fairlie.co.nz/rivendell

Double $110-$140 Single $75-$90 (Full breakfast)
Children negotiable Dinner $40pp
Visa MC accepted Children welcome
3 Queen 1 Double 2 Single (4 bdrm)
Bathrooms: 2 Ensuite 2 Guest share
Separate spa bath available

Quality country comfort and hospitality offered in a peaceful historic village on the Christchurch-Queenstown route. Joan is a well-travelled writer, passionate about mountains, literature and local history. I enjoy cooking and gardening and delight in sharing home grown produce. Take time out for fishing, skiing, walking, golf or water sports. Relax in the garden, complete with stream and cat, or come with us to some of our favourite places. Complimentary refreshments on arrival. Laundry facilities and internet available.

Lake Tekapo *40 km W of Fairlie*
Freda Du Faur House *B&B Homestay*

Dawn & Barry Clark
1 Esther Hope Street, Lake Tekapo

Tel (03) 680 6513
dawntek@xtra.co.nz
www.fredadufaur.co.nz

Double $140-$160 Single $100
(Continental breakfast)
Visa MC accepted
1 Queen 1 Double 2 Single (3 bdrm)
Bathrooms: 2 Ensuite 1 Private

Experience tranquillity and a touch of mountain magic. A warm and friendly welcome. Comfortable home, mountain and lake views. Rimu panelling, heart timber furniture, attractive decor, blending with the McKenzie Country. Bedrooms in private wing overlooking garden, two opening onto balcony. Refreshments on patio surrounded by roses or view ever changing panorama from lounge. Walkways nearby. Mt Cook one hour away. Views of skifield. Five minutes to shops and restaurants. Call for Directions.Happy hour 6:00-7:00

Lake Tekapo *43 km W of Fairlie*

Creel House *B&B*

Grant & Rosemary Brown
36 Murray Place, Lake Tekapo

Tel (03) 680 6516
Fax (03) 680 6659
creelhouse.l.tek@xtra.co.nz
www.laketekapoflyfishing.co.nz

Double $150-$160 Single $75-$80 (Special breakfast)
Off-season tariff $130 double/twin
Visa MC accepted
Children welcome
2 Queen 1 Twin (3 bdrm)
Bathrooms: 1 Ensuite 2 Private 1 private with bath

B uilt by Grant, our three storied home with expansive balconies offers panoramic views of the Southern Alps, Mt John, Lake Tekapo and surrounding mountains. All rooms are spacious and comfortable, with guest lounge and separate guest entrance. A NZ native garden adds an attractive feature. Restaurants in township. Our younger daughter, 17 years, is living with us on the ground floor with two cats, thus separate from our guest accommodation. Grant is a professional flyfishing guide (NZPFGA) and offers guided tours.

Lake Pukaki - Mt Cook *7 km N of Twizel*

Rhoborough Downs, Pukaki *Homestay*

Roberta Preston
State Highway 8 Tekapo/Twizel

Tel (03) 435 0509 or 027 621 7941
ra.preston@xtra.co.nz

Double $120 Single $70
(Continental breakfast)
Children $50
1 Double 1 Twin 1 Single (3 bdrm)
Bathrooms: 1 Guest share seperate toilets

A quiet place to stop, halfway between Christchurch and Queenstown or Christchurch and Dunedin via Waitaki Valley. 40 minutes to Mt Cook. The 10,000 acre property has been in the family 88 years. Merino sheep graze to 6000 feet, hereford cattle. Views of the southern sky. The homestead is set in tranquil gardens. Afternoon tea/drinks served on the veranda. We have a black lab. Twizel has a bank, doctor, shops and eight recommended restaurants. Please phone for bookings and directions. Cot available.

Lake Pukaki *27 km W of Lake Tekapo*

Tasman Downs Station *Farmstay*

Linda & Bruce Hayman
Lake Pukaki, Lake Tekapo

Tel (03) 680 6841
Fax (03) 680 6851
samjane@xtra.co.nz

Double $120-$130 Single $85-$100
(Full breakfast)
Dinner $45pp by arrangement
1 Queen 1 Twin (2 bdrm)
Bathrooms: 1 Private 1 Guest share

A place of unsurpassed beauty. located on the shores of Lake Pukaki, magnificent views of the lake, Mount Cook and Southern Alps. Our local stone home blends in with the natural peaceful surroundings. This high country station has been in our family since 1914 and runs mainly angus cattle. Bruce an ex-RAF pilot and Linda enjoy sharing their knowledge of farming with guests. An opportunity to experience true farm life with friendly hosts, dinner by arrangement. Meet our good natured corgi.

Twizel *1 km W of Twizel*

Heartland Lodge *Homestay Apartment with Kitchen*
Kerry & Steve Carey
19 North West Arch, Twizel, South Canterbury

Tel (03) 435 0008 or 021 230 7502
Fax (03) 435 0387
heartlandlodge@xtra.co.nz
www.heartland-lodge.co.nz

Double $200-$220 Single $130-$150 (Full breakfast)
Children negotiable
Extra adult from $30
Visa MC Eftpos accepted
Children welcome
2 King/Twin 1 King 1 Queen (4 bdrm)
Bathrooms: 4 Ensuite 3 spabaths, 1 sauna

Welcome to our friendly, comfortable homestay lodge, only 45 minutes from Mt Cook. Luxuriously appointed guest rooms feature ensuites with spa baths or sauna. Relax in our garden or sunny lounge before dining at one of several nearby restaurants. Compimentary laundry, refreshments and email services are available . The Loft is a large self-service apartment above our garage, ideal for families sleeping 2-6 people with kitchen and bathroom facilities. $120 double and $15 for each extra person.

Twizel - Mt Cook *2 km W of Twizel Info Centre*

Artemis B&B *B&B*
Jan & Bob Wilson
33 North West Arch, Twizel

Tel (03) 435 0388
Fax (03) 435 0377
artemistwizel@paradise.net.nz

Double $130 Single $105
(Special breakfast)
Visa MC Diners Eftpos accepted
Pet free home
Not suitable for children
2 Queen 1 Single (2 bdrm)
Bathrooms: 1 Ensuite 1 Private

Jan and Bob welcome you to the magnificent Mackenzie Basin and the Mount Cook National Park. Our modern home, which is situated on a hectare of land, has stunning mountain views along with space and tranquility.We are a short drive to Mount Cook National Park and a three minutes drive to restaurants.There is a guest sitting room with a balcony and tea/coffee making facilities.We look forward to sharing our home with you and are happy to discuss your New Zealand itineraries and sightseeing.

Twizel - Lake Ruataniwha *4 km SW of Twizel*

Lake Ruataniwha Homestay *Homestay*
Robin & Lester Baikie
146 Max Smith Drive, Twizel
PO Box 9 Twizel

Tel (03) 435 0532 or 027 4321 532
027 437 3294   Fax (03) 435 0522
robinandlester@xtra.co.nz

Double $120-$150 Single $75-$110 (Full breakfast)
Children negotiable
Visa MC accepted
Pet free home   Children welcome
2 Queen 2 Twin (3 bdrm)
Bathrooms: 1 Ensuite 1 Guest share

Welcome to our new home, built on four hectares overlooking Lake Ruataniwha with 360 degree views of the lake and mountains. We have travelled overseas and enjoy meeting people. All bedrooms open onto a patio. We have a variety of farm animals close to our house. Lester and his horses were extras on Lord of the Rings and he enjoys talking about his experiences. Our interests are farming, horse trekking, sport and WI. Email and fax facilities available. An ideal stopover between Christchurch and Queenstown.

Twizel - Mt Cook *0.5 km S of Twizel*
Hunters House and Hunters Cottage Self Contained

B&B Cottage with Kitchen
Anne & Matt Hunter
58 Tekapo Drive, Twizel

Tel (03) 435 0038
Fax (03) 435 0038
annehunter@xtra.co.nz

Double $150 Single $100 (Full breakfast)
Visa MC accepted
Not suitable for children
2 King/Twin (2 bdrm)
Bathrooms: 2 Ensuite

H unters House is architecturally designed for guests and features every comfort in a warm welcoming environment. It overlooks the native tussocks and trees of the Green Belt on the township boundary with the mountains as a backdrop. All rooms are tastefully decorated with all facilities and french doors opening to the peaceful outdoors sited for the sun and views. We also have a self contained cottage fully equiped with all home comforts and same views Situated in its own private setting. "Cead Mile Failte"

Twizel *1 km N of Twizel*
Pinegrove *B&B 2 Cottages with kitchens*

Al & Joh Ingram
29 North West Arch, Twizel

Tel (03) 435 0430 or 021 464 726
aljohpinegrove@xtra.co.nz

Double $140-$160 Single $100
(Special breakfast)
Children $10-$20
Visa MC Eftpos accepted
Children welcome
2 Queen 1 Double 2 Single (2 bdrm)
Bathrooms: 2 Private Walk in showers

R est a while in the beautiful Mackenzie District with its mountains and lakes. We are only 45 minutes from Mt Cook and two minutes drive to near by restaurants. We welcome you to our sunny cottages situated in an extensive garden with fishpond and tranquil areas to sit in. The cottages are fitted with modern conveniences with your comfort in mind. You can indulge in home baked goodies from the breakfast hamper. We look forward to meeting you and welcoming you to our haven.

Twizel - Mount Cook *30 km N of Twizel*
Gladstone Cottage *Cottage with Kitchen*
Peter & Margaret Hands
32 North West Arch, Twizel, 7944

Tel (03) 435 0527
info@gladstonecottage.co.nz
www.gladstonecottage.co.nz

Double $140-$200 Single $100
(Breakfast by arrangement)
Visa MC Eftpos accepted
Pet free home
1 Queen 2 Single (2 bdrm)
Bathrooms: 1 Guest share

W e are suitated in the beautiful Mackenzie Basin and are 45 minutes driving time from Mount Cook. We look forward to welcoming you to our new fully self contained cottage built on a six acre block of land that is shared with our own home.There are a good selection of restaurants and cafés within a two minute drive or 15 minute walk. Please visit our website for more photographs, information and directions at www.gladstonecottage.co.nz

Twizel *0.2 km N of Central Twizel*

Aoraki Lodge *B&B*
Ian & Sandy Darwin
32 Mackenzie Drive, Twizel

Tel (03) 435 0300
Fax (03) 435 0305
ian.sandy@xtra.co.nz
www.aorakilodge.co.nz

Double $140-$150 **Single** $100
(Full breakfast)
Visa MC Eftpos accepted
3 Queen 1 Twin (4 bdrm)
Bathrooms: 4 Ensuite

Welcome to Aoraki Lodge. If you prefer a casual informal atmosphere with friendly hosts then Aoraki Lodge is the place for you. Relax in our comfortable lodge and sunny private garden. Ian a well known fishing guide can offer helpful advice on all local attractions. We look forward to welcoming you.

Omarama *.3 km S of Omarama*

Omarama Station *Farmstay*
Beth & Dick Wardell
Omarama Station Omarama 9448, North Otago

Tel (03) 438 9821
Fax (03) 438 9822
wardell@paradise.net.nz
www.omaramastation.co.nz

Double $120 **Single** $70 (Full breakfast)
Children $20-$50 Dinner $40
2 Queen 2 Single (3 bdrm)
Bathrooms: 1 Ensuite 1 Private

Omarama Station is a merino sheep and cattle property adjacent to the Omarama township. The 100 year old homestead is nestled in a small valley in a tranquil park-like setting of willows, poplars and a fast flowing stream (good fly fishing), pleasant walking environs, and interesting historical perspective to the high country as this was the original station in the area. Swimming pool and a pleasant garden. An opportunity to experience day to day farming activities. Dinner by arrangement.

Lindis Pass *17 km W of Omarama*

Dunstan Downs *Farmstay*
Tim & Geva Innes
Dunstan Downs, Omarama, 9448

Tel (03) 438 9862
Fax (03) 438 9517
tim.innes@xtra.co.nz

Double up to $260 **Single** up to $130
(Full breakfast provisions)
Children under 12 half price
Tarrif includes dinner, bed & breakfast
Children and pets welcome
1 Queen 2 Twin 1 Single (3 bdrm)
Bathrooms: 1 Ensuite 1 Guest share 1 Family share

Dunstan Downs is a merino sheep and cattle station in the heart of the South Island high country. Our home is full of country warmth, you are welcome to join us for dinner (wine served) or bed and breakfast. The surrounding mountains and valleys are an adventure playground, tramping, mountain biking, fishing,farming activities or lazing around soaking up the peace and tranquillity.No pets inside.

South Canterbury
North Otago

Kurow *60 km W of Oamaru*

Glenmac Farmstay *Farmstay Campervan Facilities*
Kaye & Keith Dennison
RD 7K, Oamaru

Tel (03) 436 0200   Fax (03) 436 0202
glenmac@farmstaynewzealand.co.nz
www.farmstaynewzealand.co.nz

Double $90-$110 Single $45-$55 (Full breakfast)
Children under 13 half price
Dinner $25
Self-contained price on application
Visa MC accepted
Children and pets welcome
1 Queen 2 Double 2 Twin (5 bdrm)
Bathrooms: 1 Ensuite 1 Guest share 1 Family share

Peaceful location. Enjoy home-cooked meals, a comfortable bed, relax and be treated as one of the family. Explore our 4000 acre high country farm. See merino sheep and beef cattle. On farm enjoy horse riding, take a 4 wheel drive farm tour, walk some of our many tracks. Nearby fly and spinner fishing (guide available), mountain biking, golf or explore the Fossil Trail. Directions: At end of Gards Road which is 10 km east of Kurow on right or 13 km west of Duntroon on left.

Oamaru *8 km SW of Oamaru*

Tara *Homestay*
Marianne & Baxter Smith
Springhill Road, RD 30, Oamaru 9495

Tel (03) 434 8187
Fax (03) 434 8187
smith.tara@xtra.co.nz
www.tarahomestay.com

Double $110 Single $65
(Full breakfast)
Dinner $35 by arrangement
2 Single (1 bdrm)
Bathrooms: 1 Private

Want to be pampered? Tara is the place for you. Enjoy the comfort and luxuries of our character Oamaru stone home. Tara boasts all day sun and the privacy to soak up the country atmosphere, 12 acres of roses, mature trees and rural farmland. Enjoy alpacas, coloured sheep, donkeys, the aviary, burmese cat and Delphi, a Lassie collie. Not forgetting the adorable Shetland Max, plus Baxter's big horse Barney. Baxter and I will ensure your visit is an enjoyable experience. Please phone for directions.

Oamaru *3 km S of Oamaru, just off SH1*

Springbank *B&B Apartment with Kitchen*
Joan & Stan Taylor
60 Weston Road, Oamaru

Tel (03) 434 6602 or 027 403 5410
Fax (03) 434 6602
joanstanspringbank@clear.net.nz

Double $95 Single $60
(Continental breakfast)
Children $10
Visa MC accepted
1 King/Twin 1 Double (1 bdrm)
Bathrooms: 1 Private with bath & shower

We look forward to sharing our retirement haven with visitors from overseas and New Zealand. Our modern home and separate guest flat are set in a peaceful and private large garden. Feed the goldfish. Our guest flat is sunny, warm, spacious and comfortable. We enjoy helping visitors discover our district's best kept secrets! Penguins, gardens, Moeraki Boulders, beaches, pool, fishing and golf. Our interests are travel, gardening, grandchildren. Stan's are Lions and following sports. Joan's all handcrafts, patchwork, floral design.

Oamaru - Waianakarua *27 km S of Oamaru*

Glen Dendron *B&B Farmstay*
Anne & John Mackay
284 Breakneck Road, Waianakarua, RD 90, Oamaru

Tel (03) 439 5288 or 021 615 227
Fax (03) 439 5288
anne.john.mackay@xtra.co.nz
www.glenhomestays.co.nz

Double $130-$160 Single $90-$120
(Full breakfast)
Children $45
Dinner $35 with wine
Visa MC accepted
Pet free home Children welcome
2 King/Twin 2 Queen (4 bdrm)
Bathrooms: 2 Ensuite 1 Guest share Spa bath

Award Winning Homestay.Enjoy tranquility and beauty when you stay in our stylish modern home, spectacularly sited on a hilltop overlooking the picturesque Waianakarua River and surrounded by five acres of landscaped garden.

After a sumptuous farm-cooked breakfast, feed the sheep and alpacas. Then take a stroll through the forest, native bush complete with waterfalls and birds or beside the river. Play a round on our private golf course. Later, watch the seals and penguins on a beach nearby. Then, complete a perfect day with our gourmet three course dinner with fine NZ wine before snuggling down for a peaceful sleep in the fresh country air.

After a lifetime spent in farming and forestry we relish the opportunity to share our home and semi-retired lifestyle with guests. Our adult family lives overseas so we travel frequently and have a great interest in other countries and cultures. We are very keen gardeners, read widely and enjoy antiques. Anne is a floral designer and John is involved with the Lions organization.

An overnight stay is not enough to do justice to this lovely area - with so much to see, why not stay awhile! We can plan customised itineraries of the area's many attractions. Oamaru's historic architecture. Garden, heritage and fossil trails. Beaches, fishing, seals and penguins. Famous Moeraki Boulders and other interesting geological features. Use us as a base for day visits to Oamaru, Dunedin, Waitaki Valley and Mt Cook. Christchurch International Airport - 3.5 hours. We dont mind short notice!

Oamaru *1.3 km N of Oamaru Centre*

Highway House Boutique B&B *B&B Homestay*

Stephanie & Norman Slater
43 Lynn Street, (Cnr Thames Highway & Lynn Street),
Orana Park, Oamaru

Tel (03) 437 1066 or 0800 003 319
Fax (03) 437 1066 cns@ihug.co.nz
www.highwayhouse.co.nz

Double $120-$165 Single $100-$130 (Full breakfast)
Children negotiable Dinner by arrangement
Visa MC Amex accepted Pet free home
2 King 1 Twin (3 bdrm)
Bathrooms: 1 Ensuite 1 Guest share 1 Family share
Large-size showers

Our character residence on Thames Highway, (1.3 km north of town centre), has been entirely refurbished to the highest standard. We provide a full cooked breakfast and other refreshments as required. We can assist with tours of historic Oamaru or visits to the nature sites. Our courtesy car can collect or take you to nearby dining establishments. If you appreciate a quality ambiance and particular assistance from Stephanie and Norman who have travelled widely overseas, Highway House will be ideal for you. French also spoken.

Oamaru *2 km N of Oamaru Centre*

Coral Sea Cottage & Ocean View Apartments *B&B Cottage with Kitchen*

Apartments with Some Cooking Facilities

Nicola & Peter Mountain
Ocean View, 34 Harlech Street, Oamaru

Tel (03) 437 1422 or 021 659 757
021 042 6997 Fax (03) 437 1427
nmountain@xtra.co.nz

Double $145 Single $90 (Full breakfast provisions)
Children 5-16 $25 Visa MC accepted
Children and pets welcome
4 King/Twin 2 Queen 1 Single (7 bdrm)
Bathrooms: 2 Ensuite 2 Private
Ensuite is shower room Private has bath and shower

Relax on a peaceful hillside in our cosy cottage with secluded grounds or in self-contained apartments in our home overlooking the Pacific. All well equipped, most with Sky TV. Cot and high chair available. Enjoy wonderful views, pet farm animals and our son's art gallery. Resident dogs and cats! Near local shops, restaurants. 2 km to historic town centre, art galleries, famous blue penguin colony. We look forward to welcoming you and offering help with planning your visit to our area. "Best stay we had." (European Guest)

Oamaru *0.5 km W of Oamaru Centre*

Homestay Oamaru *B&B Homestay*

Doug Bell
14 Warren Street, Oamaru

Tel (03) 434 1454 or 027 408 2860
Fax (03) 434 1454
homestayoamaru@paradise.net.nz
www.bellview.co.nz

Double $75-$95 Single $45-$60 (Full breakfast)
Dinner $25
Pet free home
Not suitable for children
2 Queen 1 Double (3 bdrm)
Bathrooms: 2 Ensuite 1 Family share

Sweeping views over the town and harbour. Warm, spacious and comfortable accommodation for the travelling enthusiast, with books, maps, atlases and guides for you perusal. Quiet, private site, close to town centre. (see map on website). Off-street parking. Southern scenic walkway access at property boundary. Some of the area's attractions include sea and river fishing, historic architecture, unique geological features and eco-tourism. Host has detailed local knowledge. Site unsuitable for young children or pets.

Oamaru - Airedale *8 km NW of Oamaru*

Seadowns Farmstay *Farmstay*

Lynne & Colin Gibson
1D RD Oamaru, North Otago, Rapid No 217
Rosebery Road, Airedale, Oamaru

Tel (03) 434 9479 or 021 188 9865
Fax (03) 434 9499   lynne.col.seadowns@xtra.co.nz
www.seadowns.co.nz

Double $130-$160 Single $75 (Continental breakfast)
Children $40   Evening meal available $35pp B/A
Preferred method of payment is cash
Children and pets welcome
2 Double 1 Twin (3 bdrm)
Bathrooms: 1 Guest share 1 Family share

Seadowns is an intensive breeding property of 1100 acres of rolling hill country, with hereford, romney and dorset downs studs. The homestead built in 1939 is a relaxing home set in a peaceful country garden with coastal views. We have a fox terrier and cat. Complimentry farm tour. View or participate in shearing and farm activities. Historic sites on the property include: Oamaru stone quarrying site, limestone cliffs, lobster catching. Experience penguin colonies, historic Oamaru precinct, with 19th century architecture, Moeraki Boulders and salmon fishing.

Oamaru *8 km S of Oamaru*

Ranui Retreat Bed and Breakfast/Homestay *B&B Homestay*

Sheryl Laraman and Family
27 Woolshed Road, Totara, Oamaru, 8D RD

Tel (03) 439 5241
ranui_retreat@actrix.gen.nz
www.ranui-retreat.co.nz

Double $125-$160 Single $100 (Full breakfast)
Children negotiable
Dinner $25pp
Visa MC accepted
Children and pets welcome
2 Queen (2 bdrm)
Bathrooms: 1 Ensuite 1 Private

Welcome to Ranui Retreat. We are close to historic Oamaru and the main highway to Dunedin. Views of Otago rural landscape stretching to the Kakanui Mountains enhance the rural sense of this five acre property of mature oak, elm and ash trees. There is birdsong aplenty. Character rooms include rich, handmade quilts which add to the relaxed ambience. Join the family for the evening or you may like to retire to other spaces with music and a good book from our library selection.

Oamaru *0.5 km S of Oamaru*

Federation House Homestay Inn B&B *B&B Homestay*

Rodger McCaw
60 Tyne Street, Oamaru, 9400

Tel (03) 434 9537 or 021 0246 2418
Fax (03) 434 9537
info@federationhouse.co.nz
www.federationhouse.co.nz

Double $100-$200 Single $60-$120
(Accommodation only)
Dinner by arrangement
Off season rates: special discount from May until Oct
Visa MC accepted
Pet free home
Children welcome
3 King/Twin 1 Queen 1 Twin (5 bdrm)
Bathrooms: 3 Ensuite 1 Guest share 1 Family share

A large two storied Heritage House with a commanding site in the exclusive suburb of Cape Wanbrow. So very close to Oamaru's Historic Precinct, Harbour and Penguin Colony with views from rooms. Enjoy an era of magnificent building of Australasian Federation architecture.

Oamaru *80 km S of Timaru*

Eden Lodge Oamaru *Historic B&B Homestay*

Ian Murton
39 Eden Street, Oamaru, 9400

Tel (03) 434 6524
enquiries@edenlodgeoamaru.co.nz
www.edenlodgeoamaru.co.nz

Double $100-$120 Single $65
(Full breakfast)
Cash only
Children welcome
1 Queen 2 Double 1 Twin 1 Single (5 bdrm)
Bathrooms: 2 Private 2 Guest share

Stay in the lovingly renovated Eden Lodge, a central yet peaceful Victorian Oamaru stone house. My home retains the graciousness of a bygone era whilst offering all modern comforts. Enjoy the spacious bedrooms filled with antiques and collectables. Relax in the garden, on the terrace or in the guest library and lounge. Linger over your tasty continental breakfast before exploring the wide range of activities available in Oamaru. Walking distance to shops, Public Gardens, walking trails, museum, galleries, Historic Precinct and the Janet Frame house.

Palmerston *2 km S of Palmerston*

Mount Royal B&B *B&B*

Jo & Trevor Studholme
Mount Royal, RD 1 (Just off SH1),
Palmerston, Otago

Tel (03) 465 1884
Fax (03) 465 1440
mt.royal.bandb@clear.net.nz

Double $120-$130 (Full breakfast)
Private Sitting Room
Pet free home
Not suitable for children
1 King 1 Twin (2 bdrm)
Bathrooms: 1 Guest share

Our 1930's homestead situated in a quiet rural setting 400 meters from State Highway 1 and 1 km south of Palmerston, the gateway to Central Otago goldfields. As hosts, we enjoy making you welcome and would like you to stay to visit the Moeraki Boulders and coastal walkways, before heading central, perhaps following the gold trail: The Macraes Gold Mine is thought to be the largest open-cast mine in the Southern Hemisphere (tours by appointment).

Palmerston - Waikouaiti *40 km N of Dunedin*

Boutique Bed & Breakfast *B&B Farmstay Separate Suite*

Barbara & John Morgan
107 Jefferis Road, Waikouaiti RD 2,
Near Palmerston

Tel (03) 465 7239 or 027 224 8212
021 161 0243
Fax (03) 465 7239
info@boutiquebedandbreakfast.co.nz
www.boutiquebedandbreakfast.co.nz

Double $120-$180 Single $100-$120 (Full breakfast)
Visa MC accepted
3 Queen 1 Double (3 bdrm)
Bathrooms: 3 Ensuite

Enjoy a tranquil garden setting on a deer park. Our unique guest rooms are purpose built and designed for your comfort and pleasure. After a delicious breakfast, experience John's deer tour with dogs George and Mildred. Central location, from which to explore beautiful coastal Otago and only 30 minutes from Dunedin

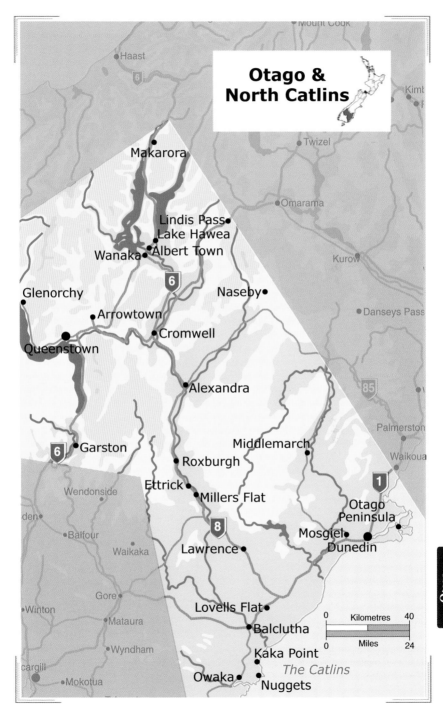

Otago & North Catlins

Haast

Kimb

Makarora

Twizel

Omarama

Lindis Pass
Lake Hawea
Wanaka • Albert Town

Kurow

6

Naseby •

Danseys Pass

Glenorchy

Arrowtown

Cromwell

Queenstown

Alexandra

85

Palmerston

Middlemarch

Waikoua

6 Garston

Roxburgh

Ettrick

Wendonside

Millers Flat

1

Otago
Peninsula

den •

8

Mosgiel

Balfour

Waikaka

Lawrence •

Dunedin

Otago
North Catlins

Gore •

Winton

Mataura

Lovells Flat •

0   Kilometres   40

Wyndham

Balclutha

0   Miles   24

cargill

Kaka Point

The Catlins

Mokotua

Owaka •

Nuggets

Makarora *65 km N of Wanaka*

Larrivee Homestay *Homestay Cottage with Kitchen*

Andrea
Makarora, via Wanaka

Tel (03) 443 9177
andipaul@xtra.co.nz
www.larriveehomestay.co.nz

Double $120 Single $80
(Continental breakfast provisions)
Children under 12 years half price
Dinner $35 BYO
Visa MC accepted
Children welcome
2 Double 2 Single (3 bdrm)
Bathrooms: 1 Ensuite 1 Private 1 Guest share

Nestled in native bush bordering Mt Aspiring National Park, our unique home and cottage are secluded, quiet and comfortable. Originally from the USA, we have lived in Makarora for over 30 years and like sharing our mountain retreat and enjoying good food and conversation. Many activities are available locally, including fishing, bird watching, jet boating, scenic flights and bush walks - including the wonderful 'Siberia Experience', fly/walk/boat trip. We are happy to help make arrangements for activities.

Makarora *65 km N of Wanaka*

Makarora Homestead *B&B Cottage with Kitchen*

Kenna Fraser & Rick McLachlan
53 Rata Road, Makarora West

Tel (03) 443 1532   Fax (03) 443 1525
bnb@makarora.com
www.makarora.com

Double $110-$120 Single $100-$110
(Continental breakfast provisions)
Restaurant in walking distance (500 m) for dinner
Visa MC accepted
Children welcome
7 Queen 1 Double 7 Twin (8 bdrm)
Bathrooms: 3 Ensuite 3 Guest share

Makarora Homestead offers a secluded retreat in the midst of the Southern Alps & is perfect for travellers looking for the peace & tranquility of the mountains. We offer a self-contained studio with kitchenette, ensuite & private balcony OR two detached bedrooms each with ensuite, tea/coffee making facilities and a sundeck. Nestled at the edge of the native forest with panoramic views of the mountains & surrounding wapiti deer farm. Hand feed our tame deer Nigel, "retired" pony Dudley & various friendly sheep.

Wanaka *1 km S of Wanaka*

Berryfarm Homestay *B&B Homestay Guest lounge*

Annette & Bob Menlove
83 Orchard Road, Wanaka, Central Otago

Tel (03) 443 4248 or 021 494 149
021 344 016
Fax (03) 443 4249
bobannette@menlove.net
www.berryfarmhomestay.co.nz

Double $150-$170 Single $150
(Full breakfast)
Visa MC accepted
Children welcome
1 King/Twin 1 Double 1 Twin (3 bdrm)
Bathrooms: 2 Ensuite 1 Private Spa and Bath

We are a small Berryfarm growing raspberries, strawberrys, boysenberries and tomatoes, on the outskirts of Wanaka just three minutes into town. Very close to very good restaurants, golf course, ski fields and fishing. We have just retired from a sheep cattle and deer farm and have been hosting for a number of years. We both enjoy meeting people. We have two cats and a labrador dog.

Wanaka *10 km N of Wanaka*

The Stone Cottage *B&B Apartment with Kitchen*
Belinda Wilson
Wanaka, RD 2, Central Otago

Tel (03) 443 1878
Fax (03) 443 1276
stonecottage@xtra.co.nz
www.stonecottage.co.nz

Double $250-$280 Single $230
(Full breakfast provisions)
Children under 12 half price
Dinner $65-$70
Visa MC accepted
1 King 1 Queen 2 Single (2 bdrm)
Bathrooms: 1 Ensuite 1 Private

5 0 years ago, a spectacular garden was created at Dublin Bay on the tranquil shores of Lake Wanaka. Its beauty still blooms today against a backdrop of the majestic Southern Alps.

Accommodation is private, comfortable and elegantly decorated.

The Stone Cottage offers two self-contained loft apartments with breathtaking views over lake Wanaka to snow clad alps beyond. Featuring your own bathroom, bedroom, kitchen, living room and balcony. Television, DVD, Video, CD player, fax and email available. Private entrance.

Enjoy breakfast at leisure, made from fresh ingredients from your well stocked fully equipped kitchen, Pre-dinner drinks, delicious three course dinner and NZ wines or a gourmet picnic hamper is available by arrangement.

Walk along the beach just four minutes from The Stone Cottage or wander in the enchanting garden. Guests can experience trout fishing, nature walks, golf, boating, horse riding, wine tasting and ski fields nearby. Only ten minutes from Wanaka, this is the perfect retreat for those who value privacy and the unique beauty of this area. Relax in the magic atmosphere at The Stone Cottage and awake to the dawn bird chorus of native bellbirds and fantails.

Wanaka *0.4 km E of Central Wanaka*

Lake Wanaka Homestay *B&B Homestay*

Gailie & Peter Cooke
85 Warren Street, Wanaka

Tel (03) 443 7995 or 0800 443 799
Fax (03) 443 7945
wanakahomestay@xtra.co.nz
www.lakewanakahomestay.co.nz

Double $120-$130 Single $85-$90 (Full breakfast)
Visa MC accepted
Not suitable for children
2 Double (2 bdrm)
Bathrooms: 1 Guest share, Great Shower

Welcome to our home. Relax and enjoy breathtaking views of lake and mountains, just five minutes walk to shops, restaurants, lake. Peter, keen fly fisherman, is happy to show guests where to find the big ones. Complimentary tea, coffee, home-made cookies during your stay. Warm home, cooked breakfast, comfortable beds, electric blankets, bedroom heaters, We have shared our home with guests for many years, making wonderful friendships. We both enjoy meeting people, fishing, golf, skiing, walking, gardening. Kate, our labrador dog is everyone's friend.

Wanaka *3 km N of Wanaka Central*

Beacon Point *B&B Homestay Apartment with Kitchen*

Diana & Dan Pinckney
302 Beacon Point Road, PO Box 6, Lake Wanaka

Tel (03) 443 1253 or 027 246 0222
027 435 4847
Fax (03) 443 1254
dan.di@lakewanaka.co.nz
www.beaconpoint.co.nz

Double up to $120 Single up to $90
(Continental breakfast)
Children $30 Dinner $40 Rolla beds available
Pet free home Children welcome
1 Queen 1 Twin (2 bdrm)
Bathrooms: 1 Ensuite

Beacon Point B&B has an acre of lawn and garden for your enjoyment. Leads to a walking track to the village around the edge of the lake. Private spacious studio with ensuite, queen and single beds (two rooms), kitchen, TV, DVD, sundeck and BBQ. Studio equipped with every need for perfect stay. We enjoy planning your days with you. Our intrests include farming, forestry, fly fishing, real estate, boating, gardening and grandchildren. Turn right at lake - Lakeside Road - then to Beacon Point Road 302.

Wanaka *1.3 km S of Wanaka*

Harpers *B&B Homestay*

Jo & Ian Harper
95 McDougall Street, Wanaka

Tel (03) 443 8894
Fax (03) 443 8834
harpers@xtra.co.nz
www.harpers.co.nz

Double $140 Single $100
(Continental breakfast)
Visa MC accepted
1 King/Twin 2 Single (2 bdrm)
Bathrooms: 1 Ensuite 1 Private
Bath & Shower with twin room

We take pride in offering a friendly, comfortable home. Share breakfast and awesome lake and mountain views with us. Also explore our extensive garden, which provides a tranquil environment for relaxing. We offer a drink and muffins on your arrival. This is a smoke-free home. Recent guests' comments: "Wonderful welcoming homestay."Friendly hosts, excellent breakfasts. "Wonderful hospitality, fantastic breakfast." "Excellent hosts, breakfasts to die for." "Very comfortable. Great hosts. Top spot." "Wonderful views. The muffins and pancakes do live up to expectations." "A home from home."

Wanaka *4 km S of Wanaka*

Stonehaven *Homestay*

Deirdre & Dennis
Halliday Lane, RD 2, Wanaka

Tel (03) 443 9516
Fax (03) 443 9513
moghul@xtra.co.nz
www.stonehaven.co.nz

Double $125 Single $95 (Full breakfast)
Children $20 negotiable
Portacots and highchairs available
Visa MC accepted
Children and pets welcome
2 Queen 2 Single (2 bdrm)
Bathrooms: 1 Private

Our home is set in two acres about five minutes drive from Wanaka. All beds have electric blankets. Tea and coffee is freely available. We have extensive views of surrounding mountains. Children are welcome and child care by arrangement. Our nearby tree collection has an accent on autumn colour. Local walks a speciality. Organic fruit both in season and preserved. We have a small dog and a cat. No smoking inside please. Please phone for directions.

Wanaka *2 km NW of Wanaka Central*

Lake Wanaka Home Hosting *B&B Homestay*

Joyce & Lex Turnbull
19 Bill's Way, Wanaka

Tel (03) 443 9060
Fax (03) 443 1626
lex.joy@xtra.co.nz
www.lakewanakahomehosting.co.nz

Double $110-$150 Single $70 (Full breakfast)
Children under 10 $25
Dinner $40
Pet free home
Children welcome
1 King/Twin 1 Double 1 Twin (3 bdrm)
Bathrooms: 2 Private

We welcome visitors to Wanaka, enjoy sharing our natural surroundings with others. We have a large peaceful home where our guests can experience not only the austerity of the lake and mountains around them, but also experience the ambience of Wanaka itself. Guest room with super king bed has adjoining TV lounge with TV, tea & coffee facilities, private bathroom. Good laundry facilities. We wish your stay in Wanaka will be a very happy one. Directions: please ring for directions. We enjoy your company.

Wanaka *2.5 km E of Wanaka*

Riverside *B&B Homestay*

Lesley & Norman West
11 Riverbank Road, RD 2, Wanaka

Tel (03) 443 1522 or 027 464 0333
Fax (03) 443 1522
n.l.west@paradise.net.nz
www.riversidewanaka.co.nz

Double $140-$180 Single $90-$100
(Full breakfast)
Visa MC accepted
1 King 1 Queen 2 Twin (3 bdrm)
Bathrooms: 1 Ensuite 1 Private 1 Guest share

We welcome guests to the quiet location of our quality home with extensive grounds. Overlooking the Cardrona River with sweeping mountain and rural views.Located 100 metres off SH84, five minutes drive from the Lake and Wanaka's excellent restaurants. Individually decorated and well appointed rooms offer high level comfort. Enjoy the open fire and central heating in winter, shady terraces in summer. Delicious continental, home-cooked breakfasts and friendly hosts ensures your stay will be enjoyable. We have two cats and a small dog (outdoors).

Otago
North Catlins

Wanaka *0.2 km E of Wanaka Central*

Te Wanaka Lodge *B&B Guest House*
Graeme & Andy Oxley
23 Brownston Street, Wanaka

Tel (03) 443 9224
Freephone 0800 WANAKA (0800 926252)
Fax (03) 443 9246
tewanakalodge@xtra.co.nz
www.tewanaka.co.nz

Double $160-$199 Single $150-$185 (Full breakfast)
Garden cottage room $230 ($250 for 3 persons)
Visa MC Amex Eftpos accepted
9 Queen 4 Twin (13 bdrm)
Bathrooms: 13 Ensuite

Owned & run by outdoor enthusiasts, the lodge is a place for active people who want to get out & explore our picturesque town and locale. Get good advice from your hosts about all the local walks and great things to do. Te Wanaka enjoys a reputation as a relaxed, fun and friendly place to stay.

After an adventurous day exploring our mountains, lake & streams, guests can soak in the private garden hot tub/spa, sit back in one of our comfy lounges or enjoy the sun in our pretty courtyard garden.

- All bedrooms with ensuite and private balcony - LCD Flat Screen TV (5 Channels Sky) - Delicious full cooked breakfast included - Vegetarian, gluten & dairy free breakfast options available - Guest Lounges with Log Fire & Library - Wireless & High Speed internet available - House Bar specialising in local beers and wines - In-house therapeutic massage - Mountain Bike Hire - Luggage storage - Laundry service - Gear drying room (Ski & other)

Wanaka *2.3 km NW of Wanaka Centre*
Peak-Sportchalet *B&B Fully Self-contained Chalet*
Alex & Christine Schafer
36 Hunter Crescent, Wanaka 9305

Tel (03) 443 6990
Fax (03) 443 4969
stay@peak-sportchalet.co.nz
www.Peak-Sportchalet.co.nz

Double $110-$155 **Single** $90-$100 (Special breakfast)
Visa MC accepted
Pet free home   Children welcome
1 King 1 Queen 1 Twin (3 bdrm)
Bathrooms: 2 Ensuite 1 Private underfloor-
heating(Chalet); hairdryer; high quality showers

Welcome at Peak-Sportchalet - your Qualmark 4 Star accommodation in Wanaka. Experience ambience and hospitality in our three guest suites and selfcontained Chalet. All are individually designed and appointed with fine furniture, ensuite or private bathrooms, TV, DVD and Sound System. Sliding doors open onto private sundecks with great mountain views. Awake refreshed after a relaxing nights sleep on our prime quality mattresses and duvets. Start your day healthy with our memorable breakfast-buffet. We also cater for special diets.

Wanaka - Albert Town *6 km N of Wanaka*
Riversong *B&B Homestay*
Ann & Ian Horrax
5 Wicklow Terrace, Albert Town, RD 2, Wanaka

Tel (03) 443 8567 or 021 113 6397
Fax (03) 443 8564
info@happyhomestay.co.nz
www.happyhomestay.co.nz

Double $140-$160 **Single** $110 (Full breakfast)
Children $25
Dinner $45pp by arrangement
Visa MC accepted
1 King/Twin 1 Queen 1 Single (3 bdrm)
Bathrooms: 1 Ensuite 1 Private

Riversong is five minutes from Wanaka Township, at Albert Town, on the banks of the majestic Clutha River. At our secluded haven all rooms have river and mountain views, with immediate access to the river. Ann's background is healthcare and Ian's law. We invite you to share the comforts and privacy of our home and garden and Ian's knowledge of the region's fishing and guidance service. We aim to provide a memorable and comfortable stay. We have two outside lab dogs. Wireless/broadband available.

Wanaka *2.4 km E of Wanaka*
The Cedars *B&B Homestay*
Mary & Graham Dowdall
7 Riverbank Road, RD 2,
Wanaka 9192, Central Otago

Tel (03) 443 1544 or 021 1208 960
Fax (03) 443 1580
thecedarswanaka@xtra.co.nz
www.thecedars.co.nz

Double $185-$215 **Single** $145-$165 (Full breakfast)
Children are very welcome.
Dinner by arrangement with 24 hours notice
Visa MC accepted
2 Queen 1 Single (2 bdrm)
Bathrooms: 1 Ensuite 1 Private with spa bath

Cead Mile Failte - One hundred thousand welcomes. A warm Irish/Kiwi welcome awaits you at The Cedars, by Mary, Graham, English Collie Nessa and cat Cara. Our stone home on 11 acres includes panoramic views, expansive gardens, guest lounge with large open fire. Nearby attractions include The Maze, Warbirds Museum, golf, ski fields, walking tracks, paragliding, lakes and rivers for water pursuits: shops and restaurants. Full breakfast is served with fresh and home-made produce. We offer evening meals or BBQ by prior arrangement.

Otago
North Catlins

Wanaka *0.5 km N of Wanaka*

Criffel Peak View *B&B Apartment with Kitchen*

Caroline Holland
98 Hedditch Street, Wanaka

Tel (03) 443 5511
Fax (03) 443 5521
stay@criffelpeakview.co.nz
www.criffelpeakview.co.nz

Double $125-$140 **Single** $90-$100 (Full breakfast)
Apartment from $180 for 4 people
Visa MC accepted
Children welcome
2 King/Twin 1 King 2 Queen (3 bdrm)
Bathrooms: 2 Ensuite 2 Private

A cosy modern cottage situated in a quiet cul-de-sac, just a short walk from the lake and town. Great mountain views, large sunny deck, friendly young hosts and a crazy cat called Splodge. We are only minutes from the stunning Wanaka Golf Course and local icon the Cinema Paradiso. Our three guest rooms look out towards the Criffel Range and are equipped with super king and queen sized beds, TVs and tea/coffee facilities. Our apartment is perfect for larger groups and families.

Wanaka *0.1 km S of Wanaka Central*

Wanaka Springs Boutique Lodge *Luxury B&B*

Lyn & Murray Finn
21 Warren Street, Wanaka, Central Otago

Tel (03) 443 8421 or 027 241 4113
Fax (03) 443 8429
relax@wanakasprings.com
www.wanakasprings.com

Double $295-$330 (Full breakfast)
Visa MC Diners Amex Eftpos accepted
Not suitable for children
2 King/Twin 5 Queen 1 Twin (8 bdrm)
Bathrooms: 8 Ensuite

W elcome to Wanaka's in-town retreat, a purpose built, boutique lodge set in the tranquility of natural springs and native gardens. It is within a five minute stroll to the lakefront, golf course and Wanaka's shops, cafés, bars and restaurants. Eight spacious guestrooms, each with private ensuite, have superior king, queen or twin beds. The guest lounge has a welcoming log fire, quality furnishings, book collection and entertainment systems. Full breakfast, afternoon tea, pre-dinner drinks and nightcaps are included in the tariff.

Wanaka *2.5 km W of Wanaka*

Wanaka Jewel *Luxury B&B Homestay Separate Suite*

Pam & Bruce Mayo
7 Foxglove Heights, Far Horizon Park, Lake Wanaka

Tel (03) 443 5636 or 027 285 6234
(03) 443 2722
Fax (03) 443 2723
wanakajewel@xtra.co.nz
www.bnb.co.nz/wanakajewel.html

Double $185-$225 **Single** $170-$210 (Full breakfast)
Visa MC accepted
Not suitable for children
2 Queen (2 bdrm)
Bathrooms: 1 Ensuite 1 Private two persons spa bath

W elcome to Wanaka Jewel - a stay in paradise. Three minutes from township. Wanaka Jewel is a newly built luxury home with purpose built bed & breakfast suites set on one acre surrounded by magestic mountains and superb lake views, close to town. Own private entrance. These suites are beautifully appointed with quality linen. Complimentary pool, spa, tennis courts, gymnasium, BBQ, pitch and putting green available to guests. Complimentary tea, coffee anytime, sumptious breakfast. Be assured of a warm welcome and a memorable stay.

Wanaka *0.2 km N of Wanaka*
Shep's Place *B&B*
Heather & Murray Sheppard
21 Hedditch Street, Wanaka

Tel (03) 443 5663 or 021 058 7742
the.sheppards@xtra.co.nz
www.shepsplacewanaka.co.nz

Double $120-$150 Single $85-$110
(Full breakfast)
Children negotiable
Visa MC accepted
Children welcome
1 Queen 2 Twin (2 bdrm)
Bathrooms: 1 Private

Shep's Place offers guests an opportunity to relax and enjoy magnificent views of Lake Wanaka and surrounding mountains. The guest sitting room with television, fridge, tea, coffee and home-made biscuits opens onto a sunny balcony. Guests only on first floor - single party bookings. Family cat in residence. Less than five minute walk to restaurants. Laundry available. We look forward to meeting you.

Wanaka *1 km N of Wanaka*
Beaconfield *Luxury B&B Homestay*
Carla & Michael Rackley
251 Beacon Point Road, Wanaka

Tel (03) 443 2737 or 021 150 5760
mikerackley@xtra.co.nz
www.beaconfieldbandb.co.nz

Double $175-$225 Single $160-$175
(Full breakfast)
Visa MC accepted
Children welcome
2 Queen (2 bdrm)
Bathrooms: 2 Ensuite

Welcome to our lovely brand new home set amidst a boutique vineyard on one acre with breath-taking lake and mountain views. We invite you to share our Kiwi hospitality and local knowledge. Your guest room with ensuite has French doors opening to a verandah with stunning views. You will never tire of the beauty and tranquility. Share our interests of food, wine, music, local art, antiques, travel. Delicious, healthy breakfast and refreshments included. Carla is a nurse and Michael was a lawyer and hospital manager.

Wanaka *5 km N of Wanaka*
Ferryman's Cottage *B&B Homestay*
Marie Lewis & Bryan Lloyd
4 Arklow Street, Albert Town, RD 2, Wanaka

Tel (03) 443 4147 or 021 144 7513
Fax (03) 443 4147
ferrymanscottage@xtra.co.nz
www.ferrymanscottage.co.nz

Double $150-$165 Single $95-$115 (Full breakfast)
Visa MC accepted
2 Queen (2 bdrm)
Bathrooms: 1 Ensuite 1 Private

Ferryman's is our lovingly restored historic cottage, located five minutes from Wanaka, on the banks of the Clutha River (famous for fishing). The warmth, peace and tranquility of our home, has been created for you to enjoy. A unique garden fresh breakfast experience from Marie's kitchen awaits you. Laze in our cottage garden. Stroll, one minute to fish, or walk riverside tracks. Bryan, lawyer by day, laidback host by night, Marie, (foodie, teacher), and our cat, Indy, invite you to our corner of Paradise.

Otago
North Catlins

Wanaka *1 km N of Wanaka Central*
Oak Tree Bed & Breakfast *B&B Homestay*
Sharlene & Ray Mulqueen
4 Little Oak Common, Wanaka, 9192

Tel (03) 443 9106
Fax (03) 443 9109
r.s.mulqueen@xtra.co.nz
www.oaktreewanaka.com

Double $130-$160
(Continental breakfast)
Visa MC accepted
Pet free home
2 King (2 bdrm)
Bathrooms: 1 Ensuite 1 Private

B ed & Breakfast accommodation with spectacular mountain views, and friendly relaxed hospitality. Situated in a quiet cul-de-sac, we are within easy walking distance or a two minute drive to town. Our home is comfortable, modern and spacious and warm. A delicious breakfast is served in the dining area, while watching the morning sun over the beautiful Southern Alps. Free email and laundry. Off-street Parking.

~

Wanaka *12 km E of Wanaka*
Kanuka Lodge *B&B*
Heather & Graeme Halliday
110 Shortcut Road, SH 8A, Luggate, RD 2 Wanaka

Tel (03) 443 7448
Fax (03) 443 7448
halldy@es.co.nz

Double $90-$120 Single $70-$90
(Full breakfast)
Children $20
Visa MC accepted
Children and pets welcome
1 Queen 1 Double 1 Single (3 bdrm)
Bathrooms: 1 Guest share

O ur home is near the Clutha river, ten minutes drive from Wanaka. It features NZ art and books. We welcome you with a glass of fine NZ wine. At breakfast you must try the Central Otago apricots and Heather's wildflower honey. You can admire the alpine landscape with geologist, photographer and fisherman Graeme, and plan your exploration of Wanaka. We have friendly cats and horses. Heather, originally from Bath in England, gives rides in her vintage buggies and grows the exotic spice saffron.

~

Wanaka *50 km NW of Cromwell*
Renmore House *B&B*
Rosie & Blair Burridge
44 Upton Street, Wanaka, 9192

Tel (03) 443 6566 or 027 434 2075
Fax (03) 443 6567
renmorehouse@xtra.co.nz
www.renmore-house.co.nz

Double $185-$210 Single $150-$170
(Full breakfast)
Visa MC Eftpos accepted
Children welcome
3 King/Twin (3 bdrm)
Bathrooms: 3 Ensuite

B lair, Rosie and Sophie the cat extend a warm welcome to guests in their home. Renmore House is a luxury, purpose built B&B just two minutes walk from Wanaka village and convenient to most Wanaka activities We are committed to ensuring your every comfort and privacy in our home including assistance with travel, complimentary laundry, guest lounge and a scrumptious breakfast menu. Sounds of springfed creeks running through our garden create a peaceful ambiance for guests wishing to barbeque or just relax with a book.

Wanaka *3 km N of Post Office*

Greystones B/B *B&B*

Dorothy & Ian McDonald
219 Beacon Point Road, Wanaka

Tel (03) 443 6362 or 027 343 8885
Fax (03) 443 6062
iandorothy@paradise.net.nz

(Full breakfast)
Pet free home
Children welcome
1 Queen 1 Twin (2 bdrm)
Bathrooms: 1 Private 1 Family share

D orothy & Ian extend a very warm and friendly
welcome to Greystones. An interesting boutique
home with art, furniture, and sound surround music. With a sumptious breakfast and pre-dinner drinks.
A casual stroll to lake and town. We come from a farming background and both enjoy Golf & bridge
- only too happy to have a game of either! Ian is a fisherman and we also tend a very interesting garden.
We take pleasure in sharing our home and hope to make your stay comfortable & memorable.

Wanaka *1.5 km N of Wanaka*

Jenny's Place *B&B Apartment with Kitchen*

Jenny
24 Old Race Course Road, Wanaka

Tel (03) 443 2063
jennyfryl@xtra.co.nz

Double $110 Single $90
(Breakfast by arrangement)
Self-catering bedroom unit $145
Children and pets welcome
1 Queen 1 Twin (4 bdrm)
Bathrooms: 2 Private

M y house is on one level with attached two
bedroom apartment at the end, it has two
bedrooms in the main house. All bedrooms open out on to own terraces with table and chairs. The one
acre of garden has a Petanque court and volleyball net. At the back of the section is a walking track to the
top of the mountain or down to the lake and shops. The garden is fully fenced and reasonably safe for
children and pets. A bright and friendly home.

Wanaka *0.8 km SE of Wanaka Central*

Golfside B&B *B&B*

Lynda & David Doolan
56 Golf Course Road, Wanaka, 9305

Tel (03) 443 4581 or 021 236 0882
ddoolan@hotmail.com
www.golfsidebandb.co.nz

Double $120-$150 Single $100
(Full breakfast)
Visa MC accepted
2 King 1 Twin (2 bdrm)
Bathrooms: 2 Ensuite

G olfside, Wanaka's only accommodation
overlooking the golf course with fantastic lake and
mountain views. 10 minute walk to town, two minute drive. Purpose built in 2005 with a separate wing
to the family home. Each room has its own private access with ample parking. Feel at home in a modern,
quality bedroom that includes tea/coffee making, fridge, TV/DVD choose from our up to date selection
or browse your emails on our laptop. Friendly hosts originally from the U.K.

Lake Wanaka *1 km N of Post Office*

Black Peak Lodge *B&B Homestay*
Helen and David Rule
38 Kings Drive, Wanaka

Tel (03) 443 4078 or 027 457 3539
Fax (03) 443 4038   hellbell@xtra.co.nz
www.blackpeaklodge.co.nz

Double $140-$200 Single $120-$140 (Full breakfast)
Children gladly welcomed
Delicious diner available by arrangement with hosts
Visa MC Diners Amex accepted
2 King/Twin 2 Queen (3 bdrm)
Bathrooms: 1 Ensuite 2 Private

Welcome to Black Peak Lodge. Unwind in comfort.... in winter by the log fire, in summer on the open deck in awe of the spectacular view. Relax in the lounge, indulging in fine wines and mouthwatering appetizers whilst listening to music of your choice. Recharge and recuperate in the spa amidst the tranquil ambiance that is ....Black Peak Lodge. Join us in our recreational activities: biking, fishing, boating, water skiing, walking or enjoying time with our gorgeous Golden Retriever, Rosa Bella.

Drift off to sleep under fine bed linens, subtle lighting and the most divine pillows in your charming room. All suites ensure top of the line comfort for you. Each offers lush spa robes, television, DVD, C.D. player, phone and Internet port, along with extra touches that will make your stay unforgettable

Awake to the tantalizing aroma of newly baked food and freshly brewed coffee. Breakfast is made from the freshest local ingredients, with a wonderful selection of gourmet delights. Indulge yourself in the breakfast room, on the deck whilst basking in the sun or in the haven of your own room.

Guest Services: Tea and coffee making facilities; Extensive CD and DVD library; Outstanding mountain views; Ski storage and drying facilities; Internet and full business facilities; Restaurant, child minding and activities reservation service; Lodge available for small private party bookings.

Wanaka *2 km S of Wanaka*

Copperwood *B&B Apartment with Kitchen & Studio with Kitchenette*

Rachel and Alan Bradbery
5 Alpha Close, Wanaka 9305

Tel (03) 443 4060
Fax (03) 443 4063
stay@copperwood.co.nz
www.copperwood.co.nz

Double $120-$165 (Breakfast by arrangement)
Delicious continental breakfast hamper $20
Visa MC accepted
2 King/Twin (2 bdrm)
Bathrooms: 1 Ensuite (studio) 1 Private (apartment)

A warm welcome, great mountain views and quality accommodation awaits you at Copperwood. Purpose built in 2006, we offer a self-contained one bedroom apartment with private entrance and garden or spacious loft studio with kitchenette. Quality bed linen and furnishings throughout. Internet lounge and sunny outdoor seating area. Friendly young hosts and Tati the cat. Just two kilometres from Wanaka's restaurants, shops, galleries and close to Wanaka Golf Course, Basecamp Mountain Adventure Centre and local favourite Café Fe. Delicious continental breakfast hamper served by arrangement.

Cromwell *1 km S of Cromwell*

Stuart's Homestay *B&B Homestay*

Elaine & Ian Stuart
5 Mansor Court, Cromwell

Tel (03) 445 3636
Fax (03) 445 3617
ian.elaine@xtra.co.nz

Double $100-$130 Single $70-$80 (Full breakfast)
Dinner $25-$35 by arrangement
Visa MC accepted
Pet free home
2 Queen 2 Single (3 bdrm)
Bathrooms: 1 Ensuite 1 Guest share

Welcome to our home which is situated within walking distance to most of Cromwell's amenities. We are semi-retired Southland farmers who have been homehosting for over 15 years. Cromwell is a quiet and relaxed town with historic gold diggings, vineyards, orchards, trout fishing, boating, walks, close to ski fields. 45 minutes to Wanaka or Queenstown. Share dinner with us or just bed & breakfast. Tea and coffee, home-made cookies available. We enjoy sharing our home and garden with visitors and a friendly stay is assured.

Cromwell *1 km N of Cromwell*

Cottage Gardens *B&B Homestay Detached Twin Studio*
Jill & Colin McColl
80 Neplusultra Street, Cromwell, Central Otago

Tel (03) 445 0628
Fax (03) 445 0628
cottage.gardens@ihug.co.nz
www.southernprofile.com/cottage.html

Double $95-$105 Single $55-$75
(Continental breakfast)
Dinner $25pp by prior arrangment
Visa MC accepted   Not suitable for children
2 Twin 1 Single (3 bdrm)
Bathrooms: 1 Ensuite 2 Private

Hospitality our speciality. For 13 years we have offered travellers good food and company, Our spacious self contained studio unit. Adjacent to private garden. Twin room with private bathroom upstairs with TV and tea making. Our home, built using local stone and natural timbers over looks an 18 hole Golf course. Cromwell, surrounded by orchards, vineyards, excellent sporting facilities. Fritter is a retired pre-school cat. Members Lions International, retired orchardists and pre-school teacher. Queenstown and Wanaka 45 minutes, Fiordland, Te Anau two hours drive. Free laundry.

Cromwell *5 km N of Cromwell*

Lake Dunstan Lodge *Homestay*

Judy & Bill Thornbury
Northburn, RD 3, Cromwell

Tel (03) 445 1107 or 027 431 1415
Fax (03) 445 3062
william.t@xtra.co.nz
www.lakedunstanlodge.co.nz

Double $110-$130 Single $80 (Full breakfast)
Children negotiable
Dinner $30 by arrangement
Visa MC accepted
2 Queen 3 Single (3 bdrm)
Bathrooms: 1 Ensuite 1 Guest share

Friendly hospitality awaits you at our home privately situated beside Lake Dunstan. We are ex-Southland farmers and have a cat Ollie. Our interests include Lions, fishing, boating, gardening and crafts. Bedrooms have attached balconies, fridge, tea and coffee facilities. Guests share our living areas, spa pool and laundry. Local attractions: orchards, vineyards, gold diggings, fishing, boating, walks, four ski fields nearby. Enjoy dinner with us or just relax in the peaceful surroundings. No smoking indoors please. Directions: 5 km north of Cromwell Bridge on SH8.

Cromwell *50 km E of Queenstown*

Cherry Tree Homestay *B&B Homestay*

Adrienne & Stuart Heal
87 Inniscort Street, Cromwell, 9310

Tel (03) 445 4094 or 027 235 8820
heals@xtra.co.nz

Double $130-$150 (Full breakfast)
Dinner encouraged to join us, price negotiable
Not suitable for children
1 Queen 1 Double 1 Twin (3 bdrm)
Bathrooms: 2 Ensuite

Come stay with us at our B&B, Its name derived from our old cherry tree. Food, wine, golf, mountain air and bikes. There's plenty to do: wonderful hikes. History, vineyards, orchards and lakes. Over dinner and chat, we'll soon become good mates. Phoebe, our spaniel, she lives outdoors. Lively and friendly, she isn't a bore!!! We escaped from the city three-years ago. We really love life-wouldn't you know. Young, fit, "retired"- we've changed our pace. Come stay with us, put a smile on your face.

Arrowtown *0.5 km SW of Arrowtown*

Jopp Inn *Luxury B&B Separate Suite*

Bev & Jim Feehly
80 Cotter Avenue, Arrowtown, 9302

Tel (03) 442 1131 or 021 267 8758
Fax (03) 442 1131
jimandbev@arrowtown-jopp-inn.co.nz
www.arrowtown-jopp-inn.co.nz

Double $150-$180 Single $120-$150
(Continental breakfast provisions)
Pet free home
Not suitable for children
1 King/Twin (1 bdrm)
Bathrooms: 1 Private

Our luxurious new fully self contained apartment, close to skifields, golfcourses and wineries has superb views over the Wakatipu Basin to the surrounding mountains. The centrally heated apartment has it's own entrance, bedroom, lounge with TV and DVD, kitchenette, and bathroom with hairdryer and robes. A speciality continental breakfast hamper is provided. Off-street parking. Ten minutes easy walk to the town centre. 20 minutes drive to Queenstown. Bev and Jim have travelled widely and Jim's family have lived in Arrowtown for over 140 years.

Arrowtown *3 km S of Arrowtown*
Peony Gardens *B&B Apartment with Kitchen*
Ian & Margaret Chamberlain
231 Lake Hayes Road, RD 1, Queenstown

Tel (03) 442 1280 or 027 436 1661
Fax (03) 442 1210
ijchamberlain@xtra.co.nz

Double $130 Single $100
(Continental breakfast)
Children welcome
1 Queen 1 Double 2 Twin (2 bdrm)
Bathrooms: 1 Guest share

Our garden was the original Peony Gardens situated at Lake Hayes, between Queenstown and Historic Arrowtown. The self-contained flat has two bedrooms, full kitchen facilities, heat pump, and opens onto a balcony which looks over to the lake and our garden. A short walk will take you to the edge of the lake with wonderful views of the mountains. Easy access to four Ski Fields and four very scenic Golf Courses. We enjoy meeting people, will do all we can to make your stay memorable.

Arrowtown *20 km SE of Queenstown*
Arrowtown Heights B&B *B&B*
Rae & Winston Wallace
6 May Lane, Arrowtown

Tel (03) 442 1726 or 027 279 1552
info@arrowtownheights.com
www.arrowtownheights.com

Double $140-$170 Single $120
(Full breakfast)
Visa MC accepted
Pet free home
1 King/Twin 1 Queen (2 bdrm)
Bathrooms: 1 Ensuite 1 Private

You are always sure of a welcome at Arrowtown Heights. Our contemporary home provides spacious and luxurious accommodation in a separate wing designed especially for guests. Step out of your bedroom to sit and relax in the garden, enjoy the panoramic views or the luxury of the outdoor spa. Join us for coffee and a chat. We are happy to assist or direct you to a wide range of local sights and activities. We look forward to your visit.

Arrowtown *0.1 km E of Arrowtown*
Arrowtown Old Nick *B&B Boutique*
Lianne & Greg Collins
70 Buckingham Street, Arrowtown

Tel (03) 442 1696
Fax (03) 442 1695
arrowtownoldnick@xtra.co.nz
www.oldnick.co.nz

Double $125-$200
(Breakfast by arrangement)
Visa MC Eftpos accepted
Children welcome
4 King/Twin (4 bdrm)
Bathrooms: 4 Ensuite

Situated on beautiful tree-lined Buckingham Street is Arrowtown's original police residence - 'Old Nick'. Set well back in spacious gardens, enjoy wonderful mountain views or explore Arrowtown's historic 'Gaol' which is directly adjacent. Perfectly located to maximise your stay, 'Old Nick' is only moments away from Arrowtown's historic centre. Offering boutique accommodation, each room is tastefully finished with private facilities including tea/coffee, fridge, toaster, sky TV and private parking. 'Old Nick' offers a unique opportunity to experience the charm of Arrowtowns' history.

Arrowtown - Queenstown *4 km W of Arrowtown*

Willowbrook *B&B Apartment with Kitchen Cottage with Kitchen*
Tamaki & Roy Llewellyn
Malaghan Road, RD 1, Queenstown

Tel (03) 442 1773 or (027) 451 6739
Fax (03) 442 1780
info@willowbrook.net.nz
www.willowbrook.net.nz

Double $150-$185 Single $125-$145 (Continental breakfast)
Cottage (sleeps 4) $315
Visa MC Diners Amex accepted
2 King 2 Queen 3 Twin (7 bdrm)
Bathrooms: 5 Ensuite 1 Private

Willowbrook is a 1914 homestead at the foot of Coronet Peak in the beautiful Wakatipu Basin. The setting is rural, historical and distinctly peaceful, and with the attractions of Queenstown and Arrowtown only 15 and 5 minutes away respectively, Willowbrook can truly claim to offer the best of both worlds. Four acres of mature garden contain a tennis court, luxurious spa pool and several outhouses. The former shearers quarters have been rebuilt and a hay barn renovated allowing Willowbrook to offer varied styles of accommodation:

BED & BREAKFAST in the MAIN HOUSE centrally heated double rooms, ensuite bathrooms, guest lounge with open fires and Sky TV.

THE BARN offers spacious accommodation with kitchenette, separate from the Main House. Super king bed, ensuite bathroom, lounge area with Sky TV and barbeque deck. Annex available for extra members of same party.

THE COTTAGE is a delightfully cosy two bedroom cottage with full kitchen and laundry facilities. Ensuite bathrooms, underfloor heating throughout, Sky TV, spacious sundecks with barbeque and private lawn.

Willowbrook is within easy reach of 4 ski fields and 3 very picturesque golf courses. Tamaki and Roy are your hosts. Expect a warm welcome, friendly advice and traditional South Island hospitality.

Arrowtown - Queenstown *4 km W of Arrowtown*

Willowby Downs *B&B Homestay Farmstay*

Pam & David Mcnay
792 Malaghans Road, RD 1, Queenstown

Tel (03) 442 1714 or 027 222 0964
Fax (03) 442 1887
willowbydowns@xtra.co.nz
www.willowbydowns.co.nz

Double $130 Single $100 (Full breakfast)
Children negotiable
Visa MC accepted
Children and pets welcome
2 Queen 1 Twin 2 Single (3 bdrm)
Bathrooms: 2 Ensuite 1 Guest share

With Pam & David you are assured of a warm and friendly welcome, ex-hoteliers they are passionate and practiced in the art of southern hospitality. With tea and coffee on your arrival you can relax in this warm and sunny home environment. Willowby Downs has lovely well appointed guest rooms, electric blankets, TV, laundry options available with guests welcome to the internet, fax and telephone facilities. Pam & David are able to arrange any extra tour or special events you may require.

Arrowtown - Queenstown *14 km N of Arrowtown*

Crown View *B&B Farmstay*

Caroll & Reg Fraser
457 Littles Road, Dalefield, Queenstown 9197

Tel (03) 442 9411 or 027 449 5156
027 476 7576   Fax (03) 442 9411
info@crownview.co.nz
www.crownview.co.nz

Double $165-$190 (Full breakfast)
Dinner by arrangement   Barbeque available
Visa MC accepted
Children welcome
3 King (3 bdrm)
Bathrooms: 1 Ensuite 2 Private
Rose Room has spa bath in private bathroom

Peaceful, relaxing rural setting. Fantastic views of Remarkable mountains and Crown Range. 15 minutes from either Queenstown and Arrowtown. Three double bedrooms two with super king-size beds, one with king. Rooms have tea/coffee facilities and TVs. Relax with us and enjoy our rural lifestyle, (a home away from home) along with our two white highland westies (Dougal & Archie) sheep, cows (Issie & Bella) Alpacas (Oscar & Jimmie) and chickens. Come as a guest leave as a friend.

Arrowtown - Queenstown *12 km SE of Queenstown*

Ferry Hotel *B&B Cottage with Kitchen*

Glenys & Kevin Reynolds
92 Spence Road, Lower Shotover, Queenstown, 9371

Tel (03) 442 2194 or 0800 111 804
027 235 6104
Fax (03) 442 2190
info@ferry.co.nz
www.ferry.co.nz

Double $185-$235 Single $185-$235 (Full breakfast)
Whole House Deals - contact for further information
Children under 12 free
Visa MC accepted
1 King 1 Double 1 Twin (3 bdrm)
Bathrooms: 1 Ensuite 1 Private

Unique Historic B&B formerly a popular hotel for over 100 years now a local landmark. Hosts Kevin and Glenys have traced the hotel's history back to 1868 - photo's display this throughout. Glenys enjoys helping you to make the most of your stay in Queenstown offering advice and information and making bookings for local attractions. Kevin will advise, guide or teach Fly Fishing, Buckley our friendly English Springer likes to walk you along our beautiful track by the river. Delightful English Cottage garden.

Queenstown *0.3 km S of Queenstown Central*

The Stable *B&B Homestay*
Isobel & Gordon McIntyre
17 Brisbane Street, Queenstown 9197

Tel (03) 442 9251
Fax (03) 442 8293
gimac@queenstown.co.nz
www.thestablebb.com

Double $180-$200 Single $150
(Full breakfast)
Visa MC accepted
Pet free home
Not suitable for children
1 King 1 Double 2 Single (2 bdrm)
Bathrooms: 1 Ensuite 1 Private

A 135 year old stone stable, converted for guest accommodation, and listed by the New Zealand Historic Places Trust, shares a private courtyard with our home.

The Garden Room is in the house, providing convenience and comfort with lake and mountain views. Our home is in a quiet cul-de-sac and set in a garden abundant with rhododendrons and native birds. It is less than 100 metres from the beach where a small boat and canoe are available for guests' use. The famous Kelvin Heights Golf Course is close and tennis courts, bowling greens and ice skating rink are in the adjacent park. All tourist facilities, shops and restaurants are within easy walking distance, less than five minutes stroll on well lit footpaths. Both rooms are well heated with views of garden, lake or mountains. Tea and coffee making facilities are available at all times.

Guests share our spacious living areas and make free use of our library and laundry. A courtesy car is available to and from the bus depots. We can advise about and are booking agents for all sightseeing tours. Do allow an extra day or two for all the activities in the Queenstown region. No smoking indoors.

Your hosts, with a farming background, have bred Welsh ponies and now enjoy weaving, cooking, gardening, sailing and the outdoors. We have an interest in a successful vineyard and enjoy drinking and talking about wine. We enjoy meeting people and have travelled extensively overseas.

Directions: Follow State Highway 6A (Frankton Road) to where it veers right at the Millenium Hotel. Continue straight ahead. Brisbane Street (no exit) is second on left. Phone if necessary.

Queenstown *0.2 km E of Queenstown Central*

Queenstown
Bed & Breakfast
NUMBER 12
.... a quiet convenient location

Number Twelve *B&B Homestay Separate Suite Apartment with Kitchen*
Barbara & Murray Hercus
12 Brisbane Street, Queenstown

Tel (03) 442 9511
Fax (03) 442 9755
hercusbb@queenstown.co.nz
www.number12bb.co.nz

Double $180-$180 Single $130-$130
(Full breakfast)
Visa MC accepted
Not suitable for children
2 King/Twin (2 bdrm)
Bathrooms: 1 Ensuite 1 Private

B&B
Approved

We would like you to come and share our conveniently situated house in a quiet no exit street. You only have a five minute stroll to the town centre. We have mountain and lake views.

Our home is warm and sunny, windows double glazed and we have central heating for the winter months. Our bedrooms have TVs, coffee/tea making facilities, hair dryers and instant heaters. Our down stairs studio apartment has a separate entrance with a view of our rose garden. Email & laundry is available.

We have a solar heated swimming pool (Dec/March) the sun deck and BBQ are for your use. Our sun room is available for your comfort. Our dining room has panoramic views.

There are several easy walking routes into the town centre, restaurants, shops and tourist centres. We are very close to the lake and our botanical gardens. We will be happy to advise on tourist activities and sightseeing and make any arrangements you would wish.

Barbara has a nursing/social work background and Murray is a retired chartered accountant. We have travelled extensively within our country and overseas. We have an interest in classical/choral music.

Directions: Highway 6A until the town centre right sign-do not turn right continue straight ahead Brisbane Street second left, very sharp turn.

Queenstown *1.5 km NE of Queenstown Central*

Birchall House *B&B*

Joan & John Blomfield
118 Panorama Terrace,
Larchwood Heights, Queenstown

Tel (03) 442 9985
Fax (03) 442 9980
birchall.house@xtra.co.nz
www.zqn.co.nz/birchall

Double $150-$170 Single $120 (Continental breakfast)
Children $50
Visa MC accepted
1 Queen 2 Twin (2 bdrm)
Bathrooms: 2 Ensuite

Welcome to our home in Queenstown, purpose built to accommodate guests in a beautiful setting. At Birchall House, enjoy a magnificent 200 degree view of lake and mountains within walking distance of town centre. Guest accommodation is spacious, private, separate entrance, centrally heated, electric blankets, smoke-free. Continental or cooked breakfast available. From Frankton Road, turn up Hensman Road, left into Sunset Lane. Or, Frankton Road, turn up Suburb Street, right into Panorama Terrace. Access via Sunset Lane. Off-street parking. Visit our website: www.zqn.co.nz/birchall.

Queenstown *0.5 km N of Queenstown Central*

Anna's Cottage & Rose Suite *Cottage with Kitchen Suite with Kitchen*

Myrna & Ken Sangster
67 Thompson Street, Queenstown

Tel (03) 442 8994 or 027 693 3025
(03) 442 8881
Fax (03) 441 8994
annas.rose@xtra.co.nz

Double $125-$145 Single $95
(Breakfast by arrangement)
Extra adult $50
Visa MC Eftpos accepted
Children welcome
1 King/Twin 1 Queen (2 bdrm)
Bathrooms: 2 Ensuite

A warm welcome to Anne's Cottage and Rose Suite. The cottage has fully equipped kitchen, living room, TV, new ensuite, hairdryer, washing machine, superking bed. Quality towels and linen. Rose Suite attached to the end of our home, self-contained with small kitchen, queen bed with new ensuite, TV, washing machine. Both serviced daily. Enjoy the peaceful mountain views. Private drive and parking at the Cottage. A few minutes from central Queenstown. Breakfast available at extra charge.

Queenstown *1 km N of Queenstown*

Monaghans *B&B*

Elsie & Pat Monaghan
4 Panorama Terrace, Queenstown

Tel (03) 442 8690
Fax (03) 442 8620
patmonaghan@xtra.co.nz
www.bandbclub.com/pages/monaghan

Double $100 Single $90
(Continental breakfast)
1 Queen (1 bdrm)
Bathrooms: 1 Ensuite

Welcome to our home in a quiet location, walking distance to town. Enjoy this panoramic view while you breakfast. One couple - personal attention. Spacious comfortable room with separate entrance and garden patio. Queen bed, own bathroom, TV, fridge and tea/coffee biscuits. Interests - music, gardening, sport, travel. We will enjoy your company but respect your privacy. Off-street parking. Directions: turn right up Suburb Street off Frankton Road which is the main road into Queenstown then first right into Panorama Terrace.

Queenstown *0.8 km NW of Central Queenstown*

Coronet View Apartments & B&B
Luxury B&B Apartment with Kitchen Guest House Private B&B Hotel

Karen & Neil Dempsey
30 Huff Street, Queenstown

Tel (03) 442 6766 or 0800 89 6766
027 432 0895
Fax (03) 442 6767
stay@coronetview.com
www.coronetview.com

Double $140-$250 Single $130-$230
(Continental breakfast)
Children by arrangement
Dinner $35-$70
Apartments from $180-$700
Visa MC Eftpos accepted
Children welcome
7 King/Twin 6 King 2 Queen 2 Twin (15 bdrm)
Bathrooms: 12 Ensuite 1 Private 2 Guest share

Centrally located just ten minutes walk from town, Coronet View enjoys superb views of Coronet Peak, The Remarkables and Lake Wakatipu.

Beautifully appointed rooms offer every comfort in either hosted accommodation or private apartments. Coronet View offers luxurious guest rooms either B&B or fully self-contained private apartments.

Guest common areas occasionally shared with gorgeous persian cats include elevated and spacious dining and living areas, outdoor decks, a sunny conservatory, outdoor barbeque, pool and jacuzzi area and computers with internet access.

Bed & Breakfast - A home away from home with true kiwi hospitality. Most rooms feature super king beds with lovely quilts, sheepskin electric blankets, tiled ensuites etc.

Your hosts are knowledgeable local people who can recommend and book your activities at no extra cost.

Apartments on site aQueenstown. 1-6 bedroomed apartments. Most configurations feature ensuites, super king beds, generous living areas, fully equipped kitchens and laundries.

Queenstown *0.5 km NE of Central Queenstown*

Delfshaven *Homestay*

Irene Mertz
11 Salmond Place (off Kent Street), Queenstown

Tel (03) 441 1447
Fax (03) 441 1383
irenemertz@xtra.co.nz

Double $200 Single $150
(Special breakfast)
Visa MC accepted
Pet free home
Not suitable for children
1 Queen (1 bdrm)
Bathrooms: 1 Private

Nestled on the lower Commonage, close to town, in a quiet street, is my warm, modern two storied home, offering great hospitality, magnificent views in all rooms over lake, mountains, and township. The comfortable guest suite, with TV, and tea making facilities, opens to the views and garden. It is a five minute downhill walk to the town.I am a retired teacher, widely travelled, enjoy good food and wine, love art, music, and meeting people. My piano waits to be played, A warm welcome awaits.

Queenstown *1.3 km N of Queenstown*

Matterhorn Chalet Lodge *Luxury B&B Homestay*

Maria & Joe Arnold
20 Wakatipu Heights, Queenstown
PO Box 1427, Queenstown

Tel (03) 441 3935
Fax (03) 441 3935
info@matterhornchalet.com
www.matterhornchalet.com

Double $230-$270 Single $220-$240
(Full breakfast)
Visa MC accepted
3 King 1 Queen 2 Single (4 bdrm)
Bathrooms: 1 Ensuite 1 Private 1 Guest share

Imagine a European alpine lodge magically moved to the shores of Lake Wakatipu. Matterhorn Chalet is a luxury B&B with views as breath-taking as any in Europe (all rooms have lake views). Only 15 minutes walk to the bustling heart of downtown Queenstown. For peace and tranquility stay; this is the place for you. Great breakfasts. Maria and Joe speak English, Swiss, German and Dutch. For the most panoramic views over Remarkables and Lake Wakatipu. We provide a courtesy shuttle to Queenstown Airport.

Queenstown *1.2 km N of Queenstown*

Campbells on Earnslaw *B&B*

Aderianne & Bevan Campbell
9 Earnslaw Terrace, Queenstown

Tel (03) 442 7783
Fax (03) 442 7784
stay@campbells.net.nz
www.campbells.net.nz

Double $175 Single $135
(Full breakfast)
Extra person $50
Children welcome
1 Queen 2 Single (2 bdrm)
Bathrooms: 1 Private

We look forward to welcoming you to our home, which has 180 degree spectacular panoramic views of lake, mountains and golf course. Guests own private living room with balcony, TV, fridge, toast, tea & coffee making facilities. Ideal for two couples or family, only one party at a time. Experienced hosts we can advise and arrange your sightseeing and activities. From Frankton Road turn up Suburb Street, right into Panorama Terrace, right into Earnslaw Terrace. We are only a ten minute stroll into town centre.

Queenstown *3 km N of Queenstown Centre*

Larch Hill B&B/Homestay *B&B Homestay Apartment with Kitchen*
Lesley & Chris Marlow
16 Panners Way, Queenstown

Tel (03) 442 4811 or 027 339 6483
Fax (03) 441 8882   info@larchhill.com
www.larchhill.com

Double $130-$180 Single $110 (Special breakfast)
Apartment (sleeps 4) $195-$275
Visa MC Amex accepted   Children welcome
2 King 1 Queen 1 Twin 2 Single (4 bdrm)
Bathrooms: 2 Ensuite 2 Private
All rooms have ensuite or private bathroom

Lesley and Chris offer you a warm welcome to Larch Hill B&B in beautiful Queenstown, purpose built on an elevated site overlooking Lake Wakatipu.

As featured in 'National Geographic Traveler Magazine' 2006 and Cathay Pacific's 'Discovery' Magazine 2004, all rooms in our comfortable and relaxing homestay have spectacular lake and mountain views, with tea/coffee making facilities. A restful theme flows through the bedrooms into the dining room with its library, opening onto a sunny courtyard surrounded by cottage gardens.

We are just three minutes drive from the centre of Queenstown and within walking distance of the lake. Public transport passes our street regularly. Breakfasts are generous with home-made bread, freshly baked croissants and pastries, fresh fruit salad, yoghurt, and freshly ground, percolated coffee.

Our self-contained apartment is ideal for families or small groups. We can provide pre-arranged complimentary pickups from Queenstown airport. Feel free to use our local knowledge to help plan your itinerary. We are booking agents for Queenstown tours and activities. We have no pets and are non-smokers, but guests are welcome to smoke outdoors. Fax, email and wireless internet facilities available.

Some guest comments: "Wonderful stay, informed hosts, excellent food!" - Tim and Karen, Arizona "A highlight of our trip. You are warm hosts, knowledgeable and great sense of humour. Thanks." - Bob & Mary, Utah "What a wonderful place! With fantastic hospitality - 5 star at least." - Elizabeth, Oxford

Directions: from Frankton drive 2.5 km on State Highway 6A (Frankton Road) towards Queenstown. Turn into Goldfield Heights at Sherwood Manor. Second left is Panners Way. Larch Hill B&B is No. 16 at the end of the accessway, _ way down Panners Way on the left.

Otago
North Catlins

Queenstown *2 km N of Queenstown*
Lake Vista Bed & Breakfast *Luxury B&B*

Lucille & Graeme Simpson
62 Hensman Road, Queenstown, 9300

Tel (03) 441 8838   Fax (03) 441 8938
bookings@lakevista.co.nz
www.lakevista.co.nz

Double $160-$220 Single $110-$175 (Full breakfast)
Children welcome
Dinner by arrangement
Wireless internet available
Visa MC Amex Eftpos accepted
1 King/Twin 2 Queen 2 Twin 1 Single (3 bdrm)
Bathrooms: 1 Ensuite 1 Guest share

Set high on Queenstown hill, a major feature of Lake Vista is our encompassing views over Lake Wakatipu to the Remarkables mountain range. You can even enjoy the view lying in bed ñ imagine that! We offer wireless internet for your laptop or use our guest computer. All rooms have their own mini-bars, security boxes, TV, hair dryers, underfloor heating, electric blankets, heated towel-rails, radio/alarms and tea/coffee facilities. Gourmet breakfasts complete the package. Be pampered with the personal attention of your hosts, Lucille & Graeme.

Queenstown *1.4 km SE of Queenstown*
Kemnay *B&B*

Heather & Fraser Ronald
57 Panorama Terrace, Queenstown

Tel (03) 442 6270
hfronald@xtra.co.nz

Double $130 Single $100
(Full breakfast)
Children by arrangement
1 Queen 1 Twin (2 bdrm)
Bathrooms: 1 Private Bath & Shower

Heather and Fraser warmly welcome you to their Queenstown Home. Wonderful views of lake and mountains, also overlooks golf course. Queen bed, plus twin, private bathroom. Small comfortable seating area with tea and coffee making facilities. One party at a time. Off street parking. 1.4 km from town centre.Directions: Approaching Queenstown along Frankton Road, turn right into Hensman Road, then first turn left inot Panorama Terrace.

Queenstown *2 km E of Queenstown*
5 Star Lane *Luxury B&B*

Merlin and Raymond Sansom
5 Star Lane, Queenstown, 9300

Tel (03) 441 8118 or 021 165 5115
Fax (03) 441 8116
stay@5starlane.com
www.5starlane.com

Double $185-$265 Single $165-$245
(Full breakfast)
Visa MC Amex Eftpos accepted
Children welcome
2 King/Twin (2 bdrm)
Bathrooms: 2 Ensuite

Enjoy all the comforts of home in a four season paradise. 5 Star Lane is a modern house built with guests in mind. We have two guest bedrooms, each with lake and mountain views, ensuite bathroom, air-conditioning and private patio. Relax in the guest lounge/dining room with a cosy fire in winter and air-conditioning in summer. We take pride in our personal service. Take advantage of our Sauna, drying room, PC with Email access or wireless LAN, TV, games, videos and extensive breakfast menu.

Queenstown *14.5 km SE of Queenstown*
Bayswater *B&B*
Marie & Angus Buchanan
4 Cedar Drive, Kelvin Heights, Queenstown, 9300

Tel (03) 441 2336 or 027 424 1890
vinnetta@kol.co.nz

Double $140-$155 Single $90-$110
(Continental breakfast)
2 King/Twin 1 Queen (2 bdrm)
Bathrooms: 2 Ensuite

We would like to welcome you to our warm sunny Kelvin Heights home, with spectacular lake and mountain views. Our rooms have comfortable beds, electric blankets, heaters and own television. Tea/coffee facilities available. We are a 15 minute senic drive to downtown Queenstown. ¹/₂ hour drive to either Coronet or Remarkables ski fields, two minute walk to the beach and amazing walking tracks. A five minute drive to the spectacular Kelvin Heights Golf course and less than ¹/₂ hour to the Arrowtown or Milbrook courses

Garston *50 km S of Queenstown*
Menlove Homestay *B&B Homestay Separate Suite*
Bev & Matt Menlove
17 Blackmore Road, Garston 9750
PO Box 39, Garston

Tel (03) 248 8516
mattmenlove@xtra.co.nz

Double $90 Single $50
(Continental breakfast)
Dinner $25 by arrangement
1 Double 1 Single (1 bdrm)
Bathrooms: 1 Ensuite

We are organic gardeners and our other interests include lawn bowls, sailing, gliding and alternative energy. Garston is New Zealand's most inland village with the Mataura River (famous for its fly fishing) flowing through the valley, surrounded by the Hector Range and the Eyre Mountains. A fishing guide is available with advance notice. For day trips, Garston is central to Queenstown, Te Anau, Milford Sound or Invercargill. We look forward to meeting you.

Garston *50 km S of Queenstown*
Naylor House *Cottage with Kitchen*
John & Avis McIver
33 Naylor Road, Garston, Southland

Tel (03) 248 8809 or 027 653 6110
Fax (03) 248 8809
naylorhouse@slingshot.co.nz
www.naylorhouse.co.nz

Double $150 (Breakfast by arrangement)
Dinner by arrangement
Visa MC accepted
Pet free home
Children welcome
1 King/Twin 1 Queen 2 Twin (3 bdrm)
Bathrooms: 1 Private

Welcome to Historic Naylor House situated in the heart of the beautiful and tranquil Garston Valley. Garston is Central to Queenstown, Te Anau, Milford Sound and Invercargill. The Mataura River which is famed for its fly fishing is on our doorstep. We look forward to sharing all our local knowledge and our beautiful location with you

Otago
North Catlins

Alexandra - Earnscleugh *6 km W of Alexandra*

Iversen *Separate Suite Orchardstay*
Robyn & Roger Marshall
47 Blackman Road, RD 1 Alexandra, Central Otago

Tel (03) 449 2520
Fax (03) 449 2519
r.r.marshall@xtra.co.nz
www.otagocentral.com

Double $150 Single $100 (Continental breakfast)
Children by arrangement
Dinner $25 by arrangement
Visa MC accepted
Children welcome
2 Queen (2 bdrm)
Bathrooms: 2 Ensuite

Our seperate guest accommodation offers you privacy and comfort. Combined with a warm welcome into our home, you can share with us, the peaceful and relaxing setting of our cherry orchard. While at Iversen you can experience the grandeur and contrasts of the Central Otago landscape, walk the thyme covered hills, visit local wineries or just relax. Directions: from Alexandra or Clyde, travel on Earnscleugh Road, turn into Blackman Road and look for our sign on the left. Advanced bookings preferred.

Alexandra *3.5 km N of Alexandra*

Duart *B&B Homestay*
Mary & Keith McLean
Bruce's Hill Lane, Rapid No. 356,
Highway 85, RD 3, Alexandra 9393

Tel (03) 448 9190 or 027 316 3569
Fax (03) 448 9190 duart.homestay@xtra.co.nz
www.duarthomestay.co.nz

Double $100 Single $80 (Continental breakfast)
Children negotiable   Dinner $25 by arrangement
Visa MC accepted   Children and pets welcome
1 Double 1 Twin 1 Single (3 bdrm)
Bathrooms: 1 Ensuite 1 Guest share

Your accredited Kiwi Hosts, Mary and Keith, welcome you to our secluded home, five minutes from Alexandra. Your privacy is assured, but we enjoy company and conversation if that is your wish. Relish the spectacular views from our extensive stone terraced garden, or relax in the sitting room, library or verandahs. Revel in the myriad activities and experiences Alexandra offers; e.g. the climate, Rail Trail, award winning vineyards, galleries, mountain biking, kayaking etc. Laundry, Sky TV. Complimentary tea, coffee, biscuits, fruit, pre-dinner drink and nibbles.

Naseby *12 km N of Ranfurly and just 200 metres from Naseby Village Green*

The Old Doctor's Residence Luxury B&B *Luxury B&B*
Jan and Grant Bean
58 Derwent Street, Naseby, Central Otago

Tel (03) 444 9775 or 027 477 3458
info@olddoctorsresidence.co.nz
www.olddoctorsresidence.co.nz

Double $245-$295 (Special breakfast)
Superb dinner menu featuring local specialties B/A
Single by arrangement
Visa MC accepted
2 Superking/Twin (2 bdrm)
Bathrooms: 1 Ensuite 1 Private

First an 1870's goldminer's cottage; then a gracious home for the local doctor; now an elegantly refurbished residence providing luxury accommodation for peaceful retreats or action-packed adventures in a region described as a World of Difference. Relax in your own guest lounge with tea and coffee making facilities, home cooking, library, Sky TV, and broadband access. Join hosts Jan and Grant for pre-dinner tasting of world renowned Central Otago wines and hors d'oeuvres. Enjoy sumptuous beds, beautiful linen and colonial antique furniture. Very special breakfasts.

Middlemarch *4 km SW of Middlemarch*

The Farm *Homestay Farmstay*
Lynley & Glynne Smith
Farm Road, RD 2, Middlemarch

Tel (03) 464 3610 or 027 436 2423
021 224 3004   Fax (03) 464 3612
glynley@xtra.co.nz
www.thefarm-homestay.com

Double $110 Single $75 (Full breakfast)
Dinner $35pp
Children and pets welcome
1 King 1 Twin (2 bdrm)
Bathrooms: 1 Guest share Spa available outside

Our charming old stone house and gardens are set amounst mature oaks, with the spectacular Rock and Pillar Range as a backdrop. Lynley & Glynne welcome you to their peaceful relaxed haven which includes a 200 acre farm, sheep, cattle, horses, two family cats and a Jack Russell dog. From high country farming background, interested in horses, hunting and a tranquil lifestyle. On the Central Otago Rail Trail, one hour from Dunedin, this is a convenient and hospitable stop for exploring this picturesque area. Guests can be picked up from Dunedin airport with their bikes, over night and then can be delivered to Clyde -cost $100 for each trip.

Roxburgh - Ettrick *17 km SW of Ettrick*

Wilden Station Homestead *B&B Homestay Farmstay*
Sarah & Peter Adam
Wilden School Road, near Dunrobin,
West Otago 9587

Tel (03) 204 8115
Fax (03) 204 8116
wildenstation@xtra.co.nz

Double $180 Single $120 (Special breakfast)
Children $20
Dinner $40
Visa MC accepted
2 Queen 2 Twin (3 bdrm)
Bathrooms: 1 Ensuite 1 Private

Experience high-country farm life with us, our two boys and two cats. Watch our dogs work the sheep. Stroll through trees to a small lake, explore our historic farm buildings, fish the Pomahaka River, tour the property by vehicle or on horseback, or simply relax in our gracious homestead. Enjoy superb meals prepared by your internationally experienced chef/hostess (all by prior arrangement). Unwind in our tranquil surroundings about two hours from Dunedin, Queenstown, Wanaka. Families most welcome. Please telephone for directions.

Roxburgh - Millers Flat *16 km S of Roxburgh*

Quince Cottage *B&B Cottage No Kitchen*
Wendy Gunn & Cally Johnstone
Rapid No 1581, Teviot Road, Millers Flat

Tel (03) 446 6889
thequince@clear.net.nz
www.quincecottage.co.nz

Double $220 Single $125
(Special breakfast)
Dinner $65pp
Visa MC accepted
1 Queen (1 bdrm)
Bathrooms: 1 Ensuite

Quince Cottage - half way between Dunedin and Queenstown/Wanaka or a destination in itself. The Cottage is set apart from the house surrounded by a big open garden dotted with trees, and lawn stretching into the distance. It is open plan with a dining table, TV, CD player, fridge, air-con and heating. Meals are served in the main house, however if you wish to dine in the cottage we are happy to deliver your meals. Dinner is $65pp - 3 courses and complimentary Central Otago wine.

Otago
North Catlins

Lawrence *30 km N of Balclutha*
The Ark *B&B*

Frieda Betman
8 Harrington Place (Main Road), Lawrence

Tel (03) 485 9328
the.ark@xtra.co.nz
www.theark.co.nz

Double $90 Single $50
(Full breakfast)
Children $15
2 Double 1 Twin 1 Single (4 bdrm)
Bathrooms: 1 Family share

My home is on the main road near the picnic ground with its avenue of poplars. The house is 100 years old, has character, charm and a lived in feeling. It's home to Ambrose & Pumpkin, my cats and Holly, a miniature Foxie. Guestrooms are restful with fresh flowers, fruit, and breakfast includes hot bread, croissants, home-made jams. Free-range eggs. There is a lovely peaceful atmosphere in our early gold mining town. Approx. 45 minutes to Dunedin airport, just over an hour to Dunedin.

Dunedin *2 km W of Dunedin*
Magnolia House *B&B*

Joan & George Sutherland
18 Grendon Street, Maori Hill, Dunedin 9001

Tel (03) 467 5999
Fax (03) 467 5999
mrsuth@paradise.net.nz

Double $120 Single $100
(Special breakfast)
Not suitable for children
1 Queen 1 Double 2 Single (3 bdrm)
Bathrooms: 1 Private 1 Family share

Our quiet turn-of-the-century villa sits in broad, flower-bordered lawns backed by native bush with beautiful, tuneful birds. All rooms have electric heating, comfortable beds with electric blanket, and antiques, while the queen room has an adjoining balcony. Close by is Moana Pool, the glorious Edwardian house Olveston, and Otago Golf Course. Our special breakfast will set you up for the day. We have a courtesy car, and a burmese cat. It is not suitable for children or smokers.

Dunedin *7 km NE of Dunedin*
Harbourside B&B *B&B Homestay*

Shirley & Don Parsons
6 Kiwi Street, St Leonards, Dunedin

Tel (03) 471 0690
Fax (03) 471 0063
harboursidebb@xtra.co.nz

Double $85-$100 Single $70-$100
(Full breakfast)
Children $20
Dinner $25
Visa MC accepted
Children welcome
1 King/Twin 2 Queen 3 Single (3 bdrm)
Bathrooms: 1 Ensuite 1 Guest share

We are situated in a quiet suburb overlooking Otago Harbour and surrounding hills. Within easy reach of all local attractions. Lovely garden or harbour views from all rooms. Children very welcome. Directions: drive into city on one-way system watch for Highway 88 sign follow Anzac Avenue onto Ravensbourne Road. Continue approx 5 km to St Leonards turn left at Playcentre opposite Boatshed into Pukeko Street then left into Kaka Road, straight ahead to Kiwi Street turn left into Number 6.

Dunedin *1 km W of Dunedin Central*
Highbrae Guesthouse *B&B Guest House*
Fienie & Stephen Clark
376 High Street, City Rise, Dunedin

Tel (03) 479 2070 or 027 4328 470
Fax (03) 479 2100   highbrae@xtra.co.nz
www.highbrae.co.nz

Double $100-$130 Single $80-$100
(Continental breakfast)   Cooked breakfast extra
Children $25 if sharing room with parents
Visa MC Amex accepted
Pet free home Children welcome
1 King 2 Queen 1 Twin 1 Single (4 bdrm)
Bathrooms: 1 Private 1 Guest share 1 Family share

Experience a taste of early Dunedin. This heritage home was built on the High Street in 1908 to provide first class accommodation to its residents. Today it is still an impressive home with spectacular views of the city and harbour. The upstairs guest rooms and self contained unit are carefully restored to preserve their character for visitors, who delight in the many features in the home. Wireless internet is available and a courtesy van can meet you at the bus or train if required.

Dunedin *1 km W of Dunedin*
Grandview *Luxury B&B Guest House*
Steve Scott
360 High Street, Dunedin 9001

Tel (03) 474 9472 or 021 101 9857
Fax (03) 474 9473
nzgrandview@msn.com
www.grandview.co.nz

Double $95-$195 Single $75-$140
(Continental breakfast)   Extra person or child $25
Visa MC Diners Amex Eftpos accepted
Children welcome
1 King 3 Queen 1 Double 1 Twin 4 Single (7 bdrm)
Bathrooms: 2 Ensuite 1 Private 2 Guest share

Grandview is centrally located! The casino, restaurants, shops, cafés and bars are only a short stroll away! Relax in luxury in this charming 1901 heritage listed Edwardian mansion. Featuring magnificent panoramic views from our viewing platforms and spa area. Television, videos, free internet, free laundry facilities and scrumptious continental breakfasts are all a complimentary part of the Grandview experience. Rooms to suit all budgets! From comfortable standard rooms to our luxury trendy spa suites for your pleasure!

Dunedin *1 km S of Dunedin Central*
City Sanctuary Bed &Breakfast *B&B*
Karen & Paul
165 Maitland Street, City Rise, Dunedin

Tel (03) 474 5002   Fax (03) 474 5006
bnbenquiry@citysanctuary.co.nz
www.citysanctuary.co.nz

Double $120-$175 Single $100-$145
(Special breakfast)   Children by arrangment
Rates for multi night on request
Visa MC accepted
Not suitable for children
3 Queen (3 bdrm)
Bathrooms: 1 Ensuite with double spa bath 2 Private

Welcome to our attractive restored villa, in an oasis of cottage gardens, yet only 1 km to the city centre and all its attractions. Three spacious bedrooms each have; Queen bed with fleecy electric blanket, bath robes, fresh flowers, oil heater, phone, TV, and free broadband internet connection. Relax in the guest living room with home theatre, and free email, or unwind on the deck amidst the organic potager garden. Enjoy a special continental breakfast. Massage available by appointment. Five cats. Not Suitable Mobility impaired.

Dunedin *0.5 km SW of Dunedin*

Deacons Court *B&B*

Neil Sutherland & Jo Howie
342 High Street, Dunedin 9016

Tel (03) 477 9053 or 0800 268 252
Fax (03) 477 9058
info@deaconscourt.com
www.deaconscourt.com

Double $100-$160 Single $80-$120 (Full breakfast)
Children $20-$30
Visa MC accepted
Children welcome
2 King/Twin 2 King 1 Queen 3 Single (3 bdrm)
Bathrooms: 2 Ensuite 1 Private

Deacons Court is a charming superior spacious Victorian villa 1km walking distance from the city centre and is on the city's heritage building register. We are only 500 meters from cafés, bars and some of Dunedin's unique attractions and offer you friendly but unobtrusive hospitality in a quiet secure haven. Guests can relax in our delightful rose garden and conservatory. Our bedrooms are large, have ensuite or private bathrooms, TV and comfortable seating. Complimentary broadband, 24 hour tea or coffee, and free parking available.

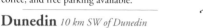

Dunedin *10 km SW of Dunedin*

Grant's Farm *B&B Apartment with Kitchen*

Tom and Jeanette Grant
151 Old Brighton Road, Fairfield, Dunedin 9076

Tel (03) 488 0336 or 027 617 3351
Fax (03) 488 0364
grantsfarm@xtra.co.nz
www.visit-dunedin.co.nz/grantsfarm.html

Double $110-$130 Single $90-$110
(Continental breakfast provisions)
Children by negotiation   Dinner not supplied
Visa MC accepted
Pet free home   Not suitable for children
1 Queen 1 Double 1 Single (2 bdrm)
Bathrooms: 1 Private

Our typical NZ woolshed on 20ha is now a unique home with private fully self contained guest accommodation. Situated on the Kaikorai Estuary we have heaps of bird life as well as sheep and cattle. We are in a peaceful rural setting with wonderful views, only 15 minutes from Dunedin Airport and eight minutes to either Dunedin or Mosgiel. Excellent restaurants and miles of beach walks are only minutes away. One loving outdoor cat only.Guests wish they could stay longer!

Otago Peninsula - Broad Bay *16 km E of Dunedin*

Chy-an-Dowr *B&B*

Susan & Herman van Velthoven
687 Portobello Road, Broad Bay, Dunedin

Tel (03) 478 0306 or 021 036 5190
021 156 0715
hermanvv@xtra.co.nz
www.chy-an-dowr.co.nz

Double $175-$245 (Special breakfast)
Visa MC accepted
1 King/Twin 1 King 1 Queen (3 bdrm)
Bathrooms: 1 Ensuite 1 Private

Chy-an-Dowr (House by the Water), a quality B&B located midway on scenic Otago Peninsula. Our character 1920's home with its harbourside location has panoramic views, is situated opposite a small beach and enroute to the albatross and penguin colonies. The upstairs guest area is spacious and private with comfortable rooms, bathrobes, tea/coffee, TV, fridge, ensuite/private facilities and sunroom. Enjoy a delicious breakfast at your leisure. Originally from Holland, we enjoy welcoming people and sharing our wonderful location with them.

Otago Peninsula - Broad Bay *16 km E of Dunedin*

Broad Bay White House *B&B Homestay*
Chris & Margaret Marshall
11 Clearwater Street, Broad Bay, Dunedin

Tel (03) 478 1160
Fax (03) 478 1159
broadbaywhitehouse@paradise.net.nz
www.broadbaywhitehouse.co.nz

Double $140-$175 (Full breakfast)
Visa MC Diners Amex accepted
3 Queen 1 Single (3 bdrm)
Bathrooms: 2 Ensuite 1 Private, showers only

Looking for peace and quiet, privacy, panoramic views over the harbour, superb meals with silver service? Look no further. We are a tranquil semi-rural hideaway located on the Otago Peninsula. Handy to albatross, penguin and seal colonies. All bedrooms enjoy spacious decks and panoramic views over the harbour. House is centrally heated throughout. Relax and wander through gardens and enjoy the abundant bird life. Have fun with a game of petanque (no experience required).

Otago Peninsula - Macandrew Bay *11 km E of Dunedin*

Mac Bay Retreat *B&B Cottage with Kitchen*
Jeff & Helen Hall
38 Bayne Terrace, Macandrew Bay, Dunedin 9014

Tel (03) 476 1475
Fax (03) 476 1975
jhall9@ihug.co.nz
www.otago-peninsula.co.nz/macbayretreat.html

Double $115 Single $100
(Continental breakfast)
Extra person $25pp
Visa MC accepted
1 King 1 Double (1 bdrm)
Bathrooms: 1 Ensuite

Mac Bay Retreat - Otago Peninsula. Welcome to your private self-contained smoke-free retreat, 15 minutes from Dunedin centre on the Otago Peninsula. Relax with the spectacular view overlooking the harbour from Dunedin City to Port Chalmers. Your cosy retreat is separate from the host's house and gives you a choice of either a super king or double bed plus an ensuite, modern kitchen and TV. Suitable for one couple, possibly two couples, travelling together. Only minutes from Dunedin's most popular attractions.

Otago Peninsula - Portobello *20 km NE of Dunedin*

Peninsula B&B *B&B*
Toni & Stephen Swabey
4 Allans Beach Road, Portobello, Dunedin

Tel 0800 478 090 or (03) 478 0909
027 634 3661   Fax (03) 478 0909
toni@peninsula.co.nz
www.peninsula.co.nz

Double $135-$185 Single $110-$130 (Full breakfast)
Children welcome, POA
Free wireless broadband internet
Visa MC accepted
1 King/Twin 1 King 2 Queen 1 Single (4 bdrm)
Bathrooms: 2 Ensuite 1 Guest share

Come and relax in the elegant and romantic Victorian ambience of our beautiful 1880's villa. Situated in peaceful gardens, enjoy wonderful views of the harbour from your ensuite room. Relish your delicious cooked breakfast in the morning, with home baking. Catch up with our complimentary newspaper and make yourself at home with tea/coffee making facilities. Keep in touch with home with our free wireless broadband internet. We are ideally located for wildlife and scenic attractions and just a minute's walk from Portobello's two restaurants.

Otago
North Catlins

Otago Peninsula - Portobello *20 km NE of Dunedin*

Captain Eady's Lookout *B&B Homestay*

Richard & Ana Good
2 Moss Street, Portobello, Dunedin 9014

Tel (03) 478 0537 or 021 478 785
capteady@earthlight.co.nz
http://capteady.co.nz

Double $130-$155 Single $120-$145
(Special breakfast)   Children negotiable
Dinner $30 by prior arrangement
Twin Room $100
Visa MC accepted
Children welcome
2 Queen 1 Twin (3 bdrm)
Bathrooms: 2 Ensuite 1 Family share

Captain Eady's Lookout is a delightful bed and breakfast on the water's edge. This character house, built early last century by Captain Eady, a ferry master, stands on a small bluff overlooking Otago Harbour. One bedroom opens onto a secluded garden, one overlooks the harbour. You may have a special breakfast in our conservatory whilst taking in the splendid harbour views. The house has many antiques and on the walls are paintings by local artists. You may sample the large jazz collection. Cats in residence.

Otago Peninsula - Portobello *20 km NE of Dunedin*

McAuley Glen Bed & Breakfast *B&B Homestay*

Mary & Pat Curtin
13 McAuley Road, Portobello Dunedin

Tel (03) 478 0724 or 021 237 1919
Fax (03) 478 0724
maryandpat@clear.net.nz

Double $155-$195 Single $135-$185
(Full breakfast)
Dinner by arrangement
Visa MC accepted
Children welcome
2 Queen 1 Twin (3 bdrm)
Bathrooms: 2 Ensuite

Peaceful, private, nestled in $1/2$ acre of trees, shrubs & rose gardens. Five minute walk to restaurants, bar & dairy, 20 minute drive to Albatross, Penguin & Seal colonies. Bedrooms have: private patio garden entrances, TV,CD, Fridge, microwave, comfy furniture, heater, quality linens, electric blankets, bathrobes, hair dryer, tea/coffee/biscuits, fresh flowers & chocs. Complimentary beer/wine, sauna, outdoor spa included. Also internet, and laundry. Mary & Pat also operate Scenic & Wildlife Tours, sea kayaking, mountain biking. We would love to share our piece of paradise with you.

Otago Peninsula - Broad Bay *15 km N of Dunedin*

Fantail Lodge *2 Self-contained Cottages with Kitchens*

Vic and Tessa Mills
682 Portobello Road, Broad Bay, Dunedin

Tel (03) 478 0110 or 027 415 6222
fantail.lodge@xtra.co.nz

Double $130-$150 Single $120-$140
(Accommodation only)
Extra adults or children $20pp
Continental Provisions extra
Visa MC accepted
Pet free home
Children welcome
1 Queen 1 Double 2 Single (3 bdrm)
Bathrooms: 1 ensuite in each cottage.

Peacefully situated on the beautiful Otago Peninsula, close to beaches, seals, penguins and albatrosses, our lush, harbourside garden contains two, delightfully rustic, self-contained cottages. Fantail Cottage has double bed accommodation with two singles on a mezzanine. Bellbird offers a queen bed and an exclusive spa pool. Both are equipped for self catering or continental breakfast hampers by arrangement. Free use of kayaks. An ideal base for touring and a great location for a romantic getaway.

Mosgiel *2 km SW of Mosgiel*
The Trees *B&B*
Jenny Blackgrove & Rex Moore
70 Main South Road, East Taieri, Mosgiel 9024

Tel (03) 489 4837 or 021 0244 2839
Fax (03) 477 1479
rex.moore@clear.net.nz

Double $120 Single $75 (Full breakfast)
Dinner $35 by prior arrangement
Visa MC accepted
Not suitable for children
1 King 1 Twin (2 bdrm)
Bathrooms: 1 Guest share Shower and separate bath

Welcome to our quiet, semirural home set on an acre of lawns and trees. We are 15 km SW of Dunedin, half-way between Dunedin and the airport. There are three golf courses in close proximity. Resident animals are two cats and a border collie dog named Dougal. Rex enjoys flying light aircraft and sailing, Jenny is a Cordon Bleu trained cook and besides cooking, Jenny's interests include gardening and reading. We both have travelled extensively. Facilities include off-street parking and make yourself tea, coffee & juice.

Balclutha *26 km W of Balclutha*
Argyll Farmstay *B&B Farmstay*
Trish & Alan May
246 Clutha River Road, Clydevale, RD 4, Balclutha

Tel (03) 415 9268 or 027 431 8241
Fax (03) 415 9268
argyllfm@ihug.co.nz
www.argyllfarmstay.co.nz

Double $130-$150 Single $65-$100 (Full breakfast)
Children negotiable
Dinner $30 by arrangement
Visa MC accepted
Children welcome
1 Queen 1 Twin (2 bdrm)
Bathrooms: 1 Ensuite 1 Private

From the moment you step onto Argyll Farm you will experience the warmth, tranquillity and hospitality extended to you by Alan and Trish; third generation sheep, deer and cattle farmers. We will make your stay a memorable one, pampering you with exquisite accommodation and cuisine. You can enjoy our day to day farm activities or enjoy quiet times. Go for walks, fish in the Clutha River bordering our property or explore. Our home is yours. Experience us for a magical stay. Directions: please telephone.

Balclutha *4 km N of Balclutha*
Lesmahagow *B&B Boutique*
Noel & Kate O'Malley
Main Road, Benhar, RD 2, Balclutha

Tel (03) 418 2507 or 0800 301 224 (NZ only)
027 457 8465
lesmahagow@xtra.co.nz
www.lesmahagow.co.nz

Double $130-$150 (Full breakfast)
Dinner $35 Lunches on request
Visa MC Eftpos accepted
Children welcome
2 Queen 2 Double 1 Single (3 bdrm)
Bathrooms: 2 Private 1 Guest share

Lesmahagow offers excellent accommodation in an historic homestead and garden setting. Centrally situated, discerning travellers can make Lesmahagow their base to explore the Catlins region, Dunedin and the Otago Penninsula or the historic goldfields of Lawrence. Centrally heated, with delightful bedrooms and gorgeous bathrooms, you can be sure of wonderful hospitality and a truly memorable stay. Evening meals are our speciality and our breakfasts will satisfy all taste buds! Come and discover this hidden paradise! You will love the experience.

Otago
North Catlins

Otago, North Catlins

Kaka Point - The Catlins *20 km SE of Balclutha*

Breadalbane House *Apartment with Kitchen*

Carolynne & Ken Stephens
3 Marine Terrace, Kaka Point, Balclutha

Tel (03) 412 8678
breadalbane@xtra.co.nz
www.kakapointaccommodation.com

Double up to $150 Single $75 (Breakfast by arrangement)
Extra Person $25
Visa MC accepted
1 Double 1 Twin (2 bdrm)
Bathrooms: 1 Private

A warm welcome awaits guests at our quality self-contained apartment which enjoys panoramic unrestricted ocean views from the balcony and both bedrooms. Quality furnishings, double glazing and central heating ensure a comfortable stay even in the cooler months. We are ten minutes from Nugget Point, seals, penguins and other birdlife and a short two minute walk to the café. Having farmed in the area all our lives, we enjoy travel and meeting people and sharing the local history with our guests over coffee.

Nuggets - The Catlins *24 km NE of Owaka*

Nugget Lodge *Apartments with kitchen*

Kath & Noel Widdowson
Nugget Road 367, RD 1, Balclutha, South Otago

Tel (03) 412 8783
Fax (03) 412 8784
lighthouse@nuggetlodge.co.nz
www.nuggetlodge.co.nz

Double $160 (Breakfast by arrangement)
Extra guests $25pp   Cooked breakfast $15pp
Visa MC accepted
Not suitable for children
1 King 1 Queen 1 Single (2 bdrm)
Bathrooms: 2 Ensuite

A small intimate business, catering for the eco-traveller. Modern , private, fully self-contained & centrally heated. Absolutely on the waters edge over looking the Pacific Ocean. Discover the enchantment of the Catlins with its, magnificent unspoilt scenery. Bush walks, seals, sealions, penguins & a bird watchers paradise. After a full day exploring the Catlins sit out on your private veranda, sipping a glass of wine. Sleep to the roar of the waves. A one day booking is not enough. Host: Wildlife Ranger/Photographer. Restaurants nearby.

Kaka Point - The Catlins *21 km S of Balclutha*

Rata Cottage *B&B Cottage with Kitchen*

Jean Schreuder
31 Rata Street, Kaka Point, South Otago

Tel (03) 412 8779

Double $70 Single $65
(Continental breakfast)
Extra person $15
1 Twin (1 bdrm)
Bathrooms: 1 Ensuite

A fully self-contained sunny bed & breakfast unit in a tranquil bush garden setting, with sea view, bell birds and tuis. Bedroom with twin beds, plus double divan in lounge. Wheelchair facilities. Five minutes from a beautiful sandy beach for swimming or long walks. Next door to scenic reserve and bush walks. You can have breakfast in the garden with the birds if you wish. Non-smoking. Laundry facilities available. Cooking facilities.

Owaka - The Catlins *15 km S of Owaka*

Greenwood Farmstay *B&B Farmstay Separate Suite*
Self-contained Beach Cottage - sleeps 8
Helen-May & Alan Burgess
739 Purakaunui Falls Road, Owaka, South Otago

Tel (03) 415 8259 or 027 438 4538
Fax (03) 415 8259
greenwoodfarm@xtra.co.nz
www.greenwoodfarmstay.co.nz

Double $130-$140 Single $120 (Full breakfast)
Children $90   Dinner $40pp (3 course)
Self-contained cottage $90 double, $15 extra person
2 Queen 1 Twin (3 bdrm)
Bathrooms: 1 Ensuite 1 Private 1 Guest share
1 Family share 2 bathrooms at Beach Cottage

Welcome ... Within walking distance to beautiful Purakaunui Falls. Alan enjoys taking people around our sheep, cattle and deer farm and you may stand on the cliffs where the movie Narnia was filmed. We enjoy evening dining with our guests. Our home offers warm, very comfortable accommodation. One guest bedroom with ensuite and day-room opens to the large garden. A private bathroom services other guest rooms. Email/phone for directions. Ask about our self-contained cottage at Papatowai Beach.

Owaka *6 km N of Owaka*

Hillview *B&B Farmstay Cottage with Kitchen*
Kate & Bruce McLachlan
Rapid 161 Hunt Road, Katea, RD 2,
Owaka, South Otago

Tel (03) 415 8457 or 027 433 4759
Fax (03) 415 8650
hillviewcatlins@xtra.co.nz

Double $105-$120 Single $60 (Continental breakfast)
Children $40   Dinner from $30, bookings essential
Visa MC accepted
Children and pets welcome
2 Queen 4 Single (4 bdrm)
Bathrooms: 2 Guest share

Our sheep and cattle grazing property is situated 15 minutes from Nugget Point, ten minutes from Cannibal Bay. Relax in our cosy private cottage set in a large developing garden, or enjoy the relaxed atmosphere of our home. Our pets usually live outside. Bruce enjoys working with horses, training sheepdogs and often works on another local farm. Kate is a school librarian who enjoys reading, gardening, and handcrafts. We enjoy our grandchildren and meeting people. Breakfast with us or in private. Phone evenings.

Owaka - The Catlins *1 km N of Owaka*

J T's Catlins B&B *B&B Homestay*
John & Thelma Turnbull
2885 Main Road, Owaka

Tel (03) 415 8127 or 027 649 7693
Fax (03) 415 8129
jtowaka@ihug.co.nz
www.jtscatlinsbnb.co.nz

Double up to $110 Single up to $80 (Full breakfast)
Dinner by arrangement
Children welcome
1 Queen 1 Twin (2 bdrm)
Bathrooms: 1 Guest share toilet, shower & bathroom,
3 seperate rooms

Welcome to our warm and comfortable home on the Southern Scenic Route, situated on a 25 acre farmlet, surrounded by colourful, peaceful gardens with splendid unspoilt views. Located in the heart of the Catlins, renowned for its wildlife and spectacular scenery, we are within walking distance of Owaka Township with its restaurants, museum and other amenities. Our guests are encouraged to dine with us for the evening meal when we enjoy quality local food and wine. We look forward to meeting you. Travel safely.

Otago
North Catlins

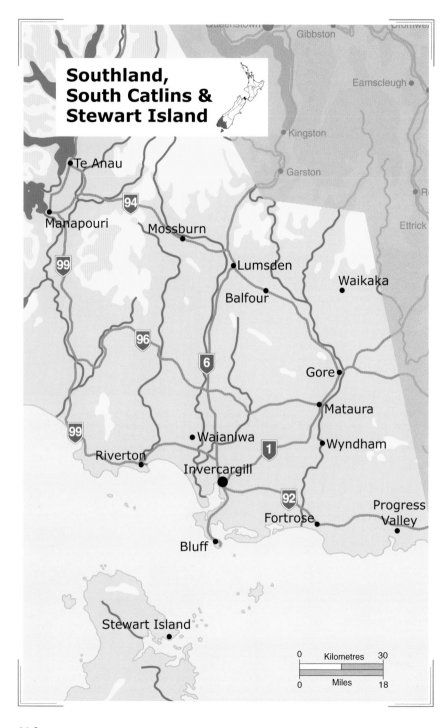

**Southland,
South Catlins &
Stewart Island**

Queenstown
Gibbston
Cromwell
Earnscleugh

Kingston

Te Anau

Garston

94

Manapouri

Mossburn

Ettrick

99

Lumsden

Waikaka

Balfour

96

6

Gore

Mataura

99

Waianiwa

Wyndham

Riverton

1

Invercargill

92

Progress
Valley

Fortrose

Bluff

Stewart Island

| 0 | Kilometres | 30 |
| 0 | Miles | 18 |

Te Anau - Manapouri *20 km S of Te Anau*
The Cottage *B&B Homestay*
Don & Joy MacDuff
Waiau Street, Te Anau - Manapouri

Tel (03) 249 6838 or 021 138 6110
don.joymacduff@xtra.co.nz
www.thecottagefiordland.co.nz

Double $120-$150 (Special breakfast)
Not suitable for children
2 Queen (2 bdrm)
Bathrooms: 2 Ensuite

Gateway to majestic Fiordland. Doubtful Sound boat only a two minute walk, beside the river through Beech trees. Our comfortable home with cottage decor is a combination of old world charm and kiwi ingenuity. Located in tranquil bush setting with lovely mountain and water views. Tea, coffee in rooms, shared fridge, microwave. Your own private outdoor area. Excellent homemade breakfasts. Enjoy our social hour most evenings. We, with Millie (our lovely dog) extend to you a warm Kiwi welcome.

Te Anau *5 km S of Te Anau*
Kepler Cottage *B&B Homestay*
Jan & Jeff Ludemann
William Stephen Road, Te Anau

Tel (03) 249 7185 or 027 431 4076
Fax (03) 249 7186
kepler@teanau.co.nz
www.fiordlandaccommodation.co.nz

Double $150-$200 (Full breakfast)
Visa MC Diners accepted
1 Queen 3 Single (2 bdrm)
Bathrooms: 1 Ensuite 1 Private

Jeff, an aircraft engineer and Jan, who works from home as a marketing consultant, welcome you to their small farmlet on the edge of Fiordland, just five minutes drive from Te Anau. Relax outdoors in the garden and enjoy the peace and comfort of our rural location between visiting Milford or Doubtful Sounds, or walking one of the many nearby tracks. Our family includes Kimba our siamese cat and Ronni our cairn terrier. We can advise tours and sightseeing and make bookings where needed.

Te Anau *1 km N of Te Anau Centre*
Shakespeare House *B&B Separate Suite*
Marg, Jeff, Kylie & Ray
10 Dusky Street, PO Box 32, Te Anau

Tel (03) 249 7349 or 0800 249 349
Fax (03) 249 7629
marg.shakespeare.house@xtra.co.nz
www.shakespearehouse.co.nz

Double $100-$130 Single $90-$110 (Full breakfast)
Children $5-$15
Self-contained, 2 bedrooms - sleeps 5
Visa MC Eftpos accepted
Pet free home
Children welcome
8 King 4 Single (8 bdrm)
Bathrooms: 8 Ensuite No Baths

Shakespeare House is a well established Bed & Breakfast, where we keep a home atmosphere with personal service. We are situated in a quiet residential area yet are within walking distance of shops, lake and restaurants. Our rooms are ground floor and have the choice of king, queen or twin beds. Each room has private facilities, TV, tea/coffee making. Tariff includes continental or delicious cooked breakfast.

**Southland
South Catlins**

Te Anau *8 km S of Te Anau*

Lynwood Park *B&B Homestay Farmstay Country stay*
Trina & Monty Joseph
State Highway 94, Te Anau

Tel (03) 249 7990 or 021 1295 626
lynwood.park@xtra.co.nz

Double up to $125 Single up to $100
(Continental breakfast provisions)
Children $40
Winter rates May-October
Visa MC accepted
Children and pets welcome
4 Queen 1 Single (4 bdrm)
Bathrooms: 2 Ensuite 1 Guest share

Kia ora - Haere mai ki ta matou kainga. We are both of Nga Puhi/Irish decent and expect to be greeted with the traditional "hongi" on arrival. Set amidst snow capped mountains (Takitimu) and surrounded by lovely green family farmland, just five minutes drive to Te Anau and all of Fiordlands unique features. Our nine year old daughter, Daniella and pets in residence. With ten years experience and local knowledge to help you book your ideal holiday attractions. All lifestyles catered for - Mauriora.

Te Anau *2 km E of Te Anau*

Rose 'n' Reel *B&B Farmstay Cottage with Kitchen*
Lyn & Lex Lawrence
Ben Loch Lane, RD 2, Te Anau

Tel (03) 249 7582 or 027 4545 723
Fax (03) 249 7582
rosenreel@xtra.co.nz
www.rosenreel.co.nz

Double $90-$110 Single $65-$80
(Continental breakfast)
Visa MC accepted
2 Queen 1 Double 1 Single (3 bdrm)
Bathrooms: 1 Private 1 Guest share

Genuine Kiwi hospitality in a magic setting five minutes from Te Anau. Hand feed tame fallow deer, meet two friendly cats and dog Meg. Sit on the veranda of our fully self-contained cabin and enjoy watching deer with a lake and mountain view. The two room cabin has cooking facilities, fridge, microwave, TV, one queen, one double plus bathroom. Our two storey home is set in an extensive garden. Two guest bedrooms. Lex is a fishing guide, I love to garden. Directions: please phone.

Te Anau *1.5 km N of Te Anau*

The Croft *B&B Farmstay Cottage with Kitchen*
Jane & Ross McEwan
Te Anau Milford Sound Road, RD 1, Te Anau

Tel (03) 249 7393 or 027 682 0061
Fax (03) 249 7393
jane@thecroft.co.nz
www.thecroft.co.nz

Double $150-$175 (Continental breakfast)
Extra person $25
Visa MC accepted
2 Queen 1 Single (2 bdrm)
Bathrooms: 2 Ensuite

Warm hospitality and quality accommodation are guaranteed at The Croft, a lifestyle farm near Te Anau. Our two modern self-contained cottages are set in private gardens and enjoy magnificent lake and mountain views. Timber ceilings, large ensuite bathrooms, window seats and elegant furnishings are highlights. Microwaves, fridges, sinks, TVs, DVDs and CD mini systems. Enjoy breakfast with Jane & Ross or served in your cottage. Pets include Dolly the sheep, Mac the Jack Russell, Kitty and Jerry. Lake and river access from our farm.

Te Anau *1 km N of Te Anau Central*
Cosy Kiwi *B&B Guest House*
Eleanor & Derek Cook
186 Milford Road, Te Anau 9681

Tel (03) 249 7475 or 0800 249 700
Fax (03) 249 8471
info@cosykiwi.com
www.cosykiwi.com

Double $140-$160 **Single** $130-$140
(Special breakfast) Children negotiable
Triple $175-$190
Visa MC Eftpos accepted
4 King 3 Queen 4 Twin 5 Single (7 bdrm)
Bathrooms: 7 Ensuite

Eleanor & Derek welcome you to our Bed & Breakfast (30 years experience in hospitality industry). Privacy with comfort, quiet spacious ensuited bedrooms, quality beds, individual heating and television. Breakfast buffet of home-made breads, jams, fresh fruits, dessert fruits, yoghurt, brewed coffee, special teas,plus mouthwatering pancakes with maple syrup or ham and cheese. Two minute walk to shops and restaurants, bookings arranged for all tours, pick-up at gate. Guest lounge with internet access, laundry, off-street parking and luggage storage.

Te Anau *5 km E of Te Anau*
Stonewall B&B *Apartment with Kitchen*
Nicky Harrison & Jim Huntington
36 Kakapo Road, RD 2, Te Anau

Tel (03) 249 8686
Fax (03) 249 8686
info@stonewallfiordland.co.nz
www.stonewallfiordland.co.nz

Double $140 **Single** $100
(Continental breakfast provisions)
Children negotiable
Children welcome
1 Queen (1 bdrm)
Bathrooms: 1 Ensuite

Come up the driveway past the pond and dry stonewalls to our self-contained guest studio, sited at our home amidst our deer farm in Kakapo Road, only 5 km out of Te Anau. You have your own private accomodation, including ensuite bathroom and kitchen. Your courtyard over looks our organic vegetable garden to the mountains of Fiordland. After a year's absence we look forward to welcoming you back to our B&B to enjoy the peaceful environment and home produce.

Te Anau *1 km N of Te Anau Centre*
Te Anau Lodge *Luxury B&B*
Matt Dagger & Chloe Marsden
52 Howden Street, Te Anau

Tel (03) 249 7477 or 021 064 9354
Fax (03) 249 7487
info@teanaulodge.co.nz
www.teanaulodge.com

Double $200-$350 **Single** $170-$270 (Full breakfast)
Visa MC Eftpos accepted
Children welcome
3 King/Twin 3 King 5 Queen 3 Twin 8 Single (8 bdrm)
Bathrooms: 7 Ensuite 1 Private
(8 Bathrooms in total, 2 with spa baths)

Experience the genuine warmth of traditional hospitality in the relaxed and peaceful environment of our 1936 relocated former convent. Set on 2.7 hectares with breathtaking lake and mountain views, Te Anau Lodge has been lovingly restored maintaining its original and delightful charm, with modern facilities. Enjoy our famous cooked breakfasts in the Chapel, spend your evenings relaxing in our library or having a drink in our sunny courtyard. Complimentary laundry facilities, luggage storage and high speed wireless internet access. A unique and special accommodation experience.

Te Anau - Manapouri *8 km S of Manapouri*

Connemara Cottage *B&B Farmstay Cottage with Kitchen*

Bev & Murray Hagen
415 Weir Road, Manapouri, Te Anau

Tel (03) 249 9399 or 027 292 3651
Fax (03) 249 9399
hagen@southnet.co.nz

Double $130-$160 (Full breakfast provisions)
Children by arrangement
1 Queen 1 Double (1 bdrm)
Bathrooms: 1 Ensuite

Yours exclusively, cosy self-contained cottage in a tranquil garden setting with magnificent mountain views. The bedroom has a queen bed while the lounge has a very comfortable double foldout sofabed. Relax and enjoy breakfast in the privacy of your cottage. Manapouri, 'The Gateway to Doubtful Sound' is five minutes from our 750 acre Deer, Sheep, and Cattle Farm, which bounds two fishing rivers. Murray's interests include Microlights, while Bev enjoys gardening, bowls crafts etc. We and Angel (cat) welcome you. Farm Tour inclusive when time permits.

Te Anau *0.4 km N of Te Anau Centre*

Antler Lodge *B&B Cottage with Kitchen*

Helen & Chris Whyte
44 Matai Street, Te Anau

Tel (03) 249 8188
Fax (03) 249 8188
antler.lodge@xtra.co.nz
www.antlerlodgeteanau.co.nz

Double $120-$155
(Continental breakfast provisions)
Visa MC accepted
1 King 2 Queen (3 bdrm)
Bathrooms: 3 Ensuite

Helen and Chris invite you to enjoy their comfortable bed & breakfast accommodation. Situated in a quiet residential area close to shops, restaurants and within walking distance of the lake. We offer three spacious self contained units, each with a private ensuite. The two cottages each have kitchen facilities, TV, electric heating and comfortable furnishings. Our third unit is an upstairs suite with private entrance and sunroom dining area. Continental breakfast provisions are provided in this unit. This suite has beautiful mountain views.

Te Anau *1 km S of Central Te Anau*

Cat's Whiskers *B&B*

Anne Marie & Lindsay Bernstone
2 Lakefront Drive, Te Anau

Tel (03) 249 8112
Fax (03) 249 8112
bookings@catswhiskers.co.nz
www.catswhiskers.co.nz

Double $175-$195 Single $130 (Full breakfast)
Children $30
Visa MC accepted
Children welcome
2 King 2 Queen 4 Single (4 bdrm)
Bathrooms: 4 Ensuite

Our peaceful lakefront home is a comfortable villa with four guest rooms all with ensuite bathrooms. Relax while you take in stunning views of Lake Te Anau. Meet fellow guests for a cooked or continental breakfast in our dining room. Opposite Department of Conservation Visitor Centre. Our cat and small Maltese dog live with us. King Queen or Twin beds. Fast internet access. TV, fridges, tea and coffee making facilities. Booking service for local trips. Off street parking. Guest laundry and short term luggage storage.

Te Anau *5 km N of Te Anau*
Lochvista B&B *B&B*
Viv Nicholson
454 State Highway 94, Te Anau

Tel (03) 249 7273
Fax (03) 249 7278
lochvista@xtra.co.nz
www.lochvista.co.nz

Double $150-$170 Single $140-$150
(Continental breakfast)
Full breakfast by arrangement $15pp
1 King 1 Queen 1 Twin (2 bdrm)
Bathrooms: 2 Ensuite

Welcome to Fiordland. Lochvista is situated on Te Anau Milford Highway 5 km from the town centre, overlooking Lake Te Anau and Murchison mountains. two rooms one with queen bed and one with king/twin with ensuite, tea/coffee making facilities, fridge, TV & hairdryer. French doors onto the patio where you can sit and take in spectacular views. Fiordland has a great deal to offer and I am more than happy to help guests with any booking to make their stay more relaxing. A cat called Mischief.

Te Anau *.2 km W of Central Te Anau*
House of Wood *B&B Homestay*
Merle & Cliff Buchanan
44 Moana Crescent, Te Anau

Tel (03) 249 8404 or 021 250 0802
Fax (03) 249 7676
houseofwood@xtra.co.nz
www.houseofwood.co.nz

Double $115-$135 Single $100-$120 (Full breakfast)
Visa MC Eftpos accepted
Pet free home Children welcome
2 King/Twin 1 King 3 Queen (4 bdrm)
Bathrooms: 3 Ensuite 1 Private

A warm welcome is assured when you arrive at our home, House of Wood. We really enjoy meeting guests from overseas (and locals). Our house is a unique architecturally designed home of native and exotic timber. Sit at the outdoor tables and enjoy the beautiful views. Our interests are boating, fishing, golf, rowing and gardening. We can help you plan your activities and book trips, with pick up at the door. We are two minutes walk from the township, five minutes to the Lake. Dinner by arrangement.

Te Anau *1 km N of Te Anau*
Dunluce *B&B Private Guest Wing*
Wendy & Roger McQuillan
Aparima Drive, Te Anau

Tel (03) 249 7715 or 027 330 2779
Fax (03) 249 7703
info@dunluce-fiordland.co.nz
www.dunluce-fiordland.co.nz

Double $185-$250 Single $155-$220
(Full breakfast)
Visa MC Eftpos accepted
Not suitable for children
4 King/Twin (4 bdrm)
Bathrooms: 4 Ensuite 1 spa bath in deluxe room

D unluce is a brand new purpose built Bed & Breakfast. Our private guest wing includes four luxury ensuite rooms and a lounge/dining room where a full breakfast is served and coffee/tea are always available. All rooms have panoramic lake and mountain views. We have laundry facilities, parking, storage, fax, and broadband connection. We are a 15 minute walk to the town centre or a two minute drive. We have an unobtrusive cat.

Southland
South Catlins

Te Anau *0.7 km SW of Te Anau*

Moptop Place Bed & Breakfast *B&B*

Yvonne & Ian Dickson
39 Luxmore Drive, Te Anau 9681

Tel (0)3 249 7206 or 027 222 1113
0800 249 720
Fax (03) 249 7206
info@moptopteanau.com
www.moptopteanau.com

Double $95-$110 Single $80-$90
(Continental breakfast)
Children negotiable
1 Queen 1 Double (2 bdrm)
Bathrooms: 1 Ensuite 1 Private

Yvonne & Ian, burmese cats MacArthur & Phoebe and labrador Zara offer a warm welcome. We are situated on Luxmore Drive the main road into the town centre and to Milford Sound. Our home has mountain views is four minutes walk to shops, restaurants and beautiful Lake Te Anau. A generous continental breakfast is provided. The two quality bedrooms have private entrances, the queen room has an ensuite, microwave and fridge both rooms include tea/coffee making facilities, TV and comfortable chairs. Fishing guide arranged.

Te Anau *0.5 km E of Te Anau*

Blue Ridge Boutique Bed & Breakfast
Luxury Separate Suite Apartment with Kitchen
Julia & Phillip Robertson
15 Melland Place, Te Anau, 9600

Tel (03) 249 7740 or 027 258 9877
Fax (03) 249 7340   info@blueridge.net.nz
www.blueridge.net.nz

Double $200-$250 Single $170-$200 (Full breakfast)
Not suitable for young children
Visa MC Eftpos accepted
2 King/Twin 2 Queen (4 bdrm)
Bathrooms: 4 Ensuite

Blue Ridge Boutique Bed & BreakfastSuperior Accommodation A warm welcome awaits you at Blue Ridge. Our three purpose built studio apartments have tiled ensuite bathrooms with underfloor heating, heated towel rails and great showers. There is SKY TV, DVD player and fast internet connection. The rooms have comfortable beds, double glazing and individually controlled heating. Our fourth guest suite is situated in a private wing within our home. Join us for a delicious gourmet breakfast using the freshest seasonal produce. We are just a few minutes walk from Te Anau town centre. Meet Latte & Meg our two friendly Birman cats

Mossburn *25 km S of Mossburn*

Turner Farmstay *Farmstay*
Joyce & Murray Turner
RD 1, Otautau, Southland

Tel (03) 225 7602
Fax (03) 225 7602
murray.joyce@xtra.co.nz
www.innz.co.nz/host/e/etalcreek.html

Double $100 Single $70 (Full breakfast)
Children under 12 $25
Dinner $35
1 Queen 4 Single (3 bdrm)
Bathrooms: 1 Private 1 Guest share

Our modern home on 301 hectares, farming sheep, is situated half-way between Invercargill and Te Anau, which can be reached in one hour. We enjoy meeting people, will provide quality accommodation, farm-fresh food in a welcoming friendly atmosphere. You can join in farm activities, farm tour or just relax. The Aparima River is adjacent to the property. Murray is a keen fly fisherman. Guiding & advice available. Pet Bichon Frise. Evening meal on request. Directions please phone/fax. 24 hours notice to avoid disappointment.

Lumsden *12 km S of Lumsden*
Chartlea Park Farmstay *Historical B&B Farmstay*

Ken & Trish MacKenzie
1 Chartlea Park Road, Balfour, 9779

Tel (03) 201 6442 or 027 285 5121
Fax (03) 201 6442
ken.trish.mack@xtra.co.nz
www.chartleaparkfarmstay.co.nz

Double $140 Single $85 (Full breakfast)
Children $45
Dinner $35pp
Visa MC accepted
4 King/Twin 1 Queen (3 bdrm)
Bathrooms: 1 Guest share
Bedrooms have own washstand facilities

Ken, Trish and Jenna MacKenzie welcome you to their 670 acre sheep beef and deer farm in Northern Southland. Enjoy tasty home cooking, a farm tour, meeting and feeding the pets or just relax in the ambience of our historic home. Nearby are excellent fishing rivers, golf courses and spectacular scenery. Our central location to the delights of Invercargill, Queenstown and Te Anau is ideal. We are committed to ensuring your time with us is THE highlight of your travels.

Balfour *3 km N of Balfour*
Hillcrest *Farmstay*

Liz & Ritchie Clark
206 Old Balfour Road, RD 1, Balfour

Tel (03) 201 6165
Fax (03) 201 6165
clarkrl@xtra.co.nz

Double $120-$150 Single $120-$150
(Full breakfast)
Dinner $40pp
Visa MC accepted
Children welcome
2 King/Twin 1 Single (2 bdrm)
Bathrooms: 1 Private 1 Family share

Welcome to our 650 acre sheep and deer farm, 3km from State Highway 94. Relax in our garden, enjoy a farm tour with mountain views or a game of tennis. Trout fishing in the Mataura, Oreti and Waikaia Rivers. Fishing guide can be arranged with notice. Enjoy a relaxing dinner with fine food, wine and conversation. Breakfast is served with fresh baked bread, yoghurt, muesli, jams and preserves. Interests include handcrafts, tennis, photography and fishing. We have two cats. Directions: please phone.

Gore *1 km N of Gore*
Connor Homestay *Homestay*

Dawn & David Connor
29 Aotea Crescent, Gore, Southland

Tel (03) 208 3598 or 0800 372 484
027 669 1362
Fax (03) 208 3598
ddconnor@esi.co.nz
www.bnb.co.nz/connororchids.html

Double $100 Single $60 (Full breakfast)
Dinner by arrangement
Visa MC accepted
1 King/Twin 1 Queen (2 bdrm)
Bathrooms: 1 Private 1 Guest share

Dawn & David invite you to enjoy quality accommodation in their modern home, situated in a quiet residential area overlooking the Hokonui Hills and farmland, close to golf course, driving range, bush walks and good fishing rivers including Mataura, well known for its brown trout. Fishing guide or advise available. We enjoy meeting people and sharing travel experiences. Laundry facilities available. Smoke-free accommodation. Please phone for directions.

Southland
South Catlins

Southland, South Catlins

Gore *3 km NW of Gore*

Hokonui Homestay *Luxury B&B Homestay Rural Lifestyle*

Brian & Shona McLennan
258 Reaby Road, RD 4, Gore

Tel (03) 208 4890 or 027 568 4835
Fax (03) 208 4890
bssm@sld.quik.co.nz

Double $100-$120 Single $70 (Full breakfast)
Children negotiable
Dinner by arrangement
Visa MC accepted
Children welcome
1 King 1 Queen 1 Twin (3 bdrm)
Bathrooms: 2 Ensuite 1 Private

Brian & Shona provide a private, spacious, modern new home on a 12 acre lifestyle property with fantastic views. Private upstairs unit, underfloor heating and full size snooker table. Close to the Mataura River, 18 hole Golf Course and Native Bush Walks. A perfect base for sightseeing Southland and attending the NZ Gold Guitar Awards, Waimumu Fieldays and the Hokonui Fashion Awards. Interests - golf, fishing, dog trialing, music and wine tasting. Horse and Dog facilities available. Phone for directions.

Gore *2 km N of Gore*

Amble In *B&B*

Richard Preston & Carolyn Moorfoot
74 Wentworth Street, Gore

Tel (03) 208 5552
Fax (03) 208 5552
moorfoot@xtra.co.nz

Double $110 Single $60 (Full breakfast)
Dinner by arrangement
Pet free home
Children welcome accompanied by adults
1 King/Twin 1 King 1 Queen 1 Single (3 bdrm)
Bathrooms: 1 Guest share

Richard and Carolyn welcome you to their home, situated amidst farmland overlooking Gore and The Hokonuis. Near by is the Mataura River, famous for Brown trout. Bush walks and art gallery's near by. Fishing guide or advice available with notice. We enjoy meeting new people, talking about New Zealand. Breakfast is served with fresh baked bread and jams and perserves, also with hot cooked bacon and eggs. Three course diners can be as kiwi as you like or perhaps venison or fish may be your choice. Laundry facilities available. Smoke Free accommodation.

Mataura - Gore *12 km S of Gore*

Kowhai Place *Farmstay*

Helen & John Williams
291 Glendhu Road, RD 4, Gore

Tel (03) 203 8774 or 027 203 8734
Fax (03) 203 8774
kowhaiplace@xtra.co.nz
www.southland-homestays.co.nz

Double $95-$100 Single $50 (Full breakfast)
Children half price
Dinner $25 by arrangement
Visa MC accepted
Children and pets welcome
4 King/Twin 2 Queen (4 bdrm)
Bathrooms: 1 Private 1 Guest share 1 Family share

John & Helen farm sheep and deer on their 50 acre farmlet. We live five minutes from one of the best brown trout fishing rivers in the world. Drive one hour south to Bluff, and 1.5 hours to Queenstown's ski fields. We both play golf and enjoy gardening. Fishing guide and garden tours can be arranged with prior notice. Children and outside pets welcome. Over the past years we have enjoyed sharing our spacious home and garden with lots of overseas guests. Enjoy the south.

Wyndham *3.65 km E of Wyndham*

Smiths Farmstay *Farmstay*

Beverly and Doug Smith
365 Wyndham - Mokoreta Road,
RD 2, Wyndham, Southland

Tel (03) 206 4840 or 027 4286 6920
Fax (03) 206 4847
beverly@smithsfarmstay.co.nz
http://smithsfarmstay.co.nz

Double $110-$150 Single $100 (Full breakfast)
Children negotiable
Dinner $40
Visa MC accepted
Children welcome
1 King/Twin 1 Queen 1 Twin (3 bdrm)
Bathrooms: 1 Ensuite 1 Private 1 Guest share

Beverly and Doug assure you of a warm welcome to the Modern Farm house set in 265 hectare sheep farm. We are situated on the hills above Wyndham only 3.65 km, set in quiet and peaceful surroundings.

Farm tour included in tarif. Feeding the animals and sheep shearing when in season. Doug will demonstrate his sheep dogs working. Beverly a registered nurse enjoys cooking, floral art, knitting, gardening and travel. We enjoy meeting people and both are of a friendly deposition, with a sense of humour.

Each bedroom has a view and is tastefully furnished to meet your needs. Genuine home cooking. Special Diets on request. Packed Lunches if required. You are most welcome to join us for the evening meal, which is $40pp. Prior booking required please.

Fishermans Retreat; The Mataura, Wyndham and Mimihau Rivers are renowned for its abundance of Brown trout. Each of these Rivers are only a short 5km away. Doug, a keen experienced fisherman is only too happy to share his knowledge of these rivers with you. Enjoy the Mad Mataura evening Rise a site to experience. Gateway to Catlins, Only two hours from Queenstown, Te Anau and Dunedin. Laundry and Fax available.

Directions: Come to Wyndham, follow signs to Mokoreta. Sign at gate, number 365.

Progress Valley - South Catlins *6 km N of Waikawa*

Catlins Farmstay B&B *B&B Farmstay*

June & Murray Stratford

174 Progress Valley Road, South Catlins, Southland

Tel (03) 246 8843
Fax (03) 246 8844
catlinsfarmstay@xtra.co.nz
www.catlinsfarmstay.co.nz

Double $180-$250 **Single** $130-$150 (Full breakfast)
Children negotiable
Visa MC accepted
Children welcome
1 King 2 Queen 1 Twin (4 bdrm)
Bathrooms: 3 Ensuite 1 Private

Ours is a great location close to fossil forest at Curio Bay. Superior guest rooms plus king self-contained suite available with private entrances. We farm 1000 acres running, 2500 sheep, 500 deer, 150 cattle with three sheepdogs. Farm tours by arrangement. Directions: turn off at Niagara Falls into Manse Road, drive 2 km. Ask about our new Waterside self-contained cottage at Waikawa . Dinner available at Niagara Falls Café. Licensed Restaurant 2 km drive from our house.

Fortrose - The Catlins *50 km SE of Invercargill*

Greenbush *B&B Farmstay Cottage with Kitchen*

Ann & Donald McKenzie

298 Fortrose - Otara Road, Fortrose, RD 5, Invercargill

Tel (03) 246 9506 or 021 395 196
Fax (03) 246 9505
info@greenbush.co.nz
www.greenbush.co.nz

Double $150-$200 **Single** $120-$130 (Full breakfast)
Children negotiable
Dinner $50 by arrangement
Visa MC accepted
Children welcome
1 King 1 Queen 1 Twin (3 bdrm)
Bathrooms: 3 Ensuite

Greenbush Bed & Breakfast is ideally located off the Southern Scenic Route from Fortrose. Within 30 minutes drive from Greenbush you can enjoy Curio Bay, Waipapa Point and Slope Point,the southern most point of the South island. Greenbush is nestled in two acres of garden. You will wake to the song of birds and magnificent views of green rolling countryside. Enjoy our beach, lake and farm tour.Ask about our self contained cottage at Fortrose. Directions:- at Fortrose take Coastal Route drive 4 km.

Invercargill *5 km N of Invercargill*

Glenroy Park Homestay *B&B Homestay*

Margaret & Alan Thomson

23 Glenroy Park Drive, Invercargill

Tel (03) 215 8464 or 027 376 2228
Fax (03) 215 8464
home_hosp@actrix.co.nz
www.bnb.co.nz/glenroypark.html

Double $110-$120 **Single** $75-$85 (Full breakfast)
Children up to 12 $12
3 course dinner $35
Children welcome
1 Queen 1 Twin 1 Single (3 bdrm)
Bathrooms: 1 Private 1 Guest share Heated tile floors

Exclusively yours, in a quiet retreat near restaurants and parks. Be our special guests and share an evening of relaxation and friendship. Our interests are golfing, meeting people, travel and cooking. We look forward to your visit. Invercargill is the gateway to Queenstown, Fiordland, Catlins and Stewart Island. Directions: from Queenstown turn left at second lights (Bainfield Road), take first left, third house on left. From Dunedin turn right at first lights (Queens Drive), travel to end, turn left, first street right, third house left.

Invercargill *5 km W of Invercargill*
The Oak Door *B&B*
Lisa & Bill Stuart
22 Taiepa Road, Otatara, RD 9, Invercargill 9879

Tel (03) 213 0633
Fax (03) 213 0633
blstuart@xtra.co.nz

Double $100 Single $80
(Full breakfast)
Children POA
Pet free home
2 Queen 2 Twin (3 bdrm)
Bathrooms: 2 Guest share

Bill (Kiwi) & Lisa (Canadian) welcome you to their warm, self-built, unique home. Enjoy attractive gardens and native bush setting; minutes from: Invercargill CBD, Scenic route amenities, airport. Coffee/tea awaits you on arrival at The Oak Door. Guests comment on a warm comfortable visit, where beds, breakfast and hospitality are quality plus! A Warm Welcome! (Nonsmoking/no pets). Directions: Drive past the airport entrance. Take first left (Marama Avenue South). Take first right Taiepa Road second drive on right (#22).

Invercargill *3 km N of Invercargill City Centre*
Gimblett Place *B&B*
Alex & Eileen Henderson
122 Gimblett Place, Kildare, Invercargill

Tel (03) 215 6888
Fax (03) 215 6888
the_grove@xtra.co.nz
www.bnb.co.nz/hosts/gimblettplace

Double $95 Single $65 (Full breakfast)
Children negotiable
Dinner by arrangement
Visa MC accepted Pet free home
1 Queen 2 Single (2 bdrm)
Bathrooms: 1 Guest share

Eileen & Alex are experienced hosts who are ex-farmers and offer comfortable accommodation in a quiet cul-de-sac close to city amenities, golf, parks, restaurants. We are pleased to assist with local and tourist information and can guide if required (ie Catlins). Alex is a vintage car and machinery enthusiast and can arrange good viewing. Close to famous trout fishing rivers. Directions: find Queens Drive, Gimblett Street is first left north of Thomsons Bush, fourth right into Gimblett Place (cul-de-sac).

Invercargill *10 km E of Invercargill on Southern Scenic Route*
Long Acres Farmstay *Farmstay Self-contained*
Helen & Graeme Spain
Waimatua, RD 11, Invercargill

Tel (03) 216 4470 or 027 228 1308
Fax (03) 216 4470   longacres@xtra.co.nz
www.longacres.co.nz

Double $120-$150 Single $100 (Full breakfast)
Children negotiable   Dinner $40
Self-contained $160-$200
Visa MC accepted   Children welcome
2 Queen 1 Double 1 Twin (4 bdrm)
Bathrooms: 1 Queen Ensuite 1 Queen Private
1 Double Guest share.

Southland hospitality. Excellent food awaits you at our friendly home. Our farm is 1200 acres carrying 5000 sheep, 80 cattle and two dogs. Native Bush Walk on farm to enjoy. Farm Tour is free. Guests Comments "Great Hospitality." Bluff is 30 minutes, you'll enjoy a day trip to Stewart Island. Home cooked meal always available. A peaceful relaxed place for a farm stay for the length of time you choose. Directions: from Invercargill, east on Southern Scenic Route approximately 15 minutes. Look for Long Acres Farmstay Sign.

**Southland
South Catlins**

Invercargill *4 km N of Invercargill Central*
Stoneleigh Homestay *B&B Homestay*

Joan & Neville Milne
15 Stoneleigh Lane Invercargill

Tel (03) 215 8921
joan@stoneleighhomestay.co.nz
www.stoneleighhomestay.co.nz

Double $95-$120 Single $70-$90
(Full breakfast)
Dinner $35
Visa MC accepted
1 Queen 3 Single (3 bdrm)
Bathrooms: 1 Private 1 Guest share

We welcome guests to share our modern home in a quiet lane five minutes from the main centre, and just off the main road to TeAnau and Queenstown. We have underfloor heating, electric blankets and guests have their own TV. We are keen golfers and members of the Invercargill club, a championship course rated in the top 10 in NZ. Our interests are golf, travel, gardening, cooking, wine and meeting people. Enjoy our hospitality, share an evening meal with us. Pick ups can be arranged.

Invercargill *6 km NE of Invercargill*
The Manor *B&B Homestay*

Pat & Frank Forde
9 Drysdale Road, Myross Bush, RD 2, Invercargill

Tel (03) 230 4788 or 027 667 0904
Fax (03) 230 4788
the.manor@xtra.co.nz
www.manorbb.co.nz

Double $100-$140 Single $70-$85 (Full breakfast)
Children negotiable   Dinner by arrangement
Visa MC accepted
Pet free home   Children welcome
3 Queen 2 Single (3 bdrm)
Bathrooms: 1 Ensuite 1 Private 1 Guest share one

Relax, enjoy our warm, comfortable home, underfloor-heating, a sheltered garden setting, ten acre farmlet (sheep, lambs, horses, hens). Private guest area, television, refrigerator, tea/coffee making facilities. We are retired farmers, golfers, enjoy gardening, harness racing, travel, meeting people. Pleasant outdoor areas, meals of fresh home-grown produce, cooked/continental breakfasts. Courtesy pick up. A stop on your way to Stewart Island, Southern Scenic Route, Queenstown or Te Anau. We would enjoy having you stay with us. Five minutes drive north east Invercargill along State Highway 1.

Invercargill *0.01 km NW of Invercargill City Centre*
Victoria Railway Hotel *Hotel*

Trudy & Eian Read
3 Leven Street, off Picadilly Lane, Invercargill

Tel (03) 218 1281
Fax (03) 218 1283
vrhotel@xtra.co.nz
www.vrhotel.info

Double $115-$140 Single $105
(Full breakfast $6-$16pp)
Children $15
Dinner $20-$30pp
Visa MC Diners Amex Eftpos accepted
5 Queen 4 Double 2 Twin (11 bdrm)
Bathrooms: 11 Ensuite 2 Guest share

Come and enjoy old world charm and southern hospitality in a boutique hotel in the heart of the city. Built in 1896 we are a Class 1 Historic Places heritage building and completed our architecturally designed upgrade and refurbishment in May 2004. We offer a variety of accommodation options including Executive, VIP, and two ground floor accessible units. Guests can relax in our bar before dining in at Gerrard's Restaurant and enjoy traditional home cooked meals and a selection of fine NZ wines.

Invercargill *0.5 km NE of Invercargill City Centre*
Burtonwood Bed & Breakfast *Boutique Bed & Breakfast*

Peter Burtonwood
177 Gala Street, Queens Park, Invercargill

Tel (03) 218 8884 or 0800 353 426
Fax (03) 218 9148   burtonwoodbnb@woosh.co.nz
www.burtonwood.co.nz

Double $125-$225 Single $125-$160
(Continental breakfast)   Children Negotiable
Dinner By arrangment
Visa MC Amex Eftpos accepted
Not suitable for children
3 Queen 2 Single (4 bdrm)
Bathrooms: 3 Ensuite 1 Private

Burtonwood, with the iconic "cat on the roof" is an elegant Edwardian house located in the heart of Invercargill. Across the road are Queens Park, Southland Museum & Art Gallery, Visitor Information Centre & golf course. Sunny, well appointed, secure guest rooms with lovely views of Queens Park. Private, off-street parking. Great restaurants, cafés, shopping and many sporting facilities (Stadium Southland & Velodrome) within a short distance. 10 minutes to beach and 5 minutes to airport. What a gorgeous stay!

Invercargill *15 km N of Invercargill*
Tudor Park Country Stay and Garden
B&B Homestay Country Stay & Garden

Joyce & John Robins
RD 6, Invercargill, 9521

Tel (03) 221 7150 or 027 431 0031
Fax (03) 221 7150
tudorparksouth@hotmail.com
http://wwwtudorpark.co.nz

Double $140-$220 Single $100-$130 (Full breakfast)
Children are welcome with parent supervision
Dinner by arrangement from $45
Visa MC accepted
1 King/Twin 2 Queen (3 bdrm)
Bathrooms: 2 Ensuite 1 Private

Tudor Park has been tastefully redecorated and refurnished with antiques and quality linens. All rooms have their own facilities and garden views. Guests privacy is respected and service is friendly and personalised. Quality accommodation, private with personalised friendly service. Guests are welcome to relax on the terrace enjoy the large garden or enjoy the attractions of the area.

Bluff *25 km S of Invercargill*
The Lazy Fish *Separate Suite Cottage with Kitchen*

Robyn & Roy Horwell
35 Burrows Street, Bluff, 9814

Tel (03) 212 7245 or 021 211 7424
Fax (03) 212 8868
horwell@thelazyfish.co.nz
www.thelazyfish.co.nz

Double $100-$120
(Continental breakfast by arrangement $8.50pp)
Children welcome
2 Double (2 bdrm)
Bathrooms: 2 Ensuite

Very homely fully self-contained unit attached to our home, in a peacefull garden setting. Sleeps 4, double bed in bedroom and sofa bed in lounge. Also double bedroom attached to house, tea & coffee making facilities and microwave. Sunny sheltered courtyard. Friendly labrador in residence. Gateway to Stewart Island and Southern Scenic Route. Take a break and absorb our Coastal and native bush walks, maritime museum, restaurants and supermarket all within walking distance. Five minutes walk to Stewart Island ferry. Continental breakfast by arrangement.

Southland
South Catlins

Riverton *45 km W of Invercargill*

Reo Moana *B&B*

Jean Broomfield
192 Rocks Highway, Riverton, Southland

Tel (03) 234 9044
Fax (03) 234 9047
alanb@orcon.net.nz

Double $150 Single $100
(Full breakfast)
Children negotiable
Pet free home
Children welcome
1 King 1 Twin (2 bdrm)
Bathrooms: 2 Ensuite

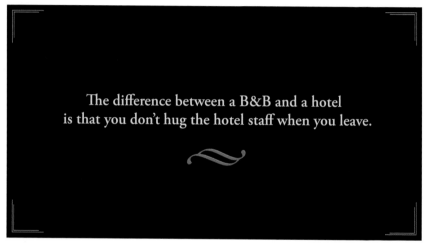

Reo Moana overlooks a beautiful secluded swimming and surfing beach with extended views to the open sea beyond, and northward to the mountains and hills of Southland. Tastefully decorated, the warm and spacious guest rooms each have ensuite bathrooms and sea views. Your host Jean has many years experience in the tourism industry. I welcome you to Riverton, on the Southern Scenic Route and just 45 minutes from Tuatapere and the Humbridge track.

> The difference between a B&B and a hotel
> is that you don't hug the hotel staff when you leave.

Stewart Island *1 km S of Oban*

Glendaruel Bed & Breakfast *B&B*

Raylene & Ronnie Waddell
38 Golden Bay Road, Oban, Stewart Island

Tel (03) 219 1092
Fax (03) 219 1092
r.r.waddell@xtra.co.nz
www.glendaruel.co.nz

Double $200 Single $100-$150 (Full breakfast)
Children by arrangement
Dinner $40 by arrangement
Visa MC accepted
1 King/Twin 1 Queen 1 Single (3 bdrm)
Bathrooms: 3 Ensuite

Peaceful bush setting, ten minutes walk from village, three minutes from Golden Bay on beautiful Paterson Inlet. Handy for water taxis, kayak hire, sandy beaches and bush walks. Large guest lounge and three balconies with bush and sea views. Colourful garden - bird lovers' paradise. Central heating. Courtesy transfers. Advice and assistance with local activities. We have travelled widely and love welcoming guests from around the world. Our friendly Cairn Terrier, Douglas, helps us provide traditional Scottish and Kiwi hospitality. "A Hundred Thousand Welcomes!"

Stewart Island *.20 km W of Oban township*

Sails Ashore & Kowhai Lane B&B *Luxury B&B*
Apartment with Kitchen Holiday Home & Self-catering Flat

Iris and Peter Tait
11 View Street & 6 Kowhai Lane, Stewart Island

Tel (03) 219 1151 or 0800 783 9278 (0800 STEWART)
Fax (03) 219 1151
tait@sailsashore.co.nz
www.sailsashore.co.nz

Double $145-$380 (Breakfast by arrangement)
Restaurants nearby for dinner
Visa MC Eftpos accepted
Pet free home
Not suitable for children
3 King/Twin 1 Queen 2 Single (2 bdrm)
Bathrooms: 6 Ensuite
Please note photos are of Sails Ashore

Sails Ashore is everything discerning guests would expect from a Qualmark 4 Star plus hosted boutique accommodation. Kowhai Lane Holiday home is 4 star self catering and available on either a room or whole of house basis. Both are situated within 4 or 5 minutes stroll of the village centre and overlook the harbour.

All rooms are fully ensuite and centrally heated. Facilities include an extensive library of books and local interest DVDs to enjoy on lazy evenings. Both are an ideal base from which to explore the magic of Stewart Island.

Hosts Iris and Peter have over 70 years combined Island life. Peter was one time Forest Ranger in Charge of Stewart Island and Iris a foundation Trustee of Ulva.

Enjoy with them Sails guided exploration of Ulva Island Open Sanctuary as well as road tours exploring Island life from days of early Maori up to the present. Tours are run on demand to suit both guests and weather on the day with a maximum party size of six per guide.

Guests at Sails Ashore & Kowhai Lane enjoy priority on tours and a discount over listed tariffs.

Index

The New Zealand
Bed &Breakfast
Book

Please help us to keep our standards high

To help maintain the high reputation of **The New Zealand Bed &
Breakfast Book** we ask for your comments about your stay.
You can simply stick a stamp on this form or save all your comment forms
and return them in an envelope.

Alternatively, leave your comment at our website
www.bnb.co.nz

Name of Host or B&B_____

Address _____

_____

Considering things such as breakfast, meals, beds, cleanliness, hospitality
and value for money, what is your overall satisfaction rating, with 1 being
the lowest and 10 being the highest rating?

1   2   3   4   5   6   7   8   9   10

Do you have any comments?

*We may display your comments on our website. The rating will be confidential
and will be kept for administration purposes.*
Fill in your details to go into our regular prize draws!
Your details will not be passed on to anyone else. If you do not have email
we suggest you use a friend's email address.

Your name _____

Your Town/city
and country _____

Email _____

Please Post this form to:
The New Zealand B&B Book,
PO Box 6843, Wellington, New Zealand

Place stamp
here or send
forms in one
envelope

Moonshine Press
PO Box 6843
Wellington
New Zealand